Barry's Books & Stuff
864-340-7376
barryadams69@yahoo.com

THE LETTERBOOK OF ROBERT PRINGLE

Inclos'd please Receive a List of what Goods are most Suitable with you for this Place, a good Asortment of them may answer, & not to have any great Quantity of any one article, but well asorted & in small Packages: I take Notice that you have been advis'd from this Place that Rice fell much in Price when Ward was Loading; doe assure you, whoever advis'd so, must beg Leave to Inform you, has advis'd what was very false, as will appear by all the Vessells that were Loaded here, all the Season, both then & before & for two or three Months after that, it was then at 50/ ℔ Ct, & was at that Price all the Season both before & then, & till the Month of July, when it grows bad in Quality, & then but few Shipping here, there was then a small Quantity; & but a small Quantity Sold at 45/ ℔ Ct: (the Chief of which I had Occasion to Purchace) but all the whole Crop that had been Exported before that Time, was Sold at 50/ ℔ Ct: & was the most Constant price for Rice, in any Crop that I have knowen; being it Usually Varies very much in price, & during the whole Season I have know it at a Different price every Week. Doe assure you it was never my Practice, nor ever shall be to Charge my Employers otherwise for their Goods, than I really paid for them, I have my Commission, & that I think is Sufficient for any Factor, & when Factors doe otherways, they ought to have no more Commissions, or be Longer Employ'd. I am at Present at a Loss who to Recommend to you at Cape Fear, for a Correspondant or Factor, Some of the Gentlemen there, have not given that Content, might be desired, but you may expect same by my Next. We have at present very fine harvest Weather & shall have a very Large Crop of Rice which is now Cutting down. This goes by Capt Atkinson in Mr Burrell's Employ, who is the only Gentleman from your place, that seems to follow this Trade pretty Constant, & sure finds his accot in it. I have not further to Communicate at present, but that I most Respectfully Remain &c

Exchⁿ to London £675 ℔ £100 Sterg

A List of Goods proper for Charles Town St Carolina, Sept 1742
White Blue & Green Plains; Cases of Knives & Forks Ivory handles; Do of Buckhorn handles; Large Clasp Knives Buckhorn handles; Stript Duffle Blanketts; Bed Blanketts, & Negro Ruggs; Suit fine Broad Cloth, of Black, Blue & Scarlet Collours; Allepines & Shalloons of same Collours for Lining; German Sergis of all Sorts; Stript Flannells; Sing: Refd Lo: Sugar; 4d 10d & 20d Clasp Nails in small Casks; Cordage of all Sorts, Ironan of all sizes; Sail Cloth & Canvas of all sorts, & Twine; Brown Ozinbriggs Gunpowder Shott & Bullets in small Caggs of 25℔ each; Writing Paper of all Sorts; Spices & Black peppor; Fruit Vizt Currans & Raisons, in 3 Gallon Juggs; Linseed Oil in 3 Gallon Juggs; Painters Collours; Course Felt Hatts for men & Boys Cheapest Sort; Bohea & Green Tea

THE LETTERBOOK OF ROBERT PRINGLE

Volume Two: October 9, 1742 – April 29, 1745

Walter B. Edgar, *Editor*

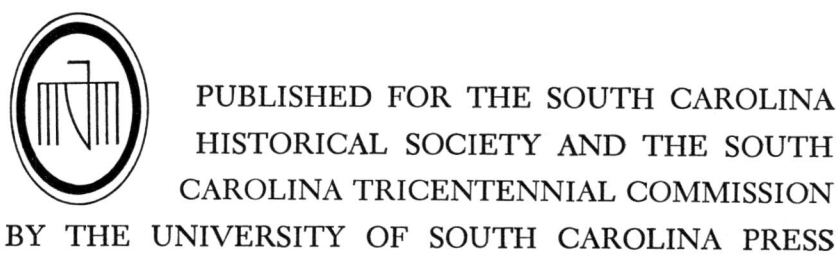

PUBLISHED FOR THE SOUTH CAROLINA
HISTORICAL SOCIETY AND THE SOUTH
CAROLINA TRICENTENNIAL COMMISSION
BY THE UNIVERSITY OF SOUTH CAROLINA PRESS

TRICENTENNIAL EDITION, NUMBER 4

This volume is published by the University of South Carolina Press, Columbia, South Carolina, on behalf of the South Carolina Tricentennial Commission and the South Carolina Historical Society

Copyright © University of South Carolina Press 1972

FIRST EDITION 1972

PUBLISHED IN SOUTH CAROLINA BY THE
UNIVERSITY OF SOUTH CAROLINA PRESS, COLUMBIA

INTERNATIONAL STANDARD BOOK NUMBER: 0-87249-241-9
LIBRARY OF CONGRESS CATALOG CARD NUMBER: 72-183905

Suggested Library of Congress classification furnished by
MCKISSICK MEMORIAL LIBRARY *of the* UNIVERSITY OF SOUTH CAROLINA:
F289.P

MANUFACTURED IN THE UNITED STATES OF AMERICA

Frontispiece:
"A List of Goods proper for Charles Town, South Carolina";
AN EXCERPT FROM A LETTER OF ROBERT PRINGLE TO WILLIAM
COOKSON AND WILLIAM WELFITT OF HULL, 25 SEPTEMBER 1742.

CONTENTS

To Thomas Hutchinson & Co.,
  9 October/429
To John Erving, 9 October/429
To Thomas Hutchinson, 12 October/431
To John Erving, 12 October/433
To John Erving, 16 October/434
To John Keith, 21 October/435
To Gedney Clarke, 21 October/436
To Andrew Pringle, 22 October/437
To William Cookson & William Welfitt,
  23 October/442
To John Wheelwright, 25 October/442
To John Erving, 23 October/443
To Thomas Hutchinson, 23 October/444
To John Erving, 25 October/445
To William Cookson & William Welfitt,
  28 October/445
To Andrew Lessly, 12 November/447
To Michael Lovell, 12 November/448
To William Pringle, 12 November/448
To Thomas Johnson & Samuel Carter,
  17 November/449
To Daniel Dunbibin, 23 November/450
To James Henderson, 30 November/451
To Adam McDonald, 1 December/453
To Andrew Pringle, 6 December/453
To Samuel Smith, 6 December/457
To Andrew Pringle, 13 December/458
To Edward & John Mayne & Edward
  Burn, 13 December/458
To Florentia Cox, 13 December/460
To James Henderson, 13 December/460
To Edward & John Mayne & Edward
  Burn, 14 December/461
To Andrew Pringle, 17 December/462

To Samuel Smallwood, 17 December/463
To Thomas Goldthwait,
  20 December/464
To Richard Partridge, 20 December/465
To William Dover, 17 December/465
To Andrew Pringle, 22 December/466
To Burryau & Schaffer, 29 December/470
To Andrew Pringle, 31 December/471

1743

To Edward & John Mayne & Edward
  Burn, 3 January/472
To Andrew Pringle, 7 January/472
To Peter Westerman, 7 January/474
To Thomas Johnson & Samuel Carter,
  7 January/475
To Andrew Pringle, 8 January/477
To James Maintru & Co., 6 January/478
To Charles & Edmond Boehm,
  7 January/478
To Andrew Pringle, 10 January/479
To Boaz Bell, 11 January/481
To John Story, 10 January/482
To Andrew Pringle, 11 January/482
To James Blount, 13 January/483
To George Honeyman, 20 January/484
To Burryau & Schaffer, 21 January/484
To Thomas Goldthwait, 21 January/485
To Andrew Pringle, 21 January/486
To John Evans, 24 January/489
To Samuel Hallin, 24 January/490
To Richard Partridge, 29 January/491
To Andrew Pringle, 27 January/492
To John Evans, 28 January/493
To Adam McDonald, 5 February/494

Contents

To Richard Partridge, 5 February/496
To Andrew Pringle, 5 February/496
To Andrew Pringle, 5 February/499
To Samuel Smith, 5 February/499
To Thomas Beswick, 10 February/500
To Andrew Pringle, 10 February/501
To John Erving, 11 February/502
To Osborne & Oxnard & Thomas Gunter, 11 February/504
To Thomas Hutchinson, 11 February/505
To John Pringle, 14 February/508
To Edward & John Mayne & Edward Burn, 17 February/510
To Thomas Hopkinson, 17 February/511
To Robert Ellis, 17 February/512
To Thomas Johnson & Samuel Carter, 23 February/513
To George Currie, 24 February/513
To Peter Baynton, 26 February/514
To Robert Ellis, 26 February/515
To Michael Lovell, 28 February/515
To Andrew Lessly, 28 February/516
To John Dunn, junior, 28 February/517
To Robert Ellis, 1 March/518
To George Lucas, 1 March/518
To Andrew Pringle, 1 March/519
To Andrew Pringle, 2 March/519
To Henry Brock, 7 March/522
To Thomas Clark, 9 March/522
To James Wimble, 9 March/523
To Thomas Burrill, 10 March/523
To William Cookson & William Welfitt, 10 March/524
To William Turner & Laurence Jopson, 10 March/525
To John Brock, 10 March/525
To Alexander Andrew, 12 March/527
To Thomas Johnson & Samuel Carter, 14 March/528
To Andrew Pringle, 15 March/529
To Andrew Pringle, 15 March/531
To Thomas Johnson & Samuel Carter, 17 March/531
To Samuel Watlington, 17 March/532
To Andrew Pringle, 23 March/533
To John Erving, 26 March/534

To Thomas Hutchinson, 26 March/535
To Osborne & Oxnard & Thomas Gunter, 29 March/536
To Andrew Pringle, 14 April/537
To Francis Dalby, 26 April/539
To Burryau & Schaffer, 25 April/539
To Thomas Goldthwait, 25 April/540
To Andrew Pringle, 27 April/541
To Andrew Pringle, 28 April/543
To Andrew Pringle, 30 April/545
To John Smith, 17 May/546
To Burryau & Schaffer, 17 May/547
To Thomas Goldthwait, 17 May/548
To Andrew Pringle, 19 May/549
To John Keith, 19 May/552
To James Buchanan, 17 May/553
To James Reid, 19 May/554
To Thomas Clark, 21 May/555
To John Dickinson, 21 May/556
To Daniel Dunbibin, 21 May/556
To Francis Dalby, 23 May/557
To Andrew Pringle, 24 May/558
To James Wimble, 24 May/559
To Charles Hay & Charles Marshall, 24 May/560
To Andrew Pringle, 31 May/561
To Andrew Pringle, 1 June/562
To James Buchanan, 1 June/562
To Peter Westerman, 6 June/563
To James Buchanan, 9 June/563
To Robert Ellis, 13 June/564
To Robert Ellis, Postscript to letter of 13 June/565
To Thomas Hutchinson & Thomas Goldthwait, 13 June/566
To Thomas Hutchinson, 13 June/567
To John Erving, 13 June/568
To James Reid, 14 June/570
To Andrew Pringle, 14 June/571
To John Keith, 14 June/572
To James Buchanan, 15 June/573
To Andrew Pringle, 22 June/574
To Jasper Mauduit, 5 July/576
To Andrew Pringle, 5 July/576
To John Bassnett, 7 July/579
To John Erving, 14 July/580
To Alexander Forsyth, 14 July/582

Contents

To Florentia Cox, 15 July/583
To Andrew Pringle, 22 July/583
To Edward & John Mayne & Edward Burn, 26 July/585
To Andrew Pringle, 19 October/587
To Andrew Lessly, 24 October/589
To Richard Oliver, 24 October/591
To Michael Lovell, 24 October/591
To John Erving, 25 October/593
To Thomas Burrill, 25 October/593
To John Story, 25 October/594
To James Henderson, 2 November/595
To John Keith, 4 November/597
To Nicholas Rigbye, 4 November/598
To Edmund Wiggins, 7 November/599
To John Bassnett, 7 November/600
To William Turner & Laurence Jopson, 7 November/600
To William Cookson & William Welfitt, 7 November/601
To William Dover, 7 November/603
To Charles, Robert, & William Campbell, 14 November/604
To Andrew Pringle, 14 November/606
To Richard Bennett, 15 November/609
To Henry Scarbrugh, 15 November/610
To Scott, Pringle & Scott, 26 November/611
To Edward & John Mayne & Edward Burn, 26 November/612
To Andrew Pringle, 1 December/613
To John Erving, 7 December/615
To William Dover, 17 December/617
To Burryau & Schaffer, 17 December/617
To Andrew Pringle, 19 December/618
To Samuel Saunders, 19 December/621
To James Archbold, 24 December/622
To Jasper King, 27 December/623
To Andrew Lessly, 27 December/624
To Gedney Clarke, 24 December/624
To Alexander Strahan, 27 December/626
To Gedney Clarke, 29 December/627
To Florentia Cox, 29 December/628

1744

To Nicholas Rigbye, 4 January/628
To Samuel Watson, 4 January/629

To Hubert Guichard, 11 January/630
To Francis Guichard, 11 January/631
To Andrew Lessly, 14 January/632
To Michael Lovell, 14 January/633
To Andrew Pringle, 21 January/634
To Samuel Storke & Son, 27 January/637
To Gedney Clarke, 4 February/638
To Andrew Pringle, 6 February/638
To Andrew Pringle, 7 February/642
To John Erving, 11 February/643
To Thomas Hutchinson & Thomas Goldthwait, 11 February/645
To John Livingston, 16 February/648
To Nicholas Rigbye, 16 February/648
To John Dickinson, 17 February/650
To Richard Rowland, 17 February/650
To John Brock, 21 February/652
To Robert Ellis, 23 February/652
To Thomas Hopkinson, 24 February/653
To Andrew Pringle, 24 February/654
To William Turner & Laurence Jopson, 25 February/657
To Samuel Watson, 25 February/658
To Michael Thompson, 27 February/659
To Andrew Pringle, 27 February/659
To Andrew Pringle, 9 March/661
To John Erving, 13 March/664
To John Erving, 14 March/665
To Gedney Clarke, 20 March/666
To Charles & Edmund Boehm, 29 March/667
To Thomas Hutchinson & Thomas Goldthwait, 31 March/668
To Andrew Pringle, 3 April/670
To Whitaker & Hannington, 11 April/670
To William Turner & Laurence Jopson, 9 April/671
To Andrew Pringle, 11 April/672
To Robert Ellis, 23 April/674
To Thomas Hutchinson & Thomas Goldthwait, 24 April/675
To John Erving, 24 April/676
To Edward & John Mayne & Edward Burn, 25 April/677
To Osborne & Oxnard & Thomas Gunter, 26 April/678

Contents

To Charles Marshall, 27 April/678
To Thomas Hutchinson & Thomas Goldthwait, 27 April/679
To Charles Apthorp, 27 April/679
To John Erving, 27 April/680
To John Webster, 28 April/681
To Samuel Storke & Son, 3 May/681
To Anthony Worland, 2 May/682
To Edward Pare, 5 May/683
To Gedney Clarke, 4 May/685
To Samuel Storke & Son, 7 May/686
To Andrew Pringle, 7 May/687
To Thomas Hutchinson & Thomas Goldthwait, 30 April/690
To Halsey & Hanbury, 16 May/691
To George Palmer, 16 May/692
To Osborne & Oxnard & Thomas Gunter, 17 May/693
To John Erving, 17 May/693
To Joseph Turrell, junior, 17 May/695
To John Erving, 18 May/696
To Thomas Hutchinson & Thomas Goldthwait, 18 May/697
To Samuel Stork & Son, 30 May/698
To Andrew Pringle, 30 May/699
To Hugh McDaniel, 30 May/702
To Thomas Hutchinson & Thomas Goldthwait, 1 June/702
To John Erving, 2 June/704
To Andrew Lessly, 9 June/705
To David Glen, 11 June/706
To Andrew Pringle, 11 June/707
To James Blount, 21 June/709
To John Dickinson, 21 June/710
To Seth Pilkington, 21 June/711
To Richard Rowland, 26 June/713
To Henry & John Brock, 28 June/713
To Gedney Clarke, 29 June/715
To Edward Pare, 29 June/716
To David Chesebrough, 30 June/717
To John Erving, 30 June/718
To Thomas Hutchinson & Thomas Goldthwait, 30 June/719
To Andrew Pringle, 30 June/722
To Michael Lovell, 2 July/723
To William Pringle, 2 July/725
To David Lewis, 9 July/726
To John Livingston, 10 July/727
To Florentia Cox, 18 July/727
To Andrew Pringle, 20 July/728
To John Falla, 3 August/730
To John Elfreth, 9 August/731
To Thomas Hutchinson & Thomas Goldthwait, 18 August/731
To John Comrin, 18 August/733
To John Erving, 18 August/733
To Nicholas Rigbye, 28 August/734
To Alexander Strahan, 29 August/735
To Henry & John Brock, 17 September/735
To Robert Ellis, 19 September/737
To John Livingston, 19 September/738
To Andrew Pringle, 21 September/739
To Andrew Pringle, 1 October/742
To John Livingston, 3 October/743
To Jacob Franks, 4 October/744
To Andrew Pringle, 9 October/745
To Edward & John Mayne & Edward Burn, 17 October/746
To Andrew Pringle, 17 October/747
To Samuel Storke & Son, 17 October/749
To Osborne & Oxnard & Thomas Gunter, 6 November/749
To John Erving, 7 November/750
To Thomas Hutchinson & Thomas Goldthwait, 7 November/752
To Roger Gordon, 8 November/755
To Boaz Bell, 14 November/756
To Isaac Duport, 15 November/757
To John Blane, 15 November/757
To Samuel Webber, 15 November/758
To James Henderson, 19 November/759
To Whitaker & Hannington, 19 November/760
To Andrew Pringle, 19 November/760
To Andrew Lessly, 22 November/764
To Richard Rowland, 22 November/764
To Seth Pilkington, 23 November/765
To James Blount, 23 November/767
To James Henderson, 29 November/768
To James Archbold, 24 December [1743]/769
To James Archbold, 5 December/769
To Fitter & Tyzack, 6 December/770

Contents

To Andrew Pringle, 6 December/771
To Gedney Clarke, 6 December/774
To Andrew Pringle, 12 December/775
To Henry & John Brock,
  12 December/777
To Alexander McKensey,
  13 December/778
To David Chesebrough,
  17 December/779
To John Erving, 17 December/781
To William Pringle, 20 December/782
To Michael Lovell, 20 December/783
To Andrew Lessly, 20 December/784
To Edward Pare, 20 December/786
To Gedney Clarke, 20 December/787
To Burryau & Schaffer, 22 December/789
To Andrew Pringle, 22 December/789

1745

To Robert Ellis, 4 January/791
To William Mackay, 10 January/791
To Burryau & Schaffer, 12 January/792
To Fitter & Tyzack, 16 January/793
To Andrew Pringle, 17 January/794
To William Cookson & William Welfitt,
  15 January/797
To Henry & John Brock, 17 January/798
To John Trenchard, 19 January/801
To Edward Pare, 19 January/802
To Gedney Clarke, 19 January/802
To Andrew Pringle, 19 January/803
To Peter Westerman, 25 January/805
To William Mackay, 25 January/806
To Edward Pare, 29 January/807
To Andrew Pringle, 2 February/807
To James Henderson, 9 February/810
To Edward & John Mayne & Edward
  Burn, 11 February/811

To Thomas Hutchinson & Thomas
  Goldthwait, 15 February/811
To Thomas Hutchinson,
  15 February/812
To Joseph Chadwick, 16 February/813
To James Henderson, 21 February/814
To Don Domingo, 21 February/815
To James Henderson, 23 February/816
To David Chesebrough, 23 February/816
To John Erving, 23 February/817
To Thomas Hutchinson & Thomas
  Goldthwait, 23 February/818
To John Hobbs, 23 February/819
To Robert Ellis, 25 February/820
To Richard Rowland, 25 February/821
To Andrew Pringle, 27 February/821
To Henry Lascelles, 27 February/823
To Fitter & Tyzack, 27 February/824
To David Glen, 6 March/824
To Edward Pare, 14 March/825
To David Chesebrough, 16 March/826
To Osborne & Oxnard & Thomas Gunter,
  16 March/826
To John Erving, 16 March/827
To Andrew Pringle, 18 March/827
To Andrew Pringle, 21 March/830
To William Pitt, 29 March/833
To Andrew Pringle, 4 April/833
To Nicholas Rigbye, 1 April/836
To Peter Westerman, 9 April/837
To Gedney Clarke, 10 April/838
To Seth Pilkington, 10 April/839
To Edward Pare, 13 April/840
To James Blount, 15 April/842
To James Henderson, 24 April/843
To William Mackay, 24 April/844
To Enoch Hall, 24 April/845
To John Erving, 29 April/845
A list of correspondents/846
Index/849

VOLUME TWO: OCTOBER 9, 1742–APRIL 29, 1745

TO THOMAS HUTCHINSON & CO.
Boston

Charles Town, 9th October 1742

Sirs:

The Last I did myself the Pleasure to write you was of the 4th September per Capt. Snelling & have not since any of your Favours which will occasion Brevity. I have lately advices from Mr. John Keith who gives over the Snow *John*, Capt. Palmer, to be taken or Lost as hearing nothing of him for a Considerable time, after Copies of my Letters by him came to hand. It is pity that he did not write per first opportunity after he put in at Boston. I hope he is Sail'd again from you Long before this.

Your Ribbons & Iron Potts remain on hand very unsaleable articles. Should be glade to have your further Directions about them, especially the Ribbons. There is also a Great part of your axes still unsold. We have a very Large Crop of Rice which it is to be hop'd will occasion it to be Low in price, as there is a Large Quantity produc'd. There are already between 20 & 30 Sail of Ships that Wait here for Freight which am of Opinion will not be high till towards the Spring, & if Shipping don't arrive then they will be wanted here, which however is Seldom the Case & we shall Continue to Ship off Rice briskly from the Middle of next Month till the Midle of May.

There is no N. England Rum here at Present, & there is a Good Dale now Consumed here, as West India Rum is high. The first N. England Rum that arrives am of opinion will fetch 20/ per Gallon if no Great Quantity happens to come together. I have not further to Offerr at present but that I am most Respectfully &c.

ADDRESSED: "Per Capt. Andrew Breading"

TO JOHN ERVING
Boston

Charles Town, 9th October 1742

Sir:

Since my Last to you of the 12th July I have not the Pleasure of any of your Favours. In my Last I advis'd you that the Spainards had made a

9th October 1742

Decent in Georgia, but they soon Left it again in a very precipitate manner after having had one Skirmish with Generall Oglethrope in which they sustain'd a Considerable Loss by an Ambuscade, nothwithstanding we have certain Information that there was 6,500 Men in the Expedition, & if it had not been thro' the bad Conduct & Cowardice of Capt. Hardy, Commander of the *Rye* & Commodore of the King's Ships here, all their Shipping had been Destroyed before they Could have gott way. He has Certainly behav'd very ill in the affair, this province having been put to a very Great Charge in Fitting out Ships & Men to assist the Generall & did nothing against the Spainards being Render'd abortive thro' his Puisilanimaty & not doeing his Duty, for which it is to be hoped he will be Broke.

[495] I am to advise you that we have a very Good Crop of Rice, & as there is a Large quantity produc'd will Occasion it to be Low in price. There are already between 20 & 30 Sail that wait for Freight & some of them have been here a Great while, & am of opinion that Freight will not be high till towards the Spring. If Shipping don't arrive then in Great numbers they will be wanted here, which however is not often the Case there being Generally a Great many Shipping here in Crop time. If you intend to send any of your Ships here this Crop, you may most assuredly depend on my Utmost & best Endeavours for your Interest, in procuring them Freight & Good Dispatch.

The Best Commodity & most Saleable that Comes from your parts is Rum of which there is now a Great Dale Consum'd here, as West India Rum is high, & as there is no N. England Rum here at present am of Opinion the first that arrives will fetch 20/ per Gallon, if no Great Quantity happens to Come in at one time. I cannot Encourage your sending any other Commodity from your Parts that will answer, Excepting some Dutch Goods if they Come Cheap, Vizt. Brandy & Ginn, Spices of all sorts, & French Claret in Bottles of which a pretty dale is sometimes brought here Via Philadelphia by the Palantine Ships that Come to Load here,[1] & of which they make a Good advantage, & those things are not taken Notice of by our Custom house officers here.

I could not prevail with the Bearer Capt. Breading's[2] Owner to take on Board 2 Barrells of Potatoes from my Wife for your Good Lady. His

---

[1] The vessels that brought the Palatines to Pennsylvania often sailed southward to Charleston to secure a cargo on the homeward leg of the voyage.

[2] Capt. Andrew Breading departed for Boston in the snow *Sarah*. SCG, 18 October 1742.

12th October 1742

Owner one Mr. Jenys a Bristoll Gentleman never takes any Goods on Freight for Boston & he is Esteem'd here as a person not very oblidging. However Capt. Breading has promis'd to Deliver Two Bushells of Potatoes for Mrs. Erving which hope will be acceptable. My Wife enjoys but a very Indifferent state of Health & is but just Recover'd from a Severe Fever. She heartaly Joins with me in best Respects & humble Service to Self, Lady, & pretty Family & Truely am with Great Respect &c.

ADDRESSED: "Per Ditto" [Capt. Andrew Breading]

TO THOMAS HUTCHINSON
Boston

Charles Town, 12th October 1742

SIR:

The Inclos'd of the 9th Inst. is what I had already writt you by this Conveyance of Capt. Breading to which please be Refferr'd & he not being yet gone gives me the Opportunity of accknlowdging the Receipt yesterday of your most Esteem'd Favours of the 21 & 23d September per Capt. Tisehurst[3] & duely Remark the Contents. Yours of the 21 Inclosing Bill of Loading & Invoice of 20 hhds. Barbados Rum & 50 Casks N. England Ditto per the *Bremin Factor*, Capt. Tisehurst, on your Account which as soon as landed shall take [496] Care to Dispose of to your best advantage, & when sold punctualy observe your Directions in Remitting the Neat Proceeds to Messrs. Burryau & Shaffer[4] in London on your Account in Good Bills of Exchange or in Gold & Silver if either to be procured or by Rice or Deer Skins, which way soever may judge most for your advantage & most Expeditious & I am in hopes to obtain 20/ per Gall. per the N. England Rum as you mention if the Large Quantity that

[3] Capt. Thomas Tisehurst. RPC, p. 508.
[4] Burryau (Bourryau) & Schaffer were merchants in Austin Friars, London. Zachariah Burryau was the son of Capt. John Burryau of St. Kitts. After moving to London, Burryau maintained his large interests in St. Kitts. His firm was concerned primarily in the West Indian trade. In the 1750's Burryau took a new partner and the firm became Burryau & Spooner. RPC, pp. 503, 684; NEH&GR, XI (1857), 236; Oliver, I, 252–254; *London Directories*.

has Come besides in Capt. Tisehurst & a pretty deal that Is just arriv'd from Barbados does not obstruct it. However you may assuredly Depend on my Utmost endeavours to dispose of it for the most it will Fetch.

I am Glad that Capt. Palmer has proceeded again on his voyage. I duely observe what you write in Relation to Capt. Blunt. His proceeding in the Manner he did you may be sensible was both against my Inclination & Interest, however am very Glad he Deliver'd the Cargoe safe after so Indiscreet & Imprudent an Action of his in Running so Great a Risque with your Cargoe & his own Vessel. Doe assure you I dissuaded him very much from attempting any thing of that Nature.

I observe that your Collector is very stiff & Riged & won't grant a Certificate in Order to Cancell my Bond here. If you cann't prevail with him, please to forward me the Certificate from the Justice of Peace, taking a Duplicate thereof. I must doe the best I can with our Kings Officers here, who am in hopes will be more Favourable Considering the Circumstances of the affair than your Collector, who I understand is but a young officer. 'Tho our officers here have insisted on their Fees for Capt. Blunts Vessell & have been oblidged to pay them £13 Currency for same which Capt. Blunt must allow, as also £8.4.6 Currency I paid him after Settling with him, which he assur'd me he would accquaint you of & pay you, if so doubt not you have given me Credit for same accordingly, & if you have not yet Settl'd with him am to desire the Favour you'll be so good as to stop same for me being in all £21.4.6 this Currency, Exchange at £700 per £100 Sterling.

If you intend any Vessells here this Crop for Freight you may depend on my best Endeavours for your Interest 'tho am of opinion that Freight wont be Encourageing 'till towards the Spring, there being a Great many Vessells already here waiting for the first of the Crop. I am most Respectfully &c.

ADDRESSED: "Per Capt. Andrew Breading"

12th October 1742

TO JOHN ERVING
Boston

Charles Town, 12th October 1742

SIR:

The Inclos'd of the 9th Instant is what I had already writt you by this Conveyance of Capt. Breading to which please be Refferr'd & he not being yet gone gives me this Opportunity of accknowledgeing the Receipt yesterday of your most acceptable Favours of the 22d September per Capt. Tisehurst & duely Remark the Contents. I am greatly oblidg'd to you for your wonted Civilities on my Account to Mr. [497] Stoutenburgh which he has accknowledg'd in a particular manner to his Father.

I observe your *John Gally* is arriv'd at Boston. As I have taken Notice to you in mine of the 9th, I cannot encourage your sending her Directly, as not knowing yet how Freights are Like to Govern & there are already as many & more Ships here Seekers that wait for the first of the Crop as will Carry off all the Rice that Can be Shipt off on this side Christmass. However you will be able best to Determine whither it may be most for your Interest to send her now, or to stay till towards Spring. No person cares to Engage a Ship at Present or offerr any Freight certain as there are so many Ships here already & a Great many more Expected & Our Rice wont begin to Come to Markett till the Middle of Nex Month.

I Receiv'd Inclos'd the Charter partie between Messrs. Thomas Hawding & Henry Wethered Owners of the Ship the *Industrious Sally*, & Crokatt & Michie[5] of this Town, also the Letter for Mr. Crokatt which I deliver'd him & Knowing what Persons you became Security for & that the Gentlemen of North Carolina, are not very Famous for being punctuall in the Performance of their Engagements, I judg'd it necessary you should be Indemnified & accordingly I drew up an Obligation which I Insisted Mr. Crokatt shoud sign for himself & Partner Mr. Michie which has accordingly done & please Receive Inclos'd Copie of same. The Original I keep by me in case there may be Occasion for it, 'tho Mr. Crokatt assures me that the Charter partie will be punctually preform'd by their Factors at Cape Fear, which it Certainly ought to be as being on Very Favourable Easie Terms.

I take notice what you are pleas'd to mention in Relation to Capt.

---

[5] The partners were John Crokatt and Kenneth Michie. Judgment Rolls, 1743–1744, 27A; *HL*, I, 94n, 130n.

434   THE LETTERBOOK OF ROBERT PRINGLE

12th October 1742

Blunt who was Guilty of a very Indiscreet Imprudent action in goeing away from this with his Vessell in the Manner he did, by which he Run a Great many Risques both with the Cargoe & his Vessell, & entirly against my Consent & Inclination, & I dissuaded him very much from attempting any thing of that Nature, as I sometime agoe advis'd Mr. Hutchinson & doubt not is well satisfied thereof as he might be sensible that I could be no sufferer by the Vessell's being stopt & Ditain'd here, & on the Contrary by his goeing as he did, I Run the Risque of Forfeiting my Bond for £1,000 Sterling. Mr. Hutchinson has made me a Very Considerable Consignment of Rum by Capt. Tisehurst being 70 hhds. & Teirces & am in hopes to obtain 20/ per Gall. for the New England Rum if the Large Quantity that has Come in the same Vessell besides & a Good deal that is just arriv'd from Barbados, does not obstruct it. Mr. Michie is Expected here in three Weeks. Capt. Breading being just agoeing, I add not but that I am &c.

ADDRESSED: "Per Capt. Andrew Breading & Copie per Capt. Walker"

[498]
TO JOHN ERVING
    Boston

Charles Town, 16th October 1742

SIR:

I have writt you per this Conveyance of Capt. Breading of the 9th & 12th Current to which please be Refferr'd, and Capt. Breading being still Detain'd in the Road by an Easterly Wind, have to advise you that on the 13th arriv'd here Two Kings Ships and Seven large Transports Ships from Jamaica with five Hundred Regular Troops to our Assistance having During the late Descent of the Spaniards in Georgia sent two Expresses from this for Assistance.[6] And it is Likely that another Ex-

[6] On October 13 seven transport ships arrived from Jamaica with 5 to 600 men under the command of Colonel Du[r]our. The ships had been convoyed by HMS *Shoreham* and HMS *Spy*. SCG, 18 October, 1742.

21st October 1742

pedition may now be Undertaken by Generall Oglethorpe against St. Augustine. I have not further to add but that I am &c.

ADDRESSED: "Did not Goe"

TO JOHN KEITH
   London
                                    Charles Town, 21st October 1742
SIR:
   My Last to you was of the 3d September to which please be Refferr'd, & about a fortnight agoe came to hand your much Esteem'd Favours of the 10th August with Inclos'd for James Ogilvie, & duely Remark the Contents. In my Last I advis'd you that Capt. Palmer had Unfortunatly Sprung a Leak at Sea & put in to Boston in N. England, where it Seems he Sheath'd his Vessell as Mr. Hutchinson advis'd me & proceeded again on his Voyage, & hope by this Time is happily arriv'd with you, which Shall be glade to be advis'd. Capt. Palmer was greatly to Blame if he did not immediatly advise you of his being put in to Boston.
   I Return you my hearty Thanks for honouring Capt. Palmer's Bill in my Favour for £53 being for Cash advanc'd him here to Defray the Charges on the Vessell, otherways he Could not have procur'd Freight & proceeded with his Vessell from this, having done it out of Freindship to you, as the Vessell was to be Consign'd to you. Mr. Hutchinson did not Ship Effects Sufficient to defray the Charges here as Capt. Palmer will make appear to you, he having an Exact Account of the Sale of the Effects & Disbursments here.
   About a Week agoe arriv'd here Two Kings Ships with Seven Transports Containing Five hundred Regular Troops from Jamaica, being by the Application of this Government Two Expresses sent from this during the Late Descent of the Spainards in Georgia, so that is Likely that another Expedition may be undertaken by Generall Oglethrope against St. Augustine. We have a very Large Crop of Rice which will occasion it to be Low in price, & we have advices of very fine Harvests in all parts

of Europe by the Last Ships from Europe. I Salute you & am most Respectfully &c.

ADDRESSED: "Per the *Minerva*, Capt. Cload, & Copie per Capt. Boyes Via Cowes"

[499]
TO GEDNEY CLARKE
London

Charles Town, 21st October 1742

SIR:

The Inclos'd of the 17th September is Copie of the Last I did myself the Pleasure to write you to Barbados & about a Week agoe came to Hand your most Esteem'd Favours of 29th August Inclosing the Account Sales of the *Susannah's* Cargoe, also Account Current, Ballance due being £43.2.9¾ which have noted accordingly. As our Crop is now Coming on, Capt. Gregory will begin to Load as soon as any Rice Comes to Markett.

I observe you had taken your passage for London & was to sail in Two Days after the Date of yours where I hope this will find you happily arriv'd after a Good passage. If the Ship that you mention in yours Should Come here you may Depend on having her dispatch'd back with Good Lumber according to your Directions, & as much Rice &c. upon Freight as can be gott for her. Barbados Rum sells here at 22/ per Gallon & Beleive wont be Lower (Shall Continue to advise your House as Conveyances offerr) & doubt not will be high in the Spring. We have a Large Consumption for it in this Province which takes off upwards of 2,000 hhds. per Annum. If you think proper to send any here in the Spring, you may Depend on my best Endeavours for your advantage.

This will be Deliver'd you by my Brother who will be heartily Glad to see you in London, & to whose good offices & Civilities have Recommended you to During your Stay there, & who will be very Glad to Coroborate Our Accquaintance & Correspondance & to Render you any agreeable Service. I Salute you & am most Respectfully &c.

ADDRESSED: "Under Cover of A.P. to London per Capt. Cload & Copie per Capt. Boyes Via Cowes"

22nd October 1742

TO ANDREW PRINGLE
London

Charles Town, 22nd October 1742

SIR:

Since my Last to you of the 20th September I have your Severall Favours of the 24th & 25 May per Capt. Macklellan[7], the 5th & 25th August per Capt. Crosthwaite[8] & Rodgers[9] & duely Notice the Sundry Contents. I observe your Continued Reflections Concerning the bad Success your Ship *Susannah* has mett with which could not be forseen, especially to be Twice Disappointed of Freight in the West Indies, 'tho She has not been Singular in that of a Great many. It appear'd according to my Judgement to be the most for your Interest to proceed as She has done as Rice was so high (& you had Limitted the Price) & Freight so Low. If your orders are possitive & Limitted Concerning your Ships proceedure you may Depend on having them punctually Comply'd with if practicable, but if they are Discretionary, I must act according to the best of my Judgement for your Interest & if the Event does not succed accordingly, The Factor cannot be Blam'd & at the worst can only be Imputed to an Error in Judgment. It is True I writt you in a postscript of the 30th March Freight for London £3 & for £3.10/ which I meant & shou'd have been worded (was Demanded) but could not be obtain'd, there being then few or no Shipping here but severall Ships Coming in prevented any from having it & if there had been any Prospect of it, you might be Certain I would not have sufferr'd the *Susannah* to proceed, & which did not happen for there was not one Ship that Loaded here Last Season for more than 40/ per Ton for London & 50/ for Holland excepting one Capt. Lemon[1] just filling up at that Nick of Time, & no other Ship than on Freight had some small part put on Board at £3 per ton & I am Certain no other, there being severall Fine Ships here still which have Layen here ever since Last March & would have Gladly accepted of 50/ for London. When Capt. Palmer Loaded there was but another Vessell besides himself in the Harbour that wanted Freight & he could

---

[7] Capt. John McClean in the brigantine *Georgia Packett* from London. SCG, 27 September 1742.
[8] Capt. Thomas Crossthwaite arrived from London in the snow *Lawrance*. SCG, 4 October 1742.
[9] Capt. James Rogers in the snow *Hector* arrived from London. SCG, 1 November 1742.
[1] Capt. John Lemon departed for London in the ship *Loyal Judith*. SCG, 1 May 1742.

not obtain more than 40/ per ton & could not have gott Loaded at all if he had not Luckely accepted of that, but I partly guess who [500] has agrevated this affair to you.

In one of your former you desir'd the whole of the *Susannah*'s Cargoe to the West Indies might be on your own Account after I had made the Invoice & enter'd it in my Books each ½ & propos'd same to you which I upon your advice alter'd the Whole to your Account accordingly & now you desire I may take the one half allowing Freight. The usuall Freight for Lumber formerly from this to the West Indies us'd to be one half of the Lumber for carrying the other, & Rice, &c. at £3 that Currency per Ton, but of Late what Vessells have gone, the Cargoes have been on the Owners Account so that there has been no settled Freight & in your next youll please advise whither said adventure must be on your Account or jointly each ½, as I advis'd you at first. It is still equal to me & shall willingly agree to which way so ever you please to order it.

As to the Exchange I advis'd in one of my Former, that it was at £700 per £100 Sterling as it has been for these Eighteen Months past, & if any alteration had happen would not have fail'd to advise you.

Capt. Palmer's Vessell unfortunatelly Sprung a Leack at Sea which oblidg'd him to put into Boston where Mr. Hutchinson writes me he Sheath'd his Vessell & proceeded again on his Voyage & hope by this Time is happily arriv'd with you as I have advis'd Mr. Keith by this Conveyance with my Thanks for honouring his Bill in my Favour.

The Sloop for North Carolina that I advis'd you for Insurance on is arriv'd there after a good Passage & have Credit your Account for £13.15 accordingly. The picture Frames & half Thicks, &c. per Capt. Crossthwaite are Landed in good order. I thank you for the acts of Parliament & Monthly Magazenes. They are allways amusing, & Usefull here, & desire I may be Charg'd in account for Same.

Mr. Home is not yet Return'd from the Northward but soon expected. Inclos'd please Receive a Letter from him there, he sent me to be forwarded you. I talk'd with Mr. Robert Steil[2] what I thought was proper in Relation to what you advise of their being Inclinable to Consign to you, who tells me that he will Contribute all in his Power for that Effect & you may always most assuredly Depend on my uttmost Endeavours to promote same whenever I can have any opportunity.

Am at a Loss to know whither it will be most for your Interest that your

---

[2] Robert Stiell and John Hume, Charleston merchants, were partners in the 1740's under the firm name of Stiell, Hume, and Co. *HL*, I, 149n.

22nd October 1742

Susannah should goe for London or Cowes as you have ommitted to give me any Directions about same, but Shall Determine as Freight Governs (of which there is not yet a Word Talkt) & may judge most advantageous. Think it may be proper to have her Dunnag'd or Floor'd with good Pitch if it Comes Low in Price & Especially as Capt. Gregory tells me the *Susannah* is always Crank with Rice only. The *Minerva* has Loaded with Old Rice at 50/ per Ton. All the other Shipping here wait for the New, of which there are upwards of 30 Sail but no Rice will be Shipt till a Month hence & it is hop'd will Break in price not higher than 40/ per Ct.

The Lisbon Markett is Likely to be the Best for Rice this Year. Am in hopes Mr. Mayne or some other gentlemen may give orders to me for Shipping some on their Account by Bills, if it Comes Low in price, as I believe it will, hope it will answer. The Bill of Exchange you sent me some time agoe for £8 Sterling on Account of Mr. Andrew of Rotterdam on one Capt. Hoare[3] here is not yet paid & am afraid never will. Hoare is very poor & Indolent, & am told his Wife & he are bad Managers & both given to Liquor, & if I was to throw him in Jail he would Swear off.

Inclos'd you have two Letters of mine for Mr. Gedney Clarke of Barbados, the Last in answer to his of the 29 August from Barbados which after perusal you'll please to Seal & deliver him. Youll observe he advises that he was then to Sail for London in two Days after, & hope he will be arriv'd before this Comes to your hands. He desired that I would write him to London. He has the Charactor of a very Honest Gentleman & Capt. Gregory tells me that he Bears an [501] Exceeding Good Character in Barbadoes, (& doubt not he may be in London before you Receive this) has Great Interest there & in very good Bussiness. He is from Boston in N. England & born there & hope you will make it your Bussiness & think it worth while to Corroborate Our Accquaintance & Correspondance with him while in London. He writes me that he Expects to be in Barbados again by February Next.

Please also Receive Inclos'd Letter of Attorney to you from Isaac Holmes[4] to Receive the Inclos'd Fire Tickett in his Favour No. 80 for

---

[3] Capt. Thomas Hoare was a Charleston pilot who died in 1743. *St. Philip's Register*, p. 273.

[4] Isaac Holmes, a South Carolina merchant, was the son of Francis Holmes who died in South Carolina in 1720. His brother Ebenezer was a Boston merchant. *HL*, I, 39n. The sum mentioned in the letter is one-third of the total loss that Isaac Holmes recorded for himself and the estate of Major Willson. In the list of the sufferers in the Charleston fire £548 sterling is recorded for ticket No. 80, but this figure had been rounded off to the nearest pound. Kenneth Scott, "Sufferers in the Charleston Fire of 1740," *SCHM*, LXIV (1963), 203–211.

22nd October 1742

£181.5 [illegible] Sterling which when Receiv'd please to Credit my Account for. You have likewise Inclos'd Copie of Account Sales from Mr. Gedney Clarke of the *Susannah*'s Cargoe at Barbados & Account Current, Balance due from him being £43.2.9¾ Barbados Currency.

This goes by Cap. Roger Cload, Commander of the *Minerva* who has promis'd to Deliver you this himself & Desir'd I ought make mention of his name to you, being desirous of being accquainted with you. He is a Clever Brisk man & a Stout Seaman, but does not seem much to like his Kinsman Mr. John Nicholeson's Employ. He was Mate of a Vessell Consign'd to me about Two Years agoe & behav'd Exceeding Well.

The Wine & Rum Trade is Likely to Turn out much Better here than the Dry Goods Trade which is much overdone, & the Credit given on Dry Goods very Long. As for your Sale Cloth per the *John & Isabella* & *Susannah*, cannot sell or Dispose of it at any Rate, & no person here will buy it. It is of so bad a Quality. Should be glad to have your orders to send it some where else. Perhaps it may goe off in Boston or Philadelphia. Madeira Wine is sold at £130 per Pipe, & not good. There is but Little in Town at present, the first that happens to arrive, if Good will meet with a Quick & Ready Sale. Salt is also Scarce. 2,000 or 3,000 Bushells could sell immediatly for 12/6 or 15/ per bushell, either Large or English salt. It might be worth while for Capt. Patton to Ballast with it at Southampton & as he Comes from Rotterdam, a Quantity of good French Claret in Bottles say 100 dozen could not be too much & sells to a very Good profitt & Runs no manner of Risque, also some Arrack, Brandy, & Ginn in Carboys[5] sell to very Good advantage, but cannot Encourage any Thing else from Holland, Excepting Cordage, White Rope, & Hamburgh Twine & Lines, & Both Cases of all Sizes. There is always a Sure Vend for these Things here & Run no Risque.

The Women here come very much into Wareing of Bone Lace if Mr. Andrew of Rotterdam could procure a Box from Flanders, well sorted from 5/ to 15/ per yard, & Two or three Suits for head Cloaths, or Lappits from 20/, 25/, & 30/ Sterling per yard, the Whole Box Value about £40 to £50 Sterling for a Tryal, might be worth While, as I observe a good Deale imported here & the Women seem to Run much upon it & it is a Commodity not perishable & goes in Little Room.

Mr. Hutchinson of Boston has made me an other Consignment of 70

---

[5] A carboy was a large, globular bottle, of green or blue glass, covered with basketwork for protection. It was used chiefly for holding acids and other corrosive liquids.

22nd October 1742

hhds. Rum the Neat proceeds thereof to be Remitted to Messrs. Bourryau & Schaffer in London.

I observe you gott a Bargain of a fine Large New Ship & goeing to Jamaica, Mr. Reids Brother, Commander & if she cannot gett Freight at Jamaica is to Come here. She may perhaps stand a pretty Good Chance for Freight to come here in the Spring, but as to her being a Ship of Force, that will be of no manner of Advantage to her as to Freight in this place, (it may as to passangers) for People here are so Unaccountable that way (of which have had Occasion to see a Great Deal of it) that if a Vessell can but Swim on the Water & tho' She goes like a Hay Stack & will take Freight but 1/ per Ton under any other Vessell, or under the Current Freight, that Vessell, I say, will be sure to have the prefferrance in getting Freight. You may Expect your Account Current & all your Account Sales that Can be Compleated by your ship *Susannah* which is this Day come down Cooper River to Town. Two of her people that Belong'd to her are Dead in Town since she went up the Freshes.

On the 13 Current Arriv'd here from Jamaica in Consequence of two Expresses that were sent there by this government Dureing the Late Decent of the Spainards in Georgia Seven Transport Ships with a Detachment of about 500 Regular Troops out of Generall Wentworth's Forces there, under the Command of Colonel Durreau & Convoy'd by the *Shoreham* & *Spy* Men of War, the officers of which are all in Town & the Souldiers keeps on board for fear of Desertion. So that is likely another Expedition may be undertaken by Generall Oglethrope who it seems happens to be the Commanding officer against St. Augustine. It is pity that Admiral Vernon & Generall Wentworth had not orders to take it rather than to Lye Idle at Jamaica distroying their Ships & Wasting their Forces. It would be vast advantage to this Province to have the Place Taken. My Wife joins in kind Love & Respects, & I Sincerely Remain &c.

ADDRESSED: "Per the *Minerva*, Capt. Roger Cload, & Copie per Capt. Boyes Via Cowes"

[502]
TO WILLIAM COOKSON & WILLIAM WELFITT
Hull

Charles Town, 23rd October 1742

SIRS:

The Last I did my self the pleasure to writt you was of the 22nd September per Capt. Atkinson with Copie to which please be Referr'd & which I now Confirm, Since have not any of your Favours. I have just time by a Ship in the Road for London to advise you that our Sessions being now Sitting & will be over this Night, & as Capt. Ward has not Come to Take his Tryal I mov'd the Court by my Lawyer,[6] that Capt. Ward may be so far Indulg'd since he is not yet Come, as to Continu'd upon his Regoginzance till next Session which begins the Second Wednesday in March next & which was Granted by the Court upon my Accquainting them that you had writt me that Capt. Ward design'd to be here by this Month (God Willing). So that if Capt. Ward has not yet sett out for this place, that you'll please accquaint he has still advis'd him to be here by March next, & if he doe not then appear here accordingly the Money will Certainly be forfeited, so thought it proper that he might have this Timely Notice.

I have Shipt the Buckrams to Mr. John Wheelwright in Boston as you Directed & have sent him Invoice & Bill of Loading for Same & advis'd him to Dispose of same to your Best advantage. In haste I Remain &c.

ADDRESSED: "Per the *Minerva*, Capt. Roger Cload, & Copie per Capt. Boyes Via Cowes"

TO JOHN WHEELWRIGHT
Boston

Charles Town, 25th October 1742

SIR:

Inclos'd Please Receive Bill of Loading & Invoice of a Case Containing Sixty Seven peices Buckrams Shipt on Board the Billander

---

[6] This may have been James Graeme who had served as Pringle's lawyer at an earlier date. Judgment Rolls, 1737, 42A.

23rd October 1742

Francis, Capt. Richard Walker, Commander for Boston, by the Directions & on the proper Account & Risque of my Friends Messrs. William Cookson & William Welfitt of Hull & to your Good self Consign'd, amount as per Invoice being £53.1.1 Sterling, which wish Safe to your Hands & which youll Please Receive & Dispose of to their best advantage & hope will meet with better Success with you, they being entirely Unsaleable here. Youll Please to Favour me with the Receipt thereof & doubt not said Gentlemen have advis'd you by this time in Relation to Same accordingly. Shall be Glad to Render you any agreeable Service here & I am most Respectfully &c.

ADDRESSED: "Per the *Francis,* Capt. Richard Walker"

TO JOHN ERVING
Boston

Charles Town, 23rd October 1742

SIR:

The preceeding of the 12th Current is Copie of what I did myself the Pleasure to write you per Capt. Breading to which please be Refferr'd. On the 13 arriv'd here from Jamaica in Consequence of Two Expresses that were sent there by this Government during the Late Decent of the Spainards in Georga Seven Transport Ships with a Detachment of about 500 of Regular Troops out of Generall Wentworths Forces there, under the Command of Colonel Durreau & Convoy'd by the *Shoreham* & *Spy* Men of War, the Officers of which are all in Town & the Soilders keept on Board for Fear of Desertion. So that it is Likely, that another Expedition may be undertaken by Generall Oglethrope against St. Augustine, & who will it seems be the Commanding Officer. If these Transports shou'd be Discharg'd here, which are all Large Ships, will help to keep down Freight, of which there is not as yet any mention made, New Rice not being yet Ready to Come to Markett. I am &c.

ADDRESSED: "Per Ditto Walker" [Per the *Francis,* Capt. Richard Walker]

23rd October 1742

[503]
TO THOMAS HUTCHINSON
  Boston

Charles Town, 23rd October 1742

SIR:
  The preceeding of the 12th Current is Copie of what I did myself the Pleasure to write you per Capt. Breeding to which Crave your Refferrance.
  Since my Last your Rum is all Landed in a pretty Good order, but Cannot obtain 20/ per Gall. for the N. England, a Considerable Quantity being just arriv'd from Barbados & Antigua. However have already dispos'd of part of the N. England at 16/ per Gall. & hope will hold that price. You may Depend on my best Endeavours in the Disposal of it to the Best advantage, & as Quick as possable, in Order to make the Remittances as you Direct.
  One Capt. Joseph Gowen[7] of your Place Who has Lately Come here from being a Prisoner among the Spaniards & being a Stranger here apply'd to me for some Relief thro' the Accquaintance he tells me that he has with you, by the Recommendation of Capt. Richard Walker, Commander of the Billander *Francis* for your Port, & I have accordingly let him have £40 this Currency to procure Cloaths & Necessaries for his passage to Boston & have taken his Bill of Exchange for £28 N. England Money on the said Richard Walker payable in Boston at ten Days Sight, being by Capt. Walker Accep'd & doubt not will be duely paid, & which please Receive Inclos'd, being to your Good self Indors'd, & for which shall Debit your account £40 this Currency accordingly, having Reckon'd £28 N. England Money, much about the Exchange for £40 this Currency.
  On the 13th arriv'd here from Jamaica in Consequence of 2 Expresses that were sent there by this Government during the Late Decent of the Spainards in Georgia Seven Transport Ships with a Detachment of about 500 Regular Troops out of Generall Wentworths Forces there, under the Command of Colonel Durreau & convoy'd by the *Shoreham* & *Spy* Men of War, the officers of which are all in Town & the Soilders keept on Board for Fear of Desertion. So that it is Likely, that another Expedition may be

---

[7] Mrs. Elizabeth Gowen, wife of Joseph Gowen, was admitted to full communion at the church in Charlestown, Massachusetts in 1727. Their three children were baptised in the same church. *NEH&GR*, XXX (1878), 169, 173, 287, 289.

Undertaken by Generall Oglethrope against St. Augustine & who will it seems be the Commanding Officer. If these Transports Shoud be Discharg'd here, which are all Large Ships, will help to keep down Freight, of which there is not as yet any mention made, New Rice not being yet Ready to Come to Markett. I am &c.

ADDRESSED: "Per Capt. Richard Walker"

TO JOHN ERVING
    Boston
                                Charles Town, 25th October 1742

SIR:
    I have already writt you of the 23d Current by this Conveyance of Capt. Walker to which please be Refferr'd, and he being still in the Road have sent you under his Care a Barrell of our Potatoes Mark't E which he has Promis'd to take great Care of and which you'll Please to make Acceptable and hope will come to hand in good Order. My Wife joins in best Respects to Self, Good Lady, and all the Pretty Family. I Remain &c.

At the same time writt the same to Mr. Thomas Hutchinson and sent him a Barell of Potatoes per Ditto.

ADDRESSED: "Per Ditto Walker" [Per the *Francis*, Capt. Richard Walker]

[504]
TO WILLIAM COOKSON & WILLIAM WELFITT
    Hull
                                Charles Town, 28th October 1742

GENTLEMEN:
    The Annexed on the other side of the 23d Current is Copie of my Last to which Refferrs, since have not the Pleasure of any of your Favour.

28th October 1742

This Serves to Convey you Copie of Invoice of One Case Quantity Sixty Seven peices Buckrams Shipt by your Directions & on your proper Risque & Account on board the Billander *Francis*, Capt. Richard Walker, for Boston in New England & to Mr. John Wheelwright, Merchant there, Consign'd which hope will goe Safe to hand & which have advis'd him to Dispose of to your best advantage, amount per Invoice being £53.1.1 Sterling. Youll please to Observe there is also annex'd to the Invoice the Charges attending same here amounting to £11.13.4 this Currency, for which have debit your Account.

As you Trade to Boston & you may sometimes be at a Loss how or in what manner to Order your Returns from thence or in what articles to be Shipt to your advantage, Am to advise you that Returns from N. England is very often made by way of this Place to Great Britain, & in particular in New England Rum, of which have had with in these four months past 100 hhds. which has answer'd very well, the Neat proceeds of which being Order'd to be Remitted to London, & that of Rum is the Only Article that Can Encourage to be Shipt from thence here as we have a Great Consumption of that Commodity.

Our New Rice is not Ready yet to Come to Markett & wont be for these three or four Weeks in any Quantity, so that there is as yet no talk of the Price nor how Freight is likely to govern. However am of Opinion that Rice must be Low this Crop as there is a Large Quantity produc'd, & if Rice & the Rate of Freights both happens to Come to your Limitation, shall take Care to follow your Orders in Relation thereto, which however is Uncertain.

I have not further to Offerr at present, but that I most Respectfully Remain &c.

ADDRESSED: "Per Capt. Boyes Via Cowes"

TO ANDREW LESSLY
Antigua

Charles Town, 12th November 1742

Sir:

My Last to you was of the 20th March per Capt. Gregory who stop'd at Barbados & Return'd here again. Since have Sundry of your most Esteem'd Favours, the Last of the 17th July per Capt. Breading with Copie thereof Conveying Bill of Lading & Invoices of Two Bales of Cinnamon on Account & Risque of the Owners of the *Loyall Judith* on Board said Breading, which happens to prove a very bad Commodity being Damag'd & Good for Little or Nothing, having open'd both the Bales & show'd it to Severalls who Distill here & are the only Persons that are Likely to buy such a Large Quantity, & who won't give any thing for it or buy any of it at any Rate. Therefore thought it most proper to Return it you per this first Opportunity of Capt. Murray, for provided it was good in Quality, such a Large Quantity Could not be Vended here for some years, there being best very Little us'd here & Generally Comes with other Spices in small Assortments which Come fresh [505] by Every Ship from London. I have sent with it the same Invoice you sent which please Receive Inclos'd & Bill of Lading for same, as also the same Certificate that Capt. Breading had, Certified here by our Collector, which have given to Capt. Murray for which I paid 15/ & for Wharfage & Porteridge 10/ is in all 25/.

If instead of the Cinnamon you had sent Rum, it would have sold off immediately at 22/6 per Gall. & I understand that it is not so high at Present with you being at 2/6 per Gall. & was at 3/6 per Gallon when you Shipt Last year per Gregory. We have a very Large Crop of Rice this year which will Occasion it to be Low in price, which happens well as we hear the Harvests are Large in Europe. I am most Respectfully &c.

P. S. I sent your Account Current per Capt. Gregory to Barbados which he told me was forwarded you from Thence. Sent him The prices of Goods.

ADDRESSED: "Per the Brigantine *Carolina,* Capt. John Murray, & Copie per Capt. Jefferies"

TO MICHAEL LOVELL
Antigua

Charles Town, 12th November 1742

SIR:

The Last I did my Self the Pleasure to write you was of the 20th March per Capt. Gregory who stop'd at Barbados, & Return'd here again, since have not any of your Favours.

In my Last I advis'd you that I would Ship your Silk Stuffs to Philadelphia per first Conveyance which I did accordingly in April Last to Mr. Attwood Shute as you Directed and at same time sent him Invoice of same, which doubt not he may have advis'd you of before this accordingly.

We have a Very Large Crop of Rice & other grain which will Occasion it to be Low in price, & hope it may be the same with you in your Island. The Prohibition on the Importation of Negroes still Continues & will so for Eighteen Months to Come. Rum & Muscovado Sugar always in good Demand there being a Large Consumption as under you have the prices of Goods. I have not further to Offerr at Present as being without any of your Favours & no Material News. Shall be allways very Glad to hear from you & to Render you any agreeable Service as being with Great Respect &c.

Rice 45/ per Ct., Pitch 45/ per bbl., Tarr 35/ per bbl., Exchange to London £700 per £100 Sterling, Corn & Pease 10/ per Bushell, Rum 22/6 per Gallon, Muscovado Sugar £10 per Ct., Madeira Wine £130 per Pipe & none Good.

ADDRESSED: "Per Capt. John Murray"

TO WILLIAM PRINGLE
Antigua

Charles Town, 12th November 1742

DEAR SIR:

My Last to you was of the 20th March per Capt. Gregory who stop'd at Barbados & Return'd here again, since have not the Pleasure of

17th November 1742

any of your Favours. Capt. Gregory told me that he forwarded my Letter from Barbados by a Sloop bound for your Island which hope you Receiv'd & hope this shall find you in perfect health which shall be Glad to be Inform'd of when ever it Suits your Conveniency.

We have a Large Crop of Rice this year & other Grain in proportion which will Occasion it to be Low in price & hope to hear your Crops are also in a Favourable Way with you. Rum & Muscovado Sugar are in Good Demand here, there being a Large Consumption for both as under you have the prices of Goods.

We have no Material News here at Present. You may perhaps have heard before this of the Spainards having made a Decent in Georgia in July Last with a Considerable Force which they soon Left again in a very pricepitate Manner, not without some Loss. I have not further to offerr at present as being without any of your Favours but that I most Respectfully Remain &c.

(The prices of Goods as above)

ADDRESSED: "Per Capt. John Murray"

[506]
TO THOMAS JOHNSON & SAMUEL CARTER
Barbados

Charles Town, 17th November 1742

GENTLEMEN:

I was Favour'd with a Letter from Mr. Gedney Clarke of the 29th August, advising that he had then taken his passage for London & was to Sail in Two Days, & that his Business would be Carried on in his absence by your Good Selves as well as if he was on the Spott, which I doe not in the Least Doubt of. I have taken the Opportunity to give a Return to his Letter to London where I hope it will find him happily Arriv'd. He Likewise advis'd me that he then Expected a Ship in Five Weeks from London in which he was one half Concern'd, & if there was no possibilaty of Getting her a Freight at Barbados, he Would order her here to me to be Dispatc'd Directly back again with Lumber, &c. Said Ship does not yet apper, but if She shoud Come here, you may Depend on her being Dispatc'd Directly back with a Cargoe of Good Lumber, &c. according to Mr. Clarke's Directions. As under you have the prices of goods. Shall be very glad to Receive your Commands, & to Render you any Agreeable Service here & I am with Great Respect &c.

P. S. We have a very Large Crop of Rice & other grain in proportion. Rice 45/ per Ct., Pitch 45/ per bbl., Tar 35/ per bbl., Corn & Pease 10/ per Bushell, Rum 22/6 per gallon, Muscovado Sugar £10 per Ct., Madeira Wine £130 per pipe & none Good at Present. Exchange to London £700 per £100 Sterling.

ADDRESSED: "Per Capt. Anderson & Copie per [*Blank*]"

TO DANIEL DUNBIBIN
Wilmington, North Carolina

Charles Town, 23rd November 1742

SIR:
I have your Favours three Days agoe of the 10th October in Return to mine of the 7th & 25th September with the Copie thereof, both by the Bearer, the Post, which Occasion'd Double Postage.

I am much oblidg'd to you for the Information you give in Relation to John Marshall. Shall send you a power of Attorney per next Conveyance, which I have not Time to doe by this. My Friend has his Bond for £100 Sterling which will admitt of no Dispute, & beleive he will not dissown the Debt, & am of Opinion with you, that doeing it in an amicable Way may be better than to Sue him, provided he Choses to doe it in that Manner. Shall take Care to advise my Freinds at Hull & Recommend you to them for a Correspondant & take Notice to them what you advise in Relation to Tar.

I have not heard any thing from Mr. Smalwood. Have given him Credit for his order on Benjamin Burleigh being for £65 Currency & he owes

30th November 1742

me the Ballance I advis'd of besides as will appear by his account which he has had Deliver'd him when here.

Shall be Glad to know when you take your Departure for the West Indies, & who has the Care of your Bussiness During your Absence. Capt. Murray sail'd a few days agoe for Antigua. He has not yet paid me for the Skins. He tells me that there is only Five pounds 10 shilling this Currency to Come to you for them, & expects to see you & pay you himself at Antigua, which is but a Trifle. I hope you will Receive the Money from Mr. Walker. I am &c.

ADDRESSED: "Per post"

TO JAMES HENDERSON
New York

Charles Town, 30th November 1742

SIR:
My Last to you was of the 19th June per my Freind Mr. James Home who is just Return'd here & who tells me that he had the Pleasure of but very Little of your good Company During his Stay at New York. I was in hopes to be Favour'd with a Line from you by him, or by some of the Late Conveyances from your port, but as yet have not the Pleasure of any of your Favours. Inclos'd Please Receive Account Sales of your Twenty One Boxes of Candles, Neat proceeds being £198.10/ this Currency which hope will be to Content. You have also Inclos'd your Account Current, Ballance in my Favour being £16.10.2 Currency which you'll please to Note accordingly.

I have at Last with much to Doe just Brought Mr. Bullock to Comply & Settle [507] the Account of Mr. Walter Henderson's Estate, Ballance as he says in his Hands being only £145.13.3 this Currency to Discharge your Debt, which I could not prevail with him to adjust & Settle till I made him Sensible that I was Determin'd to Sue him for Same, & for which Sum have been oblidg'd to take his note of Hand payable in Three Months, so that Reckoning our Exchange with your at 4½ per cent your Debt of £35.9.6 Is £159.12.9 this Currency, Our Exchange to London

30th November 1742

being at £700 per £100 Sterling, & by which you Come Short of your Debt £12.19.6 this Currency. Doe assure you I have been at no small pains to Serve you in this affair, having to Deal with a person whose Caracter here is Reckoned none of the Fairest.

We have a Large Crop of Rice & is Sold at present at 45/ per Ct., Freight to London at £3 per Ton. Shall be glad to have your Directions how the Money from Mr. Bullock is to be Apply'd when Receiv'd. I Desir'd the Favour in my Letter by Mr. Home that you woud be so good as to Send me Two Boxes of your Best Myrtle Wax Candles & Two Boxes of good Soap per first Conveyance here, being for my Own use, which I took the Freedom to doe as you were so good as to advise me that if I had Occasion for any Thing from your part you would send it & if you think proper to send them you may Depend on my Immediate Remitting for Same. Shou'd you want any thing from this or paying the Value to your Order, as under you have the Prices of Goods. I Salute you &c.

Rice 45/ per Ct., Pitch 45/ per bbl., Tar 35/ per bbl., Deer Skins 16/ per lb., Corn & Pease 10/ per bu., Rum W. India 22/6 per Gall., Madeira Wine £130 per pipe & none good, Flower £5 per Ct., Ship Bread £5 per Ct.

ADDRESSED: "Per Capt. Chapman"

Delivered Capt. Adam McDonald 1st December 1742

	Ster.
A Silk Crimson Collour'd Officers Sash Cost in London 3 Guineas	£ 3. 3.0
A Gilt Husk or Breast Plate Cost in London 15/ Sterling	15/
A Peice of very fine Holland No. 15 Containing 37 yds. Cost 7/ Sterling per yard	12.19.0
	£16.17

6th December 1742

TO ADAM MCDONALD
Charles Town

Charles Town, 1st December 1742

SIR:

Please receive the above Silk Sash, Husk, & a Peice of fine Holland the Cost of the Sash being 3 Guineas, the Husk 15/ Sterling, & the Price of the Holland Cost 7/ Sterling per yard, whish Desire you'll be so good as to dispose of to my best Advantage & rather than bring them back & not sell them, would have you lett them goe for the first Cost or under but Desire they may be Sold for Ready Cash otherwise to bring them back with you. I heartily Wish you a good Passage & Safe Return, & I am &c.

ADDRESSED: NO ADDRESS

[508]
TO ANDREW PRINGLE
London

Charles Town, 6th December 1742

SIR:

My Last to you was of the 22d October per the *Minerva*, Capt. Cload, with Copie to which please be Refferr'd, & Since have not the Pleasure of any of your Favours, neither has any Vessel arriv'd from London since Capt. Rodgers, tho one Capt. Stiles[8] from London is dayly expected Via Lisbon having put in there to Refitt. Your Ship *Susannah* is now half Loaded for London & has a Chance to be first Home with New Rice if the *Mercy*, Capt. Wright, does not gett before her. However will be the Second Ship, & if the Weather keeps fair & Rice Comes fast down to Town hope will Sail before Xmass. The price of New Rice has Broke at 45/ per Ct. Shall Ship One half of the *Susannah*'s Loading & Consign'd to your Self, the other half will be on Freight at £3 per Ton, & Could not gett higher. All the Shipping here are Engag'd at said Freight, but if Ship-

---

[8] Capt. Ephraim Styles arrived from London in the snow *Susanna*. His goods were advertised for sale by James Reid. *SCG*, 20 December 1742.

ping doe not Come In Towards the Spring Freight will be higher & So Consquently Rice Lower, as It entirely depend on Shipping, & hope your Ship from Jamaica will happen to fall in here very Luckily, if She Comes a Month or Two hence.

Youll Please therefore to gett Insur'd on Goods on Board your Ship *Susannah* from this to London, Vizt. £50 Sterling on Account the Invoice, Account Messrs. Honeyman, Sanders, & Pringle anno 1740 & £100 Sterling on Account Mr. Honeyman & your Self anno 1739 & £200 Sterling on Goods per the *Susannah* 1740 Invoice P. S. S. on Account Samuell Sanders & us each ⅓ as per Account Sales for the Whole which you may Expect per the *Susannah*. Please also to Insure £200 or £250 Sterling on Account of the Cargoe per the *John & Isabella* makes in all £550 or £600 Sterling. There is 150 BBls. of Pitch on board the *Susannah* for Flooring & Dunnidge.

About a Week agoe I Receiv'd a Letter of the 23d of October, New Style, by a Ship Charter'd from Lisbon from Messrs. Edward & John Mayne & Company advising that Rice was at 4,800 Reis per Quintal & that the first New Rice would answer Well & happening to have the Opportunity of Getting Freight for 100 Barrells on board a Vessel Loading for thence, have accordingly Shipt one hundred BBls. of New Rice in which I propose you to be one half Concern'd if you Think proper & to Messrs. Mayne Consign'd with Directions to Remitt the Neat proceeds to you by Bill of Exchange, & hope we shall make a Brave hitt of it as this will be the first Vessel there with New Rice, there being only another Small one that arriv'd from thence the other Day to be Loaded there & a small Brigantine of William Jolliffe's in Pool for Oporto.

Please therefore to Gett Insur'd on Goods on Board the Snow *Bremen Factor*, Capt. Thomas Tisehurst, Commander from this to Lisbon £180 Sterling & to receive £98 per Ct. in Case of a Loss. The Freight is at £3.5/ per Ton & part port Charges & if he had Demanded £4.5 per Ton he might have had it, as a Great many Wanted to Ship there but there are no Vessells that have a Licence. Perhaps I may be oblidg'd to Draw on you for Value of said 100 BBls. Rice, but hope not before you are in Cash for Same from Lisbon. The Vessel will sail in a Week or Ten Days hence, & please Inquire when you make said Insurance that said Vessell is not arriv'd at Lisbon before this advice which goes Via Bristoll. I thought it was pity to Let Slip the Opportunity of Embracing so good a prospect of advantage & one ought not to Loose in these Times Such good Hitts when they happen. I shall give a particular Caution to Messrs.

6th December 1742

Mayne against making bad Debts in the Sale, of which it is said here there are a Great many made on Rice at Lisbon & has happened to Mr. James Crokatt in particular. Our Friend Mr. James Home arriv'd here again, a few Days agoe from the Northward where he had been to See his Brother & I suppose will write you Soon. When he went I gave him a Letter [509] of Recommendation to Mr. James Henderson of New York & Mr. Home tells me that during his stay thereof Five Weeks Mr. Henderson never so much as ask'd him to Come to his House or to Drink a Glass of Wine with him.

I have Lately a Very pressing Letter for Remittance from Capt. Sanders of the 14th July Last & writ in a Stile that I did not Expect from him, wherein he seems to Complain of us both in Relation to Our Commission Charg'd wherein he is Concern'd with us & especially of my Commission of 12½ per cent as he makes it, & which he says both he & you thought too much & that you had promis'd him to mitigate it, tho doe assure him if he was to know the Trouble here in the Sale of Dry Goods, he would think it too Little, & did not Imagine, as he seems to profess a Sinceir Friendship for me, that he would desire me to Serve him for Less Commission then other people has here, & is Customary, 'tho at Same time he writes that he is very much oblidg'd to me for the Account Sales of Sundry things he left here with me on his Own Account & which he Says, notwithstanding the Comission Charg'd, is very much to his Satisfaction. I find as you likewise very well observe, there is no knowing a Great many People till they are try'd. He desires I should write to him to Cowes & not Via London which intend to Comply with the first Conveyance.

You may Expect all the Account Sales that are Compleated by the *Susannah* & your Account Current.

There is One Capt. James Wimble[9] here Commander of a Privateer Sloop nam'd the *Revenge* who fitted out from London in a Billander privateer of the same name, but Losst said Vessel amongst the Bahama Islands. He Once Came Consign'd to me Some years agoe & has bought goods of me, but his Money falling Short in fitting out his Vessel for another Cruize he has given me his Bills of Exchange for £74 Sterling on his Own Agent in London Lambert Ludlow, Esqr., Merchant in Crutched Fryars, & in case of his Death or that he does not honour them they are to be presented to Mr. Joseph Parker, Merchant near the Royall Ex-

[9] The exploits of Capt. James Wimble in the *Revenge* were recounted in SCG, 18, 25 October 1742.

6th December 1742

change, who is the companies Agent that are Concern'd in the privateer Sloop *Revenge*, but he has desir'd me to keep said Bills by me for three or Four Months before I forward them to London that in the Meantime he may perhaps Send in a Prize here & so Reimburse me, he having Appointed me his Attorney & Agent, & hope said Bills in case I am oblidg'd to make use of them by that Time will be Duely honour'd. Shall forward you one of his Letters of Advice to Said Gentleman per my Next. He tells me that he had the Pleasure of being accquainted with you when in London.

I hope your Goodness will excuse the trouble I give you of Delivering the Inclos'd Letter for Mr. Samuel Smith, Pewterer in Snow hill, by which you'll observe I am Drawn in & oblidg'd to pay a Debt of £93 Currency for his Wife's Brother one Edward Leapidge who Lately Came over with his Wife & Brought a Letter of Recommendation to me from him of which you have Inclos'd a Copie, being Contracter at his Lodgings which at his Request I Recommended him to & for which his Landlady & his Wife having no Money, & for which money Please Receive a Draft on Mr. Smith payable to yourself for £13.6 Sterling at the Current Exchange of £700 per £100 Sterling & am to begg you'll endeavour to Insists upon my paying & is about to Sue me for Same, the said Leapidge procure the Money of him as he cant in honour Let me Suffer for my Civility & Good Offices to his Kinsman & for the Respect & Regard I had for his Letter of Recommendation to his Friend, & I think my self in honour bound to see his Landlady paid as I Brought him a Stranger to her house. Persons in London ought to be Cautious who they Recommend here to their Freinds, they being often Lyable to Suffer thereby for their Civility & out of Respect to Their Freinds who Recommend them.

Shall Doe my self the Pleasure to writt you again soon by the Ship *Susannah* as I Beleive no Vessells will sail for London or Cowes before her & this goes Via Bristoll & hope will be in Time for the Insurances as already mention'd. My Wife joins in best Respects & having not further to Offerr at Present, I Remain &c.

ADDRESSED: "Per Capt. Smith Via Bristoll"

6th December 1742

[510]
TO SAMUEL SMITH
London

Charles Town, 6th December 1742

SIR:

I Receiv'd your Favours of the 12th June Last by your Brother in Law, Mr. Edward Leapidge, who as soon as he arriv'd here, Came to My House & Deliver'd me your Letter, & who I was very glad to See & told him I was very ready to doe him any Service here on your account, & being an Entire Stranger here, he desir'd I would Recommend him & his Spouse to Good Lodgings, which at his Request I did Accordingly to a Neighbour of mine where he & his Spouse Lodg'd & Boarded. Their Landlady (being a Widow Woman) Expected, as is Customary, that Mr. Leapidge would Settle & pay her for the Time of their being there, but to my Surprize he told her it seems that he would gett Money of me & pay her, he having No Money himself & knew no other person that he could apply to for Same. I told his Landlady that I had no particular Directions from you to Supply him with or advance any Money for him & that She must Expect the Money from himself, & I did not Imagine he would desire me to procure Good Lodgings for him, & at Same time was Conscious to himself that he was not in a Capacity to pay for them. However it Seems he has no money & Cannot pay his Landlady, So that she insists upon it, that I shall pay the Money for him as I Recommended him there, & can oblidge me to it. The Sum he Owes her is Ninty Three pounds this Currency or Thirteen pounds Six Shilling Sterling at the Current Exchange of £700 per £100 Sterling.

And as you are a Gentleman of Honour & Honesty, I make no Doubt you will pay the Money to the Bearer my Brother & his Receipt Shall be your Discharge according to My Draft I have given him on you for Same, & that you will not Lett me be a Sufferer for the Respect & Regard I had for your Letter & my Friendship & Good Offices to your Brother in Law, as I Cannot in Honour Lett his Landlady Sufferr, & She can oblidge me to pay it, as I brought him to her House, which I Expect to doe very soon. And in Expectation of your Compliamce I Remain &c.

ADDRESSED: "Under Cover of A.P. per Capt. Smith Via Bristoll"

13th December 1742

TO ANDREW PRINGLE
London

Charles Town, 13th December 1742

SIR:

The preceeding of the Sixth, i.e. 6th, is Copie of my Last Via Bristoll which this Serves to Confirm & this goes by the *Mercy*, Capt. Wright, who goes Sooner than I imagin'd being a Small Ship. Your Ship *Susannah* has 500 BBls. on Board & hope will be full in a few Days.

I Receiv'd a few Days agoe a Letter from Mr. Thomas Hutchinson & Co. of Boston with another Consignment of Rum, &c. wherein he advises that his Partner Mr. Thomas Goldthwait was to Sail from thence in Ten days from London & that he woud give him a Letter to you, having been accquainted with you in London, & Desir'd that I would Likewise write you of Same & Doubt not You'll be so good as to have a Due Regard to Said Letter, as they are Likely to prove very good Correspondants. Ships Come here Very Slowly & Freight will be high & Rice Lower if none Come Soon. Vessells to be Engag'd now might obtain £3.10/ per Ton for London. I hope your New Ship from Jamaica will happen to Come here from thence. We have Accounts that Admiral Vernon is Gone home. In haste I Remain &c.

ADDRESSED: "Per Capt. Wright"

[511]
TO EDWARD & JOHN MAYNE & EDWARD BURN
Lisbon

Charles Town, 13th December 1742

GENTLEMEN:

About three Weeks agoe have the pleasure of your most Esteem'd Favours of the 23d October per Capt. Young, & observing by yours that Rice had been sold with you at 4,800 reis per Quintal & that the first Cargoes of New Rice would answer well & happening to meet with some Freight in the first that Loaded with New Rice for your port would not

13th December 1742

omitt the opportunity of Embracing the Same. Please therefore Receive Inclos'd Bill of Loading & Invoice of One hundred Barrells of very good New Rice Ship'd on Board the Snow *Bremen Factor*, Capt. Thomas Tisehurst, Commander for Lisbon, On Account & Risque of my Brother Andrew Pringle & self Each One half Concern'd, Amount as per Invoice being £1,223.18.3 this Currency which You'll please Receive & dispose of to Our best Advantage, & as this is the first Vessel with New Rice, hope will come to Good Markett. And when in Cash for Same youll please to remitt the Neat proceeds by Bill of Exchange to my said Brother in London, having advis'd him thereof Accordingly.

I am to desire you'll be so Good as to pay Capt. Tisehurst the Freight & part of Port Charges as per Bill of Lading, as also the half Subsidy Duty due on the Rice in England. And as it is very good in Quality, as also the Casks, hope it will fetch the height of the Markett, but woud rather it should be sold for something under for Cash, thin to lett it lye on hand or to Run the Risque of any bad Debts, (by being sold on Credit) of which it is said here there are a Great many made in the Sale of Rice in your place, & which hope you'll have a particular Regard to.

We have a Large Crop of Rice this year, the New Rice broke in price at 45/ per Ct., but if a pretty many Vessells doe not come in here as usual & on which the price much Depends, it will be Lower. I was in hopes of having your Directions to Ship Some Rice for your Good selves, as you are the best Judges how the Marketts will Turn out with you, & shall be allways very Glad to Receive your Commands, as being most Respectfully &c.

P. S. From No. 51 to 80 is some of the Choicest Rice ever was Exported.

You'll please to Transmitt me Account Sales.
Exchange to London £700 per £100 Sterling. You have also 100 BBls. Rice per same Vessel Consign'd you, by Houghton, Webb, & Guyn.[1]

ADDRESSED: "Per the Snow *Bremen Factor*, Capt. Thomas Tisehurst"

---

[1] John Houghton, William Webb, and Gwyn. *HL*, I, 230n.

TO FLORENTIA COX
New Providence, Bahamas

Charles Town, 13th December 1742

SIR:

I am favour'd with yours of the 26th October in Return to mine per Capt. Marr[2] of the 18th September & observe that you have as yet sold but Seven of the Musketts, but that you were goeing to Harbour Island where you were in hopes to Sell some of them, & Doubt not of your Care to Dispose of them all, as Quick as you can & to the best Advantage. I am much oblidg'd to you for having them all Clean'd, they being very subject to take Rust in this Climate. Your Letter by Capt. Webster has not appear'd. Pray has Governour Tinker endeavour'd to assist in the Disposal of the Musketts. Please advise me. Shall be always very Glad to Render you any agreeable Service here & I am &c.

Rice New 45/ per Ct., Ditto old 35/ per Ct., Pitch 40/ per bbl., Tar 30/ per bbl., Corn & Pease 10/ per bu., Beef £7 per bbl, Rum W. India 22/6 per Gallon, ditto N. England 18/ per Gallon, Madeira Wine £130 per pipe & none Good, Brazilletto Wood in no Demand.

ADDRESSED: "Per Capt. Green"

TO JAMES HENDERSON
New York

Charles Town, 13th December 1742

SIR:

The preceeding of the 30th past is Copie of my Last per one Capt. Chapman[3] to which please be Refferr'd & about Ten days agoe have your Favours of the 30 September & 9th ulto. by the Bearer Capt. Schermer-

---

[2] Capt. Timothy Marr in the schooner *Nancy* departed to Providence, SCG, 20 September 1742.

[3] Capt. Thomas Chapman sailed for New York in the brigantine *Mary*. SCG, 6 December 1742.

14th December 1742

horn[4] by whom I Receiv'd the 2 Boxes of Bay Berry Candles, amount £4.2.6 your Currency for which have Credit your account accordingly, but think they Come dear as such candles can be made here Cheaper.

Yours that you mention of the 30th September with the Two Boxes of Soap under the Care of Mr. Thomas Baird, Surgeon of his Majesties Ship *Gosport*, has not appear'd & it is Conjectur'd said ship is gone for the West Indies. Please be Refferr'd to what I writt you in my Last in Relation to Mr. Walter Henderson's Estate & your debt as on the other side & having not further to offer at present, I Remain &c.

P. S. As the two Boxes of Soap are not Come, I have not now Occasion for any.

ADDRESSED: "Per Capt. Shermerhorn"

[512]
TO EDWARD & JOHN MAYNE & EDWARD BURN
Lisbon

Charles Town, 14th December 1742

GENTLEMEN:

Since Closing my Letter of yesterday here Inclos'd & to which please be Refferr'd, Capt. Tisehurst has had the Missfortune to fall off the Wharf where his Vessel lay & has broke his Leg which Render him incapable of proceeding the Voyage in the Vessel, So that his Mate George Edwards is appointed to take Charge, & to proceed as Master of the Vessel in his Room, which thought proper to advise you off, as the Bills of Loading are Sign'd by Capt. Tisehurst. I add not but that I am Most Respectfully &c.

& I desire that you'll please advise my Brother at the arrival of said Vessel.

ADDRESSED: "Per the Snow *Bremen Factor*, George Edwards Capt. Tisehurst his Mate"

[4] Capt. John Schermerhorn in the sloop *Mary* arrived from New York. SCG, 6 December 1742.

TO ANDREW PRINGLE
London

Charles Town, 17th December 1742

SIR:

I have already writt you of the 6th & 13th Current per this Conveyance of Capt. Wright who is on the Road & this Serves to advise you that to my very great Surprize Capt. Gregory tells me that your Ship *Susannah* is full & cannot take in any more by which means you are Shut out of 150 BBls. Rice having Shipt only 205 & I advis'd you that I woud ship one half of the Loading which is 350 Bbls. Rice & have been oblidg'd to Roll 59 Bbls. from his Ship's side & store it after it had Layen there 24 hours all mark'd & Number'd, & the Rest I Expect in Town this day or tomorrow which is a Great Disappointment & is Occasion'd entirely by Capt. Gregory's imprudence & Indiscration & Lys entirely at his door, he having always assur'd me that he Could take in 700 BBls. of Rice besides the 150 BBls. of Pitch, he having Carried before this in the *Susannah* 743 BBls. of Rice & he has now only 590 bbl. Rice & 150 bbls. Pitch. It's true he has taken on Board 15 hhds. Deer Skins & Some Madeira Plank on Freight, but he assur'd me that the skins & Plank would not Interferr with the Rice & would not obstruct or hinder One BBl. of Rice Less on Board, which it Seems has happen'd other ways, So that you have only him to Blame that you have not the Quantity that I have already advis'd & Desir'd you to make Insurance for, & now must be oblidg'd to Ship the 150 BBls. on board the Brigantine *Richard*, Capt. Samuel Hallen, Consign'd me from Boston by Messrs. Hutchinson & Goldthwaite with orders to lett her out on Freight for London if I could gett above £3 per Ton, & I am to have £3.12.6 per Ton for what I Let out, & belive Freight to London will soon be at £4 per Ton. So that you'll please to gett Insur'd 150 BBls. of Rice or £250 Sterling on Account of the Cargo per the *John & Isabella* on your & Mr. Sanders Account which I propos'd to Ship per the *Susannah* on said Brigantine.

I doe not advise this out of any ill Will or prejudice to Capt. Gregory but really think he has not acted for your Interest or had your Wellfare so much at Heart as he Ought. I ask't him again & again about the Ships Stowage & told him the Quantity I Intended to Ship you & he allways told me that he Could take it in, & in particular before I advis'd you of Insurance, & am of Opinion youll find his Management in Relation to your Ship will not merit your Approbation, & seems to make but very Light

17th December 1742

& not to Value your Employ by his Talk, as I am inform'd, & think it hard you Shoud now pay £3.12.6 per Ton Freight for your Rice, which might have Come in your Own Ship, which think the Difference he Ought to make good out of his Wages. Am of Opinion the Ship is not well stow'd. Shall Clear out the *Susannah* Tomorrow, & hope may be as soon as Capt. Wright if not before him & be the first Ship. In haste I Remain &c.

P. S. Please my humble Service to Mr. Thomas Goldthwaite, Mr. Hutchinson's Partner if arriv'd. I have not Time to write him.

The Brigantine *Richard* as mention'd, will be Loaded in 14 Days & goes Consign'd to her Owner Mr. Richard Partridge,[5] is a Single Deck'd Vessell. There is not at present Freight to be had for a BBl. of Rice in the Place, & it happens very Luckily to have this Brigantine otherwise your Rice must have Layen in Store.

ADDRESSED: "Per the *Mercy*, Capt. Wright"

[513]
TO JAMES SMALLWOOD
  Wilmington, North Carolina
          Charles Town, 17th December 1742
SIR:
  I have your Favours of the 2d Current. Mr. Burleigh paid me Sixty five pounds on your Account & there still remains a Ballance Due me of Thirty three pounds 10/Current Money, which hope you will Remitt me as Soon as it Suits your Conveniency or pay it to Mr. Daniel Dunbibin as I have already desir'd, & have given him an Order for Same. I hope you have now Surmounted all your Difficulties, & that Success attends all your undertakings, which shall be very Glad to be Inform'd of. My Wife Joyns in best Respect to your self & Mrs. Smallwood & I am &c.

ADDRESSED: "Per Dr. James Thompson"

---

[5] Richard Partridge was born in Portsmouth, New Hampshire. In 1715 he began a forty-four year career as agent for Rhode Island. His firm's address in 1744 was Water Lane, Tower Street, London. Ella Lonn, *The Colonial Agents of the Southern Colonies* (Chapel Hill, N. C., 1945), pp. 149, 294; *London Directories*.

20th December 1742

TO THOMAS GOLDTHWAIT
London

Charles Town, 20th December 1742

SIR:

I hope this will find you happily arriv'd in London after an agreeable passage from Boston, & which you will Receive at the Hands of my Brother who Doubt not will be very Glad to See you, & to Render you any agreeable Service there & to whose Good Offices have done my Self the Pleasure to Recommend you.

This Serves Cheifly to advise you that about Ten Days agoe have your & Partner Mr. Thomas Hutchinson's favours of the 9th November per the Brigantine *Richard*, Capt. Samuel Hallen, Commander from Boston, Covering Invoice & Bill of Lading for Sundry Merchandize Consign'd me on your account per said Vessel which have Receiv'd & Shall use my best Endeavours to Dispose of to your best advantage & punctually observe your Directions in Relation to Same. The Rum has Come ashoar, Some of it in very Indifferent order, oweing to the Badness of the Casks they being but in very Ordinary Condition & not Tight, which will Occasion a pretty deal of Leakage on them, & there being advice Come here of a Large Quantity intended this Way which is all make it Sell very heavily, People being in Expectation on that Account of having it Very Cheap.

You have Directed me to Let out the said Brigantine *Richard* on Freight Wholly, provided I can procure Freight with dispatch about £3 Sterling per ton for London & to keep your Effects for a Small Vessel you have Comeing hereafter. And I have Let out the Said Brig on Freight accordingly having obtain'd £3.12.6 Sterling per Ton for London & will be Loaded in Fourteen Days hence with Rice if the Weather Continues Fair, & which I have not yet had the opportunity to advise Mr. Thomas Hutchinson of, there being no Conveyance Since for the Northward.[6] Shall be very Glad to have the Pleasure of a Line from you from London & I am Most Respectfully &c.

ADDRESSED: "Per the *Susannah*, Capt. William Gregory, Under Cover of A.P."

---

[6] The brigantine *Richard*, Samuel Hallen, for London. SCG, 20 January 1743.

17th December 1742

TO RICHARD PARTRIDGE
London

Charles Town, 20th December 1742

SIR:

The Brigantine *Richard*, Capt. Samuel Hallin, Commander from Boston being arriv'd here about Ten Days agoe Address'd to me by Mr. Thomas Hutchinson & Co. of Boston with Directions that provided I could procure Freight for Said Vessel above £3 per Ton for London to Lett her out Wholly on Freight & which I have done accordingly, having obtain'd £3.12.6 Sterling per Ton & will be Loaded in fourteen Days hence with Rice if the Weather Continures fair, which I thought proper to advise you of as I understand you are part Concern'd in the Vessel & Goes to your address. Shall be very Glad to Render you any agreeable Service here & I am &c.

ADDRESSED: "Per the *Susannah*, Capt. Gregory, & Copie per Capt. Vaughan"

TO WILLIAM DOVER
London

Charles Town, 17th December 1742

SIR:

I have your Favours of the 9th of August & Copie thereof in Return to mine of the 10th of April & observe the Contents. This Goes by Capt. Gregory & Serves to advise you that I had sold your Two Chests of Indian Trading Guns to the Indian Traders (before I Receiv'd yours) & payable in May next, they having sufferr'd with the Rust by Lying so Long here, & which affects any Kind of Iron Ware, much more in this Climate than in Europe, & would have been Spoilt if they had Layen much Longer. As for the Six pair of Pistols they are all yet unsold excepting one pair, & am Reckon'd very high Charg'd. However you may Depend on my best Endeavours to Dispose of them to your best Advantage & as Quick as I can, & when sold you may expect Account Sales of the Whole,

17th December 1742

& Shall Take care to Remitt the Neat proceeds when in Cash, either in Rice or Skins as you Direct & which of the Two may Judge most for your Interest. I salute you and am &c.

ADDRESSED: "Per the *Susannah,* Capt. Gregory, & Copie per Capt. Vaughan"

[514]
TO ANDREW PRINGLE
London

Charles Town, 22nd December 1742

SIR:

My Last to you was of the 17th Current per Capt. Wright who Sail'd over the Bar the 18, & am without any of your Favours Since yours of the 25th August. This per your Ship *Susannah* & Inclos'd please Receive Bill of Lading & Invoice of Two Hundred & Eighteen Barrells of Rice & One hundred & Fifty Barrells of Pitch Ship't on board said Ship on Account & Risque as per the Severall Invoices & to your Self Consign'd, Amount of the whole being £3,083.9.6 this Currency, Exchange at £700 per £100 Sterling, which wish safe to hand & to a Good Market. Please also Receive Inclos'd a Manefest of the Cargoe and bounty Certificate for the Pitch. Since mine of the 17 Current, Capt. Gregory has thought fitt to take on board Thirteen BBls. more of your Rice, besides Fifteen more Shipt by Hopton & Smith.[7]

You have herewith Inclos'd the Severall Account Sales of all the Sundry parcells of Goods whose Sales are Compleated being in Number Twelve Separate accounts which hope you'll find Right & to Content. Have likewise sent you Inclos'd your Account Current, Ballance in my Favour as it now stands with me being £1,855.6.9 this Currency, (the Current Exchange being at £700 per £100 Sterling) which hope youll find Right. However if there should be any Errors or Omissions on either side Youll please to Remark same & advise thereof, that they be Rectified accordingly

[7] William Hopton, Charleston merchant, was appointed vendue master by Governor Glen in 1748 and 1749. Thomas Smith of Broad Street was so called to distinguish him from Thomas Smith, Sr., "on the Bay." *HL,* I, 102n, 119n, 96n.

22nd December 1742

& Transmitt me an account of what payments you have been so good to make on my account. You'll please to observe that I have not given you Credit in Account Current for Neat proceeds of your Thirty BBls. Gun powder per Trimble from Lisbon, it being still all Outstanding. The Indian Traders to whom I sold it Complain very much of the Badness of it & Decline paying for it, as insisting on an Abatment in the price, & by which I have gott much discredit from them. It is Certain Messrs. Mayne did not use you well by Shipping Such bad Powder if they knew it, & have not time at present to Transmitt you Account Sales of the *Susannah*'s Cargoe of Rum, &c. from Barbados which you may expect per my Next. It is all sold, but the Money not yet Receiv'd. Capt. Gregory Receiv'd all the Money himself for what Goods came on Freight in the Ship *Susannah* from Barbados & for which doubt not he will Account to you for.

Please to Take Notice I have Debit your Account Current Blank at the Bottom, for My ½ Neat proceeds of Rice On Our Joint Account per Greig June 1740, & for my ½ Neat proceeds of 40 BBls. Rice & some Ambergreese per the *Susannah* in October 1740, the Account Sales of both which you have hitherto Omitted to Transmitt me. I have Inclos'd sent you Thomas Gould the late Banker his Note of Hand for Five pounds Sterling. Please be so Good as to inquire for him & Learn if there is any prospect of Receiving it of him. I have also Inclos'd you Capt. James Wimble's Letter of Advice of his Bill on his own private Agent, as he Calls him, Lambert Ludlow, Esqr. for £75 Sterling in my favour as Advis'd you in One of my former, which after perusal please to Seal & Deliver him, & advise me if said Bill will be duely Honour'd in Case I should make use of it & forward it to you three or Four Months hence. As also you have my Letter to Mr. Thomas Goldthwait, Mr. Hutchinson of Boston's Partner, who I advis'd you of in my Former, & which after perusal you'll please also to Seal & Deliver him.

I am to begg the Favour you'll be so good as to pay Capt. Ayers One hundred pounds Sterling on my Account if it does Suit you. He keeps dunning of me by Letters Since he went from this, being for £1,000 this Currency he Left in my hands, & desir'd I would put out at Interest for him which the Person I Lent it to has not yet paid me, as he Expected the Lend of it for at Least Two or three years Time, & I am answerable to Ayers for it. The Ballance of Account Due him is about £100 Sterling or a Little more having Remitted him £25 Sterling per Bill by Capt. Beach in September Last.

I am also to Accquaint you, that belive must be oblidg'd to take the Liberty to Draw on you for £100 Sterling to Messrs. Bourryau & Schaffer on Account of Mr. Thomas Hutchinson of Boston & which is all I shall Trouble you for or to be in advance for me, & which will not be Long as I hope it [515] will soon be in my power to Reimburce you & to Remitt you Considerably this Season.

In case Samuel Smith the Pewterer Refuses to pay the order I have Sent you for £13.6 Sterling that I am to pay for his Brother in Law, Edward Leapidge, I am to beg the Favour, You'll please to Apply to his Own Brother John Leapidge who I am inform'd is a Stationar near the Royall Exchange, or to take it in Stationary in his Way, or in Pewter of Samuel Smith.

There is a Rumour here that Colonel Cook[8] lately gone home from this is made Governour of this Province & that Our Governour Mr. Glen is made Governour of Jamaica.

Inclos'd you have an Order I have had of One Samuel Perkins here a Chaise Maker,[9] who has very good Business & for which he agrees to give £10 Currency for £1 Sterling, which doubt not youll think worth while to Send, & which you'll please to forward per first. They are to be bought at the first hands of the Coach Founders.

I have Deliver'd the Frames &c. to the Painter according to Agreement & you may expect the Money for same Remitted you very Quickly. Let the Chaise furniture be a particular Invoice by it self & on which you are to Charge Insurance, Comission, & all other Charges. I find it a much better way to have Goods over by particular Order, or to sell them before hand at a price Certain (if I could have orders enough) than to Import them for Chance Sale.

As I am Uncertain if my affairs will permitt me to Goe to London this next year, especially if a French War happens, I have sent you Inclos'd an Assortment of Goods, Books, Prints, Plans, &c., & Silver Plate for Sale, which believe will turn out to Good Account here & meet with a Quick Sale, & which if you think proper to send on our Joint Account as Soon as you Can, Doubt not making Returns for the Whole next Crop. You'll observe there is but a Small Assortment of each article & you may pick out of it & send what you judge may be most proper that the Whole may be

---

[8] On 30 November 1739, William Cook was commissioned a lieutenant colonel in Oglethorpe's Regiment. *SCHM*, XXXIII (1932), 189.
[9] Samuel Perkins, coachmaker, died 14 April 1764 at the age of sixty-two. *SCHM*, X (1909), 161.

22nd December 1742

to the sum of £500 or £600 Sterling, but am to desire the Assortment of Books, Prints, Plans, &c. may be sent, Some of them being already bespoke, & please to Let every thing be well pack'd at put up & Exactly Mark'd & Number'd, & hope may be here in April or in May.

I had some Ground to think that Messrs. Steil & Hume wou'd have Consign'd you the 200 barrells Rice they have Shipt in the *Susannah*. Inclos'd please likewise Receive the Account of the Ship's Disbursements here & Capt. Gregory's Receipt for Money paid him, amount of the Whole being £1,554.1.6 this Currency which have plac'd to your Account Current accordingly. I don't know how Capt. Gregory has Manag'd it, but youll please to Observe that Tradsmens Bills Run very high, & as the Ship was goeing home, I Told him to put the Ship to as little Charge as Possible, but he did not think proper to accquaint or Consult me about his Tradsmen or any thing he bought or had Occasion for, but only Drew orders on me for to pay them or Demanded the Money to pay them himself. I have not been able to dispose of the Negro Boy Capt. Gregory brought over till the other Day I sold him for £160 Currency but am oblidg'd to give some time for the payment. The Wind is now very fair & hope Capt. Gregory will gett ready to embrace it, & may perhaps gett home as Soon as Capt. Wright if not before, which I heartily Wish. My Wife joyns with me in Wishing you a Merry Christmass & a Great many happy years & I Remain &c.

I am to Desire the Favour you'll be so good as to Send me the following small things for my Own use which are not to be bought here. Vizt. Six pair of Brass handles for Desks, chests of Drawers, or Scrutors to put on the Ends or Sides of them to Carry or Move them by from One place to the other of a Middling Size, Three pair Larger than the other three pair, Some being for the Top part & the other the Bottom part & Brass plates & Screws to put them on; Two handsome Locks & Keys & Two pair Brass hinges for a Mahogoney Chest; [516] One Brass Horizontal Dial for this Latitude about 9 or 10 Inches Diamater to fix on a post; One Verticle Dial for this Latitude with Two Sides to fix on the Corner or End of a House with the Letters RP: 1743 on it & a Motto or Divice in English, Vizt. this Words (about your Bussiness) or any other proper Divice for a Dial. A Square Hewen Stone of about 18 Inches Square for to Fix in the front of a House with the Letters RP: 1741 Cutt upon it & the Letters rais'd on the Stone & not Cutt in the Stone, the Same as if stampt on put on the Stone which Lasts much Longer then Cutt in the Stone; You Can have it at the

22nd December 1742

Stone Cutters. Six Tinn Dish Covers of three Different Sizes & two of each Size.[1]

P.S. My Wife has given Capt. Gregory a Silk Gown to gett Dyed which am to begg the Favour youll please to take from him & gett Dyed according to the directions given him & send it at your Conveniency.

ADDRESSED: "Per the *Susannah*, Capt. William Gregory, & Copie per Capt. Vaughan"

TO BURRYAU & SCHAFFER
London

Charles Town, 29th December 1742

GENTLEMEN:

My Friend Mr. Thomas Hutchinson of Boston in N. England has lately Shipt me Some Effects with Directions to Remitt the Neat proceeds to your Good Selvs. Youll please therefore to Gett Insur'd on Goods per the Brigantine *Richard*, Capt. Samuel Hallen, Commander from this for London Three hundred & Fifty pounds Sterling on his proper Risque & Account. The Vessell will be ready to Sail in fourteen Days hence, is a Stout New Vessell & by which I shall doe my Self the pleasure to Transmitt you Invoice & Bill of Lading for Same, & as opportunity offers you may Expect further Remittance Soon on Said Gentleman's Account. If I can be Serviceable here many Respect You'll please to Command &c.

ADDRESSED: "Per the *Susannah*, Capt. William Gregory, & Copie per Capt. Vaughan"

---

[1] The house was built on Tradd Street on portions of town lots number 87 and 88 which had been conveyed to Jane Allen Pringle and her husband by Andrew Allen. In 1774 RP built what is now known as the Judge Robert Pringle House next to the earlier three story brick residence which later was converted into law offices for John Julius Pringle. This first dwelling remained standing until the early twentieth century. Smith & Smith, p. 104.

31st December 1742

TO ANDREW PRINGLE
London

Charles Town, 31st December 1742

SIR:

I desire to be Refferr'd to what I have already writt you of the 22d Current per this Conveyance of your Ship *Susannah* which has been Clear'd out Since the 20th, & fair Winds ever Since but Capt. Gregory has been detain'd as he tells me purely for want of Hands, & is oblidg'd to goe at Last Weak handed, having two Less than his Compliment, besides Two Spainards. You'll observe the Ship's Outsett is again very high & think some money might have been Sav'd if Rightly Manag'd, but Capt. Gregory never Consulted nor advis'd with me about any thing he Wanted, but always bought of him self & Drew Orders on me for the Money, 'tho I apprehended you gave him Directions to advise with & apply to me first for any thing he Wanted. However you will be the best Judge of his Conduct & how he has Manag'd for the Ship when you Come to Settle with him. The Ship *Susannah* is old & will always want Large Repairs, & you will now best know whether it will be for your Interest to keep her any Longer or Sell her.

I Desir'd you in mine of the 17 Current to make Insurance for £250 Sterling for Goods on board the Brigantine *Richard*, Capt. Samuel Hallen, for London, on Account the Goods Shipt per the *John & Isabella*, Capt. Warden, Consign'd to your [517] Self & which I now Conferm. The Vessel will be ready to Sail in Ten Days & goes Consign'd to Mr. Richard Partridge. I was in hopes the *Susannah* might be the first for London, but there are two already Sail'd Over the Bar for London, Vizt. Capt. Wright & Commerford[2] & One Capt. Rodgers for Cowes.

No Vessell as yet appear from London, and am as yet without any of your Favours Since yours of the 25 August. Your Ship gone to Jamaica would now fall in very Luckily, no Vessels arriving so that Freight to London is at £3.15 per Ton & Rice fallen to 40/ per Ct. We have no Good Madeira Wine in the place. Some that Messrs. Stead & Evance have & very bad is Sold at £130 per pipe. If Capt. Patten is Coming with Wines he will Come very luckily if he happens to be the first. A Considerable Quantity of Rum has Come in all together from Barbados, which has Lowr'd the price from 22/6 to 20/ per Gall.

---

[2] Capt. James Commerford sailed in the ship *Success* to Falmouth. SCG, 20 December 1742.

31st December 1742

The Wind being N. W. Capt. Gregory is just agoeing Down in Order to Sail the Ship being in the Road, & hope will Soon be with you So that I add not at Present, but that I Remain in haste.

ADDRESSED: "Per the *Susannah*, Capt. William Gregory, & Copie per Capt. Vaughan"

TO EDWARD & JOHN MAYNE & EDWARD BURN
Lisbon

Charles Town, 3rd January 1742 [1743]

GENTLEMEN:

The preceeding of the 13th & 14th Ulto. is Copie of what I had the pleasure to write you per the Snow *Bremen Factor* which sail'd over the Barr about a fortnight agoe, & this per Capt. Young[3] & Serves to Convey you Copie of Invoice & Bill of Loading for the 100 bbls. of Rice on board said Snow, which hope will Come safe to hand before you Receive this. There is not another Vessell here at present for Portugal besides Capt. Young, or that has a Licence,[4] so that it is Likely to be some time before you can have any more Rice from this place. The price is now at 40/ per Ct. No Material News here at present. I Salute you with the Usual Compliments of the Season & I am &c.

ADDRESSED: "Per Capt. Young"

TO ANDREW PRINGLE
London

Charles Town, 7th January 1742 [1743]

SIR:

I Refferr you to what I have already writt you of the 22d & 31st Ulto. per your Ship *Susannah* which is still Detain'd in the Road by Southerly

---

[3] Capt. Robert Young in the ship *Young Green* departed to Lisbon. SCG, 3 January 1743.

[4] It was necessary to bring a license out from England in order to ship rice directly to a port south of Cape Finisterre.

7th January 1743

Winds & gives me the opportunity of this having lost the advantage of fine Northerly Winds a Week agoe. Have sent Copie of mine per the *Susannah* by Capt. Vaughan[5] who is now also in the Road for London, also Copie of all the account Sales, your Account Current, & Invoices. You'll please to Credit me 45/ Currency for hire of a Boat & Hands which was oblidg'd to send to the Road to Capt. Gregory Express to inform him before hand of the Man of War's Boat Goeing down to take out some of their People they had gott Information that Capt. Gregory had on board, & in Order to Sue him for Same.[6] I desir'd Cap. Gregory to pay it, & so Charg'd it, which he Refus'd.

I am under some apprehension that the Bills I have gott from Capt. Wimble on Lambert Ludlow, as I advis'd you of, won't meet with honour. In Case he don't take them up here, I must be oblidg'd to forward them. Please to advise me about it, & if you can put me in any Way to be Secure, or Can gett the Money Secur'd in London.

I am to Desire the favour you'll please to buy & send me with the other small things for myself, One dozen or one doz. & a half of Ivory handled Knives, & 1 Doz. or 1½ doz. Forks London make, Strong & fashionable in a Case being for my own use. What they send over her for Sale is poor Stuff. Also a Compleat Sett of Enamell'd China a pretty good sort.

Please Receive Inclos'd a Letter & power of attorney to your self, from Mr. Feild Cossett[7] in order to dispose of a House in Church Street Rotherheth, that Comes to him by the Will of his God Father Capt. John Field Deceas'd. He has show'd me Severall Letters (from his [518] Father John Cossett a poor Man, who Lives at the Charity House in Rotherheth for whom you have Inclos'd a Letter from him, which after perusal please to seal & Deliver him) in Relation to said House, & desiring him to send a power of Attorney to some person to take possession of the House for him, which youll observe he desires you to doe, & if you find it So as he says that the House belongs to him by said will, you'll please to dispose of it accord-

---

[5] Capt. Francis Vaughn of the ship *Hannah-Bella* sailed to London. SCG, 3 January 1743.

[6] Capt. Charles Hardy, commander of HMS *Rye*, advertised that eight men had deserted his ship at Hobcow in South Carolina. He gave notice to merchant ship captains that under the provisions of "An Act for the Encouragement of the Trade to America" a captain could be fined £20 Sterling for every deserter from the Royal Navy that he signed on board his ship. SCG, 27 December 1742; Danby Pickering, *The Statutes at Large*, vol. XI: *From the Second to the Eighth Year of Queen Anne* (Cambridge, Eng., 1764), 439.

[7] Field Cossett in the schooner *Sea Flower* arrived from and returned to Frederica. SCG, 6 May, 1 June 1745.

ingly for him for what ever it will fetch & he will Readily allow Commission & all Charges you may be at therein, & please to advise me about it, & if you Sell it & Receive the Money, Send me the Account that I may pay him the neat proceeds in Currency here, of which some part will be in Goods. He is a person that has us'd the Sea, & but in Low Circumstances here, being only in the Station of an Overseer & has a Wife & Family. You'll please to advise when you Receive Said power of Attorney if it is sufficient for you to take Possession of the House & Dispose of it for him, with out any other papers from him or Title.

The Brigantine *Richard*, Capt. Hallen, will sail in Ten or Fourteen days & by whom may expect to hear from me, So that I add not at present, as being Still without any of your Favours & Remain &c.

ADDRESSED: "Per Capt. Gregory & Copie per Capt. Vaughan"

TO PETER WESTERMAN
    Barbados

Charles Town, 7th January 1742 [1743]

SIR:

I have your favours of the 6th December Inclosing second Bill of Loading & Invoice, for four Tierces & three Barrells Rum Shipt me by the Bearer Capt. Boaz Bell on Board his Sloop *Endeavour*, which came safe to hand. I am much Oblidg'd to you for your Kind Offers of Service, and am Reciprochally to make you a Tender of mine, and to Assure you that I shall be always very glad to Render you any Agreeable Service. I am to Desire the Favour you'll Please be so good, as to use your good Offices with Mr. Daniel More in behalf of my Wifes Brother Mr. John Allen, who has lately been Oblidg'd to Trouble you with a Letter of Attorney by the Bearer Capt. Boaz Bell to bring him to Account and to pay the Ballance due to my Wifes Fathers Estate which he has kept now so many Years in his hands, and made no manner of Remittance in which think he has not acted with Honour and in doeing of which you will much Oblidge &c.

Rice new 40/ per Ct., Ditto old 30/ per Ct., Corn 10/ per Bushell, Pease Ditto, Pitch 40/ per BBl., Tar 35/ per BBl., Rum 22/6 & Falling, Mus-

7th January 1743

covado Sugar £10 per Ct., Madeira Wine £125 per pipe, Exchange to London £700 per £100 Sterling.

ADDRESSED: "Per Capt. Boaz Bell"

[519]
TO THOMAS JOHNSON & SAMUEL CARTER
Barbados
Charles Town, 7th January 1742 [1743]

GENTLEMEN:

I did myself the Pleasure to write you of the 17th November and on the 25th Ditto have your Favours per Capt. Sharnell Gravener of the Ship *Lusitania* with Invoice and Bill of Loading for Twenty Hhds. of Rum & fifteen Barrells of Sugar on the Owners Account which I have Receiv'd, also Account Current & Invoice, with Bill of Loading for Two hhds. Rum and two BBls. Sugar which Closes the Account per Gregory. In the Account Sales of said Cargoe, there are 400 hoop Poles, & Two BBls. of Tar not accounted for, their being 18 Barrels Deliver'd as per Receipt & the Tann'd Leather has fallen 45 lb. short of the Weight.

I have also a few Days agoe your Favours of the 7th Ulto. with Duplicate thereof and Duely Remark the Contents.

Capt. Gravener is gone up the River with his Ship and is takeing in his Cargoe of Lumber, and hope will have all in in ten or fourteen days hence. I am to take notice to you that a Ship to Loaded with Lumber cannot be Dispatch'd immediately or so soon as with any other Goods, as the Timber is all to be Cutt after the Ship Arrives, which take up a Considerable time before it can be taken on Board, especially such large Timber as the *Lusitania*'s Cargoe will be. However, Capt. Gravener will have all the Dispatch that the Nature of Loading will admit of, as he will be able to informe you of at his arrival and hope will be in very good time for the Crop.

I observe you order the Surplus more than the Lumber to be Shipt the one half in Rice & the other half in Corn, which shall take care to doe as you Direct Accordingly, provided the *Lusitania* can take it on Board and

7th January 1743

the price of Rice comes to be under 40/ per Ct. & Corn under 10/ per Bushell this Currency, According to your Limitation before the *Lusitania* goes. It being at present, New Rice at 40/ per Ct. and Corn at 10/ per Bushell and not under, otherwise you may expect some by the first Opportunity that Offers after.

Mr. Gedney Clark in his Letter did not order any thing to be Shipt on Board the *Lusitania* on his Account besides Lumber and to take as much Rice, &c. as I could get on Freight. But no Freight worth while seeming to Offer, I Agreed for as much Large Square Timber, before yours came to hand, as I believe will fitt the *Lusitania* pretty near.

About Fourteen Hundred Hhds. of Rum and upwards has been Imported here since August last, and a great deal of it from New England and your Island, especially since Capt. Graveners arrival, which makes it sell very heavilly, more than half of the *Lusitania*'s being yet unsold. However what I have sold has been at 22/6 per Gall. but am affraid shall not be able to Obtain so much for the Rest, as it falls in price by reason of the very large Quantity lately Imported and Continueing to come in dayly.

Please Receive inclos'd a Certificate for the Sugar per Capt. Gregory in order to Clear his Bond.

It is pity that Mr. Clarke did not give Discretionary orders in Relation to the *Lusitania* in case a good Freight offer'd here for London. Capt. [520] Gravener could now be Loaded at £4 per Ton for London with very good Dispatch and might still be back in time for your Crop. I shall have Occasion to write you again very soon. I therefore add not at Present but that I am most Respectfully &c.

Yours inclos'd for Capt. Gravener has been Deliver'd him.

ADDRESSED: "Per Capt. Boaz Bell"

8th January 1743

TO ANDREW PRINGLE
London

Charles Town, 8th January 1742 [1743]

SIR:

    I writ you yesterday per Capt. Gregory, also Duplicate thereof per Capt. Vaughan to which Crave Reffrence, and they being still in the Road have the Opportunity to Accknowledge the Receipt this moment of your most Acceptable Favours of the 5th, 12th, & 18th of October per Mr. Bowman in Capt. Scott,[8] and duely Remark the Contents.

    I am much surprized at what you writ me in Relation to Capt. Sanders. It is well we have Effects of him in our hands, and you may Depend on all the Returns being Consign'd to you, which I was Determin'd to doe, If I had not Receiv'd this very timely & Lucky Advice, happen what will as you'll observe I have already done in what have sent, & your Letter has come in good time to prevent my Shipping him about £50 Sterling In a hhd. of Skins which he desir'd me to Ship to Cowes to the Care of George MacKenzie, it being the Ballance of Account of some things he Left in my hands when here. Which shall now stop & keep for you, neither shall I write to him to Cowes as he Desir'd me, or take any further Notice of him but Shall Punctually observe your Directions in Relation to him, & hope you'll be able to bring him to Reason & its very well that I have not writ any thing to him about your Concerns with him, as he Desired me to Cowes Directly. It is pity you sent the four hhds. Deer Skins to him as he writes me you did that I Remitted & were sold there at 2/10 per lb. Round. I have been greatly Deceiv'd in him as well as you. Mr. Bowman tells me that Mr. Reid arrived in the Downs while he Lay there, but had mett with much bad weather. We have Account that Capt. Beach from this is taken in his Passage. I Ship'd the Ballance of Captain Bells Account in Rice by him & had not the Opportunity, by Reason of the Embargo, to give Advice for Insurance. In hast I remain &c.

At Nine o Clock in the Evening.

ADDRESSED: "Per Capt. Vaughan"

---

[8] Capt. Patrick Scott in the ship *Charming Susan* arrived from London. SCG, 10 January 1743.

[521]
TO JAMES MAINTRU & CO.
London

Charles Town, 6th January 1742 [1743]

GENTLEMEN:

I have your Favours of the 30th June in return to mine of the 20th February and duely Remark the Contents. I imagin'd that Gentlemen of your Consequence in the Trade of this Province were better Accquainted with the Affairs thereof than not to know that no Person that were Sufferrs by the Fire in this Town are entitled to any of the Money given by the Parliament, excepting the Sufferrers that are Inhabitants of this Town, and them only.[9] For your better information I Refferr you to the Agent for this Province, Peregrine Fury, Esqr.

I have not as yet been able to recover any of the Outstanding Debts on your Sundrie Account Sales, but as soon as I doe, or any part thereof, you may expect Returns for same accordingly. I am &c.

ADDRESSED: "Per Capt. Story & Copie Per Capt. Vaughan"

TO CHARLES & EDMOND BOEHM
London

Charles Town, 7th January 1742 [1743]

GENTLEMEN:

I have the Pleasure of your most Esteem'd Favours of the 1st June in Return to mine of the 4th March and duely Remark the Contents. I am to Advise you that I have not as yet Recover'd any of the Outstanding Debts on your Linnens, but am in hopes of Receiving a considerable part

---

[9] Other American colonials contributed £7,094 sterling in cash and provisions and Parliament contributed £20,000 for the relief of the sufferers of the Charleston fire. A committee headed by Chief Justice Whitaker was appointed to distribute the relief exactly in proportion to losses. RP's loss was set at £3,043.8.6 for which he received £45.0.4⅗ sterling from American contributions and £140 sterling from the Parliamentary grant. Wallace, I, 402; Council Journal Number 8 (15 March 1742–19 February 1743), 74, 386, S. C. Archives; Kenneth Scott, "Sufferers in the Charleston Fire of 1740," *SCHM*, LXIV (1963), 203–211.

this Crop, & as soon as I doe, you may expect immediate Returns for same in whatever may judge most for your Advantage, & duely Advise you thereof. Shall be always very glad to Render you any agreeable Service, and I Remain most Respectfully &c.

ADDRESSED: "Per Capt. Story & Copie per Capt. Vaughan"

TO ANDREW PRINGLE
London

Charles Town, 10th January 1742 [1743]

SIR:

The preceeding on the other side is Copie of what I writt you of the 8th Current & the Vessells in the Road being still detain'd by bad Weather, as it Rains & Blows very hard at North East, gives me this further opportunity that the *St. Andrew*, Capt. Steadman,[1] is also arriv'd in the Road from Cowes in which has Come passangers Mr. Houghton & his Wife[2] & Dr. John Maubray,[3] who tells me they had the Pleasure of seeing you just before they Left London, & by whom was in hopes of hearing from you, but find they bring me none of your Favours. They have been but Six weeks in their passage.

I sent you Two Letters of Attorney with two Fire Ticketts from John Keys & John Fairchild by Capt. Beach, who we have Account by the *St. Andrew*, was taken & Carried into Brest, but as I sent the Duplicates by Mr. Reid who is arriv'd hope it will be the Same thing.

I Refferr you to what Mr. Inglis[4] writes you herewith Inclos'd in Relation to what Mr. Sanders told Capt. Warden when he was at London & which Capt. Warden Related to Mr. Inglis in the passage here for your Government, & which you make your own use of which think was base, Mean, & Ungenerous in Sanders, & at sametime he gives Warden a Very

---

[1] RP had been misinformed as to the name of the *St. Andrew's* captain. The ship *St. Andrew*, Capt. Robert Brown arrived from Cowes. SCG, 17 January 1743.

[2] Mrs. John Houghton was the former Mary Sheppard. They were married on 31 August 1738, and she died late in 1744. HL, I, 17n.

[3] This is undoubtedly a slip of the pen. There is no record of a Dr. John Mowbray, but there was a Dr. Arthur Mowbray who arrived passenger in the *St. Andrew*. RPC, p. 604.

[4] George Inglis.

10th January 1743

bad Character in his Letter sometime agoe to me in Relation to the *John & Isabella*. [522] Mr. Inglis is of opinion that Mr. Sanders is Instigated & Spurr'd on by his Partner Mr. Robinson who he takes to be a subtile Crafty Man & that Sanders is entirly Directed & Ledd by him which he had occasion to See & take Notice of when at Southampton with Capt. Douglass. However I would not advise you to goe to Law with him, if possible you can make up matters & Clear with him without, which you will find both very Chargeable & Troublesome & dont know When or how it may end. As for Mr. Sanders he is but an Illiterate Man & knows nothing of Business or Merchants Accounts & those Sort of People are allways the Worst & most Troublesome to be Dealt with.

I Shall use my Uttmost endeavours to Compleat the Sale of the Goods per the *John & Isabella* & the *Susannah* Last Voyage, which is all that is unfinish'd that Mr. Sanders is Concern'd in, & it gives me Great Concern that you are like to have any trouble with him, & that he does not prove the honest & fair Dealer We took him to be, but am in hopes you will be able to Settle Matters & to Clear with him in an Amicable Manner, which shall be very Glad to be advis'd of. As for the Canvas or Sail Cloth per the *John & Isabella* & *Susannah* you have been ill us'd in it for it Still lyes on hand a dead stock & cannot gett Ridd of it at any Rate. The Manchester Goods & some of the Nails per the *Susannah* are Likewise very unsaleable. Should be Glad to gett Clear of them at prime Cost, but there is no manner of sale for them, & to Sell them at Publick Vendue may almost as well thro them in the River.

It's pity that Capt. Gregory Lost the opportunity of such fine Winds. He has been now ten days in the Road. As I shall have Occasion to write you again per the Brigantine *Richard*, Capt. Hallin, as formerly advis'd of, I therefore add not at Present but that I am.

P. S. I have not writt to Mr. Sanders since the 13th April last. It is talk'd that Generall Oglethorp has Bills of Exchange protested to the Value of £6,000 Sterling.

ADDRESSED: "Per Capt. Story"

TO BOAZ BELL
Charles Town

Charles Town, 11th January 1742 [1743]

Sir:

Inclos'd please Receive Bill of Loading & Invoice of Sundry Goods Ship'd on board your Sloop *Endeavour,* your Self Commander on my Proper Risque & Account & to your Good self Consign'd, Amount as per Invoice being £204.7.10 this Currency which desire at your arrivall at Barbados You'll be So good as to Dispose of to my best Advantage, for Ready Money, & Leave nothing behind you, but sell all off for the most it will fetch, excepting the India Sattin Work't Counterpin. If you Cannot gett £30 or £25 this Currency for it, desire you may bring it back with you.

And with the Neat Proceeds of this Small Cargoe, You'll please to purchase & bring with you for my Account, Vizt. a small Box or Pot of Preserv'd Ginger intire & no other mixture of Sweet Meats, One Pot of Sweet Meats, Two Potts of best Clay'd Sugar, & all the Rest in good Dry Muscovado Sugar in BBls. about 22/6 to 23/6 per Ct., but pray Let it be Good of the Sort & in good Casks. I desire you may not buy any Rum for me unless it is under 2/ that Currency per Gallon. For the Rest I leave to your prudent management & heartily wishing you a good passage & success I Remain &c.

P. S. Box or Pott preserv'd Ginger; a pot of Sweet Meats, Two Potts of Clay'd Sugar, all the Rest in Good Dry Muscovado Sugar in Barrells & in Good Casks.

ADDRESSED: NO ADDRESS

[523]
TO JOHN STORY[5]
  London

Charles Town, 10th January 1742 [1743]

SIR:

This goes by your Son Capt. Story & hope will find you in Good health.

I am to Desire you'll be so good as to write to Hull to Mr. Thomas Burrill there to gett a Certificate from the Customhouse for the Delivery of the Cargoe you Loaded here, in Order to Clear our Bond, the Time being now Elaps'd & I am Lyable to be Sued for the Penalty of Same, which hope You'll take Care to prevent, by getting said Certificate Sent over as soon as possible. I am Greatly Concern'd to hear of the Death of your Two Sons at Jamaica, but we must all Submitt to the Dispensations of Divine providence. Shall be glad to have the Pleasure of hearing from you & to Render you or yours any agreeable Service here. I am &c.

ADDRESSED: "Per his Son Capt. Story"

TO ANDREW PRINGLE
  London

Charles Town, 11th January 1742 [1743]

SIR:

The preceeding is Copie of what I writt you yesterday & Capt. Gregory being still in the Road have to advise the Receipt of your very agreeable Favours of the 11th November per the *St. Andrew* via Cowes, & duely note the Contents. Capt. Gregory has come up from the Road to gett some more money to buy somethings he told me he had Occasion for. Inclos'd please Receive his further Receipt for £80 this Currency, which youll please to give me Credit for accordingly. Youll observe the *Sussannah*'s outsett Comes to a great dale of Money, & how it has been Apply'd Capt. Gregory must Account.

Our Exchange Continues at £700 per £100 Sterling, but no Bills to

[5] Capt. John Story lived in Princess Street, Rotherith, London. RPC, p. 668.

be had, as there are no Orders as yet to Ship Rice per Bill. If Capt. Patton happens to arrive the first with Madeira Wine, it will meet with a Quick Sale, there being none good here at Present.

I observe what you mention in Relation to Messrs. Cookson & Welfitt, & your Directions to Ship Rice as they also Limitt. It is probable Rice may Come to 30/ per Ct., but very improbable that Freight may then likewise be obtain'd at 50/ per Ton, as Rice & Freight never happens to be both Low at the Sametime; for if one is Low, the other in Consequence is always high. I add not at present but Refferr you to all my former advices per your *Susannah*, which hope will soon be with you. I Remain.

ADDRESSED: "Per Capt. Gregory"

TO JAMES BLOUNT
Edentown, North Carolina

Charles Town, 13th January 1742 [1743]

SIR:

I have your Favours of the 3d November in Answer to mine of the 8th September & Duely observe the Contents. All Provisions are Pretty Plenty & Cheap at Present. Corn is sold at 10/ per bushell. I observe you have gott some very good Tobacco ready to Ship to London to my Brother Andrew Pringle, Merchant there. I am Inform'd there are now Severall Vessels in your Port. Hope you will be able to gett Freight & Ship it to him accordingly, but pray don't fail to advise him before hand what you intend to Ship him on my Account that he may make Insurance for same. If you send any Myrtle Wax & Tallow here, beleive it will doe very well.

I am much oblidg'd to you for your Offices to gett my Money of Peter Birst & hope you'll be able to Recover it of him. I have never yet heard a Word from Mr. Pilkington about Capt. McDowall or anything else. Shall be always very glad to hear from you & I am.

ADDRESSED: "Per Capt. Barrett"

[524]
TO GEORGE HONEYMAN
         London
                              Charles Town, 20th January 1742 [1743]
SIR:
   I have your Favours of the 6th October & I am to advise you that I have already forwarded to my Brother the Account Sales of the Two Parcells of Goods you were Concern'd in with him, as also Returns for same per the *Susannah*, Capt. Gregory, (before yours Came to Hand) which hope will Come to a Good Markett & of which doubt not my Brother will accquaint you of accordingly.
   As to Insurance on Goods there is no such thing in this Part of the World & for your Share of the Money Rais'd for the Sufferers in the Fire, You'll Please to Inform your self that none of the Sufferers are Entitl'd to any part of Said money, but only the sufferers that are Inhabitants of this Town & them only.
   Shall be always very Glad to Render you any agreeable Service. I am &c.
   ADDRESSED: "Per Capt. Hallin & Copie per Capt. Abercrombie for Cowes"

TO BURRYAU & SCHAFFER
         London
                              Charles Town, 21st January 1742 [1743]
GENTLEMEN:
   I did myself the Pleasure to write you of the 29th Ulto. with Duplicate thereof for Insurance of £350 Sterling on Goods per the Brigantine *Richard*, Capt. Samuel Hallin, for London, to which please be Refferr'd. And agreeable thereto this serves to Convey you Inclos'd Bill of Loading & Invoice of Forty Six Barrells of New Rice & Five Hogheads of Deer Skins Ship't on Board the said Brigantine on the Proper Account & Risque of Mr. Thomas Hutchinson of Boston & to your Good selvs Consign'd, Amount as per Invoice being £2,286.12.11 this Currency, which wish safe to hand, & as both are very Good in Quality hope will Come to

21st January 1743

a Good Markett. I purpos'd to have Ship't more Rice, but the Vessel has not Loaded so much as Expected. You'll Please to advise Mr. Thomas Hutchinson of said Remittance. I have not further to offerr at present, but that I am with great Respect &c.

Exchange to London £700 per £100 Sterling, Freight to London at £4 per Ton, Rice 40/ per Ct.

ADDRESSED: "Per Capt. Hallin & Copie per Capt. Abercrombie for Cowes"

TO THOMAS GOLDTHWAIT
   London
                         Charles Town, 21st January 1742 [1743]
SIR:
   I did my self the Pleasure to write you of the 20th Ultimo under Cover of my Brother with Duplicate thereof to which please be Refferr'd. And this goes by the Brigantine *Richard*, Capt. Samuel Hallin, for London & serves to advise you that a very Large Quantity of Rum has Lately been Imported here from your Place as also from the West Indies & has arriv'd almost near the same time, which has made a Glutt & makes the Sale thereof very Slow & will also Lower the Price, insomuch that I have been able as yet to dispose of but very little of Capt. Hallin's Cargoe, as he can Inform you A Quantity of Rum not being to be dispos'd of here presently, especially for Ready Money, unless when it happens to be very scarce & none in the Place which is not the Case at Present. So that it will be sometime before I shall be able or in Cash to make any Remittance on Said Account, & if your Vessel that you mention in yours, the Effects is to be Ship't on arrives here soon, must be oblidg'd to take Freight in order to Dispatch her, as I shall advise Mr. Hutchinson per first Conveyance, not having had an opportunity to write him since my Last to you. I was lately favour'd with a Letter from him of the 22d November wherein he desires me to Load the Brigantine *Richard* with Rice on your Account having Receiv'd advices that it was raising in Europe, but the Brigantine had been Lett out on Freight, according to his & your former Directions

by her & was almost Loaded before I Receiv'd his Letter, & had been Loaded sooner had it not been [525] for wett Weather. Freight is now at £4 per ton for London & Rice at 40/ per Ct., Exchange at London £700 per £100 Sterling. I have not further to offerr but that I am with Great Respect &c.

ADDRESSED: "Per Capt. Hallin & Copie per Capt. Abercrombie for Cowes under Cover of A. Pringle"

TO ANDREW PRINGLE
    London

Charles Town, 21st January 1742 [1743]

SIR:

    My Last to you was of the 11th Current per your Ship *Susannah* which sail'd over the Barr the 14th & had very near been Lost, having touch'd on the Breakers & Capt. Gregory has been oblidg'd to Leave his small Bower Anchor behind him, but whether by Capt. Gregory or the Pilot's bad Management cannot determine, 'tho the Pilots blame Capt. Gregory for it.

    This goes by the Brigantine *Richard,* Capt. Samuel Hallin, Commander for London, & Inclos'd please Receive Bill of Lading & Invoice of One Hundred & Forty Barrells of good Rice which Capt. Gregory did not take in & one BBl. old Pewter Ship't on board said Brigantine *Richard* on Account & Risque of the Cargoe of the *John & Isabella* & to your good self Consign'd, Amount as per Invoice being £1,816.19.9 this Currency which wish safe to hand & hope will Come to a good markett. I did intend to have Ship'd 150 BBls. by this Conveyance, but the Vessel has stow'd short of Expectation by upwards of 60 BBls. The Old Pewter was oblidg'd to Take in payment for a Debt, please to advise how it answers & what you sell it for. I omitted in the assortment of Goods sent you per the *Susannah* to put down in it Some Canary Wine or Sweet sack, if it Comes Reasonable in price, & perhaps some prizes with it have been Brought Into England. A pipe of it in Pint Botles well pack'd up in Casks wou'd not be too much to Send & wou'd answer very well, there being none

21st January 1743

in the Place at Present & it is pretty much us'd here especially by Sick People.

Also Some Italian Green Gauze for Pavillions for Beds would doe in the Summer such as you us'd to Send here, provided it can be afforded to be sold here at One shilling Sterling per yard, as it wou'd not fetch more in the Whole Sale way. The Green Colour is much the most us'd & most Saleable.

A Vessel of Capt. Joliffe's in Poole arriv'd here about a Week agoe from Lisbon with a Liscense in order to goe Back there again & only Two Vessels having as yet gone there this Season, & said Vessel takeing Freight, I have agreed to Ship One hundred BBls. at £4 per Ton Freight, Clear of all Charges at Lisbon, & Rice is now at 40/ per Ct. & which I propose to be on our Joint Account & to Messrs. Mayne Consign'd which youll please to advise them of, there being no Opportunity from this at Present, & to Direct them (as I shall Likewise) to sell the Said 100 bbls. Rice for Ready Cash if Possible, & rather something under the Markett than to give Credit (as I understand is often practis'd there) & so Run the Risque of bad Debts, & to Remitt the Neat Proceeds to you in Bills of Exchange or Gold.

Youll please therefore to Gett Insur'd on goods on Board the Ship *Jolliffes Adventure*, Capt. John Archer, from this to Lisbon on our Joint Account (if you think proper to be Concern'd ½ in the Adventure) about £180 Sterling or £200 Sterling the full Value of the Rice, & to Receive £98 per Ct. in Case of a Loss. The Vessel will Carry about 700 bbls. & will sail in about Three Weeks hence & hope will Come to a good markett there, as there is a better Likelyhood there than in any other part of Europe. I have Desir'd Messrs. Mayne to pay the Subsidy on the 100 bbls. Rice that I advis'd you I had Shipt there per the *Bremen Factor*, as I shall Likewise doe by this as well as the Freight.

Mr. Morson in his Account sent me Charges £2.17.3 Sterling for Freight & Insurance which was not in the Bill of Parcells sent me when I took them off from Mr. Medley's hands here to my own Account, therefore think he ought not to Demand it, especially as he Charges so much Interest on the Account being £28.15.7 Ster.

I observe what you mention in Relation to the Provincial Petition about the Three Independant Companies[6] & that you was appointed one

[6] The three Independent Companies of Foot were formed from Oglethorpe's regiment in 1749 and were disbanded with the conclusion of peace in 1763. *SCHM*, XXXIII (1932), 183.

of the Committee of Merchants to Draw up an application from the Body about Same in Order to assist in obtaining them & think you judg'd very Right in not applying or medling in it, as none of the Merchants here writt any thing to their Freinds about it, & indeed they could not as they were not Lett into the Scheme like me, or had any Knowledge of it. Our Gentlemen of the Council are of such profund Judgement & parts (& particularly that Conceited Gentleman Mr. Atkin)[7] that they doe not think it worth their While to advise [526] with, or have the Opinion of the Merchants in any thing Relating to the Welfare of the Province. Not but that some Forces Stationed here under proper Regulations wou'd be of Great Service for the Safety & Welfare of the Province, but yet think that the Merchants & Trading people ought to be Inform'd of & their Opinion ask't & advis'd with in all affairs of that Nature, & that they may advise their Freinds to assist at Home.

This Province now is Entirely Defensless in Case of a French War, as Admiral Vernon with the Fleet & Forces are gone Home, & we are apprehensive that the Spainards may pay us a Visit this Spring, Especially as we have now no help near us. Whatever People in London may think of the Strenth of So. Carolina, It is all our Opinions here on the Spott that if the Spainards had Come here Last Summer Directly instead of goeing into Georgia, they must Certainly have taken the Town, as we had neither Fortifications or People to oppose them, which are the Sentiments of the most Judicious here. This Town is a fine Bait for the French as they want a port very much on the Ocean, & especially to be Contiguous & join with their Settlements on the River Mississippi, or Louisiana as they Call it.

The Indian Blue Chelloes[8] you sent per the *John & Isabella* & per the *Susannah* prove a very Unsaleable Article. I have offerr'd them for first Cost & Cannot yett Ridd of them. I imagine they were of Mr. Sanders his Buying or advising. Most of the Saws per the *Susannah* are also still on hand & have been oblidg'd to have handles & Tillers made to them here.

This Province wants much a Good Governour & Trade will never Flourish till we have One. By the Character reported here of Mr. Glen, People dont seem fond of having him for Governour.

The Brigantine *Richard* by which this Goes is Consign'd to Mr. Rich-

---

[7] Edmund Atkin was a member of the Council and the first Superintendent of Indian Affairs for the Southern District. *SCHM*, XXXIV (1933), 213.

[8] Chello was an Indian fabric commonly used in the eighteenth century.

24th January 1743

ard Partridge, who is ⅓ Concern'd with Messrs. Hutchinson & Goldthwait in the Vessel. Inclos'd have Troubled you with a Letter for Mr. Thomas Goldthwait, not knowing how to address to him, which after perusal you'll please to Seal & Deliver him. Have Ship't 46 Barrells Rice & 5 hhds. Deer Skins by this Vessel to Messrs. Burryau & Schaffer on Mr. Thomas Hutchinsons own proper Account. I intended them more Rice but the Vessel Deceiv'd me in her Stowage. My Wife joins in kind Love & Respects & I Remain most Sincerely &c.

Exchange to London £700 per £100 Ster.

P. S. Inclos'd please Receive Copie of Invoice of the 100 bbls. Rice Ship't to Lisbon per the *Bremen Factor*.

ADDRESSED: "Per Capt. Hallin & Copie per Capt. Abercrombie Via Cowes"

TO JOHN EVANS[9]
    Port Royal, South Carolina

Charles Town, 24th January 1742 [1743]

SIR:

I Rec'd yours of the 22d this Morning at the Hands of your Passanger Mr. Gardner, & am very sorry to be Inform'd of your Missfortune. One Dinnis Chaise who tells that he's one of your People, & Came by Land, accquainted me of it yesterday. This will be Deliver'd you by the Bearer, Mr. Comeur, whose Boat have hir'd to Come to your assistance in Order to Lighten your Vessell & he has agreed to take in as much of your Cargoe as will Load his Boat. He has also engag'd to gett your Vessel off & bring

[9] The brigantine *Dolphin*, John Evans, ran ashore in St. Helena's Sound. Messrs. Osborne, Oxnard, and Gunter of Boston owned the vessel. RPC, p. 533; SCG, 24 January 1743. Thomas Oxnard, a Boston merchant, married the daughter of John Osborn. He was one of the directors of the "silver scheme." NEH&GR, VI (1852), 196, 375; XIV (1860), 263–264. John Osborn of Atkinson Street was a signer of a petition of New England merchants to the Board of Trade and a member of the Council. NEH&GR, VI (1852), 196; XVII (1863), 148; XX (1866), 31; XXI (1867), 209. Thomas Gunter was a merchant in Boston. NEH&GR, XXVIII (1874), 467.

24th January 1743

her to Charles Town Barr being the most proper Person I Could gett in the Province to goe to help you as he knows the Place perfectly well & is the Best Pilot we have for those parts. I have also hir'd & sent by Mr. Comeur's Boat Four Stout Negro Men to assist you on board & who are us'd to be upon the Water & Understand to Work on Ship board, & Desire you may Lett the Said Negros have Provisions & Drink while on board, as I have agreed with them, & hope by such Good help you will be able to gett the Vessell off without any Damage, & that youll make the best of your Way to Charlestown, & take all the Care you possibly Can of the Cargoe & to keep it free from Damage or Embezlement, & if you have Occasion for any provisions, the Country Gentlemen that Live near where your Vessell is will Supply you, upon your giving them an order on me for same which shall be duely paid. I Receiv'd advice about 14 days agoe from Messrs. Osborn & Oxnard & Mr. Gunter, your Owners, of your coming here & hoping to see you soon here. I Remain &c.

ADDRESSED: "Per Mr. Comeur"

[527]
TO SAMUEL HALLIN
Charles Town

Charles Town, 24th January 1742 [1743]

SIR:

The Brigantine *Richard* whereof you are Commander being now Clear'd and in all Respects fitted for the Sea & Ready to Sail, You are therefore to Embrace the first Opportunity that presents of Wind & Weather & make the best of your Way from this Directly for London (avoiding as it is War time as much as possible you can, Speaking with any Shipping at Sea) where at your arrival you are Immediatly to apply your Self to your Owner Mr. Richard Partridge, Merchant there. I heartily wish you a Good Passage & Success & I am &c.

P. S. I am to desire you'll put Mr. Partridge in mind to gett a Certificate from the Custom house of the Delivery of your Cargoe & to Send it over as soon as he Can in order to Discharge Our joint Bond given here for £1,000 Sterling.

ADDRESSED: NO ADDRESS

TO RICHARD PARTRIDGE
London

Charles Town, 29th January 1742 [1743]

SIR:

I did myself the Pleasure to write you of the 20th Ultimo with Duplicate thereof to which please be Refferr'd. And this per your Brigantine *Richard,* Capt. Samuel Hallin, being now ready to Sail, & Inclos'd please Receive account Sales of Boards & Bricks Shipt by Messrs. Hutchinson & Goldthwait on Account the Owners of the said Brigantine, Neat Proceeds being £188.19.1 this Currency. You'll observe the Quantity of Boards falls short of what was advis'd to be Shipt, & was mention'd in the Bill of Lading which I took notice of to Capt. Hallin, who assures me that he Deliver'd all that was put on board, excepting a small Quantity taken for the Vessel's use, & as the whole was Sold as soon as the Vessel arriv'd & measured off & Deliver'd as soon as Landed, there Cou'd be none Losst here.

You have also Inclos'd Account of Disbursements on the Vessel here & money paid Capt. Hallin, as per his Receipt Inclos'd, Amount being £459.1.0 this Currency. Likewise the Owners Account Current, Ballance in my Favour being £160.1.11 Currency for which have taken Capt. Hallin's Bill on your Good Self for £22.17.6 Ster. at the Current Exchange being £700 per £100 Sterling & Doubt not will be duely honour'd. Capt. Hallin has been at no Expence here for the Vessel but what has been necesary & has been Detain'd sometime since he has been Loaded & Clear'd at all the Offices purely for want of Sailors, having had Two Impress'd on board one of the Kings Ships with whom have had a pretty Deal of Trouble & Charge before had them Return'd, having oblidg'd them to Return them, 'tho one happen'd to be Drown'd in Endeavouring to make his Escape by Swimming a Shoar. Merchant Ships are Greatly Oppress'd here by the King's Ships Impressing their Hands,

29th January 1743

which makes Sailors Wages Run very high. It is pity that it is not taken Notice of by the Gentlemen in Trade at Home in order to have it Remidied.

Please also Receive Inclos'd a manifest of the *Richards* Cargoe on Board. I am to Desire you'll be so good as to gett a Certificate from the Custom house of the Delivery of the *Richards* Cargoe & Transmitt it me as soon as you Can in Order to Clear Capt. Hallin & my Joint Bond given here for £1,000 Sterling which have Desir'd Capt. Hallin to put you in mind of. The Wind is now fair & hope Capt. Hallin will soon be with you. Shall be always very Glad to Receive your Commands & to Render you any agreeable Service here & I Remain with Great Respect &c.

ADDRESSED: "Per Capt. Hallin & Copie per Capt. Abercrombie"

[528]
TO ANDREW PRINGLE
London

Charles Town, 27th January 1742 [1743]

SIR:

I Reffer you to what I have already writt you of the 21st Current per this Conveyance of Capt. Hallin, also Copie thereof via Cowes, & he having been Detain'd for Want of Hands, as all other Vessells are, having had Some of his people Impress'd by the Commanders of the Kings Ships with whom have had Some Dispute about same. However have oblidg'd them to Return Capt. Hallin's, & beleive am the first in the Place that has oblidg'd them to doe So, having made them Sensible that I was Determin'd to Sue them according to the Act of Parliament in that Case made & provided.[1]

Inclos'd please Receive Capt. Samuel Hallin his Bill of Exchange of

---

[1] Under the provisions of "An Act for the Encouragement of the Trade to America," the captain of a ship in the Royal Navy was subject to a fine of £20 Sterling if he impressed a mariner who was not a deserter. Danby Pickering, *The Statutes at Large*, vol. XI: *From the Second to the Eighth Year of Queen Anne* (Cambridge, Eng., 1764), 438.

28th January 1743

this Date for £22.17.6 Sterling on his Owner Mr. Richard Partridge in my Favour, payable at Twenty Days Sight, Exchange at £700 per £100 Sterling & to your good Self Indors'd which Doubt not will be Duely Honour'd & when in Cash please to Credit my Account for Same, being Ballance of Account of the Owners of the Brigantine *Richard* for Disbursement here for the Vessel & money advanc'd Capt. Hallin, which am to Desire you'll please to take Care that the Owner or Capt. pays, having been desir'd by Mr. Hutchinson of Boston to take the Capt.'s Bill on Mr. Partridge for what I advanc'd on Account of Said Vessell.

We have but few Vessels arrive here of Late so that Freight is the Same as in my Last £4 to London & £4.10/ to Holland & Rice at 40/ per Ct. We have had no Vessels from England since the *St. Andrew* & no material news at present. You'll please to make Insurance on the 100 bbls. Rice to Lisbon as mention'd in my Last & advise Messrs. Mayne thereof. I have not further to Offerr at present, but that I Remain &c.

ADDRESSED: "Per the *Richard*, Capt. Hallin, & Copie per Capt. Paterson"

TO JOHN EVANS
Port Royal, South Carolina

Charles Town, 28th January 1742 [1743]

SIR:

I Receiv'd your Letter of the 23d Inst. yesterday by John Wooley who came with the Perriagua & Deliver'd one hundred & four bbls. Flower & Two Cases & no more. I hope before this that Mr. Commeur is with you & has gott out the Rest of the Flower in his Boat & that you will be able to gett off the Vessel, that Mr. Commeur with the help I sent with him may bring her Round to this Place (if she is in a Condition) as the Carpenters work will be much better & Cheaper done than up there & in much less time, as I wou'd not have the Vessel goe to Port Royall if it can be avoided. It will be very proper that you make a Regular Protest, but beleive there is no Publick Notary up there to apply to, but must not fail that same be done as soon as you gett here.

I am in hopes soon to see you or to hear from you. I have a Letter from

28th January 1743

my Friend Capt. Beswicke[2] who tells me that he has offerr'd to supply you with what ever you may want & to take your Bill on me for the Value & Desire you may apply to him accordingly, & to whom I Likewise write by this Conveyance of Mr. Smith for that Effect. I shall take Care to advise your Owners of the Missfortune per first Opportunity & I am &c.

P. S. If your Flower is not all sent away in Mr. Comeurs Boat, & if he is Still there you may Deliver Capt. Thomas Beswicke Twenty Barrells of Flower of your Owners taking his Receipt for same, as I have advis'd him.

ADDRESSED: "Per Mr. Comeur"

[529]
TO ADAM MCDONALD
Frederica, Georgia

Charles Town, 5th February 1742 [1743]

SIR:

I Receiv'd your Favours of the 25th past at the hands of Capt. McClellan,[3] advising that you understand Mr. Kerr[4] has given his Tongue some Liberty since your absence. And there are also some others that have Done the same & in Particular Alexander Robinson at Parkers Ferry, who when I ask't him for the money for the 2 hhds. Rum he had the 17th November Last, payable in Two months, To my Great Surprize he told me that he wonder'd that I shoud ask him for the money for the Rum as he had already paid you for it at same time when he had the Rum & that he would not Pay for it twice. In answer to which I told him that I did not beleive what he said, for that Same time after he had the Rum I Paid you upwards of £100 Ballance of Account between you & I as appears by your Receipt in my Book, & if you had, you woud Certainly have Discounted it & not have taken the money then of me as I had always found you a Gentleman of Honour & Honesty. I am certain

[2] Thomas Beswicke, a bachelor from England, married in St. Helena's Parish on 23 April 1734 Deborah Haines and on 12 September 1749 Anne Wigg, a widow. He was buried on 5 June 1751. *SCHM*, XXIII (1922), 13.

[3] Capt. John McClellan in the brigantine *Georgia Packett* arrived from Frederica. *SCG*, 7 February 1743.

[4] Probably James Kerr of St. Andrew's Parish. *SCHM*, XIII (1912), 39, 157.

5th February 1743

you would never use me in that manner & told him that he us'd you ill in saying So & did you great Injustice, which I was Positive he cou'd not Doe if you was on the Spot & Mr. Kerr his Friend who was with him, Said that to his Knowledge Part of the Money for the Rum was paid you. Mr. Robinson also told me that if he had not already paid you, he would not pay me for the Rum without an Order from you, all which I thought was very Odd in him, & Resolv'd to Inform you thereof per first Opportunity. I am therefore to Desire you'll be so Good as to Send me an order on him for £255.11.3 Current Money being the amount of the Two hhds. Rum, also a Power of Attorney, otherwise the Order will not signifie & I Cann't oblidge him to pay it without a Power of Attorney in Order to Sue him, if there be Occasion, & to make him appear in his proper Colours, as I am Certain he does you Great Injustice as I Told him. And if there be any account between you & he, You'll please likewise to Send it attested by a Magistrate or Justice of Peace.

This will be Deliver'd you by Capt. Mackenzie of Mr. Jenys his Schooner who has promis'd me to Deliver this into your own hands & to bring me an answer to it from you, & will be a Witness to your Signing the Power of Attorney in Order to prove it here, & hope you'll be so good as to send it me accordingly in Order to Clear up this affair. As I apprehend that Mr. Robinson by Saying So wants only to Shuffle me off & not to Pay for the Rum.

Mr. Alexander Stewart[5] presents his Service & Desires me to acquaint you that Some People here Give their Tongues a Good deal of Liberty in Relation to a Difference that as they Say happened between you & Capt. William Wood at Port Royall, which we apprehend to be without any Ground or Foundation. I am to Desire you'll Please also to send me an Order on Alexander Moon for £85 being the Amount of a Cask Hoes you had of me for him now a year agoe, In case it may not Suit you to Come here by the Time you mention.

We have no Material News here at Present. Shall be always very Glad to Render you any agreeable Service, & in hopes of Seeing or hearing from you soon in answer to this I Remain &c.

P. S. Please advise if you have Dispos'd of the small things I gave you to Sell for me. You have heard not Doubt of a Great many of the Generall's Bills of Exchange being protested.

ADDRESSED: "Per Capt. Mackenzie"

---
[5] Alexander Stewart was an Ensign in Oglethorpe's Regiment. RPC, p. 819.

[530]
TO RICHARD PARTRIDGE
London

Charles Town, 5th February 1742 [1743]

The preceeding of the 29th Past is Duplicate of what I did my self the Pleasure to writ you per your Brigantine *Richard*, Capt. Hallin, who sail'd over this Barr the 2d Current & hope will be with you before you Receive this. I am to advise you that I have been Oblidg'd to Advance Capt. Hallin more money since my Last in Order to hire Sailors he wanted to goe the Voyage, otherways the Vessel woud not have been able to have proceeded & might have been Detain'd here a Considerable Time. Have therefore taken of him another Sett of Bills on you for £18.3.11 Sterling at the Current Exchange of £700 per £100 Ster. which Doubt not will be Duely Honour'd, & for which Capt. Hallin must account to you for, most Part of it being for Money advanc'd Sailors before he could prevail with them to goe on board. I have not further to offerr at Present but that I am with Great Respect &c.

ADDRESSED: "Per Capt. Styles & Copie per Capt. Paterson"

TO ANDREW PRINGLE
London

Charles Town, 5th February 1742 [1743]

SIR:

The Inclos'd is Copie of my Last of the 29th past per the Brigantine *Richard*, Capt. Hallin, who Sail'd over the Barr the 2d Current & Inclos'd please Receive Capt. Hallin's 2d Bill of Exchange on his Owner Richard Partridge, Esqr. for £22.17.6 payable to my Order at 20 Days Sight & to you Indors'd. Please also Receive Inclos'd another Bill of Exchange of said Capt. Hallin's on his Owner for £18.3.11 Sterling dated the first Current & likewise payable to my Order & to you Indors'd, being for more money that I was oblidg'd to advance him to hire Sailors he wanted to goe the Voyage, otherways the Vessell would not have proceeded, as I have advis'd Mr. Partridge, which doubt not will be duely honour'd, &

5th February 1743

when in Cash please to Credit my account for same. This Goes by Capt. Styles[6] to whom have given a Letter for you, Copie thereof is here Inclos'd, that in case Samuel Smith, Pewterer in Snow Hill Refuses & does not Pay Edward Leapidge his Bill to my Order for £13.6 Ster. & to Said Styles Indors'd for Value Receiv'd of him (who I have already advis'd you about) that upon his presenting the said Bill upon the others Refusal, that you'll be so good as to Pay it for my honour as I have assur'd him you will, in Case of Smiths Refusal or Leapidge's Brother, & so must have Recourse on Smith & oblidge him upon his Letter sent me by Leapidge, having been oblidg'd to pay the money for him here, & have had not a Little Trouble by it, which makes Letters of Recommendation often very Troublesome.

Capt. Styles is to allow Edward Leapidge the Drawer who Goes home with him Six Guineas for the Run home as a Sailor, so that part of the Bill will be Paid in his own Hands.

A Master of a Vessell Lately from Antigua tells me that he saw there Capt. Blackburn of your *Queen of Hungary* very well having stopt there in his way to Jamaica. If he Comes here from thence, the Sooner the better, before ships can Receive advices at other parts of a Large Crop here.

Please Receive Inclos'd Our Gazettes of the 17th & 31 past, in which you'll observe Two advertisements of Capt. Hallins in Relation to our Gallant Commodore Hardy his Conduct & Behaviour here to the Trading Interest to which I Refferr you,[7] & which hope will be taken Due Notice of by all our Merchants & Trading People at Home, & by which they may judge of how Little Service & how Little the Trading Interest is Regarded or Taken Notice of by the Commanders of the Kings Ships sent on this Station. Capt. Hallin Can inform you of the whole [531] affair.

Samuel Wragg has Trump'd up an account against my Wife's Father's estate of between £200 & £300 Sterling owed since the Year 1725, altho' Messrs. Lambol & Allen seen to be possitive that he pass'd Accounts & Gave a Discharge to Mr. William Minett in London a Good many Years since that. They have writt to Mr. Minett in Relation to same accordingly with Duplicate about a Fortnight agoe. Please to ask said Gentleman if he has Receiv'd Letters from them. Mr. Daniel More of Barbados Cries

---

[6] Capt. Ephraim Styles. RPC, p. 531.

[7] Capt. Hallin tried to get back his sailors to which Commodore Charles Hardy replied "That he had something else to mind than any little Rascally Merchant-Men. . . ." SCG, 17, 24, 31 January 1743.

5th February 1743

peccavi since a Power of Attorney has been sent against him (as I formerly advis'd you) & promises to Remitt the Money very soon.

Mr. Houghton has brought over about Sixty Pallatines & have turn'd out very well. Mr. Joseph Wragg has two Ships gone in the Trade, & Believe the Importers will find their account in it, as the Province in Generall are very Sensible of the Want of more White People, (especially in this Town of Tradesmen & Labourers in the Room of Negroes) & will be better than the Guinea Trade, & hope Our Government here will fall on Ways & Means to give Proper Encouragement for their Importation. Their are also two things that would be much for the advantage of the Trade of this Province, Vizt. Liberty to Send Our Rice from this Directly to Forreign Marketts without being oblidg'd to Stop at Cowes, or any other of the Out Ports, also Liberty to Send Rice, &c. Directly from this to Madeira, & it is pity our Gentlemen at Home in this Trade did not make application for that Effect, that we may be upon the same footing with Our Sugar Islands.

There is a Rumour that the Spainards intend us a Visit this Spring with a Considerable Force. If so, we Shall be put to it being but Indifferently provided, & no Forces now in the West Indies to Come to Our assistance.

Capt. Summersett we hear is at Antigua from Ireland & Madeira & Dayly expected here. It seems he has sold most of his Wines there at a Good Price. Have not the Pleasure of hearing from you by Capt. White in whom Came Passengers Messrs. Seaman & Stone[8] & arriv'd about a Week agoe & not a Letter from Mr. Reid which gives Mrs. Reid Great Uneasiness. Please my Service to him if still with you. I hope you'll please excuse the Trouble I give you about this affair of Edward Leapidge, & as his Brother in Law Samuel Smith Recommended him to me, think he Cannot be off from paying the Money, which I have been oblidg'd to pay for him here.

While I am Writing a Ship is Coming In which is Said to be Capt. Patton. If so, he happens to be the first with Wines & believe will meet a Good & Quick Sale, & if he has Some Wines as you advise on your Own account of about 15 pipes Seperate from the Cargoe to My Address, Doubt not of Selling it Directly for £135 or £140 per pipe if very Good in Quality. My Wife joins in best Respects, & I Remain most Sincerely &c.

ADDRESSED: "Per Capt. Styles & Copie per Capt. Paterson"

[8] William Stone was a Charleston merchant who in 1746 established himself in London "as a Merchant and also as a Factor or Agent for Storekeepers, Merchants, and others in the Province." He died in 1779 in England. *HL*, I, 134n.

TO ANDREW PRINGLE
    London
                            Charles Town, 5th February 1742 [*1743*]
SIR:

   I Refferr to what I have already writt you of this Date & this you will Receive at the Hands of Capt. Ephraim Styles to whom I have Indors'd Mr. Leapidge his Bills of Exchange for Thirteen Pounds Six Shillings Ster. in my Favour on Mr. Samuel Smith, Pewterer in Snow Hill for Value Receiv'd of him & about which have already advis'd you. And have told Capt. Styles that in Case Mr. Smith Refuses to pay him Said Bill, which am in hopes he will not, that upon his Application to you, that you will take them up & pay him the Money for My Honour, & which doubt not you will punctually Comply with accordingly, & so have Recourse upon said Mr. Smith if there shou'd be a Necessity. However hope there will not as I take him to be a Gentleman of honour, & wont Lett me be a Sufferer by his Kinsman for my Regard to his Letter & my Civility to him & having been oblidg'd to pay the money for him here. I am &c.

ADDRESSED: "Per Capt. Styles & [*Blank*]"

[532]
TO SAMUEL SMITH
    London
                            Charles Town, 5th February 1742 [*1743*]
SIR:

   I did myself the Pleasure to write you of the 6th December last with Copie thereof under Cover of my Brother in Relation to your Brother in Law Mr. Edward Leapidge who not being able to gett into any kind of Business here Goes home Passanger with the Bearer of this Capt. Ephraim Styles, & having been oblidg'd to Pay the Money for him as mention'd in my Last have taken this Bill of Exchange on you of this Date for thirteen Pounds Six Shillings Sterling Payable to my Order at 20 Days Sight which have Indors'd to the Bearar Capt. Styles for Value Receiv'd here at the Current Exchange of £700 per £100 Sterling, & which Doubt not You'll give Due honour to, & not Sufferr me to be a Looser for my Regard to Your Letter & Civility to your Kinsman. I am &c.

ADDRESSED: "Per Capt. Styles & Copie to my Brother"

TO THOMAS BESWICKE
Port Royal, South Carolina
Charles Town, 10th February 1742 [1743]

SIR:

I have your Favours of the 21st Past advising of the Brigantine *Dolphin*, Capt. John Evans, being Come into St. Helena Sound in Distress, & that you was so Good as to give him what help & Assistance you was Capable of for which I am Greatly oblidg'd to you, & Return you my hearty Thanks & the Drafts he has given you on me for what Money you advanc'd him you may Depend on it Shall be Duely honour'd.

I show'd your Letter to Mr. John Beswick who tells me that he has sent you only Six Barrels of Flower. And according to your Desire, I have sent you by the Bearer Mr. Mackay in Mr. Edward Wigg's[9] Boat Twenty barrels Flower at £4.10 per Ct., being the Lowest price I sell for ready money, & if you was to take the Whole Cargoe wou'd not sell it for Less, Amount as per Inclos'd Bill of Parcells being £207.17.2 which wish Safe to Your hands, & for which please Receive Inclos'd Mr. Mackay's Receipt. Shall be Glad also to Supply you with Good Barrel'd Beef at £6.10 per bbl., Dry'd Salt Cod at £4 per Ct., N. E. Rum 16/6 per Gall., Barbados Rum at 21/6 per Gall., if you have Occasion for any of them at Present. Shall be Glad to have the Pleasure of hearing from you & to Render you any agreeable Service & I am &c.

ADDRESSED: "Per Mr. Mackay"

---

[9] Edward Wigg (1715–1755) married Mary Hazzard on 22 February 1738 in St. Helena's parish. *SCHM*, XXIII (1922), 114, 196.

10th February 1743

TO ANDREW PRINGLE
London

Charles Town, 10th February 1742 [1743]

SIR:

My last was of the 5th Current per Capt. Styles with Copie thereof to which please be Refferr'd & this Serves to Convey you Inclos'd Capt. Hallin's Second Bill of Exchange for £18.3.11 Ster. on his Owner Richard Partridge, Esqr. payable to my Order at 20 Days Sight & to you Indors'd, which doubt not will be Duely Honour'd. Since my Last the *Andrew & Betty*, Capt. Patton, has arriv'd with 28 pipes of Wine on Account of the Owners, but none of your Proper Account as you advis'd. It seems your orders to Capt. Patton did not Reach him, & there is 31 pipes of Wine on board on Freight, as private Persons here have gone much of Late in ordering Single Pipes of Wine to be Ship'd at Madeira for their Own use however it hurts the Sale of Wine. Another Vessell with 40 pipes arriv'd. They are likely to have a pretty deal Soon. Capt. Patton tells me that Mr. Seaman has this Day Sold Some of his Wines at £120 per pipe, & that he & Mr. Stone are to Load them for Holland at £4.10/ per Ton, which is a pretty good Freight. Am of opinion that Freight will be Lower, as we are Likely to have a Good many Vessells from the Northward soon. Rice is Still at 40/ per Ct.

The *Jolliffe's Adventure*, Capt. John Archer, for Lisbon will Sail in a Week being now full & on which have already advis'd you to Insure Value of 100 BBls. Rice on our [533] Joint Account, Consign'd to Messrs. Mayne & Co. Shall send Copie of the Invoice per my next, & which wont much exceed £150 Sterling.

As I shall write Messrs. Scott, Pringle & Scott Via Lisbon, I may perhaps Desire them to Ship me a Pipe of good Madeira Wine for my Own use when they have an Opportunity of Freight for this Place & to Value upon you for the Amount & which hope you'll be so good as to honour, & that you'll Please to make mention of Same to them when you write them accordingly. This is but an Indifferent Markett for the Sale of Madeira Wine, & believe may be Plenty here till the fall of the year when is the time it is Generally Scarce & may happen to bear a pretty Good Price if not Great Quantity Comes at a Time.

I shall Desire Messrs. Mayne to Sell the 100 BBls. Rice for Ready Cash money if Possible & to Remitt the Neat Proceeds to you in Bills of Exchange or in Gold, at same time advising you in Order for Insurance. I

10th February 1743

have not further to Offerr at Present as being without any of your Favours but that I am &c.

ADDRESSED: "Per Capt. Cabot & Copie per Capt. Clarke"

TO JOHN ERVING
    Boston

Charles Town, 11th February 1742 [1743]

SIR:

    Since my last to you of the 25th October I have the Pleasure of Your most Esteem'd Favours of the 26th November with Copie & 14th December per Mr. Stoutenburgh who arriv'd here after a Pretty Good Passage. I am to Return you my hearty Thanks for your kind Recommendation to Messrs. Osborne & Oxnard & Mr. Thomas Gunter. The Brigantine Said Gentlemen order'd from Philadelphia with Rum & Flower to my address had the Missfortune to Spring a Leak soon after she Sail'd from thence, & Mistaking this Place Run ashore in St. Helena Sound, but has since gott off & is Come here, the Particulars of which have by this Conveyance advis'd said Gentlemen. Their Rum has happen'd to Come to a bad markett, the Town being Glutted with it at Present, there having upwards of 600 hhds. arriv'd here from your port & the West Indies within these two Months past, of which theirs happens to be the Last, so that there is no manner of Demand for it at Present, and am not Likely to sell it at any Rate for a Considerable Time to Come. The price is now at 15/ per Gall. & likely to be Lower. There has also a Considerable Quantity of Flower arriv'd here from Philadelphia & N. York before theirs Came to hand, which will make the Sale thereof very Slow & Tedious. I am very Sorry that the first Adventure of theirs is not Likely to prove more fortunate.

    I observe your *John Gally* was Loaded for the West Indies where I hope She will meet with Success, as I have Late advices from thence that there are Good Crops in all the Leeward Islands.

    Freight is a Lottery here, & Contrary to all Expectation very few Shipping have as yet arriv'd here this Season, which has advanc'd Freight to

11th February 1743

£4 per Ton for London & £4.10/ for Holland, but how long it may hold or Continue so is very uncertain & precarious, & entirly Depends on what Shipping may Come here this Spring, & as no Doubt advices will Goe from this to your Port as also to N. York & Philadelphia of the present Freight here, it may Occasion a Great many Ships to be sent from your Parts which may much overdoe it & so overstock the Place Especially if many Vessells shoud happen to Arrive at One time, & as it will be the Means of Rising the Price of Rice, Consequently Freight must fall & be Lower, So that You will be best able to Determine by the number of Ships that Goe from your Parts whether [534] not you will have Encouragement to send here the Large Ship that you mention will be Launch'd in March. However you may at all Times most assurdly Depend on my uttmost Endeavours for your Interest.

Mr. Andrew Lessly of Antigua has not acted with honour in Severall Concerns my Brother & I have had Occasion to address to him, So that we Shall Decline Corresponding with him for the future.

My Wife Returns Good Mrs. Erving her hearty Thanks for her very Acceptable present of Two barrels of Aples by Capt. Laws,[1] which came to hand in pretty Good Order. The other two Barrels were Deliver'd to Messrs. Wragg & Savage according to your Directions. I am to Desire the Favour that You'll be so Good as to buy for me & send me by first Oportunity (if to be had with you) a Plan or Prospect of your City of Boston Done in a Frame, & which please to Charge to my Account.

Peter Faneuil, Esqr. advises me that he has paid you on my Account & by my Direction £69.0.2 this Currency being ballance of his Account in my favour, Exchange at £450 per Ct. per £100 Sterling is £54.4.2 Currency of N. England & which Doubt not you have Credit my Account for accordingly. Please advise if Messrs. Wendell & Company have as yet paid you my Money on my account.

My Wife Joins in best Respects to your Good Lady & all your pretty Family & I am most Respectfully &c.

Rice 40/ per Ct., Pitch 35/ per BBl., Tar 30/ per bbl., Turpentine 15/ per Ct. Exchange to London £700 per £100 Sterling. This Goes by Capt. Breading who Loads at George Town, Winnyaw.

ADDRESSED: "Per Capt. Breading Via Winnyaw & Copie per Capt. Shermerhorn Via New York"

---

[1] Capt. David Law, the snow *Delight*, arrived from Boston. SCG, 17 January 1743.

11th February 1743

TO OSBORNE & OXNARD & THOMAS GUNTER
Boston

Charles Town, 11th February 1742 [1743]

GENTLEMEN:

I am by this to accknowledge the Receipt of both your most Esteem'd Favours of the 25th November & 3d January, the first advising of your ordering the Brigantine *Dolphin*, John Evans, Master from Philadelphia to my address with Rum & Flower. And it is with much concern that I have to advise you that your said Brigantine had the missfortune to spring a Leak a few Days after She Left the Capes & Mistaking the Barr, Run ashoar in St. Helena Sound, the Particulars of which I Refferr you to Copie of the Protest here Inclos'd, & on the 24th past had advices thereof from Capt. Evans & not before of his being Run ashoar there in Distress & to Send him immediate assistance in order to Lighten the Vessel & gett her off upon which I instantly hir'd a Deck'd Boat with a Pilot and Hands to Goe to him & Gett off the Vessel & bring her in to this Harbour which they did accordingly by Lightening the Vessel & arriv'd here about a Week agoe & has Landed 198 Barrells of Flower & Thirty one hhds. Rum (Four hhds. having Leak'd out in the Hold) on your account as per Invoice from Mr. Peter Baynton, & 46 bbls. of Flower on Freight.

I am also to advise that your Rum happens to Come to a very Dull markett, this Place being Glutted with it at Present, there having upwards of 600 hhds. arriv'd here from your port & the West Indies within these two months past, of which yours happens to be the Last, So that there is no manner of Demand for it at Present. I am not Likely to Gett it sold at any Rate for a Considerable Time. The price is now at 15/ per Gall. & Likely to be Lower. There is also a Considerable [535] Quantity of Flower arriv'd from Philadelphia & N. York before yours came to hand, which will Occasion the Sale to be very Slow & Tedious. I am very sorry that this first adventure of yours is not likely to prove more fortunate. However you may most assurdly Depend on my Uttmost Endeavours for your Interest, & as your Cargoe is likely to be Unsaleable for Sometime, Shall be oblidg'd to Lett out a Considerable part of the Vessel on Freight in Order to give her Dispatch back to Boston, as Rice must always be purchas'd with Ready money, 'tho are oblidg'd to Give Credit on all Goods that are Sold, especially when plenty & in no Demand.

I am to Take Notice to you that it is pity your Directions in Relation to your Brigantine *Dolphin* had not been more full & Discretionary, as I cou'd now Lett out Said Brigantine on Freight at £4 per Ton for London & £4.10/ per ton for Holland & to be Dispatch'd in a Fortnight, & So your Effects might be Remitted, as you Shou'd Direct by other Conveyances hereafter. But as your Orders are Possitive & not Discretionary I would not take upon me to Despense with them, even 'tho perhaps for your advantage. Capt. Evanes is about to gett the Vessel Haul'd a Ground in Order to find out her Leak, before she can be in a Condition to begin to Load.

Shall Doe myself the Pleasure to advise you the Needfull by all Conveyances, & be allways very Glad to Receive your Commands, & to Render you any agreeable Service. I have not further to Offerr at Present but that I am with Great Respect &c.

ADDRESSED: "Per Capt. Breading Via Winnyaw & Copie per Capt. Shermerhorn Via New York"

TO THOMAS HUTCHINSON
Boston

Charles Town, 11th February 1742 [1743]

SIR:

My last to you was of the 23d October per Capt. Walker, & since have your & Company's Sundry most Esteem'd Favours of the 23d September & 22d November, also yours of the 21 September & 8th November all per the Brigantine *Richard*, Capt. Samuel Hallin, who arriv'd here the 8th. December & by whom have Bill of Loading and Invoice of Sundry Merchandize per said Vessel which have Receiv'd. There was Landed from on board said Brigantine Three Teirces of N. England Rum more than was mention'd in the Bill of Loading & Invoice. I have also your Favours two Days agoe of the 17th past & observe the Contents. There has no Opportunity happened for your Place, since my Last of the 23d October that I know of, otherways you might have Depended on hearing from me which Shall not fail to Doe by all Conveyances that may Offerr.

I am to advise you that your Rum per Capt. Hallin has Come to a very Dull Markett, this place being Glutted with it at Present, there having

11th February 1743

upwards of 600 hhds. arriv'd here within these Two months past from your Port & the West Indies, So that there is no manner of Demand for it, & have as yet been able to Sell but very little of it, & am not Likely to gett it all Dispos'd of at any Rate for a Considerable Time to Come. The Price is now at 15/ per Gall. & Likely to be Lower. However you may most assurdly Depend on my Utmost Endeavours for your Interest. As you Directed me to Let out the Brigantine *Richard* wholly upon Freight at arrival provided I Could gett above £3 Ster. per Ton for London, & which I did immediatly accordingly, having obtain'd £3.12.6 per ton & said Brigantine has been Sail'd over the Barr since the 2d Current after having been Detain'd upwards of Fourteen Days for want of Sailors, after being Clear'd out, & did Occasion to me not a Little Trouble. Capt. Hallin did Behave pretty well till the Vessel was Loaded, & than I perceiv'd his Conduct was not Extraordinary.

Inclos'd Please Receive account of the Vessel's Disbursments [536] & money paid Capt. Hallin, Amount £586.8.6 this Currency. You have also account Sales of Boards & Bricks on Account the Owners of the *Richard*, Neat Proceeds being £188.19.1, also the Owners Account Current, Ballance in my Favour being £160.1.11 this Currency for which I took Capt. Hallin's Draft on Mr. Richard Partridge & sent him at Same time Copies of said Accounts & advice thereof. Capt. Hallin was at no Expence here but what he told me was absolutely Necessary for the Vessel, having mett with a Great dale of bad Weather in his Passage here, & which he Doubted not to Satisfie Messrs. Partridge & Goldthwaite of at his arrival in London.

In yours of the 22d November you advis'd me to Load the Brigantine *Richard* with Rice on your Own account but Said Brigantine was very near Loaded before your Letter Came to hand. Inclos'd please Receive Copie of Invoice of 46 bbls. New Rice & five hhds. Deer Skins Ship'd on board the *Richard* on your Proper Account by your Directions to Messrs. Burryau & Schaffer in London Consign'd, Amount £2,286.12.11 this Currency. I gave Said Gentlemen timely advice for Insurance on Same accordingly. I intended to have Ship't more Rice on your Account by the Brigantine after Receipt of your Letter but the Vessel Stow'd less than Expectation. Rice is still at 40/ per Ct., but are in hopes it will be Lower Especially if Freight keeps as high as it is at Present.

There is no Bills of Exchange to be had here at Present or Silver or Gold in any Quantity, otherways wou'd have Remitted Said Gentlemen in those Articles on Account Your Rum per Tisehurst, of which there are

11th February 1743

Six or Seven hhds. of the Barbados still unsold, & is Esteem'd not very Good in Quality. And altho Rum is Generally Reckoned a Ready money Commodity here yet are oblidg'd to Give Three or Four Months Credit after the Sale, Especially when there happens to be a pretty Deal in Town. Shall soon make further Remittance to Said Gentlemen, as Opportunity Offers, in whatever may judge most for your Interest always Giving due Notice for Insurance.

I observe by your Last that you Intend a Ship of yours here soon if no advice to Discourage you. And I am to advise that Contrary to Expectation very few Shipping have as yet arriv'd here this Season, which has advanc'd Freight to £4 per ton for London £4.10/ per ton for Holland, but how Long it may hold or Continue So is very uncertain & precarious & Interly Depends on what Shipping may Come here this Spring & as no Doubt advices will Goe from this to Your port as also to N. York & Philadelphia of the Present Freight here, It may Occasion a Great many Ships to be Sent from your Parts, which may much Overdoe it & so overstock this Place, Especially if many Vessels Shou'd happen to Arrive at one Time, & as it will be the means of Raising the Price of Rice, Consequently Freight must fall & be Lower. So that you will be best able to Determine by the Number of Ships that goe from your Parts whether or not you will have Encouragement to Send the Ship you mention & if you shou'd Send her, hope your Directions will be pretty full in Relation to her Dispatch & Loading, & am to Desire you may Send no more Rum, Salt Fish, Axes, Bricks, or Boards this Season, being Dull Commodities, & believe that Single Refin'd Loaf Sugar, & Molasis as you mention, if they Come Reasonable with you, may answer the best of any thing from your parts. But Desire you may Send no Double Refin'd Sugar, there being but very Little us'd here in Comparison of Single Refin'd.

I did my Self the Pleasure to write my Brother in a particular manner in Relation to your Partner Mr. Thomas Goldthwait to whom have likewise writt severall under Cover of my Brother, & by Capt. Hallin in Particular. According to your Directions have paid Mr. Levi the Ballance of your Account Current with him being £19.15.6 this Currency.

[537] Inclos'd Please Receive Capt. Joseph Gowans Second Bill of Exchange for £28 N. England Currency on Capt. Richard Walker by him accepted, in my Favour, & to your Good Self Indors'd, being Money advanc'd him here at Capt. Walkers Request, as being known to you. The first Bill I Transmitted you in my Last Letter, which you doe not Take any Notice of.

11th February 1743

Have sold part of your Ribbons Since my Last, & am in hopes to Sell off the Rest, otherwise wou'd Return them as you Direct. Most of your Iron Potts still on hand; & the Axes Sell very Slowly. Shall doe my Self the Pleasure to write you by all Conveyances & I Most Respectfully Remain &c.

Rice 40/ per Ct., Pitch 35/ per bbl., Tar 30/ per bbl., Turpentine 15/ per Ct., Rum N. England 15/ per Gall. No Demand, Ditto Barbados 20/ per Gall., Ditto Madeira Wine £120 per Pipe, Flower & Ship Bread £3.15/ to £4 per Ct., Molassis 10/ per Gall., Single Refin'd Loaf Sugar 4/6 to 5/ per lb., Deer Skins 16/ per lb.

There is no Sack or Canary Wine in this Place at Present. A pipe or Two in pint Bottles well pack'd up in a Cask might answer if it Comes Reasonable with you. A parcel of Wooden Bowls, Pales, & half Bushell measures would answer better here than Boards.

Exchange to London £700 per £100 Sterling.

ADDRESSED: "Per Capt. Breading Via Winnyaw & Copie per Capt Shermerhorn Via New York"

TO JOHN PRINGLE
    Madeira

Charles Town, 14th February 1742 [1743]

SIR:
    About a Week agoe have the Pleasure of your most Esteem'd Favours of the 7th Ultimo per Capt. Patton, by which I observe the Original of mine under Cover of Mr. John Keith of the 15th May was not Come to hand. I have advice from London, that the Vessel in which I had Ship'd the Sixty Three barrells of Rice on your & Mr. J. S. Account had been arriv'd Some time, after having been oblidg'd to put into Boston & Unload her Cargoe there, having Sprung a Leak soon after She Sail'd from this, & Doubt not you have advice thereof from Mr. Keith before this. Agree-

14th February 1743

able to your desire please Receive Inclos'd Copie of your account Current, Ballance in my Favour being £3.15.5 this Currency.

What Wines Capt. Patton brought for Sale are already sold off at £120 Currency per Pipe, which is but an Indifferent Price Considering the high Cost, & happened to be the first that arriv'd with New Wines. There is another Vessel Since arriv'd With Forty Pipes & a pritty Deal more Dayly Expected, So that believe may be Lower, & agree with you that Wine is most Likely (if at all) to bear a Good price in the months of November & December.

I Duely Remark the Hint you are so kind to Give me in Relation to Sending Rice from this Directly for your Island, & when Opportunity offerrs Shall take Care to make Due use of it Accordingly.

For the Future Shall address to your Worthy house of Scott, Pringle & Scott for which have the Greatest Esteem & Regard, & in which I heartily wish you all the Success and Felicity you Desire. I am to Desire your House may Send me when you have the Opportunity of Freight for this Port a Pipe of Very Good Wine, being for my Own use. I Doe not Limitt you as to the Price which Leave Intirely to your selvs, but am to Entreat that it may be Choice Good, & am in a particular manner to Recommend to you that the Cask it Self may be very Good. Some of the [538] Wines per Patton on Freight were Landed but in very Indifferent order, Some of the Pipes Wanting four or five Inches of being full, Occasion'd thro' the Badness of the Casks, however understand that they were not Ship'd by your House. Please likewise to Send me an Arroba or Small Box of Good Dry'd preserv'd Citron when you send the Wine. And for the Amount thereof You'll please to Value on my Brother in London & your Draft will meet with Due Honour.

I Understand by Capt. Patton that Rice is plenty with you at Present, 'tho Messrs. Mayne in their last Letters advise of its being Scarce & high in Price at Lisbon, which has Induc'd me to Ship them New Rice by the first Vessels for that Port.

Please present my humble Service to Messrs. Scotts. Shall be always very Glad to be favour'd with a Line from your house when Opportunity Offerrs & so Render you any agreeable Service as being Most Respectfully &c.

Rice 40/ per Ct., Pitch 35/ per bbl., Tar 30/ per bbl., Indian Corn 10/ per bushell, Pork £10 per bbl., Beef £7 per bbl., Exchange to London £700 per £100 Sterling.

14th February 1743

This Goes Via Lisbon under Cover of Messrs. Mayne to be forwarded you.

ADDRESSED: "Per Capt. Archer under Cover of Messrs. Mayne & Copie per Capt. Grant"

TO EDWARD & JOHN MAYNE & EDWARD BURN
Lisbon

Charles Town, 17th February 1742 [1743]

GENTLEMEN:

Above is Copie of my last of 3d January per Capt. Young, Since have not the Pleasure of any of your Favours. And this Serves to Convey you Bill of Loading & Invoice of One hundred Barrells of very Good New Rice Ship't on board the Ship *Jolliffe's Adventure*, Capt. John Archer, Commander for Lisbon, on account & Risque of my Brother & Self Each one half Concern'd, amount as per Invoice being £1,073.1.6 this Currency and to your Good Selvs Consign'd which you'll please Receive & Dispose of to Our best advantage, & as it is very Good in Quality hope it will Come to a good markett & when Sold & in Cash for same You'll please to Remitt the Neat Proceeds to my Brother in London by Bill of Exchange or in Gold, Giving him advice for Insurance accordingly.

I am to Desire You'll be so good as to pay Capt. Archer the Freight at £4 Ster. per Ton as per Bill of Loading as also the half Subsidy Duty according to the Weight Due on the Rice in England. The Rice is Exceeding Good in Quality & Greatly prefferable to some shipt on board same Ship, So hope will fetch the height of the markett. But am to Desire it may be sold for Cash if possible, Rather than to have more by selling it upon Credit or to keep it on hand, so that you'll please to Dispose of it at Arrival as there is a pretty Deal by this Ship, & a Snow that will Sail for your Port Soon after. You'll please to Transmitt me account Sales of both Parcells. Rice is still at 40/ per Ct., but if a pretty many Shipping doe not arrive this Spring it will be Lower. It is observ'd that this years Rice is better in Quality in Generall than Last Year. I most Respectfully Salute you & am &c.

Exchange to London at £700 per £100 Ster.

17th February 1743

I have taken the freedom to Trouble you with the Inclos'd, which am to beg the favour you'll be so good as to forward per first Conveyance for Madeira.

ADDRESSED: "Per Capt. Archer & Copie per Capt. Grant"

[539]
TO THOMAS HOPKINSON
 Philadelphia

Charles Town, 17th February 1742 [1743]

SIR:

I am by this to Accknowledge the Receipt of your most Esteem'd favours of the 5th November last Advising of your being so very Good & Active in my Favour, as to Recover of Mr. Richard Howell £35.6.5 your Currency & that he assur'd you of paying £9.12.5½ more before he went to Barbados, & was to give his Bond for the Residue, for which am Greatly oblidg'd to you, very much approve of your Conduct, & for which Return you my hearty Thanks.

I am equally Surpriz'd with you that my Goods were sold so Low, & as to his saying they were old Goods, Mr. Howell does not doe me justice, for he had the Choice of the Best & Freshest Goods, & which he himself thought most Suitable for Philadelphia & as he has Render'd Such an Account Sales, by which they don't near fetch the Prime Cost, am to Desire that you may insist on Interest from the time of Sale which in his last Letter to me of the 12th May 1737 You'll observe he agrees to allow me from the Sale of the Last Goods, Copie of which please Receive here Inclos'd, & am to Desire you'll please to take Notice that there are no Dates in the Account Sales, when or at what time the Goods were sold, which does not look merchant like.

I am in hopes this Spring you'll be able to Recover the Residue, & am to Desire after deducting what ever you think proper for your Trouble & Charge, which I shall with Great Pleasure very readily allow, You'll be so Good as to Remitt the Neat Proceeds in Good Ship Bread in Flower Barrels when you have the Opportunity of Freight for this Place, & that you'll please to send me Invoice & Bill of Loading for same. And on the like or any other Occasion You'll please to Command him who is with Great Respect &c.

ADDRESSED: "Per Capt. Shermerhorn Via New York"

TO ROBERT ELLIS
    Philadelphia

Charles Town, 17th February 1742 [1743]

SIR:

    I hope this will find you happily arriv'd at Philadelphia after an agreeable Journey. There has no Opportunity yet happened for your Place that I might send the Things you bought, & which Shall take Care to Doe by the first Conveyance, & if Capt. Lindsey[2] who is here at Present, Returns back for Philadelphia you may expect them by him.

    Mr. Robert Williams is lately come back here from Bristoll & gone to settle at Port Royall.[3] I Talk't to him about the Ballance of his Note of Hand & he told me to Desire you to send him the Account of a Cask of Indigo you had as also of some Salt & a Servant & untill he has them he cannot settle with you.

    I am also to Desire you'll please to send me an Account Sales of the Two Negroes we were Concern'd in togither having never had yet the Account from you. And am likewise to Desire you'll be so good as to send me, if to be had with you, a Plan or Prospect of the City of Philadelphia done in a Frame which please Charge the Cost to my Account. And hope you won't forgett the Horse & the Box for my Garden you were so Good to promise me. My Wife joins in best Respects to Self & Good Mrs. Ellis & I am & c.

ADDRESSED: "Per Capt. Shermerhorn Via New York"

[Pagination skips to page 600 without any apparent omissions]

    [2] Capt. John Lindsay in the bilander *Lucy* arrived from Philadelphia. *SCG*, 31 January 1743.
    [3] Robert Williams held lot #308 in the original plan of Beaufort. He died 3 July 1776 at the age of 90. *SCHM*, IX (1908), 158; X (1909), 223.

24th February 1743

[600]
TO THOMAS JOHNSON & SAMUEL CARTER
Barbados

Charles Town, 23rd February 1742 [1743]

GENTLEMEN:

My last to you was of the 7th January per Capt. Bell to which please be Refferr'd & since have your most esteem'd Favours of the 31st December & Duely Remark the Contents.

The *Lusitania*, Capt. Gravener, has been Longer in taking on board her Loading than Expectation, Occasion'd by the Extrordinary large Size of the Timber which has been very Tedious & attended with a Great Deal of Trouble. However all is now in, & I expect him down to Town with the Ship tomorrow or next day & beleive may Sail in a Week hence having what Rice he Can take in Ready to put on board, being now under 40/ per Ct. but Indian Corn still at 10/ per bushell, which according to your Limitation prevents me from sending any. The only thing may prevent Capt. Gravener from Sailing so soon as mention'd will be the want of Sailors. Severall of Capt. Graveners having Run away from the Vessel so that he wants hands, & which is a Great Detriment here to Trade as Capt. Gravener will Inform you. Doe assure you that Nothing has been wanting towards his Dispatch.

Rum is now at 20/ per Gall. & no Demand, the Place being Glutted at Present with a very Large Quantity Lately Imported. As I shall have Occasion to write you again soon by Capt. Gravener, I add not but that I am Most Respectfully &c.

ADDRESSED: "Per Capt. Anderson"

TO GEORGE CURRIE
South Carolina [?]

Charles Town, 24th February 1742 [1743]

SIR:

I have not been favour'd with a Line from you, nor have seen you for some years, 'tho I understand you was in Town lately or near it. I was in hopes you wou'd have Discharg'd the small Debt you Owe me Before

24th February 1743

this & now of so long a standing. Inclos'd please Receive a Letter from your Father sent under Cover to me to forward you being very Anxious to hear from you & Doubt full of your being still Living as not having heard from you for a Considerable Time past, & Desire you would write him under Cover to me, which shall take Care to forward him per first opportunity as he Directs. Shall be Glad to be favour'd with a Line from you in answer to this & I am &c.

ADDRESSED: NO ADDRESS

TO PETER BAYNTON[4]
Philadelphia

Charles Town, 26th February 1742 [1743]

SIR:
I am by this to Accknowledge the Receipt of your most Esteem'd Favours of the 3d December per Capt. Evans of the Brigantine *Dolphin* with Invoice & Bill of Loading for 35 hhds. Rum & Two hundred Casks of Flower address'd to me by Messrs. Osborne & Oxnard & Mr. Thomas Gunter of Boston. Said Brig had the missfortune to spring a Leak a few days after she left the Capes, & mistaking this Barr Run ashoar in St. Helena Sound to the Southward of this Port, where she lay Sometime, but by timely assistance & Lightening the Vessel by taking out Some of the Cargoe was gott off again, & has been arriv'd here about three Weeks agoe with the Loss of three or four hhds. of Rum Leak'd out in the Hold, of all which have advis'd said Gentlemen the Owners. The Brigantine's Cargoe happens to Come to a very Dull Markett there being a Large Quantity both of Rum & Flower here at Present & in no Demand. The Rum had better been Sold with you & not Reshipt [601] & the Flower is Esteem'd but Ordinary in Quality. Shall with Pleasure very readily Contribute all in my Power to Cultivate a further Correspondance. I Salute you & am with Great Respect &c.

ADDRESSED: "Per Capt. Coatam"

[4] Peter Baynton, Philadelphia merchant, traveled to Virginia in 1722 in pursuit of trade. He later journeyed to Charleston where he married a Miss Paris and had business dealings with John Fenwicke and Cultcheth Golightly. *PaMH&B*, VI (1882), 17n.

TO ROBERT ELLIS
Philadelphia

Charles Town, 26th February 1742 [1743]

Sir:

The preceeding of the 17th Current Via N. York is Copie of my last, & this serves to Convey you Invoice & Bill of Loading for the things you bought of me, & now Ship'd on board the Brigantine *Debby*, Capt. Thomas Coatam, for Philadelphia on your Proper Risque & Account & to your Good Self Consign'd, Amount as per Invoice being £715.6.0 this Currency together with Shipping Charges, which wish safe to hands & to a Good Markett, & the Value thereof when Due you'll please to Remitt by Bills of Exchange(if to be had with you) to my Brother Andrew Pringle, Merchant In London, but if cannot gett Good Bills, in that Case You'll please ship me some Good New Ship Bread which am of opinion will doe better than Flower, by the Return of Capt. Coatam, who tells me that he will Return here again Directly. Have also sent you per said Capt. Coatam & Included in the Bill of Loading a Bundle Quantity One hundred & Fifty Peices of Lace by the Directions & on Account & Risque, of Capt. John Murray who is here at Present & Desires as he told your Self that you'll please Receive said Lace & dispose of it to his best Advantage & Remitt the Neat Proceeds to me in what ever you may judge most for his Interest. Shall be always very Glad to hear from you & I am &c.

P. S. Have Deliver'd the Key of the Trunk to Capt. Coatam Seal'd up in Paper & Directed for you.

ADDRESSED: "Per Capt. Coatam"

TO MICHAEL LOVELL
Antigua

Charles Town, 28th February 1742 [1743]

Sir:

I have your most Esteem'd Favours of the 4th January per the Bearer Capt. Murray in Return to mine of the 12th November & am much oblidg'd to you for your kind Advices of News, &c.

28th February 1743

As I observe in yours that Rice is at a pritty Good price with you being at 20/ per Ct. Please Receive Inclos'd Bill of Loading & Invoice of Thirty Barrells of Rice Ship'd on board the Brigantine *Carolina,* Capt. John Murray, for Antigua on my Proper Risque & Account & to your Good self Consign'd, Amount as per Invoice being £202.7.5 this Currency which you'll please Receive & Dispose of to my best Advantage at arrival, & Desire it may not be keept on hand but sold off for whatever it will fetch, & the Neat Proceeds youll please to invest, half in Rum if under 2/ per Gall. & the other half in Good Muscovado Sugar. But if Rum is not under 2/ per Gallon than please to Ship the whole Neat Proceeds in Good Dry Muscovado Sugar in Barrells per Capt. Murray who Returns here Directly.

We have no Material News here at Present only that we are under Some Apprehentions of another Visit from the Spainards this Spring. Shall be always very Glad to Receive your Commands & to Render you any agreeable Service as being Most Respectfully &c.

Rum is fallen here in price & is now at 18/ per Gall.
Exchange to London at £700 per £100 Ster.

ADDRESSED: "Per Capt. John Murray"

[602]
TO ANDREW LESSLY
Antigua

Charles Town, 28th February 1742 [1743]

SIR:

Since my last to you of the 12th November per the Bearer Capt. Murray have your favours of the 30th December with Invoice & Bill of Loading for Six Casks Rum to my address for Sale on Account of the Owners of the *Loyall Judith* which has happened to come to a very Dull Markett, this place being Glutted with it at Present, as Capt. Murray can well inform you. Above 700 hhds. Rum have been imported here within these Two Months past, whereof a Great Deal from N. England, insomuch that have not been able as yet to Dispose of any of it, having a large Quantity of that Commodity by me at Present. However no time shall be lost in Disposing of it to the best advantage as soon as possible, & in Sending you accouunt Sales thereof accordingly. It's pity that you did not Ship Rum sooner, when it was Scarce and bore a Good price.

Inclos'd please Receive Copie of your Account Current sent you per Capt. Gregory Via Barbados in March last, Ballance in my Favour being £8.12.0½ Currency of Antigua & the small Charge Since on the Cinnamon makes £8.17.6½ which hope youll find Right & Please to note accordingly. I am with Great Respect &c.

ADDRESSED: "Per Capt. John Murray"

TO JOHN DUNN, JUNIOR
    Antigua
                    Charles Town, 28th February 1742 [1743]
SIR:
    I did myself the Pleasure to write you of the 20th March last per Capt. Gregory Via Barbados which hope you Receiv'd & since have not any of yours Favours. Mr. Wadge, Master of his Majesties Ship the *Flamborough*, lately come from your Island per Capt. Jeffries, tells me that you were so Good as to enjoin him to have you Remember'd to me, 'tho at same time shoud have been very Glad to have been favour'd with a Line from your Good Self. We have a pritty large Crop this year, & am very Glad to hear it is the same in all the Leeward Islands. Shall be always very Glad to hear from you & to Render you any Acceptable Service. Please to present my best Respects to Good Mrs. Dunn & I am &c.

ADDRESSED: "Per Capt. John Murray"

TO ROBERT ELLIS
Philadelphia

Charles Town, 1st March 1742 [1743]

Sir:

I Refferr you to the Preceeding of the 26th past & yesterday Came to hand your favours of the 29th January & am very Glad to be Inform'd you gott safe home, & found your Good Family all well. You'll observe I had already Shipd the Goods per the Bearar Capt. Coatam before yours Came to hand as per Inclos'd Invoice & Bill of Loading. I would Ship you Some Rice per the Sloop but you doe not mention any thing about it in Yours. I add not but that I am &c.

ADDRESSED: "Per Capt. Thomas Coatam"

[603]
TO GEORGE LUCAS
Antigua

Charles Town, 1st March 1742 [1743]

Sir:

I am honour'd with your most Esteem'd Favours of the 20th January per Capt. Jeffries, & am to Return my most Sincere Thanks for your very kind offerrs & Continuance of your Freindship, for which shall always Retain the Uttmost Regard, & be always very ambitious to Render you & your Good Family here all the Service & Good Offices I am capable of. I am greatly oblidg'd to you for your Good Inclinations to serve my Interest in your parts, & for which shall always Retain the most Gratefull Accknowledgements.

Just now there is a Report that 3,000 Spainards are arriv'd at St. Agustine from the Havanna so that we are apprehensive of another Visit from them this Spring, & are but Indifferently prepar'd for a Good Defence, as wanting both Fortifications & Men to oppose them. Shall be always very Glad to be honour'd with your Commands & to Render you any Acceptable Service & I am with Great Respect &c.

ADDRESSED: "Per Capt. John Murray"

TO ANDREW PRINGLE
London

Charles Town, 1st March 1742 [1743]

SIR:

The young Gentleman, Mr. Thomas Elliott,[5] who will Deliver you this is the Son of my Good Friend Thomas Elliott, Esqr.[6] a very Noted Country Gentleman, of a very Opulent Fortune, & bears one of the Best Characters of any Gentleman in this Province. This is his Eldest Son, who he sends to London for some years under the Care of Mr. John Hewlett (by the Recommendation of Capt. Othniel Beale here) for his Education, & further insight in Business & on which his Father is to bestow, as I am Inform'd Five hundred pounds Sterling. He goes Passenger in his Majesties Ship the *Giberalter*, Capt. Durell.[7] I therefore take the Freedom to Reccommend him to your acquaintance & Countenance, & what Civilities you are pleas'd to Show him while in London will Esteem as a Singular Favour Done to &c.

ADDRESSED: "Per Thomas Elliott, junior"

TO ANDREW PRINGLE
London

Charles Town, 2nd March 1742 [1743]

SIR:

The last I did my self the Pleasure to write you was of the 10th Ultimo with Duplicate thereof to which please be Refferr'd, & since am as yet without any of your Favours, & no Vessel from England directly since Capt. White who is again Sail'd for Cowes. Please Receive Inclos'd Copie of Invoice of 100 BBls. Rice Ship't in the *Jolliffe's Adventure*, Capt. John

---

[5] Thomas Elliott, Jr. (1724–1756) married first Mary Bellinger and second Claudia McKewn. *SCHM*, XI (1910), 60.

[3] Thomas Elliott, Sr. (1699–1760) was the son of the Quaker Thomas Elliott of Long Point plantation on Charleston neck. The senior Elliott married three times: first to Buleah Law in 1720, second to Susannah———in 1727, and third to Elizabeth Bellinger in 1744. *SCHM*, XI (1910), 57, 59.

[7] Capt. Philip Durell, commander of HMS *Gibraltar*. RPC, p. 609.

2nd March 1743

Archer, for Lisbon, on our joint account, amount as per Invoice being £1,073.1.6 this Currency & to Messrs. Mayne Consign'd as I have already advis'd you of, & on which doubt not you have made the Necessary Insurance. The Said Ship sail'd over the Barr about a Week agoe. I have writt Messrs. Mayne to sell the Rice immediatly at arrival & for Cash if possible & Rather Something under the Markett than on Credit or to keep it on hand & so [604] Remitt the Neat Proceeds to you in Bills of Exchange or Gold.

We have no Vessels as yet arriv'd with Madeira Wine excepting Capts. Patton, Jenny, & Summersett Via Antigua & these three have not brought more then about Ninty Pipes for Sale. We have an Account of a Wine Vessell taken coming here, & another with 30 pipes Run ashoar in St. Helena Sound. Severall Vessels have arriv'd lately from the Isle of May with Salt, so that its now Sold at 7/ per bushell. I have writt Messrs. Scott, Pringle & Scott of Madeira Via Lisbon to Send me a Pipe of Good Wine for my own use & some Dry'd preserv'd Citron when Freight offerrs this Way & to Value upon you for the Amount & which doubt not You'll be so Good as to Honour. They fall about 20/ Ster. in the Ballance of their Account in my Debt, which doubt not they will discount out of the Cost of the Pipe of Wine.

I writt you yesterday by a young Gentleman nam'd Thomas Elliott, Son of Mr. Thomas Elliott a very Noted Planter & has a Great Estate. He sends him to London for his Education. He is his Eldest Son & puts him under the Tuition of John Hewlett, his Father being a peice of a Quaker & is to bestow 500 BBls. of Rice on his Education, as I'm Inform'd, I hope you'll show him your wonted Civility, being a young Man who has never yet seen any of the World or ever been yet out of the Province. He goes passenger in the *Giberalter*, Man of War, Capt. Durrell lately Come in here in his Way to England.

We have but very few Shipping now left. One or Two Vessels lately arriv'd Demand £4.10/ per Ton for London & £5 for Holland but a pritty many Vessels are Soon Expected from Boston & Philadelphia. Rice is now down to 32/6 per Ct. but a Great many Planters keep up & wont Sell at that Price, there being So few Shipping at Present. Capt. Patton is loading. I very seldom See him as he keeps mostly at Mr. Seaman's.

No News as yet from Mr. Reid which makes Mrs. Reid uneasie.

As payments Come in you may assurdly depend on all the Remittance in my Power, & Shou'd be very Glad that I Could Compleat the Sales of the Goods per the *John & Isabella* & *Susannah*, which gives me great Con-

2nd March 1743

cern, a Great part of both being still on hand & very unsaleable. Capt. Bailleul[8] has come here from Guernsey with some Wine & Salt in a Vessel belonging to One James LeBay there & Consign'd to William Yeomans.[9] Your old Acquaintance Robert Gray who you knew at Lisbon is lately Dead. He keept a Store in the Country & Owes a pritty deal of money in Town 'tho he has left more than will pay his Debts. I happen to be One of his Cheif Creditors.[1] He Married, since his Wife dyed here, a young Woman She brought over with her as a Servant by whom he has one Boy & has left his Wife Bigg with Child. He Dyed Suddenly & Intestate.

About a Week agoe Mr. Arthur Mowbray[2] who came lately over with Mr. Houghton being disorder'd in his senses Stabb'd himself in the Belly with his Sword, but the Wound proves not to be Mortal & is likely to Recover. Mr. Hobbs, Surgeon of his Majesties Ship the *Giberaltar*, who Seems to be a very Clever man, & who you may Probably See in London, having been pritty well acquainted with him here Can Inform you the particulars about poor Mr. Mowbray.

My Wife joins in best Respects & have not further to Offerr at Present as being without any of your favours but that I Remain &.

ADDRESSED: "Per the *St. Andrew*, Capt. Brown, & Copie per His Majesties Ship the *Gibraltar*, Capt. Durrell."

---

[8] Captain Peter Bailleul.
[9] William Yeomans was a Charleston merchant who was buried on 5 July 1752. *Register of St. Philip's*, p. 221. His will was dated 4 February 1750 and proved 22 December 1752. Wills, VII, 49.
[1] RP, as one of the administrators of Robert Gray's estate, sued William Livingston of Colleton County. Sibella Gray and James Osmond were the other administrators. Judgment Rolls, 1743–1744, 58A.
[2] Arthur Mowbray married Mary Stanyarn on 8 November 1741. *Register of St. Philip's*, p. 176. Arthur Mowbray, "Collington County surgeon," indicated by comments in his will that he was of an irascible temper and could not get along with his father-in-law John Stanyarn. The will was written 20 September 1745. Wills, V, 547.

[605]
TO HENRY BROCK
    Guernsey

                    Charles Town, 7th March 1742 [1743]
Sir:

I have not had the Pleasure of hearing from you for some years, & I now embrace the opportunity by my Friend Capt. Peter Baileul to pay my Respects to you & to assure you that I shall be always very Glad to Receive you Commands & to render you any agreeable Service. We have a large Crop of Rice & is low in price at Present being at 30/ per Ct. Currency, So that hope Capt. Baileul will make a pritty Good Voyage for his Owner, 'tho it was higher when he Loaded. Shall be very Glad to be favour'd with a Line from you. I Salute you & am with great Respect &c.

ADDRESSED: "Per Capt. Peter Bailleul"

TO THOMAS CLARK
    Wilmington, North Carolina

                    Charles Town, 9th March 1742 [1743]
Sir:

I have not had the Pleasure of hearing from you for near these Two Years past, was in hopes that before this you would have been so good as to have advis'd me what you have done in Relation to my affair with Capt. McDowall & whither you have as yet Recover'd the Money of him, which I am to Desire the Favour you'll be so Good as to advise me by the Return of the Bearar Mr. Cater or by the first Opportunity this way, & if you have Receiv'd it, that You'll please to Ship the Value in Pitch, Tar, Turpentine, or Rice, to Mr. John Erving, Merchant in Boston, N. England or to my Brother Andrew Pringle, Merchant in London on my Account, in Case you have no Opportunity of making Remittance to this Place & Expectation of being favour'd with your answer Soon I Remain Respectfully &c.

ADDRESSED: "Per Mr. Cater, Clockmaker"

10th March 1743

TO JAMES WIMBLE
New Providence, Bahamas

Charles Town, 9th March 1742 [1743]

SIR:

I have been Inform'd that when you sail'd from this you went Directly for Providence & did not put in at Winnyaw & North Carolina, & that since you have gott your Compliment of hands & are Gone on a Cruize, in which I heartily wish you all the Success you desire. I am to advise you that the time for forwarding your Bills being Come, if I doe not hear from you in a Month longer from this Date, shall be oblidg'd to forward them to London accordingly, & which doubt not will be Duely honour'd & which I thought proper to advise you of in case this may meet you at Providence, I am &c.

ADDRESSED: "Per Capt. Smith"

TO THOMAS BURRILL
Hull

Charles Town, 10th March 1742 [1743]

SIR:

Since my last to you of the 25th September I have the Pleasure of your most Esteem'd Favours of the 27th November per the Bearar Capt. Cook[3] & Duely Remark the Contents. I am sorry our Commodity of Rice is so Discourageing in Europe, but hope it will before long take a Turn for the Better. It is very low here at Present being at 30/ per Ct. & Freight to London is at £4.10/ per Ton Their being very few Shipping here at Present & none lately from Europe, which makes us apprehensive of a French War, & if so Our produce is likely to Lye on our hands & not be Exported.

I observe you have sent Mr. Marshalls Bond to Mr. Benjamin Stead. I have talk'd with him on the affair, who tells me that he knows [606] said Marshall & was at his House when he was at Cape Fear, so that must Refferr you to what he will write you in Relation to him, as no Doubt he will advise about him, as he knows his Circumstance there, & you may

---

[3] Capt. John Cook, brigantine *Good Intent* from Hull. SCG, 7 February 1743.

524   THE LETTERBOOK OF ROBERT PRINGLE

10th March 1743

Depend on all the Service in my Power in Conjunction with Mr. Stead, as I shall be always very Glad to Receive your Commands & to Render you any Acceptable Service. I am with Great Respect &c.

ADDRESSED: "Per Capt. Cook & Copie Via London"

TO WILLIAM COOKSON & WILLIAM WELFITT
Hull

Charles Town, 10th March 1742 [1743]

GENTLEMEN:

My last to you was of the 28th October & Since have the Pleasure of your Favours of the 24th September & Duely observe the Contents. I hope all my former Advices are come to your hands which I writt you in answer to yours of the 29th June, Vizt. of the 2d September per Capt. Smithson & 25th Ditto per Capt. Atkinson with Duplicate of the 23d October to all which please be Refferr'd.

I am to advise you that for want of Ships Rice is at Present low in Price being at 30/ per Ct. but than on the other hand Freight is very high being at £4.10/ for London £5 per Ton for Holland, so that altho the Price of Rice comes to your Limitation Freight does not, otherways wou'd have taken up a Vessell & Loaded for you according to your Directions of the 29th June, & am of Opinion that there will be but few Shipping here now & that Freight will keep high all the Season. I am also to advise you that your Colchester Bays still Remain on hand quite unsaleable as formerly advis'd not having been able to dispose as yet of One peice thereof, being not at all us'd here & have as yet Dispos'd of but of Six or Seven peices of your Broad Cloaths, as there are large Quantitys of ready made Cloaths imported from London, hinders much the Sale of such Cloths here & as I have already advis'd, you sent too large a Quantity of the Cloths, as also of the Lead shott most part of which is also still unsold. There is not Variety enough of the Sizes, & for the Gloves both Men & Womans, they are so ordinary & so much inferrior in Quality to London Gloves (which comes as Chap) that makes them also stick on hand. Am sorry you have happen'd to Send such unsaleable Goods & so ill sorted for this place, the Chief part of the Cargoe being still unsold. Shall be Glad to have your

10th March 1743

further particular Directions in Relation to them per first Opportunity, & hope you'll give me orders to Ship all that Remains on hand for Boston in New England or Philadelphia as you did the Buckrams where am of Opinion they can be soon Vended, & Doe much better than here, the Woolens especially being a Very perishable Commodity in this Warm Climate & very lyable to be spoilt by the Moth, & are Wore only one half of the year, so that no Great Quantity is us'd here of Wearing Apparell.

Our Sessions Comes on next Week, & as Capt. Ward has not Come to make his appearance [607] the Money will be forfeited & must be paid in Court accordingly. I am glad you have been so Good as to secure it for me, for which I am much oblidg'd to you. I was in hopes of having the Pleasure to hear from you by the Bearar Capt. Cook, from your port, who is loaded entirely with Pitch & Tar which is also low here at Present. We being in Want of Shipping, & none has arriv'd from Europe for sometime past which makes us apprehensive of a French War. If so, Our Produce is likely to Lye on Our hands & not be Exported. I have not further to offerr at Present, as being without any of your Favours, which however am in hopes of having soon, in the Meantime I Remain Most Respectfully &c.

Rice 30/ per Ct., Pitch 35/ per bbl., Tar 30/ per bbl., Turpentine 14/ per Ct., Deer Skins 16/ per lb., Freight to London £4.10/ per ton, Ditto to Holland or Hamburg £5 per Ton, Exchange to London £700 per £100 Ster.

ADDRESSED: "Per Capt. Cook & Copie Via London"

TO WILLIAM TURNER & LAURENCE JOPSON
Hull

Charles Town, 10th March 1742 [1743]

GENTLEMEN:

The preceeding of the 2d September per Capt. Smithson is Copie of my Last & by whom Return'd your Goods According to your Directions which hope are come safe to hand, Since have your Favours of the 12th November per the Bearar Capt. Cook & Duely observe the Contents.

10th March 1743

I have dispos'd of your Woolens, & you might have expected Account Sales thereof by this Conveyance but that I happen to be pritty much hurried at Present with severall Vessells that are agoeing, which however shall be Transmitted you by my next. I would have Shipd you the Deer Skins as you Desir'd by Capt. Cook if any had Come to Town in his Time as I expected, there being none in Town at Present as I told him, 'tho most of the money for the Woolens is still Outstanding, but Expect to Receive Same this Crop, & shall be Glad to have your Directions in what manner You'll have it Remitted in Case I cannot procure Good London Bills of Exchange they being very Scarce here at present, as there are no orders this Season to Ship Rice on Bills, there being it Seems no Encouragement for that Commodity in Europe this Year. We have but few Shipping here at Present, which makes all Our Produce Low in price & Freight high being at £4.10/ per Ton for London & £5 to Holland. I have not further to Offerr at Present but that I Remain Most Respectfully &c.

Rice 32/6 & 30/ per Ct., Pitch 35/ per bbl., Tar 30/ per bbl., Turpentine 15/ per Ct. Exchange to London at £700 per £100 Sterling.

ADDRESSED: "Per Capt. Cook & Copie Via London"

TO JOHN BROCK[4]
Guernsey

Charles Town, 10th March 1742 [1743]

SIR:

I embrace the opportunity by my Friend Capt. Peter Bailleul to pay my Respects to you, & to assure you that I shall be always very Glad to Receive your Commands & to Render you any Acceptable Service, & as I had the Good Fortune to Corrospond with your Late Worthy Mother Mrs. Mary Brock Deceas'd, so shall be very Glad to Cultivate & Improve an agreeable Corrospondence with your Good self. I Refferr you to Capt.

[4] John Brock was the brother of Henry Brock, merchant in Guernsey. RPC, pp. 704, 745.

12th March 1743

Bailleul for the present Occurrences here & affairs in Trade, Shall be very Glad to be Favour'd with a Line from you, I Salute you and am with Great Respect &c.

I am to Reccommend to your acquaintance my Brother Andrew Pringle, Merchant in London who will be very Glad of your Correspondence & to Render you any agreeable Service There.

ADDRESSED: "Per Capt. Peter Bailleul"

[608]
TO ALEXANDER ANDREW
   Rotterdam

Charles Town, 12th March 1742 [1743]

SIR:

The last I did my self the Pleasure to write you was of the 30th March last per the Bearar Capt. William Patton, Since have your most Esteem'd Favours of the 15th February & Duely Remark the Contents. Capt. Patton arriv'd here Via Madeira five weeks agoe & is now ready to Sail Loaded with Rice at £4.10/ per Ton Freight for your Port which is a pritty good Freight, being Loaded entirely by Messrs. Seaman & Stone, & if he getts safe to You, hope will make Good Voyage, having had very Good Dispatch, & Beleive the Small Quantity of Wines here for Sale are mostly Dispos'd of, as Mr. George Seaman Doubt not will adivse. We have very few Shipping here at Present, which makes Rice low being at 30/ per Ct. having had a Very Good Crop. A Small Vessel lately arriv'd has obtained £5 per Ton for Holland.

The Young Gentleman, your Son Mr. Patrick, left this place sometime before Mr. Seaman went for England, & has not been here Since. I am very much Concern'd that I Cannot give you a Satisfieing Account of him, & that he did not follow the advice of your Friends here, and as Mr. Seaman has had the Pleasure since of being with you Doubt not he has given you an Account in Relation to him. We have had no Vessels from Europe for sometime past which makes us apprehensive of a French War.

12th March 1743

If so, Our Produce is likely to Lye on Our hands & not be Exported. And there are Reports that the Spainards intend us Another Visit from Havanna, & St. Augustine this Summer, & we are as yet but Indifferrently prepar'd for them. My Wife joins with me in Our best Respects to your Good Lady & Miss Andrew, & having not further to Offerr at Present, as being without any of your Favours per your Ship *Andrew & Betty*, Capt. Patton, I most Respectfully Salute You & am &c.

Exchange to London at £700 per £100 Ster.

ADDRESSED: "Per Capt. William Patton & Copie under Cover of A.P."

TO THOMAS JOHNSON & SAMUEL CARTER
Barbados

Charles Town, 14th March 1742 [1743]

GENTLEMEN:

The last I did my self the Pleasure to write you was of the 23 past & this per the *Lusitania*, Capt. Sharnell Gravener, & Inclos'd please Receive Bill of Lading & Invoice of Eighty Six Barrells of Rice, 40,600 Cypress Shingles & a parcell of Timber & Plank ship'd on board said Ship *Lusitania* on Account & Risque of the Owners & to your Good Selvs Consign'd, Amount as per Invoice being £1,421.4.8 this Currency which wish safe to hand & to a Good Markett. The Ship is quite full. I woud have ship'd more Rice, but Capt. Gravener told me that he Could not take it in for fear of making the Ship too tender. Youll observe there is Ten Barrells of Old Rice which came low in price, the Rest is all New Rice of very Good in Quality, & hope will bear a Good price Accordingly. The Shingles are from the best maker in the Province & hope youll also find all the Timber very good according to the Different Sizes. Inclos'd please also Receive Account Sales of the Fifteen Barrells of Muscovado Sugar, Neat Proceeds being £362.3.0 this Currency. You'll observe it has lost a pritty Deal of the Weight in the Invoice, as Muscovado Sugar Generally Does. Have not yet Compleated the Sale of the Rum, there being still Seven or Eight hhds. Unsold, it being a Drugg here at Present, & no Demand. I happen to have a pritty large Quantity by me at Present & is now Sold under 20/

15th March 1743

per Gall. in Town as I am inform'd, So that [609] cannot at Present send you Account Sale thereof as I expected, but hope soon to Compleat same & by the next Opportunity of Freight for Your Island Shall ship what Ballance may be Remaining as formerly Directed in Rice, & in Corn if it shoud happen to be under 10/ per bushell as you Limited, which it is not Likely to be this Season.

Capt. Gravener has been Detain'd sometime for want of Sailors & which has given him a pritty Deal of Trouble, Severalls of them having Run away from the Ship since he has been here, & Two were Impress'd on board one of the Kings ships here, which however I have oblidg'd the Capt. to Return again to Capt. Gravener. The Freight of what Goods came here per the *Lusitania* besides the Owners, has been Receiv'd by Capt. Gravener & which doubt not he will Account for. His Mate makes by his Account the Quantity of Shingles something less than were Deliver'd on board, & which I understand has been Occasion'd by his Reckoning the Narrow Shingles at two for One, & are all Reckon'd alike here the Narrow as well as the Broad.

I hope by the Time you Receive this that Mr. Gedney Clarke may be Return'd from London. If so, please my best Respects to him & Congratulation upon his happy arrival. I have not further to offerr at Present but that I am most Respectfully &c.

Please Receive Inclos'd Capt. Graveners Receipt for £703.11.7 this Currency being the Amount of his Disbursments. Exchange to London £700 per £100 Ster.

ADDRESSED: "Per the *Lusitania*, Capt. Gravener, & Copie per Capt. Edward Evans"

TO ANDREW PRINGLE
    London
                            Charles Town, 15th March 1742 [1743]
SIR:
    I Refferr you to what I have already writt you of the 2d Current & Copie per his Majesties Ship the *Giberalter*, Capt. Philip Durell, who not being yet gone gives me the Opportunity of this per Mr. Hobbs, Surgeon

15th March 1743

of Said Ship, who seems to be a very good Sort of a Man, & who I Recommend to Your acquaintance, & am to advise that am as yet without any of Your favours & no Vessell yet from England, which makes us apprehensive of a French War. We have no Vessells hardly now left in the Place & no Freight to be procur'd any where, so that the Planters keep up their Rice, & wont send it to Town, there being no Sale for it at Present. There has some small parcells been sold at 30/ per Ct., but most of the Planters Refuse to Sell or engage at that Price in Expectation of a Good many Vessells arriving here soon, & so have a better price. Trade is very Dull here at present & payments very backward, a Scarcity of Money being much Complain'd of & Dry Goods Selling Daily at Publick Vendue.

Mr. Robert Steil Partner with Mr. Hume here has taken his passage in One Capt. Jeffries for Cowes. I understand he intends to Continue in London, & his Partner here.

Capt. Peter Bailleul desires his best Respects may be presented you. He Sails for Falmouth & Guernsey under the Convoy of Capt. Durell, as does also under said Convoy Captains Summersett, Jeffries, & Staple[5] for Cowes and MClellan for London, after whose Departure there won't be Six Topsail Vessells Left in the Harbour. A Small Brigantine Lately arriv'd from Boston has obtain'd £4.15/ Ster. for London which is the highest Freight I have known given Since I have been in the Province. A Snow arriv'd Two Days agoe with 180 pipes of Wine from [610] Madeira to Benjamin Savage & Company.

Capt. Gregory left his small Bower Anchor in Five Fathom Hole when he went over the Barr, & Since gott One of Our Pilots to Look for it but Cannot be found, so imagine that it is either taken up or intirely Lost.

Capt. Patton Sail'd over the Barr for Cowes the 13th Current having had Good Dispatch being Loaded by Messrs. Seaman & Stone at £4.10/ per Ton for Rotterdam, So that hope you will make a Good Voyage of it.

Inclos'd is a Letter for Mr. Alexander Andrew, being Copie of mine to him per Capt. Patton, which after perusal You'll please to Seal & forward him. I was not favour'd with a Line from him per Patton.

There are Reports that the Spainards intend us another Visit from Havanna & St. Augustine this Summer, & we are as yet but Indifferrently prepar'd for them. My Wife joins in Kind Love & Respects & I Remain &c.

ADDRESSED: "Per Mr. Hobbs, Surgeon of His Majestie's Ship *Gibralter* & Copie Via Cowes per Capt. Jeffries"

[5] Capt. Samuel Staples, ship *Jenny* to Cowes. SCG, 28 February 1743.

TO ANDREW PRINGLE
London

Charles Town, 15th March 1742 [1743]

SIR:

I have already writt you of this Date per Mr. Hobbs, Surgeon of his Majesties Ship the *Giberalter,* to which crave Refferrence. And this will be Deliver'd you by Mr. John Wragg, Eldest Son of Joseph Wragg, Esqr. of this Place, who goes passenger with Capt. Summersett to England in Order to spend some time there. I therefore take the Liberty to Recommend Mr. Wragg to your Acquaintance, being a Very pritty agreeable Good Humour'd Young Gentleman & what Civilities you are pleas'd to Show him while in London, will Esteem a Very Singular Favour Done to &c.

ADDRESSED: "Per John Wragg"

TO THOMAS JOHNSON & SAMUEL CARTER
Barbados

Charles Town, 17th March 1742 [1743]

GENTLEMEN:

I have already writt you of the 14th Current per Capt. Gravener to which please be Refferr'd & since Settling, severall of his Sailors have again left the Ship, which has detain'd him, & have been Oblidg'd to Lett Capt. Gravener have Fifty Six Pounds more in Order to Defray the Charge of procuring his Hands that the Ship may be Dispatch'd, & for which please Receive Inclos'd Capt. Gravener's Receipt. I am Most Respectfully &c.

ADDRESSED: "Per Capt. Gravener"

TO SAMUEL WATLINGTON
London

Charles Town, 17th March 1742 [1743]

SIR:

I Receiv'd your Esteem'd Favours of the 17th September at the Hands of Capt. Summersett, & am very sorry to be Inform'd of Your bad State of Health & Heartily wish You a happy Recovery, & a Perfect State of health.

According to Your Desire I have Ship'd on board the *Carolina Packett,* Capt. Summersett, Commander for Falmouth Eighteen Barrels of Rice on Your Proper Risque & Account & to said Summersett Consign'd, & for which please Receive Copie of Invoice & Bill of Lading for Same which wish safe to hard & to a Good Markett, Amount as per Invoice being £174.11.8 this Currency. Please also Receive Inclos'd your Account Current, Ballance in my Favour being £6.1.11 Currency which if you think proper you may pay to my Brother in London. Youll Please observe that there are Still Debts Outstanding on the Account Sales sent you, & Due by James Wathen, Richard Dale,[6] & Abraham Didicott, Amount £98.3.6 Currency, which am [611] afraid will never be Recover'd, Didcott being Dead & his affairs much Involv'd, & the other two are Gone off the Province, but if they ever can be Recover'd, or any part thereof you may expect immediate Remittance, & to be duely advis'd thereof Accordingly.

I have Deliver'd Capt. Summersett a Copie of the Invoice, who is Clear'd Out & Ready to Sail. Shall be always very Glad to have the Pleasure of hearing from you & to Render you any agreeable Service. I heartily wish you, Your Health & all Felicity, & am with Great Respect &c.

Exchange to London at £700 per £100 Ster.

ADDRESSED: "Per Capt. Summersett & Copie per Capt. Bailleul for Falmouth"

---

[6] Richard Dale, a weaver from England, was buried 17 December 1757. *SCHM,* XXIII (1922), 59.

23rd March 1743

TO ANDREW PRINGLE
London

Charles Town, 23rd March 1742 [1743]

SIR:

My last was of the 15th Current per Mr. Hobbs in his Majesties Ship *Giberalter*, Capt. Philip Durell, who has been detain'd in the Road ever since, also Duplicate of same Via Cowes & this per Capt. Dennis also Via Cowes, & have nothing matterial to advise since my last, only that am as yet without any of Your Favours & no Vessells from England, neither from anywhere else excepting Two Vessells from the Northward.

Beleive Shall have no Occasion to Draw on You as I mention'd in one of my Former to Messrs. Burryau & Schaffer. Two of our Gentlemen of the Council are goeing home, Vizt. Mr. Colleton[7] with Capt. Staple & Mr. Hill[8] with Capt. Jeffries both for Cowes under Convoy of the *Giberalter*. There also Goes Passenger with Capt. Jeffries Mr. George Austin, Merchant[9] who goes home Cheifly for his Health. He has been here about Thirteen or Fourteen Years & bears one of the best Characters of any person in this Place, & who you will find Worthy of Your Acquaintance being a Clever good humour'd Man.

Your Ship *Queen of Hungary* would happen well to fall in now from Jamaica, if Freight is not Encourageing for her to Stay & Load there. There is no Freight to be procur'd here at Present, there being few or no Vessells in the Place & what are, were engaged before they arriv'd, & no Bills of Exchange, so that Rice & Deer Skins will be the Only Commodities that Can be Remitted, unless sometimes a little Gold & Silver.

Two Privateers from Jamaica nam'd the *Hawk* & *Eagle* are arriv'd here a few Days agoe, Capt. Edward Fennell, Commander of Both. They have taken Two small prizes in the Bay of Mexico which are not yet arriv'd.[1]

---

[7] John Colleton was appointed a member of the Council on 16 June 1736. BPRO-SC,, XVIII, 31–32.

[8] Richard Hill's appointment was dated 4 August 1741. BPRO-SC, XX, 378–379.

[9] George Austin, a native of Shropshire, came to Charleston in 1730. He was a successful merchant and retired to his estate Aston Hall, in Shropshire, where he lived from 1763 until his death in 1774. HL, I, 176n.

[1] The sloop *Eagle*, Capt. Cornish, arrived on 17 March. The brigantine *Hawk*, Capt. Edward Fennell, arrived on 21 March. The two Jamaica privateers had been out only three weeks. They had captured on 25 February a Spanish sloop of 10 guns and 22 men, bound for the Havannah and laden with salt, skins, hides, red leather, hammocks, shoes, and some silver. On 27 February they had captured a Spanish brigantine of 10 guns and 20 men bound as the former with a similar cargo. SCG, 21 March 1743. The two prizes arrived later. SCG, 28 March 1743.

23rd March 1743

Times are very Dull here at Present for want of Shipping. My Wife joins in best Respects, & have no further to offerr at Present but that I Remain &c.

ADDRESSED: "Per Capt. Dennis Via Cowes & Copie per Capt. Macklellan"

TO JOHN ERVING
   Boston

Charles Town, 26th March 1743

SIR:

My last to You was of the 11th February per Capt. Breading & Duplicate thereof via N. York, to which please be Refferr'd, & since have not the Pleasure of any of your Favours. This goes by Capt. Evans of the Brigantine *Dolphin* belonging to Messrs. Osborne & Oxnard & Mr. Thomas Gunter, Loaded with Rice, Pitch, &c. part whereof is on Freight at £10 per ton Boston Money for Rice being the highest Freight ever known as I am inform'd from this to Boston. I have not been able yet to make Sale of their Effects for so much as the Charge of the Vesel Amounts to here, so that what I have Ship'd you per the Brigantine is all advance. Their Cargoe of Rum & Flower proves very unsaleable, this Place being still Glutted with both these Commodities, so that there is no Demand, as I have advis'd them.

We have had but very few Shipping here this Season hitherto & what may Come hereafter is very uncertain. A few Days agoe arriv'd One Capt. Ford[2] in a Brigantine from your Port which is lett out on Freight at £4.7.6 per Ton for London, tho severall [612] have of Late obtain'd £4.10/ per Ton for London & £5 for Holland. But as more Vessells arrive it is Expected that Freight will rather be Lower than higher, & yet more than half of Our Crop of Rice is still in the Province not exported. Rice is now at 32/6 per Ct., but as the Freight is high it is Thought will not answer in Europe. If you intend the Ship here that you mention'd in your last, would not advise her to be here latter than a Month hence of the 1st of May. There has no Vessells arriv'd here from any part of Europe

[2] Capt. Robert Ford, brigantine *Dove*, arrived from Boston. SCG, 28 March 1743.

26th March 1743

for a Considerable Time past, which makes us apprehensive of a French War.

I intended you a Turtle by Capt. Evans but there is none in the Place at Present. My Wife joins in best Respects to Your Good Lady & all your pritty Familly & I Remain Most Respectfully Dear Sir &c.

ADDRESSED: "Per Capt. John Evans"

TO THOMAS HUTCHINSON
 Boston

Charles Town, 26th March 1742 [1743]

SIR:
 The last I did my Self the Pleasure to writt you was of the 11 February per Capt. Breading, also Duplicate thereof Via New York to which please be Refferr'd, & since have not any of Your Favours. Since my last have Sold but very little of your Rum per Capt. Hallin, this place being still Glutted with that Commodity, so that there is no manner of Demand & is now sold a 14/ per Gall. As I am in Expectation of the Dayly arrival of the Ship you mention'd in Your last, Shall Ship what ever is dispos'd of Your Effects per said Ship according to Your Directions. Some hhds of the Barbados Rum per Tisehurst are still unsold, being Esteem'd but very Indifferent in Quality, which has hitherto prevented the Sale of it, having a pritty Deal of West India Rum by me at Present.
 We have had but very few Shipping here this Season hitherto, & what may Come here after is very uncertain. If Your Ship happens to arrive soon will obtain a very Good Freight. A few Days agoe arriv'd one Capt. Ford in a Brigantine from Your Port, which is lett out on Freight at £4.7.6 per ton for London, 'tho Severall Vessells have of late obtain'd £4.10/ for London & £5 per ton for Holland. But as more Vessells arrive it is Expected that Freight will rather be Lower than higher Tho' more than half of Our Crop is still in the Province, not yet exported. Rice is now at 32/6 per Ct. but as the Freight is So high, it is thought will hardly answer in Europe. We have had no Vessells from any part of Great Brittain for a Considerable Time past, which makes us apprehensive of a

26th March 1743

French War. I have not further to Offerr at Present, as being without any of your Favours. I Salute you & Most Respectfully Remain &c.

ADDRESSED: "Per Capt. John Evans"

TO OSBORNE & OXNARD & THOMAS GUNTER
   Boston
                              Charles Town, 29th March 1743
GENTLEMEN:
   I did myself the Pleasure to write you of the 11th February by Capt. Breading, also Duplicate thereof via N. York to which please be Refferr'd, Since have not any of your Favours. This per your Brigantine *Dolphin*, Capt. Jonathan Evans being now Loaded & Ready to Sail, & Inclos'd please Receive Bill of Loading & Invoice of One hundred Barrells of Rice, One hundred Barrells of Pitch, & Fifty nine Sides of Tann'd leather Ship'd on board said Brigantine on your proper Risque & Account & to Your Good Selvs Consign'd, Amount as per Invoice being £1,230.7.6 this Currency which wish safe to hand & to a Good Markett. The Rest of the Lading is on Freight at £10 per Ton Boston Money for the Rice which is at the highest Freight ever known from this to Boston, as I am inform'd. Inclos'd please Receive a Manifest of the Cargoe. I Recommended to Capt. Evans to make as Good Stowage in the Vessell as possible he Could. And Doe [613] assure you I have not yet made Sale of Your Effects for so much as the charge of the Vessel come to here, So that what I have ship'd You is all advance. Your Rum & Flower prove very Unsaleable, this place being still Glutted with both these Commodities so that there is no manner of Demand. The Flower seems to be but very Indifferrent in Quality, some of it that has been sold has been Complain'd of & fault found with it, as being Musty, & not Fresh Flower.
   You'll please observe that I have ship'd 100 bbls. of Pitch which is 40 bbls. more than you order'd, & which I was persuaded to by Capt. Evans in Order to Compleat the Flooring or Dunnidge of the Vessell, as none than Offerr'd on Freight, & as it is very Good & Comes low in price, hope will be no Disadvantage, expecially as Capt. Evans told me that he could not doe without it & that the Vessel is still Inclinable to be a little Leaky.

14th April 1743

Have also ship't the Tann'd leather thro' Capt. Evans his persuasion that it would answer very well at Boston & help the Stowage of the Vessel, as taking up no Room.

I am to Desire You'll please to forward a Certificate from your Customehouse for the Delivery of the Cargoe, as soon as you Conveniently can, in Order to Clear my Bond given with Capt. Evans for £1,000 Sterling.

Capt. Evans took Two BBls. of Flower of the Cargoe for the Vessel's use before he arriv'd here, & he has Receiv'd for Freight of Goods from Philadelphia £71.6 this Currency for both which doubt not he will Account for.

We have had but very few Shipping here this Season hitherto & what may Come hereafter is very Uncertain. A few Days agoe arriv'd here One Capt. Ford in a Brigantine from your Port, which is Lett out on Freight at £4.7.6 per ton for London, tho severall Vessels have of late Obtain'd £4.10/ for London & £5 per Ton for Holland. But as more Vessels arrive it is Expected that Freight will be rather lower than higher, 'tho more than half of Our Crop of Rice is still in the Province, not yet Exported. There has no Vessells arriv'd here from any part of Great Brittain for a Considerable Time past, which makes us to be apprehensive of a French War.

Please also Receive Inclos'd an account of the Vessells Disbursements here, & Money paid Capt. Evans, for which you have Inclos'd his Receipt, Amount £643.8.8. this Currency & for which shall Debit your account. I have not further to Offerr at Present, Capt. Evans being just agoeing, the Wind being fair so hope will soon be with you. I Salute you & am Most Respectfully &c.

ADDRESSED: "Per the Brigantine *Dolphin*, Capt. John Evans"

TO ANDREW PRINGLE
London

Charles Town, 14th April 1743

SIR:

The last I did my self the Pleasure to write you was of the 23d past with Copie thereof, and am as yet without any of your Favours which

14th April 1743

will Occasion Brevity, & not a Line from you since the 11th November. No Vessells as yet from Europe, & we find there has been none from thence to the Northward or at the Islands, which makes us Conjecture that there must be an Embargo at home or that Something Extrordinary has happened. We have very few Shipping here still & the Planters keep up their Rice & won't sell at 32/6 per Ct. As there are few Shipping & no Rice sold so Consequence no Trade, So that the Place is as Dull as in the middle of Summer when no Trade is Stirring. There is just arriv'd from Boston from Mr. Thomas Hutchinson to my Address a new Ship about 200 Tons Nam'd the *Good Hope*, Capt. Joseph Turell, Commander to be Loaded on Freight for London & am in hopes of Obtaining £4.10/ or £4.5/ per Ton. No Word of your Ship *Queen of Hungary*, if she Comes at all here the Sooner the Better. Very few Vessells have gone this Season as yet for Portugal & none here at [614] Present for that Kingdome which makes me imagine that it must be the best Markett for Rice & that it must bear a Good price there. If so, Shou'd think it worth Messrs. Mayne's While to Charter a Vessell or Two at London for to Send here for Rice to be Loaded on Bills of Exchange if none Can be had at Lisbon, as Rice will be very low here, there being still above half the Crop in the Province, & no great Likelyhood of many Vessels Coming here this Season, but you will be the best Judges in Europe whether it will answer there. This I only Offer as a hint for your Government.

This goes by Capt. Hallyburton[3] for London who came here from Jamaica & has a fine Ship for this Trade, but beleive will be Sold or at Least the Capt. Turn'd out for his bad Management here. Am told the Ship is Own'd by the Metcalfs at Hamburg.

Have been Oblidg'd to Sell Mr. Robert Ellis of Philadelphia, who was here lately, 20 pieces of the Russia Canvas at £17 per piece pay'ble in Six months & have Desir'd him to Remitt the Value to you in Good Bills of Exchange if he Can procure them. If not, he is to make Remittance here in Bread & Flower. A good Deal of the Canvas still on hand which Cannot make Sale of at any Rate. My Wife joins in best Respects & I Remain.

ADDRESSED: "Per Capt. Hallyburton & Copie per Capt. Ford both for London"

---

[3] Capt. William Halliburton, the ship *St. George*, to London. SCG, 11 April 1743.

25th April 1743

TO FRANCIS DALBY[4]
    London

Charles Town, 26th April 1743

SIR:

The Ship *Good Hope*, Capt. Joseph Turell, Commander from Boston, arriv'd here about twelve or fourteen days agoe Address'd to me by Mr. Thomas Hutchinson & Company of said place with Directions to procure a Freight for said Ship for London or Holland, and Freight Offering more readily for London, I have procured a Freight Accordingly for London part at £4.5/ per ton and part at £4 per Ton. I was in hopes of Obtaining £4.5/ for the whole, but severall Vessells having arriv'd before I had Compleated her Loading that struck for £4 per Ton, was Oblidg'd to accept of the same in order to get her Dispatch'd. The Ship will be ready to sail in three weeks from this Date, if the Weather keeps fair, and as Mr. Hutchinson Accquaints me that you are Chiefly concern'd in said Ship, thought proper to Advise you thereof. He has Ship'd a small Quantity of Rum which is very Dull Commodity at Present, Axes, &c. on Account of the Owners, in order to Defray the Vessells Charge here and which doubt not he has Advis'd you of. The Ship will make a very good Freight if gets safe Home, and by which shall do my self the pleasure to writ you again. In the meantime I remain with great Respect &c.

ADDRESSED: "Per Capt. Jauncey & Copie per Capt. Johnson"

[615]
TO BURRYAU & SCHAFFER
    London

Charles Town, 25th April 1742 [1743]

GENTLEMEN:

The last I did myself the Pleasure to writ you was of the 21st January per Capt. Hallin, with Copy, to which please be Refferr'd. And this is to Desire you'll please to get Insur'd on Account & Risque of Mr. Thomas Hutchinson of Boston, N. England on Good on Board the Ship *Good*

[4] Francis Dalby of London owned ¾'s of the ship *Good Hope*. RPC, pp. 616, 625.

25th April 1743

Hope, Capt. Joseph Turell, Commander for London, Two hundred & Fifty Pounds Sterling. The Ship will be ready to sail in three or four Weeks at furthest from this Date, and by which shall Transmitt you Invoice & Bill of Loading for said Goods. I have not further to Offer at Present, but that I am most Respectfully &c.

ADDRESSED: "Per Capt. Jauncey & Copie per Capt. Johnson"

TO THOMAS GOLDTHWAIT
London

Charles Town, 25th April 1742 [1743]

SIR:

The last I did myself the Pleasure to writ you was of the 21st January per Capt. Hallin with Copy, to which please be Referr'd. And this serves to Advise you that about 14 days agoe arriv'd here the Ship *Good Hope*, Capt. Joseph Turell, from Boston Address'd to me by your Partner Mr. Thomas Hutchinson with Directions to procure a Freight for said ship for London or Holland, and Freight Offering more Readily for London then for Holland, I have Procur'd a Freight Accordingly for London, part at £4.5/ per Ton and part at £4 per Ton. I was in hopes of Obtaining £4.5/ for the whole, but severall Vessells hapening to Arrive before I had Compleated her Loading that struck for £4 per Ton, was Oblidg'd to Accept of the same in order to get her Dispatch'd. The Ship will be ready to Sail in three Weeks if the Weather proves fair. You'll please therefore to get Insur'd on Goods on Board said ship, Two hundred Pounds Sterling on yours & Partners Risque & Account being on Account of the Rum, &c. per the *Richard*, Capt. Hallin, of which a great part still remains unsold and Payments are very Backward, otherways you might have Expected a larger Remittance by the said Conveyance. By my next shall transmit you Invoice and Bill of Loading of said Goods, & by Capt. Turell shall doe myself the Pleasure to write you again who if he getts safe Home will make a Very good Freight, and will have good Dispatch. I add not at Present but that I am Most Respectfully &c.

ADDRESSED: "Per Capt. Jauncey & Copie per Capt. Johnson under Cover of A.P."

27th April 1743

[616]
TO ANDREW PRINGLE
London

Charles Town, 27th April 1743

SIR:

My last to you was of the 14th Current with Copie to which please be Referr'd & am still as yet without any of your Favours. Capt. Ayers arrived here about a Week agoe, by whom was in hopes of having the Pleasure of hearing from you. He has its true been long from London, but lay at Portsmouth & Plymouth where there was letters sent that came by him for this Place.

About a Fortnight agoe arriv'd here from Boston the Ship *Good Hope*, Capt. Joseph Turell, Commander, Burthen about 200 Tons, a New Ship to my address from Mr. Thomas Hutchinson there, with Directions to Procure a Freight for said Ship for London or Holland & I accordingly procur'd a Freight for London part at £4.5/ per Ton & part at £4 per ton. I was in hopes of Obtaining £4.5/ for the Whole, but severall Vessells happening to Arrive before I compleated her Loading that Struck at £4 per ton, was Oblidg'd to Accept of the same. Mr. Francis Dalby is ¾ & Messrs. Hutchinson & Goldthwait ¼ part Concern'd & Goes to Mr. Dalby's address. The Ship will be ready to Sail in three Weeks hence. And am to Desire if think proper Youll please gett Insur'd on Goods on board said Ship One hundred & Fifty Pounds Sterling on your Own proper Risque & Account which I purpose to Ship in Rice for your Account.

Please Receive Inclos'd Generall Oglethorpe's Bill of Exchange for Fourteen pounds Sterling on Mr. Harmon Varelst payable to Thomas Hunt on Order Dated in Frederica February 21st 1742/3 and Indors'd by Thomas Jenys, having Receiv'd of him for Sixteen pounds Ster. Ballance of his Note of hand to Mathew Brown you lately sent me, & when in Cash you'll please to pay him Sixteen pounds Sterling & Debit my Account with the Difference. At Same time Deduct Sixteen Shillings Sterling being my Commission of 5 per cent for Receiving & Remitting. Inclos'd please also Receive Letter of advice for said Bill.

About a Week agoe I Receiv'd a Letter from Messrs. Mayne of Lisbon of the 4th March by a Vessell arriv'd at George Town Winyaw advising of the arrival of the *Bremin Factor*, & Contrary to my Expectation that the 100 barrells Rice was sold, a half at 3$600 reis & a half of it at 3$400 reis only & that they had Acquainted you of same, so that we are likely to gett no Profit by that Adventure.

The Act of this Province against the Importation of Negroes expires in about fourteen months hence but whether it will then be Renew'd for a longer time is yet uncertain. Shall be Glad to know if any attempts are like to be Concerted or promoted from London to Carry on the Guinea Trade to this Province as formerly, & if you are Inclinable to be anyways Concern'd, as I am in hopes of Coming in for a Share of this Business when the Trade is open again.[5]

Our Auditor & Land Surveyor Generall, James St. John Dy'd about Three Weeks agoe[6] & Left Mr. Richard Hill & his Own Son[7] his Executors who are both gone to England. His Son went about Three months agoe in Order as it's said to obtain his Father's Place thro' the Interest of his Freind the Bishop of Salisbury, tho' he seems very unfitt for that or anything Else. There will be no Doubt Candidates for St. John's Place, if his Son has not already gott it, & there is no person as yet appointed here by Our Governour pro tempore. Surveyor Generall is not worth much now. The Place of Auditor is in the Gift of Horatio Walpole, is the better place of the Two, for St. John had both. We don't hear a word of a Governour coming yet amongst us. All the Plantations have the Governours sent them Excepting this Province, which Shows that we are but a Little Consequence.

Mrs. Reid Receiv'd a Letter from Mr. Reid by Capt. Ayers of the 7th January in which he advises that he wont be here till the fall. He has writt to no other person that I know of. Inclos'd is a Letter for Mr. Thomas Goldthwait (as I dont know how to address to him) which after perusal please to Seal & deliver him. We hear One Capt. Widerburn is coming here & Daily Expected. Am in daily Expectation of your Favours which I Long much for. My Wife Joins in kind Love & Respects & having not further to Offerr at Present I Remain.

ADDRESSED: "Per Capt. Jauncey & Copie per Capt. Johnson"

---

[5] Passed 5 April 1740 for 5 years. *Statutes*, III, 556–568.
[6] James St. John was buried 6 April 1743. *St. Philip's Register*, p. 272.
[7] Miller St. John was his father's executor. Wills, V, 196.

28th April 1743

[617]
TO ANDREW PRINGLE
London

Charles Town, 28th April 1743

SIR:

I Writt you of Yesterday with Duplicate thereof to which Please be Refferr'd, & wou'd not omitt this Opportunity of Accknowledging the Receipt last neight of Your Most Acceptable & Long wish'd for Favours of the 17th & 23d November & 3d December, 15th, 18th, & 23d February & Duely Remark the Various Contents which I have not time to give a Return to per this Conveyance.

Inclos'd please Receive Generall Oglethropes 2d Bill of Exchange on Harmon Varelst for Fourteen pounds Sterling Indors'd by Thomas Jenys on Account of Mr. Mathew Brown, also the Original Letter of Advice with it. I am not a Little Surpriz'd & Concern'd that Capt. Wimble has impos'd upon me in such a Manner & that I am likely to be so Considerable a Sufferer by him. He went from this in December for Providence & from thence on a Cruize, & has not been heard of Since. Shall send a power of Attorney to Providence that in case he goes in there I may endeavour to Secure the Money. In the meantime please Receive Inclos'd his Bill of Exchange for Seventy five Pounds Sterling on Lambert Ludlow, Esqr. in London payable to my Order at Thirty Days Sight & to your good Self Indors'd, which please to present to Said Ludlow, & in case of none Acceptance & payment to gett it Regularly Noted, & Protested, & send back to me with the first Bill, that he may have no Occasion to Dispute the payment; in Case the Bills are not sent home & presented & Refus'd to be Honour'd, as I hope to be able to Come at him if Alive, Some where or other. The Charge of Noting & Protesting, please to Charge it to my Account & hope you'll forgive the Trouble. Inclos'd is also 2d Letter of Advice for said Bill. The Other Person the Bill was to be Presented to, is Joseph Parker, as he calls him, & not Perkins as you mention in yours.

Mr. Caw[8] lives here, and in Good Business. He came here from London just after Our Fire happened, keeps a Shop in the Druggist & Apothecary Way, & he practises Phisick & Surgery, and as soon as you Transmitt me

---

[8] David Caw, Charleston druggist and doctor, was church warden for St. Philip's in 1747, a member of the Charleston Library Society, and a justice of the peace. He died 20 Septembr 1758. Waring, p. 187.

28th April 1743

the Proper Accounts & Vouchers Shall use my Uttmost Endeavours to Recover the Money & follow your Directions punctually therein.

I am Glad you have Receiv'd Leapidge's money for which am greatly oblidg'd to you. I took his Bill on Samuel Smith for the Money & Indors'd it to Capt. Styles for the Value paid me, as I advis'd you by him, so Doubt not Youll Please Return him the Money.

I Observe Messrs. Cookson & Welfitt were to send you some Brazilletto Shipt them by me to be Sold on my Account as being Ship't without their Order, but said Gentlemen are Mistaken, for it was by their particular Order to Ship either Logwood or Brazilletto, otherwise wou'd have Ship'd neither, as appears very plain by their Letter now before me, as I shall advise them, & Observe the hint you are so good to give me about them.

As the Powers of Attorney from Messrs. Kay & Fairchild for their Fire Ticketts have misscarried by Capt. Beach shall gett fresh Ones from them & send you, as you think it necessary, 'tho I am inform'd Severall Ticketts have been paid without Powers, 'tho in the meantime hope payment of he Money won't be Stop'd on that Account.

I am very sorry that you have so much Trouble & are us'd so ill by that Deceitfull man Sanders. I have not writt him since I formerly advis'd you about him, neither doe I intend to have any further Correspondance with him.

I have a Short Letter from Mr. Reid by Capt. Wedderburn of the 21st February advising Cheifly about the *Griffen,* Capt. Sutherlands Cargoe. I have never yet had a Line from any of the Gentlemen Concern'd & Mr. Reid does not write me particularly who I must make Remittance to, which however I apprehend [618] to be Mr. James Buchanan. Please to advise me about it. Shall take Care to Deliver Lord Andovers Letter to Mr. Millechamp.[9] The person nam'd Fletcher, he writes of is still alive, & lives with his Family at Dorchester about 24 miles from Town. I have known him for these Eight Years past. His Wife practises Midwifry & is the most noted of her Profession in the Province, & beleive maintains the Familly by her Business.

I am again to pray You'll be so good as to send me the most material News papers by all Conveyances which please to Charge to my Account & in haste I Remain.

ADDRESSED: "Per Capt. Johnson & Copie per Capt. Stevenson"

[9] Mr. Timothy Millechamp was rector of St. James, Goose Creek, from 1732 to 1746 when he sailed to England because of his health. He tried to keep his cure at St. James, but was sent of letter of dismission, 21 May 1748. *HL,* I, 181n.

TO ANDREW PRINGLE
London

Charles Town, 30th April 1743

SIR:

The annexed of the 28th Current is Copie of my last & Since have your most agreeable Favours of the 28 February & 1st March per Capt. Young & Duely Note the Contents. Inclos'd please Receive Capt. James Wimble his Second Bill of Exchange in my Favour of £75 Ster. on Lambert Ludlow. Inclos'd please also Receive Copie of Account Current sent Mr. Humphrey Hill under Cover to you the 17th January 1739, Ballance due me being only £5.10 Sterling for which begg leave to Refferr you to my said Letter, paragraph relating to which please Receive Inclos'd, also Copie of my Letter to Mr. Hill about same. I shall not have Occasion to Trouble you with my Draft to Messrs. Burryau & Schaffer as I have already advis'd you, being I now Remitt them Considerably by Capt. Turell. Have Credit your Account £6.12.3 Ster. for my ½ of £200 Insur'd on the *Bremin Factor* to Lisbon.

I Duely Remark that you are to send the assortment of Goods on Our Joint account & the Sooner they are Ship't the better, & wish there was more Tea & China Ware being both scarce here at Present, as is also Womens bone Lace, Single Refin'd Loaf Sugar & 100 lb. or 200 lb. of Good Rich Indigo wou'd answer very well none being in Town, also Brown Ozenbriggs. If you learn that there is no Quantity of those Articles already Ship'd here before you Receive this you may Depend on their answering, as also 1,000 lb. Single Fine of very Good Gunpowder in half Barrells there being little Good here at Present. I also Note that you are so good as to Oblidge me with the small Orders for my Self.

I Observe what you are pleas'd to Hint about Gedney Clarke. His Ship went back sometime agoe to Barbados According to his Orders. He takes no Notice in his Letters to me of my kind Letter to you in his Behalf, & which you are so very Good to pay so much Regard to on my Account, which think does not agree with his Character in Barbados.

Severalls have told me that they have sent over their fire Ticketts to their Corrospondants without Letters of Attorney & only Indors'd them, as likewise those that bought Ticketts here had them only Indors'd.

I am Inform'd that the *Susannah*'s Anchor Capt. Gregory left near the Barr is taken up by One of our Pilots, unknown to me, & he wont Deliver it unless I can prove it to be his Anchor. His Name is Thomas Harden,

30th April 1743

Pilot. Please to gett Capt. Gregory to write him & Discribe the Marks of it & Weight, with an Order to Deliver it to me. The Anchor lyes on the Wharf, & he calls it his till an Owner appear to Claim it. When I Expostulated with Capt. Gregory about his Shutting out your Rice out of the *Susannah,* & that you wou'd pay a higher Freight by its goeing in another Vessell, he told me with an air that it was only his paying the Differrence of Freight, & which hope he will make no Objection to Doe if you insist on it.

My Wife & I are Greatly Oblidg'd to you for your most kind Invitation to your House when we Come to London, & in which I most heartily wish you, perfect health, Success & all the Felicity you Desire. I have advis'd you that my affairs would not permitt us to pay Our Respects this Summer but hope (God willing) to have that Pleasure the next. My Wife joins in kind Respects & I truely am with most Tender Regard &c.

[619] P. S. Inclosed please also receive Mr. H. Hills' Letter to me of the 5th October 1739 which explains the account Current & the said Ballance of £5.10 Ster. due to me.

ADDRESSED: "Per Capt. Stevenson & Copie per a Sloop Capt. Hall"

TO JOHN SMITH
London

Charles Town, 17th May 1743

SIR:

I Receiv'd about three Weeks agoe your Favours of the 24th February & Observe my Brother has paid you the Money I Receiv'd from the Executors of Mr. Green on your Account according to my Directions. I Show'd Mr. Seaman the Paragraph in your Letter in Relation to Mr. Johnston's Bond to you (who has not yet paid me one Farthing of it). His Answer was that, as he had told you in Lloyd's Coffee house, he woud pay it as soon as he was in Cash on Said Estate, which as yet he was not, & when he would, he Cou'd not Determine, which was all I coud gett out of him.

I have also talk'd with Mr. German Wright[1] about the Money you mention, who tells me that he is Surpriz'd you are not paid before this, & that it is your Own Fault in not making your application to his Friend, having made Remittance for that Effect. However he says he has lately Remitted some Bills of Exchange, & in particular made mention of your Debt, so that he Reckons you are paid before this Time, which if so, it is well, if not Please to Advise me. My affairs will not Permitt me to Goe for London this Summer, but hope (God willing) to have the Pleasure of seeing you the next. My best Respects attend Good Mrs. Smith & I am.

ADDRESSED: "Per Capt. Turell & Copie per Capt. Young"

TO BURRYAU & SCHAFFER
London

Charles Town, 17th May 1743

GENTLEMEN:

The last I did my Self the Pleasure to write you was of the 25th Ultimo with Duplicate thereof Advising for Insurance of Two hundred & Fifty pounds Sterling on goods per the Ship *Good Hope*, Capt. Joseph Turell, Commander for London to which please be Refferr'd. And Inclos'd please Receive Bill of Loading & Invoice of One hundred Barrells Rice & Two Hogsheads Deer Skins Shipt on board the Said Ship *Good Hope* on the proper Account & Risque of Mr. Thomas Hutchinson of Boston & to your good Selvs Consign'd, Amount as per Invoice being £1,705.7.7 this Currency which wish safe to hand & to a Good Markett. The Ship is Clear'd out & Ready to Sail & hope will soon be with you. You'll please to Advise Mr. Hutchinson of the said Remittance. Shall be very Glad to have the Pleasure of a Line from You, & to Render you any Acceptable Service here, as being Most Respectfully &c.

ADDRESSED: "Per Ditto Turell & Copie per Capt. Young"

---

[1] Jermyn Wright, Charleston merchant, became a partner in the firm of Stiell and Hume in the 1750's. *HL*, I, 149n.

TO THOMAS GOLDTHWAIT
London

Charles Town, 17th May 1743

SIR:

My last to you was of the 25th Ultimo with Duplicate thereof to which please be Refferr'd. And this per the Ship *Good Hope*, Capt. Joseph [*Turell*], for London & Inclos'd please Receive Bill of Loading & Invoice of Sixty Six Barrells of Rice & Two hogsheads Deer Skins shipt on board said Ship on the Joint Account of your Partner Mr. Thomas Hutchinson & Your Good Self & to you Consign'd, amount as per Invoice being £1,349.17.10 this Currency which wish Safe to hand & hope will Come to a Good Markett. I fully Intended to have Ship'd you 100 Bbls. Rice per Capt. Turell, & he only is to blame you have not said Quantity, having Assur'd me that his Ship would Certainly Carry 800 bbls. of Rice, & You'll observe falls Greatly Short [620] of that Number. The Remittance is on Account of the Rum, &c. per Capt. Hallin of which a Great part is still on hand, being very slow in Sale, there having been a Great Deal of that Commodity lately Imported from the West Indies which has Greatly Overdone this Markett, insomuch that N. England Rum is now sold at 12/6 per Gall. there being still a very Considerable Quantity of it Still in Town. There has been a Great Deal too much of it Imported here & pritty near all at One Time.

Mr. Thomas Hutchinson in his last Letter to me advises that as there is nothing at Boston that Gives a Prospect of advantage at this Markett, he imagines Something may be done from London, & if I woud send you an Invoice of what Goods May be Suitable for this Place to the Amount of Five hundred pounds Sterling You woud readily send them. Please therefore Receive Inclos'd an Invoice of Goods accordingly, which if think proper to send here per first Vessell for this Place Shall use my Utmost Endeavours to Dispose of to your best advantage, & Doubt not may be able to make Returns for Same next Spring as you Shall Direct, The Goods mention being a Suitable assortment for this Place. Capt. Turell is ready to Sail & hope will soon be with you. I have not further to Offerr at Present but that I am most Respectfully &c.

ADDRESSED: "Per Ditto Turell & Copie per Capt. Young"

TO ANDREW PRINGLE
London

Charles Town, 19th May 1743

SIR:

My last to you was of the 30th past with Duplicate thereof to which please be Refferr'd, & a few Days agoe came to hand your most acceptable Favours of the 9th & 11 March per the *Minerva,* Capt. Cload, & Duely Note the contents. I am very Glad to observe by Yours of the 11 that your *Susannah* was at last arriv'd off Dover, also that Capt. Hallin was arriv'd who must have had a Quick passage. Have Credit your Account £32.7/ Ster. you have been so good as to Pay David Glen on my Account. I have Recover'd for you Hans Springs Money, being £56 Currency for which please to Debit my Account being £8 Ster., Exchange at 7 per 1.

Please Receive Inclos'd Bill of Loading & Invoice of One hundred Barrells of very Good Rice shipt on board the Ship *Good Hope,* Capt. Joseph Turell, Commander for London (by whom this Goes) on your proper Account & Risque & to you Consign'd, Amount as per Invoice being £979.7.0 this Currency which wish safe to hand, & hope will come to a Good Markett being Choice Rice & very good in Quality. I have also Ship'd to Messrs. Burryau & Schaffer on Account of Mr. Thomas Hutchinson of Boston, & to Mr. Thomas Goldthwait on their Joint Account as youll Observe by the Inclos'd Manefest of the Cargoe. Mr. Hutchinson advises me as there is nothing he can send from Boston that will answer here, that I woud send an Invoice of about £500 Sterling of what Goods would doe here to Mr. Goldthwait & he will send them on their Account in Order to have Returns made them next Spring & which I have done accordingly by this Conveyance, in what things I have thought will be Most Suitable & attended with the Least Trouble, being not fond of Dry Goods on Commission.

Please Receive Inclos'd The Reverand Mr. John Fordyce[2] his Bill of Exchange for Fifteen pounds Ster. on Messrs. William & Thomas Tryon[3] payable to William Fleming at 30 days Sight & to your Good Self In-

---

[2] John Fordyce, A. M., was ordained in 1730 by the Bishop of St. David's. In 1736 the SPG sent him as a missionary to Prince Frederick Parish where he remained until his death in 1751. Dalcho, pp. 319–320; George C. Rogers, Jr., *The History of Georgetown County, South Carolina* (Columbia, S. C., 1970), pp. 80–84.

[3] Thomas Tryon, a West India merchant, was a Director of the Royal Exchange Assurance Co. He and his brother, William, were treasurers to the SPG. He died 8 October 1747. *HL*, I, 124n; *RPC*, p. 683.

19th May 1743

dors'd, which doubt not will be Duely honour'd, on which please to doe the Needfull, & when in [621] Cash Credit my Account for same.

I made your Compliments to Our Chief Justice Mr. Whitaker as you Desir'd, who seem'd well Satisfied that the Merchants take Notice of his good Offices in Relation to preventing the Emission of Paper Currency, which is an Injury to the Province & especially to Trade, 'tho most of Our Country People here are for having a Great Deal of Currency.

The Worthy Mr. Manigualt has Resign'd the Place of Publick Treasurer for the Province & Mr. Jacob Motte is appointed by Our Assembly in his Room, 'tho it is said George Saxby, & severall others intend to make Application for Treasurer at home, that One may be appointed from England for the Future. It is worth about £200 Ster. per Annum.[4]

I Deliver'd my Lord Andovers Letter to Mr. Millechamp, who since tells me that he is soon to Send My Lord Authentick Papers of Henry Fletcher's being alive here & well.

Samuel Wragg has Fild a Bill in Chancery against my Wife's Father Mr. Allen's Estate about an Old Account of Anno 1725 & the Executors are of Opinion that he was paid in full by Mr. William Minett in London long since. Inclos'd is Copie of their Letter to Said Gentleman, which after perusal please to Seal & Deliver him, & at same time ask him if he has already Receiv'd Copie from them of said Letter, & that he'll be so Good as to write them an answer to it as soon as he Can, or give his Letter to You to forward me. The Sum Mr. Wragg demands is about £300 Sterling.[5]

I Observe what you are pleas'd to mention about Madeira Wine. It is now from £120 to £115 per pipe a pretty Deal having come in, but not Likely to Come to your Limitation of £80 or £90 per pipe at least what is fitt for the London Markett, which must be very Good, but if it shoud so happen You may Depend on having your Directions punctually Comply'd with.

---

[4] Gabriel Manigault, a wealthy Huguenot merchant, was reputed to be the richest man in South Carolina. He was active in public affairs, serving in the Commons House and as Public Treasurer (1735–1743). Jacob Motte succeeded Manigault as Public Treasurer and remained in office until 1770. *HL*, I, 191n; Marion Eugene Sirmans, *Colonial South Carolina: A Political History, 1663–1763* (Chapel Hill, N. C., 1966), p. 252.

[5] Samuel Wragg filed the bill in chancery on 10 May 1743. The bill was not dismissed until May 1747 when the court decided that the complainant had "his Remedy at Common Law." *Records of the Court of Chancery of South Carolina, 1671–1779*, Anne King Gregorie, ed. (Washington, D. C., 1950), pp. 397, 402, 407, 412–13.

19th May 1743

There has lately come over here a printed Paper by way of Satyre or Invective, & it is Suppos'd to be on James Crokatt Calling him a Scotch Jew Lately Come from So. Carolina, & it is Said was handed about at the Coffee houses in London. If you have not sent the Verticle Dial before this Comes to hand, please to Lett it be a South Verticle Dial to put on the End of my House to the South.

Please Receive Inclos'd Account Sales of the Rum, &c. ship'd by Mr. Clarke per your Ship *Susannah* from Barbados in Return of the Cargoe Shipt there, Neat Proceeds being £2,600.7.2 this Currency for which have Credit your Account.

You have also Inclos'd another Letter of Attorney to You from John Keys in Order to Receive the Fire Tickett formerly sent you. As for John Fairchild[6] he Lives up in the Country & has not been in Town since to gett another from him, but hope you won't need it. However if Can gett Another from him, Shall send it you.

We have had no Turtle here as yet this Season, otherways you might have Expected one by Capt. Turell.

On the 14th Current arriv'd here Capt. Alexander Keith of the Snow *Caesar* from Madeira, Recommended to me by Messrs. Scott, Pringle & Scott there who advise me that Capt. Keith has come Chiefly in hopes of procuring a Good Freight for London. He has On board Twenty Pipes of Wine on account of his Kinsman Mr. John Keith of London who is also Concern'd with him in the Vessell. He has apply'd to me & put the Wines under my Care for Sale, & I have accordingly Lett out his Vessell on Freight at £3.15/ per Ton for London & will be Loaded in Three Weeks which is the highest Freight at Present, Freight having fallen insomuch that Capt. Wedderburn from London & some others have taken in Some at £3.5/ & £3.10/ for London. I intend to advise Mr. John Keith of Capt. Keith by this Conveyance, & I purpose to Ship Mr. James Buchanan 100 or 150 barrells Rice on account the Owners of the *Griffen* per Capt. Keith & advise him [622] thereof Accordingly.

Rice has been sometime & is still at 35/ per Ct. Shall also Write Mr. Reid in answer to his per next Conveyance.

Inclos'd please also Receive an assortment of Goods for the Indian Trade which I had of Two Indian Traders & who will take them off my Hands Deliver'd here at the Current price for Such Goods & if you think proper to Send them on Our Joint Account, Let them be Shipt as Soon

[6] John Fairchild was a deputy surveyor. *SCHM*, VIII (1907), 95.

as you Can that they may be here if possible in November next or Sooner, & Lett the Whole Assortment be of about £500 Ster. Value of which the Strouds will be about ⅓d Value of the Whole, & if you have any Freind in Bristoll, it will be most proper to have them from thence from the Same person that Samuel Eveleigh[7] has his, which are Esteem'd the best & are most Saleable, & London Duffle Blanketts are Esteem'd better than Bristoll, as are all the Other Articles excepting the Strouds only. My Wife joyns in best Respects & I most Affectionately Remain &c.

ADDRESSED: "Per the *Good Hope,* Capt. Joseph Turell, & Copie per Capt. Ayers"

TO JOHN KEITH
London

Charles Town, 19th May 1743

SIR:

My last to you was of the 21st October with Duplicate thereof to which please be Refferr'd, Since have not the Pleasure of any of your Favours. I am to advise you that on the 14th Current arriv'd here the Snow *Caesar,* Capt. Alexander Keith, Commander from Madeira & Recommended to me by Messrs. Scott, Pringle & Scott who advises that you are part Concern'd in the Vessell with Capt. Keith who is your Relation, & who I shall very Readily & with Pleasure Render all the Assistance & Good Offices I am Capable of, as well on yours as on Said Gentlemen's Account. As Capt. Keith has come here for a Freight he has happen'd to Come at a Time to meet with a pritty Good One & will have very Good Dispatch, having obtain'd £3.15/ per ton for London, & will be Loaded in Three Weeks. It's true Freight has been higher here, but at Capt. Keith's arrival it was only at £3.5/ per Ton & as I cou'd raise it 10/ per ton, thought it most for your Interest to strike in Time, especially as a Great Many Vessells are Dayly Look't for, when it is Expected Freight will be at £3 per Ton & under.

[7] Samuel Eveleigh of Bristol and Charleston, merchant, was involved in the Indian trade in South Carolina longer and more extensively than any other merchant in the colony. Crane, pp. 108, 121–23.

Capt. Keith has put under my Care Twenty Pipes of Wine on your Account, but as a pretty Deal has happened to Come in here of Late, am affraid will Come but to an Indifferent Markett, being sold at Present at £115 per pipe by the Quantity. However you may Most assurdly Depend on my Utmost Endeavours to Dispose of them to your best advantage & as Quick as possible, & in makeing Returns in what Ever may Judge most for your Interest.

Capt. Keith writes you by this Conveyance, to which please be Refferr'd, & as I shall doe my Self the Pleasure to write you again Soon by him, I add not at Present but that I am with Great Respect &c.

James Ogilvie presents his best Respects to you.

Exchange to London at £700 per £100 Sterling.

ADDRESSED: "Per Capt. Turell & Copie per Capt. Ayers"

[623]
TO JAMES BUCHANAN
London

Charles Town, 17th May 1743

SIR:
I have not had the Pleasure of being favour'd with a Line from Any of the Gentlemen Concern'd in the Ship *Griffen*'s Cargoe, but as I understand by Mr. James Reid that the Returns are to be made to Your Self, You'll please therefore to gett Insur'd on Goods on Board the Snow *Caesar*, Capt. Alexander Keith, Commander for London Two hundred & fifty pounds Sterling being on Account of the Owners of the *Griffen* which I purpose to Ship in Good Rice & to you Consign'd. The Vessell will be ready to Sail in Three Weeks & by which shall doe my Self the Pleasure to Write you again, & at same time Transmitt you Bill of Loading & Invoice. In the Meantime I Remain most Respectfully &c.

ADDRESSED: "Per Capt. Turell & Copie per Capt. Ayers"

19th May 1743

TO JAMES REID
London

Charles Town, 19th May 1743

SIR:

About three Weeks agoe came to hand your Esteem'd Favours of the 21st February & am very Glad to be Inform'd of your Recovery from your late Illness, & hope this will find you in perfect Health. I Duely Remark what you are pleas'd to advise in Relation to Mr. Fryar & the *Griffen*'s Cargoe.

I have by this Conveyance given advice to Mr. James Buchanan to gett Insur'd on Goods on board the Snow *Caesar*, Capt. Alexander Keith, for London Two hundred & fifty pounds Sterling being on Account of the Owners of the *Griffen* which I purpose to Ship in Good Rice & to Said Gentleman Consign'd, as I apprehend it is your Meaning that what ever we Remitt on Our part on Said Account Shou'd goe to Mr. Buchanans address, & to him Only.

Our Planters have been this Crop, hitherto, very Backward in pay & have keept up their Rice from Sale in Expectation of a higher price for it all this Season. It is now & has been for Sometime at 35/ per Ct. & Freight for London is at £3.15/ per Ton.

Mr. Edward Thomas has not paid any further part of his Bond, Since the Bills you had which I Observe by yours are paid. Mr. Peter Du Plissis[8] of Santee is Dead whose Bond is very Considerable & am afraid, by what I Understand, there wont be Sufficient to pay his Debts. There are also a Good many other Bonds yet unpaid having Receiv'd as yet but Little since you have gone. However you may Depend on my Doeing my best to gett the Bonds paid & to make Remittances to Mr. James Buchanan Accordingly, in what ever may Judge most for the Interest of the Owners of the *Griffen*. Have never yet been favour'd with a Line from any of the Gentlemen Concerned.

We have no Material News here at Present. Mrs. Reid & Miss Reid are both in perfect Health.[9] Shall with Great Pleasure Render you & yours

---

[8] Peter DuPlessis had arrived in September 1736 to be the rector of the parish of St. James Santee. Arthur Henry Hirsch, *The Huguenots of Colonial South Carolina* (Durham, 1928), p. 66; Deeds, AA, 153.

[9] No record has been found of a daughter of Reid's or of any other female relative in South Carolina at this time, so presumably the reference to "Miss Reid" was a slip of the pen and RP meant to refer to Reid's son, Thomas. On 21 February 1737, Thomas, son of James Reid and Dorothy his wife, was baptized. *St. Philip's Register*, p. 80.

21st May 1743

all the good Offices & Service I am capable of. I heartily wish you a Good Passage Over, & I am &c.

ADDRESSED: "Per Capt. Turell & Copie per Capt. Young under Cover of A.P."

[624]
TO THOMAS CLARK
Wilmington, North Carolina

Charles Town, 21st May 1743

SIR:
I have yours of the 9th Current per post in Return to mine of the 9th March, in which you advise that All that You Know of McDowalls affairs is that you Caus'd arrest him, & had agreed with a Lawyer to prosecute him, & about Eighteen months agoe you was Told that I had Recall'd (as you Express it) my Power of Attorney to you & Given it to another. The Recalling my Power you allow, to be only hear say, by being told so & in fact it was no more than hear Say, for I gave no power to any other person. It is True indeed about Fourteen months agoe & not Longer I gave an Order to a person to Receive the money of Capt. McDowall in Case you had not Receiv'd it, or done any thing in it, which I think I had very good Ground for to Doe, as not having heard from you in So long a Time, & as you have had the Power ever Since the 1st August 1740 & never advis'd me of Late about it. If you had no Inclination to Doe any Thing in it you Ought to have been So Candid as to have acquainted me thereof, & I woud not have Troubled you. However by what I understand I am at no Loss as it has happened, & that I am still equally in as Good a Situation, by its being in *Statu quo* than if it had been otherways. When you think to Send the small Account of Charges which you Say is Due to you in that Affair properly attested, I am very ready to pay it, & I am &c.

ADDRESSED: "Per Post"

TO JOHN DICKINSON
Beaufort Town, North Carolina

Charles Town, 21st May 1743

SIR:

I have been favour'd with severall of yours the Last of the 24th September advising of your being than bound to Philadelphia & so from thence here to this Place, & was in hopes of Seeing you here before now accordingly. I am by this to advise you that as your Bond has been now Due sometime, I am in hopes youll be so good as to take proper measures to Discharge it & if You don't Come here soon your self, You'll please order the Payment Some way or other, Either by way of Philadelphia in Bread & Flower or by Way of the West Indies in Rum & Sugar, & if this Does not find you in North Carolina, hope you are Gone to the West Indies & that you will Call in here from thence.

All Sort of Provisions are Plenty here at Present Excepting Pork, which is Scarce & would fetch £12. per bbl., but than it pays a Duty of Two pounds or Forty Shillings this Currency per barrell. I hope You'll be so good as to Let me have the Pleasure of hearing from you as soon as you Can in answer to this; & when I may Depend on payment of Your Bond & youll Oblidge &c.

ADDRESSED: "not Sent"

[625]
TO DANIEL DUNBIBIN
Wilmington, North Carolina

Charles Town, 21st May 1743

SIR:

My last to you was of the 23d November last, Since have not any of your favours. Am Glad to hear of your Safe Return from the West Indies. Capt. Murray Sail'd for Antigua in February last, & hope you had the Good luck to meet with him there, & that he paid the Demand you had on him for the Skins. He is not yet Return'd from thence.

I am to Desire the Favour youll be so good as to forward the Inclos'd

Letter for Capt. John Dickinson of Beaufort Town in Core Sound & please inquire if he is there now or if he is gone to Sea, as he has a Sloop & Goes a Voyaging. He advises me that he has Lately bought a Plantation at Core Sound & intends to Settle there. He formerly Liv'd in Road Island. Please advise me if you have any Knowledge of him or can gett any Information about him.

All Sorts of Provisions are Plenty here Excepting Pork. Good Pork would fetch £12 per barrell but than it pays a Duty of Forty Shillings Currency per bbl. from your parts. Shall be always Very Glad to hear from you & Render you any agreeable Service, Please Excuse this Trouble, I am with Due Respect &c.

ADDRESSED: "Per post"

TO FRANCIS DALBY
London

Charles Town, 23rd May 1743

SIR:

I did my self the Pleasure to write you of the 26th Ultimo with Duplicate thereof to which please be Refferr'd. And this per your Ship *Good Hope,* Capt. Turell, being now ready to Sail & who has been Detain'd some days for want of hands, Some of his Sailors having run away here. Inclos'd pleasure Receive account Sales of the Rum, &c. Ship'd per said Ship by Messrs. Hutchinson & Goldthwait on account of the Owners in Order to Defray the Charges of the Ship, Nett proceeds being £476.2.10 this Currency. You have also Inclos'd account of Disbursments on the Ship here & money paid Capt. Turell as per his Receipt Inclosed, amount being £729.16.8, which was oblidg'd to advance for Sailors, &c. otherways the Ship Cou'd not have been Dispatch'd.

Please also Receive Inclos'd the Owners Account Current, Ballance in my Favour being £325.13.10 Currency for which have taken Capt. Turells Bill of Exchange on you for £46.10.6 Sterling at the Current Exchange of £700 [*per*] £100 Ster. According to Messrs. Hutchinson & Goldthwait Their Directions, & which Doubt not will be Duely honour'd.

23rd May 1743

Inclos'd you have also a Manifest of the Cargoe. The Ship has had very Good Dispatch her Loading having been put on board as fast as Coud be taken In, & will make a Good Freight, but was in hopes woud have Carried 800 bbls. Rice, as Capt. Turell seem'd to assure me the Ship Certainly woud & had Engag'd that Quantity, however falls as youll observe by the Manifest Short of it Considerably.

I am to Desire youll be so good as to gett a Certificate from the Custom house of the Delivery of the *Good Hope*'s Cargoe & please to Transmitt it me as Soon as you Can in Order to Clear Capt. Turell's & my Joint Bond for £2,000, which have Desir'd Capt. Turell to put you in mind of. The Wind is fair so hope Cap. Turell will soon be with you. Shall be always very Glad to Receive your Commands & to Render you any agreeable Service as being Most Respectfully &c.

ADDRESSED: "Per the *Good Hope*, Capt. Joseph Turell, & Copie per Capt. Young Via Cowes"

[626]
TO ANDREW PRINGLE
London

Charles Town, 24th May 1743

SIR:

My last to you was of the 19th Current per Capt. Turell with Duplicate thereof to which I crave your Refferrence, since none of your Favours. Capt. Turell having been Detain'd for want of hands gives me still this Opportunity by him. And please Receive Inclos'd, John Fordyce his second Bill of Exchange for Fifteen pounds Sterling on William & Thomas Tryon & to you Indors'd. Please also Receive Inclos'd Capt. Joseph Turell his Bill of Exchange for Forty Six pounds Ten Shillings & Six pence Sterling on Mr. Francis Dalby his Owner payable to my Order at Twenty Days Sight of Yesterdays Date & to your Good Self Indors'd which Doubt not will be Duely honour'd, being for money advanc'd to Defray the Ship's Charge here on which please to Doe the Needfull, & when in Cash please to give my Account Credit for Same. I have writt Mr. James

24th May 1743

Buchanan by this Conveyance to gett £250 Sterling Insur'd, on Goods to be Ship on board the Snow *Caesar*, Capt. Keith, for London, on Account of the Owners of the Ship *Griffen*.

Have troubled you with the Inclos'd Letter for Mr. Reid, which Desire the Favour after perusal You'll please to Seal & have left or Deliver'd to him. I Refferr you to the Contents.

Have advice from Messrs. John Mayne & Edward Burn of Lisbon of the 19th April by Capt. Rodgers just arriv'd that their Uncle & Partner the very Worthy Mr. Edward Mayne Dyed there the 11th March & that they shall keep up the House & Business without any alteration & Doubt not You'll Continue to Correspeond with them. If otherwise, youll please to advise me. I understand they bear very Good Character. They also advise of the arrivall of the *Jolliffe's Adventure*, Capt. Archer, five Days before from this Place, & as a Vessell before her whose Cargoe of Rice was sold at 3$600 Reis, they were in hopes of obtaining the same for Ours in Archer, if so hope will turn out pretty well. Our Rice per the *Bremen Factor* was all sold at 3$600 reis per Quintal as they advise. Capt. Turell being just agoeing & the Wind fair, I have not further to Offerr at Present but that I remain &c.

ADDRESSED: "Per Capt. Turell & Copie per Capt. Young Via Cowes"

TO JAMES WIMBLE
New Providence, Bahamas

Charles Town, 24th May 1743

SIR:

I forwarded to my Brother in London One of your Letters of advice of your Sett of Bills of Exchange for £75 Ster. you gave me on Lambert Ludlow, Esqr. in London, & my Brother advises me that when he Deliver'd Mr. Ludlow your Said Letter to my Great Surprize, he gave him for answer that he woud not accept or pay any of your Bills upon no Account whatever, & that he had nothing to Doe with you upon which my Brother acquainted Mr. Parker thereof as you Desir'd, who likewise gave him the same answer, & at sametime told him that he was then under Missfortunes on Your Account. I did not imagine you woud have us'd me in this manner as you know I have advanc'd Most of the money of my pockett purely to Serve you. I am therefore by this to acquaint you that I have given a Letter [627] of Attorney to Messrs. Charles Hay & Charles Marshall of New Providence to Receive the money of you & whose Receipt shall be your Sufficient Discharge. Your Compliance will oblige &c.

ADDRESSED: "Per Charles Hay"

TO CHARLES HAY & CHARLES MARSHALL
New Providence, Bahamas

Charles Town, 24th May 1743

GENTLEMEN.

I am to Desire the Favour that youll please Receive herewith a Letter of Attorney to Receive from Capt. James Wimble, Commander of the Privateer Sloop the *Revenge*, Seventy five pounds Sterling. He is indebted to me for money, &c. advanc'd him here for his Vessell, & for which he gave me Bills of Exchange on Lambert Ludlow, Esqr. in London, with Letters of advice of same, One of which Letters I immediatly forwarded my Brother in London having promis'd Capt. Wimble to keep his Bills by me three or four months after Date before I sent them to London that perhaps in that Time he might take a Prize & so take them up here himself. But having been gone since the beginning of December & as yet no Account of him, I have lately sent his Bills to London accordingly, but as I had before hand sent one of his Letters of advice to my Brother & who since advises me that he Deliver'd said Letter to Lambert Ludlow & he gave him for answer that he had nothing to Doe with Capt. Wimble, & wou'd not Accept or pay any of his Bills upon no Account whatever, I am therefore to Desire youll be So Good as to Recover for me the Said money of Capt. Wimble who hope will make no Scruple to pay it as he knows it is justly Due, being most part of it Money advanc'd him out of my Pockett purely to Serve him, & what Charge & Trouble you may be at in the affair will with Pleasure alow you, & allways Greatly Accknowledge the Favour & on the like or any other Occasion you may freely Command.

31st May 1743

P. S. I hope youll be so Good as to advise me the Success of this per first Conveyance after Capt. Wimble's arrivall at Providence & if he Cann't pay in money am to Desire you may take the Value in any kind of Goods, but pray don't Lett him goe away from the Island on any Account, without paying the Money.

ADDRESSED: "Delivered to Charles Hay himself here"

TO ANDREW PRINGLE
London

Charles Town, 31st May 1743

SIR:

The Preceeding on the other side of the 24th Current per Capt. Turell, who Sail'd over the Barr the 25th is Copie of my last, to which please be Refferr'd. And this Serves Chiefly to advise you that I have of this Date Drawn a Sett of Bills of Exchange on you for One hundred Pounds Ster. payable to the Order of Capt. Jacob Ayers at 40 Days Sight which Doubt not you will be so Good as Duely to honour & to Debit my Account for Same, Exchange at £700 per £100 Sterling. And in Case you have already paid the said Sum of One hundred pounds Sterling as I formerly advis'd you, to his Order, then Said Bills are to be Void & not to be Honour'd, or Capt. Ayers is to Return you the Money again, it being Ballance in full of all accounts Due to him, having this Day Settled with him. Please Receive Inclos'd Capt. Joseph Turell his Second Bill of Exchange for £46.10.6 Ster. on Mr. Francis Dalby payable to my Order at 20 Days Sight & to you Indors'd.

There has been no Ships from London Since Capt. Cload & no material News here at Present. The next Ship Expected from London, We hear is one Capt. Campbell.[1] My Wife joins in best Respects & I Remain with the Greatest Regard.

ADDRESSED: "Per Capt. Young Via Cowes & Copie per Capt. Ayers"

[1] Capt. Joseph Campbell, the ship *Carolina Galley*, arrived from London. SCG, 4 July 1743.

[628]
TO ANDREW PRINGLE
London

Charles Town, 1st June 1743

SIR:

The above of Yesterdays Date is Copie of my Last per Capt. Young & this per Capt. Ayers under whose Care have sent you a Turtle which please to make acceptable. Am sorry it is not a Large One, but coud gett no Larger at Present & hope will Come safe to Hand, Capt. Ayers & Capt. Bradford having both promis'd to take Great Care of it having sent on Board a Large Tub & Some Indian Corn for its sustenance & which they Generally Like to Eat. We begin to be again Scarce in Shipping & Great Deal of Rice still in the Country. I add not at Present but that I Remain &c.

ADDRESSED: "Per Capt. Ayers & Copie per Capt. Wedderburn"

TO JAMES BUCHANAN
London

Charles Town, 1st June 1743

SIR:

The Preceeding is Copie of what I did my Self the Pleasure to write you of the 17th Ulto. to which please be Refferr'd. And this is to Advise you that being Dissappint'd in Shipping the whole Quantity of Rice I intended per the Said Snow *Ceaser*, the Vessell not Carrying near so much as Expected, You'll Please therefore to gett One Hundred Pounds Sterling of said Insurance alter'd from the Snow *Ceaser* to the Ship *Menerva*, Capt. Roger Cload, London, which I purpose to Ship in good Deer Skins (as I cannot gett any more freight at Present for Rice) & hope will come to a good Markett, & as I shall have Occasion to write you again soon I add not at present but that I am &c.

ADDRESSED: "Per Capt. Ayers & Copie per Capt. Wedderburn"

9th June 1743

TO PETER WESTERMAN
   Barbados
                                    Charles Town, 6th June 1743
Sir:
   I have your Favours of the 25th April Inclosing Account Sales of Twenty Four Barrells Rice &c. per Capt. Bell, Neat Proceeds being £17.12 which renders a poor Account. However am much Oblidg'd to Capt. Bell for his Care in the Disposal thereof. I have also Invoice & Receipt for (say three) 3 Barrells Muscovado Sugar, Two Potts Clay'd Sugar, & a Box with Two Potts of Sweet meats per Capt. Lightwood which Came safe to hand & in Good Order, Amount as per Invoice £17.4.9¼.
   Messrs. Lamboll & Allen were in the Expectation of the Pleasure of hearing from you, & Write you by this Conveyance in very Strong Terms to Desire You'll be so Good at Receipt of theirs immediatly to make a Demand of Mr. Daniel More of the Debt, & if he does not than pay the Money that You'll please to Sue him Directly without further Ceremony as they are Sensible he merits no Longer forbearance or Indulgence, especially Considering how he has us'd Mr. Allens Estate & which at their Desire I Take the Liberty to Recommend to you very heartily & hope your Good Offices & Endeavours won't be wanting to Serve them all you Can in that Affair which will Greatly Oblidge him who is with Great Respect.

ADDRESSED: "Per Capt. Paterson"

[629]
TO JAMES BUCHANAN
   London
                                    Charles Town, 9th June 1743
Sir:
   My last to you was of the 1st Current with Duplicate thereof, & this per the Snow *Caesar*, Capt. Keith, for London, & Inclos'd please Receive Bill of Loading & Invoice of One Hundred & Twenty Barrells of very Good Rice Ship'd on board said Vessell on Account & Risque of the Owners of the Ship *Griffen* & to Your Good Self Consign'd, Amount as

9th June 1743

per Invoice being £1,189.7.2. this Currency which wish safe to hand & hope will Come to a Good Markett, both the Freight & price of Rice happening to be Low. The Rice is Very Good in Quality. Per my next may Expect Bill of Loading & Invoice of Two hhds. of Good Deer Skins on Board the Ship *Minerva* on the Same Account as advis'd in my Last.

The Planters have this Season hitherto been very Backward in Discharging their Bonds, having keept up their Rice in Expectation of a high price for it, & now they are Disappointed few Shipping having Come here this Season. You may assuredly Depend on my best Endeavours to gett in the Debts in Order to make you further Remittances as Speedily as possible. I have not further to Offerr at Present, but that I am with very Great Respect &c.

ADDRESSED: "Per Capt. Keith & Copie per Capt. Geare"

TO ROBERT ELLIS
Philadelphia

Charles Town, 13th June 1743

SIR:

My last to you was of the 1st March per Capt. Coatam & Since have your Sundry Favours, the last of the 26th May, which Receiv'd a few Days agoe with Inclos'd Bill of Loading for a Black Gelding per Capt. Chad, which is Landed in Good Order & hope will prove to my Satisfaction, being a Large Likely Horse.[2] Capt. Chad had the Good Fortune of a Quick Passage with him. I Observe the Amount of the Cost & Provision put on Board for him per your Account to be £24.0.6½ Philadelphia Currency for which shall Credit your Account accordingly. I notice that you wou'd have sent some Bread & Flower, but that the Markett is low & that you

---

[2] Ellis paid £20 Philadelphia currency for the horse. His account with RP was considerably in arrears and he promised to make remittances from time to time. In November 1743 he sent apples on account and "sundry goods" in March 1744, but he was plagued with business misfortunes, and in 1746 he wrote RP that he was "very much obliged for your long forebearance" and once more promised to make additional remittances in the future. Robert Ellis to RP, 26 May, 15 November 1743; 20 March, 14 December 1744; 12 November 1745; 25 May 1746. *The Robert Ellis Letterbook*, Historical Society of Pennsylvania, Philadelphia, Pa.

13th June 1743

will Remitt the Ballance in the fall of the Year, if you doe not Come Yourself & if it shoud suit you to make Remittance by Bill of Exchange to my Brother Andrew Pringle in London it woud be equally the Same.

I hope You'll Please to send me the Chimney Stove & the Garden Box you were So good to Promise me in the fall. My Wife & I Return Good Mrs. Ellis Our hearty Thanks for her kind present of a Ham per Capt. Collock.

I Remark what you are pleas'd to mention in Relation to Andrew Bankson's Bond to George Messlin for Twenty pounds Philadelphia Currency. I Cannot give you much Encouragement to Buy the Bond or to have anything to doe with it, it being very uncertain when the Money Cou'd be Recover'd, & if ever it Can, & if he Shoud happen to Dye before he could pay it the money would be Entirely Losst, which is a great Risque & if you was to give half the Value of the Principal Bond, which is Ten pounds, it is my Opinion You'll give full enough, & if it Can be Receiv'd of him at all, beleive there is no person in this Province stands so Good a Chance to Receive it of him as my Self, & shall be Glad to Render you all the Service I Can in it in Case you Doe make a purchase of Said Bond.

Believe Capt. Chad is lett out on Freight at £4 or £4.5/ per Ton for London & Capt. Collock is Ready to Sail. My Wife Joyns in Best Respects to Good Mrs. Ellis & Self & I am &c.

P. S. Since Writing the Preceeding I understand the Horse you sent me has Gott the Botts[3] which he has Voided in his Dung, which gives me Some Concern as most of the Horses in this Town Dye of the Botts.

ADDRESSED: "Per Capt. Hall"

[The following was a separate unattached sheet inserted in the copybook.]

Charles Town, 13th June 1743

A Postscript to Mr. Robert Ellis' Letter of this Date

I am to desire that You'll be so Good as to Send me a Plan or Prospect of the City of Philadelphia in a Frame if not, without One. If any such this is [be had] with you, the Charge of which please to Debtor my Account with & You'll much Oblidge Yours &c.

---

[3] A bott is a parasitical worm which inhabits the digestive organs of a horse.

13th June 1743

[630]
TO THOMAS HUTCHINSON & THOMAS GOLDTHWAIT
Boston

Charles Town, 13th June 1743

GENTLEMEN:

My last to you was of the 26th March, & Since have your Esteem'd Favours without a Date per Capt. Trenn, & Duely Remark the Contents. Inclos'd please Receive Copie of Invoice of (say sixty six) 66 Barrells of Good Rice & Two hhds. Deer Skins Ship'd on board the Ship *Good Hope*, Capt. Joseph Turell, Commander for London on Your proper Risques & Account & to Mr. Thomas Goldthwait Consign'd, Amount as per Invoice being £1,349.17.10 this Currency which wish Safe to hand & hope will Come to a Good Markett both being Very Good in Quality. I purpos'd to have Shipt One hundred Barrells of Rice, but Capt. Turell's Ship did not Stow so much Rice in Quantity as he persuaded me the Ship woud Carry. He Sail'd Over the Barr the 25th past having had very Good Dispatch his Cargoe being tender'd to him faster than he Cou'd take it on Board, but was Detain'd Sometime (as most Ships are) for want of hands. His Freight was One half at £4.5/ & One half at £4 per Ton which hope will Turn out a Good Freight if he getts safe to London. Please also Receive Copie of the Owners of the Ship *Good Hope* their Account Current, Ballance in my Favour being £325.13.10 this Currency, for which I took Capt. Turells Draft at the Current Exchange on Mr. Francis Dalby as you Direct'd & Doubt not will meet with Due Honour. At Same time I Transmitted him Account Sales, Account Current, & Account of Disbursements on the Ship *Good Hope*, & Capt. Turells Receipt for the Hole.

Freight is high again here & not to be had, there being but few Shipping. As Soon as I can procure Freight may Expect further Remittances to be made on Account of Capt. Hallins Cargoe & Your own Account either in Rice or Deer Skins, or both, as may Judge most for your Interest, but am at a Loss to whom same on account of Hallins Cargoe must be Consign'd in Case that Mr. Goldthwait may be parted from London. You have given me no particular Directions in Relation thereto, & if I have not Same before I Remitt on Said account, shall still Consign to Mr. Goldthwait, & in his absence to My Brother Andrew Pringle. As you Desir'd in your Last, I have sent Mr. Goldthwait by Capt. Turell an Invoice of Goods Copie of which please Receive Inclos'd on your Account to the Amount of about Five hundred Pounds Sterling to be here in the fall of

13th June 1743

the Year, & if Rightly Bought hope will meet with a Quick sale & Turn to Good Account & may be able to make you Suitable Returns for Same next Spring as you shall Direct.

A Good part of Hallin's Cargoe is still on hand notwithstanding my uttmost Endeavours for the Speedy Sale thereof. There has a Good Deal of West India Rum been Lately Imported which makes the Sale of N. England Rum very Slow & tedious but hope that it will Turn out a Pritty Good Sale at Last, there has been Severall small parcells Come in here Lately & Sold as I am inform'd very Low. Shall doe my Self the Pleasure to advise you the needfull by all Conveyances & Truely am with very Great Respect.

Exchange to London at £700 per £100 Ster.

ADDRESSED: "Per His Majesties Ship *Rose* & Copie per Capt. Liddall"

[631]
TO THOMAS HUTCHINSON
   Boston
                              Charles Town, 13th June 1743
SIR:
   I Refferr you to what I have already writt you to your Good Self & Mr. Goldthwait in Company of this Date & per this Conveyance & Inclos'd please Receive Copie of Invoice of One hundred Barrells of Very Good Rice & Two hhds. Deer Skins Shipt on board the Ship *Good Hope*, Capt. Joseph Turell, Commander for London on your proper Risque & Account & to Messrs Burryau & Schaffer Consign'd, amount as per Invoice being £1,705.7.7 this Currency which wish safe to hand & hope will come to a Good Markett. Have Compleated the Sale of your Rum per Tisehurst & per my next may Expect Account Sales thereof, which have not Time to Forward you per this Conveyance. A Good part of the Axes are still unsold being but Slow in Sale unless was to Sell them to a Disadvantage. The Iron Potts are Render'd entirely unsaleable by their Out of the Way Size, being near all the Same Size & all almost still on hand & Cannot gett

13th June 1743

Ridd of them on any Terms as I formerly advis'd you, also a Good part of your Ribbons still unsold. They Stick on hand the Women having alter'd their Fashions which are very Changeable in those Sort of things. As Soon as I Can procure Freight you may Expect a further Remittance on your Own Account to Said Gentlemen in what ever may Judge most for your Interest. N. England Rum won't be wanted here till the fall of the year, 'tho Loaf Sugar is in Good Demand & has been for Sometime past & woud Sell well. I have but a pritty Deal of it in the Invoice sent Mr. Goldthwait.

This Goes by his Majesties Ship the *Rose* on the Bahama Station & Goes to be Refitted at your Port.[4] I add not a Present but that I am most Respectfully.

ADDRESSED: "Per His Majesties Ship *Rose* & Copie per Capt. Liddall"

TO JOHN ERVING
Boston

Charles Town, 13th June 1743

SIR:

Since my Last to you of the 26th March I have a few Days agoe your sundry most Esteemed Favours per Capt. Check[5] of the 11th, 12, & 20 April & Duely Observe the Contents. I Return you my hearty Thanks for your very kind present of Fish which have Come to hand in pritty Good Order Considering now the hot Season is Come on, as also the Plan of the Town of Boston, which is very Acceptable, & for which am Greatly Oblidg'd to You.

Inclos'd please Receive Account Sales of Sundries, Neat Proceeds being £1,420.0.3 which hope will be to Content. You have also Inclos'd your Account Current here, Ballance in your Favour being £1,458.1.10 this Currency which waits your Directions how You'll please to have the Same Apply'd. Also Inclos'd is your Boston Account Current, Ballance Due me

---

[4] The *SCG*, 13 June 1743, carried a notice that the *Rose* was sailing for Boston. The *SCG*, 20 June 1743, stated that several vessels had sailed with the *Rose* under convoy.

[5] Capt. John Chick, ship *Dispatch*, from Boston. *SCG*, 13 June 1743.

13th June 1743

being £54.13.5¼ N. England Currency. All which after perusal You'll please to Note in Conformity accordingly.

I Observe the Paragraph in your Letter of the 12th April in Relation to the Young man Named Robert Forsith on board his Majesties Ship the *Rye*, Capt. Hardy, (being One of Our Station'd Ships. Said Ship is just Come in to the Road from a Cruize for a few Days & is Goeing Out again to Sea. I took the Opportunity the other Day to enquire of the Purser who was ashoar about Said Mr. Forsith, who tells me that he Enter'd Some time agoe a Vountier & on that Account Capt. Hardy has preferr'd him to the Station of a Middshipman, & believe it's the Young man's Inclinations to Remain on Board, & that it will be a hard matter on said account to Gett Capt. Hardy to part with him, who is not very Oblidging, especially to Trading People, by whom he is not well lik'd or Regaurded, & indeed his Behaviour here has been such as not to Meritt their Esteem or Respect on which Account he & I happen not to be on very Good Terms togither. He has acted but very Indifferently Since he has been on this Station. However I have this Day sent a Letter to Mr. Forsith on Board to know his Own Inclinations from himself, & as soon as I have his answer, Intend to make my [632] Application accordingly, & you may Depend on it that my uttmost Endeavours shall not be wanting to Obtain his Discharge provided it is his Own Inclinations to Leave the Ship & to Goe Home to his Father,[6] & if it Cannot be Done before the Ship Goes Out to Sea again which will be in a few Days, hope to Effect it at her Return.

I take Notice what you mention in Relation to Charles Dunbar, Esqr. of Antigua, the Gentleman happens to be an Entire Stranger to me, So that I cannot give you any advice in Relation to him. I Duely Remark what you are pleas'd to advise with Respect to Shipping & Freight. We have had but few Shipping here all this Season, otherwise Freight would have been Low & is now at £4 for London, but if three or four Vessells more was to arrive Soon it woud be much Lower.

This Goes by his Majesties Ship the *Rose*, Capt. Frankland, who Goes to your Port to be Reffitted & which has a Good many Passangers on Board & amongst the Rest Goes Mr. Benjamin Savage. Mr. Allen,[7] Lieutenant

---

[6] Capt. Alexander Forsyth, Boston merchant, subscribed to Prince's Chronology. *NEH&GR*, VI (1852), 193. The story of Robert Forsyth is told in W. E. May, "Capt. Charles Hardy on the Carolina Station, 1742–1744," *SCHM*, LX (1969), 15–16.

[7] Lt. James Allen (Allan). May, 164.

of the *Rose* has promis'd me to take Care to Deliver you this. He tells me you & he were Born only a few miles Distant from one Another. He was formerly Master of a Ship here & has always Behav'd well & Doubt not You'll find him Worthy of your Acquaintance. My Wife joins in Best Respects to Self, Good Lady, & all your pritty Familly & I am with very Great Respect &c.

ADDRESSED: "Per Ditto & Copie per Ditto" [Per His Majesties Ship *Rose* & Copie per Capt. Liddall]

TO JAMES REID
    London

Charles Town, 14th June 1743

SIR:
    I did my Self the Pleasure to write you of the 19th Ulto. with Duplicate thereof to which please be Refferr'd.

I have Ship't per the Snow *Caesar*, Capt. Keith, for London, One hundred & Twenty Barrells of very Good Rice on account & Risque of the Owners of the Ship *Griffen* & to Mr. James Buchanan Consign'd, and as the Freight & Price of Rice happen both to be pritty Low, hope will Come to a Good Markett, the Rice being very Good in Quality. I did intend more Rice on board Said Vessell, but was Shut out, not having Stow'd near what was Expected & have been Oblidg'd to advise Mr. Buchanan to alter the Insurance for One Hundred Pounds from Said Vessell to an Other, & I purpose to Ship Deer Skins as I Cannot gett Freight for any more Rice at Present. I have advis'd Mr. Buchanan that I shall use my best Endeavours to gett in the Debts in Order to make him further Remittances as Speedily as possible.

We have now but few Shipping here at Present & it is Reckoned that a Good part of this Crop won't be Exported this Season. Mrs. Reid has some Rice to Ship but Cannot procure Freight at Present, who has been a little out of Order, but now upon the Recovery. Miss Reid is very well. My Wife joins in best Respects & I am.

We have no material News here at Present.

ADDRESSED: "Per Capt. Quarm under Cover of A.P."

14th June 1743

TO ANDREW PRINGLE
London

Charles Town, 14th June 1743

SIR:

My last to you was of the 1st Current per Capt. Jacob Ayers with a Turtle, & Copie thereof per Capt. Wedderburn. They both Sail'd Over the Barr the 7th to which please be Refferr'd, Since have not any of Your Favours & no Vessells from England Since the *Minerva*, Capt. Cload.

Have Shipt per the Snow *Caesar* 120 bbls. Rice on Account of the Owners of the *Griffen* & to Mr. James Buchanan Consign'd. I intended to have Shipt more per Said Vessell but was Shut out by Capt. Keith, who is a very Troublesome Scrub Fellow and Mr. John Keith has no Credit in his Relation. I procur'd him a Good Freight & assisted him in the Sale of his Wines, but he has ill Requitted me. He intended to Reship his Wines & Carry them with him unless he Could obtain Such a price, notwithstanding his Vessell was all Lett out [633] on Freight & he had Orders to Sell them if he Could at a Saving Price, & I told him I Could Sell them so & for more than a Saving price Ready Cash, which he Refus'd, & yet afterwards alter'd his mind & went himself to the Same People & Offerr'd them & for Less money than I Could Obtain'd for them Ready Cash, which I think was not useing me well, & not acting for Mr. Keith's Interest, which has Sufferr'd by his ill Conduct. But it was purely I suppose in his mean Way of Thinking to Save my Commission, altho I Enter'd his Wines, paid the Duty for them, & had them in my Store, so that he has not Managed or Acted for his Owner Mr. Keith's Interest, as I Could have been of a Good Deal of Service to him here. But as he did not Seem to Regard my Advice I did not Trouble my Self further about him, but Let him goe on in his Own way being an Ignorant Fellow entirely Unacquainted with Business & has had Disputes with every Person that he had any thing to Doe with. I did all I Could to Serve him on his Kinsman Mr. Keith's Account & Messrs. Scott of Madeira who Recommended him to me, having enter'd & Clear'd his Vessell & Given in Bond with him both in the Customehouse & Naval Office & yet the Fellow is not Sensible of it, nor so much as Thinks it Deservs Thanks, which I hope You'll be so Good as to Endeavour to make Mr. Keith Sensible of, 'tho I imagine he will Endeavour to make his Own Story Good to his Kinsman. He has prefferr'd Messrs. Watson & Wooddrop who were the other Freighters by taking in all their Quantity of Rice, & Shutt mine Out, altho' I procur'd him the

14th June 1743

Freight from them. It Seems Capt. Wooddrop is an Old Acquaintance of his & on that Account he gave him the preferrance. As I am excluded of the Quantity I purpos'd to Ship Mr. Buchanan by Said Keith, have advis'd him to gett £100 Ster. of the Insurance alter'd, which I purpose to Ship in Good Deer Skins to make up the Insurance advis'd for, as I Cannot gett Freight for anymore Rice at Present.

The *Rose* Man of War is goeing to Boston to Refitt being Worm Eaten. Inclos'd is a Letter for Mr. Reid which after perusal please to Seal & have Deliver'd to him. You may soon Expect further Remittances which you may Depend on all possibly can & Speedily. Having not further to Offerr at Present, I Remain &c.

P. S. I have writt Mr. Keith about his Kinsman's Behaviour per this Conveyance, & have not Charg'd Commission on procuring Freight, which I might have Done, but what I Did was purely to Serve Messrs. Scott & Mr. Keith.

ADDRESSED: "Per Capt. Quarme & Copie per Capt. Cload"

TO JOHN KEITH
   London

Charles Town, 14th June 1743

SIR:

My last to you was of the 19th Ulto. with Duplicate thereof to which please be Refferr'd. Capt. Keith has had very Good Dispatch in Loading, his Cargoe being Tender'd To him Faster than he Cou'd Take it on Board, but wish I Cou'd give you a more Satisfieing Account of his Conduct here which has been none of the Best. I was very Willing on your Account & Messrs. Scott of Madeira who Recommended him to me to doe him all the Service in my Power and assist him in the Sale of your Wines that they might be Dispos'd of to the Best Advantage, but as he Seem'd not to approve of my advice & took his Own measures, I did not give my Self any further Trouble about him & let him goe on in his Own Way. He seems to be very fickle & unsteady in his Temper. After he Land-

15th June 1743

ed all his Wines & Lett out the Vessell entirely on Freight & had taken a Good part of his Loading on Board, he than propos'd to Reship or take on Board again all the Wines unless he Cou'd gett such a price, & would not Sell them, as I told him they Could be Sold for Ready Cash, & was more than a Saving Price, which Messrs. Scott advis'd me he was to Sell here if at a Saving Price Rather than Carry them home that so he might have the Advantage of the Freight here. Yet afterwards he alter'd his mind & went to the People I had been in Terms with for the Wines & Offerr'd them for Sale & at last Sold them for Less money than I Could have Obtain'd for them, which think was not useing you or me well [634] & notwithstanding I was at a Good Deal of Trouble in procuring him a Freight & in Entering & Clearing his Vessell at all the Offices, & in being his Security by Giving in Bond Jointly with him both at the Customhouse & Secretary's Office. Yet he has been so unhandsome as to Shutt me Out of a pretty Deal of the Quantity of Rice I agree'd with him for to Ship on Board & had writt for Insurance for Same on his Vessell accordingly & has Lett the other Freighters have their full Compliment on Board. I am Sorry that Capt. Keith by his Behaviour here prevented me & did not give me the Opportunity of Serving your Interest According to my Inclination, & am of Opinion You'll have Reason in Some Respects not to Approve of his Conduct, & he may tell you what he pleases at meeting, but what I now write you is matter of Fact. I have not further to Offerr at Present but that I am with very Great Respect &c.

P. S. The Snow *Caesar* is in the Road Wind Bound.

ADDRESSED: "Per Capt. Quarm & Copie per Capt. Cload"

TO JAMES BUCHANAN
    London
                                              Charles Town, 15th June 1743

SIR:

    The last I Did my Self the Pleasure to write you was of the 9th Current with Duplicate thereof Conveying Bill of Loading & Invoice of 120 bbls. Rice on Board the *Caesar*, Capt. Keith, for London to your Address.

15th June 1743

Said Vessell Sail'd yesterday. And this Serves to Convey you Bill of Loading & Invoice of Two hhds. Deer Skins Ship'd on Board the Snow *Hector*, Capt. James Rodger, Commander for London on Account & Risque of the Owners of the *Griffen* & to you Consign'd, Amount as per Invoice being £727.0.11 this Currency which wish safe to hand & hope will come to a Good Markett, being the Deer Skins I writt you of the 1st Current that I intended to have Ship't on Board the Ship *Minerva*, Capt. Cload, for London & for which advis'd you to make Insurance, but since said Letter the Ship's Voyage has been alter'd for Holland. Am very Sorry Shou'd give you so much Trouble in having the Insurance alter'd so often, which Cou'd not be forseen, & for which must ask your Pardon. There are So few Vessells here at Present that Freight is very hard to be procur'd & has Occasion'd the Disappointment on Same & Oblidg'd me to Ship them per Capt. Rodger who will Sail in 10 or 14 Days at furthest, on which You'll please, if think proper to make the necessary Insurance. I Salute you and am Most Respectfully, &c.

ADDRESSED: "Per Capt. Rodger & Copie per Capt. Cload & Quarme"

TO ANDREW PRINGLE
   London

Charles Town, 22nd June 1743

SIR:

   The last I did my Self the Pleasure to write you was of the 11 Current with Duplicate thereof, & am as yet without any of your Favours. I am in hopes that Goods I writt for per the *Susannah* are on the way, as you advis'd me & which am in Daily Expectation of. This Serves to Desire you to gett Insur'd on Goods on Board the Ship *Grayhound*, Capt. Thomas Perkins, Commander at & from this for London One hundred & Fifty Pounds Sterling on Your Own proper Risque & Account which is Value of One hundred Barrels of Good Rice I purpose to Ship you per Said Ship which will Sail in a Fortnight or three Weeks at furthest.

Inclos'd Please Receive Mr. Edward Thomas his Discharge to his Brother Samuel Thomas of Lavenham in the County of Suffolk, Physi-

22nd June 1743

cian for the Receipt of Fifty Pounds Sterling which you'll Observe is to be paid to you & which Doubt not will be Duely Comply'd with & when Receiv'd please to advise of Same accordingly, Exchange at £700 per £100 Sterling. Both Said Remittances being on your Own Account for the proceeds of the Gun powder from Lisbon & the *Susannah's* Cargoe from Barbados & which You'll please to Note Accordingly. I am as yet prevented from making further Remitances on Account of the *John & Isabella* for want of getting Debts, People are so very Backward & payments So hard to be gott. I very much Desire to have that Cargoe, as also the Last per the *Susannah* brought to a Conclusion. You may Depend on it my Uttmost Endeavours are not wanting for that Effect.

As Vessells often Come here from Holland & bring Claret which the Custom house Officers take no manner of Notice, it would be well worth while if you Cou'd gett a Correspondant in Rotterdam & Amsterdam to Ship for you by way Vessell they Can gett to bring it on Freight Twenty or Twenty Four Doz. by Every Vessell, Say about one Hundred or One hundred & Fifty Dozen per annum of a Light Neat Small Wine that Could afford to be Sold here with a Good Proffit at £8 or £9 this Currency per Dozen, for which what is Brought from Holland is Commonly Sold & beleive woud Turn to Account as it can be purchas'd Low in Holland & it Runs no Risque in being Imported here, provided Masters of Vessells can be persuaded to Take it on Freight. What is brought here being Generally Imported by Masters of Vessells, who I understand make a Good Proffitt of it, it being very much lik'd here & a Good Deal of it us'd when it Can be had. Please to write me Your Thoughts on this.

By my Next you may Expect Bill of Loading & Invoice for 100 bbls. Rice. My Wife Joins in best Respects & I Remain &c.

P. S. I have Shipt per this Conveyance of Capt. Rodger Two hhds. of Deer Skins to Mr. James Buchanan on Account the Owners of the *Griffen*, Capt. Sutherland, Commander. The Freight per Perkins is £4 per Ton & Rice at 30/ per Ct. which hope will Doe pritty well.

James Home Sail'd a few Days agoe in the *Rose* Man of Warr for Boston being gone again to See his Brother in the Jerseys. Inclos'd you have also Mr. Edward Thomas his Letter of Advice to his Brother of his Discharge for Said £50 Sterling to be paid you, which please to have Deliver'd to him.

ADDRESSED: "Per Capt. Rodger & Copie per Capt. Cload"

5th July 1743

TO JASPER MAUDUIT
London

Charles Town, 5th July 1743

SIR:

I have your Favours a few Days agoe of the 8th April last. I did not know but that the Ballance Due you had been paid you by my Brother, otherwise you might have Expected it long before this, & which I have Desir'd him by this Conveyance to Discharge with what ever Interest you think proper thereon & upon your application to him Doubt not you will Receive the Same Accordingly. I am Sorry that it has not been paid before this. I Respectfully Salute you and am &c.

ADDRESSED: "Per Capt. Perkins & Copie per Capt. Chad"

[636]
TO ANDREW PRINGLE
London

Charles Town, 5th July 1743

SIR:

My last to you was of the 22d past with Copie, & about a Week agoe came to hand your most Acceptable favours per Capt. Glegg[8] of the 12th, 19th, 26th, & 27th April, and Duely Remark the Contents. Yours of the 19th Covering Account Sales of 208 BBls. Rice on our Joint Account per Capt. Greig 1740, Neat Proceeds being £158.1.9 Sterling my ½. As for the Account Sales you now sent of 200 barrells Rice per the *Susannah* in January 1739 that I receiv'd long agoe, and you'll Observe is Charg'd to your Debit in Account Current sent you. But what I still want is Account Sales of 40 Bbls. of Rice and 25¼ Ounces Ambergreaze Ship'd per the *Susannah* on our Joint Account in October 1740, which have not yet Receiv'd as youll Observe by your Account Current last sent you. I am sorry to observe so many Errors in the severall Account Sales sent you, and all

---

[8] Capt. John Glegg, ship *Friend's Goodwill*, arrived from London. SCG, 4 July 1743.

5th July 1743

to your Disadvantage which shall pass to the sundry Credits, and has happen'd thro the oversight of Mr. Inglis, being all Errors as you advise excepting the 9/ in Account Sales of Goods in Company per the *Susannah* 1739 and 3/9 in the 7th article, which upon further Persual, believe youll find to be right as in the account Sales Sent.

As I advis'd in my last please receive Inclos'd Bill of Loading and Invoice of One Hundred BBls. of good Rice Shipt on Board the Ship *Grayhound*, Capt. Thomas Perkins, Commander for London, on your own proper Risque and account & to your Good self Consign'd, Amount per Invoice being £812.12.7 this Currency which wish safe to hand and hope will come to a good Markett being at the lowest Price that Rice has yet been this Crop and very Good in Quality Considering the Season of the Year.

I hope by this time you have certain advices that the Apprehentions we were under Relating to an Invasion from the Spainards was Groundless and that you have before this Ship'd the Goods, especially the Books and other things that I writt were Engag'd, otherways it may affect my Credit and hinder me from having any Orders for the future. I observe what you mention in Relation to Field Cossett. If you can get his Property to the House proved and the House Sold without much Trouble, it will be as so much money in your hands as I shall pay him the Value here in Currency, Goods, &c. Inclos'd is a Letter for his Father which after Perusal please seal and Deliver him. You'll observe he Desires his Father to come over and live with him here, but am of Oppinion the Old Gentleman had better stay and End his Days in London, his Son having no fix'd or Certain abode of his Own, being in Low Circumstances, and in the Station only of an Overseer, and Obildg'd often to Shift and move about.

I also Remark what you are Pleas'd to mention about Mr. Rodger Kelstahl. Inclos'd please Receive Copy of a Paragraff of my Letter to you [637] about him the 11th August 1740. He was a Clergyman in Virginia and not in this Province and Dyed there a good many years agoe, but that he has a Son still allive here that was an Overseer to our Lieutenant Governour Bull, and believe he is so still and has Issue. However shall Enquire of Mr. Bull when he comes to Town further about him and advise you all the Particulars I can.

Our Publick affairs will never goe well here till we have a Good Governour which is greatly wanted. Our assembly think that their agent Mr. Fury is more a Friend to Generall Oglethorpe than to this Province and they find fault with him for not Publishing the Report of Our Committee

5th July 1743

of Assembly of the Seige of St. Augustine sent him under the Broad Seal of the Province on Purpose to publish,[9] and Instead thereof it seems he Quash'd it. If so think he did not Deal Candidly by them and acts too much like a Courtier.

I would have you be as Circumspect as you can in whatever Business you Transact with Mr. Andrew Lessly of Antigua, and am of Opinion the sooner you are Cleare of him and the Less you do with him the Better, for he is a Person I have no Opinion of, and what I may have Occasion to have done in Antigua shall be always with Mr. Michael Lovell who I believe is perfectly honest.

Hope that both Capt. Hallins Bills on Mr. Partridge are Paid. Hallin is a very simple plain Man and am affraid is too much given to Liquor which had Occasion to observe here.

Mr. Jasper Maduit writes me for a Ballance of Account still due to him of about £15 Sterling which I did not know but that you had paid him, and which am to Desire the Favour youll be so kind as to Discharge, and Charge to my account with Interest if he requires it, I have advis'd him thereof per this Conveyance.

I am sorry to be inform'd that our Commodity of Rice is so Discouraging at home which you are Sensible is our Chief Return. And as it turns out so poorly hope it will Lessen the great Numbers of Importers of Dry Goods here as well as the very large Quantity thereof Imported, as well as prevent the very Long Credit given thereon and put this Trade on a better Footing which it had much need of.

I writt you lately in one of my former of Capt. Gregorys leaving his small Bower Anchor by the breaking of the Cable at the Ring of the Anchor in Five fathom hole just when they were geting over the Barr and that one of our Pilots Detains and keeps Possession of it as his own for want of Proof of its being the Anchor left by the *Susannah*. I am therefore again to Desire you, you may get from Capt. Gregory & send me over the Exact marks & weight of the Anchor as also of the Buoy it had, the Hoops of the Buoy, and Buoy Rope, and the particular marks thereof, in short every thing as plain and particular as can be to prove the property of its being the *Susannah*'s in Order that I may Recover it.

Inclos'd I return you the Letter for Mr. [638] Robert Steil as I imagine

---

[9] "The Report of the Committee of Both Houses of the Assembly of the Province of South Carolina," printed by Peter Timothy at Charleston in 1742 and reprinted in London in 1743. Robert J. Turnbull, *Bibliography of South Carolina, 1563–1950* (Charlottesville, Va., 1955), I, 103.

7th July 1743

he is arriv'd in London before this. I have lately a Letter from Giberalter from Messrs. Charles, Robert & William Campbell's there advising that they shoud be glad a Correspondance could be kept up to any Mutuall profitt, and that some of the Wines there and Fruits might answer here which am Inform'd come very Cheap but are prohibited Importing here. However they run no Risque if any Vessells comeing here can be prevail'd on to bring a small Quantity of Mountain Wine in Hhds. or Quarter Casks and some Fruit, Vizt. Raisins and Currants in Earthen Juggs or Jarrs for a Trial on Freight in the fall of the Year doubt not would answer very well here. Please to writ them about same and if Rice, Indian Corn, or Navall Stores would answer at Giberalter. My Wife joyns in kind Respects & I am &c.

ADDRESSED: "Per Capt. Perkins & Copie per Capt. Chad"

TO JOHN BASSNETT[1]
Williamsburg Township, South Carolina

Charles Town, 7th July 1743

SIR:

I Receiv'd yours of the 27th past by the Bearer Mrs. Gladoe, Inclosing one from Mr. John McIver which gives me but little satisfaction as he is to Serve you; but as he mentions, not till sometime next Winter, & which perhaps may not be till next Spring, as it was to have been this last Spring, according to Your usual assurances, & which can put no Great Dependance on unless Mr. McIver gives me some more Satisfeing account himself when he Comes to Town which he writes me will be in a Month, & so I don't think it needfull to write an answer to his Letter. I am to Desire you'll advise me if I may tell him the full Sume you Owe me, being

---

[1] John Bassnett, a planter of Williamsburgh, South Carolina, borrowed £4,000 from RP. He gave 400 acres on the Black River in Williamsburgh Township and Lot number 5, near the King's Tree, in Williamsburgh as security. Bassnett defaulted and RP sold the town lot in 1747. Deeds, T, 308; Y, 533; DD, 258. John Bassnett had been elected in 1739 to represent Prince Frederick parish in the Commons House of Assembly. George C. Rogers, Jr., *History of Georgetown County, South Carolina* (Columbia, 1970), pp. 59, 60, 518.

7th July 1743

you advise that you are afraid he wont exceed £1,100 or £1,200 which is far Short of the Debt, & am to advise that You cannot Expect I will give him up all the Securitys I have, if he advances no more than Said Sume or Less than £2,000. It being but Reasonable that I ought to have some Security for the Remainder as well as Mr. McIver, which thought proper to Inform you of that you may have a Right Understanding Togither, especially as he seems to hint in his Letter of having all the Securitys I have of you. I Shoud be very Glad we Cou'd Settle togtiher Speedily & without any Trouble which woud be much more agreeable to me, as well as to You, but must be Done soon & not give Occasion to put Our Selves to so much Trouble by Writing to One another so much and so often on the Same Subject to no purpose. Shall be Glad to hear from you in answer to this before Mr. McIver Comes to Town & I am &c.

P. S. I hope you may be able to prevail with Mr. McIver to join with you in a Bond for what is Over what he may advance, that he may take up all the Security.

ADDRESSED: "Per Mrs. Mary Gladoe"

[639]
TO JOHN ERVING
   Boston

Charles Town, 14th July 1743

SIR:
My last to you was the 13th June per his Majesties Ship *Rose*, also Duplicate thereof to which please be Refferr'd. And this I hope you will Receive at the Hands of Mr. Robert Forsyth who I have gott Releas'd from his Majesties Ship the *Rye* according to Your Desire, tho' attended with a pritty Deal of Trouble & a Considerable Charge as You'll Observe by the Inclos'd account being Seventy Pounds 15/ this Currency which have been Oblidg'd to advance on the affair, & unless I had taken the Method I did, Mr. Forsyth must Still have been Detain'd on Board, as Capt. Hardy was not so Good Natur'd to Discharge him for all the En-

14th July 1743

treaty & Application that was made to him in a Civill way. I took all the pains I Could to have Application made to Capt. Hardy by Friends to Release him in an amicable Manner, But I found him a Person of that Disposition that the more he was Court'd & Entreated on the affair the more Stiff and obstinate he was to keep him on Board. And Mr. Forsyth by his Letters to me from on Board inform'd me that he was forc'd on Board & Detain'd very much Contrary to his Inclination & Importun'd me to gett him Discharg'd, being very Desirous to goe Home to his Father, all which Determain'd me to Oblidge Capt. Hardy to Release him, & to take the Measures I did, & which immediatly had the Desir'd Effect. For Notwithstanding the Airs Capt. Hardy gave him Self, Soon after the Marshall had Serv'd the Writt upon him & that he found him Self Ty'd Down to give Spicial Bail in an Action for £2,000 to be Try'd at next Court for False Imprisonment, There Came a Person to me, as also a Letter from Mr. Forsyth from on Board to Acquaint me, that if I woud Drop the Action against Capt. Hardy, Mr. Forsyth Sould be immediatly Releas'd & sent up to Town, the Ship being in the Road & was to Sail on a Cruise the next Day & which at Mr. Forsyth's Request, I did agree to accordingly, upon his Being Releas'd & paid all his Wages for the Whole Time he had been on Board, & which was immediatly Comply'd with & has gott a Tickett for his Wages. I at Same Time insisted that Capt. Hardy Shou'd pay the Charges I had been at in the affair, or at Least half thereof, & which I Expect he'll Comply with at his Return, & which shall advise you of, he having Sail'd over the Barr the Same day that Mr. Forsyth was Releas'd & put on Shoare.

You'll please present my Best Respects to the Gentleman Mr. Forsyth's Father & Inform him of the Affair & which hope will be agreeable to him, as I was Determin'd to Spare no pains to Obtain his Son's Liberty on your account, & had no other way left to accomplish it besides the Metheod I took which hope will meritt his Approbation, as I always take the Greatest Pleasure to Serve You or any Friend of Yours to the Uttmost of my Power. Inclos'd please also Receive Mr. Forsyths Receipt for what Money I have Supply'd him with here being Fifty Nine pounds Currency which Shall Carry to your account Accordingly. I think Capt. Clark that Brought Mr. Forsyth here Ought to Suffer for his ill usage of him. He takes his Passage to Road Island, there benig no Opportunity here at Present for Your Port Directly. I have writt to his Father Capt. Alexander Forsyth by him.

Freight to London is at Four pounds Per Ton, & but few Shipping here

14th July 1743

at Present, a pritty Deal of our Crop of Rice not yet Exported & hitherto a very Good Prospect of a Large Crop ensuing. My Wife Joins in Best Respects to your Good Lady & all the pritty young Ones & I most Respectfully Remain &c.

Exchange to London £700 per £100 Ster., Rice 30/ per Ct., Pitch & Tar 30/ per bbl., Deer Skins 16/6 per lb.

ADDRESSED: "Per Robert Forsyth in Capt. Murray for Road Island & Copie per Capt. Harramond"

[640]
TO ALEXANDER FORSYTH
    Boston

Charles Town, 14th July 1743

SIR:
    This I hope you will Receive at the Hands of your Son Mr. Robert Forsyth who I have gott Releas'd from the *Rye* Man of Warr according to my Good Friend Mr. John Erving's Request on your & his behalf, Tho' Capt. Hardy was not so Good Natur'd as to give him his Discharge till I was Obildg'd to Compell him to let, by taking Out an Action against him. The Particulars Relating to the Affair I have advis'd Mr. John Erving to whom please be Refferr'd as also to the Young Gentleman your Son. And if I had not taken the Measures I did your Son must Still have been Detain'd on Board, there being no other way Left to Effect it besides the Metheod I took & has been attended with a Pritty Deal of Trouble as well as a Considerable Charge, the Account of which have Transmitted Mr. Erving being £70.15 this Currency. Doe assure you I spar'd no pains to Obtain your Son's Liberty on my Friend Mr. John Erving's Account as also all your sons Request by his Letters to me from on Board (he not being permitted to Come on Shoar) which hope will merit your approbation.
    I have likewsie Supply'd your Son with what money he had Occasion for according to Mr. Erving's Desire being Fifty Nine Pounds Currency for which have taken his Receipt & Transmitted same to Mr. Erving. He

has gott his Tickett for his Wages for the whole Time he has been on Board the *Rye*, & Think Capt. Clark, who your Son Came here with Ought to Sufferr for his ill usage of him. He takes his Passage to Road Island, there being no Opportunity from this at Present, for your Port Directly & hope will soon be with you. Shall be very Glad to Cultivate a Mutual Correspondance & be always very Ready to Render you or yours any agreeable Service, & I am most Respectfully &c.

Exchange to London at £700 per £100 Sterling, Rice at 30/ per Ct., Pitch & Tar 30/ per bbl., Deer Skins 16/6 per lb.

ADDRESSED: "Per his Son Robert Forsyth & Copie per Capt. Harramond"

TO FLORENTIA COX
    New Providence, Bahamas

Charles Town, 15th July 1743

SIR:

My last to you was of the 13th December per Capt. Green & Since have not any of your Favours. You'll please advise me if you have near Compleated the Sale of the Musketts, & hope you Dispos'd of Some of them at Harbour Island, where you advis'd me you was agoeing, And that the Privateers that have been lately at your Island have been Chapps for them. Your Answer at your Conveniency will much Oblidge &c.

ADDRESSED: "Per Capt. Paul"

[641]
TO ANDREW PRINGLE
    London

Charles Town, 22nd July 1743

SIR:

My last to you was of the 5th Current with Copie & since have not the Pleasure of any of your Favours. This is Chiefly to Desire you'll gett

22nd July 1743

Insur'd on Goods on board the Ship *Ackworth*, Capt. Samuel Jones, Commander at & from this to London, One hundred & fifty pounds Sterling being on Account of the Cargoe per the *John & Isabella* Value of three hhds. Deer Skins which I purpose to ship per Said Ship to you Consign'd & hope will be a better Return than Rice at this Season. The Ship will Sail in a Fortnight or Three Weeks at furthest & by which you may expect Bill of Loading & Invoice for said Skins. Inclos'd please Receive Copie of Mr. Edward Thomas his Discharge to his Brother Samuel Thomas for the Receipt of Fifty pounds Sterling to be paid to you & Forwarded you the 22d June, in Case the said Original may not be come to hand.

Please also Receive Inclos'd Copies of Accounts Current of Pringle & Reid & my particular Account Current with Messrs. James Hunter & Co. that I have Deliver'd Messrs. Stead and Evance by Vertue of Powers of Attorney sent them by Mr. Nickleson the Assignee of Messrs. James Hunter & Co. by which youll Observe the Ballance Due me at Present to be £934.18.10 this Currency till the Outstanding Debts are gott in being £3,171.4.6 on the Account with Pringle & Reid & £348 on my proper Account Current with them & you'll Observe I have been greatly in Advance before their Goods per the *Eagle*, Capt. Long, were sold & in Cash, for which have Charg'd £600 on the Account Current with Pringle & Reid, being the Lawfull interest of £3,000 for 2 years, & youll perseive by perusing the Account that I was more in Advance, & Mr. Reid did not advance one Farthing.

Mr. Stead goes to London by this Conveyance & carries all the Accounts I have Deliver'd him to give Mr. Nickleson & Tells me that he does not Beleive the assignees will allow the Article of £600 for Interest which think is very justly Due me, being Advanc'd for Goods I Shipt them to Dispatch their Ship *Eagle* of the Faith of the Goods they Sent here per said ship, & if Mr. Nickleson (who I understand you are well accquainted with) Shou'd say anything to you about it, Doubt not youll use your Good Offices to Convince him of the Reasonableness of it, & is what I think any Impartiall Judges or Indefferent Persons would allow of, & which accounts as given in, I am Determin'd to stand by & Don't Think I can be Oblidg'd to give it up, if they Dispute it. However could willingly agree to any Condesention, if they insist on it & you Desire it, & think it for my Interest so to Doe. I have told Mr. Stead I am ready to give him Orders on the Persons that Owe the Outstanding Debts upon his giving me a proper Discharge, which he has not thought proper to Doe.

I am to Desire you'll please to send me, when you have an Opportunity

26th July 1743

a Copper Cooler or Cistern for holding of Botles & Glasses to Contain about 3 or 4 Gallons of an Oval Shape, they are very Necessary here to keep Liquors Cool & pray lett it be thick & Strong, also 3 doz. of Wire Bird Cages from Two Shillings to Six Shillings per price of Different Sorts, & one Dozen of Trapp Cages for Catching Birds.

Just now I am told by a Person from the Island of Providence that Capt. Wimble of the *Revenge* Privateer from whence he Sail'd last, has in a Cruize in Consort with a Road Island Privateer one Capt. Allen, Commander taken a Considerable Prize & Carried her in to Road Island, & from thence Capt. Wimble is gone for England, & if you have not before this Comes to hand already Return'd me his Bills of Exchange I sent you for £75 Ster. on Lambert Ludlow, beleive it will be best to keep them with you, & if he is Gone for London, doubt not you'll hear of him, & that you'll be so Good as to gett my money Secur'd for the Bills, & Considering how he has us'd me hope you'll show him no favour. As I shall have Occasion to writt you soon again I add not at Present But that I Remain.

I understand Capt. Wimble was Born at the Town of Baccle in Sufix where perhaps he may be gone.

ADDRESSED: "Per the *Princess Amelia*, Capt. Haurney, & Copie per Capt. Cheek Via Bristoll"

[642]
TO EDWARD & JOHN MAYNE & EDWARD BURN
Lisbon

Charles Town, 26th July 1743

GENTLEMEN:

Since my last to you of the 17th February per Capt. Archer, I have the Pleasure of your most Esteem'd Favours of the 4th March & 19th April and most Heartily Condole with you on the Death of the very Worthy Mr. Edward Mayne your Uncle and Partner, pray God Comfort you under the Great Loss.

I Observe by yours that the *Bremen Factor* & Capt. Archer were both arriv'd and that you had Sold the 100 BBls. Rice per the first at 3,600

26th July 1743

reis per Quintal & hop'd to Obtain 3,400 reis for the Parcell & per Archer, which will turn out to but an Indifferent Account and Did not Imagine that the Price would so Suddenly have fallen so low, as from 4,800 reis to 3,600 reis per Quintal. I hope you will soon be in Cash so as to make Remittance to my Brother in London for the Neat Proceeds of both Parcells of Rice as formerly Directed.

There are two Vessells for your Port. Rice at 30/ per Ct., but not Good in Quality, a good part of the Crop still not Exported, & a good Prospect hitherto of a very large Crop Ensueing. When any Vessells happen to goe from your Port for this Place in the Cold Season, as they always come in Ballast, & that Lemmons are Cheap & Fresh, should be Oblidg'd to you to ship me by two or three Vessells at Different Times Fifteen or Twenty half Chests of Lemmons (very well Pack'd & put up in Paper) in each Vessell provided the Freight comes Easie as the Vessells are in Ballast. The Captain & Vessell will runn no manner of Risque from the Custom house in bringing them here, & for the amount please to Value on my Brother in London which will be Duely Honour'd.

We have no materiall News here at Present. Mr. Robert Gray formerly of your Place Dyed here in the Month of February last. He Burried his Wife and Daughter here, and married again and has left a Widow and two young Children. He kept a Store in the Country. Generall Oglethorp of Georgia Sail'd from thence for England about ten Days agoe, being as it is said Order'd Home.[2] I salute you and am most Respectfully &c.

Exchange to London £700 per £100 Ster.

ADDRESSED: "Per Capt. Phillips & Copie per Capt. Glegg"

[643–666 missing]

---

[2] Charges had been made against Oglethorpe's handling of provisions for his troops and bills of exchange. Amos Aschbach Ettinger, *James Edward Oglethorpe, Imperial Idealist* (Oxford, 1936), pp. 249–251.

19th October 1743

[667]
TO ANDREW PRINGLE
London

Charles Town, 19th October 1743

SIR:

The Last I did myself the Pleasure to write you was of the 3d Current per Capt. Diamond[3] Via Cowes, also Copie thereof to which please be Reffer'd, Since have not any of your favours. In my Last I Desir'd you to gett Insur'd on the Ship *Charming Susan*, Capt. Patrick Scott, & from this to London One hundred Pounds Sterling Value to be Shipt you in Spanish Silver on Account & Risque as per my Last. Said Ship will sail in a fortnight or three Weeks hence by which may Expect Invoice & Bill of Loading for same & which I confirm. I also intend to Ship a hhd. Deer Skins per said Scott & to you Consign'd on Account & Risque of Capt. Sanders for Ballance of his own proper Account of £357.18.9 this Currency which imagine may not be worth wile to make Insurance for Value about £50 Sterling & Inclosed please Receive Copie of his last Letter to me per Capt. Rice & also Copie of mine Answer to same per Ditto Rice of this Date to which please be refferr'd. I thought it proper to Remitt him said Ballance thro your hands that you may Stop it in case your still in Advance for him & to prevent his sending a power of Attorney here to Receive it, & so goe throw a Nother Chanell.

Inclosed Please also Receive David Caws Letter to your self in Relation to his Kinsman William Caws Account as I advis'd in my Last & to which please be Refferr'd. About a week agoe Arrived here his Majesties Ship the *Loo*, of 40 Guns. Capt. Ashby Hutting, Commander by way of New York (having Landed their New Governour Clinton[4] there) & in which came passanger Mr. Abercomby[5] (pray how has our Governour & he Settled their Affair). Said Ship *Loo* is to be Station'd at Port Royall & will be a safe gaurd to that part of the Province.[6] The *Loo* brings Account

---

[3] The snow *Barum*, John Daymund, to Cowes. SCG, 3 October 1743.
[4] George Clinton, through the influence of his friend, the Duke of Newcastle, received the governorship of New York. Although he supposedly profited to a great extent from his administration (1743–1753), the alleged dishonesty was never proved. DAB, IV, 225–26.
[5] The Attorney General of South Carolina, James Abercromby.
[6] HMS *Loo*, Ashby Utting, arrived on the Carolina station 18 October 1743 and was wrecked 5 February 1744. May, 164.

19th October 1743

of a great Likelyhood of a french Warr before they Left England which will be Bad for this Province.

About Two months agoe about forty persons here, have Enter'd into Contract, & are Concerned in Carrying on a Silver mine said to be found out in the Cherrokee Mountains on the Back of this Province.[7] There are Seventy Shares at £500 this Currency per Share & have Petetion'd home to the King for a Grant & to be Allow'd to goe on with it, & have as I am inform'd Offerr'd a Share or two to the Duke of New Castle[8] & our agent Mr. Fury that they may Stand their friends.[9] I for my Part am no ways Concern'd in it. Neither Desire to be, tho' three or four of our Councill & as many of our Assembly are Concern'd or Proprietors & all the Rest of our Assembly & Councill are Unamiously against it & the whole Body of the Province Except those persons Concern'd as it will be a great Detriment both to Trade & Planting & Improving the province. [668] Our assembly have taken it into Consideration & have sent home a Memorial to the King & Councill against it in Order to get a Stop put to it & Doubt not all the Merchants & Gentlemen Concern'd in the Carolina trade will join in having a Stop put to it, as it will Certainly Ruin the Trade of the Province & the Province it self if it Should goe on & prove a Silver mine as is thought & may Engage the Province, in a Warr with the Indians as well as with the French. I am Endeavouring to gett a List of the persons Concern'd in Order to send you, tho' since the Assembly have taken Notice of it they Endeavour to Carry on every thing Relating to it very Private. All the Planters Cry out Loudly against it & they have a good Reason for so doeing, as would Render their Estates & Interest worth Nothing.

Shall Doe my self the Pleasure to write you again by Capt. Scott. My Wife joins in best Respects & having not further to Offerr at present as being without any of your favours I Remain &c.

---

[7] In 1743 James Maxwell and Cornelius Doharty, two Indian traders, purchased 30,000 acres of land and drew other men into their company on the reported discovery of a silver mine in the Cherokee Nation. The planters opposed the venture because it would draw off their labor, create a few excessively rich men, and probably cause an Indian war. Some merchants did favor the scheme, although RP was not among them. All the furor was unnecessary, as Governor Glen reported in 1749 that there were no mines in the province. Wallace, I, 389.

[8] Thomas Pelham-Holles, Duke of Newcastle (1693–1768).

[9] This memorial has not been found. Another memorial, dated 14 October 1743, sent by George Saxby, Receiver General of the Quit Rents in South Carolina, requested information on the portion that His Majesty would expect from the profits of the mine. Council Records, CO 5/444, 219. Public Record Office, London.

P. S. We hear our Governour Glen is coming at Last & is Expected very soon here. No new Rice as yet come to Town & it is thought will Breake in price not under 40/ at first.

I am Concern'd that my affairs should Occasion me to be so Often troublesome to you & I am to pray the favour youll be so good as to Speake to Mr. John Keith to desire he will send over a Certificate from the Custom house in London for the Delivery of the Cargoe of the Snow *John*, Capt. George Palmer, in 1742 & for the Cargoe of the Snow *Ceaser*, Capt. Alexander Keith, in May Last, Also to Mr. Richard Partridge for a Certificate for the Brigantine *Richard*, Capt. Samuel Hallin, in December Last, & to Mr. Francis Dalby for the Cargoe of the Ship *Good hope*, Capt. Turell, in April Last. I am also to Desire youll be so good as to write to Mr. Thomas Burrell of Hull for a Certificate for the Ship *Friendship*, Capt. John Story, in February 1740/1 & Expires February Next in Order to Clear & take up my Bonds given for said Vessells, most of them the time is near Expir'd. Capt. Story lives in Princes Street, Rotherith ought to Exert himself to gett a Certificate. I expect to be sued for Capt. Drummonds Bond to Antigua being Expir'd & Mr. Lessly has never yet sent a Certificate for the Cargoe. Yours &c.

ADDRESSED: "Per Capt. Sweetman & Copie per His Majesties Snow the *Swift*, Capt. Bladwell"

[669]
TO ANDREW LESSLY
  Antigua

Charles Town, 24th October 1743

SIR:

Since my Last to you of the 28th February I have your Esteem'd Favours of the 6th April & Observe the Contents. Inclos'd please Receive Account Sales of the Six Casks Rum per Capt. Murray on account of the Owners of the *Loyall Judith*, Neat Proceeds being £349.6.3 this Currency which Hope you'll find Right & to Content. It being Sold at the height of the Markett, Large Quantitys of Rum having been Imported from

24th October 1743

Barbados has keep it Low here & is now at 14/ per Gall. & has been Lower. Have Credit the Account of the Owners of the *Loyall Judith* with the Neat Proceeds of said Rum & there Remains still a Ballance Due as per account Current formerly sent you which Doubt not youll Remitt as soon as you have an Opportunity, as also the small Ballance of your Own proper Account Current due me being £9.17.6½ Antigua Currency.

We have a very Large Crop of Rice & Corn this year & in about a Month hence New Rice will begin to Come to Markett, it being Reckoned the Largest Crop that has ever yet been produc'd in the Province & Computed at 120,000 bbls.

You have hitherto Omitted to send here a Certificate from your Custom house for the Delivery of the *Loyall Judith*'s Cargo at Antigua, & the Time of three years being Expir'd, the Bond I gave in with Capt. Drummond is put in Suit and will cost me Five or Six pounds Sterling Charge to the Kings Attorney Generall to allow Some Longer time to have a Certificate for the Delivery of the Cargoe, being Ennumerated Goods. I am therefore to Intreat youll be so good, as not to fail Sending a Certificate per the Return of this Opportunity of Capt. Murrays Brigantine, One Capt. Hutchins, Master who goes for St. Kitt's & Returns here Directly, or by the first Conveyance for this Place, as also a Certificate for the Delivery of the Ship *Susannah*, Capt. Gregory's Cargoe in August 1741 which has not been yet Sent, & the time of said Bond Expires in May next when it will Likewise be put in Suit & which hope youll be so kind as to prevent by forwarding it per first. I have not further to Offerr at Present but that I Remain Most Respectfully &c.

Rum 14/ per Gallon, Muscovado Sugar £10 per Ct., Cocoa £50 per Ct., Coffee 7/ per lb., Exchange to London at £700 per £100 Ster.

ADDRESSED: "Per Capt. Williams & Copie per Capt. Hutchins Via St. Kitts"

TO RICHARD OLIVER[1]
Antigua

Charles Town, 24th October 1743

SIR:

I have the Pleasure of your most Esteem'd Favours of the 3d March last Inclosing Bill of Lading & Invoice of Six hhds. Rum per the *Two Sisters*, Capt. Rice, which came safe to hand, & want of any Conveyances your Way has prevented my giving you advice of same before this. Please Receive Inclos'd account Sales of said Six hhds. Rum, Neat Proceeds being £385.14.5 this Currency which hope youll find Right & to Content being sold at the heighth of the Markett, Large Quantitys of Rum having been Imported from Barbados has keept it Low here & is now at 14/ per Gall. & has been Lower.

I have not as yet been able to meet with a Bill of Exchange for the Value, they being very Scarce here at Present, but as soon as I can procure a Good One shall take Care to Remitt Same on your account to Messrs. Fitter & Tyzach in London as you Direct, the Exchange being at £700 per £100 Ster.

We have a very large Crop of Rice & Corn this year & in about a Month hence Rice will begin to Come to Markett, it being Reckon'd the Largest Crop that ever has yet been produc'd in the Province & Computed at 120,000 BBls. Shall be always very Glad to Receive your Commands & to Render you an acreptable Service & I am most Respectfully &c.

ADDRESSED: "Per Ditto Williams & Hutchins"

[670]
TO MICHAEL LOVELL
Antigua

Charles Town, 24th October 1743

SIR:

Since my Last to you of the 28th February I have the Pleasure of your most Esteem'd Favours of the 23d May, 22 & 29 August & Duely

[1] Richard Oliver of Antigua and later of London and Leyton, county Essex, was a West India merchant. He was a member of the Assembly (1721–1738), a major of the militia (1723), and a member of the Council (1739). In 1750 Oliver purchased the Great House in Leyton and died there 10 June 1763. Oliver, II, 318.

24th October 1743

Remark the Contents. Yours of the 22d August Inclosing Invoice & Bill of Lading for a Box & Chest of Linnens, which have Receiv'd & shall Take Care to Dispose of to your best advantage. If the Cambricks had been finer & from 30/ to 60/ Ster. per piece they wou'd be much more Saleable, ¾ & ⅞ Garlix from 14/ to 24/ Ster. per piece happen to be more wanted here at Present than any other Linnens and China Ware, Vizt. of Bowls, Dishes, & Plates are a Very Saleable Commodity in Case you happen to be Over Stockt.

What good Offices I can Render Capt. Ougier[2] here on your Account Doe assure you shall not be wanting, or any other Person you are Pleas'd to Recommend. Have also Receiv'd by Mr. Carroll a Small Box, quantity Nine pieces of Spainish Ribbon which happen to be very Unsuitable for this Place, & shall be at a Loss how to gett them Dispos'd of, the Newest Fashions of Ribbons being Imported fresh by Every Ship from London.

I observe the Rice per Capt. Murray proves very Unsaleable thro' the Badness of the Quality thereof. If you have not got Ridd of it before this Comes to hand, youll Please Dispose of it at Vendue (which hope you have already done as you advis'd me in your former) or otherwise as you Please, being a Perishable Commodity Especially in a Hott Climate. It had been good Rice, but keept too Long on hand. We have a very Large Crop of Rice & Corn this year, & in about a month hence New Rice will begin to Come to Markett, it being Reckon'd the Largest Crop that has ever yet been produc'd in this Province and Computed at 120,000 BBls.

We have no Material News here at Present, only that a Forty Gun Ship arriv'd here from England to be Station'd at Port Royall for the safe Guard of the Southern part of this Province it being a New Station. I heartily Salute you and am most Respectfully &c.

Rum 14/ per Gallon, Muscovado Sugar at £10 per Ct., Cocoa £50 per Ct., Coffee 7/ per lb., Exchange to London at £700 per £100 Sterling.

ADDRESSED: "Per Capt. Williams Via Port Royall & Copie per Capt. Hutchins Via St. Kitts"

---

[2] Capt. Peter Ougier, snow *Mary*, to Cowes. SCG, 19 December 1743.

25th October 1743

TO JOHN ERVING
   Boston

Charles Town, 25th October 1743

SIR:

The preceeding of the 13th Current is Copie of my Last to which Please be Refferr'd, & this Serves to Convey you Copie of Invoice & Bill of Loading of Sundries Ship'd on your Account per the Brigantine *Prosperity*, Capt. Priam Selew, for Boston who sail'd over the Barr four or five days agoe & not before being Detain'd by Contrary Winds, but hope will now be soon with you. I ommitted in my Last to Accknowledge the Very great Obligations my Wife & I are under for your hearty & very kind Offerr & Invitation to take our Passage to London in one of your Ships, which I doubt not will Suit to Accomodate us if they happen to be here, as I perpose to goe in April or May, at furthest, if a favourable Opportunity then Offerrs. My Wife presents her Compliments, to you, Good Lady, and all the pretty Young Ones & I Remain with most perfect Regaurd &c.

ADDRESSED: "Per Capt. Thornton"

[671]
TO THOMAS BURRILL
   Hull

Charles Town, 25th October 1743

SIR:

The Last I did my self the pleasure to write you was of the 10th March Last & since have not any of your favours. This is to Request youll be so good as to send over per first a Certificate from the Custom house at Hull for the Delivery of Capt. Storys Cargoe there, which you have hitherto Ommitted, in Order to discharge my Bond given here with Capt. Story, the time of which Expires in February next against which time I expect to be Sued for Same, & which will be a Considerable Charge, in Order to Obtain a Longer time to gett a Certificate sent Over, & am in hopes youll be so good as to have a Certificate sent by the time the bond expires & be pleas'd to send a Duplicate of your Letter with it in Case of Misscarriage.

John Marshall at Cape Fear is Dead, as perhaps Mr. Stead may have Advis'd you before he went for England, & as no Doubt you will see him at Hull, he can inform you about his Circumstances.

We have a very Large Crop of Rice this year & which will begin to come to Markett in about a Month hence, it being Reckon'd the Largest that has ever yet been produc'd in the Province & beleive will breake in price at about 40/ per Ct.

We have no Material News here at present only that we are Under Apprehensions of a Warr with France. I am again to Entreat you wont Omitt to Send over the Certificate per first, & youll greatly Oblidge him who is most Respectfully &c.

Rice 40/ per Ct., Pitch 40/ per bbl., Tarr 35/ per ditto, Turpentine 10/ per Ct., Deer Skins 16/6 per lb., Rum Barbadoes 20/ per Gallon, Madeira Wine £120 per pipe.

ADDRESSED: "Per the *Swift*, Capt. Bladwell, Via London & Copie per the *Hawk*, Capt. Forest"

TO JOHN STORY
London

Charles Town, 25th October 1743

SIR:

Above is Copie of what I writt per your Son the 10th of January Last which hope you Receiv'd but Since have not heard any thing from you, neither have I as yet Receiv'd a Certificate of the Delivery of your Cargoe Loaded here for Hull, in Order to Discharge the Bond given in with you here & for which I expect to be Sued for very Soon, which will be a considerable Charge & which you must Expect to pay. For as you did not bring a Plantation Certificate for bond given in London, your Chartie partie would have been Void as you Could not have Loaded your Cargoe Unless I had been Security in the Plantation Bond with you. I am therefore again to Desire you may Procure a Certificate from Hull as quick as

2nd November 1743

possible you Can & send me over. I have writt to Mr. Thomas Burrill for that Effect. What Charge I am put to in said Affair I must desire my Brother to Receive of you in London as you are Oblidge to Indemnifie your Security & which hope youll Endeavour to Prevent by sending Over a Certificate as soon as possible. I am &c.

ADDRESSED: "His Majesties Snow the *Swift*, Capt. Bladwell"

[672]
TO JAMES HENDERSON
New York

Charles Town, 2nd November 1743

SIR:

I Receiv'd your favours of the 22d January, but happening to be in the Country when it came to hand, I miss'd the Opportunity of Shipping the Rice, otherwise you might have depended on same, according to your Directions & no Other Conveyance happening your way for a Considerable time after, I imagin'd it might then be too Late for you. I have also your favours of the 4th past which I Receiv'd about a fortnight agoe at the hands of Mr. George Lesslie, Purser of his Majesties Ship *Loo*, & what good Offices I am capable of doeing him here, doe assure you shall not be wanting on your Account.

I heartily Condole with you on the Loss of the Young Gentleman, your Son, & hope by this the Severe Sickness you have had will be entirely abated. As to the few Goods Mr. Lesslie had to Sell, I Advis'd him to Carry them with him to Port Royall where the Ship is Station'd & which he has done Accordingly being gone with the Ship & where he can Dispose of them to a better advantage then here. Mr. Lesslie, seems to be a very Agreeable Clever Gentleman & with whom have had the pleasure to Drink to your & famillys good health. Shall take care to send the Quantity of Rice as you Direct & to be with you by the time Mention'd here, being None but Old Rice to be had at Present which is not good, & in about a month hence. New Rice will begin to come to Markett, of which we have the Largest Crop that has ever yet been Produc'd in the Province.

2nd November 1743

I have not as yet been Able to procure payment from Mr. Bullock of his Note & find that I must be Oblidg'd to sue him before I can Recover it, being as I Understand a Person of that Disposition that he pays no Person till he is Oblidg'd to it in that Maner. I could Obtain no Abatement on the Tea but the Person that I had it of cannot Expect that I should ever Deal with him for the Future. I went to our Custom house in Order to gett a Certificate for the Loaf Suger you Shipt me, & the *Abany*, Capt Clarke, August 1740, & the Officers upon Looking over there Books found that a Certificate had been granted to Cancell the Bond given in for said Goods the 24th September as appears by their Books, & which they Desired me to Accquaint you, which hop'd will Satisfie your Custom house Officers.

I am to Desire you'll please be so good as to send me by the Return hereof, the Bearer Capt. Shermerhorn who comes back here Directly or the first Conveyance this way, Twenty Boxes of good Tallow Candles provided they come Reasonable with you & dont exceed 6½ or 7d. per lb., also Twelve Barrells of good Strong Beer Say Twenty Barrells such as Capt. Shermerhorn brings here for Sale, but pray Lett the Casks be tight & well hoop'd that they may come in good Order, but would not have the Beer to be here Latter than the first of January otherwise not to send it & Please to gett the Freight as Easie as you can.

I am to desire the favour youll please to be so good as to enquire & Advise me per your next if one John Smith Lives in New York. He came here from Boston where he Liv'd some time & from this about four years agoe went to Georgia & from thence to New York as I am inform'd he formerly Us'd the Sea & has been Master of a Sloop. I have not further to Offerr a present but that I Remain with Best Respects to you & yours &c.

P. S. I Receiv'd Two Boxes of Soap & for which have Credit your Account Current £3.7.2 Our Currency.

ADDRESSED: "Per Capt. Shermerhorn"

4th November 1743

[673]
TO JOHN KEITH
  London

          Charles Town, 4th November 1743

SIR:

 My Last to you was of the 11th August per Mr. Ogilvie, who I hope is by this safe Arrived, & since have your Esteem'd favours of the 26th May. I am Surprized to be advis'd that the Rice Ship you per Capt. Palmer on Account of Messrs. Pringle & Scott of Madeira prov'd so bad. Am certain it was good Merchantable Rice when Shipt here, but by being so Long a time on Board it might Perish, which it is very Apt to Doe in the Hott Season & when it is long keept & has been Long Clean'd, & some Rice will keep much longer than some other Rice Seemingly to the Eye. There was no better Rice in the Cargoe than it was when Shipt, which I took Notice to you of in my Letter to said Palmer.

 This is to desire youll Please to gett a Certificate from the Custom house for the Delivery of Capt. Palmers Cargoe at London & send me over in Order to Discharge my Bond given in here for said Vessell, the time of the Bond being near Elasp'd, & you have hitherto Omitted to forward the Certificate, as also be pleas'd to send a Certificate for the Delivery of Capt. Keiths Cargoe, having Likewise been his Security, both which Certificates Doubt not youll be so good as to forward without Loss of time.

 We have a very Large Crop of Rice this Year & about a Month hence will begin to come to Markett, it being Reckon'd the Largest that has ever yet been Produc'd in the Province. Shall be always very Glad to Receive your Commands & to Render you any Agreeable Service as being with great Respect &c.

Please my Service to Mr. Ogilvie, the Letter for him has been sent back to him.

 ADDRESSED: "Per His Majesties Snow *Swift,* Capt. Bladwell, & Copie per the *Hawk,* Capt. Forest"

4th November 1743

TO NICHOLAS RIGBYE[3]
Savannah

Charles Town, 4th November 1743

SIR:

Since my Last to you of the 21st September, I have Both your favours of the 5th & 24th past & Remark the Contents.

I was in hopes you would have been so good as to have made me a Remittance by this Opportunity as you Promis'd, especially as Quarter Day is now past & as you are Sensible the Suger I bought was money Advanc'd out of Pockett without any Advantage. As to Allowing me Interest, think it is no Eqivalent, & had much Rather have my Money, even at 10 per cent as is Customary here much Less at 5 per cent as it is with you. However doubt not of your good Inclinations to Remitt me as Quickly as you can, & which hope youll be able to Effect in a very Short time according to the Assurances you give me & doubt not of your Endeavours for that Effect. We had Advice from London that some of the Trustees Bills had been Stopt but are now Current again & punctually Paid. You advis'd me in yours of the 5th that you Expected Daily to Receive one or Two of the Generalls Bills. If you think Proper may send them to me & I will take Care to forward them to London in Order to procure payments of them & will Credit your Account for same accordingly.

I Observe in what Manner you have Agreed to Settle my Affair [674] With Mr. Dormer, & as I beleive you have done it in the Best Manner you Could for me, I must be Satisfied, & desire you may make an End of it as Propos'd, for which I thank you, & very willingly Confide in you to Negotiate & Receive same for me accordingly. Tho as it is Settled, I hardly Receive more than half my Debt besides Lying out of my Money so Long, & it is a Little hard that I should Loose what Money I paid out of my Pockett for Endeavouring Legally to Recover my Own, which is always Allow'd of in all Courts that ever I heard of, & I should be at no Loss at any time here, (if so Disposed) to Lett out £10,000 Sterling at 10 per cent Interest & on very good Security, which is the Lawfull In-

---

[3] Nicholas Rigby arrived in Georgia in 1737 as the indentured servant of William Stephens, Secretary to the Georgia Trustees. Freed of his indenture in 1742, he was appointed Clerk to the President and Assistants in 1743 and served until 1749 when he was appointed Secretary for Indian Affairs. Coulter & Saye, pp. 36, 43; *Col. Recs. Ga.*, VI, 63; XXV, 174; XXVII (unpublished, MS in Georgia Historical Society, Savannah), 387–388.

7th November 1743

terest in this Province, by a Law Confirm'd in England,[4] therefore a persons Money must Certainly be worth so much to them as it will fetch & ought to bear the Lawfull Interest of the Place where the Debt is Contracted. If Mr. Dormers Debt to me had been Contracted in England or in Georgia, I should be well Satisfied with 5 per cent the Lawfull Interest there. I Receiv'd inclosed Mr. Dormers Account against Mr. Thomas Christie for £5.16.2 Sterling which was presented to him for Payment & he gave for Answer that he would not Pay it, or have any thing to Say to it, & seem'd to be affronted, & withall, that he had a great Deal of Money oweing to him in Georgia & was going there in a Short time in Order to Recover it, & which Account I herewith Return you again Inclosed. I hope youll Continue to Lett me hear from you as often as it Suits your Conveniency. I add not a present but that I am &c.

ADDRESSED: "Per Mrs. Emery"

TO EDMUND WIGGINS
Williamsburgh Township, South Carolina

Charles Town, 7th November 1743

SIR:

I writt you about a Month agoe directed for you at Mr. Treageagles[5] in George Town, but have no Answer as yet from you, which makes me imagine that the Letter has not come to your hands.

I am again to Desire to know if you will Undertake to Secure JB.s[6] Negroes & I will send you up a proper Power for that Perpose, & how soon you can goe about it as he is Like to make me no Satisfaction & where & in what Manner you propose to Sell them & if it will be Needfull for me to send up any person from Town to be Present & assistant to you in the Sale of them. I again Desire youll Lett me have your Answer as soon as this comes to your hands by the first Opportunity I am &c.

ADDRESSED: "Per Alexander Anderson"

---

[4] A 1720 law limited the interest rate to 10%. Previously, it had been as high as 25%. Wallace, I, 398. In 1748 the rate was lowered to 8%. *Statutes*, III, 709–712.
[5] Nathaniel Tregagle kept a well-known tavern in Georgetown. SCG, 21 July 1746.
[6] The "JB" was John Bassnett.

7th November 1743

TO JOHN BASSNETT
    Williamsburgh Township, South Carolina
                              Charles Town, 7th November 1743

SIR:

My Last to you was of the 16th September & since have yours of the 27th Ditto & since that am Inform'd by Mr. Barry by your Direction that Mr. McIvar would be in Town Latter end of Last Month, but as yet doe not hear any thing of him. It being now above three Months since he was to be in Town, as you Advis'd, so that imagine he has Alter'd his mind. Inclosed pleas Receive the Account of the Thirteen Barrells Rice you sent, Neat proceeds being £75.6.9 Currency for which have Credit your Account I am &c.

Mr. Plowden[7] has sent me Two firkens Butter but does not yet Discharge his Bond.

ADDRESSED: "Per John James"

[675]
TO WILLIAM TURNER & LAURENCE JOPSON
    Hull
                              Charles Town, 7th November 1743

GENTLEMEN:

I receiv'd about two Months agoe your favours of the 27th April & Duely Remark the Contents. I Observe your goods Return'd you per Capt. Smithson were come to your hands but that they had Receiv'd some Damage which am Sorry for. They were Reshipt here in the same good Order as I Receiv'd them. Inclosed Please Receive Account Sales of your goods, the Neat Proceeds being £1,178.18.0 this Currency which hope youll find right & to Content for doe assure you I spar'd no Pains to Dispose of every thing to your Best Advantage. As to Remitting Bills of Exchange for the Ballance of Account, they are very Scarce & none to be had here at Present. However you may soon expect same in good Deer Skins as you Direct & If no Opportunity happens soon for your Port shall Ship

---

[7] Edward Plowden lived in Prince Frederick parish. *Register Book for the Parish Prince Frederick Winyaw*, pp. 9, 10, 11, 18, 22, 158, 163; *SCHM*, XXVI (1925), 124.

7th November 1743

them by way of London as you Order & Should have been glad to have been Advis'd to whose Address they must goe to there, but as you have given no particular Directions shall Ship them to my Brother Andrew Pringle there & transmitt you Invoice thereof Accordingly & if you think proper may give Directions for the Necessary Insurance.

I Receiv'd your Letter & Order to Messrs. Jones & Oliver[8] to Deliver to me an Account Sales of the Books, Chairs, &c. you sent them & to pay me the Neat proceeds thereof which I Deliver'd to them accordingly, & have waited ever since I Receiv'd yours in expectation of Receiving said Account in order to transmitt you, but could not Obtain the same of them, altho often ask't for, till two days agoe with a good Deale to Doe, & which please Receive here Inclosed. I Observe by said Account they doe not Allow you for the goods the first Cost thereof in London, altho order'd as Saleable Goods. As for the Money when I shall Receive it of them is very Uncertain, altho they promise Payment soon, and as I have no power of Attorney from you cannot Oblidge them.

We have a Large Crop of Rice this Year & begin now to come to Markett it being Reckon'd the Largest Crop that has ever yet been Produc'd in the Province & has broke in price at 40/ per Ct. I have not further to Offer at Present but that I Remain most Respectfully &c.

Rice 40/ per Ct., Pitch 40/ per barrell, Tarr 35/ per barrell, Turpentine 12/6 per Ct., Deer Skins 17/6 per lb., Rum 20/ per Gall., Madeira Wine £120 per Pipe, Exchange to London £700 per £100 Sterling.

ADDRESSED: "Per His Majesties Snow the *Swift*, Via London"

[676]
TO WILLIAM COOKSON & WILLIAM WELFITT
   Hull

Charles Town, 7th November 1743

GENTLEMEN:

I have your favours of the 30th March Last, also Copie thereof & Duely Remark the Contents. According to your Directions please Re-

[8] Possibly Samuel Jones and Thomas Oliver. Thomas Oliver, shopkeeper, who died late in 1744, appointed Samuel Jones, planter, one of his executors. Wills, V, 326–327.

ceive Inclos'd Copie of Invoice of your Goods Shipt on Board the Brigantine *Prosperity,* Capt. Priam Selew, for Boston In N. England on your Proper Risque & Account & to Mr. John Wheelwright there Consign'd which hope will goe Safe to hand & which have Advis'd him is by your Orders & to Dispose of same to your best Advantage, Amount as per Invoice being £185.12.6¾ Sterling. You have also Annex'd to Said Invoice the Charges in Shipping same, Amount £15.16.6 this Currency also Storage at 2½ per cent of £31.7.8 for which have Debit your Account. They were very Unsaleable here as I Advis'd you in my former & hope will meet with better Success at Boston than they have had here, & I have not had an Opportunity to Ship them sooner since I Receiv'd your Orders for so doeing & by which youll Observe a Considerable part of your goods are Ship'd to Boston tho there still Remains Unsold part of your Cordage & Lead Shott, the Cordage being much higher Charg'd than any that comes from London which has Occasion'd it to Stick so Long on hand. There was too Large a Quantity of the Small Shott. However hope soon to Compleate the Sale of the Whole & to Transmitt you Account thereof & Shall be glad to have your Directions in Relation to the Returns to be Remitted you & in what Manner in case the Price of Rice & Freight doe not both happen to be at Same time according to your Limittation which has not as yet ever happen'd. It is True that Rice has been some time in Last Season at 30/ per Ct. but then at Same time Freight was not to be Obtain'd under £4. & £4.10/ for London all Last Crop & to an Out Port as yours is Considerabley more & Freight is not Likely to be Less this Season as we have this year a very Large Crop of Rice & Shipping will be Scarce & Freight high As Long as the Warr Continues & more especially if a French Warr should happen which seems to be very Likely.

 I am Surpriz'd at what you are Pleased to Express in your Last Letter, Vizt. that in your Letter per Capt. Ward, Brazilleto was never Mention'd or Spoke of. To Convince you of the Contrary, I herewith Inclose you an exact Copie of your said Letter the Original of which is now before me in which is the following Paragraph Relating to the Brazilleto, Vizt. (as the Ship cannot Stow full of Casks, may put into her Logwood or Brazilletto which ever is the Cheapest & Best). And as no Doubt you keep Exact Copies of all your Letters, I Refferr you to your Own Copie Book of [677] Letters where youll find it the Same if Copied exact According to the Original & therefore think Appears Very plain to be your particular Orders, & I did not think I had to Deale with Gentlemen that would Deny or goe from there own Letter & Directions, espeicially for a

7th November 1743

thing of so trifling a Value & of so Little Consequence as Six Tons of Brazilleto which I again Repeat that I would by no means have Shipt it If it had not been Order'd by you in your said Letter & which If I had not it by me to Show it Looks as if you would have thrown any Loss that might have Accrued by it on me which think is not honourable & a Factor to be so Dealt by had better be without such Commissions. I shall expect your Orders in whatever youll have the Ballance of your Account Invested & how & in what Manner Remitted you, there being no great Matter of yours now Remaining in my hands.

As to Capt. Wards Affair here, as he has not come & Appear'd to take his trial the Money is forfeited being £80 Ster. which I Expect Daily to be Call'd upon to pay Accordingly, besides a Considerable Charge in getting it put off so Long from Court to Court till I had your Advice of his not Coming, the Account of which shall send you in Order that Capt. Ward may make the same good, said affair has been Attended with a great Deal of Trouble to Me. I have not further to Offerr at Present but that I am Respectfully &c.

Rice 40/ per Ct., Pitch 40/ per Barrell, Tarr 35/ per barrell, Turpentine 12/6 per Ct., Deer Skins 17/6 per lb., Rum 20/ per Gallon, Madeira Wine £125 per pipe, Exchange to London £700 per £100 Sterling.

ADDRESSED: "Per His Majesties snow the *Swift*, Capt. Bladwell, Via London & Copie Via Bristoll.

TO WILLIAM DOVER
    London

Charles Town, 7th November 1743

SIR:

Since my Last to you of the 17th December I have your Sundry favours, the Last of the 28th February & Inclosed please Receive Account Sales of your Trading Guns & Pistolls Receiv'd per Capt. Gregory, Neat Proceeds being £301.4.6 this Currency which hope youll find right & to Content, as I did my Utmost Endeavours in the Disposal of them, to best

7th November 1743

Advantage. They had Suffer'd by Lying so Long here Unsold, & was Oblidg'd to be at the Charge of having them all Clean'd otherwise would have Losst the Sale of them. And by the Ship *Charming Susan*, Capt. Patrick Scott, Commander which will be the first Ship for London & will Sail in about a Month hence you may Expect Returns for the full Neat Proceeds thereof (which I Delay'd till I could Compleat the Sale of the Pistolls) either in good Deer Skins or New Rice of which we have this Year Largest Crop that has ever yet been produc'd in the Province & is begining now to come to Markett. I say in either of which Commodities may Judge most for your Advantage, & on which if you think proper may make the Necessary Insurance.

We have no Material News here & having not further to Offerr at Present I Remain Respectfully &c.

Exchange to London at £700 per £100 Sterling.

ADDRESSED: "Per His Majesties Snow the *Swift* & Copie per [*Blank*] Via Bristoll"

[678]
TO CHARLES, ROBERT, & WILLIAM CAMPBELL
Gibraltar

Charles Town, 14th November 1743

GENTLEMEN:

I have your Agreeable favours of the 8th April Last Old Style with Inclosed a Letter for Doctor Edward Knott, but by all the Enquiry I have been Able to make, I cannot find out that there is any Such person or of that Name in this Province. However if upon further Enquiry I can learn that there is any Such person in being & in these Parts, Shall take Care to have the Letter safe Deliver'd to him.

I Remark what you are pleas'd to Mention in Relation to a Mutual Correspondence & as there are frequent Opportunitys of Vessells that come here from your Port in Ballast for to Obtain Freight & that would bring things Easie. I am of Oppinion, that your Mountain Wine in Quart

14th November 1743

Bottles Pack'd up in Casks or Barrells, quantity Six or Seven Dozen Each Barrell, allso Canary Sack if to be had in pint Bottles, Raisons & Currans put up in three Gallon Stone Juggs or Jarrs, Olives in Quart or three pints Bottles, Anchovies in Botles or Stone potts, Florence Oyle & Wine in Betties[9] in half Chests, also Bourdeaux Clarrett & Frontenai Wine in Botles, & Itallion Silk Gauze of Blue & Green Colours only for Pavilions for Beds. All these Artikles would turn to very good Account, Provided they come Cheap with you & you can gett Commanders of Vessells to bring them here on an Easie freight. As for our Custom house, they Run no Manner of Risque that Way, this being Accounted the Easiest Port in America for anything of that Nature, & no Notice taken of any thing what Ever, all these things being put on Shoar & Sold here publickly.[1]

Shall write to my Brother in London Relating to your Proposal who has been at your Port, as Likewise here on the Spott, therefore a better Judge than I can be of those things & if he finds they will Answer, doubt not will give you directions for a Small Assortment of about One hundred & Forty or Fifty Pounds Sterling of the said things Assorted & to Value on him in London for the Amount thereof, & shall be glad to know if you are Inclinable to be part Concern'd yourselves in the Trade, which will be to our Mutual Profitt, & a pretty deal may be Vended here as Opportunitys happen to send but not to Exceed £100 or £150 Sterling in one Vessell & at one time, & perhaps you may have Opportunity this Way three or four times per Annum. Please Advise if there are any Other Artickles to be had with you besides those I have Mention'd that you think would Answer here. I would not have any Raisons or Currans sent here Unless to be here in the fall of the year & wont Doe to be here Latter than the Month of January. They must be here always between August & January by Reason they are not Saleable & perish in our hott Season, as for the other things they will Doe at any time of the Year.

We have a very Large Crop of Rice this year, there being Reckon'd upwards of One hundred thousand Barrells Produc'd, but if we should have a french War are afraid we shall want Shipping to Carry it off. Please Advise if any of our Produce from this will Answer at your Port, Vizt. Rice, Pitch, Tar, Turpentine, Indian Dress'd Deer Skins, Brazelleto, Logwood,

[9] A betty was a pear-shaped bottle covered with straw.
[1] RP's comment was contrary to what Governor Glen reported: "No Country in this part of the World hath less illegal Trade than *South Carolina*; at least, so far as I can learn; though if there was any, it would be difficult to prevent it, by Reason of the great Numbers of Rivers and Creeks, and the small Number of Officers of the Customs." [James Glen], *A Description of South Carolina* (London, 1761), p. 48.

& Mahogony Plank. Shall be always very glad to have the Pleasure of hearing from you by all Conveyances this Way & to Render you any Acceptable Service & Doubt not but that a Correspondence may be Carried on between us & Continued to our Mutual Advantage & I am most Respectfully &c.

Rice 40/ per Ct., Pitch 40/ per barrell, Tarr 35/ per barrell, Turpentine 12/6 per Ct., Deer Skins 17/6 per lb., Brazilleto Wood £30 per ton, Logwood £30 per ton, Mahogony Plank £25 per 100 ft., Rum 20/ per Gallon, Madeira Wine per pipe £125, Exchange to London £700 per £100 Sterling.

ADDRESSED: "Per His Majesties Snow the *Swift* under cover of A.P."

[679]
TO ANDREW PRINGLE
    London

Charles Town, 14th November 1743

SIR:

My Last to You was of the 19th Ultima of which you have Inclos'd Copie thereof to which please be Refferr'd & since have not any of your Favours & no Ships from England for a Considerable time past. I advis'd you in my Last to gett Insur'd on the Ship *Charming Susan*, Capt. Patrick Scott at & from this to London on Goods on Board said Vessell One hundred Pounds Ster. which you may make up to One Hundred & Thirty or Thirty five pounds Sterling, whereof £70 on Account the Cargoe per the *John & Isabella* & £60 on my Own proper Account. As Capt. Scott is not ready to Sail being he now waits for New Rice, not having been able to gett Loaded with Old Rice. However will be the first for London & Sail in a Month hence. The New Rice which now begins to Come to Markett has broke in price at 40/ per Ct. but beleive wont hold that Price Long, there being the greatest Crop that has ever yet been produc'd in this Province. Freight to London is at £3.15/ per Ton, & if more Vessells doe not Come in soon will be higher.

14th November 1743

I have advertis'd in Our Gazette[2] my goeing off the Province the ensueing Spring, in Order to gett in Debts, & hope to Settle my Affairs as to have the Pleasure of Seeing you next Summer if any favourable Opportunity happens. Mr. Erving of Boston has given my Wife & I an Invitation to take our Passage in any of his Ships that may happen to be here if we should like them & may Suit to Accommodate us to our Satisfaction.

I am Greatly Concern'd to Observe in our advices from Philadelphia of the 29th September of a Hurricane at Sea that happen'd to Some Homeward Bound Ships from Jamaica, amongst which was your Ship *Queen of Hungary*, Capt. Blackburn which had Lost all her Masts, excepting her Main mast, but what became of her after have no account. Hope you are fully Insur'd, & perhaps you may have advice thereof before this Comes to hand.

One Capt. Bowler in a Ship about 170 Tons bound from Jamaica To London is put in here very Leaky, & a Great part of her Sugars wash'd out. The Capt. is out of his Sensis, the Sailors having Left the Vessell on the Coast & Came all ashoar in the Boat, & Mr. Joseph Wragg takes Care of the Vessell.

You may Depend on my Utmost Endeavours to Sell off Everything in Order to Compleat the Sales per the *John & Isabella* & per the *Susannah* very Speedily & to make you all the Remittances that I am Capable and as Quick as possible.

Upon Recollecting I find that you Transmitted a Certificate for Capt. Hallin's Cargoe & that the Bond is Cancell'd. I have writt to Mr. Burrill at Hull & to Capt. Story about his Certificate, to Send it Over, as also to Mr. John Keith for to Send me Over Capt. Palmer's & Capt. Keith's as soon as possible, the want of which in Due time Occasions a Good Deal of Trouble.

If a Warr with France happens am afraid we shall have but few Shipping here, so that Our produce will Lye on hand unexported. No ships will Sail for England after this Conveyance for this Fortnight or three Weeks to Come, as they will all Load now with new Rice which am afraid will be a poor Commodity in Europe, then is so much produc'd here.

[2] "Whereas Robert Pringle intends off the Province the ensuing Spring, he therefore requests all Persons that have any Demands on him to bring in their Accounts in order to be discharged; and all those who are any way indebted to him, either by Bond, Note, or Book Debt, to be so kind, as to discharge or settle the same, to his Satisfaction, by the first of January next, that he be not obliged to take any Measures that may not be agreeable." SCG, 7 November, 14 November 1743.

14th November 1743

This Goes by his Majesties Snow the *Swift*, Capt. Bladwell,[3] on the Cape Fear Station which is Order'd Home. The Capt. whereof beleive to be as Errand a Coward as Ever Commanded a King's Ship, has us'd all his Officers & People ill & it is thought that it will be in the Power of Mr. Rawlins his Lieutenant to gett him Broke with Ignominy. His Majesties Ship the *Loo*, Capt. Utting, of 40 Guns has gott safe into Port Royall Harbour & where there is found Water Sufficient for Ships of 60 or 70 Guns which Doubt not Capt. Uting will Report to the Admiralty.

My Wife who is often Sickly, Joyns in Kind Love and Respects & I add not at Present as being without the Pleasure of your favours, but that I most Sincerly Remain &c.

Rice 40/ per Ct., Pitch 40/ per bbl., Tar 35/ per barrell, Turpentine 12/6 per Ct., Deer Skins 17/6 per lb., Rum Barbados 20/ Gallon, Madeira Wine £120 per Pipe, & not Good, Exchange to London at £700 per £100 Ster.
Mrs. Reid tells me, that She looks for Mr. Reid Daily.

P. S. Inclos'd please Receive a Letter I have writt to Messrs. Charles, Robert, & William Campbell of Giberalter being in Return to One I had of them, to which I Refferr for your Perusal and approbation. Youll Observe that I have writt them about Opening a Branch of Trade [680] this way which am of opinion may turn out to Our mutual advantage, as frequent Opportunitys of Vessells happens coming from thence in Ballast for Freight here & no manner of Notice is taken of Such things by Our Custom house So that there is no Risque that Way. I have known Commanders of the Ships that have brought Such things from thence & made a Very good Profitt on them here, as they have told me, being purchas'd at Very low Rates there, and as those things always fetch ready Money here, Can be Enabled thereby to make very Quick Returns for them. If you approve of Same and are inclinable to be jointly Concern'd, You'll please to Seal and Forward them said Letter, & write them what you think proper on the afair, and at Sametime to propose to them, to be part Concern'd if you judge it proper, Such by hitts often turn out to better Account than things in the Common Course of Trade. I am *ad Supra* yours &c.

---

[3] Capt. William Bladwell, commander of HMS *Swift*. May, 164.

15th November 1743

I have writt Messrs. Cookson & Welfitt about the Brazilletto & Sent them a Copie of their Own Letter, in which appears plain, their Order for it.

ADDRESSED: "Per His Majesties Snow the *Swift*, Capt. Bladwell, & Copie Via Bristoll"

TO RICHARD BENNETT
   Queen Anne's County, Maryland

Charles Town, 15th November 1743

SIR:
   I have the Pleasure of the Duplicate of your most Esteemed Favours of the 20th December, which did not Come to hand till June Last, advising of the Receipt of mine per your Schooner *Hopewell*, which am very Glad was safe arriv'd. As for your Original Letter it has never yet appear'd. Since the Receipt of yours no Opportunity has happened Your way Before this that I know off in Order to give a Return to Yours & to Transmitt you Account Sales of the Cargoe per said Schooner, 'till this, & Inclos'd please Receive Account Sales thereof, Neat Proceeds being £1,397.19.3 this Currency which hope will be to Content as I us'd my Uttmost Endeavours to Dispose of Every thing to your Best advantage. Inclos'd Please also Receive your Account Current, Ballance in your Favour being £308.17.0 this Currency which I Observe you Direct to be Remitted on your Account to Colonel Alexander Mackenzie at Hampton in Virginia, or if Freight Offerrs there in Pitch, Tar, Turpentine, or Rice, or part of either, which shall be punctually Comply'd with.
   But I am to take notice to you that no Opportunity has yet happened, & it is very seldom that any does from this to Virginia in any manner of way, excepting Sometimes when Corn is Scarce here, We send Vessells there for that Commodity, which will not be the Case this year, as we have a Large Crop Both of Corn & Rice, it being Reckoned the Largest that has ever yet been produc'd in this Province. If in Case that I can have no Opportunity of Remitting the Ballance of Account to Virginia as you Direct, Youll Please advise if it may not Suit you to have same Remitted to London, Philadelphia or Boston in N. England, or to Antigua or Bar-

bados in any or Some of all the Articles of the Produce of this Province as you mention, Vizt. Rice, Pitch, Tar, Turpentine, & Corn. If so, You'll please to Lett me have your Orders & which shall be punctually Comply'd with Accordingly.

I am Greatly Oblidg'd to you for your kind advice Relating to Richard Howell who I understand has Lately been at Philadelphia & where I have gott a Freind to Negotiate my affair with him there to my Satisfaction. I Receiv'd Inclos'd William Medcalf's Account & who I have made it my Business to inquire for all I Can, but Cannot Learn that there is any such Person, or of that name in this Province, unless perhaps he may have Chang'd his Name. However if I shou'd happen to hear off or meet with him, You may Depend on my Utmost Endeavours for the Recovery of your Money, & I shall be always very Glad to Receive your Comands & to Render you or your Friends any agreeable Service & in Expectation of your further Directions I Remain Most Respectfully &c.

Exchange to London £700 per £100 Sterling.

ADDRESSED: "Per Mr. Ross Via North Carolina"

[681]
TO HENRY SCARBRUGH[4]
Accomack, Virginia

Charles Town, 15th November 1743

SIR:

I herewith Inclose you a Letter for Richard Bennett, Esqr. on Wye River in Maryland which he Desir'd me to Send him Directed under Cover to you & which you'll Please be so Good as to forward him per the first Opportunity. Shall be very Glad if at any time I Can Render you any agreeable Service here, & I am most Respectfully &c.

ADDRESSED: "Per Mr. Ross Via North Carolina"

[4] Col. Henry Scarbrugh of Accomack, Virginia, was the collector of customs on the eastern shore. He was Richard Bennett's correspondent in Virginia. *VaMH&B*, I (1894), 363; II (1895), 2, 3; *RPC*, p. 818.

TO SCOTT, PRINGLE & SCOTT
Madeira

Charles Town, 26th November 1743

Gentlemen:

I have the Pleasure of your most Esteemed Favours of the 15th April per Capt. Keith & Out of Respect to your Recommendation of him doe assure you I Did him all the Service & Good Offices that I was capable of, having immediatly upon his arrival procur'd him a very Good Freight & very Good Dispatch, his Loading being tender'd to him Faster than he Could take it on Board. But he happened to be a person of that Temper & Disposition that instead of being Gratefull for any Service Done him, he us'd me ill by Shutting me Out part of the Goods that I at first agreed to Load on Board him in Order to Give him the Better Dispatch & had Order'd Insurance for, which he Did it Seems to Oblidge some Old Acquaintance here, & who I had gott to Ship on Board him & if it had not been for the Respect that I had for Your Good Selvs & Mr. John Keith, I would have Oblidg'd him before he went from this to have made Good the Dead Freight & Insurance. I was also very assistant to him in Order to Gett his Wines Dispos'd of to Good advantage, but he likewise Behav'd so ill in that Respect, that I at Last Did not give my self any further Trouble about him, but Left him to take his Own Measures (being of a very odd Fickle Temper) which prov'd to his Owner Mr. Keith's Disadvantage, by his ill Management in the Sale & Returns, so that Mr. Keith's Interest Sufferr'd, thro' his ill Conduct, Ignorance & Indiscretion.

I am likewise to accknowledge both your Esteem'd Favours of the 8th June (as also that of Same Date from your J. P.[5]) per the *Lewis*, Capt. Francis, with Bill of Loading for One pipe of Wine per said Vessell which Came to hand in pritty Good Order 'tho it wanted Six Inches of being full. It is very Good Wine, but Dear. Your Wines have Greatly advanc'd in price within these few Years past, & am to take Notice to you for the future that the Wine of a Deep Amber Colour is more in Esteem here than the Pale Colour, also that Wine be of a very Good Flavour. And am to Desire that youll Please to Ship me an Other Pipe to be here between the midle of April next at furthest, Valueing on my Brother for the Amount thereof, & Doubt not youll Lett me have it Choice Good, of a Deep Amber Colour, & pray Lett the Cask be Good & Tight (the Last was but Indifferent) & four Good Iron hoops on it. What Wines Remain here

---

[5] This was John Pringle.

on hand for Sale are Very Indifferent and Sell at £120 per pipe, about 700 Pipes have been Imported here Since February Last & not much Left.

I Observe that all sorts of Provisions are in Plenty with you & Rice very Low & we have a Very Large Crop this year both of Rice & Corn, it being Reckon'd the Greatest Ever Yet Produc'd in the Province & if a French War Should happen, of which we are apprehensive, are affraid we shall be in want of Shipping to Export it.

Capt. Patton has not been heard of Since he Sail'd from this in March Last. We have had no Vessells from London for these Two Months past & no Material news here at Present. This Goes Via Lisbon, under Cover of Messrs. Mayne, & having not further to Offerr at Present I Remain with Very Great Esteem &c.

Rice 40/ per Ct. & like to be much Lower, Exchange to London at £700 per £100 Ster.
Please be so good as to Inform me what number of Pipes of Wine is produc'd and Exported Annually from your Island *Communibus Annis.*

ADDRESSED: "Under Cover of Messrs. Mayne"

[682]
TO EDWARD & JOHN MAYNE & EDWARD BURN
Lisbon

Charles Town, 26th November 1743

GENTLEMEN:

My Last to you was of the 9th September per Capt. Rose with Copie & a few Days agoe Came to hand your most Esteem'd Favours of the 30th September per Capt. Gelly. Yours that you mention of the 20th July has not Come to hand. I Duely Remark your kind advices in Relation the Price of Rice at your Markett which is not very Encouraging at Present. This is the first Vessell with New Rice for your Port, by which this Goes, & there are two for Oporto. The Exportation of Rice for your Markett will be according to the Quantity of Shipping that arrive of which we have but few at Present, & if a French War happens, are afraid We Shall want

1st December 1743

Ships to Carry off Our Rice of which we have a Very Large Crop. I hope you have been so Good as to make a Remitt to my Brother in London as you advis'd me in yours of the 22d May. In his Last of the 20th July, he advises that he had not than Receiv'd any from you. We have no material News here at Present & no Ships from London for Sometime. I have not to add at Present but that I Remain Most Respectfully &c.

Rice 40/ per Ct., Exchange to London £700 per £100 Sterling.

P. S. I am to Desire the Favour Youll Please be so good as to forward per first the Inclos'd Letter for Messrs. Scott, Pringle & Scott of Madeira.

ADDRESSED: "Per Capt. Bellgarde Via Oporto & Copie per Capt. Boone for Oporto"

TO ANDREW PRINGLE
  London

Charles Town, 1st December 1743

SIR:

The Last I Did my Self the Pleasure to write you was of the 14th Ultimo per his Majesties Snow the *Swift*, also Copie thereof Via Bristoll to which Please be Refferr'd. Am as yet without any of your Favours which will Occasion Brevity & no Vessells from England since my last. The Last of your Favours was per Capt. Rice of the 20th July.

I Take the Opportunity of this per the Bearar Mr. Patrick Reid,[6] who has promis'd to Deliver it to you himself. He was Bookeeper to Messrs. Crokatt & Michie & has left them, & Goes Passenger in His Majesties Snow the *Hawk*, Capt. Arthur Forrest, Commander[7] whose Father Doubtless is known to you, who keeps Forrest's Coffee house at Charring Cross. He Came Dispatch'd in Said Snow from England by the Admiralty with Packetts for most of the Governments its said to be upon Our Guard

---

[6] Patrick Reid, Charleston merchant, was first the partner of Henry Kennan and later a partner in the firm of (John) Stuart & Reid. *HL*, I, 42n, 61n.
[7] HMS *Hawk*, Arthur Forrest, departed the Carolina station on 4 December 1743. May, p. 164.

1st December 1743

in Case of a French War & has been at Newfoundland, Bermuda & Providence. He went first to Boston.

Inclos'd Please Receive Account Sales of One Teirce of Rum Barbadoes on Account the Owners of the *John & Isabella,* Neat Proceeds being £70.15.6, also Account Sales of Two hhds. Rum & Two Barrells Muscovado Sugar on Account the Owners of the *Susannah* both Shipd by Gedney Clarke, Neat Proceeds being £232.6.2, Account Sales of Sundries Remaining on the Cargoe P S S per the *Susannah* 1740, Neat Proceeds £97.10.8, Account Sales of One Case Writing Paper per Capt. Harramond on your Own proper Account, Neat Proceeds £51.12.9 & Account Sales of Sundries per Capt. Crossthwaite on your Own Proper account, Neat Proceeds being £274.9.7½ this Currency. All which hope you'll find Right & to Content & which youll Please to note in Conformity accordingly, & which is the Sale of Every Thing Excepting the Cargoe per the *John & Isabella* [683] and the *Susannah's* Last from London, both which hope soon also to Compleat & To Your Satisfaction.

Inclos'd Please also Receive the Reverand Mr. John Fordyce his Bill of Exchange for £15 Ster. on Messrs. William & Thomas Tryon the Treasurers to the Society for the Propagation of the Gospell Payable to my Order at Thirty Days Sight & to your Good Self Indors'd which Doubt not will be Duely Honour'd. You have also Two Georgia Sola Bills, One of the Generall's No. 3753 & the Trustees No. 7355 for Twenty Shillings Sterling Each & for both which youll Please to Credit my Account & you may assuredly Depend on all the Remittances I am Capable & as Quick as possible.

Capt. Scott beleive will be Ready to Sail in a Week or Ten Days for London. New Rice is at 40/ per Ct. and Freight to London has been Engag'd at £3.15/ tho' Capt. Scott I hear has £4 for some & now Refuses £4 for what he wants, which is a Small matter. Beleive the first Vessell that arrives a Seeker will easily Obtain £4 per Ton for London or more, there being no Freight to be Obtain'd at Present, for want of Shipping & am afraid Rice wont answer at Said Rate.

I hope Messrs. Mayne have made you Remittance from Lisbon as they advis'd me a Considerable time agoe. I had advice from them Lately that Rice is Low there & a Good Deal had been Sent from London as also from Oporto to Lisbon.

You have also Inclos'd a Letter for you from Field Cossett & One for his Father to which Refferr You. Hope you have Dispos'd of his Old house & the Pew in Rotherith Church that belongs to it, being he wants the Mon-

7th December 1743

ey Pretty much, & wants to Run more in my Debt in Expectation thereof. Have Likewise Inclos'd you my Letters to Mr. Thomas Burrill of Hull, John Keith, & Capt. Story, about sending Over Certificates in Order to Discharge my Bonds, which after perusal You'll Please to Seal & have Deliver'd to them in Case the Copies I have already sent them may not have Come to Hand, all which I have Inclos'd by this Opportunity in Order to Save Postage.

Shall doe my Self the Pleasure to writt you again by Capt. Scott or next Ships with Invoice of Silver, &c. & Long much for your Favours. Capt. Warden, Mr. Reid, Capt. Stiles, Cap. Ayers, Capt. Wedderburn, & Capt. White We hear are all soon Expected from London, but none of them Does yet Appear. My Wife joins in Kind Love & Respects & I Remain most Affectionatly &c.

Prices of Goods as in my Last.

P. S. I hear Capt. Wimble was lately at Providence and gone again on a Cruize well Mann'd. I hope you have sent over One of his Bills & Protest, as I hope to Catch him in America. If he getts a good Prize I imagine he will bring it in here.

Exchange to London at £700 per £100 Ster. Inclos'd Please Receive Copie of my Last of the 14th Ulto.

ADDRESSED: "Per Patrick Reid in the Snow *Hawk,* Capt. Arthur Forrest, & Copie per Capt. Scott"

TO JOHN ERVING
Boston

Charles Town, 7th December 1743

SIR:

I have just time by a Sloop agoeing Down for Road Island to Acknowledge the Receipt of your most Esteemed Favours of the 5th, 16th September & 11th November per Mr. Benjamin Savage in the *Rose,*[8] &

---

[8] The *SCG,* 12 December 1743, announced that "on Monday last," 5 December, the *Rose* had arrived from Boston completely refitted.

7th December 1743

Duely mark the Contents. I Refferr to what I did my Self the Pleasure to write you of the 13th October per the Brigantine *Prosperity*, Capt. Priam Selew, who Sail'd about the 22d Ditto & by whom I ship'd you according to your Directions on your Proper Account Eighty Barrells Very Good Rice, & a Hhd. of Choice Deer Skins, Amount as per Invoice Sent £1,084.11.8 this Currency which hope is Come Safe to hand, also Two Barrells of Potatoes for your Acceptance, & Copie thereof & of the 25th October per Capt. Thornton[9] who hope is also Safe Arriv'd.

I Observe you intend Severall of your Ships here this Season & hope they will meet with Good Encouragement, & the Sooner you send them beleive will be the better. Freight is now at £4 per Ton for London & £4.10/ for Holland or Hamburg. We have had but few Vessells as yet arriv'd this fall, & beleive Freight will hold up as we are apprehensive of a Scarcity of Shipping this Season, Especially if no [684] great numbers Come from your Parts, and am of Opinion Freight will be higher than is at Present as we have the Greatest Crop of Rice ever yet Produc'd & Expected will be Low in price. It has broke in Price & is at Present at 40/ per Ct. As to what Goods you may Purpose to send in your Ships, as I advis'd in my Former am of Opinion Rum & Loaf Sugar are most Likely to Answer the Best, Some Hay, & for Ballast, Stone, will be preferable to Bricks which are unsaleable & never exceed £3.10/ per mille & may Lye a Considerable Time on Our Wharfs, Lyable to be Lost or Stolen before they Can be Dispos'd of.

Capt. Arthur Forrest, by Whom had the Pleasure of hearing of Your & Good Familly's Welfare, Receiv'd the Things you Sent for him from Doctor Rind of the *Rose*,[1] just in Goeing Over the Barr. Capt. Forrest seems to be a Very Worthy Agreeable Gentleman & Doubt not Justly merits the Good Character you Give him. I am Surpriz'd that I have not heard of Late from Mr. Thomas Hutchinson in Return to Severalls of mine. Please my Best Respects to him as I have not the Opportunity of writing him by this Conveyance.

My Wife Joyns in her best Respects to Good Mrs. Erving & all the Pritty Familly, most heartily wishing you a Merry Xmass & a Great many happy Years, & I Remain in haste with very Great Respect &c.

ADDRESSED: "Per Capt. Monro Via Road Island"

---

[9] Capt. Christopher Thornton, brigantine *Good Intent*, from Boston. SCG, 29 August 1743.
[1] Dr. William Rind was to remain in the province. Waring, p. 60.

TO WILLIAM DOVER
London

Charles Town, 17th December 1743

SIR:

My Last to you was of the 6th November with Copie thereof Via Bristol to which please be Refferr'd, & agreeable thereto Please Receive Inclosed Bill of Lading & Invoice of one hhd. very Good Deer Skins Shipt in the *Charming Susan*, Capt. Patrick Scott, for London on your Proper Risque & Account and to your Good Self Consign'd, Amount as per Invoice Being £296.7.2 which wish Safe to hand & hope will Come to a good Markett, the Skins being of the Best Sort in Quality. You have also Inclos'd your Account Current, Ballance in your Favour being £4.7.4 this Currency, & the Current Exchange to London at £700 per £100 Is 12/6 Ster. which if you Please apply to my Brother for, he will pay you Said Ballance Accordingly, being the hhd. would not hold any more Skins without being Over Packt. Capt. Scott by which this Goes is now Ready to Sail & will soon be with you. I am with Due Respect &c.

ADDRESSED: "Per Capt. Scott & Copie per Capt. Branscombe"

TO BURRYAU & SCHAFFER
London

Charles Town, 17th December 1743

GENTLEMEN:

The Last I did myself the Pleasure to write you was of the 17th October, with Copie advising for Insurance of the £100 Ster. on the Ship *Charming Susan*, Capt. Scott, for London on Account of Mr. Thomas Hutchinson of Boston, Said Scott having been Oblidg'd to wait for New Rice has Detain'd him here till this Time, but is now ready to Sail first Opportunity of Wind. Please Receive Inclos'd Bill of Loading & Invoice of Three hundred & Seventy five Ounces Spanish Silver Ship'd on Board the above Vessell on the proper Account & Risque of the Said Mr. Thomas Hutchinson & to your Good Selvs Consign'd, Amount as per Invoice being £708.15.0 this Currency which wish Safe to hand & hope

17th December 1743

will Come to a Good Markett, & which You'll be pleas'd to Advise Mr. Hutchinson of Accordingly. As I Understand your Z. Burryau, Esqr. has a Considerable Interest in the Island of St. Kitts, Shou'd be very Glad to Receive his Comands if he Shoud have Occasion to Ship any of the [685] Produce thereof here, as Rum & Sugar are always very Saleable Commodities in Good Demand. Am of Opinion he might find it Turn Out to Good Account to Order Some for this Markett, the Sugar in Barrells & Rum in hhds. & Teirces. I Salute you and am most Respectfully &c.

Exchange to London at £700 per £100 Ster. Rice 37/6 per Ct.

ADDRESSED: "Per Capt. Scott & Copie per Ditto Branscombe"

TO ANDREW PRINGLE
London

Charles Town, 19th December 1743

SIR:

Inclos'd please Receive Copie of my Last of the 1st Current per his Majesties Ship *Hawk* to which please be Refferr'd. And about Ten Days agoe have the Pleasure of your Most Acceptable Favours per Capt. Warden of the 1st, 6th, 9th, 15th, & 19th September as also Two Days agoe yours of the 1st & 4th October per Capt. White & Same Day yours of September 11th & Copie of the 4th October per Capt. Wedderburn & Duely Remark the Various Contents which have not the Opportunity at Present to give a Due Return to by this Conveyance.

Our Governour James Glen, Esqr. arriv'd in his Majesties Ship *Tartar* the 17th in the Afternoon & Yesterday Morning I had the Pleasure to Kiss his hand, who told me that he Left you well & was very Glad to See me.[2]

I Receiv'd all the Accounts & Invoices per Capt. Warden & the Goods Accordingly which have all Come in very Good Order (excepting the Pickles, Some of which are Spoilt, the Pickle have Leak't out, by not being Corkt tight) And for all which you have my Sincere Thanks. Mr. Birt the

---

[2] For the announcement of Glen's arrival, see *SCG*, 19 December 1743.

19th December 1743

Book Seller,[3] it seems was not at much pains to Gett all the Books, otherwise am inform'd that he might have mett with them all at One Mr. Paul Vallaint's Book Seller in the Strand.

I am much Oblidg'd to you, for you Receiving £31.10.6 of Mr. Dalby in Part of Capt. Turrils Bill & hope youll be able to Recover the Remaining £15, as I am under no Obligation to Give my Time & Trouble to him who is a Stranger to me for Nothing, & Especially as his Ship Brought no Cargoe here worth while. If Messrs. Hutchinson & Co. had not been ¼ Concern'd wou'd have Charg'd £20 Sterling, and as for Capt. Turells Saying that he Could have Engag'd all his Freight on his arrival at £4.5/ was absolutely false & shows him to be an old Knave (tho I Question if he said so & take it to be made up by Mr. Dalby himself) as well as a Very Weak Ignorant Man interly unfitt to take Charge of any Vessell, as hardly Knowing stem from Stern, for if I had taken his Council & hence Delay'd & stood off from Engaging he had not have gott £4 per Ton, which appear'd plainly by the Freight I gott for him the Part I engag'd first being at £4.5/ & the Remainder being Only at £4 by Waiting & Endeavouring to Compleat the whole at £4.5/ but Cou'd not be Done for more than £4 & Presently after, while he was here, Freight was at £3.12.6. You'll please to Credit my Account with the Neat Proceeds of Field Cossetts House being £65.17.6 Ster. which shall make good to him here & Take his Discharge Accordingly.

I have not had the Opportunity to Talk much to Mr. Reid Since his arrival but on Generall Things, he being Very Busie about his Goods. He Introduc'd the Young Man[4] to me Yesterday that is Come Over to be his Partner.

The Rascally Fellow nam'd Harding One of Our Pilots has put the *Susannah*'s anchor in the Admiralty, being as he Says found & without any Owner & so Consequently Comes to the King, which he Did out of Spite because he found that he Could not make it his Own as he Intended, tho threatn'd to arrest him if he Did not Deliver it up, altho' I Offerr'd him what ever Salvage [686] was Reasonable and Customary & it will Cost as much as the Value to Claim it in the Admiralty. Mr. Graeme the Judge[5] who is my Friend & Knows the Case, Let's it Lye Dorment till I Can have

---

[3] Samuel Birt. *HL*, I, 79.
[4] Henry Kennan was James Reid's partner. *RPC*, p. 809.
[5] James Graeme, Charleston lawyer, was a member of the Council, Judge of the Court of Vice-Admiralty, and Chief Justice of the Court of Common Pleas. He died in 1752. *SCHM*, XXXIII (1932), 148n.

19th December 1743

the Marks & Proofs of it's being the *Susannah's* which Pray Delay not if Possible to Gett of Capt. Gregory & send Over otherwise you will Loose £20 Ster. the Value of it.

Beleive it wont be worth Capt. Robert Thompson's while to Come Over here for any thing he Can Expect from Mr. Gray's Estate.[6] The Creditors have Receiv'd but 15/ per pound as yet of the Debts & when the whole Debts are paid, there will be but a Small Reversion for his Widow & son that Mr. Gray had by her here & who are next Heirs to what ever they may be both of Real & Personal Estate, & it will be a Considerable Time before all the Debts are Gott in.

I Receiv'd Inclos'd my Account Current in Sterling Money with you in London & upon perusal Remark Some Small Oversights for which have Debit you, & Please Receive Inclos'd the Account Stated, as it appears to me to stand between us at present, Ballance in your Favour being £654.6.7¼ Sterling which if you find without Errors youll please to Note in Conformity Accordingly, & for Said Ballance (being indeed a Considerable Sum) You maybe assur'd of being Reimburs'd as Quick as possibly I am Capable. I am again to Desire Youll Please Send Over One of Capt. Wimbles Bills with the Copie of the Protest. I had a Letter from him Lately from Providence. He has gone on other Cruize well mann'd & Expect him here Soon, or at Rhoad Island if he getts a Prize. He Owes no Person here but Trifles besides my Self.

As I still Continue my Intention of Seeing you in London (God Willing) the next Summer, provided my affairs will Permitt, & Can gett in Debts. I writt you for the Copper Cooler as it will be very usefull on Board the Ship, not Lyable to be Broken, or to Leake, & the Bird Cages I intend for Some Birds that I purpose to bring & may be Esteem'd Rare & Curious in England. I have no Account of any Goods for me per Capt. White or Wedderburn that you mention was to be Shipt per Capt. White, Value about £200 Ster. on Account of Messrs. Hutchinson & Goldthwait. I am very Willing to be Concern'd as you advise in a Ship with you & said Gentlemen, & will always very readily Concurr with you in that or any other Schame or Branch of Trade & you may Desire of me, & that I Can afford to be Engag'd in.

Please Receive Inclos'd Bill of Loading & Invoice of 250 Oz. Spanish Silver On Account & Risque of the Owners of the *John & Isabella*, Amount as per Invoice being £472.10.0 this Currency which wish Safe to

---

[6] Robert Gray's estate.

19th December 1743

hand also Ditto of 220 Oz. Ditto on my Own Proper Account, Amount £415.16/ Currency, The Neat Proceeds youll Please to Give Credit to my Account. You have also Bill of Loading & Invoice of One hhd. Deer Skins On account & Risque of Capt. Samuel Sanders, Amount as per Invoice being £361.2.5 this Currency all Ship'd on board the Ship *Charming Susan*, Capt. Patrick Scott, for London & to your Good Self Consign'd. Inclos'd please also Receive Copie of Capt. Sanders his account Current which I send him per this Conveyance, Ballance in my Favour Over Remitted him being £3.3.8 or 9/ Ster. which have Desir'd him to Pay to you And am to Desire youll be So good as to Pay to Mr. William Dover Twelve shillings & 6d per Sterling Ballance of Account Due him, having Remitted him 1 hhd. Skins per this Conveyance for Some Arms he Consign'd per Capt. Gregory.

My Wife presents her best Respects & kind Thanks for your present of Walnutts which are Exceeding Good & in the Best Order of all Articles & most heartily wishing you a Merry Xmass & a Great many happy years, I Most affectionatly Remain &c.

P. S. Exchange to London at £700 per £100 Ster. Rice 37/6 per Ct., Freight to London at £4 per ton, Pitch 40/ per bbl., Tar 35/ per bbl.

ADDRESSED: "Per Capt. Scott & Copie per Capt. Branscombe"

[687]
TO SAMUEL SAUNDERS
Southampton

Charles Town, 19th December 1743

SIR:

My Last to you was of the 19th October per Capt. Rice with Copie thereof to which please be Refferr'd. And agreeable thereto Please Receive Inclos'd Copie of Invoice of One hhd. of Very Good Deer Skins, Ship'd on Board the Ship *Charming Susan*, Capt. Patrick Scott, Commander for London, On your Proper Risque & Account And to my Brother Consign'd, Amount as per Invoice being £361.2.5 which wish Safe to

19th December 1743

hand & hope will Come to a Good Markett. This being the first Ship for London & no Opportunity Like to be Soon for Cowes. Please also Receive Inclos'd Your Account Current, the Ballance in my Favour being £3.3.0 this Currency or 9/ Ster., Exchange 7 per 1 which you'll Please to Pay to my Brother. Capt. Scott by which this Goes Sails in a Day or Two hence.

We have no material News here at Present, only that Our New Governour James Glen, Esqr. arriv'd here four days agoe in his Majesties Ship the *Tartar*. Freight is Pretty high at Present And we are afraid if a French War that we Shall want Shipping to Carry off Our Crop, of which We have the Largest Ever yet Produc'd. My Wife joyns in Best Respects to Mrs. Sanders, pritty Miss, & Good Self & Heartily wishing you a Merry Xmass & a Great many happy Years, I Remain most Respectfully &c.

Rice 37/6 per Ct., Freight to London £4 per Ton & to Holland or Hamburg £4.10/, Exchange to London at £700 per £100 Sterling.

ADDRESSED: "Per Capt. Scott & Copie per Capt. Branscombe"

TO JAMES ARCHBOLD[7]
  Oporto
           Charles Town, 24th December 1743

SIR:

I receiv'd Two Days agoe Copie of your Esteem'd Favours of the 24th August Via New England. The Original has not yet Appear'd. I Duely Remark what you are Pleas'd to Advise in Relation to Our Commodity of Rice & when I have Occasion & there is Encouragement of Shipping Rice to your Port, you may Expect Same to Your Address, as I have Great Reguard for my Brothers Recommendations & Shall be always very Glad Reciprochally to Contribute in Encouraging any Branch of Trade that has a Prospect for Our Mutual Interest, & when your Markett is Encouraging, & you may think Proper to Give Directions for Shipping any Rice for your Port, Shall be Willing to Goe Part Concern'd in the Adven-

[7] "Brother A. P. in his letter of the 26 June 1743 advises to Consign Rice to Mr. James Archibold, Merchant in Oporto...." RPC, p. 819.

27th December 1743

ture, as I doubt not my Brother will Likewise take part therein. At Present Our Markett does not Seem to be Encouraging, for by Late advices from my Friends at Lisbon, they acquaint me that a pritty Deal of Rice has been Shipt from your Port for Said Place.

Shall take it kind as Opportunity Offers that youll be so good as to Favour me with your advices Relating to your Markett, & be always very Glad to Render you any Acceptable Service. I Salute you with the usual Compliments of the Season, & I am Most Respectfully &c.

Rice 37/6 per Ct., Exchange to London at £700 per £100 Ster. We have the Largest Crop of Rice this Year that has ever yet been Produc'd in the Province.

ADDRESSED: "Per Capt. Bellegarde & Copie per Capt. Boone"

[688]
TO JASPER KING[8]
Prince Frederick Parish, South Carolina
Charles Town, 27th December 1743
SIR:
I Receiv'd Yesterday yours of the 20th Inst. and in Answer Doe not think it Proper to Give up all the Securitys that I have on Mr. Bassnetts Estate upon your Advancing for him Only the Sum you mention, Unless that I Can have Sufficient Security for the Remainder of the Debt, which is Very Considerable. As it is but Reasonable & just that I Ought to be Secur'd as well as You & Mr. McIver. And I Doe not think the Obligation Done Mr. Bassnett so Great, when you have Good Security & Interest for your Money. If Satisfieing Resolution is not Come to Very Soon, Must give me Leave to take proper Measures for the Recovery of my Money. I am &c.

ADDRESSED: "Deliver'd Mrs. Bassnett at Mr. Berry's"

[8] Jasper King, a small South Carolina planter, served on the vestry of Prince Frederick Winyaw between the year 1743 and his death late in 1749. John Bassnett was one of the executors of his will. The will was dated 4 September 1749 and proved 11 January 1750. Wills, VI, 438; *The Register Book for the Parish of Prince Frederick Winyaw* (Baltimore, 1916), pp. 93–109.

624   THE LETTERBOOK OF ROBERT PRINGLE

27th December 1742

TO ANDREW LESSLY
Antigua

Charles Town, 27th December 1743

SIR:

The Preceeding of the 24th October is Copie of the Last I Did my Self the Pleasure to write you which this Serves to Confirm & have not further to Offerr at Present, as being without any of your Favours. Only am again to Intreat Youll be So good as to forward the Certificates as Directed per first Conveyance. I Salute you with the usuall Compliments of the Season And Most Respectfully Remain &c.

Rice 35/ per Ct., Corn 10/ per Bu., Pork £10 per bbl., Rum 15/ per Gall., Muscovado Sugar £9 to £11 per Ct.

ADDRESSED: NO ADDRESS

TO GEDNEY CLARKE
Barbados

Charles Town, 24th December 1743

SIR:

I have the Pleasure of your Sundry most Esteen'd Favours of the 10th December & 20th February from London, the 29 January from Bristoll, & the 9th July from Madeira. And hope this Shall find you happily arriv'd in Barbados which Shall be very Glad to be Advis'd of.

My Late Indisposition has Occasion'd my Missing an Opportunity to Give a Return to your Said Letters & forwarding you account Sales & Account Current per the *Lusitania* before this. Your Sundry Letters from England all Came to hand a Great Deal too Late to prevent the *Lusitania*'s goeing back to Barbados according to Your Directions Sent me in Relation to her before you Left Barbados, being Sail'd from this Long before I Receiv'd any of yours, & which I often wish'd (as I told Capt. Gravener) had been more Discretionary, as I Could certainly have procur'd him a Good Freight for London & Very Good Dispatch & am Sorry it happen'd so unlucky. Please Receive Inclos'd account Sales of the Rum

24th December 1743

per the *Lusitania*, the Neat Proceeds being £1,918.3.6 which hope will be to Content. A Great Deal of Rum, happening to Come in from time to time soon after the *Lusitania* (as Capt. Gravener Can inform you) which Could not be forseen, Lower'd the price very much, however Can Venture to Say that it was Sold the best of any Parcell of Rum that was here at that Time or of any Since.

Please also Receive Inclos'd your Account Current, Ballance in your favour being £99.10.3 this Currency, which you might have Expected before this to have been Remitted in Corn, as Messrs, Johnson & Carter Order'd per theirs of 2d June, but Could not obtain any Freight for your Island, neither Could I prevail on Capt. Anderson, by which this Goes, to Lett me have any Freight which is not at Present to be Procur'd for Your Island on any Terms. However may Expect Same per [689] the first I Can procure Freight to Your Island in Corn, unless I have your Orders to the Contrary.

We have a Very Large Crop of Rice this year, being the Largest ever yet Produc'd in the Province & We are afraid (especially if a French War happens) that we Shall want Shipping to Carry it off. Freight is now at £4 per Ton for London and £4.10/ per Ton for Holland or Lisbon. As Under you have the Current prices of Goods, but little Rum has yett arriv'd here this fall from your Island & Muscovado Sugar pretty Scarce as also Coffee. Shall be allways very Glad to Receive your Commands & to Render you any Acceptable Service. I Salute you with usual Compliments of the Season & I am most Respectfully &c.

Rice 35/ per Ct., Tar 35/ per bbl., Turpentine 10/ per Ct., Corn 10/ per bu., Pease 10/ per bu., Beef £7 per bbl., Pork £10 per bbl., Rum 20/ per Gallon, Muscovado Sugar £9. to £11 per Ct., Coffee 7/ per lb., Madeira Wine £130 per pipe, Exchange to London at £700 per £100 Ster.

ADDRESSED: "Capt. Anderson's Scooner & Copie per Capt. Hinson"

TO ALEXANDER STRAHAN[9]
Kingston, Jamaica

Charles Town, 27th December 1743

Sir:

I have your very agreeable favours of the 20th June last & am very Glad to be Inform'd of your Health & Wellfare On the Score of Old Acquaintance & heartily wish you every thing agreeable in Life.

In Answer to yours, I never heard of any Such Vessell as the Snow *St. Lucas*, neither Such a Person here as Capt. Robertson as you mention to the best of my Knowledge, otherwise would have been very ready to have Render'd you all the Service & Good Offices in my Power, & if Capt. Robertson did Come here, he never made himself known to me. It is very Seldom that we have any Conveyances from this for your Island, unless sometimes small Vessells with Provisions Such as the Vessell by which this Goes, & but Rare any Vessells Comes here from thence, unless Sometimes for Freight when they happen to Miss of a Loading at Jamaica & the Only Commodity that answers here is Muscovado Sugar & Molassis. Your Rum Comes too high priced for this Place, Barbados Rum being Most in use here of which this Province takes off about 1,200 hhds. annually.

We have a Very Large Crop of Rice this Year, being Reckon'd the Largest ever yet Produc'd in the Province, & are afraid, Especially if a French Warr happens, that we Shall want Shipping to Carry it off. If in anything I can be of Service to you here, you may always freely Command me. I Salute you with the Usuall Compliments of the Season & am very Respectfully &c.

Rice 35/ per Ct., Corn 10/ per Bushell, Pease 10/ per bu., Beef £7 per bbl., Pork £10 per bbl., Muscovado Sugar £9 to £11 per Ct., Molassis 10/ per Gall., Coffee 7/ per lb., Exchange to London at £700 per £100 Ster.

P. S. Shall be always very Glad to have the Pleasure of hearing You.

ADDRESSED: "Per Capt. Webster"

---

[9] Alexander Strahan was a merchant in Kingston, Jamaica. RPC, p. 818.

29th December 1743

[690]
TO GEDNEY CLARKE
Barbados

Charles Town, 29th December 1743

SIR:

I have already writt you of the 24th Current per this Conveyance Inclosing Your Account Sales & Account Current to which please be Refferr'd. And this Day have the Pleasure of your Very agreeable Favours, Copie of the 16th August, & yours of the 29th November & Duely Remark the Contents. The Original of yours of the 16th August has not yet appear'd.

I was very much out of Order with a Flux During the whole month of September & Part of October which prevented me from sending the Account & Giving a Return to your Favours But (thank God) am & have been Sometime perfectly Recover'd. And there has not for a Considerable Time before this that I Coud hear off been any Conveyance for your Island, otherwise you might Certainly have Depended on hearing from me, & to have had the Ballance of Account Remitted in Corn as Directed, if Possibly I Could have Obtain'd Freight which Could not be had at any Rate. I Should be very Sorry if I have Given any Reason or Occasion for you to Change your Correspondance here, being Conscious to my Self that I have Acted in all Respects the Best I Could for your Interest, and Shall be always very Ready to Execute Your Commands with the Utmost Integrity & Punctualy.

I Refferr you to what have already advis'd you per this Conveyance in Relation to the Prices of Goods here & Freight. If you Send the *Lusitania* here for a Freight, Doubt not may find good Encouragement as it is Thought that Freight will keep high all this Season, And it may be Proper that your Directions may be full & Discretionary. The Vessell being just agoeing, in haste I Remain with very Great Respect &c.

ADDRESSED: "Per Capt. Anderson's Scooner & Copie per Capt. Hinson"

TO FLORENTIA COX
New Providence, Bahamas

Charles Town, 29th December 1743

SIR:

I have your Favours of the 16th October & Observe you had than Sold no more than 27 (i.e. Twenty Seven) of the Small Arms & that you was Collecting Plank in Order to Remitt for the Same which you expected to Doe in a Short time, as hope Soon to have them accordingly. I am to Desire the Favour You'll be so Good as to use your best Endeavours to Dispose of the other Twenty Small Arms without Loss of Time which hope by this Time you have pretty near Effected & Transmitt me Account Sales thereof. I heartily Wish you a Merry Xmass & a Great many happy Years & I am &c.

ADDRESSED: NO ADDRESS

[691]
TO NICHOLAS RIGBYE
Savannah

Charles Town, 4th January 1743 [1744]

SIR:

I have your Favours of the 15th Ulto. per the Bearar Capt. Grant[1] in Return to mine of the 4th November & Remark the Contents. I was in Great hopes of a Remittance at Least, if not the whole Account, by this Conveyance, it being now near Six Months Since you had the Goods & you assur'd me you woud make Returns for Same at most in three or four Months, especially did at Least Expect you woud have Reimburs'd me for the Cash I Advanced out of Pockett for the Sugar Sent you, as you have a Certain Sallery Coming In & Doubt not according to the Repeated Assurances you now Give me in your Last that you will very Speedily, & I hope by next Opportunity, make Remittance for your whole Account, & as it is the first of Our Dealing was in hopes you woud have been Punctual in Order to have Encourag'd a further Correspondance. Messrs.

[1] Ludowick Grant was a trader in the Cherokee nation. Coulter & Saye, p. 76.

Grant & Habbersham[2] from your Place are very Punctual in their Returns & have Establish'd a Very Good Credit in this Place, & money Can be no Scarcer to you than to them.

As the Time for the 1st payment of Mr. Dormers Account is now Come, hope he has paid it, & Doubt not you will Remitt it per first Opportunity. In Expectation of your Compliance I Remain (heartily wishing you a Great many happy Years) &c.

ADDRESSED: "Per Mrs. Emery"

TO SAMUEL WATSON
    Hull

Charles Town, 4th January 1743 [*1744*]

SIR:

I Receiv'd about three Weeks agoe, & not before at the hands of Mr. James Reid, your Very angry Letter of the 22d June Last about your Small parcell of Manchester Goods which I wish I had never anything to Doe with, and of which a Good part still Remain unsold, being as I formerly advis'd you Very Unsaleable here & could not Encourage or Desire your sending any such Goods, but more especially are so very high Charg'd in your Invoice, being 25 per cent higher Charg'd than the Same sort of Goods I have had Ship'd from London, & which has been the Occasion of their Lying so long on hand, as I Cannot Sell them for so much as they are Charg'd in your Invoice. However as you insist on Account Sales to be Sent, I shall without Loss of Time, Dispose of them at Publick Vandue or Sale, or otherwise for the most they will fetch & transmitt you Account Sales thereof & Remittance for what may be in Cash accordingly.

But as for Remittance by Bill of Exchange, it will be Impracticable, there being no Such thing to be had here at Present as Bills of Exchange, So that you must Give me Your further Directions how and in what Com-

---

[2] James Habersham came to Georgia in 1740 with the Rev. George Whitefield. He served as president of Whitefield's Bethesda Orphan Home, Secretary of the Province, a member of the King's Council, President of the Council, and for a brief while as royal governor. He and his partner, Charles Harris, established the first commercial house in Georgia. *Historical Collections of the Joseph Habersham Chapter*, DAR, I (1901), 185–186.

4th January 1744

modity & in what manner You'll have the Neat Proceeds Remitted, which must be Done by Way of London in Rice or Deer Skins, &c., either or both as may judge most for your Interest or as you may think proper to Order, unless an Opportunity of Freight may happen for your Port of Hull Directly from this which is Very unlikely. Either way as you think proper & your Directions shall be Duely Comply'd with, & which I Desire you may Lett me have by the first Opportunity. Doe assure you your Goods was a Commission I did no ways Desire & as you sent them of your Self without any advice or Encouragement from me you have the Less Reason to make so great Complaint, especially about an affair of so small Consequence. I am &c.

ADDRESSED: "Per Capt. Branscombe & Copie per Capt. Abercrombie"

[692]
TO HUBERT GUICHARD
   St. Kitts

Charles Town, 11th January 1743 [1744]

SIR:

My last to you was of the 25th June 1741 to which Please be Refferr'd, Since have not the Pleasure of any of your Favours. Since my Last have never yet had the Opportunity of any Freight for your Island, otherwise you might have Depended on the Ballance of Account in my hands being Remitt'd you Long before this, there being but very few Conveyances from this & those small Vessells that goe won't take in any Goods on Freight. Shall be Glad you'll Please to Order Said Ballance to be Remitted by way of London or any other way you may think Proper, in Case no Opportunity happens soon from this to your Island. You might have expected Said Ballance to have been Remitt'd you by the Bearar Capt. Webber[3] for your Island in Rice, Corn or Pease, but Could not prevail on him to take any Goods on Freight, being Loaded Interely by his Owner.

We have a very Large Crop of Rice & Corn, & all other Provisions in Great Plenty. Shall be very Glad to be favour'd with a Line from you with

[3] Capt. Samuel Webber, sloop *William*, for St. Christopher's. *SCG*, 2 January 1744.

11th January 1744

your Directions about Said Ballance of Account. I Salute you with the usual Compliments of the Season & I am most Respectfully &c.

ADDRESSED: "Per Capt. Webber & Copie per Mr. Hanson"

TO FRANCIS GUICHARD
 St. Kitts

Charles Town, 11th January 1743 [1744]

SIR:

My Last to you was of the 25th June 1741, Since have not the Pleasure of any of your Favours. Since my Last have never yet had the Opportunity of any Freight for your Island that I might Remitt your Uncle Mr. Hubert Guichard the Ballance of his four hhds. Molassis, neither Could I prevail with the Bearar Capt. Webber to let me Ship either Rice, Corn or Pease, otherwise he might have Expected Said Ballance by this Conveyance, as I have writt him by Said Webber, & that in Case no Opportunity of getting Freight soon for your Island, I have Desir'd him to give me his Directions to Remitt Said Ballance by way of London or Philadelphia. We have a very Large Crop of Rice & Corn & all other Provisions in Great Plenty.

Please advise me if there is any Likelyhood of ever Getting Payment from Mr. Valentine French of his Note of Hand that you were So good to take of him on my Account. Shall be always very Glad to have the Pleasure of hearing from you & to Render you any agreeable Service. I Salute you with the usual Compliments of the Season & I am Most Respectfully &c.

ADDRESSED: "Per Capt. Webber & Copie per Mr. Hanson"

14th January 1744

[693]
TO ANDREW LESSLY
   Antigua

Charles Town, 14th January 1743 [1744]

SIR:

I have a few Days agoe your much Esteem'd Favours of the 11th December per Capt. Lavers[4] in Return to my Last of the 24th October with Inclos'd the Certificates for the *Loyall Judith's* Cargoe & Capt. Gregorys & Shall Credit your Account 12/ Antigua Currency for the Last. As for the *Loyall Judith's* Certificate, Our Attorney Generall has Charg'd me Six Guineas for His Indulgence in not putting the Bond in Suit.

Inclos'd please Receive Copie of the account Sales of the 6 HHds. Rum, Original sent per Capt. Williams, the Neat Proceeds being £349.6.3 this Currency.

I am sorry your Crop is like to prove so short. I observe that Rice & Lumber is in pritty Good Demand with you. I would have shipt some Rice but no Freight is to be Obtain'd for your Island. Capt. Webber by which this Goes would take no Goods on Freight, being Loaded interely by the Owner. I make no Doubt of your Remitting both the Ballances of Accounts as you are Pleas'd to mention the first of your Crop, which hope will prove better than Expectation. I Remark your taking a Young Gentleman in Company with you in which I Heartily wish you all the Success you Desire & I Remain with very Great Respect &c.

Rum 16/6 per Gallon, Muscovado Sugar £9 to £11 per Ct., Coffee 7/ per lb. & Scarce, Rice 35/ per Ct., Corn 10/ per bu., Pease 10/ per bu., Pork £12 per bbl., Exchange to London £700 per £100 Ster.

The Bearar Capt. Webber being a Stranger in Your Island, If it Suits you to be any ways servicable to him Shall Esteem it a Favour. He has a Suitable Cargoe of Provisions.

ADDRESSED: "Per Capt. Webber & Copie per Mr. Hanson"

---

[4] Capt. Hercules Lavers, ship *Planter*, arrived from Antigua. SCG, 16 January 1744.

14th January 1744

TO MICHAEL LOVELL
Antigua

Charles Town, 14th January 1743 [1744]

SIR:

I have a few Days agoe your much Esteem'd Favours of the 17th December per Capt. Lavers in Return to my Last of the 24th October with Inclos'd Account Sales of the Thirty BBls. Rice, the Neat Proceeds being £45.5.3 Currency of Antigua and am Greatly oblidg'd to you for your Good Offices & Care in so bad & Troublesome a Consignment.

I Observe you have some thoughts of sending a Small Schooner here Soon, & if I doe not hear from you in a month to Ship you Six or Eight Bbls. of Broken & as many Bbls. of Whole Rice & two or three Bbls. of Pease, which Shall be punctually Comply'd with, provided any Freight Can be Obtain'd for your Island. Capt. Webber by which this Goes would take in no Goods on Freight being Loaded by his Owner Intirely, otherwise woud have Shipt you Some Good Rice by this Conveyance.

I have sold part of your Linnens but Oblidg'd to give a Considerable Credit on them as we doe on all Dry Goods, & hope soon to Compleat the Sale thereof & to your Satisfaction. I heartily wish you a Great many Happy Years, & I am with very Great Respect &c.

Rum 16/6 per Gall., Muscovado Sugar £9 to £11 per Ct., Coffee 7/ per lb. & Scarce, Rice 35/ per Ct., Corn 10/ per bu., Pease 10/ per bu., Pork £12 per bbl., Exchange to London at £700 per £100 Ster.

The Bearar Capt. Webber being a Stranger in Your Island, if it Suits you to be any ways Serviceable to him, shall Esteem it a Favour. He has a Good Suitable Cargoe of Provisions.

ADDRESSED: "Per Mr. Webber & Copie per Capt. Hanson"

21st January 1744

[694]
TO ANDREW PRINGLE
   London

Charles Town, 21st January 1743 [1744]

SIR:

My Last to you was of the 10th December per Capt. Scott with Copie thereof per Capt. Branscombe to which please be Refferr'd, And about a Week agoe has come to hand your very acceptable Favours of the 19th & 25 October per Capt. Hayden[5] & 3d November per Capt. Miznard,[6] & Duely Observe the Contents. In Particular with Relation to the Wine Adventure you advise of, in which I joyn in Opinion with you that it will be a Good Scheme & you may Depend on my Uttmost Endeavours for the Effecting thereof here to the best advantage & for the Dispatch of the Vessell to Porto, & in which adventure am very willing to Accept of your kind Offerr of being Concern'd the Proportion as you Desire, but am to take Notice to you that as the Vessell is to be Dispatch'd here for Opporto, & all the Wines She brings to be Reship'd besides a Quantity of Wines as you Advise to be purchas'd here to be mix'd up with same, am afraid Cannot be able to raise money to Effect Same without being Oblidg'd to Draw Bills on you, as you mention, & which you may Depend on will be as Sparingly as possible without hurting my Credit, & there is no Such thing as putting off Dry Goods here for Wine at any Rate, they being a Drugg & Wine is always a Ready Money Commodity & purchas'd with Money only & is sold now at £120 per pipe & but small Wines.

Youll please to send over a Fresh power of Attorney to me, as it is proper to be Recover'd whatever may happen.

Shall Ship the Canvas to N. York or Boston as you Direct, as it is not like to meet with Sale here & wish I had had your Orders for so Doing Long agoe. I Remark what you are Pleas'd to mention about Mr. Elliotts Son, & have talk'd with his Father about him. I Desir'd him to write you & to Lett you have his Directions about him which he tells me that he will very soon & Desires that after his Son has done with the Academy he may take a Tour over England & Goe over & See Holland if he Inclines to it.

Mr. Stead's Partner Mr. Evance tells me that he has lately a Letter from Mr. Nickleson,[7] wherein he advises that he wont allow the Article of

---

[5] Capt. James Hayden, ship *Ulysses*, arrived from London. SCG, 23 January 1744.
[6] Capt. Stephen Meshard, ship *Carolina*, arrived from London. SCG, 23 January 1744.
[7] John Nickleson of London.

21st January 1744

£600 Currency I Charg'd for Interest for my Advance on James Hunter & Co. Their Account which think is unjust in him, as it is but Reasonable & we intend to Insist on it, & if they shoud Sue for it & is brought to a Tryal, if we should happen to be Cast in Common Law we Can thro it into Chancery & keep them out of the whole money these seven Years to Come. However would much rather to have it Settled Amicably & hope you have Spoke to him of it before this, which please to Advise me of.

I Observe that Messrs. Mayne have Remitted 430$500 Reis, my Neat Proceeds per the *Bremen Factor* Exchange 67 ⅛ d, & they Gave me Credit in the Account the Exchange at 67 ⅞ d per Milreis.

The Pool Captains Report in Yours of the 3d November of the Damage Done by the Hurricane here is entirely false, there being very Little or no Damage Done by it Either in Town or to the Crop of Rice as I have already advis'd, & there is Certainly the Greatest Crop of Rice that has ever yet been produc'd & Computed at 120,000 barrells.

[695] Field Cossett Desires you may Give the Old man his Father no more money, as it would be of no Service to him for if you was, he would give it all to his worthless Sister.

You advise of Chartering a Ship on me which if you have not already Done, I shall not have Occasion for as I Expect Two or three from Boston that will Accomodate me with what I shall have Occasion to Ship. It is pity but that we had forseen to have Charter'd Some Vessells to Come here at the Low Freight of £3.5 per ton as a pritty many have been Especially by Steill & Hume, who have gott 20/ Ster. per Ton Clear on Severalls they Charter'd at £3.5/ & have Lett them out again at £4.5/ per Ton to £4.10 per Ton, but before this Can reach you, it will be too Late am afraid to Try now any thing of that Nature this Season.

Inclos'd please Receive paragraph of a Letter, & Copie of Mr. John Erving's Last Letter to me from Boston, by which youll Observe I happen to be pritty much in his Good Graces, & that his Corrospondant in London Mr. Hodshon has Greatly Disoblidg'd him, so that hope there may be an Opening in your Favour for his Business there, & you may Depend on it no Stone shall be Left unturn'd by me for that Effect, when Opportunity & a Favourable Occasion Offerrs.

I have Receiv'd by Capt. Hayden a parcell of Goods Ship'd by Mr. Samuel Storke in London on account of Messrs. Hutchinson & Goldthwait of Boston, Amount as per Invoice being £256.9.0 Ster., but are not so well assorted as I Coud wish, neither according to the List I sent Mr. Goldthwait, Loaf Sugar, Tea, & China being three of the Principall Ar-

21st January 1744

ticles, Especially the Loaf Sugar, & they have Sent none of them, & they Coud never have happen'd to Come at a better Time being all of them very Scarce at Present in Town, but I imagine the Reason was these Articles Cost ready Money & the Other things that they have sent they have a Considerable Credit for.

A Good many Traders & others of this Place are proposing to fitt out Two Privateers under the Command of One Capt. Mark Anderson[8] who Some time agoe Brought in a Spanish Privateer & Since has been taken himself in a Privateer belonging to this Place & Carri'd to the Havannah, & lately Return'd here again. I was not Concern'd in the Last, but intend to be Concern'd in this, if it is brought as propos'd to Maturity. Capt. Anderson is to Goe to London to purchase a Suitable Vessell there with the Assistance of Two Managers who can be Appointed in London. Each Person to be £50 Ster. Concern'd & if it can be brought to Bear, I mean if there can be gott Fifty or Sixty Subscribers, it will be undertaken. If so, I am to be one of the Managers here & Beleive Your self will be appointed with Capt. John Nickleson the Two Managers in London. In case it Succeeds, shall send you per my next a Copie of the Proposalls & a List of those Concern'd. The Adventure is propos'd to Amount to three Thousand Pounds Sterling.

I hope your Directions by the Wine Vessell will be full and Particular for my Government. My Wife joyns in kind Love and Respects & I most Sincerely Remain &c.

P. S. Our Governour Glen by his Behaviour in the Introduction to his Government Seems to Gain the Love & Esteem of the People.

ADDRESSED: "Per Capt. Willson & Copie per Capt. Brown both Via Cowes"

---

[8] Capt. Mark Anderson had commanded the privateer sloop *Eagle* and the privateer brigantine *Loyal William*. SCHM, XXV (1924), 6.

27th January 1744

[696]
TO SAMUEL STORKE & SON
Ⅼondon

Charles Town, 27th January 1743 [1744]

Gentlemen:

I Receiv'd 14 Days agoe your Esteem'd favours of the 28th October with Inclos'd from Mr. Thomas Goldthwait, also Invoice & Bill of Loading for Sundry Goods per the Ship *Ulysses*, Capt. James Hayden, for Account of his Company as per Invoice being £256.9.0 Ster. which have Receiv'd in prity Good Order, Excepting the Case of Pickles, Severall of the Bottles being Broke by Reason of the bad Package & which Pickles have been Shipt too Late in the Season for Sale at this Place. I am to take Notice to you that three of the most Material Articles I writt to Mr. Goldthwait for have been Omitted to be Sent, Vizt. Tea, China Ware, & Loaf Sugar which Could never have Come here in a better Time & Could have fetch'd present money, especially Loaf Sugar, of which I Desir'd one third in Value of the whole Assortment to be in that Article, & as most of the Goods you have Sent are Usually Sold on Credit, will not turn out so much for their Advantage as the others in Case they had been Sent as Desir'd.

I have no Directions from Messrs. Hutchinson & Goldthwait to make you any Remittance on their Account as you advise. On the Contrary Yesterday arriv'd here from Boston a Sloop from them with the Orders to be Loaded back for Boston on their Account with what Effects I have at Present of theirs in my hands. I am Receprochally to make you a Tender of my best Services here & to assure you that I am Most Respectfully &c.

addressed: "Per Capt. Willson & Copie per Capt. Brown Via Cowes"

4th February 1744

TO GEDNEY CLARKE
    Barbados
                            Charles Town, 4th February 1743 [1744]
Sir:
    My Last to You was of the 29th December with Copie thereof, Since have not the Pleasure of any of Your Favours. Please Receive Inclos'd Bill of Loading & Invoice of Twelve Barrels of Very Good New Rice Ship'd on Board the Sloop *Posstillion*, Capt. Edward Lightwood, for Barbados on Account & Risque of the Owners of Ship *Lusitania* & to Your Good Self Consign'd, Amount as per Invoice being £108.11.1 which hope will Come safe to hand & to a Good Markett. I Could not Gett freight for Corn & as the Rice is Low in Price hope it will answer better, tho' youll Observe the Freight is high, but was Oblidg'd to give it & Embrace the Opportunity as it is very uncertain when Freight Could be Obtain'd again for your Island on any Terms.
    Inclos'd please also Receive Account Current, Ballance in my Favour being £9.-.10d this Currency. Freights are still pritty high & much the Same as in my Last, being at £4 per Ton for London, & £4.10/ for Holland or Hamburg. If the *Lusitania* Comes here to Load for Europe Doubt not may Obtain a Good Freight. I have not further to Offerr at Present, but that I Remain Most Respectfully &c.

Exchange to London at £700 per £100 Ster., Rice 32/6 per Ct., Rum 20/ per Gall., Madeira Wine £130 per pipe.

ADDRESSED: "Per Capt. Lightwood & Copie per [*blank*]"

[697]
TO ANDREW PRINGLE
    London
                            Charles Town, 6th February 1743 [1744]
Sir:
    The last I did my Self the Pleasure to write you was of the 21st Ulto. per Capt. Willson & Copie thereof per Capt. Brown both Via Cowes, since have not the Pleasure of any of your Favours.

6th February 1744

I mention'd to you in my last that a good many Persons here in Trade & Others were proposing to Fitt out Two privateers from this Province under the Command of Capt. Mark Anderson & since that they have agreed & Determin'd on Said undertaking, & accordingly Capt. Anderson takes his passage in his Majesties Ship the *Rye*, Capt. Hardy,[9] & by whom you will Receive this, & who has also a Packett Directed to Alderman Baker,[1] Mr. James Crokatt, & your Self, you three being jointly appointed Managers in London for all the Concern'd & who we are Directed to apply to, as being Managers for the Rest here. Capt. John Nickleson & your Self only we pitch'd on to be the Managers for us, but his Brothers Messrs. Shubricks[2] desir'd to have him Excus'd by Reason of a Disorder in his eys that renders him unfitt for Business & a Division arising whither Alderman Baker or James Crokatt shoud be join'd with you in the Room of Capt. Nickleson, it was Judg'd proper, for the Satisfieing the whole Concern'd, to join both of them with you & I am apprehensive that you will have the Labouring Oar in the Affair, as well as I have had here, and most of the Gentlemen seem to put their Cheif Dependance on you for the Managment & Conducting the Undertaking being Sensible of your being best Qualifi'd for same.

I Refferr you to Our Packett by the Bearar Capt. Anderson about the whole Affair, being Directed to you Jointly as Our Agents and Managers, & by whom we have Sent Inclos'd Bills of Exchange, Amount £1,070 Ster. which hope will be all Duely Honour'd, & as the Country Gentlemen who are Concern'd propose to Deliver us Rice to be Ship'd by us on their Account for their Proportions, & as Soon as we Can Collect it together, we intend to Ship it to your joint addresses in Order to apply the Neat Proceeds to their Credit for their Proportions being Fifty Pounds Ster., the Sum which each has Subscrib'd for.

Inclos'd please Receive for your Own Private use & Satisfaction a Copie of the Proposalls, also a List of the Subscribers, being as yet only Thirty five in Number at Fifty Pounds Sterling each, so that we want only five Persons more to take the Subscription up to £2,000 Ster. which we Judge may Doe for the Cost of the Privateer to be purchas'd in London & by the Time that Capt. Anderson arrives there, Doubt not of Getting

---

[9] HMS *Rye*, Charles Hardy, departed the Carolina station on 7 February 1744. May, p. 164.
[1] Alderman William Baker (1705–1770) was one of the foremost London merchants trading to America. Namier & Brooke, II, 39–41.
[2] Richard and Thomas Shubrick were brothers-in-law of John Nickleson.

6th February 1744

the Subscription made up to Sixty Subscribers which will Compleat the Sum of £3,000 Ster. which we imagin will be Sufficient for the Cost & Outsett of the Privateer & a Sloop for a Tender to her that is to be Purchas'd here. I accordingly, as I advis'd you in my Last, am one of the Subscribers for £50 Ster. which am to Desire youll please to Advance for me as my Said Proportion, & which I have told Capt. Anderson & the Gentlemen here will be readily Supply'd by you for Said undertaking on my Account, there being no Occasion as I Told Capt. Anderson & them to Draw a Sett of Bills on you for it & hope will be as ready Comply'd with by you without. And shou'd be very Glad you will take on half of my said Share of £50 Ster. from off my hands to Your Own Account & So Credit me for £25 Ster. especially as you are So Considerably in advance for me at this Time.

I am in a Particular manner to Recommend Capt. Anderson to your Civilities & Good Offices, whose meritt doubt not will gain him your Countenance & Esteem, as it has Diservedly all those who have had the Good Fortune of his Acquaintance here, altho' he Came here but Lately & a Stranger in the Place. Tho he makes no Great Appearance as to his Person Youll find him a Man of Good Sens & Parts, & tho' modest has given Convincing Proofs both of his Good Conduct & Personal Bravery & as I have told him, am of Opinion that he will have more Occasion to make his application to you in the undertaking he goes upon than to the other Two Managers.

Colonel John Fenwick[3] an old Stander here, & his Family Goe home [698] Passengers for Good and all in the *Rye,* Capt. Hardy, who Leaves this Station with perhaps as Little or Less Reputation than any before him ever Did, being a Person of no Activity or Spirit as indeed few of Our Commanders of Kings Ships are now a days.

Our Friend Mr. Thomas Elliott (who youll observe makes one with us in the Privateer) tells me that he has writt to you & His Son by Colonel Fenwick, & who hope will take Care to Deliver your Letter Accordingly. Colonel Fenwick has accquir'd a Very Opulent Fortune here by his Own Industry & has a Good Deal of Money as is said in England, 'tho has not been a very popular man here & is a Person of no Extraordinary Parts or Education.

[3] John Fenwicke, Charleston merchant, retired to England. In his will proved in 1747 he left his daughters and grandson several hundred pounds sterling, but the funds were to be invested in the New South Sea Company. Andrew Pringle was one of the witnesses to Fenwicke's will. *SCHM,* VII (1906), 27-28.

6th February 1744

A pretty many Ships are in the Road Wind bound for Europe. Freight is at £4 per Ton for London & £4.10/ for Holland. Rice is at 32/6 per Ct., Pitch 35/ per bbl. As there Seems no Great Likelyhood of a French War & having no advice from you in your Late Letters about Purchasing Pitch, Did not Judge it Proper to buy up any Especially Since you Communicated the Intended Scheme about the Madeira Wine of which there is none Good in Town, a Good Deal of it being Prickt, & believe wont Doe to Buy it to Blend with the other, as you propose, & is now Sold at £130 per pipe, Wine being Generally Scarce here between the Old & the New.

All or Most of the Gentlemen in Town that are Subscribers for the Privateer give Bills of Exchange or Orders on their Friends in London for their Proportions excepting Branfield Evance, Mr. Stead's Partner, who 'tho they make a Great Show here in Trade & his Cousin the Alderman Baker is One of the Managers, yet when I ask'd him the other Day for his Proportion to be Remitted with the Rest, he told me that he Could neither Draw nor Raise Currency to purchase a Bill of £50 Ster. & that he must be Oblidg'd to pay it in Rice, which looks as if his Credit was but Low with his Cousin Baker & his other Friends in England. Capt. Anderson being just agoeing Down, I have not further to Offerr at Present, but that I Remain in haste &c.

Exchange to London at £700 per £100 Ster.

Youll Observe in the List of Bills Remitted the Managers that John Houghton, one of the Subscribers, has Drawn a sett of Bills of Exchange for £50 Ster. being his Proportion on Messrs. John Steedman & Co. Merchants in Rotterdam payable to my Order, which I have Indors'd to the Order of the Managers or either of them & which you'll please to take notice of.

ADDRESSED: "Per Capt. Mark Anderson in His Majesties Ship *Rye*"

7th February 1744

TO ANDREW PRINGLE
London

Charles Town, 7th February 1743 [1744]

SIR:

I writt you yesterday by Capt. Mark Anderson who goes in his Majesties Ship *Rye*, & being still in the Road gives me the Opportunity of Accknowledging the Receipt just now of Copies of your most agreeable Favours of the 19th, 25th, October & 3 November also Inclos'd yours of the 19th November all per Capt. Sandwell.

I Observe mine of the 2d September per Capt. Breading was not to hand by whom sent you Mr. Thomas Elliotts Letter of Attorney to you to Receive his Fire Tickett, as also I sent you my Account Current with Mr. Michael Thompson, Ballance in my Favour being £47.9.8½ Sterling, & as we apprehand that Capt. Breading has been taken, So the Letters have miscarried which gives me Great Concern, especially as Mr. Elliott did not send a Duplicate of his Letter of Attorney, & which shall acquaint him of at Meeting.[4]

I Duely Remark you have bought a Handsome small Vessel for Capt. Douglas of about 120 Tons which you intend to send here Directly, & that you desire I may be one third part Concern'd with you & Capt. Douglas in Same which very kind Offerr I willing Embrace, especially as you have been so good to name her the [699] *Robert & Jane* in Compliment to my Wife & I, & Doubt not Desires the Good Qualities you give of her & will have Success Accordingly. You may Depend on my Uttmost Endeavours in giving her all the Dispatch here & to Our best Advantage that She may answer Our Good Expectations, & hope She will make a Very Good Voyage.

I Take notice that your Intention of sending to Giberalter is Frustrated, but no help for it, must submit to the Times. However I hope your Directions will be ample & at large in Relation to Said Vessel that same may be punctually Comply'd with. Some are of Opinion that Rice will bear a Price in Portugul as none will be permitted to be Imported from the Straits on Account of the Plague. One William Jones & Co. of Bristoll has Order'd Mr. Savage to Buy up 3,000 bbls. of Rice on Bills of Exchange, but what can be their Scheme therein none can Comprehend.

---

[4] Fire ticket No. 47 was for the estate of Thomas Elliott and No. 48 for Thomas Elliott. The first was for £363 and the second for £1,328 sterling. Thomas Elliott would be collecting one-third of each sum. *SCHM*, LXIV (1963), 210.

11th February 1744

My Wife joyns in kind Respects & I add not at Present but that I Remain in haste &c.

P. S. We have Remitted William Baker, Esqr., Mr. James Crokatt, & your Good Self as Managers for the Privateer £670 Ster. in Bills of Exchange by Capt. Anderson & Orders by Letters for £400 Ster. more, makes £1,070 Ster. which hope will be all Honour'd.

ADDRESSED: "Per Capt. Gould Via Topsham"

TO JOHN ERVING
Boston

Charles Town, 11th February 1743 [1744]

SIR:

My Last to you was of the 7th December Via Rhoad Island, & about three Weeks agoe have the Pleasure of your most Esteem'd Favours of the 27 Ditto per Capt. Raitt,[5] who had the missfortune in Coming here to Runned ground on Cape Romain Shoal,[6] but by Good help gott off again without any Considerable Damage.

I am Glad Capt. Selew arriv'd safe & that the Rice & Skins came to hand in Good Order. Am in hopes that Rice is again in Demand with You, that Messrs. Hutchinson & Goldthwait of your Place has sent a Small Sloop, which have Loaded Back to them with that Commodity & by which this Goes.

I am Greatly oblidg'd to you for your good Offices, to Secure my Debt due from Capt. Wimble, & as it is likely he may Return after this Cruize to Rhoad Island, if he should bring any Effects there, doubt not You'll be kind enough to Oblidge him to Pay his Bill & all Charges, & if you can Learn that there is any Effects of his Lodg'd in Mr. Bours of Rhoad Island his Custody (which I have been Inform'd he has) You'll please to Order the Same to be Attach'd for the Satiefieing my Debt.

I am Sorry to Observe that Mr. William Hodshon has been so Over-

---

[5] Capt. Alexander Raitt, snow *George*, arrived from Boston. SCG, 23 January 1744.
[6] Cape Romain was about forty miles to the north of the entrance to Charleston harbor.

seen in Letting out your *John Galley* (which is a fine Ship) at such an under Rate, & on so bad Terms, to that part of the World. It is Great Pity, that she had not Come here instead of goeing there.

I am again to Accknowledge the Obligations I Lye under for your Repeated very kind Invitation & Offerr of my Wife's & my Passage to England in your Ship *Cromwell* & as I doubt not of Our being very well Accomodated in said Ship, So no Commander could be more Agreeable for us to take Our passage with than Capt. Nickelson for whom have always had a very Particular Reguard & if said Ship Comes here, & my Affairs will Permitt, we Intend to Embrace your kind Offerr & be passengers Accordingly.

Freight keeps still prity high, One Capt. Mackay[7] Lately from your Part has Obtain'd £4.5/ per Ton for London which is the highest Freight has been yett given this Season. If your Ship that you Mention is to Goe to Antigua Don't Succeed there & should Come here, am of Opinion she wont be Disappointed.

Capt. Raitt was oblidg'd to thro' all his Horses & Hay Over Board in his Passage.

My Wife joins in Best Respects to Good Mrs. Erving, all the pritty Young Ones, & I most Sincerly Remain with very Great Respect &c.

Rice at 32/6 per Ct., Pitch 32/6 per bbl., Tar 35/ per bbl., Deer Skins 17/ per lb., Rum W. Indies 20/ per Gallon, Ditto N. E. 15/ per Gallon, Exchange to London at £700 per £ Ster.

ADDRESSED: "Per Capt. Blunt"

---

[7] Capt. Aeneas Mackay, ship *Friendship*, arrived from Boston. RPC, p. 109; *SCG*, 13 February 1744.

11th February 1744

[700]
TO THOMAS HUTCHINSON & THOMAS GOLDTHWAIT
Boston

Charles Town, 11th February 1743 [1744]

GENTLEMEN:

My last to you was of the 14th October & about a Fortnight agoe have your Esteem'd Favours of the 7th January per the Bearar Capt. Blunt with One hhd. & Two BBls. Cocoa & Eight BBls. of Blubber. And according to your Directions Please receive Inclos'd Invoice & Bill of Loading for One Hundred & Fifteen BBls. of very good New Rice & Fifty BBls. of Pitch, Ship'd on Board the Sloop *Bonaventure*, Capt. Samuel Blunt, for Boston on your Proper Risque & Account And to Your Good selves Consign'd, Amount as per Invoice being £1,132.2.3 this Currency, which hope will come safe to Hand & to a Good Markett. The Sloop Could not take three Heights of Rice & there was no Tar to be had without Detaining the Sloop, & indeed am apprehensive if Tar had been put in the Bottom under the Rice it had been Greatly Damag'd. So was oblidg'd by Capt. Blunt's advice to Ship the Pitch that the Vessel might not be Detain'd. As it is Low in Price hope you'll be no Sufferers by it, especially so small a Quantity & which is Very Good.

Shall sell off the Ribbands, Potts, & Axes at Publick Vendue as you Direct as soon as I Can have an Opportunity, which have not had time to Doe since Capt. Blunt's arrival, & then Transmitt you Account Sales of Capt. Hallin's Cargoe. I am to take Notice to you that the Cocoa & Blubber per Capt. Blunt happen to be the Two worst Commodities you could possibly have sent here. As for the Blubber, it is always so very Bad that there is Great Discredit in the Sale of so bad A Commodity & really not worth sending here. Train Oyl[8] would answer much better. And there happens to be a Great Deal of Cocoa in Town at present lately Imported from Diferent Parts which makes it a Drugg. Shall be Glad to have your Orders to Sell both off at Publick Vendue, otherways may Lay a Long time on Hand before they Can be Dispos'd of & Cannot Encourage your sending any Commodity from your Place excepting Rum & Loaf Sugar, & as the Crops fall short in the West Indies your Rum is Likely to be in Demand here.

I Observe you have Receiv'd Some Goods Ship'd by my Brother on his & my Account, Amount £255.4.9½ Ster. which doubt not of your Dis-

[8] Train oil is obtained by boiling whale blubber.

posal of to Our best Advantage, & in following his Directions in the Remitting of the Neat Proceeds to London. I Receiv'd about Three Weeks agoe per Capt. Hayden a parcell of Goods shipt by Messrs. Samuel Storke & Son per Order of Your T. G. when in London, on your joint Account, Amount as per Invoice being £256.9.0 Ster. which shall use Uttmost Endeavours to Dispose as Quick as possible & to your best advantage. They were all Landed in Good Order except the Case of Pickles, Severall of the Bottles being Broke Occasion'd by the bad package thereof & the Pickles spoilt which have happen'd to Come too Late in the Season for Sale, having expected those Goods here early in the fall of the Year. And I am to take notice to You, that three of the most Matterial Articles that I writt to your T. G. for have been Omitted to be Ship'd by Messrs. Storke, Vizt. Tea, China Ware, & Loaf Sugar, which could never have Come here in a better Time & would have fetch'd present money especially the Loaf Sugar of which You'll Observe I Order'd Considerable Value of the Assortment, to be in that Article, & which I have advis'd Messrs. Storke of as said Goods have happen'd to Come So Late, & must [701] give Credit in the Sale thereof. I shall not be able to make any Returns for Same till next fall of the Year. The Indian Trading Guns, Powder, & Bulletts Ought not to have been Ship'd without Strouds & Duffle Blanketting which are the most Material Articles for the Indian Trade, & there ought always to be a Compleat assortment of said Indian Trading Goods.

As to what you are pleas'd to mention in Relation to Mr. Dalby, Mr. Yeomans Case Differs Greatly from mine he having had a Great many very Valueable Consignments from him whereas Mr. Dalby was a Stranger to me & under no Obligation to him & the Ship Brought Nothing of a Cargoe here, & if you had not been Concern'd would have Charg'd him £20 Ster., having procur'd his Ship a Very Good Freight, & I think I was under no Obligation to give him my Trouble for Nothing, especially as the Freight & Dispatch Could well afford Commission. I Charg'd him no Commission on the Disbursments paid out on the Ship here, which was upwards of £100 Ster. & so Consequently a third part of the Money Charg'd him, & which Reduces it to only £10 Ster. As to any of my Friends, I never did Charge them in such Case. However think Mr. Dalby had no Reason to Complain till he had paid the money, my Brother having advis'd me that he was oblidg'd to take payment of Capt. Turills Bill on him by Deducting said £15 Ster. out of it, & have no advise from him as yet of said Money being paid. I have Charg'd £20 Ster. on Procuring Freight here in such a Case as Mr. Dalby's where a Large Ship has Come here to Seek without a Cargoe from Strangers, & have been very Thankfully allowed it as the Owners have found their Account in it.

I am to Desire you'll please to send a Certificate for the *Bonaventures* Cargoe as soon as you Can in Order to Discharge my Bond with Samuel Mason, in whose name the Sloop was Enter'd & Clear'd. As for the Bond given for the former Sloop *Good Intent*, Capt. Blunt, am afraid shall have some Trouble about my Bond when the Time expires in Case no Certificate can be Obtain'd. Please advise me if you Receiv'd payment of Capt. John Gowan's Bill for £28 Boston Currency on Capt. Richard Walker in your Favour & Remitted you in October 1742 in said Walkers Vessell, who was than here, & with whom Capt. Gowan went Passenger from this to Boston.

Inclos'd please Receive Copie of Invoices of 375 Oz. Spanish Silver Remitted Messrs. Burryau & Schaffer on Account of your T.H. in December Last, Amount as per Invoice being £708.15.0 this Currency which have plact to his Account accordingly. You have also Inclos'd the Account of the Sloops Port Charges here, Amount being £49.18.9 this Currency for which shall Debit your Account. The Sloop has had all the Dispatch could be Desir'd, Capt. Blunt having had his Loading tender'd to him as fast as he Could take it in, who has Lost no Time for Dispatch, who seems to be a Sober Dilligent man & to have his Imployers Interest at Heart. Capt. Blunt is just agoeing & as the Wind is fair hope he will soon be with you. I add not but that I Remain most Respecfully &c.

ADDRESSED: "Per Capt. Blunt"

16th February 1744

[702]
TO JOHN LIVINGSTON[9]
New York

Charles Town, 16th February 1743 [1744]

SIR:

By the Direction of my Brother Andrew Pringle of London, Merchant, Please Receive Inclos'd Bill of Lading for 20 pieces Russia Canvas Shipt in the Sloop *Carolina*, Capt. John Schermerhorn, for New York & to your Good self Consign'd being on Account & Risque of my said Brother & Mr. Samuel Sanders, which you'll Please to Receive & Dispose of Same to their Best Advantage, being at Present Unsaleable here. My Brother advises me that you have already Dispos'd of some of the Same Sort of Canvas Consign'd you on his Account. I shall advise him of Shipping You said Canvas accordingly & Doubt not youll follow his Directions in making Returns for the Neat Proceeds as formerly. Youll please to advise me of the Receipt of the Canvas, & if in any thing I can serve you here, you may always freely Command &c.

P. S. I have Deliver'd Capt. Schermerhorn a Cockett from the Custom house for the Canvas.

ADDRESSED: "Per Capt. Shermerhorn"

TO NICHOLAS RIGBYE
Savannah

Charles Town, 16th February 1743 [1744]

SIR:

I have yours of the 5th Current per Mr. Rae in Return to mine of the 4th Ulto. & did not Expect you would give me the Occasion to be making a Continual Demand of money from you (as you are pleas'd to express it) as I did not imagine, being a Stranger to me, you would have

---

[9] John Livingston was a New York merchant. Because there were several persons with the same name living in New York, it was not possible to determine which John Livingston was Andrew Pringle's correspondent there. RPC, p. 818.

16th February 1744

Desir'd to take Goods from me, unless you were sensible that your Circumstances were so as to keep your Credit by performing your Engagements, especially as you order'd Considerable Quantities after those you had first & which I had not to Supply you with. However doubt not of your good Inclinations of Discharging the Debt with Honour as soon as possibly you can & according to your Own Proposal. Please Receive Inclos'd your Account, also a Bond fill'd up for the Amount being £50.5.3¼ Sterling. Mr. Rae does not goe back your way, so have sent it by the Bearer Mr. Johnson, his Patroon of the Boat, who will see you execute the Bond, the same as Mr. Rae, & which youll Please to Return. I have made it Payable the first of May, it not being material when payable as it bears Interest from the 1st December.

Have advice from London that the Generall's Bill for £16 Ster. you sent me is not paid & very uncertain when it will there being Likelyhood as yet. Was in hopes that money was now pretty Plenty with you in Georgia as the Parliament granted the Collony £12,000 Sterling last session which Doubt not has been sent Over before this. Youll Please advise me in what time you may with Certainty assure me of Discharging your Debt which will be Satisfieing.

I Remark what you mention in Relation to Mr. Dormers affair, who I find has not Complied with the first payment according to Agreement which is postpon'd till the first of April by Mr. Charles Watson,[1] his note for £10.18.8 Ster., which Doubt not will be paid when Due, & hope therein you have Done for the Best. You did not advise me whether Mr. Dormer had given any Security for the Moneys being paid according to his agreement as I have Reason to be of Opinion that his word is not much to be Depended on, & am thereby in no better Situation, than formerly. [703] Whereas if he had been Sued, he must have paid the money or given Security for it's being paid in a Time Certain.

I hope youll Favour me with your answer & that youll Return the Bond executed as Drawn, being done According to your Own Proposal. I add not but that I am Respectfully &c.

ADDRESSED: "Per Mr. Johnson"

---

[1] Charles Watson, Clerk of His Majesty's Council, died in Savannah in 1771. SCHM, XXXIV (1933), 149.

17th February 1744

TO JOHN DICKINSON
St. Kitts

Charles Town, 17th February 1743 [1744]

SIR:

Your last to me was of the 25th August Last from St. Christophers, wherein you advise that you hop'd to be here by Xmass at furthest, & not hearing anything from you since, or any Likelyhood of your coming here, or of your making any Remittances in Order to Discharge your Bond & Note now so long Due, I have by this Conveyance sent your said Bond & Note of hand to my worthy Friend Richard Rowland, Esqr. with a Power of Attorney to Receive the Money of you, & as you may be sensible it ought by agreement to have been paid a great while agoe. I make no doubt of your punctual & Ready Compliance, & therefore Desire you may pay your Bond & Note at the Current Exchange to the Said Gentleman accordingly. I am &c.

ADDRESSED: NO ADDRESS

TO RICHARD ROWLAND
St. Kitts

Charles Town, 17th February 1743 [1744]

SIR:

I have not had the Pleasure of hearing from You for some Years past, & was very Glad to be Inform'd by Capt. Hutchins lately from your Island of your Good Health.

I take the Liberty to Trouble you with this, which hope your Goodness will excuse, being to request your Friendship & Good Offices to obtain payment of the Inclos'd Bond from Capt. John Dickinson formerly of Rhoad Island & now of North Carolina, who I understand by Capt. Hutchins is at Present & has been for some time past at your Island of St. Kitts. You'll observe he Is Indebted to me per Bond £818.3.6 also his Note of hand for £17.17.6, Amount with Interest as per Inclos'd Account to £947.10.5 this Currency which at this Current Exchange of £700 per £100 Ster. is £135.7.2¼ Sterling.

And Inclos'd please Receive a Power of Attorney and am to Desire the favour you'll please be so Good, at the Receipt of this, as to oblidge Capt. Dickinson to pay the Money, or by any manner of way to Secure the Debt, as I am Inform'd he has Effects in the Island, not to Sufferr him upon any Account to Goe off without Discharging the Same or at Least giving good Security for the Debt. As youll observe the Bond was to have been paid a Considerable Time agoe, am to pray the Favour you may show him no Indulgence, but insist on the Immediate payment as it may be the best Opportunity I may have of Recovering it, & whatever Charge or trouble you may be at in the affair will with Great Pleasure very thankfully repay it. Please Receive Inclos'd his Last Letter to me from your Island and as I am apprehensive he wont come here at all, so hope you wont Trust to him or Depend if he Should say he is coming here to Discharge the Debt, but Oblidge him to pay it to you in St. Kitts, it being for a Parcell of Goods Sold him when here in June 1742, & he has never been here since, neither made me any Remittance whatever.

Capt. Dickinson in Person is a pretty Large Bodied man about Fifty Years of Age & has a Blemish in One of his Eyes, however make no Doubt you may know him as he has been for some time at St. Kitts. If Contrary to Expectation before you Receive this he shou'd be gone interely off the Island & no Likelyhood of his Returning, Youll Please to Return me the Bond & Note by first Opportunity, & if you Recover the money of him, I am to Desire youll Please to Remitt it to [704] my Brother Andrew Pringle, Merchant In London by Bill of Exchange or in Sugars giving him privious advice for Insurance.

This goes by your Sloop *Susannah*, Capt. Joseph Willson, who with his Mate Andrew Schuyler are Witnesses to the Letter of Attorney in Order to prove it. We have the Largest Crop of Rice & Corn ever yet produc'd, & all other Provisions in Plenty.

I hope your Goodness will pardon the Trouble I give you in this affair, & if on the Like or any other Occasion I can be of any Service to You here, You may always most freely Command him who is with very Great Respect &c.

P. S. Inclos'd is a Letter for Capt. Dickinson which please to Deliver him or not as you judge Proper.

ADDRESSED: "Per the Sloop *Susannah*, Capt. Joseph Willson"

TO JOHN BROCK
Guernsey

Charles Town, 21st February 1743 [1744]

SIR:

I have the Pleasure of your most Esteem'd Favours of the 17th August in Return to mine of the 10th March per the Bearar Capt. Peter Bailleul, & am to Return you my hearty Thanks for your kind Offerrs of Service & Correspondance & to assure you that I shall be always very Glad to Receive your Commands & to Render you any agreeable Service. I am Glad this Trade is so encouraging as to engage Capt. Bailleul's Owners to Continue him in it. We have no material News here at Present. Please present my best Respects to your Brother Mr. Henry Brock, & beleive me to be with very Great Respect &c.

ADDRESSED: "Per Capt. Peter Bailleul"

TO ROBERT ELLIS
Philadelphia

Charles Town, 23rd February 1743 [1744]

SIR:

My last to you was of the 13th June, and since have only Two Lines from you of the 15th & 27th November & both writt in haste, as indeed your Letters always are to me, & of Two Lines only.

I Receiv'd per Capt. Mason your very kind & acceptable present of a Barrell of Apples in pritty Good Order, for which my Wife & I return you & Mrs. Ellis Our joint Thanks. I was in hopes, as you have advis'd in severall of yours that you woud have been so Good as to have made some Remittance last Fall, but as yet have not been favour'd with any from you. However expect the same per first Conveyance, as you advis'd me in your Last, and you may be sensible the whole ought to have been paid sometime agoe. Please to advise me if you have made any Remittance by Bill of Exchange to my Brother Andrew Pringle in London, which should be Glad you could doe, & will be the same thing as Remitting it here.

I sent you with the other Goods per Capt. Coatam One hundred &

Fifty peices of Lace for Sale on Account of Capt. Murray, & the Neat Proceeds thereof to be Remitted me in Bread & Flour. Please advise if said Lace is sold & am to acquaint you that said Murray is Lately Dead, & Mr. James Reid has administred on his Estate, & Desires if the Lace is Sold that you may Remitt the Neat Proceeds thereof to him or to me as you think proper.

Inclos'd please Receive a Packett Directed for Richard Bennett, Esqr. on Wye River in Maryland, which am to Desire the Favour You'll be so Good as to have forwarded to him by the first sure hand. I am again to remind you, of the Garden Box that you were so good as to promise to send me, as also a Prospect in a Frame of the City of Philadelphia & Charge the Cost thereof to my Account.

I hope youll please to be more Particular when you write me & more at Large as youll [705] Observe I am to You. Freight is at £4 per Ton to London & £4.10/ to Holland & Rice 32/6 per Ct. & not likely to be Lower this Season. My Wife joins in Best Respects to Mrs. Ellis & Self & I am Respectfully &c.

Rice 32/6 per Ct., Pitch 32/6 per bbl., Tarr 32/6 per bbl., Turpentine 10/ per Ct., Deer Skins 16/6 per lb., Madeira Wine £120 per pipe, Rum W. Indies 20/ per Gallon, Ditto N. England 15/ per gallon.

ADDRESSED: "Per Capt. Bird & Copie per Capt. Hutchins"

TO THOMAS HOPKINSON
Philadelphia

Charles Town, 24th February 1743 [1744]

SIR:

I have the Pleasure of your most Esteemed favours of the 27th May & Copie also yours of the 31st Ditto which I have not had an Opportunity since that I know off to give a return to. Your Last Convey'd me Bill of Loading & Invoice of Forty Nine Barrells Flour per the Ship *Argyle*, Capt. Charles Stedman, Amount as per Invoice being £42.4.3 which came safe to hand & was to my entire Satisfaction.

I Observe you have been so good as to Receive of Mr. Howell £45.5

24th February 1744

& that he has given his Bond for the Residue & for which you have my most hearty thanks & what ever you may think Proper to Charge for your Trouble in said affair will with great Pleasure most Readily Allow. I doubt not youll be so good as to write me when he Discharges his Bond & that you'll make him pay Interest for the Long time he has keep't me out of my money. I have According to your Desire Enquir'd after the Price of Barr Iron & find that what comes from your Province is Low here at Present & wont fetch more than £6 per Ct. or £120 per Ton this Currency, the Sizes are Square & Flatt Barrs & are both a Like suitable for this place.

Shall be very glad if at any time I can have it in my Power to render you any Acceptable Service & to Retaliate your favours as being with very great Respect &c.

Exchange to London £700 per £100 Sterling.

ADDRESSED: "Per Capt. Bird & Copie per Capt. Hutchins"

TO ANDREW PRINGLE
London

Charles Town, 24th February 1743 [1744]

SIR:

Inclos'd please Receive Copie of my Last of the 7 Current which miss'd the Opportunity by Capt. Mark Anderson & which Confirm. Since have your most kind & acceptable Favours of the 19th, 25th, & 29 November & 3d December per Capt. Kitchinman[2] & Copies of the 13th December with Invoice of Mr. Elliotts Bricks & Stones per Capt. Atkinson, as also the Bird Cages & Chillingworth's *Works*[3] per Ditto which have Receiv'd in prity Good Order, & for which am very Thankfull being all I writt for, excepting the Copper Cooler. Your of the 20th & 29th November advising in Relation to Capt. Murphy, concerning whom shall

[2] Kitchingman from London. *SCG*, 20 February 1744. Capt. Joseph Kitchingman, ship *Blacker & Fenwicke*, for London. *SCG*, 19 March 1744.
[3] *The Works of William Chillingsworth* went through numerous editions with the tenth being published in 1742. His theology "rested upon Scripture interpreted by reason...." *DNB*, IV, 253–255, 256.

24th February 1744

follow your Last Directions & procure him a Freight rather than Load him on your & Owners Account especially as a Great many Vessels have gone for the Portugal Markett, & if you had retain'd the Charter in your hands to be Loaded him Discretionary, you might have gott 20/ per Ton in your Pockett by the Freight as I expect to Lett out said Vessell for 20/ per Ton more than your Charter of £3.5/ per Ton.

I duely Remark what you are pleas'd to mention relating to Capt. Atkinson who I take to be a very honest brisk man, but at this Time it does not so well suit me to take a part in his Ship till I can gett in my Debts here of which I have still very Considerable Outstanding. He is Charter'd on Crokatt and Michie at £3.5/ per Ton. If you have an Inclination to take part with Capt. Atkinson in his Ship, beleive you are very safe with him, & is a very Active Stirring [706] man. I am much Concern'd that mine of the 2d September per Capt. Breading did not come to your hands in which was Mr. Elliotts Power of Attorney to you to Receive his Fire Money, & also an Order to Mr. Inns, Executor to Mr. Hewlett to Deliver you his Tickett. He now sends another power to you, Duplicate thereof by the first Ships for London, & to Reimburse Your Self out of said Money for the Bricks & Stones you sent him which are very much to his Satisfaction, & for which you have his hearty Thanks. He writt you in Relation to his Son of the 2d September & has again at Large as he tells me, by Colonel Fennwick. Inclos'd please Receive a third Bill of Generall Oglethrops for £25.4 Ster. payable to Patrick Graham, which is on Mr. Elliotts Account & which he desir'd me to forward you, in Order to use your Endeavour to Procure payment thereof for him. He sent the first & Second Bill of Same per Capts. Breading & Moss who have both been taken & has Losst £11 Ster. in Georgia Sola Bills sent to his Son by Capt. Breading.

I have according to your Directions shipt to Mr. John Livingston of New York Twenty pieces of the Russia Canvas which is all remaining of it on hand & hope soon to transmitt you the Account Sales per the *John & Isabella* & per the *Susannah* that you may Clear with that Deceitfull man Sanders. I am much Concern'd that we had ever any thing to doe with him. I hope you have Receiv'd the Hhd. Skins I shipt you per Capt. Scott, for the Ballance of his Account.

I Remark your very kind Offices to George Pringle in London. Have never heard a Word from him since I Left London, & hear but an Indiferent Character of him. Hope he'll have gratitude enough thankfully to Repay you.

24th February 1744

All Vessels from Giberalter are now oblidg'd to perform here a Quarantine of Fourteen Days. Capt. Douglas hope will come here in Good time in all March, Capt. Murphy does not yet appear. Freight to London is now at £4 per Ton & Rice at 32/6 per Ct. & not likely to be higher this Season.

I duely take notice of your kind hint in Relation to Mr. Nickolson who is assignee to Mr. Hunters Estate, as Mr. Crokatt has given it in my Favour, shall insist upon it, and am ready to settle with Stead & Evance as I have told them, upon their allowing said Articles of Interest as Stated in the Account, & Giving me a proper Discharge, they having gott Powers of Attorney from Messrs. Nicholson & Hunter, & Mr. Evance, as he says now waits Mr. Nicholsons final Orders to him to allow said Interest or not.

This Conveyance Goes via Cowes otherwise would have sent Mr. Elliotts Power of Attorney to you by this Opportunity & beleive One Capt. Mackay will be the first for London. We are about taking up a Vessell to Load with Rice on Account of the Country Gentlemen that are Concern'd in the Privateer to be Shipt to your & the other Managers address. We only wait to Obtain Freight for 500 or 600 BBls. to be sent you.

There is but little Encouragement at Present to Ship Rice & other Provisions to the W. Indies & Rum & Sugar very high there. Our Planters send no small Rice to Markett, Rice being Low in Price. They keep the small Rice for their Negroes. I shipt the Musketts per the *John & Isabella* to Providence to One Florentia Cox there, but he advises that he has not yet Compleated the Sale of them, & I dont find that Governour Tinker has been any ways aiding or assisting therein, notwithstanding his Promise. My Wife joyns in Kind Respects, & I add not at Present, but that I am &c.

ADDRESSED: "Per Capt. Steinson Via Cowes & Copie per Capt. Miznard for London"

25th February 1744

[707]
TO WILLIAM TURNER & LAURENCE JOPSON
Hull

Charles Town, 25th February 1743 [1744]

GENTLEMEN:

My Last to you was of the 7th November, also Copie thereof, Conveying you Account Sales of your Goods to which please be Refferr'd. And about a Month agoe have your Favours of the 12th October per the Bearar Capt. Agars for your Port of Hull & by whom you might have expected Good Rice to the amount of the Ballance of Your Account Current according to your Directions, but could not prevail on Capt. Agars & the Gentleman he came Consign'd to, to take on board any Goods for you on Freight on any terms whatever, he having Loaded Capt. Agars on the Owners Account.

There are no Bills of Exchange to be procur'd here at Present, & it is now very rare to obtain any Good ones on London, and no Deer Skins have come to Town since my Last, as they seldom doe in Winter. But in a very Short time there will be Considerable Quantitys & if I cannot procure them very stout & Good as you advise, shall Ship you Good Rice by way of London in Case no Opportunity of Freight happens soon for your Port.

I sent you per my Last Messrs. Jones & Oliver Their Account Sales of your Chairs, &c. & since the Receipt of yours have again made a Demand of the Neat Proceeds according to your Order sent me, but they have not paid the Money, and am of Opinion you will find it needfull for you, to send over a Power of Attorney before it can be Receiv'd. Shall be always very Glad to render you any agreeable Service, & having not further to Offerr at Present, I Remain &c.

Rice 32/6 per Ct., Pitch 35/ per Barrell, Tarr 35/ per Barrell, Turpentine 12/6 per Ct., Deer Skins 17/ per lb., Exchange to London at £700 per £100 Ster., Freight to London at £4 per Ton & to Lisbon & Holland £4.10/ per Ton.
Inclos'd please Receive Copie of your Account Sales.

P. S. Have sent per the Bearar Capt. Atkinson the following Things I Receiv'd of Thomas Oliver Left here by Nathaniel Blyth, which Please

25th February 1744

Receive & Deliver to him, Vizt. 1 Cloth Coat, Jackett & Breeches, 1 White Linnen Shirt, 4 Stocks, 5 Printed Books. Yours &c.

ADDRESSED: "Per Capt. Agars for Hull & Copie per Capt. Atkinson"

TO SAMUEL WATSON
    Hull

Charles Town, 25th February 1743 [1744]

SIR:

The Preceeding on the other side of the 4th January is Copie of my Last. And about a month agoe have your Favours of the 20th October per the Bearar Capt. Edmund Agars, Commander of the Ship *Providence* for your Port, & according to your Directions Please Receive Inclos'd Bill of Lading & Invoice of Fifty Barrells of very Good New Rice Ship'd on Board said Ship *Providence* for Hull on your Proper Risque & Account & to your Self Consign'd, Amount as per Invoice being £453.12.0 this Currency which wish safe to Hand & hope will come to a Good Markett. Have had no Opportunity of advising you for Insurance since Capt. Agars arrival. You might have expected more Rice, but could not prevail on Capt. Agars to take any more for you on Board, & as to Freight he tells me you must Settle that with his Owners according to the Agreement you had made with them.

A Pretty many of your Goods as Advis'd in my Last still remain unsold. I delay'd as yet to put them up at Public Sale as they will render a better Sale towards the approach of the Summer than in Winter, especially the Dimittys, &c. as the Spring now advances Shall very soon Sell them off [708] at Publick Sale accordingly, & transmitt you Account Sales thereof, & wait your Orders for the Remitting that may be Remaining Due to you. I have not further to Offerr at Present but that I am &c.

Exchange to London at £700 per £100 Ster.

ADDRESSED: "Per Capt. Agars for Hull & Copie per Capt. Miznard for London & Copie per Capt. Atkinson"

27th February 1744

TO MICHAEL THOMPSON
London

Charles Town, 27th February 1743 [1744]

SIR:

The Preceeding on the other Side is Copie of what I did my Self the Pleasure to write you of the 1st September Last, which by advice from my Brother I understand has not come to hand, the Vessel by which it went as also the Copie having both been taken by the Spainards, to which please be Refferr'd, & which this Serves to Confirm. I make no doubt upon perusal of your Account Current Youll find it right & that youll be so Good as to pay the Ballance to my Brother being £47.9.8½ Ster. according to the order given him on You for Same. I add not but that I Remain with very Great Respect &c.

ADDRESSED: "Per Capt. Miznard under Cover of A. P."

TO ANDREW PRINGLE
London

Charles Town, 27th February 1743 [1744]

SIR:

I writt you three days agoe of the 24th per Capt. Steinson Via Cowes of which you have Inclos'd Copie thereof, & meeting with the Opportunity of the Bearar Capt. Stephen Miznard for London sooner than Expected & Mr. Elliott happening to Come to Town, Please again to Receive Inclos'd his Letter of Attorney to you in Order to Receive the Money for his Fire Tickett & hope will have better luck than the Last Sent & of which you have Inclos'd the Duplicate thereof amount being £439.5.2 3/4 Ster. Mr. Inns who is Mr. Hewletts Executor has the Orignial Tickett which was sent some time agoe & doubt not he will Deliver it on Demand, or upon Showing said Letter of Attorney & when you have Receiv'd said money, Mr. Elliott desires you may pay yourself the amount of the Bricks & Stones & for what you have Disburs'd for his Son, & for the Remainder to wait his Directions in Reguard to Same. Inclos'd please Receive a Let-

27th February 1744

ter from him wherein he tells me he has again writt you fully in Relation to the Disposal of his Son under your Direction, which doubt not you will punctually Observe.

Mr. Elliott intends to Sell all his Crop of Rice here so that he wont ship you any on his Own Account. Capt. Stephen Miznard, Commander of the Ship *Carolina* is witness to Mr. Elliotts Power of Attorney to you in Order to prove it. He has promis'd to Deliver you this Packett with his Own hands. He may be heard of at the New York Coffee House,[4] (being a New York Man) & upon his Delivery of it, I have told him you will pay him five Shillings Ster. which Please to Charge to Mr. Elliotts Account. Inclos'd please also Receive another Copie of my Letter to Mr. Michael Thompson of the 1st September Last per Capt. Breading, & his account Current with me, Ballance in my Favour being £48.9.8½ Ster. about which youll please Observe [709] I have again writt him of this Date, & to pay the Inclos'd Order to you for said Ballance which Letter & Accounts after perusal & Copieing the Accounts I am to Desire the Favour you'll Please to Deliver him, & hope he will make no Dispute or delay to pay the Same honourably.

I have taken the Liberty to writt Messrs. Scott, Pringle & Scott for another Pipe Good Madeira Wine, which I purpose to bring to London with me, in Case I goe as I intended.

The Silk Gauze ready made Pavillions you sent here per Capt. Warden am afraid wont answer. They are a Great deal too Small for Beds as us'd here & are fitt only for Field Beds, which will make a Slow & Tedious Sale. It had been better you had sent Gauze in peices to be made up. There has a Great Deal of Salt been Imported here Lately, in so much that it has been Sold at 4/ per Bushell.

George Austin arriv'd here three Days agoe from Bristoll who brings Account that there is a Great Likelyhood of a French War.[5] I have not further to Offerr at Present, but that I most Sincerly Remain &c.

P. S. Since Writing the preceeding Capt. Miznard tells me that he has the Good Fortune to be known to you, so that you need take no Notice of the five Shillings I mentioned to be paid him.

ADDRESSED: "Per Capt. Miznard & Copie per Capt. Steinson Via Cowes"

---

[4] Lillywhite does not list a New York Coffee House for this early date. Bryant Lillywhite, *London Coffee Houses* (London, 1963), pp. 407–408.
[5] Austin had arrived in the ship *Brislington*, John Purnell, from Bristol. SCG, 27 February, 2 April 1744.

9th March 1744

TO ANDREW PRINGLE
London

Charles Town, 9th March 1743 [1744]

SIR:

My last to you was of the 27th Ulto. per Capt. Miznard & Copie thereof per Capt. Steinson[6] Via Cowes, to which please be Reffer'd, & yesterday have your most Esteem'd Favours of the 31st December & 3 January per Capt. Lester, & duely Remark the Contents.

Mr. Elliott being in Town, I this day deliver'd him your Letter & who is very thankfull to you for all Favours & especially for your Goodness to his Son. Inclos'd please Receive his Letter to you, as also One to his Son, to which Refferr you. You have also Inclos'd another Power of Attorney to You, to Receive his Fire Money, in Case the Power sent you per Capt. Miznard, shoud happen to misscarry, & doubt not Mr. Inns will deliver You the Tickett on Demand being for £439.5.2 ¾ Ster. Mr. Elliott desires you may pay your Self out of said Money for the Bricks & Stones & for what ever you may have Disburs'd for his Son & the Remainder of the Money to Lye in your hands to supply his Son with as you may see Occasion. He also desires that Generall Oglethropes Bill for £[torn]5.4.0 Ster. may Remain with you to wait the Event for payment.

This Goes by Capt. Æneas Mackey who is witness to Mr. Elliotts signing the Letter of Attorney in order to prove it. He has promis'd to deliver this into your Own hands. He is a very Cliver Brisk man. His Ship belongs to the Wendells at Boston & Mr. Hodshon in London.

A few days agoe arriv'd here the Ship *Lusitania*, Capt. Sharnell Gravener, from Barbados Address'd to me by Mr. Gedney Clarke to procure a Freight for London, there being a very bad Crop this year in barbados. Said Vessell has brought no Rum or Sugar, and is Own'd by Mr. Gedney Clarke & Messrs. Whitaker & Hannington in London. Youll please to gett £100 Ster. Insur'd on Goods on Said Vessel, which I purpose to Ship you on Account of Messrs. William Turner & Laurence Jopson in Hull, & perhaps on your & my Account as may best Suit.

A pritty many Vessels have arriv'd here within these 10 days past which has put a Damp upon Freight, & I have not as yet been able to Lett out Capt. Gravener on Freight as I Cannot at Present Obtain £4 per Ton, & if any more vessels arrive soon beleive it will be under, So that if Capt. Douglas does not arrive 'till a month [710] hence beleive it may happen

---

[6] The snow *Friendship*, John Steinson, to Cowes. SCG, 5 March 1744.

9th March 1744

better than if he was here at Present for Freight. I am inform'd by Capt. Gravener, who was lately at New Castle upon Tyne, that Mr. Erving of Boston had a fine large Ship nam'd the *Cromwell*, Capt. Nicholson, Commander that unhappily Oversett in the Harbour for want of Ballast in November last which is a Great Missfortune. Mr. Erving advis'd me of his sending said Ship here for Freight & make my Wife & I an Offerr of Our passage in her to London. I am very thankfull for your Good Office & Care in Speaking to the severall Gentlemen to transmitt the Certificates to Clear my Bonds. Mr. Dinnwidie[7] the Inspector Generall is now very strickt on the Customhouse Officers in America.

Please to advise me who is your Correspondant in Jamaica as also in Antigua & St. Kitts,[8] in Case I may have any Occasion of Corresponding that Way.

I duely Remark your Good Offices to have the Companies & Gallies Granted to us, for which this province is Greatly Oblidg'd to you, and if all the Gentlemen in this Trade has as just a Concern for it as you, things would goe better here than they doe.[9]

I Omitted in my last to Acquaint you that His Majesties Ship the *Loo* of 40 Guns, has lately been unhappily Losst on the Rocks Call'd the Martyrs on the Coast of Florida in a Cruize, & Capt. Utting & most of his Officers goe home Passangers with Capt. Mackey.[1]

The Persons Concern'd in the mine here are so close & Shy about it that there is no coming at the Knowledge or Condition of it, neither can I obtain a List of those who are Concern'd. They keep it so private so as that I may enquire about it in Order to Procure a Share if to be Obtain'd, & in Case may find it worth while. However Great Britain & Our Dominions in America are better without mines than with them, as it wou'd put an End to Trade & Our Manufactures. Wittness the Spainards who were the most Polite & Powerfull Nation in Europe before the Discovery of their Mines & Ever since, that Nation have been upon the Decline & are now become

---

[7] Robert Dinwiddie (1693–1770) was appointed in 1727 collector of customs in Bermuda and in 1738 Surveyor-General for the Southern Part of America. In the latter office he uncovered frauds in Barbados and dismissed a number of officials. In 1751 he was appointed lieutenant governor of Virginia. DAB, V, 316–17.

[8] Andrew Pringle's correspondents were James Henderson in Jamaica, Isaac Duport in St. Kitts, and John Blane in Antigua. RPC, p. 818.

[9] Andrew Pringle had obviously been using his influence to obtain more galleys for the Carolina station and more companies of soldiers for the southern frontier.

[1] The entire story of the shipwreck of the *Loo* on 5 February 1744 on Las Martyrs, "the Martiers," was given in SCG, 20 February 1744. Part of the crew arrived in Charleston via Providence. SCG, "Postcript," 5 March 1744.

9th March 1744

Lazy & Poor, & would make us the Same, especially in America, as it coud put an End to Industry & Planting & make Our Collonies Deserts as all the Spainish settlements are, tho' they have the best Lands in America. How much Sugar, &c. might be produc'd in the fine Island of Cuba, much exceeding all our Islands put together & Instead thereof all their Lands lye Uncultivated, & not a Fifth of the People there that otherwise might be by reason of their mines which keeps them from Industry & Improvements.

I find it very hard & Dufficult to gett in Debts in Order to make Remittances & Goe for London as I intended, So that must be Oblidg'd to Sue Some Persons which is very disagreeable,[2] & my not being able to make Remittances According to my Inclination, will be the only thing that will Obstruct my not seeing you this Summer as I still intend, however have hopes of Effecting Same, by the Month of June next.

The Managers here have writt to you & Messrs. Baker & Crokatt of the 2d Current, also Copie thereof, to make Insurance for £650 Ster. on the Ship *John & Thomas*, Capt. Edward Brooks, for London which we are Loading with Rice on Account of the Privateer We writt you for & to your Good Selvs Consign'd. The Vessel will be ready to Sail in Ten Days & by whom shall forward Invoice & Bill of Loading. You may also expect some more Bills & Orders on Said Account by Said Vessel.

Mr. Elliott tells me he Sent (Six) £6 in Georgia Bills to his Son by Mr. Thomas [711] Lloyd,[3] who went passenger in His Majestys Snow the *Swift*.[4] It Seems Admiral Ogle[5] Lyes very Quiet at Jamaica, for the Spainish Admiral Torres is at Sea with some Large Ships Cruizing.[6] Capt. Frankland in the *Rose* fell in with them in his Station & Retook a Vessel from them belonging to Boston with Logwood, having Admiral Torres Lieutenant on Board with twelve Spainards who came ashoar here this

---

[2] RP seldom took his debtors to court. During the period covered by the copybook, he sued only two persons. In 1737 he sued Edward Bullard, Charleston merchant; in 1744 as an administrator of Robert Gray's estate, he sued William Livingston, Colleton County, planter. Judgment Rolls, 1737, 42A; 1743-1744, 58A.

[3] Thomas Lloyd was a Charleston merchant who died 2 September 1766. HL, I, 101n.

[4] HMS *Swift*, William Bladwell, had been on the North Carolina station. May, p. 164.

[5] Sir Chaloner Ogle (1681?-1750) joined Admiral Vernon at Jamaica in January 1742 and took part in the ill-fated attack on Cartagena. He and Vernon quarreled constantly until the latter left in October 1742 at which time Ogle replaced him. He returned to England in the summer of 1745. DNB, XIV, 928-29.

[6] Admiral Don Rodrigo Torres brought out a Spanish fleet to the West Indies during the winter of 1739-1740, and in 1744 he escorted home the only treasure fleet that returned to Spain from the West Indies during the war. Pares, pp. 86, 111.

9th March 1744

Day. Capt. Frankland gott from them in the Night, being 60 to 70 Gun Ships.[7] My Wife Joyns in Kind Love & Respects & I Remain &c.

P. S. Having had Occasion to wait on Our Governour Mr. Glen the other day, he desir'd his kind Service might be presented You.

ADDRESSED: "Per Capt. Aeneas Mackay & Copie per Capt. Sandwell Via Cowes"

TO JOHN ERVING
Boston

Charles Town, 13th March 1743 [1744]

SIR:

The Preceeding of the 11th Ulto. is Copie of my Last per Capt. Blunt & Since have your most Esteemed favours of the 7th January & Duely Observe the Contents. I am greatly Concern'd to be Informed by Capt. Gravener Lately from New Castle of the missfortune that has there befallen Your fine Ship *Cromwell*, Capt. Nicholson, Commander which he Informs me Oversett in the Harbour & Could not be gott up without a great Charge & Trouble for which am heartily Sorry & which Doubt not you may have advice of before this. In Case the Ship had come here with a Loading of Coals it would have been a Dificult matter to have Dispos'd of such a Large Quantity soon, a great Deal haveing been Lately Imported & never Exceed in Price £10 this Currency per Chalder.

A Pretty many Vessells having Arriv'd here within these ten Days Past insomuch that Little freight is Wanted at Present & Seekers Cannot Obtain more than £3.15 per ton for London & £4.5 per ton for Holland but if no more Vessells appear soon Freight will still keep up & beleive wont be Under £4 per ton for London this Season Unless more Shipping Arrive here than is Expected.

We are Inform'd they are like to have good Crops in the Leeward Islands but none in Barbadoes. I am again to Entreat the favour youll use

---

[7] Capt. Thomas Frankland had brought back three prizes this time. *SCG*, 12 March 1744.

14th March 1744

your good Offices to Secure my Debt with Capt. Wimble If he has any Effects in Rhoad Island, being Credibly Inform'd by Capt. Allen, Commander of a Rhoad Island Privateer who touch'd here a few Days agoe & is Sail'd again. He told me that he was Consort with Wimble in a Cruize & they Carried Two good Prizes Last Summer in to Rhoad Island & that Wimble has Left a good Part of his Share of the Effects in the Hands of Mr. Peter Bours there (as I formerly advis'd you) till his Return & he has not been there since, & I am Also Inform'd by said Allen that Wimble has Taken no Prize this Cruize & has Lost his Sloop near Cape Francois & Since is gone to Jaimaica, so that Doubt not youll be so good as to Endeavour to Attach his Effects or Order some Friend to Attach his Effects in said Mr. Bours his hands for my Debt if Rhoad Island is not out of Reach. My Brother writes me that he is to send you over one of said Wimbles Bills with Protest & Doubt not your good Endeavours to Recover it with the Re-Exchange & all other Charges as Customary. Re-Exchange is 15 per cent here on Bills.

My Wife joins in hearty Respects to your good Lady & all the Pretty Young ones & I Remain Very Respectfully &c.

ADDRESSED: "Per Capt. Davis"

[712]
TO JOHN ERVING
Boston

Charles Town, 14th March 1743 [1744]

SIR:

I did my self the Pleasure to write you Yesterday by this Conveyance of Capt. Davis to which please be Refferr'd, & he not being yet gone gives me the Opportunity to advise you that I Receiv'd this Morning an Express sent me from Sewee[8] with a Letter from Capt. James Hodges, Commander of the Ship *Panther* from Boston, advising that he mett with a Rhoad Island Privateer off this Barr which he Took for a Spainard & having but Six Men that Cou'd either Fight or Work the Ship He Run into

[8] Sewee Bay, north of Charleston near Bull's Bay, is entered through Price's Inlet.

14th March 1744

Sewee Harbour, a little to the Northward of this Place & desir'd that I would immediately send him four or five good hands to help assist him to gett out the Ship & bring her Round to this Place, Sewee being a pritty hazardous place in Case of bad weather. I according to his Request have immediatly dispatch'd a Boat with Six able Seamen to his assistance & hope will soon bring out the Ship without any Damage & bring her Round safe to this Place.

I Receiv'd Inclos'd from Capt. Hodges your most acceptable Favours of the 17th February & Messrs. Apthorp, Hancock & Wheelwright,[9] who Capt. Hodges advises me are his Owners may Depend upon all the Good Offices & Services I am Capable of to Capt. Hodges & their Ship *Panther* on Your Recommendation & to which Gentlemen please my best Respect. I am very Glad to be Inform'd, that your Ship *Cromwell* is likely to be gott up again at New Castle with little Damage, & am afraid if said Ship was to Come here now with Coals on Board they would not Sell, being now too late in the Season for that Commodity.

Am Greatly Oblidg'd to you for the four Bundles of Hay per Capt. Hodges, who also Informs me in his Letter that his Chief Mate Mutined on Board & he Cannot depend on him. He was oblidg'd to give him the Point of his Sword in his Own Defence. In Haste I Remain &c.

ADDRESSED: "Per Capt. Davis"

TO GEDNEY CLARKE
Barbados

Charles Town, 20th March 1743 [1744]

SIR:

The Preceeding on the other side of the 4th February is Copie of my last per Capt. Lightwood to which please be Refferr'd, & Inclos'd you have Copie of Invoice & Bill of Lading for Twelve Barrels of Rice shipt You on Board said Lightwood on Account of the Owners of the *Lusitania* as also Copie of Account Current. Since my last have your most Esteem'd Fa-

---

[9] Charles Apthorp, eminent Boston merchant, and John Wheelwright were among the signers of a petition of the merchants of Boston to the Board of Trade. *NEH&GR*, XII (1858), 281; XX (1866), 31.

29th March 1744

vours of the 6th February as also Yours of the 12th Ditto per the *Lusitania*, Capt. Gravener who arriv'd here the 5th Current & agreeable to Your directions have procur'd him a Freight of Rice for London at £3.15/ per Ton. He is now prity forward in his Lading & if the weather continues fair hope he will be ready to Sail in Ten days. I was in hopes of Obtaining £4 per Ton, but a pritty many Vessels happening to arrive at the Same time with Capt. Gravener, Lowerd Freight 5/ per Ton, & Judg'd it more for his Owners Interest to Embrace said Freight with Quick dispatch than the Vessel should be detain'd upon an Uncertainty.

The Butter & Grindstones happen both to be very unsaleable articles here at Present. Am oblidg'd to Retail the Butter by the single Firkin at 2/6 per lb. & for the Grindstones they are Likely to Lye on hand for Sometime. There was Landed only ninty Eight Grindstone two having been broke.

It is well you did not send the Sloop here with Salt, a Great Deal having been Lately imported, So that it is very Low at Present. Shall Try to Engage a Freight for Capt. Gravener to return here from London Directly, & advise Messrs. Whitaker & Hannington[1] thereof Accordingly, but it is uncertain whither or not it Can be obtain'd. I am Most Respectfully &c.

Prices of Goods the same as in my Last.

ADDRESSED: "Per Capt. *[Blank]*"

TO CHARLES & EDMOND BOEHM
London

Charles Town, 29th March 1744

[713] SIR:

I have your Favours of the 16th March 1742/3, & not having been able to Recover any of the Outstanding debts as advis'd you in my Last, according to my Expectation has been the Occasion of my Silence till now. Please Receive Inclos'd Bill of Loading & Invoice of Fifteen Barrels

---

[1] Whitaker and Hannington, merchants in Dolphin Court Tower Hill, London, were co-owners of the *Lusitania* with Gedney Clarke of Barbados. *London Directories*; RPC, p. 716.

29th March 1744

of very Good Rice Shipt on Board the Ship *Lusitania,* Capt. Sharnell Gravener, Commander for London on Your proper Risque & Account & to your good selves Consign'd, Amount per Invoice being £132.17.0 this Currency which wish safe to Hand & hope will come to a Good Markett, both the Price of Rice & Freight being Pritty Low & is for the Outstanding Debts Recover'd of Robert Gray & that of Abraham Didcott. As for the others, it is very uncertain if any of them can be Recover'd, some of them being dead & others gone off. Doe assure you my uttmost Endeavours has not been wanting to Recover the whole & am Concern'd that it has not been in my Power to Effect it. I am greatly oblidg'd to you for your Good Inclinations towards me & shall be always very Glad to Receive your Commands, as being with very Great Respect &c.

P. S. The Ship will sail in a Week or ten Days.

ADDRESSED: "Per Capt. Lee & Copie per Capt. Gravener"

TO THOMAS HUTCHINSON AND THOMAS GOLDTHWAIT
Boston

Charles Town, 31st March 1744

GENTLEMEN:

I have your Favours two days agoe of the 2d Current advising of Capt. Blunts arrival, & Inclosing a Certificate of his Cargoe. This serves to advise you that about three Weeks agoe Capt. Frankland, Commander of His Majestys Ship the *Rose,* brought in here a Square Stern'd Ship Burthen about One Hundred & Sixty Tons Loaded with Logwood & taken by said *Rose* in a Cruize near the Havannah & having only Spainards on Board, but suppos'd to have been lately before, One of Our Ships by them taken, & a Spainish Lieutenant that Commanded on Board said Ship when taken says, that all the English belonging to said Ship were taken out of her & put on Board the Spainish Admiral Torres then at Sea, so that there is no English Left on Board or any Papers to prove what Ship she is, & whereto belonging.[2]

[2] HMS *Rose* had recently secured three prizes. One was a ship laden with logwood, belonging to Boston, but had been taken on her way home from the Bay of Honduras by a large Spanish man of war. SCG, 12, 19 March 1744.

31st March 1744

One Capt. Abraham Remick here at Present belonging to Boston, Commander of a Ship lately from Jamaica, Informs me that he was master lately of said Prize ship which was nam'd the *Sarah*, & belonging to One Mr. Clarke of Boston lately Dead, & after his Death said Ship was sold to One Mr. Hubbard & your Mr. Thomas Hutchinson & by them sent Last Summer to the West Indies with Lumber from thence to proceed to the Bay of Honduras, One David Lewis, Commander. And as said Ship will soon be Condemn'd as a Lawfull Prize to the *Rose* if no Claimant Appears, And as I am Credibly inform'd by said Capt. Remick that you are Concern'd in Said Vessel, Out of Reguard to your Interest I intend to Lay Claim to the Vessel on your Behalf in Order to prevent her being Condemn'd as an Entire prize to the Captors. I am therefore to desire youll please per first Conveyance to advise me if it is so as Capt. Remick informs me & Let me have your full & ample Powers & directions Relating to said Ship in Case said Vessel proves to be your & Mr. Hubbard's Property, & if she happens not to be a prize, the Captors will have only one Eight part of Ship & Cargoe Clear of all Charges, which one Eight part might be immediatly paid down with all the Charges attending the Claim, &c.

The Blubber & Coca per Capt. Blunt Remains still unsold. Shall be Glad to have your directions to put both up at Publick Vendue or to Return you the Cocoa. [714] A Great deal of Cocoa has been lately Sold here at Vendue. Freight is Lower then it has been & is now at £3.10/ per Ton for London, a pritty many Vessels, having lately arriv'd here.

This Goes by a Sloop Via Rhoad Island & in Expectation of your particular advice in Relation to said Ship per first Conveyance, I Remain in haste &c.

P. S. I have some Thought of taking a Trip to London this Summer. However my Business will be Carried on in the Same manner, as if here present.

ADDRESSED: "Per Capt. Johnson Via Road Island"

TO ANDREW PRINGLE
London

Charles Town, 3rd April 1744

SIR:

My last to you was of the 9th Ulto. per Capts. Mackey & Sandwell[3] & since have not the Pleasure of any of your Favours. In my last I desir'd you to make Insurance of £100 Ster. for Goods on Board the Ship *Lusitania*, Capt. Sharnell Gravener, Commander at & from this to London, & am now again to desire that youll please to gett Insur'd £100 Ster. more on Said Ship which makes Two hundred Pounds Sterling, whereof Seventy Five pounds on Account of Messrs. Turner & Jopson of Hull & the Remaining £125 Ster. on Account of the Last Cargoe per the *Susannah* between you & Capt. Sanders. The Ship will Sail in ten Days, is a Good Ship & the Commander, Gravener, a very Clever man. I Lett him out at £3.15/ per Ton Freight for London, a pritty many Vessels have arriv'd Lately, & now Freight is at £3.10/ per Ton for London & Rice at 30/ per Ct. I shall ship part Rice & part Deer Skins per said Ship on Account as above, & as I shall doe my Self the Pleasure to write you again soon by said Ship, I add not at Present but that I Remain in haste, with most Tender Reguard &c.

No word as yet of Capts. Murphy or Douglas.

ADDRESSED: "Per Capt. Purnell Via Bristol & Copie per Capt. Mackellan"

TO WHITAKER & HANNINGTON
London

Charles Town, 11th April 1744

GENTLEMEN:

This you will Receive by your ship *Lusitania*, Capt. Sharnell Gravener, Commander for London being address'd to me by Mr. Gedney Clarke of Barbados to Procure for said Ship a Freight to London which

---

[3] Capt. Stephen Sandwell, ship *Union*, arrived from London. SCG, 13 February 1744.

9th April 1744

agreeable to his desire I have Effected accordingly & Goes Loaded with Rice at £3.15/ per Ton. The Ship has had very Good Dispatch & hope will soon be with you. Capt. Gravener Brought here Thirty Firkins of Irish Butter & Ninty Eight New Castle Grindstones for Sale on Account of the Owners of the *Lusitania* for which please Receive Account Sales Inclos'd of what has been sold, Neat Proceeds Being £171.7.5 this Currency & by which Youll Observe a pritty deal still Remains unsold being both very dull Commodities here at Present.

According to Mr. Gedney Clarkes directions, I have Taken Capt. Gravener's Bills of Exchange on your Good Selvs for £41.10 Ster. payable to my order at Twenty days Sight, being for money advanc'd Capt. Gravener here for the Ship, &c. which doubt not will be duely honour'd. I have endeavour'd to Engage a Freight Certain for the *Lusitania* back here directly, but Cannot be Obtain'd as it is Thought there will be Shipping enough for what Freight there may be wanted in the fall of the Year, & at a Lower Rate than at Present.

[715] Freight has fallen Since Capt. Gravener's Arrival & is now at £3.5/ per Ton. Shall be very Glad to be Favour'd with a Line from you at Capt. Gravener's Arrival & to Render you any agreeable Service here, & I am with very Great Respect &c.

Exchange to London at £700 per £100 Ster. The *Lusitania*'s Lading Consist of 543 Barrells Rice, One hhd Deer Skins & Fifty Madeira Plank. I have deliver'd the Account Sales of the Butter & Grindstones to Capt. Gravener.

ADDRESSED: "Per Capt. Gravener & Copie per Capt. Stedman Via Cowes"

TO WILLIAM TURNER & LAURENCE JOPSON
Hull

Charles Town, 9th April 1744

GENTLEMEN:

The last I did my self the Pleasure to write you was of the 25th February per Capt. Agars & Copie thereof per Capt. Atkinson both for your

11th April 1744

Port, Since none of Your Favours. As no Good Bills of Exchange are to be had at any Rate or Good Stout Deer Skins, neither any Freight for your Port or Likely to Offer soon, & happening to Procure Freight for London pritty Low (in Respect to what has been all this Season) as well as Rice, Inclos'd please Receive Invoice of Sixty Barrels Good New Rice, I have Shipt on Board the Ship *Lusitania*, Capt. Sharnell Gravener, Commander for London on your proper Risque & Account & to my Brother Andrew Pringle, Merchant there Consign'd amount as per Invoice being £536.10.6 this Currency which wish Safe to hand & hope will Come to a good Markett, both the Freight & Price of Rice being Low, Freight at £3.15/ per Ton. I have given my Brother previous advice for Insurance on Said Ship for Value of your Rice, & who doubt not will advise you of Same.

Inclos'd Please also Receive your Account Current, Ballance in my Favour being £39.16.9 this Currency, you'll please to Observe there is £141.14.6 debts still Outstanding by three Persons as mention'd in the Account to be made Good when Receiv'd. Have not yet Receiv'd the Neat Proceeds of your Chairs, &c. from Messrs. Jones & Oliver. As I mention'd in my Last, beleive it will be proper for you to Send a power of Attorney before it Can be Receiv'd. Shall be always very Glad to Receive your Commands & to Render you any agreeable Service. I am Most Respectfully &c.

Exchange to London at £700 per £100 Ster.

ADDRESSED: "Per Capt. Gravener & Copie per Capt. Stedman Via Cowes"

TO ANDREW PRINGLE
London

Charles Town, 11th April 1744

SIR:

Since my Last of the 3d Current have not the Pleasure of any of your Favours. My Last was to desire you would please to make Insurance of £200 Ster. on the Ship *Lusitania*, Capt. Sharnell Gravener, Commander at & from this to London, & whereof £75 on Account of Messrs. William

11th April 1744

Turner & Laurence Jopson of Hull & £125 Ster. on Account of the Last Cargoe per the *Susannah*. And Inclos'd please Receive Bill of Lading & Invoice of Sixty Barrels Rice ship'd on Board the Ship *Lusitania* by which this Goes on the Proper Account & Risque of Messrs. William Turner & Laurence Jopson of Hull & to Your [716] Good Self Consign'd, Amount as per Invoice being £536.10.6 this Currency, Copie of which I have sent them per this Conveyance. Youll please to advise them of Receipt of Same & follow their directions there anent, being for Goods formerly sent here for Sale, & have had no Opportunity of Shipping them for Hull directly so thought it proper to Consign Same to Your address, as having no particular Directions from them, & of which have advis'd them per this Conveyance.

Please also Receive Inclos'd Bill of Lading & Invoice of One Hhd. Deer Skins, Forty One Barrels Rice, & Forty Pistoles & half in Gold Ship'd on Board the Ship *Lusitania* for London & to you Consign'd, being on Account of the Goods Ship't here Last on your joint Account per your Ship *Susannah*, Amount as per Invoice being £943.10.9 this Currency which wish Safe to hand & hope will Come to a Good Markett, & as the Rice is Low in price & likewise the Freight Lower than any as yet this Season, hope will be no Loss on it, being to fill up Capt. Gravener. I would not Ship any Quality having your Directions Rather to Ship any thing else than Rice if to be had. Have also by this Conveyance Shipt Seventy Seven Barrels More of Rice to your self & the other Managers of the Privateer & Transmitted a Bill of Exchange for £50 Ster. & advice of Mr. Daniel Laroche[4] One of the Subscribers his Remitting £50 Ster. more on the Said Account & to which Letter of Ours per this Conveyance Relating to Same Please to be Refferr'd, & hope soon to Remitt the full sum of £2,000 Ster. You have not advis'd whither James Blount of Edentown in North Carolina has made you any Remitances from thence, which I am in hopes he's done before this, not having heard from him for Some Time. He bears a Good Character here. Shall be Glad Mr. Dalby has paid the Remaining £15 Ster. of Capt. Turell's Bill on him.

Messrs. Hutchinson & Goldthwait writes me that he makes great Complaint to them of Same, notwithstanding, he had not paid the Money as I have advis'd them. In mine of the 9th March I advis'd that Capt. Frankland, Commander of his Majestys Ship *Rose* had Retaken from the Spainards near the Havannah & brought in here a Square Stern'd Ship,

---

[4] Daniel LaRoche was a Georgetown merchant. *HL*, I, 4n.

11th April 1744

Burthen about One Hundred & Sixty Tons Loaded with Logwood & belonging to Boston, & Since have been Credibly Inform'd that the Said Ship belongs to Our Friend Mr. Thomas Hutchinson of Boston, so that I have Claim'd here on his Behalf that She may not be Condemn'd as a prize to the Captors. There was none of the Ship's Company left on Board when Retaken, but only Spainards who Say that all the English & their Papers were all carry'd on Board the Spanish admiral when Taken.

The Ship *Lusitania*, Capt. Gravener, Goes address'd to Messrs. Whitaker & Hannington who are Owners of her with Mr. Clarke of Barbados & who adress'd said Ship to me for Freight & Inclos'd please Receive Capt. Graveners Bill of Exchange on said Gentlemen for £41.10/ Ster. payable to my Order & to your Good Self Indors'd which doubt not will be duely Honour'd & when in Cash please to pass it to the Credit of the Cargoe per the *Susannah*'s Last Voyage between you & Capt. Sanders the Same as the other Remittances per this Conveyance. A Snow, One Capt. Gibbon, Commander Lately from London & Madeira has been just taken up upon Freight by Mr. Reid & Self to London On account the Owners of the *Griffen* at £3.5/ per Ton, so that Freight is Fallen & am of [717] opinion wont be higher now this Season.

No word as yet of Capt. Murphy or douglas. It is pity they had not been here sooner before Freight fell. About 55,000 Barrels of Rice has been already exported of which a pritty Deal to Portugal. By a Vessel a few days agoe from Lisbon we have the Surprizing News of the Empress of Rushia & a French Embassador's being assasinated which if True no doubt may Occasion an alteration in the affairs of Europe. I am &c.

ADDRESSED: "Per Capt. Gravener & Copie per Capt. Stedman Via Cowes"

TO ROBERT ELLIS
   Philadelphia

Charles Town, 23rd April 1744
SIR:
   My last to you was of the 23d February also Copie thereof, & about a Fortnight agoe came to hand your Favours of the 20th March per the Ship *Delaware*, Capt. Joseph Rivers, from Philadelphia Covering Bill of

24th April 1744

Lading & Invoice of Sundry Merchandize, Amounting to £75.17.0 Currency of Philadelphia on your Proper Account which have Receiv'd in Good Order excepting the Beer, some Barrels of which had Leak'd out on Board thro' the Badness of the Cask, & am to acquaint you that all sorts of Provisions happen to be very low in price here at Present, & as for the Beer it has Come a Great Deal too Late in the Season, Our hott Weather being already Come in, a Great deal Lately Imported, insomuch that am Oblidg'd to sell it at Eight pounds by the Single Barrel. However you may Depend on my Utmost Endeavours to dispose of every thing to Your best Advantage. I have also Receiv'd the Bundle of Lace which have deliver'd to Mr. Reid. Hope per next Conveyance to Receive further Remittances as you mention in Yours in Order to Ballance your Account.

My Wife Joyns with me in best Respects to you & Good Mrs. Ellis & I am in haste &c.

ADDRESSED: NO ADDRESS

TO THOMAS HUTCHINSON & THOMAS GOLDTHWAIT
Boston

Charles Town, 24th April 1744

GENTLEMEN:

The Preceeding of the 31st Ulto. is Copie of my Last Via Rhoad Island, since none of your Favours. Since my Last having Certain Information & proof from Capt. Abraham Remick & Others here that the Prize Ship Loaded with Logwood, Retaken & brought in here by His Majestys Ship *Rose* does belong to your Mr. Thomas Hutchinson & Mr. Thomas Hubbard, I have accordingly Laid Claim to said Ship on your & Mr. Thomas Hubbard's Behalf in the Court of Admiralty, & hope in a few days to have a decree for Said Ship as Your Agent, paying One Eight part according to Act of Parliament. Youll please therefore per first Conveyance to Lett me have Your Orders & directions at Large about Said Ship, & her procedure in Case she is deliver'd to me. As she will want a Master, Hands, & Fitting out accordingly, & the One Eight part Salvage of Vessel & Cargoe must be paid down to the Captors immediatly free of all Charge which with the Outsett will be Considerable.

Your Cocoa & Blubber still Remains on hand unsold, & as our hott Season now begins to Come in, the Blubber wont keep, so must be Oblidg'd to expose to Publick Vendue. Pray never send any more of it. Freight is Lower than it has been & is now at £3.5/ per Ton for London. In Expectation of hearing speedily from you I Remain &c.

P. S. Rice 30/ per Ct.
By a Ship Yesterday in Seven Weeks from London, there appears Great Likelyhood of a French Warr.

ADDRESSED: "Per Capt. Monroe Via Road Island"

[718]
TO JOHN ERVING
   Boston

Charles Town, 24th April 1744

SIR:
My last to you was of the 14th March advising of Capt. Hodges in the Ship *Panther* being put in to Seewee a Little to the Northward of this, & who a few days after gott safe into this Harbour, Since have not any of Your Favours. Capt. Hodges is now Loaded with Rice for Cowes & Holland, having Engag'd his Freight at £3.15/ per Ton by my advice, & by which he has acted in the best manner he Coud here for his Owners Interest, & if he had not Accepted of said Freight when he did, he might have waited till this & Could not now have Obtain'd even that. Freight has fallen here since my Last and is now at £3.5/ per Ton for London & not Likely to be higher this Season, a pritty many Vessells have arriv'd here of Late, & a Good part of the Crop already Shipt off. So that as you have not before this sent here any of your Ships, am afraid it will be now too Late for any to Come to have a Tolerable Freight or Good Dispatch, especially as Vessels are dayly dropping in from different parts.

By a Ship Yesterday in Seven Weeks from London there appears a Great Likelyhood of a French War.

My Wife joyns in best Respects to your Good Lady & all the pritty

25th April 1744

Young Ones & having not further to Offerr at Present as being without any of your Favours I Remain with very Great Respect &c.

This Goes Via Rhoad Island.

ADDRESSED: "Per Capt. Monroe Via Road Island & Copie per Capt. Ward for Boston"

TO EDWARD & JOHN MAYNE & EDWARD BURN
Lisbon

Charles Town, 25th April 1744

GENTLEMEN:

My last to you was of the 26th November with Copie, & since have your most Esteem'd Favours of the 5th October, 17th & 25th January & duely Remark the Contents. The Original of yours of the 17 January wherein you mention my Account Current was Inclos'd has never yet appear'd & which youll please to Transmitt me per your next. I Observe you have been so good as to Remitt the Ballance of the Two parcells Rice to my Brother in London for which am very Thankfull.

I Receiv'd per Capt. Steinson a Chest of Lemmons in pritty Good Order which he told me you were so Good as to send me in a present & for which Return you my most hearty Thanks. Am sorry to Observe that our Commodity of Rice is so Low with you, as it is every where else. It is now at 30/ per Ct. Capt. Swayne[5] by which this Goes is at the Lowest Freight that has as yet been for your Port this Season being at £3 per Ton. By a Ship Two days agoe in Seven Weeks from London, there appears a very great Likelyhood of Our having very soon a War with France. I have not further to Offerr at Present but that I Remain Most Respectfully &c.

Exchange to London £700 per £100 Ster.

ADDRESSED: "Per Capt. Swayne & Copie per Capt. Tillidge"

[5] Capt. John Swain, brigantine *Charming Betty*, cleared for Lisbon. SCG, 30 April 1744.

[719]
TO OSBORNE & OXNARD & THOMAS GUNTER
Boston
Charles Town, 26th April 1744

GENTLEMEN:

I have your Favours of the 20th January And Inclos'd please Receive Account Sales of your Cargoe per the *Dolphin*, Neat Proceeds being £3,140.16.4 which hope youll find right & to Content. Inclos'd please also Receive your Account Current, Ballance due you being £1,209.16.4 this Currency & per first Opportunity by which I can procure Freight you may Expect same to be shipt you in Good New Rice being now at 30/ per Ct. as you Direct, which would not have fail'd to have done per Capt. Fadree provided he had taken Freight back for Boston. And as I understand Severall Vessels are soon expected from Your Port, doubt not of their taking Freight back again for Boston as Freight for Europe has fallen Considerably, being now at £3 per Ton for London & but few Shippers at Present. I Could not Obtain any Freight per this Conveyance at any Rate & there is no Gold or Silver to be had here at Present. I am &c.

ADDRESSED: "Per Capt. Ward"

TO CHARLES MARSHALL
New Providence, Bahamas
Charles Town, 27th April 1744

SIR:

I Receiv'd Sometime agoe a Letter from Capt. Wimble Deliver'd me by Mr. John Crokatt Open. Shoud have been Glad at Same time to have been Favour'd with a Line from You Inclosing the Same.

I am to desire You'll be so Good as to advise me by the Bearar Capt. Webster or the first Conveyance if Capt. Wimble has been since at Providence or any Likelyhood of his Coming Soon. I understand by Capt. Webster that he is gone Cruizing in a fine Brigantine Privateer from Jamaica & upon advice of your Expecting him will Transmitt you his Bill of

Exchange to me & Protest, as you have my Power of Attorney. Hope you'll Excuse this Trouble & if in the like or any thing else I can serve you here may Freely Command &c.

ADDRESSED: "Per Capt. John Webster"

TO THOMAS HUTCHINSON & THOMAS GOLDTHWAIT
Boston

Charles Town, 27th April 1744

GENTLEMEN:

The Preceeding on the other side of the 24th Current is Copie of my Last, & since the Court of Admiralty after Tryal have Decree'd your Ship *Sarah* or *Thomas* & Cargoe to be Restor'd to the Owners upon paying one Eight part of the True Value for Salvage to the Captors, free of all Charge. Youll please therefore per first Conveyance to Lett me have your ample & full directions about said Ship, which shall be punctually Comply'd with as the Ship will be Detain'd till I have same from you. I add not but that I Remain in Haste &c.

ADDRESSED: "Per Capt. Ward"

[720]
TO CHARLES APTHORP
Boston

Charles Town, 27th April 1744

SIR:

I have your most Esteem'd Favours of the 6th Current. Your Ship *Panther*, Capt. James Hodges, is now Loaded with Rice for Cowes & Holland he having Engag'd his Loading by my advice at £3.15/ per Ton, & in which he has Acted in the Best manner he Could for his Owners Interest as Times have happen'd here, & if he had not Accepted of Said Freight when he did he might have waited till this, & Could not now obtain £3.10/ per Ton. Freight has Fallen Considerably & not Likely to be higher this Season being now at £3 per Ton for London, & but few Shippers. Capt. Hodges is detain'd from Sailing for want of Some Hands being unfortunate in his Mate, who has Left him, & been the means also of severall others Leaving the Ship as doubt not Capt. Hodges will advise you per this Conveyance. What Service I have been capable of Rendering Capt. Hodges has not been wanting, & shall be allways very ready to Render you any acceptable Service, as being with very Great Respect &c.

ADDRESSED: "Per Capt. Ward"

TO JOHN ERVING
Boston

Charles Town, 27th April 1744

SIR:

The Preceeding on the other side of the 24th is Copie of my Last Via Rhoad Island & at the hands of Capt. Henry Aithen in your Snow *Thistle* & shall take Care to Load back said Snow on your Account according to your directions tho' the Article of Pitch is now pritty much in Demand here, which Occasions it to be Scarce & Rises in price. However you may depend upon my Loading your Snow Back with all possible dispatch. The Rum you sent will turn out but poorly, being very Low here at Present. Its well you did not send more being there is no Likelyhood of its bearing a better Price. I Return you my most hearty Thanks for your kind presents per Capt. Aithen.

I have no Letter from Mr. Hugh McDaniel as you advise. I am to desire the Favour that per your next, youll be so good as to enquire & advise me if Capt. Wimble has any Effects in the Hands of Mr. Bours of Rhoad Island, as I am Inform'd he has, that so the same may be attach'd for payment of his Bill. Freight for London is now at £3 per Ton & few Shippers. Mr. James Reid tells me that you have writt him that I am to pay him a small Ballance of £4.16.6 N. England Currency on your Account which shall be duely Comply'd with.

As the Times & affairs in Europe seem in so much Confusion at Present, am in Suspence with Reguard to goeing for London this Summer. Next advices from England may probably determine whither a War with France or not. In Haste I am Respectfully Remain &c.

Exchange to London £700 per £100 Ster.

ADDRESSED: "Per Capt. Ward"

[721]
TO JOHN WEBSTER
   Charles Town

Charles Town, 28th April 1744

SIR:

I have Shipt on Board your Sloop *Peggy* & to your Self Consign'd, Two Negro Men named Jack & Coudjoe on Account & Risque as per Bill of Lading which at your Arrival at New Providence youll please to Sell to the best Advantage for Silver Money & bring the Returns with you. And if you cannot Sell them during your Stay there, Leave them there with your Friend behind you as you may be Sensible that they Cannot be brought in to stay or to be Sold here. I put no Price or Value on the Two Negroes, but Leave them to your Prudent Management to Dispose of them for the most they will Fetch. I heartily wish you a Good Voyage & Success & I am &c.

ADDRESSED: NO ADDRESS

TO SAMUEL STORKE & SON
   London

Charles Town, 3rd May 1744

The Last I did my self the Pleasure to write you was of the 27th January with Copie & since have not any of your Favours. I am by this to ad-

3rd May 1744

vise you that Messrs. Hutchinson & Goldthwait of Boston, N. E. have directed me to Value on you for the Salvage of their Ship *Thomas* & Cargoe of Logwood Lately Recover'd here for them in Our Court of Admiralty being Retaken from the Spainards & brought in here by his Majestys Ship *Rose*, Capt. Frankland, Commander. Having had Occasion to make them Remittances to Boston in Rice by their Order And by next Conveyance you may Expect by Bills of Exchange on you accordingly which will not Exceed One Hundred Pounds Sterling & doubt not will by Duely Honour'd, as you will have Directions about same from said Gentlemen. They have Directed me to dispatch the Vessell with her Cargoe of Logwood for Hamburgh & to be address'd to Messrs. Halsey & Hanbury, Merchants There. The said Ship *Thomas* is burthen about 150 Tons Capt. George Palmer, Commander & is Fitting out & will be Ready to Sail in Ten or Fourteen days hence & Order'd to goe north about[6] & doubt not you will have Directions from Messrs. Hutchinson & Goldthwait for the neccessary Insurance on the Ship & Cargoe as also in Relation to the disposal of her Cargoe in Hamburgh & the Ships Procedure from thence, which the Gentlemen advise me is to be from thence to New Castle for Coals & so to Boston. I have not further to Offerr at Present but that I Most Respectfully Remain &c.

ADDRESSED: "Per Capt. Remick & Copie per Capt. Summersett"

TO ANTHONY WORLOND
  Barbados

Charles Town, 2nd May 1744

SIR:

By the directions of Capt. Sharnell Gravener who sail'd from this the 13th past, Please Receive Inclos'd Bill of Lading & Invoice of Eight Barrells & One half Barrell very Good Rice Ship'd on board the Schooner *Charming Sarah*, Capt. John Davison, Commander for Barbados on Account & Risque of said Capt. Gravener & to you Consign'd, Amount as per Invoice being £68.2 this Currency, which wish safe to Hand & to a Good Markett which he desir'd might be sent Mrs. Gravener. Freight being now

---

[6] To sail north of Ireland and Scotland.

5th May 1744

low here, I could not engage another here for Capt. Gravener directly. Inclos'd please also Receive Copie of Capt. Gravener's disbursments & Please present my best Respects to Mrs. Gravener & I am &c.

ADDRESSED: "Per Capt. Davison"

[722]
TO EDWARD PARE
Barbados

Charles Town, 5th May 1744

SIR:

This hope will be handed you by Capt. John Davison of your Schooner *Charming Sarah*, who by the Recommendation of Capt. Sharnell Gravener Apply'd himself to me for the Disposal of what small Cargoe he Brought here & to Obtain for him a Freight back to Barbados, which have accordingly procur'd for him with very Good Dispatch being Loaded Chiefly with Rice on Freight at Three Pounds per Ton Barbados money which hope will be more for your Interest than if he had brought here Salt, which is at Present a meer Drugg & very Low in Price.

Please Receive Inclos'd Account Sales of the Rum, &c. per the Schooner *Charming Sarah*, Neat Proceeds being £470.3.11 this Currency which hope You'll find Right & to Content. You have also Inclos'd Invoice & Bill of Lading of Sundries Ship'd on Board your said Schooner *Charming Sarah* on your proper Risque & Account & to your Good self Consign'd, Amount as per Invoice being £196.16.5 this Currency which wish safe to hand & hope will Come to a Good Markett as every thing is very Good in Quality.

As for the Lime juice Cannot dispose of it at any Rate, there being no manner of demand or Sale for it at Present, the People here of Late having gone very much into the Custome of Drinking Toddy & no Souring & at Capt. Davison's desire shall Ship it for Boston Consign'd to a Friend of mine there which Capt. Davison judges will be more for your advantage than to Carry it back with him.

The Two Negroe Men you Order'd Capt. Davidson to dispose of here Could not be Sold by Reason of a Law that has Subsisted for these Three

5th May 1744

Years past Prohibiting the Importation thereof & which expires the 5th July next, so that by my advice they have been Shipt to the Island of Providence where hope they will be sold to Good advantage, as Capt. Davison Tells me that he had Orders from you not to bring them back again upon any Account & when I have Account Sales shall Transmitt you Same accordingly & wait your Orders for Remitting the Neat Proceeds. As Our Negroe Act for Prohibiting the Importation of Negroes expires the 5th day of July next the First Parcells of Negroes that are Imported will Sell to very Good Advantage, expecially Boys & Girls of about 15 or 16 years of Age of which ⅔ Boys & ⅓ Girls to Say Thirty or Forty in a Vessel. They must be new Negroes from Africa & a Certificate of Same, otherways will be Lyable to an Extraordinary Duty of £50 per head the Common duty being Ten Pounds Currency per head for Men & Woman & Five per head for Boys & Girls.

If Barbados Rum Comes Cheap & Low in Price with you it will always answer here being the best Lik'd & most in Esteem of any Sort of Rum Imported & of which there is a Great Consumption, this Province Taking off & Consuming yearly Two Thousand hhds. of said Commodity, also Good Muscovado Sugar when Cheap is generally in Good Demand, Rum & Sugar being the Two most Suitable Commoditys from your Island for this Markett.

Youll Please to Return [723] a Certificate for the Delivery of the Schooners Cargoe in Order to Clear the Bond Given with Capt. Davison at Our Custom house. Freight to Europe has been very Low since Capt. Davisons Arrival & is now at 50/ per Ton for London & few Shippers. He intimated your Letters to Me, Ordering him to Take Freight to Europe, but it arriv'd too Late being then Loaded & Freight very Low, neither could he procure the Sundry things you Order'd in your Last to him not having Time to have them gott ready, being oblidg'd to have them sent for from the Country. Capt. Davison seems to have your Interest very much at heart & is very Sober diligent Man. Inclos'd please also Receive your Account Current, Ballance in your Favour, when the Money for the Rum is Receiv'd (being Oblidg'd to give Three Months Credit) £157.13.1 this Currency which youll please to Order to be Remitted as you Judge Proper. Shall be always very Glad to Render you any acceptable Service here & to Receive your Commands & I am with very Great Respect &c.

Exchange to London at £700 per £100 Ster.

4th May 1744

P. S. Inclos'd Please Receive Capt. Davisons Receipt for Money paid him for Disbursments being £115.14.5 this Currency for which have debit your Account.

ADDRESSED: "Per the Schooner *Charming Sarah,* Capt. John Davison, & Copie per Capt. Kilner"

TO GEDNEY CLARKE
Barbados

Charles Town, 4th May 1744

SIR:

The Annexed of the 20th March is Copie of my Last & three days agoe have your Esteem'd Favours of the 4th past & duely Remark the Contents. Capt. Gravener Sail'd Over this Barr the 13th past a full Ship with 543 BBls. Rice, Fifty Madeira Plank, & 1 hhd. Deer Skins for London, Rice at £3.15/ per Ton, Plank at 2½ d. per Foot, & Skins at 35/ per hhd. Freight having fallen after the *Lusitania*'s Arrival Could not Obtain another Freight for her to Return here Directly & Freight is now at 50/ per Ton for London & few Shippers.

Inclos'd please Receive Copie of Account Sales Deliver'd Capt. Gravener of what Butter & Grindstones were dispos'd of during his stay here Copie of which have also forwarded Messrs. Whitaker & Hannington, by which you'll Observe a good part of Both Remain'd on hand unsold & does still to this Time there being no Demand for either. The Butter being now almost spoilt & the weather having already Come in very hott, must be oblidg'd to put it up at Publick Vendue, as also the Grindstones as they wont pay store Room.

According to your directions I Took Capt. Gravener's Bill of Exchange for £41.10/ Ster., Exchange at £700 per £100 Ster. on Messrs. Whitaker & Hannington, being Ballance of money paid him here for his disbursments after deducting the Neat Proceeds of Butter & Grindstones & which doubt not will be duely honour'd.

As you desire I am to acquaint you that the act of this Province prohibiting the Importation of Negroes expires the 5th day of July next &

4th May 1744

will not be Renewed or Lay'd on again & than the Former duty will take Place of £10 per head for Men & Woman & £5 per head for Boys & Girls. Boys & Girls of about 15 & 16 years Old will answer the best ⅔ Boys & ⅓ Girls & am of opinion the first Parcells that are Imported here will sell to Good advantage, say Thirty or Forty at a Time in a Vessel, but Cannot be dispos'd of immediatly for Bills of Exchange being Cheifly sold to the Planters who dont ship their Produce as in the Islands [724] 'tho part may be dispos'd of for Ready Cash which will Purchase Bills, & what is sold on Credit Goes on Bond at 10 per cent Interest after become Due. There must be a Cocket or Certificate if any are sent to Certifie their being Imported Lately from Africa, otherways those that have been for any Time exceeding Three months in any of Our Islands are Lyable to an Extraordinary Duty of £50 per head.

There is little or no Pork now to be had, it being already Chiefly exported.

We have no matterial News here at Present, but that we are under daily Apprehensions of the News of a War with France. I Salute you & Remain Most Respectfully &c.

P. S. I Give you Joy of the Rich Prize brought in to your Island. Rum Barbados new 15/ per Gallon, Muscovado Sugar £10 to £12 per Ct.

ADDRESSED: "Per Capt. Davison & Copie per Capt. Kilner"

TO SAMUEL STORKE & SON
    London

Charles Town, 7th May 1744

GENTLEMEN:

The above of the 3d Current is Copie of my Last which Confirm & yesterday have another Letter from Messrs. Hutchinson & Goldthwait of the 6th April in which they Desire me to advise you to gett Insur'd for the Owners Six Hundred Pounds Ster. on the Said Ship *Thomas* & Cargoe at & from this to Hamburgh, George Palmer, Master. I have advise from my Brother in London in his Last to me that the Price of Logwood is advanc'd to £6.15/ per Ton. If so, am of Opinion that the said Ship & Cargoe of Logwood is worth £1,000 Ster. provided it is their Sentements that the Ship & Cargoe may be fully Insur'd. This I only offerr for your Government that you may act as you judge most proper for said Gentlemens Interest. I add not at Present but that I am with very Great Respect &c.

Exchange to London at £700 per £100 Sterling. Rice 30/ per Ct.

ADDRESSED: "Per Capt. Summersett & Copie per Capt. Rivers"

TO ANDREW PRINGLE
London

Charles Town, 7th May 1744

SIR:

My Last to you was of the 11th Ulto. with Copie & about a Fortnight agoe have the Pleasure of your most acceptable Favours per Capt. Mackenzie of the 15th, 28th February, 1st & 3d March, as also about a Week agoe Your Favours of the 19th January, 10th, 15th, & 23d February per Capt. Ayers & duely Notice the Contents. You advise that Mr. William Cookson of Hull has given me Orders to make his Returns into your Hands of about £400 Ster. I shou'd be very Glad it was so, for your sake. But so far from that, said Gentleman has given no such Orders to me & in his last Letter of the 25th February by Capt. Mackenzie, he Orders what Effects in my Hands Remitted to himself by Bill of Exchange. And as to his Effects in my Hands doe assert it is nothing near the Sum he has advis'd you & very little exceeds £400 this Currency of which I shall very soon make him Sensible by Transmitting him account Sales & Account Current & I am by this to give you a Caution to be very Circumspect in having any manner of dealing with him, for he appears to me to be a Person that I desire to have nothing to Doe with.

Capt. Atkinson sometime [725] agoe gave me a hint of his Character & told me that he was the Sharpest Man in Hull & indeed his Letters since & way of acting seems to Confirm & Corroborate the Same. As I have been on my Guard he has not had the Opportunity to take me in, & hope his Cunning won't be abble to gett the advantage of you to your Prejudice,

7th May 1744

but wou'd advise you to be very Cautious in having any Dealing with him. He Notoriously contradicted his Own Letters & Orders to me for Brazilletto he Order'd to be Ship'd, by endeavouring to thro' Six Tons of it on me pretending as ship'd without his Order & after having sent him an exact Copie of his own Letter in which he Order'd it, he has the modesty to own it was a mistake of his & now he wants to thro 1½ Tons Sasafras, Value £22.10/ this Currency on me, as ship't without order which I shall by no means agree to.

I have Receiv'd Inclos'd Messrs. Mayne's Account Current for the Last parcell of Rice per Archer, but not the account of the first per the *Bremen Factor.* I am greatly oblidg'd to you for the Inclos'd Certificates. Pray endeavour to gett that of Capt. Storys from Hull. I am dunn'd for it by Mr. Abercrombie, a King's Attorney, who is very tenacious of his Fees & Perquisites. I Receiv'd Mr. Caws Power of Attorney against David Caw, & Mr. Moore the Apothacary has also sent a Power of Attorney against him to Stead & Evance to Sue him for the Same Debt to Them, so that he is to be sued for the Same by both. However he tells me if I will Indemnifie him against Mr. Moore & Partner,[7] he will pay me the Ballance of his Account very speedily being £183.9.10 Ster. & which I told him am willing to doe upon his paying the money, & which I apprehend I may safely doe.

The India Pictures you have sent per Capt. Ayers are some of them damag'd in the Case, & happen not to be the Sort I meant. Those I meant are about a foot Square in Frames Glaz'd, however hope to dispose of them without Loss.

Mr. Elliott has Receiv'd his Gun & Pewter Water Plates. Hope one of his Letters of Attorney Last sent to you to Receiv'd his Fire money is Come to your hands before this. I Observe Mr. Elliotts Son directs his Letters to his Father to the Care of Colonel Othniel Beale which I imagine is by his Father's Order said Beale being his Friend in Town.

Messrs. Hutchinson & Goldthwait have not advis'd me about their Order of Goods to you for £500 Ster. in China, &c. Mr. Hutchinson advises me of sending Sixty hhds. of N. E. Rum on his Own account which will turn out very poorly being a Drugg here at Present & sold at 10/ per Gallon so that there will be a Loss on it. As I advis'd in my Last, I

---

[7] William Moore and William Huthwaite, London druggists, sued David Caw of Charleston for non-payment of his debts. RP entered the case in behalf of Caw and James Graeme was his attorney. Despite their efforts, Caw lost the judgment. Judgment Rolls, 1746 Oversize Box, 42A; see also RP to Andrew Pringle, 2 February 1745.

7th May 1744

have Claim'd & Recover'd the Logwood Ship (which appears to belong to Mr. Hutchinson & One Mr. Hubbard in Boston) in Our Court of Admiralty paying ⅛ of the Value of Ship & Cargoe to the Captors. Messrs. Hutchinson & Goldthwait have Order'd me to draw on Messrs. Storke & Son in London for the Salvage, as not being in Cash for them & which will be about £100 Ster. & have Order'd the Ship to be sent to Hamburgh & address'd to Messrs. Halsey & Hanbury there. The said Ship is fitting out & will sail in Ten days. George Palmer formerly of the Snow *John* Goes Master, having been dispatch'd from Boston for that Purpose with a Power of Attorney to me to Claim the Ship, but as it happened I had already done it for them before their Letters Came to Hand, & for which hope to meritt their Thanks, & as Logwood advances in Price hope they will make a Good Voyage of it. They have Desir'd me to advise Messrs. Storke & Son for Insurance of £600 Ster. on Ship & Cargoe of 150 Tons Burthen & which I Reckon to be worth £1,000 Ster.

I Remark your kind hint about Remittances & the Low Price of Rice about which shall observe your directions & ship none of said Commodity, so that you will have only the 41 Barrells gone in Capt. Gravener. If at any Time any Prize Goods shoud happen to Come here to be sold a Good Bargain will endeavour to Purchase & draw on you when Shipt, for what may [726] not be in Cash before the Bills become due, & Please keep me advis'd of the Price of Goods.

I Receiv'd Inclos'd Account Sales of 220 Oz. Silver per Scott on my Account Which turns out very well, Neat Proceeds £60.2.6 Ster. Have Credit you £2.10/ for Insurance on Same. I have also Wimble's Bill & Protest. Have not been able to Lay hold on him yet. I hear he Losst his Privateer Sloop lately at Cape Francois & has now another Brigantine fitted out at Jamaica. I wish I knew your Correspondant there that I might send his Bill & Protest. Please to advise & Lett me know who are Your Friends in all Our Islands. Please Receive Inclos'd Field Cossett his Receipt to you, for the money paid him for his House you sold. Am sorry you had so much Trouble about said affair.

Mr. James Osmond[8] & his Fammilly are Goeing this Summer to live at Exetor for Good. He always bore a Good Character here & very well Respected. He is Partner with One Mr. Binford in Exeter. Mr. Ham-

---

[8] James Osmond, Charleston merchant with a house on the Bay, had been a partner of Thomas Binford in the firm of Binford & Osmond. *HL*, I, 6n; *SCG*, 16 January 1744; Deeds, O, 6.

merton[9] Our Secretary Goes by this Conveyance of Summersett for London, & Mr. Abercrombie[1] is also goeing for London soon. I am greatly Oblidg'd to you for the News Papers you so Constantly send me & your own advices of News about the affairs of the World which are always very Acceptable, & not only Diverting, but may sometimes be of use even in affairs of Trade.

I am Hurried at Present having a pretty deal of Business on my hands, haveing the Logwood Ship to Fitt out & Dispatch for Hamburgh, also a Snow from Mr. Erving which am Loading back to him on his Own Account with Pitch & Rice, & I look daily for a Vessel with Rum from Mr. Hutchinson, to Load back with Rice to Boston on his Own particular Account.

I begin now to be apprehensive that my affairs will not now permitt me the Pleasure of Seeing you in London this Summer as I intended. And we Imagine there is by this Time a War with France for Certain which will make it very hazardous, & no Opportunity of a Man of War Goeing from this this Summer, & as yet have very Considerable Debts to gett in in Order to make Returns, as I purpose to make all my Remittance (before I Leave this) to every Person I have any Concerns with. My Wife joyns very heartily with Kind Love & Respects & I Remain most Truely &c.

ADDRESSED: "Per Capt. Summersett & Copie per Capt. Rivers"

TO THOMAS HUTCHINSON & THOMAS GOLDTHWAIT
Boston

Charles Town, 30th April 1744

GENTLEMEN:

The above of the 27th is Copie of my Last, & Last Evening have your Favours of the 2d Current per Capt. Palmer. You'll observe I have already Recover'd your Ship *Thomas*, paying One Eight part of the Ship & Cargoe to the Captors for Salvage as apprais'd, & have this day put Capt. Palmer in Possesion of the Ship & Shall follow your directions Re-

[9] John Hammerton.
[1] James Abercromby (1707–1775) would later represent Clackmannanshire in the House of Commons. Namier & Brooke, II, 2–3.

16th May 1744

lating to her & her procedure which hope will be more particular & per your next before she is Ready to Goe to Sea. I Have also your T. H.'s. Favours of the 26th March and am sorry he Is sending so much N. E. Rum at this Time, being very Low at Present & no demand, a Great deal having been Imported, insomuch that it is sold at 10/ per Gall. & Contrary to Expectation there is advice of Good Crops in the Leeward Islands tho' Late. Rum is now in Barbados at 13/ shillings per Gallon.

Shall Endeavour to dispatch the Schooner you [727] advise of as soon as Can be with Rice which is all yet to be purchas'd & Brought down from the Country, & there are now many Buyers. A Pritty many Vessels have arriv'd lately which am afraid will make it Scarce to be had & advance the Price. In Haste I Remain &c.

P. S. Shall be Oblidg'd to give a Bill of Exchange for the ⅛ Salvage of the Ship *Thomas*. You'll Please give directions to Mr. Samuel Storke & Son to Honour my Bill accordingly which will be about £100 Sterling.

ADDRESSED: "Per Capt. Shermerhorn Via New York & Copie per Capt. Woodwell"

TO HALSEY & HANBURY
Hamburg

Charles Town, 16th May 1744

GENTLEMEN:

This hope will be Deliver'd you by Capt. George Palmer, Commander of the Ship *Thomas* Loaded with Logwood & which by Directions to me from her Owners Messrs. Hutchinson & Goldthwait, Merchants in Boston, N. England Goes to your Good Selvs Consign'd & which hope will arrive safe & to a Good Markett as I have Advice Lately from London that Logwood is Considerably advanc'd in Price. Messrs. Samuel Storke & Son Merchants In London are said Gentlemen's Friends there & from which doubt not Youll have Directions in Relation to the Disposal of the Cargoe & the further procedure of Said Ship, which was Retaken from the Spainards by his Majestys Ship *Rose* and Brought in here & by me Claim'd in Our Court of Admiralty in Behalf of the Owners, & Decree'd to be Restor'd to them upon paying One Eight part Salvage of Ship & Cargoe free of all Charge, & which has been done accordingly. Capt. Palmer takes his Passage North about in Order to be more Safe from the Enemy.

Shall be very Glad to be Favour'd with a Line from you of Said Ships Arrival & to Render you any acceptable Service here & I am with Great Respect.

ADDRESSED: "Merchants in Hamburg Per Capt. Palmer & Copie Via London under Cover of S. Storke & Son"

TO GEORGE PALMER
Charles Town

Charles Town, 16th May 1744

SIR:

You Being Appointed by your Owners Messrs. Hutchinson & Goldthwait, Merchants in Boston, N. England Commander of the Ship *Thomas* Retaken from the Spainards & Brought in here by his Majestys Ship *Rose* & Claim'd & Deliver'd up to me in the Behalf of your said Owners by a Decree of the Court of Admiralty of this Province, A Copie you have herewith Deliver'd you. And the said Ship *Thomas* being in all Respects now fitted for the Sea, Clear'd & Ready to Sail. You are therefore to Embrace the first Opportunity that Presents of Wind & Weather & make the best of your way from this Directly for the Port of Hamburg (avoiding as it is War Time as much as you Can Speaking with any Shipping at Sea) where at your arrival you are immediatly to apply your Self to Messrs. Halsey & Hanbury, Merchants there, & deliver them my Letter herewith given you, & to whom by the Particular Directions of your Owners you Goe Consign'd & to follow their Directions or what Orders you may Receive from Messrs. Samuel Storke & Son of London in Relation to further procedure. I heartily wish you a Good Passage & Safe arrival & I am &c.

ADDRESSED: NO ADDRESS

17th May 1744

[728]
TO OSBORNE & OXNARD & THOMAS GUNTER
 Boston

Charles Town, 17th May 1744

GENTLEMEN:

The Above of the 26th Ulto. is Copie of my Last & agreeable thereto please Receive Inclos'd Bill of Lading & Invoice of One Hundred & Fifty Barrells of good Rice Ship'd in the Snow *Sea Horse*, John Woodwell, Master for Boston by which this Goes on your proper Risque and Account and to Your good Selvs consign'd, Amount as per Invoice being £1,205.1.0 this Currency which wish safe to hand & hope will Come to a Good Markett, the Rice being very Good in Quality, Low in Price and at a Reasonable Freight of £8 per Ton N. England Money. There is a Small Ballance You'll Observe of £4.14.6 still due you which with the Outstanding Debts, Amount £56.14.1 when Receiv'd, Shall be immediatly Remitted you.

I am to desire youll be so Good as to Transmitt me per first Conveyance a Certificate from your Custom house of the Delivery of the *Dolphin*'s Cargoe at your Port in Order to Cancell my Bond given in here with Capt. Evans, which you have hitherto Omitted. Shall be always very Glad to Receive your Commands & to Render you any Acceptable Service as being with very Great Respect &c.

Exchange to London at £700 per £100 Sterling.

ADDRESSED: "Per Capt. Woodwell & Copie per Capt. Aithen"

TO JOHN ERVING
 Boston

Charles Town, 17th May 1744

SIR:

My last was of the 27th Ulto. advising of the arrival of your Snow *Thistle*, & Since have Your Favours of the 28th March per Capt. Boutin which did not Come to hand till some days after the arrival of Your Snow. Since her arrival there has been a very Great demand for Pitch, every Person here being Buyers at Present which makes it very Scarce to be had & has already advanc'd the Price from 35/ to 40/ per Barrell & Cannot be Obtain'd for that & Likely to be higher, & very hard to be purchas'd at any Rate.

It is pity that I had not had previous notice of your Intention of sending your Snow to Load Back on your Own Account, the Cargoe might have been all Ready to put on Board at Arrival, & also wish you had been pleas'd to have given me more particular or Discretionary Orders in Relation to the Price of Pitch and Rice as the prices of Our Produce are very Fluctuating. As for Rice I have the Quantity you Mention ready to put on Board, but Cannot procure Pitch which must be put on Board before the Rice, there being only 200 BBls. thereof as yet on Board, & am of Opinion as Pitch rises & is so difficult to be gott, it will be more for your advantage to put Less Pitch & more Rice than you Order'd being at 30/ per Ct. As I Conceive it will be agreeable to your Sentiments to Load your Snow with whatever may be most for your Interest, & the Dispatch of the Vessel altho' Contrary to Your directions. Pitch having been Low in Price Sometime agoe & no Buyers, But is at this Time more in demand [729] than I have Known it for those Seven Years past. You may assuredly depend on [my] giving Capt. Aithen all possible Dispatch, & if Pitch can be gott hope to have him Dispatch'd in a Week or Ten Days hence, as there is a pritty deal of Pitch expected soon in Town from Winnyaw where it is Chiefly made.

Shall follow Your Directions to draw on you for the Amount of the *Thistles* Cargoe after Deducting the Neat Proceeds of Your Rum & Ballance of Account Current. Am of Opinion it will be most for your Interest to Sell off the Rum for what it will Fetch at Present altho very Low & there is no Likelyhood of its bearing a Better price, as Large Quantitys are Daily Coming in from the West Indies & a Great Deal more expected. To keep it any time it Inleaks a Great Deal in Our Hott Season by the keeping it in Store, besides the Charges of Cooperage for Hoops, &c.

Freight is now very Low here being offerr'd at 40/ per Ton for London & Severall Vessells are preparing to Goe up the Freshes So that there is no manner of Encouragement for any Shipping to Come here for Freight for this Season. As I shall doe myself the Pleasure to write you again soon by your Snow *Thistle*, I Add not at Present but that my Wife joyns in

17th May 1744

best Respects to your Good Lady & all the pritty Young Ones & I am Most Respectfully &c.

Exchange to London at £700 per £100 Sterling.

ADDRESSED: "Per Ditto Woodwell & Copie per Capt. Aithen"

TO JOSEPH TURRELL, JUNIOR[2]
Boston

Charles Town, 17th May 1744

SIR:

I Receiv'd yours of the 16th December and Inclos'd Please Receive Bill of Lading & Invoice of Eighteen Barrels very Good New Rice Ship'd on Board the Snow *Sea Horse*, Capt. John Woodwell, for Boston by which this Goes On Account & Risque of Your Father Capt. Joseph Turell & to you Consign'd, amount as per Invoice being £159.–.3d this Currency which wish safe to hand & hope will Come to a Good Markett, & which you might have expected Long before this, but had not the Opportunity of Freight for your Port. You have also Inclos'd your Fathers Account Current with me, Ballance in my Favour £13.–.3d this Currency which youll Please pay to Messrs. Hutchinson & Goldthwait, being as Youll Observe Over Remitted by Said Rice. I am &c.

Exchange to Boston at 25 per Ct.

ADDRESSED: "Per Capt. Gatman alliis per Capt. Woodwell & Copie per Capt. Aithen"

---

[2] Joseph Turrell, Jr., clerk of the court in Massachusetts, was indicted as a Royalist in July 1776 along with John Erving and Stephen Greenleaf. NEH&GR, XXX (1876), 442; XIV (1860), 149–51.

18th May 1744

TO JOHN ERVING
Boston

Charles Town, 18th May 1744

SIR:

I Did my self the Pleasure to write you per this Conveyance of Yesterday & have just now your very acceptable favours of the 15th April per Capt. Watson & Observe the Contents. I duely take notice of the News you are so good as to Communicate. We had much the Same by a Ship with a Good Passage from London now near a Month agoe, & which makes as yet no alteration in any thing here, excepting it may be in Pitch, there being a Great demand for it which Raises the Price. West India Rum is Offer'd at 12/6 per Gallon & Cannot gett more for your Rum than 10/ or 10/6 per Gallon which is very Low, it being a Glutt here & no Likelyhood of being better for Some time. Bills of Exchange I find are not wanted at Present on Boston & Mr. Perroneau[3] just now having Occasion for to Remitt £723.10/ this Currency, have given him a Sett of Bills on your Good Self for £570.10/ Currency of N. England, Exchange at 25 per Cent, payable at 30 days Sight [730] to the Order of Messrs. Ebenezer Newell, Senior & Ebenezer Newell, Junior[4] which are to be forwarded by Your *Thistle*, & doubt not will meet with due Honour.

Capt. Aithen presents his best Respects. This Goes by a Vessell of Salem that Came for Freight, but not having Obtain'd any Returns to Boston with what Freight Offerr'd. In haste I Most Respectfully Remain &c.

ADDRESSED: "Per Ditto Woodwell & Copie per Capt. Aithen"

---

[3] Henry Peronneau, wealthy Charleston merchant of Huguenot ancestry, married Elizabeth Hall 30 July 1728. He died in 1755. Alexander Peronneau, brother of Henry, married Mary Pollock in the Congregational Church in Charleston. He died in 1774. *SCHM*, V (1904), 218–220; XII (1911), 30, 217; XIII (1912), 25; XXXIV (1933), 214.

[4] Ebenezer Newell was a partner in the Land Bank of 1740. He signed a petition as a subscriber of the Parish at Roxbury to change the psalm version used from the New England to the Tate and Brady. In 1750 Capt. Ebenezer Newel was listed as a settler in Brookfield. *NEH&GR*, III (1849), 132–133; XX (1866), 160; L (1896), 310.

18th May 1744

TO THOMAS HUTCHINSON & THOMAS GOLDTHWAIT
Boston

Charles Town, 18th May 1744

GENTLEMEN:

My last to you was of the 30th Ulto., since have your Favours of the 6th ditto Via Winnyaw & Observe the Contents. Since my Last have gott your ship *Thomas* fitted out & Ready for the Sea in Order to proceed on her Voyage to Hamburg according to your Directions with her full Loading of Logwood of which she is very full, & has not been Touch'd here, & the Ship is now in the Road Wind Bound, Capt. Palmer having been pritty Brisk in getting her Ready for the Sea. Her Outsett has been pretty Considerable altho' nothing has been bought, or Lay'd out on her, but what Capt. Palmer told me was absolutely necessary.

As I Advis'd you in my last, shall according to your Directions Draw on Messrs. Samuel Storke & Son in London One Hundred Pounds Sterling for the Salvage paid the Captors, &c. And I have already advis'd said Gentlemen thereof & doubt not You'll give directions to them that my Bills may meet with due Honour as the One Eight part Salvage (Court Charges which run high) & Outsett of the Ship Come to a Considerable Sum for which am not in Cash for you, and by next Opportunity Shall Transmitt you account of the Appraisment & the whole Charge attending the Ship. I have according to your Directions also advis'd said Messrs. Storke & Son that you Desire them to make Insurance on said Ship *Thomas* & Cargoe on your Accounts, Six Hundred Pounds Sterling at & from this to Hamburg, & at Sametime I took Notice to them that as I have late advice from my Brother in London that the Price of Logwood had advanc'd to £6.15/ per Ton & was Rising, therefore it was my Opinion that the Ship *Thomas* and Cargoe is worth £1,000 Ster. provided it is your Sentiments & Intention that said Ship & Cargoe may be fully Insur'd especially as there is very Great Likelyhood of a War with France which I Mention'd for his Government.

Have also as you Direct address'd the Ship *Thomas* & Cargoe to Messrs. Halsey & Hanbury in Hamburg. Capt. Palmer Intends to Goe North about where he will be more Safe from the Enemy, as you have Order'd him. Freight has Fallen very much here of Late. It has been Offerr'd at 40/ per Ton for London & Cannot be Obtain'd even at that. I Remain Most Respectfully &c.

18th May 1744

P. S. I have Desir'd Joseph Turell, Junior to pay into you on my Account Thirteen Pounds 3d this Currency being Ballance of Account over Remitted him in Rice by this Conveyance on Account of his Father Capt. Turell, for which Please to Credit me Accordingly.

ADDRESSED: "Per Capt. Woodwell & Copie per Capt. Aithen"

[731]
TO SAMUEL STORKE & SON
London

Charles Town, 30th May 1744

GENTLEMEN:

The last I did my self the Pleasure to write you was of the 7th Current with Copie Desiring you to make Insurance of £600 or £1,000 Sterling on the Ship *Thomas* and Cargoe, Capt. George Palmer, Commander at & from this to Hamburg by Order & on Account of Messrs. Hutchinson and Goldthwait of Boston. Said Ship Sail'd from this the 25th Current, After being detain'd sometime in the Road by Contrary Winds & hope you will soon hear of her arrival at Hamburg.

I am Now to advise you that agreeable to my former I have of this Date Drawn a Sett of Bills of Exchange on you for One Hundred Pounds Sterling payable at forty Days Sight to the Order of Mr. John Watsone, agent for His Majestys Ship *Rose*, Capt. Thomas Frankland, Commander being for Salvage for the said Ship and Cargoe on Account Messrs. Hutchinson and Goldthwait which doubt not will meet with due Honour, & which You'll please to Charge to their Account accordingly.

Inclos'd is a Letter for Messrs. Halsey and Hanbury, Merchants in Hamburg which youll Please be so good as to Forward them per First. I have not further to Offerr at Present & I am with very great Respect &c.

ADDRESSED: "Per His Majestys Ship *Scarburough*, Capt. Tucker"

30th May 1744

TO ANDREW PRINGLE
London

Charles Town, 30th May 1744

SIR:

The last I did my self the Pleasure to write you was of the 7th Current with Copie, & Since have not any of your Favours. Since my Last have Receiv'd of David Caw the Ballance of his Account with William Caw being £183.10.9 Ster. and Inclos'd please Receive George Seaman his Bill of Exchange for One Hundred and Twenty four Pounds Ster. on Mr. James Crokatt payable to my Order at Two Months Sight, Exchange at £700 per £100 Sterling and to your good self Indors'd which doubt not will be duely honour'd being in part of said Ballance of Account Receiv'd of David Caw. The Ballance still Remaining due after deducting the Charges and my Commission being £349.5.6 this Currency which shall ship in Deer Skins or Silver as Shall judge most advantageous in Case no Bill of Exchange can be Obtain'd for Same. As I advis'd in my Last I have given David Caw my Bond of Indemnity against Messrs. Moore and Hurthwait their Debt for £217.10 Sterling. They Charge David Caw to Refund to them the money. In case he is Oblidg'd to pay them after being Sued & Oblidg'd to it by Law, which youll please have Regaurd to & take Care not to part with the Money or to make a Dividend of it, but keep it in your hands, unless you have Security given you to be Refunded in Case Said Caw is Oblidg'd to pay Moore & Hurthwait as they have sent a Power of Attorney to Sue him for it here.

I have of this Date drawn a Sett of Bills of Exchange for £100 Ster. on Messrs. Samuel Storke & Son in London payable to John Watsone who is Capt. Frankland's agent by Order & on Account of Messrs. Hutchinson & Goldthwait being for Salvage of the Ship *Thomas*, Loaded with Logwood, Claim'd by me, & Recover'd for them in Our Court of Admiralty, as mention'd in my Last, & which doubt not will meet with due Honour. Said Ship Sail'd a Few days agoe for Hamburg address'd by their Order [732] to Messrs. Halsey & Hanbury there. The Charge I have paid out on Said Ship here Comes to upwards of £2,000 Currency.

I am to Acquaint you that Our Generall Assembly have Yesterday pass'd a Tax Bill[5] very pernicious & Injurious to Trade, done in a very

---

[5] The "tax law" was the revival of a 1734 statute that placed an additional duty on Madeira (£4 per pipe), rum (5d per gal.), molasses (2d per gal.), flour (2/6 per bbl.), Muscovado sugar (2/6 per ct.), clay'd sugar (5/ per ct.). The duties were to

30th May 1744

arbritary manner, & doubt not when it becomes to be known at Home may make some noise, especially as Goods Imported are thereby Lyable to pay Duty or Tax three or Four severall ways before any profitt or Returns can be made which Greatly affects the Interest of British Subjects Trading here who reckon themselvs a free People & not Subject to such Arbritary Taxes at Home, much Less ought to be Suffer'd in new Collonies or Plantations. For your better Idea thereof I have Inclos'd sent you a Copie of the Oath we are oblidg'd to take by this Law which is Levell'd interily against the Trading People of this Town & which no Trading Person can Clearly swear to. We have Petition'd the Governour against it, as soon as we heard the Nature of it (who is very partial in the Affair, & seems very obsequious to the Country members of assembly who are the Majority, on Account of his Sallary, they have given him £600 Ster. this year, which in a Great measure is to Come out of Trading Peoples Pocketts, & them only). With much adoe we obtain'd a hearing before the Governour by a Lawyer against the Bill, but he Rejected all Our Arguments & by his Conduct & Behaviour to us, when all before him in the Council Chamber, it appears he is no Friend to Trade & am affraid he wont answer Our Good Expectation of him. The Merchants here intend to apply Home to the King & Council by an Agent or agents to be apply'd to in Order to have the Law Repeal'd, tho it will take place Instantly & we shall be affected by it this Year before Redress can be Obtain'd. This Present Law (We have good reason to apprehand) being only a Prelude or Introduction for Our Assembly to Tax & Cramp the Trading Interest for the future more & more. Beleive every person here in Trade will write to their Friends at Home about said Tax Bill.

We have no Ships from London since Capt. Mackenzie & no word as yet of Capt. Douglas. Freight has been offer'd for London at 40/ per Ton & no Shippers. Severall Vessels have been Oblidg'd to goe up the Freshes, & yet Pitch has advanc'd from 35/ to 45/ per bbl. & Rice from 30/ to 35/ per Ct. there being severall Large Charter'd Ships here, & there not being likely to Turn out so Large a Crop as was at First Imagin'd, but little as it is said Remaining unexported. Seventy Two Thousand Barrels being already Exported from this Port & upwards.

As I have had a pritty deal of Business lately on my hands, I find it will be impracticable for me to See you this Season as I hoped before it

---

be in effect for seven years. Nicholas Trott, *The Laws of the Province of South Carolina* (Charleston, 1736), Part II: "The Temporary Laws," II, 56–57. For the laws passed 29 May 1744 see *Statutes*, III, 629.

is too Late to Goe off, & indeed no Good Opportunity of a Ship Offers to goe in So I must Remain Content till next Year if it Pleases God.

We hear from Antigua that Capt. Warren takes all the French Vessels he meets with, & had already Carri'd in Eight Sail there.

This Goes by his Majestys Ship *Scarbourgh*, Capt. Tucker,[6] Commander who call'd off this Barr from Jamaica to take what Shipping are goeing for England under Convoy. Mr. Abercromby Goes passinger in said Ship. He has not so much as ever askt Me if I had a Letter for you. These Gentlemen in Posts & Places behave quite diferent here to what they doe to you in London & think themselvs all very Great Men here. My Wife joyns in best Respects & I Remain most Affectionatly &c.

P. S. The Guinea Traders especially will be Greatly Affected by our Tax Bill. Mr. Seaman has advis'd Mr. Crokatt of his draft on him for £124 Sterling.

[733] A Postcript to the afore goeing Letter. The Chief motive for Our Application at Home against the Tax Bill will be that Our Governour may have a Particular Injunction not to pass any Bills for the future that may be Injurious to the Trade of Great Britain and this Province, & some are of Opinion that he has no Such an Instruction, but takes no notice of it, therefore such Intructions ought to be made Known to Trading People.

ADDRESSED: "Per His Majestys Ship *Scarburough* & Copie per Mr. Osmond"

---

[6] Capt. Thomas Tucker, commander of the hospital ship *Scarbourgh*. SCG, 21 May 1744.

30th May 1744

TO HUGH MCDANIEL[7]
Boston
Charles Town, 30th May 1744

SIR:

    I received a Letter in your behalf from Mr. Thomas Kilay Inclosing James and William Wright[8] their bond for £160 also John Davis his Account, Ballance £62.1.8 Currency of new England with your Letter of Attorney to Recover same & which Capt. Boutin has proved. Said three persons are here. I have acquainted them of your power of Attorney to me to Demand & Recover from them the money. They all acknowledge their debt but tell me that at present there are not able to Discharge the same, & desire to have time allowed them. Inclosed please Receive a Letter from James Wright who keeps A Store for a Person in the Country to which Refer you. His Brother William Wright Lives in town & works at his Trade. As for John Davis he is master of a small Coasting vesell employed to Carry Rice, Pitch, &c. to town. It is my opinion it will be proper to allow them some time rather than to Sue them as it might not answer the end, they being all as I am informed but in Low Circumstances.

    You may depend upon all the Service I am Capable of in the affair on the Recommendation of my Good friend Mr. John Erving, & I am, Sir, your most Humble Servant

ADDRESSED: "Per Capt. Aithen & Copie per Capt. Batchelder"

TO THOMAS HUTCHINSON & THOMAS GOLDTHWAIT
Boston
Charles Town, 1st June 1744

GENTLEMEN:

    The preceeding on the other side of the 18th past is Copie of my last, since none of your Favours. Your ship *Thomas*, Capt. Palmer, sail'd

---

[7] Hugh McDaniel of Boston. RPC, p. 735.

[8] William Wright was working as a silversmith in Charleston before 1740. His shop was on Tradd Street opposite Mr. Savage's store. But Wright did not prosper and after 1751 was not heard of again in Charleston. Burton, pp. 198–200; Cohen, p. 54.

1st June 1744

over the Barr the 25 Ultimo for Hamburg & all well on board after having lain ten days in the Road Wind Bound & hope will have a Good passage. I have drawn a Sett of Bills of Exchange for One hundred pounds Sterling on Messrs. Samuel Storke & Son of London on your account as you Directed for Salvage, &c. of the said Ship & which doubt not you have Before Given them advice to Honour. I intended to have sent an account of the whole Charges on the Ship per this Conveyance but there are severall small Bills on the Ships account that Capt. Palmer did not gett in before he went, otherwise you might Have expected it accordingly as I intended to send the whole together & which will amount to upwards of £2,000 this Currency. The appraisment of the Ship & Cargoe being £4,887.10/ Currency, having with a pretty deal of trouble obtain'd a Second apraisement after the Ship was Decreed to be Restored to the Owners, the first Appraisement being amount to £6,672.10/ Currency, they having Overvalued the ship as also the Quantity of Loggwood on Board.

One of Capt. Palmers Seamen broke his Arm when the Ship was Going down to the Road so he was obliged to leave him in sick [734] Quarters at the ships Charge till his arm is well as he Cannot be admitted a Charge on the publick. No word as Yet of the Scooner you mentioned. Have had two Vessells on my hands to dispatch with Rice but have not been able to procure any for the Scooner, there being but very little for sale, a Great many of the planters not careing to Sell it at the Low price it has been & keep it up and wont send it to town in expectation of a much better price for it. As pitch has lately advanced from 35/ to 50/ per bbl., so they Imagine Rice must also Rise & has got to 35/ per Ct. & none can be purchased under & Likely to be higher being very Scarce neither any Likely Hood of its being Lower this Season. When your Scooner arrives you may depend on my Given her all the Dispatch can be Desired & hope no accident has happened to her.

West India Rum is imported daily so that I am afraid that N. England rum will meet with a very dull & tedious sale. When West India rum is plenty & Cheap here N. England rum wont sell at any rate.

I have given over thoughts of Going for London this summer as I some time agoe intended. I have not Further to offer at present as being without any of your favours, & I remain most respectfully &c.

ADDRESSED: "Per Capt. Aithen & Copie per Capt. Batchelder"

2nd June 1744

TO JOHN ERVING
Boston

Charles Town, 2nd June 1744

SIR:

The preceeding of the 18th Ulto. is Copie of my Last, And this per your Snow *Thistle*, Capt. Henry Aithen, which is Compleatly Loaded, Clear'd out, & ready to Sail, and Inclos'd please Receive Bill of Lading & Invoice of Four Hundred & Two Barrells of very Good Pitch & Two Hundred & Twelve bbls. Rice Ship'd on Board your said Snow for Boston on your proper Risque & Account & to your Good Self Consign'd, Amount as per Invoice being £2,678.8.2 this Currency which wish safe to hand and to a Good Markett. Was oblidg'd to Ship more Rice than you Order'd to Dispatch the Vessel for want of Pitch, there being none to be had being all bought up & perhaps Could not have procured 100 or 200 Barrells more for this Month or Two to Come, there being still a Great Demand for Pitch as also now for Rice, Pitch being advanc'd to 50/ per Barrell & Rice is now at 35/ per Ct. & begins to be pritty Scarce. Have been oblidg'd to pay ready Cash down for both Pitch and Rice as soon as Deliver'd otherways Could not be Obtain'd. You'll observe both are at Different Prices, having rise from time to time before could be purchas'd, & some that had Vessels here before Capt. Aithen arriv'd are still buying & oblidg'd to give 50/ for Pitch & 35/ per Ct. for Rice. Hope both Rice & Pitch will be to Content being very Good in Quality. There is no ordinary or Old Rice at Present to be purchas'd, & if there was it would not Come for Less than the Good, unless it is sometimes Small parcells fitt only for the West Indies.

Please also Receive Inclos'd Account Sales of your Rum, Neat Proceeds being £701.4.0 which turns to a very poor Account, but there is no Likelyhood of its being better for a Considerable Time, & if it was to have Layen all the Summer perhaps might not bear a Better price in the Fall, a Great deal of West India Rum daily arriving & when it is plenty & Cheap N. England [735] Rum wont Sell at any Rate. Have not as yet dispos'd of any of the Axes, this not being the Season that they are Saleable. As we hear nothing as yet of a French War & no Danger between this & Boston did not think it needfull to write to Mr. Hodshon in London for Insurance.

I have Receiv'd a power of Attorney from Mr. Hugh McDaniel against three Persons here who are Indebted to him. I have writt him about Same

9th June 1744

by this Conveyance, & beleive it will be a Considerable Time before the money Can be Recover'd, they being all in Low Circumstances. You have also Inclos'd Capt. Aithen's Receipt for Money paid him here for the Ship's use £145.5.0 Currency, also Your Account Current, Ballance in my favour being £1,125.10.9 Currency for which there is no Opportunity of Valueing on You there being none here at Present that want to Remitt to Boston.

Have sent by Capt. Aithen a Small Barrell of Rice which youll Please to make Acceptable & my Wife desires Mrs. Erving to Accept of Two Red Birds.[9] Was in hopes to have sent some Turtle but none has arriv'd since your Snow has been here.

My Wife has had the Missfortune to Misscarry Lately, & is at Present in the Country for her Health, otherways wou'd have done her Self the Pleasure to have writt Mrs. Erving by Capt. Aithen, to whom please my humble Service & to all the pritty Young Ones. Capt. Aithen is just agoeing & hope will Soon be with you, So that I add not at Present but that I Most Respectfully Remain &c.

ADDRESSED: "Per Capt. Aithen & Copie per Capt. Batchelder"

TO ANDREW LESSLY
Antigua

Charles Town, 9th June 1744

SIR:

I have your Esteemed favours of the 29th February in Return to mine of the 14th January and since my last have been Oblidg'd to pay our Attorney Generall Three Guineas before Could have our Bond per the *Loyall Judith* Delivered up. If it had been Put in Suit (which he Certainly might as a Certificate was not return'd) it would have been a Considerable Charge for Retaining Fees to defend it even altho' he could not have Recovered the penalty. It is the first that I have been put to

---

[9] The Eastern cardinal was the best-known of the Carolina birds. It was noted for "a beautifully clear, melodious whistle" and brilliant plumage. It was a popular cage bird. *HL*, I, 79n.

9th June 1744

any Charge about, & I am not Singular, a Great many persons in Trade here have been obliged to pay often & more Considerably & altho there may be no such practice with you, doe assure you what I advise is Matter of Fact here. We are informed your Crop is like to prove pretty good tho late which am Glad off. We have no material News here. I add not at Present but that I most Respectfully Remain &c.

ADDRESSED: "Per Capt. John James"

[736]
TO DAVID GLEN
    London

Charles Town, 11th June 1744

SIR:

I hope this shall find you and Familly in good Health. I have not had Occasion for anything in your way for a Consdierable time past neither any Cloaths from London since the last I had from you. I am now to desire that as soon as this comes to your hand You'll be so Good as to gett made for me and deliver to my Brother to be Shipt per first Opportunity: A suit of Cloaths for my Own Ware, Vizt. Coat Jackett and two pair of Breeches, the Cloath to be of the best Super fine Broad Cloth of a Grave Fashionable Colour, not a heavey thick Cloth, & Mounted with the best plain Mohair or Hair Buttons of the same Colour full made & full trimm'd, & lin'd with the best & strongest Mazarine[1] Blue Alapine. Pray let the Suit be full made & fashionable & according to the Measure here Inclos'd for your Guidance & Directions (the Last Cloaths you sent me were too short & Scanty). Let the work be all very neat & the Body of the Jackett lin'd with Garlix as also the Breeches & but two pocketts lind also with Garlix, & a Fobb to each of the Breeches, & doubt not all the Furniture will be of the best of the Kind & every thing Charg'd at the Lowest Rate. Pray Let them be put up in a Box, & put some spare Buttons & some of the Cloth & Lining up with it, for perhaps they cannot be match'd here if any should be wanted, which hope You'll not Neglect, & Send me an Account of the whole with them.

[1] Mazarine is a deep rich blue.

11th June 1744

I hope to have the pleasure of Seeing you in London next Spring, which I intended this summer, but my affairs doe not permitt till it will be too late in the Season to goe, & if I doe not Come in the Spring as I intend, You may however depend on having the Money Remitted you by that Time for the Cloaths. Please present my best Respects to Mrs. Glen & I am &c.

P. S. I hope You'll send the Cloaths with all the Dispatch you can that I may have them here by Winter.

ADDRESSED: "Under Cover of A.P. & 2 Copies per Capt. Mackenzie & Capt. Ayers"

TO ANDREW PRINGLE
London

Charles Town, 11th June 1744

SIR:

My last was of the 30th Ulto. per his Majestys Ship *Scarburough* with Copies thereof to which please be Refferr'd, Since have not any of your Favours neither any Ships from England. We are anxious to know whether a French war is Declar'd of which we are very Apprehensive, as having no Ships for sometime. This Goes by the Opportunity of Mr. James Osmond Via Topsham who goes home with his Wife & three Children in Familly to settle for Good at Exeter. You may Remember he was a member of Our Club[2] when you was Last here & Goes off the Province with a Good Fortune gott with a Fair Character, being a very Good sort of a Man. I have told him you would be very Glad to keep a Friendly Correspondance with him & to Render him any agreeable Service in London where he intends A Trip to the next Spring. He has ap-

[2] It is not certain to which "Club" RP was referring. In its early years, the St. Andrew's Society was called a "club." RP was elected a member of that organization in 1736 or 1737, but Osmond's name does not appear on its rolls. The "club" could have been any one of a number of small groups which flourished in the city during this period, but of which there is little or no record extant. J. H. Easterby, *History of the St. Andrew's Society* (Charleston, 1929), p. 21; *Rules of the St. Andrew's Society* (Charleston, 1892), p. 31.

11th June 1744

pointed Capt. Othniel Beale his Attorney and is to be Concern'd with his Partner Mr. Binford & him in Trade to this Province.

I am at the Desire of my Friend Mr. John Beswicke, Merchant here to Acquaint you that his Kinsman Mr. Thomas Beswicke who Goes Passanger in Capt. McKenzie for London has been prosecuted by our Chief Justice, Mr. Whitaker with a Great deal of Rigour & has Layen a Considerable Time Confin'd in Jail & with much to doe admitted to Bail in a very Considerable Sum of Money to be allowed to goe to London, there to appear at the Kings Bench Barr next Michaelmass Term in October next. And all the Crime & Offence that is alledg'd against him (is upon the Oath of a Sailor) that when he was Lieutenant of One of our Country Gallies & went with a Flagg of Truce to Carry Prisoners to St. Augustine about a Year agoe, an Old Negroe Fellow & some dry goods on Board had been Sold to the Spainards. It is Thought by a Great many persons here in Trade that he has been very Cruelly & Ridgidly us'd by our Chief Justice & it is to be hop'd that the Gentlemen in Trade at Home will befriend Mr. Beswicke in the Affair & doe him any Service they Can, as it is thought it will not be taken any Notice of & he will be Discharg'd. Mr. Beswicke has spoke to all his Friends to write to their Friends in London in his Kinsman's behalf, having been thrown out of Business thereby, & put to a Great deal of Trouble & Charge. Mr. John Beswicke Imagines that the Cheif Justice his Severity to his Kinsman proceeds from a Resentment he has to him, Mr. Beswicke having married Lately one of Mr. Richard Hill's Sisters & Neice to the Chief Justice Contrary it Seems to his Inclinations tho' all her other Relations were for the Match.[3] Mr. Beswicke & I have had pritty Considerable Dealings togither & who bears a Good Character here & is Considerably Concern'd in Trade & doubt not You'll be so good, as to take some Notice of his Kinsman & doe him any Good Offices in your way.

As I have now given over thoughts of Seeing you this Summer as it would be too Late in the Season before I could goe, tho' hope early next Spring if it pleases God, I am to desire the Favour you'll be so good as to send me the Inclos'd assortment of Books of Accompts & Stationary, &c. being for my Own use the Town being unsorted at Present, and there are few or none of any of those things to be had here at Present. A pretty many articles are wanted in Town being scarce and Dear in particular

---

[3] John Beswicke had married Mary Hill, sister of Richard Hill. *SCHM*, IV (1903), 233.

21st June 1744

Loaf Sugar, Tea, China Ware, & if a French War happens all sort of Dry Goods it is Thought will be scarce & Dear.

I am also to pray the Favour you'll please after perusal to Seal & Deliver the Inclos'd Letter for David Glen my Taylor being for a Suit of Cloaths, not having had any Cloaths made here but One Suit since I had the Last from him in 1738 or 1739, and there is no good Cloth or Furniture to be had here, & the workmanship very bad. I have sent Inclos'd my measure for his Guide & if he should be Dead You'll please to employ who ever you Think proper.

The Commander of his Majestys Ship *Scarborough* Declin'd letting Mr. Abercrombie & one Alexander Murray[4] who is Our Naval Officer have their passage with him, & they now goe with Capt. Campbell[5] who was sent here from Virginia to Mr. Reid by his Brother. My Wife joyns in best Respects, & having not further to Offerr at Present as being without any of your Favours, I Remain most truely &c.

ADDRESSED: "Per James Osmond Via Topsham & Copies per Capt. Mackenzie & Campbell"

[738]
TO JAMES BLOUNT
Edentown, North Carolina

Charles Town, 21st June 1744

SIR:

I am much surpriz'd that I have not heard from you for a Considerable time past, & that you have not by some means or other taken care to Discharge your Bond Long before this, it being now two Years agoe since you had the Goods. The Last I writt you was of the 18th January by one Mr. Houston for your Town, but since not a Word from you. Mr. Pilkington of Bath town writes me that he saw you in October last & that you told him that you Design'd for this Place this Spring. I am

[4] On 28 September 1746, Alexander Murray, Naval Officer of Charleston, was buried. He died of a fever at the age of 32 after a short illness. *SCHM*, XXVI (1925), 28.
[5] Capt. William Campbell, ship *George*, to London. *SCG*, 11 June 1744.

in hopes youll now very soon Discharge your Bond, if you have not already made Remittance for Same to my Brother in London, as I take you to be an Honest Man, & not oblidge me to take any measures that may not be agreeable to you or my Self. Pray have you heard of Capt. Dickinson Lately or where he is. I have not heard from him for sometime, neither has he yet Discharg'd his Bond. This Goes by one Mr. William Stephens who has lately come from your Parts with Horses & Returns again, & hope to have a Speedy answer from You to this & to my Satisfaction in Expectation of which I Remain &c.

P. S. We have very dry weather at Present, & if we have not Rain very soon will occasion a Scarcity of Corn in the Province.

ADDRESSED: "Per William Stevens"

TO JOHN DICKINSON
Beaufort Town, North Carolina

Charles Town, 21st June 1744

SIR:

I writt you the 30th September last to Corse sound and since had your Letter from St. Kitt's advising that you would be here by Christmass, but since have heard nothing from you neither any Remittances in Order to Discharge your Bond now so Long due. If this finds you at Corse Sound, hope youll take some measures to Discharge Your Bond very Speedily as you may be sensible it has been now a Long time due & not Oblidge me to take any measures that may not be agreeable to you or to my Self and as I take you to be an Honest Man, doe not think, as I was so generous as to Trust you tho a Stranger, that you would take my Goods without you were determind and in a Capacity to pay for them. And if you think proper to send a Cargoe of Pork, Tallow, Myrtle Wax, Pitch, Tarr, Turpentine, am willing to take it of you on my own Account & pay the Duty here for them so that you may soon have an opportunity to discharge your Bond that way. This goes by a Person from your Parts with

21st June 1744

Horses & who Returns again and hope to have a Speedy answer from you to this, & to my Satisfaction, in Expectation of which I Remain &c.

P. S. We have very dry weather here at Present, & if we have not Rain very soon will Occasion a Scarcity of Corn in the Province.

ADDRESSED: "Per William Stevens"

TO SETH PILKINGTON
Bath Town, North Carolina

Charles Town, 21st June 1744

SIR:
  I have your Favours of the 17th May, by the Bearer Mr. William Stephens with his Receipt for a Stallion, but have no Occasion for him at Present or the Gelding which I told Mr. Yeomans, as you mention'd in your Letter & which I show'd him, but he refuses to take up your Note & paying the Money, & tells me if he Sells all the Horses he will give you Credit for them, but will not Discharge your Note out of them, so hope You'll Order payment thereof Some other way Soon. As for the Gelding you mention I think him Dear at £100 this Currency, & if I was to take him & pay Mr. Yeomans £60 & Sell him, he would not fetch more than £60 or £70 this Currency at most. I am much oblidg'd to you for your advices in Relation to Capt. McDowall. You'll please to Observe that upon looking into his Account Deliver'd you (& Copie of which please Receive Inclos'd, Amount £140.17.8 this Currency) I say youll find that he has Credit there for £39.10/ for the Two Casks of Tobacco sent here & in my Letter to him Deliver'd you, You'll please to take notice that I by said Letter Revoke My Power of Attorney to Mr. Clarke, & upon Capt. McDowalls paying the Money to you it shall be a Sufficient & full Discharge to him, & Desire that Mr. Clarke may deliver up his Note, & may be paid by him what Charge he may have been at, if any. And as to an Abatement on the Interest, if he Requires it, I Entirely leave it to you to make him what allowance You judge proper, tho' think as he has keept me so long out of my Money, it is but Reasonable that he

ought to pay Lawfull Interest. However I am to Desire the Favour You'll be so good as to Settle with him in the Best manner you can, & for which shall be Greatly oblidg'd to You, & be always very Glad to have it in my Power to Retaliate your Favours.

I have not heard from Mr. Blount of Edentown since my Last to you, neither has he been here this Spring as he told You. I intimated to Mr. Brunett[6] what you mention Relating to Capt. Lipelly, who thinks him Guilty of the highest ingratitude as he advanc'd the Money for him out of his Pockett, & thereby freed him from the Common Jail where he was Confin'd, & as Mr. Brunett has no Friend or Acquaintance in your parts, & you were so Good as to Accept of the Papers, he hopes You'll still be so kind as to doe him what Service you can (if not too much Trouble) in Order to Recover his Money of said Lepelley, if he is in a Capacity to pay, & if he was to write Mr. Brunett & to show his Intentions are Honest, but that he is not in a Condition at Present; Mr. Brunett would be very willing to indulge him & be easie by giving him a Longer time if he Requires it, & acknowledge the Debt.

We have advices of the Intended Expedition from the Havannah to Invade Georgia or this Province or both, & as we hear of a very Considerable Force to Come. Shall be always very Glad to hear from you, and to Render you any acceptable Service & I am &c.

P. S. Pray advise me if you know one Capt. John Dickinson that Lives at Corse Sound & if he is there now he is master of a Sloop. We have very Dry Weather here at Present & if we have no Rain very soon, will Occasion a Scarcity of Corn in this Province.

ADDRESSED: "Per William Stevens"

---

[6] Although there was an Isaiah Brunet in Charleston at this time, RP undoubtedly meant "Burnett" as he had written earlier to Pilkington about Henry Burnet, a carpenter. See RP to Seth Pilkington, 8 September 1742.

[740]
TO RICHARD ROWLAND
    St. Kitts

Charles Town, 26th June 1744

Sir:

I have your most Esteem'd favours of the 26th March last with Inclos'd John Dickinson's Bond & Note Return'd me, and am Greatly Oblidg'd to you for your Goodness and Readiness to Serve me in Said Affair, & if he shou'd happen to your Island, hope you'll be so kind as to Serve him or his Effects, and upon advice from you (if Occasion be) will immediatly Transmitt you his Bond and Note. And am to Desire youll be so Good as not to Sufferr him to goe off the Island without Securing my Debt. I am Sorry the Trade between your Island and this is not more Encouraging. Shall be always very Glad to embrace every Opportunity of holding a Friendly Correspondance with you, & to Render you any acceptable Service. We have Receiv'd Information of another Expedition Intended this Summer from Hananna against Georgia or this Province. I Salute you and am Most Respectfully &c.

Rice 30/ per Ct., Corn 12/6 per Bu., Rum 17/6 per Gal.

ADDRESSED: "Per Capt. Mulryne Via Mountserrat & Copie"

TO HENRY & JOHN BROCK
    Guernsey

Charles Town, 28th June 1744

Gentlemen:

I have your much esteem'd favours of the 24th March per your Sloop *Ann Galley*, Capt. Mathew Bernard, who arriv'd here the 23d Current, & it is with much Concern that I have to Acquaint you that your said ship has happened to arrive here in the worst time of the Year that she possibly could have Come, there being no Freight to be obtain'd at Present at any Rate, far less at Your Limitation of £5 per Ton which at the

28th June 1744

highest did not atain to that in all the Season of Shipping off. The highest Freight to London being at £4 per Ton, & to Holland at £4.10/ per Ton & of late Freight has been Offerr'd at 50/ per Ton for Holland or Hamburg and could not be obtain'd. Neither is there at Present any Pitch or Tar to be purchas'd, it having of Late been all Bought up & Exported, there having been a Considerable Demand for Naval Stores for these Two Months past on Account of the War with France[7] & which has Occasion'd the Prices, especially of Pitch, to advance Considerably & there will be none ready for Markett till two or three months hence. So that there is nothing to be done with your *Ann Galley* at Present, & must be oblidg'd to goe up one of our Fresh Rivers for Two Months to be free from the Worms or Hurricanes & where she will Lye at a Small Charge, as Provisions are Cheap and Plenty. And if any Likelyhood of obtaining a Freight at Five Pounds according to your Directions will not fail to embrace it. If not shall Load her with Pitch and Tar according to your Orders & take the Captains Bills on You which doubt not will be Duely Honour'd.

It is also with much Concern that I have to acquaint you that Capt. Bernard has the missfortune to be disorder'd in his head, and is entirely out of his sensis, in which Melancholy Condition the Mate John Falla tells me that he has been for these Six Weeks past. I have provided a Lodging for him on Shore and put him under the Care of the Best Phyician in the Place & hope in a Short time he may be Brought to the use of his Reason & Judgement. So that Mr. Falla the Mate has the whole Charge of the Ship upon him, & has gone to the Custom house & other offices to enter the Ship Inwards. It is pity that you had not been better advis'd about your ship, which ought to have been here, three or Four Months sooner in the Year, or three [741] or Four Months Later, and not at this unseasonable time of the Year when neither Freight or Goods are to be had. If Capt. Bernard had been in his Right Sensis, it would have been Impracticable for him to have purchas'd a Cargoe to Load the Ship here, as being an Intire Stranger, without applying & Valueing himself upon Some Merchant here to Supply him with Money & Purchase the Cargoe & to take his Bills on the Owners. If Capt. Peter Bailuel had been

---

[7] The declaration of war against France was proclaimed in Charleston in July with elaborate ceremonies. The declaration was read in four public places: at the end of Broad Street near the Council Chamber, in the center of the Great Market Square in Old Church Street, at Broughton's Battery, and at Granville's Bastion. SCG, 23 July 1744.

29th June 1744

at Home doubt not he woud have been able to have Disuaded you from sending the *Ann Galley* here at this Time of the Year.

There has been for these Ten Days past an Embargoe Laid here on Shipping, by reason of advices Receiv'd of an Intended Expedition at the Havanna, against Georgia or this Province.[8] You may Depend on all the Service & Good Offices I am capable of to your Ship *Ann Galley*, And shall be always very Glad to render you any acceptable Service as being with very Great Respect.

P. S. Shall be very Glad to have the Pleasure of hearing from you Via London which it is probable I may before your ship *Ann Galley* sails from this.

ADDRESSED: "Per Capt. Campbell under Cover of A.P. & Copie per Capt. Ayers"

TO GEDNEY CLARKE
Barbados

Charles Town, 29th June 1744

SIR:

The Inclos'd of the 4th May is Copie of my Last to which please be Refferr'd, & since have not the Pleasure of any of your Favours. An Embargo has been Laid on here on all Shipping since the 17th Current till this Day on Account of Advices Receiv'd of an Expedition from Havanna Intended against Georgia or this Province, but we have no Information of Late of any Certainty thereof. We imagine there is nothing in it or that it is Laid aside. Rum and Muscovado Sugar has advanc'd in Price since we had advice of a French War & Single Refined Loaf Sugar in Particular is very scarce & dear at Present. A Large Quantity could be sold off presently at 10/ per lb. this Currency. Freight will be probably high here next Crop, as we expect but few Shipping here during the War here with France, especially if any Continuance thereof.

Our Negroe Act Expires the 5th of next Month and we doe not hear

---

[8] The council on 16 June ordered the embargo to be laid and on the 29th ordered the embargo to be lifted. CO 5, 450, pp. 334, 369. The embargo was in effect from the 18th of June to the 28th. *SCG*, 20 June, 4 July 1744.

of any Negroes coming this way. The first that happen to arrive will come to a Good Markett. You'll be able to know if any Negroes are bound here as they Generally touch first at your Island. I have not further to Offerr at Present as being without any of your Favours, & I most Respectfully Remain &c.

Rum 17/6 per Gall., Muscovado Sugar £12.10/ per Ct., Madeira Wine £120 per pipe, Rice 30/ per Ct., Corn 12/6 per bu., Pork none, Shingles £4 Per Mille, Single Refin'd Loaf Sugar 10/ per lb., Double Ditto 15/ per lb., Exchange to London at £700 per £100 Ster.

ADDRESSED: "Per Capt. Kilner"

TO EDWARD PARE
    Barbados

Charles Town, 29th June 1744

SIR:

The preceeding on the other side of the 5th May is Copie of what I did my self the Pleasure to write you by your Scooner *Charming Sarah*, Capt. John Davison, which hope is safe arriv'd with you after a good passage, & since have not any of your Favours. An Embargo has been Laid on here on all Shipping since the 17 Current till this Day on Account of advice Receiv'd of an Expedition from Havanna Intended against Georgia or this Province, but as we have no Information of Late of any Certainty thereof, we Imagine there is nothing in it or that it is Laid aside. Rum and Muscovado Sugar has advanc'd in Price since we had advice of a French War, and Freight will be probably high here next Crop as we expect but few Shipping here during the War with France. Your Two Negroes are Safe arriv'd in the Island of Providence & by my next you may expect the Account Sales of them. I Cannot dispose of your Lime Juice at any Rate, there is now no manner of Demand for it here. I have not further to Offerr at Present, but that I am most Respectfully &c.

P. S. the prices of Goods as above in Mr. Clarke's Letter.

ADDRESSED: "Per Ditto Kilner"

30th June 1744

[742]
TO DAVID CHESEBROUGH[9]
Newport, Rhode Island

Charles Town, 30th June 1744

SIR:

I have the pleasure of your favours of the 9th & 10th May per the Sloop *Abigail*, Daniel Batchelder, Commander by which this goes, who arriv'd here the 20th Current & not before, Conveying Bill of Loading & Invoice of Sixty Hhds. of N. England Rum Shipt by Order & on Account of & Risque of Mr. Thomas Hutchinson of Boston, which has been Landed in tollerable good Order tho' some of the Casks appear to be verry Old which will occasion a Great deal of Cooperage, as being Subject to leake. The Rum happens to Come to a Dull Markett being verry Low at present, there being a Great deal of West India Rum Lately Imported, but as we have now a Warr with France hope it will bear a better price. Yours of the 10th May inclosing Bill of Loading & Invoice of Twenty Boxes of Soap on your own Account which have received, but Happens to be a very Dull Commodity at present, not having been able as yet to Dispose of One Box of it, and seems to be but Indiffrent in Quality & verry Soft. However you may depend on my Best Endeavours to dispose of it, in the best manner I can for your Interest and to Remitt you the Neat proceeds in Spanish Dollars or pieces of eight if to be had at 30/, or to Mr. Stephen Greenleaf in Boston as you Direct. I am to return you my thanks for your kind offers of Service and Correspondance & am Reciprochally to Assure you that I shall be verry ready to Contribute all my power towards Cultivating a Lasting & Agreeable Correspondence with you.

The Commodities usually Imported here from your Island are most in Demand in the fall of the year from the Month of October to the Month of March, & the most Saleable Commodities are Rum & Single Refin'd Loaf Sugar, a Quantity of the Last would be a verry Good article here. I could dispose of Several Tons Weight at present at 10/, being verry scarce at present and Like to Continue so for Some time as the Insurance and other Charges from Europe run now verry high.

An Embargo has been Laid here on all the Shipping since the 17th Current till this day on Account of advices received of an Expedition from

[9] David Chesebrough was a merchant in Newport, Rhode Island. *NEH&GR*, VI (1852), 191.

Havannah Intended against Georgia or this Province, but as we have no information of Late of any Certainty thereof, we Imagine that there is nothing in it or that it is Laid aside. Shall be always verry Glad to hear from you & to render you any acceptable Service, & I am most Respectfully &c.

Rum N. E. 11/6 per Gall., Ditto West India 15/, Single Refined Loaf Sugar 10/ lb., Ditto Double 15/ lb., Maderia wine £120 per pipe, Exchange to London £700 per £100 Sterling.

ADDRESSED: "Per Capt. Batchelder Via Boston & Copie per Capt. Kingsloe"

[743]
TO JOHN ERVING
    Boston

Charles Town, 30th June 1744

SIR:
    The Annexed of the 2d Current is Copie of my last per your Snow *thistle,* Capt. Aithen, who sail'd over this Barr on said Day & hope before this is safe with you, to which Please be referr'd, & since have not any of your favours.
    An Embargo has been Laid on all Shipping here since the 17th Current till this day on Account of Advices Receiv'd of an Expedetion from Havanna Intended against Georgia or this Province, but as we have no Information of Late of any Certainty thereof, we Immagine that there is nothing in it or that its Laid Aside.
    This Serves to Advise you that I have of this Date Drawn a Sett of Bills of Exchange on you for £800 Currency of New England payable To the Order of Messrs. Henry & Alexander Perroneau at 30 Days sight, Exchange at 25 per Ct. Is £1,000 this Currency which Doubt not will meet with Due honour & for which have Creditt your Account Current. Said Gentlemen Remitt the Bills to your good self As they have Likewise

30th June 1744

Loaded Capt. Barns[1] his Sloop with rice to your Address & by which this goes.

We have had no Ships from London for these two Months Past & no advices as yet of a Warr with France, but what we have had from your Parts so that the War has not yet been Declar'd here. We have had a pretty Deal of Dry Weather of Late which has Affected our Corn but the Crop of rice has a good Prospect. It is very Probable that Freight will be high next Crop as few Shipping are Expected here during a Warr with France which has made as yet no Alteration in the Prices of Goods here but Doubt not it must before Long. Rum is Still Low a great Deale has come in from the West Indies. The Only Scarce Commodity here at Present is Single Refin'd Loaf Suger has been Sold by the Quantity at 10/ per lb., there being but Little in Town at Present.

My Wife Joyns in Best Respects to your Self, good Mrs. Erving, & all the Pretty Young Ones & I most Respectfully remain &c.

ADDRESSED: "Per Capt. Batchelder & Copie per Capt. Barns & Copie per Capt. Kinsloe"

[744]
TO THOMAS HUTCHINSON & THOMAS GOLDTHWAIT
Boston

Charles Town, 30th June 1744

GENTLEMEN:

My last to you was of the 1st Current of which you have Inclos'd Copie thereof, & this per your Sloop *Abigail*, Daniel Batchelder, Master who arriv'd here the 20th Current from Rhod Island, & not before, & by whom have your Esteem'd Favours of the 27th April & duely notice the Contents. Have also a Letter from Mr. David Chesebrough there Conveying Bill of Lading & Invoice of Sixty hhds. of Rum on Account & Risque of your Mr. T. H. which has been Landed in Tolerable Good Order, 'tho some of the Casks are very old & Indifferent. Shall observe your Directions in the Disposal of same which happens to Come to a

[1] Capt. Thomas Barnes, sloop *Midnight*, arrived from Antigua. SCG, 11 June 1744.

30th June 1744

Dull Markett, as I formerly advis'd, Large Quantitys having Come in from the West Indies so that it has been sold for 10/6 per Gall. & wont fetch more than 11/6 at Present. But as we have now a French War, hope it will bear a Better Price soon. You may depend on my uttmost Endeavours to dispose of it to your best advantage.

Inclos'd please Receive Bill of Lading and Invoice of One Hundred and Twenty Barrels of Good Rice and Seventy One Barrells of Turpentine shipd on Board the said Sloop *Abigail* for Boston for Account & Risque of your Mr. T. H. & to himself Consign'd, amount as per Invoice being £1,250.3.1 this Currency, which hope will come safe to hand & to a Good Markett, the Rice being very Good in Quality considering the Season of the Year & was all ready in Store for the Sloop when she arriv'd & with which is entirely full & not capable to take one BBl. more on board. Rice has fallen since my Last, & since the Embargo has been Laid on the Shipping has been offerr'd at 30/ per Ct. but now no Buyers. An Embargo has been Laid here on all shipping since the 17th Current till this Day on Account of Advices Receiv'd of an Expedition from Havanna intended against Georgia or this Province, but as we have no Information of Late of any certainty thereof we imagine that there is nothing in it, or that it is laid aside.

I have Return'd you per the Sloop *Abigail* the Cocoa you sent per Capt. Blunt which is Included in the Bill of Lading & put in Seven bbls. for the Conveniency of Stowage. It is a perfect Drugg here. A Large Ship Loaded with Cocoa has been Carried in a Prize to Cape Fear, which has Glutted this Place with it.

I have never yet been favour'd with a Letter from Messrs. Burryau & Schaffer accknowledging any of the Remittances made them on Account of your T. H. I have not yet been able to Dispose of all the Goods shipt per Messrs. Storke & Son. Some things are but Indifferent in Quality. If instead of so much Rum you had sent a Quantity of Single Refin'd Loaf Sugar, it would have been very Good Commodity. I could now sell at this Time severall Tons Weight of it at 10/ Currency per lb., being very scarce & Little in Town & will be so for a Considerable Time. Am of Opinion that a Quantity in the fall will certainly answer very well, and the sooner you send it the Better, & it would be no bad Scheme to Contract for a Quantity as soon as you Receive this, if Reasonable with you, as I apprehend there will be a Considerable Demand for it from this Place & Orders to Buy up. The Insurance, &c. being now very high from England will make it Come dear from thence.

30th June 1744

Please Receive Inclos'd Account Sales, &c. of Sundries, Vizt. Account Sales of Rum per the *Richard*, Capt. Hallin, Neat Proceeds being £3,007 this Currency; Account Sales of a Box Ribbands per Capt. Snelling, Neat Proceeds being £369.2.6; Account Sales of Sundries Remaining on hand per Capt. Blunt, Neat Proceeds being £451.16.1; Account Sales of Eight Barrells Blubber per Capt. Blunt 2d Voyage sold at Vendue, having keept it on hand till it woud keep no longer, Neat Proceeds £15.18.11; fitting out the Ship *Thomas* for Hamburg, Amount £853.1.7, also the Account of the whole Charge in Claiming and Recovering said Ship for the Owners & [745] paying the Salvage, Amount £2,204.17.2, Ballance of your Account due me on said ship being £1,504.17.2 for which have Debit your Account Current, likewise Inclos'd Ballance in my Favour being £819 this Currency. Likewise please Receive Inclos'd your Mr. T. H. his own particular Account Current, Ballance in my favour being £1,155.9.0 this Currency, all which hope you'll find Right & which youll please to note in Conformity accordingly. Have also Inclos'd you Account of the Port Charges and Disbursements on your Sloop *Abigail*, Amount £111.6.4 this Currency.

Have sent you under the Care of Capt. Batchelder a small BBl. of Rice Markt T. H. which youll please to make Acceptable. Was in hopes of sending you a Turtle by him but none has been in the Place since the Sloops Arrival. Freight it is probable will be high here this next Crop, as few Shipping are Expected here during the War with France, & so in Course our Produce will be Low. Capt. Batchelder being Clear'd out & just agoeing, & hope will soon be with you, I add not at Present but that I most Respectfully Remain &c.

Rum N. England 11/6 Gallon, Ditto W. India 15/ per Gallon, Muscovado Sugar £12.10/ per Ct., Single Refin'd Loaf Sugar 10/ per lb., Ditto Double 12/7 per lb., Madeira Wine £120 per pipe, Canary none, Rice 32/6 per Ct., Pitch none, Tar 40/ per bbl., Turpentine 15/ per Ct., Corn 12/6 per bu.

ADDRESSED: "Per the Sloop *Abigail*, Capt. Daniel Batchelder, & Copie per Capt. Kinsloe."

TO ANDREW PRINGLE
London

Charles Town, 30th June 1744

SIR:

The Last I did myself the Pleasure to write you was of the 11th Current with Two Copies, as yet am without any of your Favours. No Ship from London since Capt. Mackenzie, & Capt. Douglas does not yet appear. Hope he has not again had the Missfortune to fall into the Hands of the Spainards, or the French. We have advices from the Northward & by a Vessel of Capt. Jolliff's by way of Pool that War has been Declar'd on both sides between Great Britain and France, which am afraid will be detrimental to this Province. We have also Receiv'd Information by way of Providence and Georgia of another Expedition intended this Summer from Havanna against Georgia or this Province, or both which has Occasion'd an Embargo to be Laid on all the Shipping here since the 17th till this Day. Our Governour Glen gives no manner of Credit to the Report of an Invasion, & will not beleive there can be anything in it, or take any pains to put the Town & Province in a Posture of Defence, altho' very much wanted. He seem'd to sett out very well when he came first Over amongst us, but now begins to loose himself not a Little.

Severall things have advanc'd in price here since the French War was known, & in particular Loaf Sugar has Rise to 10/ per lb. by the Quantity as also Tea & China Ware & Black pepper, there being but Little in Town at Present of said Articles. Mr. Hutchinson of Boston has shipt me since my last Sixty hhds. N. E. Rum on his own particular Account, but nothing yet on Account of the Goods shipt them in Company with us. I am Loading the Sloop that brought the Rum back to them with Rice per their Order. The Rum comes to a poor Markett, being very Low here at Present.

A few days agoe arriv'd here from Guernsey directly the Ship *Ann Galley*, Capt. Mathew Bernard, Commander, Burthen about 160 Tons in her Ballast in Expectation of Obtaining a Freight for Europe at Five pounds per Ton & failing of that the Capt. is Recommended to me by Messrs. Henry & John Brock of Gurnsey to have her Loaded with Naval Stores & to take the Capt.'s Bills on them for the Amount. Said Ship has Nine Owners in Gurnsey, but the three Dobrees & the Two Brocks are the Chief. [746] The Capt. Bernard, poor man, is in a fitt of Melancholy & interely out of his Sensis. Please be Refferr'd to the Inclos'd Letter that

2nd July 1744

I have writt said Gentlemen in Relation to the Capt. & Ship, which after perusal You'll please to seal and forward them to Gurnsey. The Ship must be oblidg'd to goe up the Freshes for Two or three months, there being neither a Freight nor Pitch to be had for her at Present, & Rice is now Down again to 30 / per Ct.

Several of the India Pictures you sent me per Ayers are pretty much Damag'd by being Wett, & he tells me that they Receiv'd Damage before they Came on board, being shipt in Rain. Am afraid they will prove very unsaleable, as I cannot dispose of any of them. I Intended to have made you a Remittance of some Gold by Capt. Ayers, but as I have had no Opportunity of advising for Insurance thought it not proper to Risque it. Capt. Ayers has been oblidg'd to Leave some Gold he had himself behind him. The Embargo now being taken off, all the Vessels are now hurrying to gett away, & we shall have very few Remaining here, excepting what Lye up Cooper River at Childsbury[2] where there is already Eight or Ten Sail that Lye till next Crop.

My Wife joyns in most hearty Respects and in Haste I Remain.

ADDRESSED: "Per Capt. Campbell & Copies per Capt. Ayers & Capt. Mackenzie"

TO MICHAEL LOVELL
Antigua

Charles Town, 2nd July 1744

SIR:

My last to you was of the 17th January per Capt. Webber & Since have your most esteemed favours of the 3d February, 2d March, & 9 May, the Last per Capt. Webber & Duley Remark the Contents. Mr. Robert Williams of Port Royal Did not apply to me for any money on your account otherwise would with great pleasure very Readily have Supplyed him. I had no Opportunity in the Season of sending you any hogs Lard as you desired & there is none to be had till the fall of the year when shall

---

[2] For a description of Childsbury on the Cooper River see Henry A. M. Smith, "Childsbury," *SCHM*, XIV (1913), 198–203.

2nd July 1744

take Care to send you some or any thing else that you may have Occasion for & that this province affords. I am Greatly oblidged to you for your Civilities & Good offices to Capt. Webber & shall be always verry Glad to have it in my power to Retaliate your many favours. Have not yet Quite Compleated the Sale of your Linnens. The Cambricks stick on hand being verry Course. If they had been a Better sort they had Gone off long before this. However hope soon to send your Account Sales of the Whole & shall be glad to have your Directions how the Neat proceeds is to be applyed.

An Embargoe has been Laid on all Shipping here for the fortnight past on Account of advices received of an Expedition from Havanah Intended against Georgia or this Province, but as we have no Information of late of any Certainty thereof, we Imagine that there is nothing in itt or that it is laid aside. Rum & Muscovado Sugar has advanced in price since we had advice of a Warr with france, & Loaf Sugar in particular is verry Scarce and Dear at present. A Large Quantity of Single Refind especially could be sold of presently at 10/ per lb. & 11/6 & Double Ditto at 14/ this Currency & is like to be higher.

Our Negro Act prohibiting the Importation of Negroes here Expires the 5th Instant so that it is Likely that we may have some Guinea Vessells before long.

This Goes by Mr. George Lucas, Son to your Governour, Colonel Lucas, with [747] whom have had the pleasure to Remember all absent Friends. His Sister Miss Lucas[3] was married about a fortnight agoe to the Honourable Charles Pinkney, Esqr., one of our Councill & a verry popular Gentleman here. I salute you & am most Respectfully &c.

Rum 17/6 per Gall., Muscovado Sugar £12.10 Ct., Loaf Sugar Single Refined 11/6 per lb., Double 14/, Rice 30/ per Ct., Pitch 45/ per bbl., Corn 12/6 per Bushell, Pork none, Beef none, Madeira wine £120 per

---

[3] Eliza Lucas was probably born in Antigua where her father, Lieutenant-Colonel George Lucas was stationed. He brought his family to South Carolina in the 1730's, but he returned to Antigua leaving the teen-aged Eliza in charge of the family's plantation, "Wappoo." In 1744 she married Charles Pinckney, with whom she had had a close relationship for a number of years. She is best remembered for her experiments with indigo which provided Carolina with a second cash crop prior to the revolution, but at "Wappoo" she also experimented with flax, hemp, and attempted to revive silk culture. Following Pinckney's death in 1758 she devoted the remainder of her life to her books, her garden, and her children. DAB, XIV, 616–617; *The Letterbook of Eliza Lucas Pinckney*, South Carolina Historical Society, Charleston, South Carolina, *passim*.

2nd July 1744

pipe, Shingles £4 per Mille, Exchange to London £700 per £100 Sterling.

ADDRESSED: "Per George Lucas, Junior, Esqr. in the Brigantine *Rigby Hole*, Capt. Mulryne"

TO WILLIAM PRINGLE
   Antigua

Charles Town, 2nd July 1744

SIR:
I have not had the pleasure of hearing from you for a Considerable time past. I was verry Glad of being Inform'd by Capt. Lee of your Health & Wellfare. This is purely to pay my Respects to you after so Long silence, & to assure you that I shall be always verry glad to hear from you, & to keep up a Friendly & Lasting Correspondance.

An Embargoe has been Lay'd on all Shipping here for this Fortnight past on Account of advices Received of an Expedition from Havannah Intended against Georgia or this Province, but as we have no Information of late of any Certainty thereof, we Imagine that there is nothing in it or that it is Lay'd aside. Rum & Muscovado Sugar has advanced in price since we had advice of a Warr with France, & Likely to be higher.

This Goes by Mr. George Lucas, Son to your Governour, Colonel Lucas with whom have had the pleasure to Remember all absent Friends. His Sister Miss Lucas was Married about a fortnight agoe to the Honourable Charles Pinkney, Esqr., one of our Council & a verry popular Gentleman here. I Salute you & am most Respectfully, &c.

Rum 17/6 per Gallon, Muscovado Sugar £12.10/ per Ct., Single Refind Loaf Sugar 11/6 per lb., Double Ditto 14/ per lb., Rice 30/ per Ct., Pitch 45/ per bbl., Corn 12/6 per Bushell, Pork none, Madeira Wine £120 per pipe, Shingles £4 Mille, Exchange to London £700 per £100 Sterling.

ADDRESSED: "Per George Lucas, Junior, Esqr."

9th July 1744

TO DAVID LEWIS
Havanna

Charles Town, 9th July 1744

This hope will be Deliver'd you by Capt. John Webster who goes from this for the Havanna with a Flagg of Truce[4] with the Spanish Prisoners taken in your Ship *Thomas* which had the good fortune to be Retaken by his Majestes Ship *Rose*, Capt. Frankland, Commander in four Days after you was taken and Brought in here, & I being Inform'd by Capt. Remick who was Commander of the *Thomas* Last Voyage (& who happen'd to be here) that the Ship Belong'd to my Friend Mr. Thomas Hutchinson of Boston, I enter'd a Claim in his Behalf & Recover'd the Ship & Cargoe in the Court of Admirality, Paying One Eight Part of the Value for Salvage to the Captors, which Ship I fitted out here by Mr. Hutchinsons Directions, & sent her with her Cargoe of Logwood for Hamburgh One George Palmer, Commander, sent here by Mr. Hutchinson from Boston & sail'd for thence in April.

As Capt. Webster will bring here in his Sloop all the English Prisoners he can Doubt not youll be one of the Number & have recommended you to the Spanish Leiutenant Don Gasper Ruiz (who was Commander of your Ship after taken) as also to Capt. Webster & shall be glad to see you after your Arrival here. Inclosed is a Letter for you from Mr. Thomas Hutchinson, he imagineing you might be come in here with the Ship. I wish you a good Passage here & I am &c.

ADDRESSED: "Per Capt. Webster"

---

[4] "Since our last, sail'd the Sloop *St. Andrew*, John Webster, Master, for the Havanna with a Flag of Truce, and all the Spanish Prisoners that were here." SCG, 16 July 1744. The Council ordered an advertisement for a vessel to carry the flag of truce on 30 May. John Crokatt won the bid by payment of £100 sterling. CO 5/450 pp. 309, 313–14. Public Record Office, London.

18th July 1744

[748]
TO JOHN LIVINGSTON
New York

Charles Town, 10th July 1744

SIR:

I have your favours of the 14th April, per Capt. Waddle Advising Receipt of Twenty pieces Duck, Sent you per Capt. Schermerhorne on Account of Mr. Sanders & my Brother, which doubt not youll Dispose of to their Best Advantage And Advise my Brother of same Accordingly.

Have had the Pleasure to drink to your good health with Capt. Waddle, & doe assure you what good Offices I am capable of rendering him shall not be wanting. He is gone up the Freshes with his Ship Not having been Able to Obtain a Freight for Europe & where he must Remain till our next Crop which Doubt not he has Advis'd you of. Shall be always very Glad to Render you any Agreeable Service & I am &c.

Provisions Plenty. Rice 30/ per Ct., Rum West India 17/6 per Gallon, Rum N. England 12/6, Madeira Wine £120 per pipe, Loaf Suger very scarce, Single Refin'd at 12/6 per lb. by the Quantity, Exchange to London £700 per £100 Sterling.

ADDRESSED: "Per Capt. Leacraft"

TO FLORENTIA COX
New Providence, Bahamas

Charles Town, 18th July 1744

The above of the 29 December is Copie of my Last to which Refferr, since none of your favours. I am in hopes by this you have Compleated the sale of the Small Arms which shall be glad to be Advis'd of & to have the account of same. Your answer will be much Oblidge &c.

ADDRESSED: "Per Capt. I'on"

20th July 1744

TO ANDREW PRINGLE
London

Charles Town, 20th July 1744

Sir:

My Last to you was of the 30th past with three Copies thereof to which please be Refferr'd and since have not the Pleasure of any of your Favours neither as yet any Ship from Europe excepting his Majesty's Ship *Swallow* dispatch'd to the severall Governments with the Declaration of War against France, which was proclaim'd here Yesterday, & not before.

We have now no Shipping here excepting what Lye up the Freshes, & therefore no Opportunity of making any Remittances. This goes by a Vessel that came here from Barbados and bound for Bristoll, being a Charter'd Vesell and a Stranger. I writt you in my Former about Our Tax Bill, & that the Inhabitants of this Town Intended to send Home a Remonstrance against it in order to have it Repeal'd, but since a Great many draw Back & wont subscribe to it, so that am afraid will Drop & that here will be nothing done in it, & is like all the Rest of Our Carolina affairs where People are never steady or Unanimous in any one thing. As for the Silver Mine beleive it is Come to nothing, and am inform'd is like to turn out no better a[t] Last than an Iron Mine & not worth the Charge of Carrying it on.

We have not been able as yet to Remitt the Compleat Sum of £2,000 Sterling to you, and the Other Gentlemen, who are Managers, for our Privateer, for want of Two or three more Subscribers, and none of the managers here besides my Self take any pains to Compleat the Sum propos'd by endeavouring for more Subscribers. However hope you have been able before this to procure a Good Ship for Capt. Anderson & that we may expect same here Soon, & as we have now a War with France doubt not of Getting Subscribers enough, & perhaps some Gentlemen in London may have desir'd to be Concern'd with us in Said Two Privateers, as we purpose to have a Sloop to be with the Ship. The Accounts of an Expedition from the Havannah to Invade Georgia or us is Come to nothing. It seems there was no Such Design. We have [749] lately sent a Flagg of Truce there with some Spainish Prisoners & to bring back what can be gott of Ours there.

Mr. Stead's Partner Mr. Evance has not it seems heard from Mr. Nicholson of late or had further Orders about Messrs. Hunter & Co. Ac-

20th July 1744

counts Deliver'd them that he has said nothing to me about it for Sometime past. I Tender'd to him the Ballance upon his giveing me a Proper discharge for the Accounts as Stated, which he has Declin'd doeing, & we Intend to stand by the Accounts.

A Vessel to arrive now with a Good Assortment of European Goods would sell well & for Ready Money, a pretty many articles being wanted in particular Loaf Sugar which is sold by the Hhd. at 10/, Single Refin'd & Double at 12/6 per lb., Tea, especially Green Tea, China Ware, Spices, Ozenbrigs, Superfine Broad Cloths, & furniture Suitable with a Good many other things of which there is none in Town at Present. You may now soon expect Account Sales per the *John & Isabella* & *Susannah*, this being now our Leizure Time. Tho' the season is now very Hott, We have Good Seasonable Weather for the Crop of Rice and a Great deal planted as usual, but whither it will answer the Charge of Exportation (by reason of high Freight & Insurance) this next Season is a Question.

If it had now Suited me to have gone to London this Summer would had no Opportunity & it would have been a Great Risque to have gone as Times are in Europe. When you was last here in Carolina you may Remember I gave you a Petition to Deliver to the Trustees of Georgia about Thomas Causton their Agent and Manager there, his Seizing & taking into his Own Possission my Effects sold Dobree & Harris, and who are Largely Indebted to me. Inclos'd please Receive a Copie of said Petition and my Affidavit of said Debt to which please be Refferr'd.[5] I understand said Causton is now in England having gone there as am Inform'd for Good having gott Money during his stay in Georgia, but Honestly I will not say. And please God if I gett to London next Year, Intend to inquire after Causton & if Possible to bring an Action against him in order to Make him Refund the Money for my Effects that he has by his Roguery Converted to his Own use. Pray be so good in the meantime to enquire after him, if it Lyes in Your Way. He may be heard of very Likely at the Georgia Office in Westminster, & I hope Your Goodness will excuse the Trouble I so very often give you.

I am likewise to Desire the Favour Youll please to send me over a Fashionable Light Periwigg for my own ware, price about three Gueneas either a Good neat Bobb or a Tail Wigg, I mean a Bob Major. I have had none but One since the Last you sent me which were very Good, & there

---

[5] There were many complaints lodged against Thomas Causton, the storekeeper for Georgia. Amos Aschbach Ettinger, *James Edward Oglethorpe, Imperial Idealist* (Oxford, 1936), pp. 209–211.

are none Good for any thing to be had here & are very dear. We have no Material News here at Present and are in Daily expectation & Long much to hear from Europe. Now above three Callendar Months, since the Last ship we had arriv'd from London.

My Wife joyns in most kind Love and Respects. I have not further to Offerr at Present as being without any of Your Favours, but that I most Affectionatly Remain &c.

ADDRESSED: "Per His Majesty's Snow *Spy*, Capt. Newnham"

TO JOHN FALLA
    Charles Town

Charles Town, 3rd August 1744

SIR:

Capt. Mathew Barnard, late Commander of the Ship *Ann Galley* of Guernsey whereof you are Chief Mate, having on the 29th past unhappily Laid Violent Hands on himself whereby he Dyed Instantly, I am therefore to Desire in Behalf of the Gentlemen who are Owners of the Ship *Ann Galley*, that you take the Charge & Command of the said Ship in the Room & Place of Capt. Barnard Deceas'd, & Doubt not Your Behaviour & Conduct in said Station will be such as to Meritt their Approbation. And I doe hereby as Factor or Agent for all the Owners appoint you Commander of the said ship *Ann Galley* accordingly. I heartily wish you Success & I am &c.

ADDRESSED: NO ADDRESS

18th August 1744

[750]
TO JOHN ELFRETH
Frederica, Georgia

Charles Town, 9th August 1744

SIR:

I Receiv'd yours by the Bearar Mr. Cossett, and am Inform'd by him that after he had Legally Seiz'd the Negro Boy according to the Mortgage expir'd long agoe, You Forcibly Rescued him and threat'nd Mr. Cossett by which you have Render'd your Self Lyable to the Penalty of the Law in that Case. Your Debt to me is One Hundred & Fifteen Pounds, & if it is such a Trifle as you mention I am Surpriz'd you dont discharge it, & which if you think Proper to pay the Bearar, Mr. Cossett, his Receipt shall be Your Sufficient Discharge, and upon paying the Money your Bond & Mortgage shall be Deliver'd to your Order. If not, Mr. Cossett has a full Power from me to Seize the Negro Boy and bring him to Town. Expecting your Complyance, I am &c.

ADDRESSED: NO ADDRESS

TO THOMAS HUTCHINSON & THOMAS GOLDTHWAIT
Boston

Charles Town, 18th August 1744

GENTLEMEN:

The last I did my self the pleasure to write you was of the 30th June per your Sloop *Abigail*, Capt. Batchelder, who sail'd from this the 1st of July and Copie thereof per Capt. Kinsloe for Boston Via New York to which please be Refered & since have not any of your Favours. This hope will be delivered you by Capt. David Lewis, Late Master of your ship *Thomas*, who has Come here in a flagg of truce from the havannah with Several of his Ships Crew & being Destitute of Cloath's, &c. did apply himself to me & who I have Supply'd with what he had occasion for amount being £126.3.6 this Currency & have Taken His Bill on your good selves for £94.12.8 Boston Currency at the Current Exchange of 25 per Ct. for which you'l please to Creditt my account & which please Receive Inclosed & to you Indorsed.

18th August 1744

I have sold about half the Rum per the *Abigail*. It is now at 12/6 per Gallon & hope it will still Rise in price and be Higher tho' there is Still a great deal of West India Rum in Town. We have had but one Ship from London for these four months past which arriv'd about three Weeks agoe & Brought no loaf sugar, So that it is still very scarce & Dear & Likely to Continue So and to be higher in price than at present being from 10/ to 12/6 per lb. by the Quantity Single Refin'd and double from 12/6 to 15/ per lb. The first that Happens to Come from your port will turn to good account.

We have a Good prospect of a very large Crop of Rice, But wether it will answer the great Charge of Exportation this next Season is a Question. As this province has been for some years past Improving in the Planting of Orange Trees[6] Especially in this Town & about it, So now they have Brought them to such maturity that this year a verry considerable Quantity of Oranges are produc'd, insomuch that a pretty many will be export'd This Fall to the Northward, provided Freight Can be obtain'd & on Reasonable Terms. If you have any Small Sloop or Vessel Coming here soon beleive you may have her Loaded Back with Oranges in Chests on Freight & to your good selves Consign'd, or if you think proper to send a small Sloop or Schooner to be here in all next month or in October to be Loaded back on our joint Account should be Glad to Go half Concern'd as I am sincible It would turn to good Account as Oranges will be sold Low here, & I intend to Ship you Some [751] The First Freight that can be procured for your port. The Oranges produced here are Esteem'd verry good and large & much Exceed any in Europe or the West Indies being of the Sour or Seville Kind.

I am to desire the favour you'll please to be so good to forward the Inclos'd Letter for my Brother by the first Conveyance for London there being none here at Present for England neither will for some time to Come. I have not further to offer at Present as being without any of Your favours, & I most Respectfully Remain &c.

ADDRESSED: "Per Capt. David Lewis in Capt. Harramond with Inclosed for my Brother"

---

[6] In 1745 Governor Glen reported that Carolinians were making "large plantations of Orange Trees" which he hoped would enable the province to supply the London market within a few years. In 1747–1748, the colony exported 296,000 oranges, but all the trees were destroyed by a severe frost during the winter of 1747. BPRO-SC, XXII, 100; Wallace, I, 384; *HL*, I, 166.

18th August 1744

TO JOHN COMRIN
Boston

Charles Town, 18th August 1744

Sir:

The preceeding on the other side of the 24 August 1743 is Copie of my last per Capt. Seavey[7] By whom sent you Four Barrels of Rice which hope Came safe to hand & Since have not the pleasure of any of your favours. This Hope will be deliver'd you by Capt. David Lewis who Came Here in a Flagg of Truce from the Havannah & hope this shall find you & Mrs. Comrin in good health, to whom my wife joyns with me in our Best Respects. Shall be glad to have the pleasure of hearing from you & having not Further to offer at present as Being without any of your Favours I Remain &c.

P. S. Loaf Sugar is very scarce and dear here at present a Large Quantity Could be Imediatly disposed of at 10/ per lb. & Likely to be higher.

ADDRESSED: "Per Capt. David Lewis in Capt. Harramond"

TO JOHN ERVING
Boston

Charles Town, 18th August 1744

Sir:

My Last to you was of the 30th June with Two Copies thereof advising Cheifly of my Draft on you in Favour of Messrs. Henry & Alexander Peronneau for £800 Boston Currency at the Current Exchange of 25 per Ct. is £1,000 this Currency which Doubt not will meet with Due Honour & since have not the Pleasure of any of your Favours which will Occasion Brevity at Present.

We have a very Good Prospect of a Large Crop of Rice, but whither it will answer the Great Charge of Exportation in this Times is a Question,

---

[7] Capt. Stephen Seavey, schooner *Portsmouth*, arrived from Boston. SCG, 25 July 1743.

18th August 1744

& Our Crop of Corn is likely to turn out much better than was at first Apprehended.

We have had but One Ship from London for these four Months past which arriv'd about three Weeks agoe, which being put ashoar in the Downs in January Last and Repair'd at Portsmouth, brought no material News, & we have none at Present in these Parts. As we apprehend a Scarcity of Shipping here next Crop by reason of the War with France & Spain, it is Thought Freight will be high tho at Sametime Our Produce being of but Small Value wont afford it.

My Wife joyns in best Respects to Mrs. Erving & all the pritty Young Ones & I most Sincerly Remain &c.

ADDRESSED: "Per Capt. David Lewis"

[752]
TO NICHOLAS RIGBYE
    Savannah

Charles Town, 28th August 1744

SIR:
    I have your favours of the 5th & 20th May. The first Brought me Inclosed your Bond for £34.5.3¼ Sterling, payable the 1st September & want of Material Subject has been the Occasion of my Silence. Since I had not the Good fortune to see the Gentleman your Brother in Law having been in the Country when he was so good as to Call on me with your Letter & am Sorry that I had not the Pleasure of seeing him while in Town. As your Bond becomes Due the 1st of next Month Doubt not you'll be so good as to make Remittance in Order to discharge it as soon as you Can, & that Cash has come to hand by this time from England so that am in hopes Likewise of having Remittance for James Dormer's Note very Soon. Shall be glad to have the Pleasure of hearing from you & I am &c.

ADDRESSED: "Per Mr. Grant"

17th September 1744

TO ALEXANDER STRAHAN
Kingston, Jamaica

Charles Town, 29th August 1744

Sir:

The Annex'd of the other side of the 27th December last is Copie of what I did my self the Pleasure to write you per Capt. Webster & since has come to hand your favours of the 21st May by which I Observe you have not Receiv'd mine per Capt. Webster, who told me at his Return here that when he was at Jaimaia you happen'd to be in the Country but that he Deliver'd my Letter to you to Messrs. Prioleau & Crokatt[8] who Promis'd to take Care & give it you when you Came to town, which if they have not been so good as to Doe the Blame Lyes at their Door. I intimated to Mr. William Woodrope what you mention in yours to him who tells me that Capt. Robinson Losst his Vessell & Cargoe among the Bahama Islands & sav'd Nothing, And that he will Advise you himself of same Accordingly. Shall be always very Ready to Render you any Agreeable Service & I am &c.

ADDRESSED: "Per Capt. Wood"

TO HENRY & JOHN BROCK
Guernsey

Charles Town, 17th September 1744

Gentlemen:

I did my self the Pleasure to write you at the arrival of your Ship *Ann Galley* of the 28th June with Two Copies thereof which hope you have Receiv'd & to which please be Refferr'd, Since have not any of your Favours & no Ships of Late from Europe, neither has there been an Opportunity from this of writing you since my Last in which I advis'd you of the Bad Season of the Year in which your Ship had arriv'd here & that She must be Oblidg'd to goe & Lye up the Freshes for Two or three Months to be free of the Worms & Hurricanes [753] & where the Ship went accord-

---

[8] Samuel Prioleau and John Crokatt.

ingly a few days after, & still Remains there as yet but Intend to have her come down to Town in a Week hence, 'tho as yet no Freight Offerrs, Our Crop of Rice, being now only cutting down & won't be ready to be Shipt till towards November & there is no Naval Stores to be purchas'd as yet at any Rate.

I likewise took notice to you in my Last that Capt. Mathew Barnard was out of his Sensis & had been so for a Considerable Time before the Ships arrival here, & it is with very Great Concern that I have to Acquaint you of His Melancholy Fate. For on Sunday the 29th July about noon Said Capt. Barnard being alone in his Cabin on board his Ship at Childsbury, he laid Violent hands on himself & Shott himself thro' the Head with a Pistoll, whereby he dyed Instantly without ever Speaking One Word, & Inclos'd please Receive Copie of the Verdict of the Coroners Jury who sett on his Body & Certyfied by the Coroner Upon the Decease of Capt. Barnard.

I appointed Mr. John Falla, the Mate, Commander of your Ship *Ann*, in his Room, & who on the 10th of August Dyed at Childsbury, where the Ship Lyes, of a Strong Nervous Fever after a Few Days Illness, So that your Ship has had the Missfortune to be Depriv'd of both Commander & Mate, & at Present Peter Bonamy together with the Boatswain has the Cheif Care of the Ship where she Lys up the River, & should be glad that Mr. Bonamy was Capable & Qualifi'd to take Charge of the Ship as Capt. for her Voyage to Europe, which am affraid he is not, & that I must be Oblidg'd to provide a Commander here, who must be a Person well Qualified for such a Charge & you may assuredly depend on my acting in the best manner I can for your Interest, as having the same very much at heart. Some of the Ship's Company have been Sickly where the Ship Lyes, & One of them has Dyed there, & am apprehensive that their making too free with Spiritous Liquors in this hott Season (as I am Inform'd) may in a Great measure have been the Occasion thereof.

As we are likely to have a very Large Crop of Rice I am in hopes of procuring a Good Freight for your Ship either for Holland or London if no Great Number of Shipping happens to Come here this Fall, & perhaps more than your Limitation of Five pounds per Ton, & which I will not fail to Embrace as soon as possible I can, that the Ship may goe with all the Dispatch to Europe that Can be Desir'd. In the meantime I am to advise you may not Omitt to Order the needfull Insurance on your Ship *ann*, as well as on the Freight which hope may Come to Seven or Eight Hundred Pounds Sterling, & for my Disbursments on the Ship, &c. here, shall draw

Bills on Your Good Selvs payable at the House of Mr. William Dobree, Merchant in London, which doubt not You will give Direction to have Duely Honour'd.

As you sent your Ship here in Order to Obtain Freight, it is pity that you Omitted to gett a Licence for Portugal which would have Cost but a Small matter in London, & Freight very often happens here to be better & more ready to Portugal for a Vessel of the *Ann Galley*'s Burthen than any where else. This goes by his Majesty's Ship the *Spy*, Capt. Newnham, which hope will Come safe to Hand, being under Cover to my Brother in London.[9] I shall Continue to advise you in Relation to your Ship as Conveyances Offerr & having not further to Offerr at Present, I Remain most Respectfully &c.

ADDRESSED: "Under Cover of A.P. per His Majesty's Snow the *Spy*"

[754]
TO ROBERT ELLIS
Philadelphia

Charles Town, 19th September 1744

SIR:

My Last to you was of the 23d April, since have not any of your Favours. Inclos'd please Receive account Sales of the Goods Shipt on your Account per the Ship *Delaware*, Capt. Rivers, Neat Proceeds being £234.5.1 and hope will be to Content. The Beer Came a Great deal too Late & thro' the badness of the Casks has Occasion'd a Great deal of Leakage as well as the Charge of Cooperage. The Neat Proceeds have Carried to your Credit in Account Current.

This Goes by the Sloop *Postilion*, Capt. Duthy, who Returns here Directly. He will take in Freight and as he has promis'd me he will take on Board whatever you have a mind to Ship for me, So it will be a Good Opportunity for you to Remitt by Said Conveyance the Ballance of Your Account. And am of Opinion that Some Good Matlock's Beer,[1] Midling

---

[9] HMS *Spy*, James Newnan, departed the Carolina station on 20 September 1744. May, p. 164.
[1] Matlock's Best Beer of Philadelphia.

19th September 1744

Bread Such as you sent Last, & some Good Tallow Candles in Boxes may answer very well, it being now the Proper Season of the Year for those things, & some Single Refin'd Loaf Sugar if made & to be had reasonable with you. My Wife joyns in best Respects to Good Mrs. Ellis & Self & I most Respectfully Remain.

ADDRESSED: "Per Capt. Duthy"

TO JOHN LIVINGSTON
New York

Charles Town, 19th September 1744

SIR:

I have the pleasure of your Esteemed Favours of the 4th Current per Capt. Romme[2] in Return to mine of the 10 July & duely note the Contents. I observe what you are pleas'd to mention in Relation to the French Prizes Carried into your Port, & do much approve of your Scheme in making a purchase of the said Vessels to send here for a Freight to Europe. And as we have a Verry large Crop of Rice, freight will Certainly be high if no great number of Shipping happens to come here, which is verry improbable in these Times, & the Ships that have arriv'd here this Summer, which are about Ten in number, expect Five or Six pounds per Ton Freight for Europe, So that a good Freight may Clear the Cost of the Vessell, & one of about 150 or 160 Tons would be a good size for this place & the smaller the more Readily to be Taken up or Freighted.

Good Muscovado Sugar as it is sold verry Cheap with you would answer very well here put up in flour Barrels, provided you perseive there is no great Quantity thereof shipt here, & it will be verry proper to send a Cocquett with it from the Custom house to prove that the Kings duty which is Five Shillings Sterling per Ct. on French sugars has been paid at Importation which Imagine the Captors were obliged to pay or give Security to the Collector for Before the Sugars Could be Landed or exposed to sale, our Custom officers being of late very Strict here.

[2] Capt. Cornelius Roome, sloop *Carolina*, arrived from New York. RPC, p. 758; SCG, 16 July 1744.

21st September 1744

As this province has been for some years past Improving in the planting of Orange Trees Especially in this town & about it, so now they have brought them to such maturity that this year a Considerable Quantity of Oranges are produced, insomuch that a pretty many will be Exported this fall to the Northen Collonies if Freight can be obtain'd & on Reasonable Terms, & if I can procure Freight per Capt. Romme intend to ship some to your Address for Sale as a Tryal, put up in Chests, & hope may turn to pretty good account.

I am glad to hear the Privateers from your port are so successfull. Provissions of bread & flour may probably be in demand here this fall, & Loaf Sugar is still very Scarce, having had no Ships from Europe for a Considerable Time past. I am most Respectfully.

ADDRESSED: "Per Capt. Duthy Via Philadelphia"

[755]
TO ANDREW PRINGLE
London

Charles Town, 21st September 1744

SIR:

The last I did my self the Pleasure to write you, was of the 20th July, by Capt. Trenchard for Bristoll, but miss'd the Opportunity, & which please Receive Inclos'd. Indeed said Vessel happened to be taken goeing from this & Carried into St. Augustine, Value of Vessel & Cargoe £7,000 Sterling. There was 101 hhds. Deer Skins on board, & Since there has been no Conveyance from this for Europe, neither have I as yet any of your Favours so much long'd for. The Latest from you being of the 3d March, & as yet no London Vessels excepting Capt. Glegg who arriv'd the 6th August from Spithead & by whom the Managers of the Privateer *Recovery* had Copie of your & Mr. James Crokatts most Acceptable Favours of the 12th May in Relation to the Privateer, & all the Concern'd are exceeding well pleas'd therewith, & think themselves greatly oblidg'd to you in particular, but wish in your Letter you had been more particular to have advis'd when the Vessell might Reasonably have been provided with Sufficient Hands, & Ready to Sail, as she does not yet appear, & that you had been pleas'd to mention the Burthen of the Vessel & whither a Ship or a Snow.

The Managers write the Gentlemen in London by this Conveyance to which please be Refferr'd. We were in hopes to have made Remittance in Bills of Exchange by this Conveyance to have Compleated the £2,000 Sterling as propos'd, but People are so backward have Disappointed us, but none of them give themselvs much Trouble about it. I have the Labouring Oar myself. Indeed Good Bills of Exchange are very Scarce at Present, but hope to Compleat same per next Conveyance. The Concern'd begin to be dubious of the *Recovery* as She does not yet appear. There is a very Clever New Snow getting ready to joyn the *Recovery* on the Same Concern & to be in Consort together. The Vessel is almost ready to Launch & will soon be fitted. Capts. Scott & Ham doe not yet appear, & as for poor Capt. William Douglas am afraid that he has had the Misfortune to fall into the Enemeys hands the Third time.

We have no shipping here at Present, excepting eight or Ten that have Layen the Summer up the Freshes, so that Freight is likely to be high provided that Rice is worth exporting of which we have again this Year a very Large Crop & is now Cutting down.

We are now in a fair way to have a New Produce & better than Rice, Vizt. Indigo,[3] some of which has been made & accounted by those that understand it to be very Good. A pritty many Persons are goeing upon it to make it, & it likely that next year a pritty deal may be produc'd. It is planted and made easier & with fewer hands than Rice & very easily done, & the Weed it Is made of grows & thrives very well. Intend to send you some of it from the Person who is the first projector & maker of it here.

This will be Deliver'd by Mr. Michael Pickering, Purser of his Majestys Snow the *Spy*, Capt. Newnham, & Inclos'd please Receive his Receipt for Sixty Spainish Pistolls in Doublloons in a Small Bagg Markd AP (say A P) & Seal'd, at £5.17 Currency each is £351 Current Money being Ballance of the Account of the assignees of William Caw as already Sent & On their Account & Risque. Mr. Pickering is Son of Mrs. Pickering who is married to Mr. Benjamin Savage & born here. He belong'd formerly to his Majestys Ship *Loo*, Capt. Uting, who is his Friend. I told him that you would be very Glad to See him & to Render him any Service. You'll Please

---

[3] Although Eliza Lucas Pinckney was credited with perfecting the processing of indigo in the colony, Andrew De Veaux, a planter in St. Andrew's Parish, claimed that he had completed the experiments successfully first. Wallace, I, 384–385.

21st September 1744

to pay him a Pistoll for Freight as Mention'd in the Receipt, as I would not Miss this Opportunity of Remitting, Good Conveyances being Rare & Seldom to be mett with.

[756] Please also Receive Inclos'd Forty Six Shillings Sterling in Nine small Georgia Bills which are not worth Sending, but have no other way of Remitting them without a Considerable Charge if any Quantity, & are often oblidg'd to take them in payments & for which please to give me Credit, Exchange at £700 per £100 being a Trifle on my Risque. I am to pray the Favour You'll be so good as to Speak to the Gentlemen I already writt you of, to send over the Certificates to Clear my Plantation Bonds, especially that of Capt. Storys at Hull, & Mr. John Keiths for that of Capt. Keiths. Our Governour has gott a very Strict Instruction Relating to Plantation Bonds. Please likewise Speak to Messrs. Samuel Storke & Son to Gett a Certificate for the Goods he Ship'd me per Capt. Hayden in account of Messrs. Hutchinson & Goldthwait, the Cocketts being burnt or Losst on board Said Hayden in the Passage here & the Custom House Officers Require Copies or a Certificate for the Same from London. I am sorry it has not been in my power of Remitting hitherto so Considerably as it was my Inclination and uttmost endeavours for that Effect, & You may Depend on all that Possibly I can this Fall and with the Greatest expedition. I find Debts are extreamly Difficult and Troublesome to be gott in. I have had no Remittances as yet on Our Account from Messrs. Hutchinson & Goldthwait of Boston. Capt. Glegg will be the first for London, and will Sail soon, by whom shall doe my Self the Pleasure to write you again.

My Wife joyns in best Respects & having not further to Offerr at Present, as being without any of your Favours I most Sincerly Remain &c.

P. S. Inclos'd is a Letter for Messrs. Brock of Guernsey which after perusal please to seal and forward them. You'll Observe their Ship has been very unfortunate here.

ADDRESSED: "Per Michael Pickering in His Majesty's Ship the *Spy*, Capt. Newnham"

TO ANDREW PRINGLE
London

Charles Town, 1st October 1744

SIR:

The preceeding of the 21st past is Copie of my Last per Mr. Michael Pickering, Purser of his Majestys Snow *Spy*, who Sailed Over the Bar the 22d Ulto. & to which please be Refferr'd, since have not as yet the Pleasure of any of your much Long'd for Favours, & no Ships from Europe which will Occasion Brevity. Inclos'd please Receive Copie of Mr. Pickering's Receipt for the Gold Deliver'd him as advis'd in my Last. This Goes by Capt. Glegg being the only Ship that has arriv'd here from London Since Last Spring, being Charter'd by Mess'rs. Steill & Hume & Loaded with Naval Stores Interely. And Inclos'd please Receive Bill of Loading for Two Chests of Oranges the Produce of my Own Garden, Contents 450 Oranges each Chest, which thro Mr. John Hume's means I prevail'd with Capt. Glegg to take on Board, & hope will Come to Hand in Good Order. One of which Chests you'll please to make acceptable for your Self & the other youll be so good as to Sell to any of the Orange Merchants, being for a Trial, to know what they would give for such Oranges per Chest or per 100 to have them Deliver'd in London annually by the first or middle of the month of December & if they keep & will answer, a Great many may be Sent Home Yearly when [757] Peaceable Times Come & Freight is Low. This Province having been for Some years past improving in the Planting of Orange Trees, especially in this Town & about it, so now they have brought them to Such Maturity that this Year a Very Considerable Quantity of Oranges are produc'd, insomuch that a Pritty many may well be exported this fall to the Northern Collonies for Sale as a Tryal & there is a Sloop now Goeing to New York which will have 200 Chests of Oranges on Board on Freight for Sale, whereof which I am One of the Adventurers, My Garden having produc'd Ten thousand Oranges & Upwards.

I Inclos'd in my Last a Letter for Messrs. Henry & John Brock of Guernsey, Relating to their Ship *Ann* & to Order Insurance on the Ship's Freight Home which may Come to £700 or £800 Ster. in Case of being taken. And it being most Likely to Obtain a Freight for London, & Sooner than to Holland and as there are a Great Many Owners & I am Likely to be very Considerably in Advance for the Charge & Disbursments on the Ship here for which I must Draw Bills of Exchange on Messrs. Brocks & have only their Honour to Trust to in Case the Ship shou'd be taken, So that I want

3rd October 1744

to Secure my Self on the Ship's Freight for the Money I advance, & Intend to Consign the Ship to You to Receive the Freight & in Case my Bills shou'd not be honour'd (which shall make payable to your Self) than you can Secure me by having the Freight in Your Hands. Therefore if this getts to Hand, as soon as the Letter to them in my Last, You may stop it for some time & advise them that I have Desir'd you to write them for you to have their Orders to make Insurance on the Ships Freight Home. The Capt. & the Mate both being Dead, have been Oblidg'd to appoint One Capt. Trenchard, Commander & I had no particular Directions from the Brocks or any of the Owners to advance any Money. Inclos'd Please also Receive Copie of the Owners Instructions to their Capt. Barnard, also Messrs. Brocks their Letter to me. I only want to be safe & to Secure my Self. If I thought my Self not Safe, woud have the Ship Bottom'd for my Security & Order Insurance accordingly. The Messrs. Brocks beleive are Men of Honour, but for the other Owners I have no Knowledge of them, 'tho am Inform'd Some are Top Men in the Island. And they are in Generall a Pretty Close People & esteem'd Litigious as most of the Normans are.

The Privateer *Recovery* does not yet appear which makes the Concern here apprehensive that Some accident or bad Fortune has befallen her. Freight has not yet broke neither the Price of New Rice, there being none yet ready to Come to Markett.

I add not a Present but Remain in haste with most Tender Regaurd &c.

P. S. Mr. John Hume Shipt Four Chests of Oranges by Capt. Glegg for Mr. Steill.

ADDRESSED: "Per Capt. Glegg & Copie per Capt. Jacks"

[758]
TO JOHN LIVINGSTON
New York

Charles Town, 3rd October 1744

SIR:

The preceeding of the 19th Ulto. is Copie of my Last Via Philadelphia to which please be Refferr'd. As I advis'd in my Last I intended by

3rd October 1744

this Conveyance of Capt. Romme to have Consign'd You some Chests of Our Carolina Oranges as a Tryal for Sale, but the Two Gentlemen that took up the Sloop on Freight would not permitt me to put any on Board unless I Lett them goe with theirs to their Friend & to which I have been Oblidg'd to Comply with rather then Loose the Opportunity, it being the only one we are Likely to have to the Northward this Season. We have not as yet any Vessells from Europe. I have not further to Offerr at Present but that I Remain with very Great Respect &c.

ADDRESSED: "Per Capt. Romar"

TO JACOB FRANKS[4]
New York

Charles Town, 4th October 1744

SIR:
Above is Invoice of Twenty Four Chests Oranges Ship'd per the Sloop *Carolina*, Cornelius Romme, Master for New York on my Account & Risque & to your Good Self Consign'd as per Bill of Lading in Company with Messrs. Jarmain & Charles Wright[5] whose Directions youll be pleas'd to follow in Relation to the Sale thereof. The Oranges are very Good & Sound & will keep a Great while & doubt not will Come to a Good Markett, This being the first Essay of a Tryal for Exportation from this Province, & hope will meet with Good Encouragement so as an annual Exportation of same may be Continued.

You'll please to forward me Account Sales & with the Neat Proceeds to Ship me Two Barrils Esopus Flour, Two Barrils of Middling Bread, Two Boxes Good Soap, Two Boxes best Moulded Tallow Candles of Mutton Suet, Twelve Horns, & Twelve pieces smoak'd Beef & the Ballance you'll please to Invest in Good Single Refin'd Loaf Sugar if to be had with you. But if not to be purchas'd, youll please to Ship Said Ballance in Middling & Ship Bread in Small Barrils & Good Esopus Flour.

Shall be very Glad to Render you any agreeable Service here & I am most Respectfully &c.

[4] Jacob Franks was a New York merchant. RPC, p. 819.
[5] Sons of Robert Wright, chief justice of S. C. and brothers of James Wright, later royal governor of Georgia.

9th October 1744

[*Mark*] " P " No. 1 to 24: 24 Chests Oranges, whereof No. 1 to 11 quantity 600 each, & no. 12 to 24 quantity 500 Oranges each.

ADDRESSED: "Per Capt. Romar & Copie per Capt. Bangs Via Boston"

TO ANDREW PRINGLE
London

Charles Town, 9th October 1744

I have already write you by this Conveyance of Capt. Glegg of the 1st Current & being still in the Rhode give me the agreable Opportunity of acknowledgeing the Receipt yesterday of all your most welcome & much wished for favours per Capt. Scott, of the 8th & 29 May, the 7th, 8th, 15th, & 27th June whose sundry Contents most duely observe but have not Time by this Conveyance to give a due Return to same, only that last evening after Sealing your Letter for our Governour Mr. Glen, had the Oppertunity of waiting on him & delivering it to him & Company Coming in before he had quite Read it, had not the Oppertunity of Discoursing with him on the Contents but as you Rightly Observe I find him a person of that Disposition that he is not much to be [759] Depended on and seems to beguile & want Resolution.

Shall after sealing, Deliver yours for Mr. Elliott First Oppertunity. Think his Chaise Comes very Cheap both in Respect to the Cost & Charge attending it in Comparison to most that Come here & doubt not will give intire content. Said Gentleman is under great Obligations to you & doubt not is sensible of same and hope you have Received the money for his Fire Tickett.

I am supprised at what you write in Relation to Michael Thomson & that I am like to be a sufferer by such an oversight but as it is a debt of Honour he must have no principal if in his power to discharge it. If he is so ungreatfull as to lett me loose the said £46.9.8 Sterling for Recovering for him near £400 Sterling I need not Recommend your best Endeavours to Recover it if possible and without delay.

The Concerned in the the privateer *Recovery* are greatly obligded to you in particular as the whole fatigue & Conducting of that afair so heavily has Layn on you as is also the whole province in General for your Exerting your self so vigourously & in so Conspicious a manner for the wellfare thereof & wish they may be sencible of the great service done them as you thereby have Incurred the malice & Resentment of a person whose Caracter & principles are not to his Honour & of a Crew whose Fortunes Depend intirely on him & on said account Render him a most Submissive and blind obedience, but hope it will not be in their power to act any thing to your prejudice or Disadvantage.

I understand yesterday the Shubricks gave themselves some Airs in Company after Receipt of Mr. Nicholsons Letter in Relation to Mr. Crokatt & your Conduct of the privateer pretending you had given him orders to goe a Cruizing before he Came out, Contrary to the Intentions of the Concerned & his Instructions, but your Letter of the 27th June makes plainly the Contrary appear & will give Content to all the Concerned (notwithstanding the Sinister insinuations of the said Gentlemen to Create Divisions) especially as we are informed by Capt. Scott of Capt. Andersons Carrying in a prize or Two to Fallmouth & which Mr. Nicholson takes notice of to the Shubricks in a Letter dated in July. As Capt. Glegg is preparing to Sail must begg leave to Conclude in hast &c.

ADDRESSED: "Per Capt. Glegg & Copie per Capt. Jacks"

TO EDWARD & JOHN MAYNE & EDWARD BURN
Lisbon

Charles Town, 17th October 1744

GENTLEMEN:

The last I did my self the pleasure to write you was of the 25th April, & three Days agoe have your most Esteemed Favours per Capt. Douglas, Copie of the 28th August, the Original has not come to hand, also yours of the 2d September & Observe our Comodity of Rice is Low with you & Freight here is verry high being at Six pounds per Ton which Discourages Shipping to your port. We have this year a Verry large Crop of Rice, but the Dulness of the Marketts every where for the sale, will be a hindrance to its Exportation.

17th October 1744

Shall pay to Messrs. Simmons & Smith[6] 5$400 reis for the Chest of Lemmons Delivered me by Capt. Steinson thro mistake. This province produces now Oranges in great Plenty, & this Season a Considerable Quantity is Exported to the Northen Collonies, So that Lemmons wont be much wanted here in Time to Come. Should be greatly oblidged to you if you'll be so good as to send me some young Olive Trees or plants from the Kingdom of Algarve when any Conveyance offers. Olive Trees thrive Exceeding well here.

My account Current has hitherto Miscarried, so that must still desire the Favour of your sending another Duplicate thereof.

There being no Conveyance from this at present for [760] England, have taken the Freedom to Trouble you with the Inclosed for Messrs. Samuel Storke & Son & my Brother which am to pray the Favour you'll please be so good as to forward per first. We have no material News at Present, & no Ships Lately from Britain. I am most Respectfully &c.

Rice 30/ per Ct., Exchange to London £700 per £100 Sterling.

ADDRESSED: "Per the *Jolliff's Adventure*, Capt. John Archer, & Copie per Capt. Philips"

TO ANDREW PRINGLE
London

Charles Town, 17th October 1744

SIR:

The preceeding of the 9th Current is Copie of my last per Capt. Glegg for London, & there being no Conveyance here at present for England I Embrace this Oppertunity Via Lisbon under Cover of Messrs. Mayn to advise you of the arrival of the Snow *Robert & Jane*, Capt. William Douglas, from Lisbon after a passage of Seven weeks & all well on board, & has happen'd to Come in a verry good Time for the first new Rice & at a Time that there are few Shipping here & freight high so that

---

[6] Ebeneezer Simmons and Benjamin Smith were partners in Charles Town 1738–1745 under the firm name of Simmons, Smith & Co. Rogers, *Evolution of a Federalist*, pp. 10–11.

17th October 1744

Capt. Douglas and I have thought it most Advantageous to take a freight back to Portugal, as a good one offers & especially as Rice is verry low there & accordingly have lett out said Snow at Six pounds Sterling per Ton for Porto to be Loaded in Six weeks (or a month, if new Rice can be gott Ready in that Time) which is the highest Freight that has yett been given here this warr and is to be Loaded by Mr. Steils partner Mr. John Hume who assures us of being imediately at her arrival there Loaded with wine on Freight for London, so that if pleases God the snow getts safe hope will make a Good voyage of itt, & you'll please to make the needfull Insurance, both on the Vessel & Freight at & from this to Porto.

I am to desire you'll please to gett Insured on Goods on board the Sloop *Rebecca*, Benjamin Bangs, Master at & from this to Boston, New England One hundred pounds Sterling which you'll please to charge to my account. The said Sloop will sail in a fortnight or three weeks hence is about 80 tons a Stout Vessel & Well Mann'd.

Alderman Baker has writ to his Freind Mr. Colcock[7] here in a plausible manner in excuse of his Declining being Concerned in the Privateer as has also Mr. Nichleson to his Brother & the Shubricks, which seems to Influence them to make as it were a party matter of it in their behalf & to insinuate of it Capt. Anderson had Directions or Leave from Mr. Crokatt to take a Cruize before he Comes here Contrary to his instructions. Which if he does and any accident should happen to him it will make a great Clamour here, but hope Capt. Anderson when he arrives will Clear up every thing of that nature to intire Satisfaction, & this if you please to your self. Capt. Douglas likewise writes you by this Conveyance. Am at present oblidged to attend our Court of Sessions being a Jurryman so that I have not to add at present but that I am &c.

ADDRESSED: "Per Capt. Archer Via Lisbon under Cover of Messrs. Mayne"

---

[7] John Colcock married Deborah Milner on 13 July 1732. *St. Philip's Register*, p. 163.

[761]
TO SAMUEL STORKE & SON
London

Charles Town, 17th October 1744

GENTLEMEN:

My last I did my self the pleasure to write you was of the 30th May & since have not the pleasure of any of your favours. Messrs. Hutchinson & Goldthwait of Boston, N. E. Direct me to advise you to gett Insured on their proper account on Goods to be Shipt on board the Sloop *Rebecca*, Benjamin Bangs, Now in this Harbour, at & from this to Boston Three hundred pounds Sterling. The Sloop will sail in a fortnight or Three weeks, & is a Good new Vessell, well mann'd, burthen about 80 Tons. This Goes via Lisbon there being no Conveyance here at present for England, neither will be before said sloop sails. I have not further to offer at present but that I am &c.

ADDRESSED: "Per Capt. Archer Via Lisbon under Cover of Messrs. Mayne"

TO OSBORNE & OXNARD & THOMAS GUNTER
Boston

Charles Town, 6th November 1744

GENTLEMEN:

My last to you was of the 17th May last with Copie Conveying you bill of Lading & Invoice of 150 barrils Rice per the Snow *Sea Horse*, Capt. Woodwell, for Boston on your account and which hope Came safe to hand, Since have not the pleasure of any of your Favours. This is again to desire you'll be so good as to transmitt me a Certificate from the Custom house of the Delivery of the Brigantine *Dolphin's* Cargoe from this in order to Clear my bond given with Capt. Evans the time being now Elasp'd, which am to Request you may not fail to forward per first Conveyance.

We have a very large Crop of Rice this Year & but few Shipping at present, So that freight is likely to be verry high, & in Cource Rice low in Price. I am with verry Great Respect &c.

New Rice 27/6 per hundredweight & likely to be lower, Rum N. E. 14/ to 15/ per Gallon, West India ditto 17/6 & 20/ per Gallon.

ADDRESSED: "Per Capt. Bangs & Copie per Capt. Hilton Via Rhode Island"

TO JOHN ERVING
Boston

Charles Town, 7th November 1744

SIR:

My last to you was of the 18th August & about a month agoe have the pleasure of your most Esteem'd Favours of the 4th September via winyaw. I note your due Honour to both my setts of Bills on you in favour of Messrs. Peronneau. Please Receive Inclosed a Letter from said Gentlemen. They tell me they have writ you to Charter a Sloop for them to be loaded back to your good self on their account to which Refer you.

We have the largest Crop of Rice it is thought ever has yett been Produced in this province, & but few Shipping here at Present so that Freight is likely to be high, tho' no Ships yett take up on freight excepting for Portugal at Six pounds per Ton & it is thought wont break lower than £6 or £7 per ton for London. If you Incline to have any Rice purchased here the most Certain & Venable [762] Commodities to send from your port for that Effectt are Rum & Single Refin'd Loaf Sugar. New Rice of which verry little is yett Ready for Markett broke at 30/ per Ct. & is now at 27/6 per hundred weight & likely to be much lower. Naval Stores are high & Scarce, Pitch 47/6 per bbl., Tarr 35/ per ditto, Turpentine 12/6 per hundredweight.

This goes by a Sloop Hired by Messrs. Hutchinson & Goldthwait to my Addres & loaded back on their account with new Rice & Oranges for Sale per their Order, being the Produce of this Province. For one Chest of which please Receive Inclosed Capt. Bangs his Receipt being marked J E

7th November 1744

No. 1 which is some of the Produce of my Garden & which you'll be pleased to make acceptable. A great number of Orange trees have of late being planted in this town & Near it & are now Come to such maturity that a Large Quantity of Oranges has been produced this Season & beleive what I have Shipt per this Sloop is the first Essay of a Tryall for Sale from this Province in any Quantity & hope will meet such encouragement so as an Annual Exportation to our Northen Collonies may be Continued, the Oranges being verry Good of the Kind & will keep for a Considerable Time.

I am to pray the favour you'll be so good as to purchase for me a Copper water Cooler or Cistern to Put Bottles in & to Contain about Seven or Eight Gallons, I mean such a one as Mr. Joseph Wragg bought at your place when there, as also a New Prospect of your Town of Boston which am informed is lately Publish'd & Exceeding well done, & the Two Volumes of Mr. Thomas Prince his *Cronologil History of New England*[8] the first Volume of which you was so kind as to send me some time agoe & which had the misfortune with all my other Books to be burnt in our fatal fire 1740.

I hope your Goodness will pardon the Freedome I take in troubling you with things of so little Consequence, the Cost whereof you'll please to advise me & Charge to my account.

My Wife still enjoys but a verry Indiffrent state of Health who presents her most Kind respects to your good Lady & all the Rest of your pretty familly & beleive me to be with verry Great Respect &c.

ADDRESSSED: "Per Capt. Bangs & Copie per Capt. Hilton Via Rhode Island"

---

[8] The book was Thomas Prince's *Chronological History of New England*, the first volume of which was published in 1736. RP wanted the second volume, but it was not even begun until 1755. Charles Evans, *American Bibliography*, II: 1730–1750 (Chicago, 1904), 104.

7th November 1744

TO THOMAS HUTCHINSON & THOMAS GOLDTHWAIT
Boston

Charles Town, 7th November 1744

GENTLEMEN:

My last to you was of the 18th August per Capt. Lewis and since have your Esteemed Favours of the 18th September per the Bearer Benjamin Bangs, Master of the Sloop *Rebecca* who arrived here the 14th past Inclosing Bill of Loading & Invoice of sundry on board the said Sloop on your account & to my self Consign'd which have received & Shall dispose of without Loss of Time to your best advantage. The Sugar proves the Best article, which have sold at 7/6 per lb. & some of itt at 8/, a pretty Deal having Come in lately in Two Ships from London which is Esteemed preforable in Quality to what is made with you. There has also been several parcells from New York where it seems that Comodity is verry plentifull at present & from whence a Good deal is soon expected as also from London, so judg'd it more for your Interest to Sell it in Case it may be lower. Have also Disposed of most of your Clarett at £55 per Hhd. It is a Small wine & Green, One hhd. whereof is prict & am afraid wont fetch any thing. A pretty large Quantity of prize Clarrett had arrived here sometime before yours from Antigua & Sold at £40 per Hhd., Said wine having been sold there at 40/ per hhd. that Currency. As for your Brandy it will [763] Turn out but poorly being not much in use here and Cannot obtain More than 25/ per Gall. and will be verry slow sale tho at Same time Lyable to a high Duty of 2/ per Gallon so that it happens to be the worst article you sent.

Inclosed please Receive Capt. David Lewis his Second Bill of Exchange to me on your good selves for £94.12.8 Boston Money & to you Indorsed for £126.3.6 this Currency advanced him here. You'll please to observe my Bookeeper made a mistake in Calculating the Exchange at 25 per Ct. & Should have been £100.18.10 instead of £94.12.8, the Diffrence being £6.6.2 Boston Money which you'll please to Receive of Capt. Lewis.

It is not without Supprize that I observe you Seem to object to my Commission Charged on your Ship *Thomas* & Cargoe which doe not think Equivalent to the Customary Commission on other Bussiness, & verry few persons here Care to Undertake or to be Concern'd in an afair of that Nature or to be in advance especially in a place where the Interest of Money is at 10 per Cent unless for particular freinds & under Singular obligations. Your ship *Thomas* happens to be third that I have had ocas-

7th November 1744

sion to Claim in that manner since the Commencement of the warr & have always most thankfully been allowed said Commission by the Owners and at Same time acknowledged themselves under verry particular Obligations to me for same, One of which was a Large Virginia Ship belonging to London of verry Considerable Value, & I Cannot omitt taking notice of to you that it was with no Small trouble & address that I gott the First appraizers & appraizement appointed & Return'd into the Court of Admiralty sett aside & other appraizers appointed by which you were gainers upwards of £200 Sterling & which perhaps another person might have sitt down with being a thing uncommon if I had not hadd your Interest very much at Heart. There are but few Persons here would Care to undertake a thing of that nature for the Commission I have Charged & doe assure you it is a Commission I should at all times desire to be Excused from, Unless to Serve particular Friends therefore hope you Cannot Require any Deduction on said Charge.

Please receive Inclosed account Sales of the goods Shipt per Messrs. Samuel Storke & Son from London on your Account, Neat Proceeds being £2,066.6.6 this Currency which hope will be to Content as I observed in my former the goods were but ordinary in the Quality & high Charged. Some of the sail Cloth had Received some Damage & the Pickles being all put up in one large Case are verry ill pack'd (as I advised Messrs. Storke) had occasioned the Damage & Breaking Several Bottles.

You have also Inclosed account Sales of the Rum per the Sloop *Abigail*, Capt. Batchelder, on account of your Mr. T. H., Neat Proceeds being £3,381.15.8 this Currency. Shall take Care to Remitt the Ballance of your account Current as also of your Mr. T. H. as you have particularly Directed & am to Desire you'll be so good as to transmitt me my account Current with you that same may be Noted in Conformity with each of yours already sent you.

Inclosed please Receive Bill of Loading & Invoice of One hundred & forty Seven bbls. of good New Rice Shipt per the Sloop *Rebecca*, Benjamin Bangs, Commander for Boston on your proper account & to your good Selves Consign'd, it being the first & only New Rice yet Shipt this Crop, amount as per Invoice being £1,328.14.2 this Currency, which hope will Come safe to hand & to a Good Markett. You have also according to your Directions Bill of Loading & Invoice of One hundred & Eighty five Chests of Oranges Shipt on board said sloop *Rebecca* on our Joint account each one half Consern'd & to your good selfs Consign'd, Amount as per Invoice being £1,226.8.9 this Currency which wish safe to hand &

7th November 1744

hope will Come to a verry [764] Good Markett & in good order, being all pack'd up with great Care & verry sound & Good of the Kind, & will keep for a Considerable Time if preserv'd from the Cold, & as it is the first Essay of a Tryall for Exportation for Sale from this Province hope will meet with good Encouragement, So as an annual Exportation of same may be Continued. You'll please to Charge my half part of freight of the Oranges in proportion to the Freight or Hire of the Sloop, & for my one half Neat Proceeds of Same, please Remitt me in Single Refin'd Loaf Sugar & Rum of each one half. If there happens no Great Demand for the Oranges at arrival, you may Depend on it they will keep verry well for Some Time, provided they are taken Care of from the Cold.

According to your Directions I writt to Messrs. Samuel Storke & Son in London Via Lisbon (there being no Conveyance for England since Capt. Bangs his arrival) to gett Insured on goods on your account on board the Sloop *Rebecca* at & from this to Boston Three hundred pounds Sterling, which if said advise getts to hand, doubt not will be punctually Executed. Inclosed please Receive a Certificate for Loaf Sugar per the Snow *John*, Capt. Palmer, as also a Certificate for the Sugar per this Sloop *Rebecca* as there is no Likelyhood of Rice being higher in price than at present, but Rather much lower, there being a verry large Crop. I shall not provide any before hand on your account Unless I have your further Directions.

I am to Return you my thanks for your kind present of apples and Cramberries. Have sent you under Capt. Bangs his Care a Rice Barrel of Potatoes Markt H No. 1 & One of the Chests of Oranges No. 186, or any other which desire you'l please to make acceptable. I would have Shipt the Quantity of 120 to 140 thousand Oranges as you order'd but the Sloop has Disappointed me in her Stowage & altho quite full does not Carry so much as I imagined.

Please Receive Inclosed Capt. Bangs his Receipt for One hundred & Twenty pounds this Currency paid him here for which he is to account to you & for which have Debit your account. Capt. Bangs has also Received £17.10 for freight for a Boat &c. but Cannot gett the freight of the Two Grave Stones. When I Receive itt shall give you Creditt for Same.

I am to Desire you'll please to send a Certificate for the Delivery of Capt. Bang's Cargoe. Just now I understand that an officious Person here having heard that I was to Ship a Quantity of Oranges to Boston has privately sent a Small Quantity of Oranges in flower barrils from this to be put on board a Sloop at Winyaw which it seems is bound for Boston, as thinking to be before hand with us in the Markett, So that hope the

8th November 1744

Quantity Shipt per Capt. Bangs may be sufficient. The Sloop is just agoing & hope will soon be with you. I Remain Most Respectfully &c.

P. S. Just now we hear that his Majestys Ship *Flamborough*, Capt. Hamor,[9] one of our Station'd Ships is Come to our Barr with a Rich French Prize.

Exchange to London £700 per £100 Sterling.

ADDRESSED: "Per Capt. Bangs & Copie per Capt. Hilton Via Rhode Island"

[765]
TO ROGER GORDON[1]
Williamsburgh Township, South Carolina

Charles Town, 8th November 1744

SIR:

I Received this Day your Favours by the Bearer Mr. Buckles[2] and am Surprized the Gentlemen who are Collecters of the Tax should have Acted in so Imprudent a Manner as to order my Negro to be Seized for another persons Tax Contrary to Law or Justice. I have this day taken advise of a Gentleman of the law on the affair, & Esteem'd one of the Best Councill of this Province Who Tells me that I have a verry Good acction against the Collecters of the Tax & that they might with as much Right have Seiz'd a Negroe of yours or of any other Persons of this Province, the said Negroe being my sole Right & Property & that Mr. Bassnett has no Manner of Right, Interest, or Concern in him.[3] I am to desire the favour

---

[9] On 10 November HMS *Flamborough*, Joseph Hamar, brought in the ship *La Sendre* of Rochelle, Sieur Elias Seguinard, bound from the Mississippi and Havanna for France with a cargo valued at £20,000 sterling. SCG, 12, 19 November 1744.

[1] Roger Gordon owned land in Williamsburg Township where he lived and in Boggy Swamp. Moore & Simons, II, 136.

[2] Thomas Buckle, the elder of Charles Town, "gentleman," had an account with the cabinet-maker Thomas Elfe. SCHM, XXXVII (1936), 29; Wills, XXII, 187.

[3] In 1761 RP sued Bassnett's estate for a debt contracted in 1739. Judgment Rolls, 1761, 177A.

you'll be so good as to send me down the names of the said Gentlemen Collecter and of what Parish (who doubt not are verry good men) that I may enter my action against them, being Determin'd to prosecute them & to make them pay for their Indiscretion. As for Mr. Moony the Constable I desire you may make a Demand of my said Negro from him to be Deliver'd to you according to my order, & at his Perill to keep or detain him or to Sell him to any Person whatsoever, as I have Likewise a verry good action both against him & who ever may dare to Buy him, & they may Expect to be Imediately Prosceuted with the utmost Rigour of the Law, which desire you'll be so good as to acquaint him of accordingly, & if the Negroe is not Imediately Deliver'd to you, pray be so kind as to Inform me thereof as Speedily as you Can that I may take Proper Mesures to bring them to Justice. Your Compliance & answer will greatly oblige &c.

ADDRESSSED: "Per Mr. Buckles"

TO BOAZ BELL
    Bermuda

Charles Town, 14th November 1744

SIR:
    I am verry Glad to hear by Capt. Cooper of your health & Welfare. This is to putt you in mind of an India Sattin Workt Counterpin for a Bed delivered you with some Rice on my account & Consigned to your self, when here in January 1742, to Sell for me which you have not accounted for or Returned me. Mr. Westerman Shipt me Rum by your Order for the Proceeds of the Rice. I am therefore to Desire you'll be so good as to Return said Counterpin or send me the Value being Charged at £30 this Currency or Remitt the Value on my account to Mr. Gedney Clark in Barbadoes of Mr. Michael Lovell in Antigua, if no Oppertunity this way, or by Capt. Cooper if he Touches att your Island in his Return here or by any other Oppertunity you think proper. I heartily wish You all Happiness and I am &c.

ADDRESSED: "Per Capt. Beek for Bermuda & St. Kitts"

15th November 1744

[766]
TO ISAAC DUPORT
    St. Kitts

Charles Town, 15th November 1744

SIR:

    Being Informed by my Brother Andrew Pringle of London Merchant that he Coresponds with you for what Bussiness he has Occasion to have transacted at your Island, I take the Oppertunity by this to make you a Tender of my Best Services here, & to assure you that I shall verry much Esteem your Commands & be always very Glad to Render you any agreeable Service. We have the Largest Crop of Rice this Year ever yett produced in the Province. Please Receive as under the prices of Goods here at present. I Salute you & am Most Respectfully &c.

P. S. Rum 20/ per Gallon, Muscovado Sugar £12 to £14 per hundredweight, New Rice 25/ per hundredweight, Pitch 47/6 per bbl., Tarr 35/ per bbl., Corn & pease 8/6 per Bu., Beef £8 per bbl., Pork £12 per bbl., Shingles £3.10/ per thousand, Exchange to London £700 per £100 Sterling.

ADDRESSED: "Per Capt. Beake & Copie per Capt. Cooper Via Antigua"

TO JOHN BLANE
    Antigua

Charles Town, 15th November 1744

SIR:

    Being Informed by my Brother Andrew Pringle of London Merchant that he Coresponds with you for what Bussiness he has occassion to have transacted at your Island, I take this Oppertunity to make you a Tender of my Best Servises here, & to assure you that I shall verry much Esteem your Commands, & be always verry Glad to Render you any agreable Service. We have the Largest Crop of Rice this Year ever yett produc'd in the Province. Please Receive as under the prices of Goods here at present. I Salute you & am most Respectfully &c.

P. S. Rum 20/ per Gallon, Muscovado Sugar £12 at £14 per hundredweight, New Rice 25/ per hundredweight, Pitch 45/ per bbl., Tarr 40/ per bbl., Corn & pease 8/6 per Bushell, Beef £8 per bbl., Pork £12 per bbl., Exchange to London £700 per £100 Sterling.

ADDRESSED: "Per Capt. Beake Via St. Kitts & Copie per Capt. Cooper for Antigua"

TO SAMUEL WEBBER
St. Kitts[4]

Charles Town, 15th November 1744

SIR:

I Ommitted before went from this to Desire the favour you would be so good as to Enquire at Jamaica for One Capt. James Wimble formerly Commander of the Privateer Sloop *Revenge*, & am Informed is lately dead at Jamaica where he Commanded a Privateer Brigantine belonging to Jamaica. I had a Bill of Exchange of him on London for £75 Sterling for Money advanced When here about Two Years agoe, which has been Return'd Protested. Please be so good as to enquire wether he is Alive or Dead, & if dead wether he has any Effects in Jamaica, that I may send a power of Attorney in order to Recover my Money. I heartily wish you a prosperous Voyage & safe Return. Your Compliance with the above will greatly oblidge &c.

P. S. This goes by the Sloop *March*, Capt. David Conyers of Bermuda, Freighted by Mr. Manigault.

ADDRESSED: "Per Capt. Conyers"

[4] Capt. Samuel Webber, the sloop *William*, for St. Kitts. SCG, 12 November 1744.

19th November 1744

[767]
TO JAMES HENDERSON
Kingston, Jamaica

Charles Town, 19th November 1744

SIR:

I hope this Shall find you safe arrived from London. Being Informed by My Brother Andrew Pringle, Merchant there that he Corresponds with you & that you are to transact for him what Bussiness he may have occasion at Jamaica. I therefore take the Liberty to Trouble you with the Inclosed power of Attorney to your good self & am to Request the favour youll be so good as to use your best Endeavours to Recover of the Effects or Estate of Capt. James Wimble Late Commander of a Privateer Belonging to Jamaica who I understand dyed lately at Sea after taking a pretty good prize which is Carry'd into your Island of Jamaica.

You'll please observe he is Indebted to me £75 Sterling as per his Bill of Exchange on Lambert Ludlow, Esqr. in London for said sum and protest, herewith Inclosed, which he gave me when here about Two Years agoe it being for Cash I advanc'd him out of my Pockett towards fitting out his Privateer Sloop *Revenge* with Provissions & amunition otherways he Could not have proceeded to Sea, which Bill I Remitted to my Brother in London & was Return'd protested & Capt. Wimble has never been here since. The Bill you'll please Observe with Charges & Interest due thereon, to this Time as per account, Amount to £98.6.4 Sterling & am to begg you'l lose no Time to Recover Same or any part thereof & as Spedily as you Can, as beleive there may be other Demands on his Effects from Providence where he likewise owes Money, & if you Recover Same or any part thereof (am to desire you may take what you Can gett more or less Rather than lose the whole) & which you'll please to Remitt to my Brother in London on my account in any manner you may Judge proper or in Muscovado Sugar if any Conveyance offers for this Place. Inclosed please Recieve a Copie of Capt. Wimbles last letter to me being from New Providence of the 27 October 1743. I hope your Goodness will excuse the trouble & if in the like or any other occasion, I can be of any Service to you here, you may always verry freely Command &c.

P. S. Capt. David Conyears the Bearer of this & his mate are Witnesses to the power of Attorney and will attend for the Proof of it.

ADDRESSED: "Per Capt. David Conyers of the Sloop *March* & Copie per Abraham Snelling"

TO WHITAKER & HANNINGTON
London

Charles Town, 19th November 1744

GENTLEMEN:

I have your most Esteem'd favours of the 2d July per Capt. Scott In Return to mine of the 11th April per the *Lusitania* which am glad arrived safe & Remark your Due Honour of Capt. Graveners Bill in my favour for £41.10/, also your delivering a Certificate for the *Lusitanias* Cargoe to my Brother which expect per next Conveyance from London, & for all which am verry thankfull. By the Directions of Mr. Gedney Clarke am to advice you of the safe arrival here the 17th Current of the Sloop *Merrimack*, Francis Donovan, Commander from Barbadoes & I Embrace this Conveyance for Bristoll which is the first & only Oppertunity for England that will be from this for these three Weeks or Month to Come in hopes of Saving the Insurance on said sloop here.

We have this Year the Largest Crop of Rice that has ever yett been produced in the province, & but few Shipping here at present, so that freight will be high but is not yett broke, £7 per ton is Demanded for London, but not yett obtain'd. Shall be always verry glad to Receive your Commands & to Render you any acceptable Service being with verry Great Respect &c.

ADDRESSED: "Per Capt. Bartlett Via Bristol & Copie per Capt. Hunt"

[768]
TO ANDREW PRINGLE
London

Charles Town, 19th November 1744

SIR:

The Inclosed of the 17th October is Copie of my last Via Lisbon under Cover of Messrs. Mayne, & Since has Come to hand per Capt. Ham[5] Copies of all your favours as advised in my former, also yours of

---

[5] Capt. Peter Ham, ship *Priscilla*, arrived from London. *SCG*, 12 November 1744.

19th November 1744

the 12th May & Duely Remark the Contents. Mr. Thomas Elliott has Received all his letters & is verry thankfull for his Chaize & Watch. I did not think it to be needfull to Deliver him his account you sent, as I hope you have before this Received the Money for his Fire Tickett. He has writ you by this Conveyance as also to his Son & Sent him a Bill for £20 Sterling Drawn by one Mr. Mitford here on One Mr. McDonald at the Jamaica Coffee house[6] being at his Sons Request to purchase for him a Tickett in the state Lottery being Desireous as he has writ his Father to take his Chance or Try his Fortune in the Lottery & in Case the Bill on Mr. McDonald is not Honour'd desires you may Supply him with said sum of Ten pounds Sterling for a Tickett.

Some persons here Concern'd in the Privateer *Recovery* begin to Complain greatly of her not being as yett arrived & Seem to Insinuate that Mr. Crokatt & you have advised Capt. Anderson to go a Cruizing in Europe instead of Coming here Directly, & thereby breaking through his Instructions & which they say frustrates our Intentions with Respect to said privateer, especially as there is another Privateer Snow new Built of the Stocks and purchased here for a Consort & now Ready to put to Sea & only waits the arrival of the *Recovery*.[7] The Managers here talk of writing to you & Mr. Crokatt that in case Capt. Mark Anderson is still in Europe to turn him out of the Command of said privateer for Breach of orders & to put the Lieutenant or any other person you may Judge proper in the Command of said Privateer in order to proceed here with her Directly.

Your observation on Raizing a fund for the Defraying the Expence of Publick Opperations in Behalf of Trade or other Merchants in the Plantation Trade is Certainly verry good & Just & which Could I prevail on People here in Trade To join & agree on would be greatly for the advantage of this Province & the Trade thereof. Butt there is not a place perhaps in the Brittish Dominions where there is so little Good Harmony, Sociableness, & Unaminity amongst Persons in Trade as in this Town of Charles Town. I for my part have taken a Good deal of pains to make them Sociable & to have a Good understanding amongst themselves but all to no purpose & will be a hard task to bring them to a thing of that nature, altho so verry much for their Interest, there being some

---

[6] The Jamaica Coffee House was in St. Michael's Alley, London. Bryant Lillywhite, *London Coffee Houses* (London, 1963), pp. 282–285.
[7] This is the snow *Assistance* to be captained by Richard I'On which is described in *SCG*, 3 September 1744.

19th November 1744

persons here who you have knowledge of that are so Dogmaticall & verry opinionated.

I duly take notice what you are pleased to mention about Messrs. Turner & Jopson of Hull, who I think doe not use me well as I had a General order from them in Relation to Remittances and shall take Care to Secure my self in £16.4.0 Sterling Insurance on £75 at £21 per Cent per the *Lusitania* & Creditt your account for Same accordingly. Shall duely Honour your Draft to Capt. Nicholas Wadge for £10 Sterling whenever it appears. He is master of his Majestys Ship *Flamborough*, Capt. Hamar, on this Station which about a week agoe brought in here a French Prize Ship from Havannah with 80,000 peices of Eight on board, the Rest of the Cargoe being Hydes, Snuff, & Tobacco, the whole Value betwen Twenty & Thirty thousand pounds Sterling. If the Cargoe is Sold here and any bargains to be had at the Sale Intend to purchase what may think there Can be Something worth wile gott by.

We have the Largest Crop of Rice this Year that has ever yett been produced in the Province & is at 25/ per hundredweight new Rice. There are but few Ships here & Freight for England is not yett broke or Settled, £7 per Ton is Demmanded for London, but has not been yet obtain'd.

The *Robert & Jane*, Capt. Douglas, is half Loaded for Porto at £6 per Ton as I advised in my last & will be Ready to sail in Ten Days if Weather permitts, & hope you'll not omitt to take the [769] needfull Insurance on the Vessell & freight at & from this to Porto & advise your Friends thereof her Coming so that she may have a Good prospect at her arrival for a full Load of wine to London where at her arrival I shall interely leave to you to project her further procedure & Employs. As the planting of Rice is much overdone & a verry dull prospect for the Sale thereof it obliges our Planters to bestirr themselves to endeavour to Raise & produce other Comoditys, & in particular Indigo has been Try'd & the first Esay of a Tryall has been made by a person who has produced 50 lbs. weight & by those who pretend to be Judges is Esteem'd to be verry good which Incourages a Good Many others to try & proceed on the Planting & making of it next spring & which doubt not in a Short Time may come to great perfection & hope will not be soon overdone as Rice has been.

I duely Remark what you are pleased to hint of Messrs. Hutchinson & Goldthwait & which shall observe accordingly & take Care to be safe with them. I am to pray your best Endeavours to Recover the money due from Michael Thomson, & if he has the least spark of Gratitude or

19th November 1744

Honour in him, he Cant but pay itt if able, especially as you are Sencible he has taken a Good deal of my Money. Suppose I was to Draw a Sett of Bills of Exchange on him for the money, payable to his partners Wats & fuller in favour of Michael Lovell as a Remittance which he Desires me to make them on his account when in Cash for some Effects I have of his.

This Goes by Capt. Bartlett for Bristol who Came here with a Cargoe of Negroes to Hill & Geurrard. They & Messrs. Savage have had two Vessels each, with Negroes from Affrica all belonging to Bristoll since the Expiration of our Negro act in July last, & have all sold at verry good Rates & Verry Quick Sales.[8] I have not yett obtain'd a freight for the Ship belonging to Guernsey, which I would Rather have to London than Holland in order to Secure my self for my advance on her here as advised you in my former.

I am informed Capt. Wimble dyed lately at Sea, Commander of a Privateer belonging to Jaimaica where he had sent in a prize, & am now sending a power of Attorney to your Correspondent there Mr. James Henderson in order to Recover his Bill which I send him & the Protest by a Sloop now a Going there, & Shall advise him in Case he Recovers the Money or any part to Remitt same to you & am to desire you may advise him of Same & Send him the Second Bill & Copie of the Protest in Case the first I now send should Miscarry, this being the only Chance I may now have for the Money & perhaps may Recover Something if Mr. Henderson is Vigourous in the affair & pushes it.

My Wife Joyns in Kind love & Respects & I Remain most Truly & with the greatest Regaurd, &c.

P. S. I Still Continue my Resolution of paying my Respects to you in London when my affairs will permitt but when, or if next Summer, is Still as yett uncertain. Capt. Douglass writes you by this Conveyance.

I have at Several Times made Remittances to Messrs. Burryau & Schaffer on account of Thomas Hutchinson of Boston, but have never yett been favour'd with a Line from them.

ADDRESSED: "Per Capt. Bartlett Via Bristol & Copie per Mr. Jermyn Wright"

---

[8] Capt. John Bartlett, ship *Jason Galley*, cleared for Bristol. SCG, 26 November 1744. The cargo of the snow *Tryal*, William Jefferies, was sold by Hill & Guerard, while that of the snow *Nancy*, Joseph Beaver, and that of the snow *Africa*, Joseph Hunt, were sold by John Savage & Co. Donnan, IV, 296. SCG 6 August, 17 September, 22 October, 29 October 1744.

TO ANDREW LESSLY
Antigua

Charles Town, 22nd November 1744

SIR:

My last to you was of the 9th June per Favour of Mr. George Lucas. Since have not the Pleasure of any of your Favours. I have Just Time by this Conveyance to advise you that a Few days agoe arrived here the Sloop *Merrimack*, Capt. Francis Donovan, Commander from Barbadoes to my address belonging to Gedney Clark, Esqr. with directions from said Gentleman to Load the Sloop with Pitch, Tarr, & Turpintine to be delivered to your Good self at Antigua.

Naval Stores happen to be verry Scarce & dear here at present, there being a Great demand for Same. However Shall take Care to dispatch the sloop as Speedily as possible if I can procure a Load for her, according to Mr. Clarks directions. And hope will be with you in Ten days [770] After you Receive this. I have not Further to offer at Present as being without any of your Favours & I Remain With verry great Respect &c.

P. S. Capt. William Douglas is here bound for Portugal in a Vessel belonging to my Brother and who Presents you his Best Respects.

ADDRESSED: "Per Capt. Cooper & Copie per Capt. Dunovan"

TO RICHARD ROWLAND
St. Kitts

Charles Town, 22nd November 1744

SIR:

The Preceeding of the 26th June is Copie of my last, & Since have not the Pleasure of any of your Favours. Having the Following paragraph in a Letter from a Person in North Carolina who knows Capt. Dickinson, I am in hopes it is your good self that has Secured him in Order to oblidge him to discharge his Bond & Note due me & that you have secur'd my debt or the best Part of it, for which shall always Rekon my self under the greatest obligations. Paragraph, Vizt. Capt. Dickinson was last May

23rd November 1744

put in Jail at St. Kitts for Money he owed in So. Carolina. He Mortgag'd some Lands he had at Core sound, Sold his Sloop to gett at Liberty, & is gone a Privateering in a Sloop belonging to that Island.

If so youll please be so good as to advise me thereof by the Return of Capt. Cooper bound for Antigua who Returns here Directly, & if there is any occasion to send you again his Bond & Note, it shall be duely Comply'd with per first Conveyance. What you may have Recover'd of said Dickinson you'll please (after Deducting for what Charge & Trouble you have been at in the affair) To Remitt same to my Brother Andrew Pringle, Merchant in London, By bill of Exchange or otherwise as you Judge proper, giving him previous Notice for Insurance if worth while.

We have a Verry large Crop of Rice & all provisions in great plenty, as under please Receive the Prices of Goods. I Most Respectfully Salute you & am &c.

Rum 17/ per Gallon, Muscovado Sugar £12.10 per Ct., Rice 25/ per hundredweight, Pitch 50/ per bbl., Tarr 40/ per bbl., Beef £8 per bbl., Pork £12 per bbl., Shingles £3.10/ per Mille, Exchange To London £700 per £100 Sterling.

ADDRESSED: "Per Mr. Hanson in Capt. Cooper Via Antigua & Copie per Capt. Dunovan Via Antigua"

TO SETH PILKINGTON
Bath Town, North Carolina

Charles Town, 23rd November 1744

SIR:

I Received your kind favours of the 2d Current by the Bearer of this, John Hardison, and am greatly oblidged to you for your kind Advices & Especially for your good offices in Recovering my debt of Mr. McDowall, who it Seems proves a Great knave. When you Receive the Money for said McDowalls debt, if no oppertunity this Way, you'll please to Remitt itt in any of your Country produce of Pitch, Tarr, or Turpintine, &c. to Boston on my account, Consigning it to Mr. John Erving, Merchant there, or to St. Christophers to Mr. Isaac Duport, Merchant there, or to

23rd November 1744

Antigua to Mr. Michael Lovell, Merchant there, or to Barbadoes to Mr. Gedney Clarke, Merchant there. As also for your own note which Mr. Hardison tells me it does not suit him to discharge, so that he has not paid me the money.

I am Suprized I never hear, neither have had any Remittances, made by James Blount of Edentown (who bears a Verry good Charracter). I have his Bond for Goods he bought of me when here last, for Eighty four pounds Sterling Due now near three Years agoe & he has not made any Remittances in Tobacco to My Brother Andrew Pringle, Merchant in London as he he writ me he would, nether any where else which think is not using me Well & hope he wont put me or him self to the Trouble of Sending a power of Attorney to Sue him Which must be oblidg'd to do If he does not Verry Soon discharge his Bond, which you'll observe is [771] for a Considerable Sum & if in Case I am oblidged to take such measures Contrary to my Inclinations shall be glad to know if you'll be so good as to accept a power of Attorney from me to put His Bond in Suit & Will Send you his Bond by the first Sure hand after Receipt of your Answer in Case he does not take proper Measures to discharge it & the Interest due thereon Very Speedily.

Inclosed please Receive a Letter for him which after perusal you'll please to Seal & deliver him your Self, & at Same time desire him to lett you have his positive Answer in Writing to Send me & am to pray the Favour you'll Give me your opinion of Mr. Blunt & his Circumstances & your advice in What Manner to proceed with him & the Likelyest way to Recover My Money which you'll be so kind as to acquaint me off by the first oppertunity this way. I have writ him a Great Many letters & Can never hear a Word from him. I hope your Goodness will Excuse this Trouble I Give you & if in the like or any other occasion I can be of any Service to you here you may always Verry freely Command &c.

P. S. Please Receive as under the Prices of goods here at present.
Rum West India 17/6 per Gallon, Ditto New England 15/, Muscovado Sugar £12.10 per hundredweight, New Rice 25/ per hundredweight, Pitch 50/ bbl., Tarr 40/ bbl., Turpintine 15/ per hundredweight, Beef £8 barrell, Pork £12 per barrell, Corn & pease 10/ bushel, Myrtle Wax 5/ per lb., Madeira Wine £120 per pipe, Loaf Sugar Single Refin'd 8/ per lb., Deer Skins 16/ per lb., Flower £4 per Ct., Ship Bread £4 per Ct., Exchange to London £700 per £100 Sterling.

P. S. You may also if you please Remitt to New York to Mr. John Livingston, to Philadelphia to Mr. Robert Ellis or to Rhode Island to Mr. David Chesebrough, Merchants there, &c.

ADDRESSED: "Per John Hardison"

TO JAMES BLOUNT
Edentown, North Carolina

Charles Town, 23rd November 1744

SIR:

I have writ you a Great Many Times the last of the 21st June last by one William Stevens, but to my great Suprize Cannot hear one Word or have one line from you Which think does not answer the good Character I always Entertain'd of Mr. Blount. My Brother Andrew Pringle, Merchant in London, advises me in his last letter from thence that as yett he had Received no Remittances in Tobacco, Bill of Exchange, or any thing else you promised and advis'd me you would make to him. You may be Sencible your Bond has been now due a Very Considerable Time & is for a Considerable Sum & you have not yett discharg'd any part of itt. I hope you wont give me Reason & oblidge me to take Measures which will not be agreeable to me no more than to you & Contrary to my Inclination to have your Bond put in Suit, which must be the Case if you doe not take proper measures to discharge it in a Short Time. This will be delivered you by my Freind Mr. Seth Pilkington who I have desired the Favour to deliver you this himself & to gett from you your Positive answer in Writing to send me, & to know When I may Certainly depend on payment of your Bond which desire you will not fail to do as Soon as this Comes to your hand. And if you have not yett made any Remittances to my Brother as aforesaid, hope you'll take Care to do same without any further delay & if no oppertunity to London desire you may Remitt to the West Indies in Beef, Pork, &c. to Antigua Consign'd to Mr. Michael Lovel, if to St. Christophers to Mr. Isaac Duport, if to Barbadoes to Mr. Gedney Clarke, Merchants there, or to Boston, N. E. in

23rd November 1744

Pitch, Tarr, or Turpintine Consign'd to Mr. John Erving, Merchant there. So that you May make Remittances as Conveyances offers to any of the places which hope for your own Interest you will not fail to Embrace as soon as you can giving me advice thereof. I desire your full & Speedy answer to this, to be Delivered to My freind Mr. Pilkington aforsaid in order to be sent me as soon as possible, and which hope will be to my satisfaction so that I may take my measures accordingly, & in Expectation of which I Remain &c.

P. S. You may also Remit to New York to Mr. John Livingston, to Philadelphia to Mr. Robert Ellis, or to Rhode Island to Mr. David Chesebrough, Merchants there.

ADDRESSED: "Under Cover of Seth Pilkington to be Deliver'd by him"

[772]
TO JAMES HENDERSON
Kingston, Jamaica

Charles Town, 29th November 1744

SIR:
The preceeding on the other side is Copie of mine of the 19th Instant per Capt. Coneyears which this Serves to Confirm & Inclosed please Receive Copie of Capt. Wimbles 1st Bill of Exchange in my favour for £75 Sterling with Copie of the Protest and account of the whole amount, also another power of Attorney to your Good self in Case of Miscarriage of the other & Witness'd by the bearer Mr. Abraham Snelling[9] who will wait on you to prove itt. He brings a Cargo of provissions to dispose of and being a Stranger in Your Island Shall Esteem it a favour for what Civilitys or Good Offices you may be pleased to Show him. I most Respectfully Salute you and am &c.

ADDRESSED: "Per Abraham Snelling in Capt. Wells"

---

[9] Capt. Abraham Snelling, ship *Venus*, to London. SCHM, III (1902), 216n; SCG, 29 December 1739.

TO JAMES ARCHBOLD
Oporto

Charles Town, 24th December 1744 [1743]

SIR:

I Received Two days agoe Copie of your Esteem'd Favours of the 24th August Via N. England. The Original has not yett appeared. I duely Remark what you are pleased to advise in Relation to our Commodity of Rice, & when I have occasion & there is Encouragement of Shipping Rice to your port you may expect same to your address, as I have great Regard for my Brothers Recommendation, & shall be always verry Glad Reciprochally to Contribute in Encouraging any branch of Trade that has a prospect for our mutuall Interest & when your markett is encouraging, & you may think proper to give directions for Shipping any Rice for your port, shall be willing to goe part Concern'd in the adventure, as I doubt not my Brother will likewise take part therein.

At Present our Markett does not Seem to be Encouraging, for by late advices from my Freinds in Lisbon they acquaint me that a pritty deal of Rice has been Shipt from your port for said place. Shall take it kind as oppertunity offers that you'll be so Good as to favour me with your advices Relating to your Markett & be always verry Glad to Render you any Acceptable Service. I Salute you with the usual Compliments of the Season & I am Most Respectfully &c.

ADDRESSED: "Per Capt. Douglass & Copie per Capt. Phillips Via Lisbon"

TO JAMES ARCHBOLD
Oporto

Charles Town, 5th December 1744

SIR:

The Preceeding on the other Side of the 24 December last is Copie of what I did my self the Pleasure to write you in Return to yours & since have not any of your favours. This will be Deliver'd you by Capt. William Douglass of the Snow *Robert & Jane*, who Came here from Lisbon & is bound for Oporto, and as our Comodity of Rice bears but a Low Price in

5th December 1744

Portugal, & being offered a Good freight for your place thought it most for the Interest of the Concern'd to embrace the Opportunity & Goe Loaded with Rice accordingly. My Brother & I are Concern'd with the Vessell. I therefore take the Liberty to Recommend Capt. Douglas to your good offices while at Oporto, & am to Request the Favour you'll be so good as to be assistant to procure him a Load of Wines on freight for London.

We have a Verry large Crop of Rice this Year & is now at 25/ per hundredweight & but very few [773] Shipping. Shall be verry glad to have the pleasure of hearing from you & to Render you any acceptable Service, & I am with verry Great Respect &c.

Exchange to London £700 per £100 Sterling.

ADDRESSED: "Per Capt. Douglass & Copie per Capt. Philips"

TO FITTER & TYZACK[1]
London

Charles Town, 6th December 1744

GENTLEMEN:

Richard Oliver, Esqr. of Antigua Sometime agoe Consign'd me 6 Hogsheads Rum, & the Neat Proceeds thereof he Directed me to Remitt to your Good Selves per Bill of Exchange which he might have Expected before this, but in the Cource of this Trade at present good Bills are verry scarce & Seldom to be obtain'd, which has been the occasion of my not Remitting long agoe. However please now Receive Inclosed Mr. John Lightfoot his first Bill of Exchange for Fifty pounds Sterling on Mr. Richard Boddicott, Merchant in London Dated in Antigua July 14th, 1744 payable at 30 days sight to the order of Messrs. Benjamin King, Thomas Sommers, Andrew Lessly, and Charles Dunbar, & to your Good Selves Indorsed, & which doubt will be duely Honoured.

Please also Receive Inclosed Mr. Olivers Account Current, Ballance

[1] Fitter & Tyzack were merchants in Tower Hill, London. RPC, p. 774; *London Directories*.

6th December 1744

Due him being £18.4.5 this Currency which at the Current Exchange of £700 per £100 Sterling Is £2.12 Sterling for which Ballance desire you'll please to apply to My brother Andrew Pringle at the Carolina Coffee house who will pay you said small Ballance & for both which you'll please to Creditt the account of Richard Oliver, Esqr. accordingly, who I understand is lately gone from Antigua for England, to whom please to present my best Respects & acquaint him of said Remittance. I am most Respectfully &c.

P. S. You'll please be so good as to favour me with a Line of the Receipt of said Bill. The account Sales of the Rum I forwarded Some time ago to Mr. Oliver himself to Antigua.

ADDRESSED: "Per Capt. Hunt & Copie per Capt. Bartlett both for Bristoll"

TO ANDREW PRINGLE
London

Charles Town, 6th December 1744

SIR:

My last to you was of the 19th Ulto. with Copies to which please be Refered & am Still without any of your Favours, the last being of the 7th June. This per the Snow *Robert & Jane,* Capt. William Douglas, being now Compleatly loaded & Ready to Sail for Oporto having on board One hundred Baggs & four Hundred & fifty Barrils New Rice. I have writ by Capt. Douglass to Mr. James Archbold at Porto Requesting his good offices in favour of the *Robert & Jane,* & hope he wont be wanting to assist Capt. Douglas in procuring a Load of Wines on Freight for London.

The privateer *Recovery* does not yett appear on which account there are now great Complaints & Reflections & which is like to Create great Disputes & Confusion amongst the Concern'd by Reason of the *Recovery*'s not Coming here Directly without Cruizing as Directed & according to our Instructions to Capt. Anderson who has broke his Instructions & think has Us'd the Concern'd here verry Ill & has acted with the Greatest Indiscretion & Ingratitude. You'll please observe the Let-

6th December 1744

ter from the Managers here of the 30th past to your self & Mr. Crokatt Relating thereto by which you'll observe they have given you positive directions to turn out & displace Capt. Anderson from the Command of the *Recovery* if still in England in Case does not Come away or does not proceed here directly, & which if he does not Instantly Comply with. Think he is a verry great Villain & ought to be exposed for his Ingratitude & ill usage to those who have been the making of him. Inclosed please Receive Copie of the 3d, 4th, 5th, & 6 Article of his Instructions by which you'll observe that he has most notoriously broke thro' Same by not [774] Coming here directly, & hope your best Endeavours wont be wanting to turn him out of the Command according to his Deserts, & to Dispatch the *Recovery* here as there is no Dependence nor no faith to be putt in such a Man, & am of opinion it will be Necessary for you to Exert your Self in this afair for the Interest of the Concern'd, both for your own Honour & Reputation as well as mine, which are both Concern'd in the afair.

I engag'd in it being of opinion it would Redound both to your Reputation & mine, but instead of being of any Service to us is likely to prove the Reverse & am like to have nothing but Reflections & Ill will on said account, Especially from the freinds of Alderman Baker & Who seems to Snear at our Disapointments & Andersons Villany & to insinuate that Mr. Crokatt & you have Countenanced him & advised him to Detain the Ship by going a Cruizcing in Europe, as appears by his letters to us of the 16th June. Therefore say they you are more Blameable than He, tho' Doubt not Mr. Crokatt & you are able to Clear your Selves with much Honour. However the *Recoverys* not Coming has intirely frusterated the Scheme & Intentions of the Concern'd & have Render'd the whole undertaking in a Manner abortive. A fine new Snow Built here & now fitted for a Consort for the *Recovery* at a Great Expence Lying Ready & of no Use being in Dayly expectation of Andersons arrival, & dont know what to doe with her or where to send her on a Cruize without a Consort, & Several of the Concern'd Refuse to pay us their Subscriptions, so that the Burthen is like to fall on the Managers, & am dayly hearing so much Clamour & Reflections that I heartily wish I had Never desired you, nor been any ways Concern'd in the afair myself.

Thomas Elliott, Esqr. Desires you may send him as soon as Conviently you Can a Chair for a Single horse with an Iron Axle Tree, the Carriage to be fixed on the Shafts, the Wheels to be five feet high, & the seat three feet in the Clear, & to make Insurance for the Value.

6th December 1744

The *Robert & Jane* has happen'd to gett a Verry good freight. It was Lucky that Capt. Douglass had a Licence with him which all Vessells that Come here any Time for freight ought never to be without. Freight is not yett broke for London or Holland, & altho' but verry few Shipping are not yett Taken up, the Shippers keep off. I would take £6 per Ton for London for the Geurnsey Ship but cannot obtain it neither any Ship here & may Insure on said Ship *Ann Galley*, Capt. John Trenchard, Commander for London One hundred or One hundred & fifty pounds Sterling but in Case I Cannot obtain Freight for said ship for London & oblidge to lett her out on Freight for Holland. In that Case the Insurance must be alter'd from her to Some other Vessel that I can gett freight on for London. Rice is at 25/ per hundredweight, pitch 50/, & Tarr 40/, Turpintine 15/ per hundredweight.

I am to Request you'll please be so good as to pay to Messrs. Fitter & Tyzack, Merchants in London, £2.12/ Sterling (say fifty Two Shillings Sterling), being ballance of account Current of Richard Oliver, Esqr. of Antigua which have Remitted them by his order & which have Desired them to aply to you for being so much Short of the Remittance made them for Ballance of his account. I understand Mr. Oliver is gone for England to live there for good, & by Character is a Verry worthy man. Have Sent you under the Care of Capt. Douglas Two Dozen of Clarett & Two Dozen of good Barbadoes Rum, also a Cage with Two Birds Called Non pareils,[2] a Cock & a Hen, which are Esteem'd Curious to bring round with him to you, & which you'll please to make acceptable.

Inclosed please Receive Account of Capt. Douglass his Disbursments here on the *Robert & Jane*, Amount £642.5/ this Currency also his Receipt for money paid him here, amount £390 Currency which you'll please to note accordingly. [775] Capt. Douglass proposes to Sail tomorrow & as the wind is at N. W. hope he will gett over the Barr & have a good passage. I add not at present as being without any of your Favours but that I most Respectfully Remain &c.

P. S. Several of the Concerned in our Privateers want to Sell out their Shares but Can find no Buyers.

ADDRESSED: "Per Capt. Douglass & Copies per Capt. Hunt & Capt. Bartlett both for Bristoll"

[2] The painted Bunting was a bird of gorgeous colors which summered in South Carolina and wintered in Yucatan and Panama. Locally, it was called the "non-pareil," "without an equal." *HL*, I, 264n.

6th December 1744

TO GEDNEY CLARKE
Barbados

Charles Town, 6th December 1744

SIR:

My last to you was of the 29th June, & on the 17th past arrived here your Sloop *Merrimack*, Francis Donovan, Commander from Barbadoes By whom have your Esteem'd Favours of the 26th October with Bill of Loading & Invoice of Fifteen Hhds. Rum, & three Teirces & Six barrils Sugar on your account which have Received in pretty Good order, also your directions to Load with dispatch your said sloop with about 130 bbl. Turpintine, 400 bbls. of Pitch, & the Remainder of her Loading in Tarr to be delivered to Andrew Lessly, Esqr. in Antigua.

I am to acquaint you that your Sloop has happened to arrive here at a Time when all manner of Naval Stores are verry Scarce & dear there being a verry great Demand for them at Present & Esteem'd the best Return for Europe (our Rice of which we have a verry great Crop being a Verry dull Commodity all over Europe & America) which has prevented me from dispatching your Sloop by the Time you order'd. There can not a bbl. of Naval Stores to be purchased in Town since her arrival at any Rate & little or none Ready up in the Country to bring to Town, having sent up one of My Clarks on purpose who mett with verry little ready but what had been Engag'd a Considerable Time agoe. However the Sloop has now about 250 barrils on board & may depend shall not Lose one Moment in giving her all the Dispatch possible, tho' am afraid must be obliged to Ship more or less of some of the Commodity's you ordered to give the Sloop the More dispatch & wish you had been more full & Discretionary in your Orders, as the Sloop might have been Loaded & dispatch'd within the Time you Limited, provided that naval Stores Could be purchas'd at any Rate.

Shall per my next Transmitt you Invoice of the Cargoe which I had not your directions to Send to Mr. Lessly. I immediatly advised Messrs. Whitaker & Hannington of the Sloop's arrival as you Directed by three Difrent Conveyances So that am in hopes you will Save the Insurance. Have sold your Sugar at £12.10/ per hundredweight & the bbl. of Clay'd for £14 per hundredweight. As for the Rum there is a great deal in Town at present & a Slow Sale not having as yett disposed of any of it & wont fetch more than 17/6 per Gallon. I Received Two bird Cages per Capt.

Philips[3] which you may expect with Birds as you desire per Capt. Donovan.

Inclosed please Receive account Sales of the Remainder of the Grindstones & Butter per the *Lusitania* which was obliged to put up at Publick Vendue, Neat Proceeds being £67.8.11 this Currency which have plac'd to the Creditt of the Owners & wait your orders how Same is to be Invested & Remitt'd

I have advise of the 2d July from Messrs. Whitaker & Hannington of the *Lusitanias* safe arrival. Freight is Likely to be high here this Season but not yett broke, there are but few Shipping at present, & we have the Largest Crop of Rice ever yett produced & is at 25/ per Ct. I try'd to Dispose of your Sloop *Merrimack* at the price you mention'd but find no person Inclinable to purchase.

Four Vessells have arrived here with Negroes from the [776] Coast of Africa since the Expiration of our Negro Act in July last & were all immediatly sold of at Verry Good Rates. About three weeks agoe his Majesty's Ship the *Flamborough* on this Station brought in here a French Prize from the Havannah Value about £20,000 Sterling. Shall doe myself the pleasure to write you again soon by your Sloop *Merimack*, meantime I most Respectfully Remain &c.

ADDRESSED: "Per Capt. Hutchins & Copie per Capt. Dunovan Via Antigua"

TO ANDREW PRINGLE
London

Charles Town, 12th December 1744

SIR:

I have already writt you of the 6th Current (with two copie thereof via Bristoll) per this Conveyance of the Snow *Robert & Jane*, Capt. Douglass, who since my Last has been Detain'd in Our Road by N. E. Winds, to which begg Leave to be Refferr'd, & am as yet without any of your Favours. Since my Last have lett out on Freight the Ship *Ann Galley* of Guernsey, Capt. John Trenchard, Commander for London at £5.15

---
[3] Capt. Samuel Philips, ship *Indian King*, arrived from Antigua. SCG, 28 May 1744.

per Ton to be Loaded in Three Weeks or a Month. The Ship is London built, about 150 Tons, well Fitted and Mann'd, & agreeable to my Last You'll please to gett Insur'd on Goods to be Ship'd on board said Vessel, at & from this to London Two hundred Pounds Sterling, One Hundred Pounds whereof On Account of the Owners of the *John & Isabella* in Company with S S[4] which I purpose to Ship in Deer Skins, & the other One Hundred Pounds on my Own Proper Account which I intend to Ship in Rice, & to Receive 98 per cent in Case of a Loss. I am to Desire you'll please to advise Messrs. Henry & John Brock of Guernsey of my letting out their Ship accordingly, which I am afraid I shall not have time to doe by this Opportunity, & that they may Order Insurance on the Ship, as also on the Freight from this to London.

As I advis'd in my former most sorts of European & India Goods are very scarce & much wanted in Town at Present, particularly Single Refin'd Loaf Sugar, Gun powder Single Fine, Tea of Both Sorts, China Ware, Spices, Ozenbriggs, Course ¾, & Middling Garlix, Florence Oyl, & Middling Cambricks, & Diaper, ¾ Cheq Linnens & Yard-Wide, most of which wou'd fetch ready Pay, also Sail Cloth, Cordage & Twine, &c. I Refferr you to an Assortment of Goods I sent you Last Year, most of which wou'd now answer very well, especially the aforesaid Articles; also men & Womens Cotton & thread Stockings.

Our Assembly have been upon an Act of Parliament which is to be pass'd at Home to prevent the Issueing of Paper Money in America & which it is thought will greatly Affect all the Collonies on the Continent, & are about Giving Directions to the Agent, Mr. Fury, to make Application to prevent the Said Act from Passing, & am told they are to Join Colonel John Fenwick with the Agent as an Assistant (being Diffedent of him) & who I take to be a very unfitt Person, as being but a Weak Man & in his Dotiage.[5]

I have not further to Offerr at Present, but Remain in Haste.

P. S. Inclosed please Receive a Letter which have writt Since for Messrs. Henry & John Brock in Guernsey, which after perusal please to Seal & Forward them.

ADDRESSED: "Per Capt. Douglass & Copies per Capt. Philips Via Lisbon & Capt. Hunt Via Bristoll

[4] SS was Samuel Saunders.
[5] The currency act when passed in 1751 applied only to New England.

12th December 1744

[777]
TO HENRY & JOHN BROCK
   Guernsey

Charles Town, 12th December 1744

GENTLEMEN:

My Last to you was of the 17th September with Copies And as Yet have none of your Favours. In my Last I Advis'd you of the Unhappy Death of Capt. Bernard, as also of Mr. Falla the Mate, & since all the Ships Company have been sick, & two of them are Dead, Vizt. John Dubois & Daniel Parker the Carpenter. And am now to Advise you that since my Last, finding Peter Bonamy not Quallified to take Command of your Ship *Ann Galley*, I did Appoint Capt. John Trenchard, Commander thereof, a very Capable Person well known in this Place & of a very good Character & who had the Misfortune to be taken in goeing Commander of a Ship from this Last Summer to Bristol & Carry'd in to St. Augustine & since Mr. Bonamy is mate of your Ship *Ann* which have gott fitted for the Sea, having wanted Considerable repairs & been very much out of Order, & have waited till now for a Freight which have just Engaged at £5.15/ Sterling per Ton for London to be Loaded with Rice & Some Deer Skins in a Month, & will be the first Ship Loaded this Season with New Rice, & which is the Largest Freight has been yet obtain'd to England or Holland since the Commencement of the Warr & hope will be to your Approbation.

As I Advis'd in my Last no Doubt you have Order'd what Insurance you judge Proper both on Ship & also on the Freight, which my Brother in London will take Care to Negotiate for you if you have not already given Directions otherwise, & to whom shall Address your Ship *Ann* at Arrival there as having no Directions Relating to Same from your good Selves. As for my Disbursments on your Ship here which you may be sensible must be Considerable having been here now for near These Six Months past. You may Expect my Drafts on You payable at the house of Mr. William Dobree, Merchant in London which doubt not Youll give Directions may be Duely honour'd.

It happens well that Provisions are Cheap here, & that your Sailors are on Easie & Low wages & stay by the Ship. There being now Fifteen & Twenty Guineas given to Sailors for the Run to Europe, Seaman are so very Scarce & Difficult to be Procured here. As I shall write you again soon by your *Ann Galley*, I have not Further to Offer at present but that I am most Respectfully &c.

ADDRESSED: "Under Cover of A.P. per Capt. Douglass & Copies per Capt. Philips & Capt. Hunt"

TO ALEXANDER MCKENSEY
Hampton, Virginia

Charles Town, 13th December 1744

SIR:

Having Occasion to have some Correspondance with Richard Bennett, Esqr. of Wye River Maryland, who acquainted me that he Corresponds with Your Good Self, & directed me to Consign to you some of the Produce of this Province on his Account, but have never been able since to meet with any Freight Your Way, which I Advis'd Mr. Bennett of & Since he has Order'd Same Otherways. And altho unknown to you I Take the Liberty to Recommend to your Acquaintance the Bearar of this, Mr. Alexander Abercrombie,[6] a very worthy Agreeable Gentleman, who Comes to Your Place, with a Small Cargoe of New Rice & Oranges the produce of this Province. This Year being the first Essay of a Tryall for Exportation of Oranges from this Province, & hope will meet with Good Encouragement in Your Parts, so as an Yearly Exportation of Same may be Continued. Orange Trees having been brought to great Maturity here, & a very Considerable Quantity of Oranges has already this Fall been Exported from this to Philadelphia, New York, & Boston.

What Civilities & Good Offices you are Pleas'd to Show Mr. Abercrombie, shall esteem a very Particular Favour, & if in any thing I can be of any Service to You or Friends here, You may always most freely Command him who is Most Respectfully &c.

[6] Alexander Abercromby, brother to James Abercromby, the Attorney General of South Carolina, was one of the sixty-eight English prisoners returned by the *St. Andrew*, flag of truce, from Havanna. SCG, 29 October 1744.

17th December 1744

P. S. Shall be very Glad to be Favour'd with a Line from you by Mr. Abercrombie who Returns here Directly & that some Branch of Trade could be Carry'd on between your place & this to Mutual Advantage.

ADDRESSED: "Per Mr. Alexander Abercrombie"

TO DAVID CHESEBROUGH
Newport, Rhode Island

Charles Town, 17th December 1744

SIR:

I have your Favours of the 13th October in Return to mine of the 30th June & observe the Contents. Inclosed please Receive Account Sales of your Twenty Boxes Soap, Neat Proceeds being £119.3 this Currency which hope will be to Content. Those I sold It to Complain of its having shrunk very much in the weight as it dry'd up Greatly in our Hott Season. Inclosed please also Receive your Account Current, Balance in your Favour being £114.6/ Currency for which is Inclosed Bill of Loading for Seventy Six Dollars at 30/ & one Pistareen at 6/ Is £114.6/ Currency Deliver'd Dudley Hilton, Master of the Sloop *Olive Branch* for your Island which wish safe to Hand & Ballances Your Account Current. Shall be Verry Glad to Continue a Correspondence with you which the War Seems at Present to obstruct & which ought to make us wish for a Speedy but Honourable Peace.

Indigo is a Commodity that is Verry uncommon in this Place & none has been brought in here since the War So that I cannot with any Certainty advise you what It woud Sell for here, but am of opinion a Quantity would Sell verry well & be a Good Article for a Return to Europe provided it Comes Reasonable & Especially as our Comodity of Rice is So Verry dull in Europe & freight here So high being at Six pounds per Ton for London, So that Rice wont bear a freight that a Comodity of Value Will, & for your Return you may have Dollars being now pretty plenty here & Current at 30/ a peice.

As for Cocoa it will not am afraid Answer there having been

17th December 1744

a pritty deal Imported & Sold at Publick Vandue at £25 & £30 per Ct. Currency. Good muscovado Sugar in Barrels & Loaf Sugar would Answer very well & florence Oyl, but no Clarett or Brandy, a Pretty deal of both being lately Imported. New England Rum has taken a Sudden Rise & is now at 15/ Gal. & West India Rum at 17/6 per Gall. Shall be always verry Glad to have the Pleasure of hearing from you & to Render you any agreeable Service & I am most Respectfully &c.

P. S. Rice 25/ per Ct., Pitch 50/ per bbl., Tar 40/, Muscovado Sugar £12.10/ per Ct., Loaf Sugar Single 7/6 per lb., Exchange to London £700 per £100 Sterling. I am to pray the Favour You'll be so good as to Enquire & advise me if One Capt. James Wimble lately Commander of the Privateer Sloop *Revenge* at your Island left or has any Effects in hands of Mr. Peter Bours of Your Island, said Wimble being Indebted to me, & I understand was Commander of a Privateer from Jamaica & is Since dead. Should take it verry kind if you Can put me in a Way to Recover my Money.

The Following Goods besides what I have already mention'd if Reasonable & Come low with you will answer very well here at present, Vizt. Coffee, Gun powder single Fine, Tea of both Sorts, China Ware particularly Bowles, Dishes, & Plates, Spices of all sorts.

Just now We Have an account that his Majestys Ship *Rose*, Capt. Frankland, is Come off our Bar it is said with a Register Ship, being a Large Ship, & Esteem'd a very Rich Prize Taken Near the Havanah after a Very Smart Engagement.[7] The 76 Dollars are in a Bagg Mark't. D. C. & Sealed with wax.

ADDRESSED: "Per the Sloop *Olive Branch*, Capt. Dudley Hilton"

---

[7] For an account of the capture of the ship *Conception*, De Marcan and Piedro DeLessagrate, commanders, and its incredibly rich cargo, see *SCG*, 24 December 1744. This prize was worth £80,000, perhaps the greatest prize ever brought into Charleston harbor. For a description of the goods aboard see George C. Rogers, Jr., *Charleston in the Age of the Pinckneys* (Norman, Okla., 1969), pp. 33-34.

TO JOHN ERVING
Boston

Charles Town, 17th December 1744

SIR:

The preceeding of the 7th November per the Sloop *Rebecca*, Capt. Bangs, is Copie of my last & about three Weeks agoe Received your most Esteem'd Favours of the 27th October at the hands of Mr. Osborne, & are heartily Concern'd, my Wife & I to be Informed of the Indisposition of good Mrs. Erving. Hope this shall find her, your self, & all the pritty Young Ones in the Most perfect State of Health. I shall with great Pleasure Render Mr. Osborne all the good offices in my power, or any other Friend that you may be pleased to take Notice of to me.

Freight has just broke here at £5.15/ & £6 per Ton for London & there are but Very few Shipping here at present. Rice is now at 25/ per hundredweight, & Naval Stores Scarce & dear, Pitch being at 50/ per bbl., Tarr 40/, & Turpintine 15/ per Ct. & all of them much in Demand, but will be in plenty in the Spring as our Planters find it will answer much better for them now to goe on making of Naval Stores than Rice which is now a Verry dull Comodity. Several European Goods are very Scarce & Dear here at Present particularly Gun powder, Florence Oyl, Tea of both Sorts, China Ware, Spices, & Loaf Sugar.

This Goes by a Sloop Via Rhode Island. My Wife joyns in most kind Respects to your good Lady, & all your pritty Family, Most heartily Wishing you a Merry Xmass & a great many happy Years & truely am with very Great Respect &c.

Rum N. E. 15/ per Gall., West India at 17/6, Muscovado Sugar £12.10/ per Ct., Loaf Sugar Single 7/6 per lb., Madeira Wine £125 per Pipe, Brandy 25/ per Gall. P. S. Just now we have account that his Majestys ship *Rose*, Capt. Frankland, is Come off our Barr it is said with a Register Ship, being a Large French Ship & Esteem'd a very Rich Prize Taken near the Havanna after a Verry Smart Engagement.

ADDRESSED: "Per the Sloop *Olive Branch*, Capt. Dudley Hilton Via Rhode Island"

[780]
TO WILLIAM PRINGLE
    Antigua
                        Charles Town, 20th December 1744
Sir:
    Since my last to you of the 2d July I have your Very Kind Favours of the 28th August, as it is always very agreable to me to have the Pleasure of Hearing from you, & to be inform'd of What passes Remarkable in your parts.
    I am Very Glad to hear that your Island has been so successfull in Distressing our Most Formidale Enemies the French, & thereby Contribute so much to the advantage of Antigua for which, as I have Some Very worthy Friends there, I Shall always have the greatest Reguard. We in this part of the world have been hirtherto pretty much out of the way in making advantage by the war, & this Province has profitted nothing thereby till of late. One of the Kings Ships stationed here Named the *Flamborough*, Capt. Joseph Hamar, Commander about 6 Weeks agoe brought in here a large french Ship bound from Havanah to France after a Pritty Smart Engagement in Value about Twenty thousand pounds Sterling & a few Days agoe arrived of this Bar His Majesty's Ship *Rose*, Capt. Frankland, Commander with a Large Ship burthen about 300 Tons taken Near the Havanna bound from Cartagena after a Long & Bloody Fight & proves to be an exceeding Rich Prize in gold & Silver the Value not yett known.
    Am Glad to hear the Crop is like to Prove so good in Your Island this Year & we have the largest Crop of Rice that has ever yett been produced, & which proves a Very dull Comodity. We have had No news from London for these four or five months past & but few Shipping here at present so that our Produce of Rice is likely to be Very Low, tho' Naval Stores are much in Demand. I heartily wish you a Merry Xmass & a Great many Happy Years & I most Respectfully Remain &c.

Rum 17/6 per Gall., Muscovado Sugar £12.10 per hundredweight, Rice 25/ per Ct., Pitch 50/ per bbl., Tar 40/, Madeira Wine £125 per pipe, Exchange to London £700 per £100 Sterling.

ADDRESSED: "Per the Sloop *Merrimack*, Capt. Francis Dunavan"

20th December 1744

TO MICHAEL LOVELL
Antigua

Charles Town, 20th December 1744

SIR:

 Since my last to you of the 2d July per Mr. Lucas, I have your Esteem'd Favours of the 11th September & according to Richard Oliver, Esqr. & your Directions I have Remitted Ballance of his account per Bill of Exchange to Messrs. Fitter & Tyzack, Merchants in London which doubt not will be Duely Honour'd. I shall likewise Take Care as you Direct to make a Remittance to Messrs. Watts & Fuller on Your account after Charging you with the Ballance of my account as you Desire, at the Current Exchange, having Dispos'd of your goods per Capt. Ougier. I am heartily Concern'd to be Informed of your Indisposition & if you are not already gone to the Northward as you advised hope this shall find you Restored to a perfect State of Health, which I most Heartily Wish.

 Am Glad to Hear that the Crop is like to prove so Very good in Your Island this Year, & we have the largest Crop of Rice that has ever yett been produced in the Province which proves a Verry Dull Commodity Every where. We have had No News from London for these four or five Months past & but few Shipping here at present So that Rice is Likely to be very low, & Naval Stores are much at present in Demand.

 A few days agoe His Majesty's Ship *Rose*, Capt. Frankland, brought of this Barr a Very large Ship taken by him, (being bound from Cartagena to Havanna) after a Long & Bloody Fight & which proves an Exceeding Rich Prize in Gold & Silver. I heartily wish you a Merry Xmass & a Great many Happy Years & Remain most Respectfully &c.

Rum 17/6 per Gall., Muscovado Sugar £12.10/ per Ct., Rice 25/ per Ct., Pitch 50/ per bbl., Tarr 40/ per barrell, Madera Wine £125 per pipe, Exchange to London £700 p £100 Sterling.

P. S. If European & India goods are plenty with you & Come Reasonable they would answer exceeding well at present, being very Scarce & in great Demand here, particularly Middling Bag, Hollands, Cambrick, ¾ Garlix, Silesias, Cheq Linnens, Ozenbrigg, Tea of both Sorts, China Ware, Gun powder Single Fine, Single Refin'd Loaf Sugar, Florence Oyl, Black Velvett, Silks for Womens Ware, & Lace, Gold & Silver Lace, Mens Castor & Beveritt Hatts. I hear that Clarett & Brandy is Very plenty with you, but wont doe here, being also plenty here. Per my next you may expect Account Sales of your Dry goods, per Capt. Ougier, &c.

ADDRESSED: "Per Ditto Dunavan" [Per the sloop *Merrimack*, Capt. Francis Dunavan]

TO ANDREW LESSLY
   Antigua

Charles Town, 20th December 1744

SIR:
   The Preceeding of the 22d Ultimo is Copie of my last & Since have Copie of your Esteem'd Favours of the 16th June & yours of the 28th September Via Port Royall, the first with Bill of Loading & Invoice of Six Hogshead Rum upon your account to my address per the Sloop *Royall Ranger*, Edward Burroughs, Master, also said Burroughs his Receipt for £9.17.6½ in money for the Ballance of my account.
   Am sorry your Rum had the Misfortune to be Taken, Chiefly owing to the Obstinary & Indiscretion of the Master who ought to account for the Loss. I Received Inclosed in yours of the 28th September John Lightfoots first Bill of Exchange for Fifty pounds Sterling on Richard Boddicot of London payable to the agents at 30 days Sight which doubt not will be Duely Honoured & Shall Creditt your account Current per the *Loyall Judith* (£350 this Currency being at the Current Exchange of £700 per £100 Sterling) which have not Time to Transmitt you per this Conveyance. There is Still a Ballance Due on said account as you may be Sensible have been in Advance now for these four years past & Doubt not you'll be of opinion that it is but Reasonable there ought to be some allowance for Lying out of the Money During said Time agreable to my last.
   Please Receive Inclosed Bill of Loading for 159 barrells Pitch, 43 barrells Turpintine, 238 barrells Tarr, & 4,000 Shingles Shipt on Board the Sloop *Merimack*, Francis Donovan, Commander for Antigua by order & on account of Gedney Clarke, Esqr. of Barbadoes & to your good self Consign'd which wish safe to Hand & Hope will Come to a Good Markett everything being verry good in Quality. I have had a Great Deal of

20th December 1744

Trouble to procure the Cargoe, all Naval Stores being exceeding Scarce at this Time & in great Demand which (with a good Deal of bad Weather) has Detained the Sloop much Longer than Expectation. We have a very Large Crop of Rice which is a Dull Comodity Every Where, & but few Shipping here at Present, so that Rice is likely to Be Very low. Freight to London is at £6 Sterling per Ton. I am Very Glad to Hear that your Island has been so Successfull against the Enemy & been so fortunate in prizes.

A few days agoe his Majestys Ship *Rose*, Capt. Frankland, [782] Arrived here With a Very large French Ship bound from Cartagena to Havannah having 315 Men on board & Taken by said *Rose* after a Long & Bloody fight, in which the French had 121 Men Killed outright & which proves an Exceeding Rich Prize in Gold & Silver. I Salute you with the Ussual Compliments of the Season & am Most Respectfully &c.

P. S. Rum 17/6 per Gall., Muscovado Sugar £12.10/ per hundredweight, Rice 25/ per Ct., Corn & Pease 10/ per bu., Madera Wine £125 per pipe, Pitch 50/ p bbl., Tar 40/ p bbl., Turpintine 15/ per Ct.

If European & India Goods are plenty with you & Come Reasonable they would doe verry well here at present, being very Scarce & in great Demand, particularly Midling Cambricks, Holland, ¾ Garlix, Siliseas, Cheq Linnens, Tea of both Sorts, China Ware, Silks for Womens ware, & Bone Lace, Gun powder Single Fine, Single Refin'd Loaf Sugar, Florence Oyl, Black Velvett, Gold & Silver Lace, No Clarett or Brandy being plenty Here as well as with you. I am to Request you'll not omitt to Send a Certificate of the Delivery of Capt. Donovans Cargoe by the first Conveyance to prevent any Trouble on account of Bond given, having had not a Little by the omission of the *Loyall Judith*'s not being Sent, & which I have Recommended to Capt. Donovan to gett done before he leaves the Island.

ADDRESSED: "Per the Sloop *Merrimack*, Capt. Francis Dunavan"

20th December 1744

TO EDWARD PARE
Barbados

Charles Town, 20th December 1744

SIR:

My last to you was of the 29th June, & Since have your most Esteem'd Favours of the 15th ditto, also yours of the 12th July. Your first advising of the arrival of your Scooner *Charming Sarah*, I am Supprized at the Six Barrells Pitch being left out of Capt. Davisons Clearance which find was in the Manifest given in at the Custom house here, as is likewise in the Copie of the Clearance Entered in their Books & my Clark who Shipt Capt. Davisons goods seems to be Pritty positive that it was put on board, having Seen it Roll'd down to the Vessell but Cannot account how it Came to be omitted if on board unless thro' the Oversight & Neglect of my said Clark. However please Receive Inclosed a Letter from our Naval Officer to your Naval Officer, which hope will Satisfie your Gentlemen about it, if Necessary, & which you may deliver or Not as you see Proper. I have gott up my Bond with Capt Davison upon Delivery of the Certificate you sent & am heartily Concern'd that Capt. Davison should have Come to any Trouble about so trifling an affair, as there Could be no Intention of Fraud in the Case by Capt. Davison, who I take to be a Very Honest good Man. Youll please advise per your next Wether Capt. Davison found that the Six Barrels Pitch were Shipt on board or Not.

I have Still four Casks of your Limejuice on Hand which Cannot Dispose of at any Rate, & beleive must be obliged to Sell it at Publick Vendue where it will fetch Little or Nothing, Oranges being now Produc'd here in great Plenty makes it no ways Saleable. I did Intend to ship it to Boston but found that it would not answer there Neither. Shall per my next Transmitt you account Sales of your Two Negroes which have not Time to do per this Conveyance, & as for Bills of Exchange am Sorry there is none or verry Rare here now to be purchased that I might make Remittance in Same as you Direct. You'll please therefore advise me in what Shape or manner you'll have your Effects Remitted to your Island & if in [783] any thing that Can be sent from this & Shall be duely Comply'd with. I could have no opportunity of Shipping any thing by this Conveyance being bound to Antigua & did not take in any thing on freight.

We have a Very large Crop of Rice which is a Dull Commodity Every where & there is but few Shipping here at Present So that Rice is Likely to be Very low.

20th December 1744

A few Days agoe his Majesty's Ship *Rose*, Capt. Frankland, arrived here with a Very large French Ship bound from Cartagena to Havannah having 315 Men on board & Taken by said *Rose* after a Long & Bloody Fight in which the French had 121 Men killed outright, & proves an Exceeding Rich prize in gold & Silver. I Salute you with the Ussual Compliments of the Season & I am Most Respectfully &c.

P. S. Rum 17/6 per Galls., Muscovado Sugar £12.10/ per Ct., Rice 35/ per Ct., Pitch 50/ per bbl., Tar 40/ per bbl., Turpintine 15/ per Ct., Corn & pease 10/ per busshel, Madera Wine £125 per pipe, Beef £8, Pork £12 per bbl., Exchange at £700 p £100 Sterling.

ADDRESSED: "Per Capt. Francis Dunavan"

TO GEDNEY CLARKE
Barbados

Charles Town, 20th December 1744

SIR:

The preceeding of the 6th Current is Copie of my last per Capt. Hutchins[8] to which please be Refered. This per your Sloop *Merrimack*, Francis Donavan, Commander being Compleatly Loaded with Naval Stores, & Inclosed please Receive Invoice of 159 barrells Pitch, 43 barrells Turpintine, 238 barrells Tar, & 4,000 Shingles Shipt on board your said Sloop on your account & Risque & by Your Order to Andrew Lessly, Esqr. in Antigua Consign'd, Amount as per Invoice being £1,080.16.3 this Currency which wish safe to Hand & hope will Come to a Good Markett, every thing being Exceeding good in Quality. You'll please observe there is More Pitch & Turpintine than you ordered, which Could not possibly be avoided without Detaining your Sloop much Longer, there not being Tar enough to be purchased at any Rate for Love or Money, & which was obliged to Ship to dispatch the Sloop, & has been the Ocasion of her being detain'd so much Longer than your Limitation of time. I have had not a Little Trouble in purchasing your Sloops Cargoe as Capt. Donavan Can

---

[8] Capt. Joseph Hutchins, schooner *Swanzey*, to Barbados. SCG, 17 December 1744.

20th December 1744

well inform you, Naval Stores being not only in great Demand but exceeding Scarce & not be purchased at this Time at any Rate, but as the Demand Encourages our planters to goe upon making of them it is Thought will be pretty plenty next Spring.

The Rum is not Saleable at Present & have as yett disposed of but Two Hhd. at 17/6 there being a great Deal in Town at Present. I have not sent Mr. Lessly Invoice of the Sloop *Merrimacks* Cargoe, as not having your Directions So that have only Transmitted him Bill of Loading of the Contents, which hope is agreable to your Intentions.

Have Sent in your Bird Cages under the Care of Capt. Donavan Ten Cock Red Birds & Two Nonpareil Birds Reckon'd very Curious Birds here, & proper food for them Which you'll please to make acceptable, & Shall be glad to know if there is any thing else here that may be agreable to you & will Take Care to Send it. You have also Some live Stock sent of fowls, Geese, Turkies, & Shoats which Capt. Donavan told me you have Given Directions might be sent you, the Charge of which is Included in the Disbursments & of which Capt. Donavan has the account thereof. Please also Receive Inclosed Account of [786] Capt. Donavans Disbursments & his Receipt for Same amount being £306.9.3 this Currency for which have Debit your account.

A few days agoe his Majestys Ship *Rose*, Capt. Frankland, Commander arrived here with a Large French Ship bound from Cartagena to Havanna having 315 Men on board & Taken by said *Rose* after a Long & Bloody Fight in which the French had 121 Killed out Right, & which proves an Exceeding Rich Prize in Gold & Silver, the Value not yett known, Three Hundred & fifty thousand Dollars being already found besides a great Quantity of Gold. I Salute You with the Ussual Compliments of the Season & Most Respectfully Remain &c.

Rice 25/per Ct., Pitch 50/ per bbl. & Tar 40/ (both very Scarce), Turpintine 15/ per Ct., Corn & Pease 10/ per bu., Beef £8 per bbl., Pork £12 per bbl., Madeira Wine £125 per pipe, Exchange to London £700 per £100 Sterling.

P. S. If European & India goods are plenty with you & Come Reasonable, they will answer very Well here at present being Very Scarce & in great Demand particularly Hollands, Cambricks, Garlix, Silesias, Cheq Linnens, Tea of both Sorts, China ware, Bone Lace, Silks for Womens Ware, Black Velvett, Gold & Silver Lace, Gunpowder Single Fine, Single Refin'd Loaf Sugar, & Florence Oyl, No Clarett or brandy it being Plenty here &c.

ADDRESSED: "Per Capt. Francis Dunavan"

TO BURRYAU & SCHAFFER
    London
                               Charles Town, 22nd December 1744

GENTLEMEN:

My last to you was of the 17th December 1743, Since have not the Pleasure of any of your Favours. This is to advise You'll please to gett Insured on goods to be Shipt on board the Ship *Ann Galley*, Capt. John Trenchard, Commander at & from this to London One hundred pounds Sterling on account & Risque of Mr. Thomas Hutchinson of Boston, New England, which I intend to Ship in Deer Skins. The Ship is about 150 Tons, a Stout Vessel, & Well man'd, & will be Ready to sail in about a Fortnight or three Weeks hence, & by which you may Expect Invoice & Bill of Loading. I Salute you & am Most Respectfully &c.

ADDRESSED: "Per Capt. Hilton Via Lisbon & Copie per Capt. Ham Via Cowes"

TO ANDREW PRINGLE
    London
                               Charles Town, 22nd December 1744

SIR:

The Annexed on the other side of the 12th Current is Copie of my last per the Snow *Robert & Jane*, Capt. Douglas, who sail'd Over the Barr the 16th Instant for Porto which I Confirm, & as yett none of your Favours which will occasion Brevity. No Appearance as yett of the Privateer

22nd December 1744

Recovery. There are News Papers in Town from the West of England that make mention of Some Prizes Taken by the *Recovery* however that dont give Content here, & now they decline making any Further Remittance to make up the Defeciency of £2,000 Sterling as at first proposed & Intended till they have further advice from Mr. Crokatt & self & Insist on having the Ship Sent out here at all Events, as her not Coming they say has broke the Scheme proposed & will be obliged to send out the Snow *Assistance* now Ready for a Cruize Single & without a Consort.

Benjamin Whitaker, Esqr. was pleased at a Meeting to Read to us a paragraph [785] of his Friend in London his Letter to him setting forth his Reasons for not paying to Mr. Crokatt & your self his Subscription for £50 Sterling which were that Alderman Baker had Declin'd being Concern'd as not liking your Conduct & Management & withal mentions that it was his Opinion it was the better for him that he did not pay the Money for him & that he was not Concern'd as he did not like those who had the Conducting of the Affair. I answer'd that it was an unjust & unhandsome Refflection & desired to know his Friends Name (as he Call'd him). He said it was Capt. Curruthers. I thereupon Told him before them all that his Friend was greatly Mistaken & that I did not Doubt but that the Gentlemen, meaning Mr. Crokatt & Self, would give Intire Satisfaction as to their Whole Conduct in the affair to all Concern'd. I well know that said Reflection was Level'd Cheifly against Mr. Crokatt & not you, Curruthers & J.C. having an old Grudge from a Quarrell here between them. This I thought proper to acquaint you of & desire it may be to your self for you to make the proper use of it & has been a Pretence for Mr. Whitaker to Decline paying his Subscription here Likewise.

A few Days agoe his Majestys Ship *Rose*, Capt. Frankland, arrived here with a Large French Ship bound from Cartagena to Havanna having upwards of 300 Men on board & Taken by said *Rose* after a Smart & Bloody Fight in which the French had upward of 100 Men killed out Right & which proves an exceeding Rice Prize in Gold & Silver there having been already Found it is said to the Value of One hundred thousand Pounds Ster. & Great Deal more on board, the Captains of kings Ships having Certainly too large a Share of Prizes especially when they happen to be of so great Value. The Prize Money ought to be Limitted & some proper fund appointed to appropriate Same.

My Wife Joyns in Wishing you a Merry Cristmass & a Great many happy Years & having not further to offer at Present I Remain &c.

P. S. Several of Mr. Crokatts Friends were at the Meeting when the affair hapen'd but said Nothing.

ADDRESSED: "Per Capt. Ham Via Cowes"

TO ROBERT ELLIS
   Philadelphia
                              Charles Town, 4th January 1744 [1745]
SIR:
   The above of the 17th September is Copie of my last per Capt. Duthy who Tells me that he Delivered it to Your Young man, Since have not any of your Favours. I was in hopes you would have been so good as to have let me heard from you by Capt. Duthy by whom Expected Some Remittance, which would have turn'd Out Very well, most Goods from your parts being in Demand here, and hope You'll be so Good as to Ship Some of the things as Mention'd in my last by Capt. Mason or Wilson, or any other of the Palatine Ships bound this Way as the freight will Come easie. My Wife Joyns in Best Respects to Mrs. Ellis, I Salute you with the Ussual Compliments of the Season, & I am &c.

ADDRESSED: "Per Sloop *Indian King*, Capt. Gilbert Albertson"

[786]
TO WILLIAM MACKAY[9]
   Cape Fear, North Carolina
                              Charles Town, 10th January 1744 [1745]
SIR:
   I hope your Goodness will excuse the Freedom I take in Troubling you with the Inclosed Power of Attorney, & am to desire the Favour youll

[9] William Mackay lived at Cape Fear, North Carolina, RPC, p. 794.

10th January 1745

please be so good as to Accept of Same in Order to Recover of One Richard Caulton by Trade an Upholsterer Lately gone from this Considerably Indebted & who I understand by Capt. Frazer now Lodges at Robert Harveys, a Carpenter in Brunswick. Inclosed please Receive his Note of hand to me for One Hundred & Sixty Eight pounds this Currency with the Proper afidavits for Same & hope You'll have the Good Fortune to Recover it of him, as it is said he has Carry'd of a Good Deal of Money with him & Effects, some of which are Still here (it is Suspected to be sent to him, he having been Industrious to Impose on people here), So that he Meritts no favour. I never had any Dealings with him but once, & never Received a penny of money of him. He was in Very Good Bussiness here & gott Money, but am told he has been Too Extravagent & It Is thougt would have Stay'd & taken the Benfitt of our Late Act, & have Swore off had it not been that he had Carry'd Money & Effects with him. Mr. James Thomson, who does me the Favour to be the Bearer of this, has been so Good as to Witness the Power of Attorney for the Proof of it.

I heartily wish you a Happy Meeting with good Mrs. Mackay & Familly. I ask pardon for this Trouble & if in the Like or any other occasion, I can be of any Service to you or yours here, You may always most Freely Command &c.

What Charge & Trouble you may be at in this afair will with great Pleasure most thankfully allow.

ADDRESSED: "Per Mr. James Thomson & Mrs. Mackay"

TO BURRYAU & SCHAFFER
London

Charles Town, 12th January 1744 [1745]

GENTLEMEN:

The above of the 22d Ulto. is Copie of my last, having forwarded three Copies thereof & Inclosed Please Receive Bill of Loading & Invoice of two hhd. deer Skins Shipt on board the Ship *Ann Galley*, Capt. John Trenchard, Commander for London (by which this Goes) on the Proper

16th January 1745

account & Risque of Mr. Thomas Hutchinson of Boston, N. England and to your good Selves Consign'd, Amount as per Invoice being £699.11.9 this Currency which wish safe to hand & to a Good Markett being very good in quality. You might have Expected Remittance on said Gentleman's account per Bill of Exchange but there are none to be had here at any Rate, our Rice being a Dull Comodity Every where & in no Demand, which occassions Bills to be Very Scarce. Youll please advise Mr. Hutchinson of said Remittance. The Ship is Ready to Sail as Soon as the Wind & Weather Permitts. I am most Respectfully &c.

ADDRESSED: "Per Capt. Trenchard & Copies per Capt. Addis & Capt. Waddel"

TO FITTER & TYZACK
   London

Charles Town, 16th January 1744 [1745]

GENTLEMEN:

The preceeding on the other side is Copie of what I did my Self the Pleasure to write you of the 6th December with three Copies therof & this Serves to Convey you Inclosed Mr. John Lightfoot his Second Bill of Exchange on Mr. Richard Boddicott in London for Fifty Pounds Sterling since forwarded me from Antigua & to your Good Selves Indorsed & when the third Bill Comes Shall Likewise be sent you. I have not further to offer at Present but that I most Respectfully Remain &c.

ADDRESSED: "Per Capt. Trenchard"

17th January 1745

[787]
TO ANDREW PRINGLE
London

Charles Town, 17th January 1744 [1745]

SIR:

The Inclosed of the 22d Ulto. is Copie of my last per Capt. Ham Via Cowes, & am still without any of your Favours. This per the Ship *Ann Galley* of Geurnsey, Capt. John Trenchard, to your address, being now Compleately Loaded & Ready to Sail, &c. Inclosed please Receive Bill of Loading & Invoice of Two hhds. Good Deer Skins Shipt on board said Ship on account & Risque of your Good self & S. Sanders & to you Consign'd, Amount as per Invoice being £687.9.2 this Currency which wish safe to hand & hope will Come to a Good Markett. You have also Invoice of One hhd. Deer Skins & Fifty barrells of New Rice, Shipt in said Ship as per Bill of Lading on my Proper Account, amount as per Invoice being £724.3.11 Currency which you'll please dispose of to my best Advantage & the Neat Proceeds thereof Pass to the Credit of the Cargo per the *John & Isabella* in Company with S. Sanders.

You have also included in said Bill of Lading a Cake, quantity 34 lb. Myrtle Wax sent you in a present from Mr. Thomas Elliott & a Barrel of 46 deer Skins he sends to his Son at his desire, Which you'll please to Enter at the Custom house with the others & have delivered him. Inclosed is a Letter from Mr. Elliott for you & one for his Son.

Please also Receive Inclosed, Account Sales of the Cargoe per the *John & Isabella*, Neat Proceeds being £9,785.0.11 Currency, also account Sales per the *Susannah*, Capt. Gregory, Neat Proceeds being £3,099.2.0 both in Company with S. Sanders. The Sale has been Very Tedious & have had not a Little Trouble to dispose of everything to your best advantage. You'll observe there are Still Considerable Debts outstanding, & when they will be Received is uncertain, which shows on how bad a footing the Trade in dry Goods has been here for some Years past, but is like to be better for the time to Come.

Please also Receive Manifest of the Ships *Ann Galleys* Cargoe for London which has only 492 barrels Rice & 14 hhd. deer Skins & some Plank & yett is Chock full. She is not a Ship that Burthens well & very unfit for this Trade. I have directed Capt. Trenchard at his arrival to apply himself to you (having never heard from the owners since the ships arrival here) and that you are to Receive all the Ships freight & pay him his Wages as Com-

17th January 1745

mander of the Ship from the 26 September last at Six Pounds Ster. per month, & Inclosed is his Receipt for Seven pounds Seven Shillings Ster. paid him in part thereof being to Leave the Ship & to be Discharg'd in London, so that the Ship will be under your Care till you have directions from the owners in Guernsey in Relation to her.

Inclosed is a Packett for Messrs. Henry & John Brock some of the owners of said Ship (who Recommended the Ship to me). I Reffer you to the Contents thereof which after perusal you'll please to Seal & forward them. You have also Inclosed my Bill of Exchange for £200.9.7 Ster. on said Messrs. Henry & John Brock payable to your Good self at thirty days sight at the House of Mr. William Dobree in London which doubt not they will give directions may be duely Honoured, being for my Disbursment advanced for their Ship here as per account sent them Inclosed, Copie of which you have also Inclosed. I have Charged them only 5 per Cent Commission altho' the Interest of the money since I have been in advance would Come to the Commission Charged, & have Likewise Charg'd them 5 per Cent on the Amount of the Ships freight to London for procuring & Engageing same & which I [788] Compute to be £600 Ster. which doubt not you'll be of opinion is but Reasonable, having had a great deal of Trouble with the Ship & People belonging to her, both the Capt. & Mate having dyed. The whole Trouble of every thing lay to me, insomuch that I would not have the Trouble again for Ten Times the Commission I Charge, & hope as the Guernsey People are Honest men of Honour Doubt not they will Readily allow everything & duely Honour my Bill on them but in Case they should not, hope You'll have it in your power to Secure me, as you'll Still I hope Receive all the Ships freight in Case she getts safe home to London, or you Can make the Ship it self Lyable for my money if the ship should have the misfortune to be taken, as doubt not they have ordered full Insurance both on the Ship & also on the Freight. They will make no dispute to Honour my draft which when paid please also to Carry to the Creditt of your adventures in Company with S. Sanders. I have inclosed you a Copie of the owners of the said ship *Ann Galley* their Instructions to their Capt. Barnard deceas'd, also Copie of Messrs. Henry & John Brock their Letter to me about their Ship as also all the Tradesmen Bills upon the Ship to send to the owners if needfull.

I advised in mine of the 17th October Via Lisbon to gett Insured on Goods on Board the Sloop *Rebecca*, Benjamin Bangs, Master from this to Boston One Hundred Pound Ster. & in Case that said Insurance has not been already affected Desire it may not be done having advice of the said

17th January 1745

Vessel's arrival. Your Bill on me for £10 Ster. to Mr. Nicholas Wadge, Master of the *Flamborough*, has not yet appear'd & Mr. Wadge Now desires that you may Repay the said money back to his Freind, he having now no occasion for it here as having Receiv'd near £1,000 Ster. for his share in the Late prize which he wants to Remitt to England. I have herewith Inclosed you a packett for Messrs. Cookson & Welfitt of Hull with their account Sales & account Current, the Contents of which Refer you to, & which after perusal please to Seal & forward them. I wait their orders how & in what manner the Ballance of their account is to be Remitted having no orders to Remitt Same to you as you formerly advised. Mr. John Keith has never yett sent me a Certificate for the Delivery of his kinsmans Capt. Keiths Cargoe. I am to Request youll be so good as to procure it of him & Transmitt me. I Charged nothing for All the Trouble I had of his Kinsman. Youll please also to send me a Certificate for Capt. Trenchards Cargoe as soon as you Can, our Governour being Very Strict on Plantation Bonds as having a verry strict Instruction in Relation to them. If Capt. Douglas should Come out this way again after his arrival from Porto, am to pray the favour you may send me by him Thirty or Forty Tons of Black heath Gravel for my Garden such as you sent me per the *Susannah* but am to observe that they give Very bad measure. The last I had did not Turn out half the quantity Charg'd. As it is thought we shall have but very few Shipping Here so in Course there will be pretty Good freight for what Shipping may happen to Come & if the *Robert & Jane* Comes again soon may be pritty Certain of a Freight especially if Capt. Douglas brings a Lincence with him as he did last, which pray dont let him Come without.

The Prize advised of in my last that has been taken by the *Rose* And brought in here Turns out a Very Rich Ship.

I am yet uncertain wether I shall see you in London next Summer. I am in great want of the Cloaths I writt for Last Summer, all kinds of Goods being very scarce & dear here at Present. My Wife joyns in best Respects & I most Truely Remain &c.

[789] P. S. We have a Report here Via New York that our Privateer *Recovery* has Taken several Rich French Prizes & the Concern'd here long to have advices about her. We are agoing to send the New Privateer Snow *Assistance* built here, on a Cruize in Consort with a Jamaica Privateer Sloop as the *Recovery* dont yett appear.

I am to desire that for the future when Conveyances dont offer from

15th January 1745

London, You'll be so good as to Write me Via Bristoll as the Bristoll Vessels dont stay for Convoy & there is One just now arrived after a Quick passage & a great many letters by her from London (but none of your favours) particularly from Mr. Kenneth Michie[1] & News Papers to his Freinds here. Inclosed is also your Account Current in Company with S. Sanders, Ballance due you being £894.16.8 which hope you'll find right & which the Remittance now made will pretty near Ballance & as soon as possible the Outstanding Debts can be gott in, shall Likewise be Remitted.

ADDRESSED: "Per Ship *Ann Gally*, Capt. Trenchard, & Copies per Capt. Waddle & Capt. Scott & Copie per Capt. Baber Via Bristoll"

TO WILLIAM COOKSON & WILLIAM WELFITT
Hull

Charles Town, 15th January 1744 [1745]

GENTLEMEN:

Since my last to you of the 7th November 1743 I have One from your Mr. William Cookson of the 25th February & Remark the Contents. I delay'd giving a Return to yours till I could Transmitt you an Account Sales of your Goods Which has been Very Tedious on account of the Price and Quality thereof, & which please Now to Receive Inclosed Neat Proceeds thereof being £2,301.14.6 this Currency which hope will be to Content. They have proved a pretty Troublesome Commission, Most of the Goods, Especially the Lead Shott, being Landed in a Very Indifferent order & obliged to Sort & put it up in New Bags, having broke out of the Casks in the Hold. Youll observe part of the debts are Still outstanding. Inclosed please also Receive your account Current, Ballance in your Favour being £809.12.8 this Currency.

You advise to have Remittance made in Bills of Exchange but am to Inform you that there are No Bills to be procured, the Course of our Trade here being Intirely Alter'd since the French Warr & our Rice no Where in Demand being now 20/ per hundredweight & freight to Lon-

---

[1] A Scottish merchant of Charleston. *HL*, I, 94n.

15th January 1745

don at Six pounds Ster. per Ton & there are but few Shipping here at present & Very few more Expected. As no Bills of Exchange Can be had as you ordered, You'll please give directions in What manner You'll have Ballance of Your account Remitted & it shall be duely Comply'd with. My Brother Andrew Pringle in London advised me some time agoe that you had Writt him that you had given me orders to Remitt the Ballance of your account to him, which order however has not yett appeared & desire you may give me your particular Directions If I must Remitt the Ballance to my Brother or how you will have the Same Remitted, as Bills of Exchange are Not to be procured.

As to Capt. Wards affair, was obliged to pay the money in Court according to his forfeiture & also the Charge attending it for postponing it in expectation of his Coming here as you advized. Youll please to favour me with your Directions, as Soon as you can, I am most Respectfully &c.

ADDRESSED: "Under Cover of A.P. per Capt. Trenchard & Copies per Capt. Waddle & Capt. Scott"

TO HENRY & JOHN BROCK
    Guernsey
                        Charles Town, 17th January 1744 [1745]

GENTLEMEN:

The last I did myself the Pleasure to Write you was of the 12th Ulto. with three Copies thereof to which please be Refered & as yett have not any of your favours. This per your Ship *Ann Galley*, Capt. John Trenchard, Commander for London being now Compleately Loaded with Rice & Deer Skins, &c, Cleared out & Ready to Sail & is the first Ship as yett Loaded & Cleared out this Season. Several Ships that arrived here before your Ship *Ann* being here still & not yett Loaded, & freight is much more Wanted for London than for Holland at present there being but one Vessel freight for Holland this Season. I have addressed your Ship *Ann* at her arrival to my Brother Andrew Pringle, Merchant in London, as having no advice or [790] directions from your Good selves who to Consign her to there & Who I am Well assured will give you intire Satisfaction, as to his

17th January 1745

Management for your Interest. I am to take Notice to you that your Ship Ann is not a proper Ship for this Trade as She does not Burthen Well enough nor Carry neer the Quantity of Goods would be Imagined, having only 492 barrells Rice, 14 hhds. Deer Skins, & some plank & wood for Dunnidge & Stowage, So that She is not a profitable Ship for freight, yett She is very well stowed & Chock full as Mr. Bonamy Can inform you.

Please Receive Inclosed Account of the Whole Charge which I have disbursed on your Ship Since her Arrival here, Amount being £1,521.7.7 Currency and doe assure you have managed every thing with the best Oeconumy I was Capable of for Your Interest & with the Least Expence possible which has occasion'd me not a little trouble & have Charged only the Customary Commission of 5 per Cent Which indeed is not the Interest of the money for the Time I have been in Advance for a Good part of It, the Interest of Money being Here at 10 per Cent per Annum & have Charged 5 per Cent on the Freight of the Ship for procuring & Engageing the Same which is Always Customary here, especially when the Ship brings No Cargoe of Goods on Consignment & both which doubt not You'll allow to be Very Reasonable. And agreable to my Former advices this is also to advise you that I have of this date drawn a Sett of Bills of Exchange on you for £200.9.7 Ster. at the Current Exchange of £700 per £100 payable at thirty days Sight to my Brother Andrew Pringle at the House of Mr. William Dobree, Merchant in London & which doubt not will be duely Honoured Inclosed please also Receive the Sailors Receipts for Money advanced them here being Cheifly To pay for their Sickness, most of them having been Very Ill, The Amount being £229.2.6 Currency to be deducted out of their Respective Wages. You have also inclosed Peter Bonamy his Bill of Exchange for £12 Ster. on his Father Peter Bonamy payable at 10 days Sight to Your Good Selves for money that I have been obliged to advance him here & Which he assures me will be duely Honoured. He has Received no Wages here so that his Wages due from the Ship will Come to Near the Money. He Goes now in the Ship as mate but as to his Wages in that Station, I have left him to Settle it with you as you may Judge proper.

Inclosed is also Account Sales of Capt. Barnards Adventure of Wines, &c. in the Ship, Neat Proceeds being £292.0.11 Currency also his account Current, Ballance due him being £303.0.4 this Currency & for which you'll observe I have Creditt your account Current, Ballance Due me being £1,403.7.3 Currency being Value of my draft on you as Mention'd above. Capt. Barnard left by a Sort of Will made at Sea (& sent you with

17th January 1745

other papers under the Care of Mr. Bonamy) the Neat Proceeds of his Adventure of Wines, &c. in your Ship *Ann* to his Mother, which doubt not you'll Take Care to let her have accordingly.

Inclosed is also the Account of Capt. John Trenchards Disbursments here on the Ship & his Expences paid him of 20/ per day as Customary & always alowed here, Amount being £127.1.3 Currency. I agreed with him at £6 Ster. per month & to be discharg'd at London & have paid him Seven Guineas advance Wages as per His Receipt Sent to my Brother & have also allow'd him Two Tons priviledge on the Freight as Customary. You'll please observe that I have Creditt your Account Current for Eight Water Butts £48 Currency sold here to make more Room in the Ship for Stowage, also for a Grapling & Some old Junk as being useless & only taking up Room in the Ship. The Ships Bell happen'd to be Indiscretly brok't by [791] a Master of a Ship when the Ship Lay up at Childsbury & being left to Arbitration, it was agreed that he Should pay Three pounds Ster. for damage & for which have Creditt your Account accordingly. As to the Ships Long Boat it has been Condemm'd here as good for Nothing, being so bad that it was not worth the Charge of Repairing, & no person here will give any thing for the Boat as Mr. Bonamy Can well inform you, being an entire wrack.

Naval Stores are Still very Scarce here & high in price. I should have been Glad to have had the Pleasure of hearing from you, before your Ship *Ann* Sail'd.

We have had no Vessels from London for these three Months otherwise was in hopes of having the Pleasure of your favours which am in dayly Expectation of, & hope you'll be so good as to favour me with a Line from you at the arrival of your Ship *Ann Galley* which hope will have a Safe and Quick passage & make a Good Voyage. I Salute you & am most Respectfully &c.

Please to present my best Respects to all the Gentlemen Concern'd & Shall be always very Glad to Render them any agreable Service.

ADDRESSED: "Under Cover of A.P. per Capt. Trenchard & Copies per Capt. Waddle & Capt. Scott"

TO JOHN TRENCHARD
Charles Town

Charles Town, 19th January 1744 [1745]

SIR:

As you are appointed Commander of the Ship *Ann Galley* of Guernsey in the Room of the Late Capt. Mathew Barnard, Deceased & the said ship being now Loaded & in all Respects fitted for the Sea, Clear'd Out & Ready to Sail. You are therefore to Embrace the first oppertunity of wind & weather & make the best of your way from this directly for the Port of London (avoiding as it is War Time as much as you Can Speaking with any Shipping at Sea) where at your arrival desire You may Imediately Apply your Self to my Brother Andrew Pringle, Merchant to be heard of at the Carolina Coffee house or at his house in Fan Court Fan Church Street to whom you go Consign'd & who will Report & Enter the Ship at the Custom House & who I have desired to pay you at the Rate of Six pounds Ster. per month Since you have been Commander With Two Tons priviledge as per Agreement. And as you discharge your Self from the Ship at London, my Brother will Take Care of her Till he has Directions from the owners in Relation to her further proceedure. If you should happen to be put in to any out port, desire you may advise my Brother thereof as Soon as you Can & Send him a Manifest of your Cargoe on board, & if you should have the Misfortune to be Taken by Enemies (which God forbid) in Such Case may thro' all your Letters overboard & advise my Brother as Soon as You Can to what port you are Carried to. I heartily wish you a safe Passage and Success & I am &c.

P. S. You enter'd on board as Captain of the *Ann Gally* the 26 September last & I have Deliver'd into your Charge all the Papers belonging to Said Ship.

ADDRESSED: NO ADDRESS

19th January 1745

[792]
TO EDWARD PARE
Barbados

Charles Town, 19th January 1744 [1745]

SIR:

The preceeding of the 20 Ulto. is Copie of my last per Capt. Donavan Via Antigua & Since have your Favours of the 2d December & duely Remark that you have Turn'd your Schooner *Charming Sarah* into a Brigantine of the Same Name & that you intend her for this place as Soon as possible & to be Loaded back with Sundry Goods as you have therein Directed, & which in Compliance with your orders I have purchas'd & Gott Ready to be putt on board your said Brigantine at her arrival accordingly every thing you have ordered excepting the Cedar, which is of that Extraordinary Large Size & Dimensions that I am afraid it Cannot be procur'd in the Province. However my Utmost Endeavours shall not be wanting in that Respect to obtain it if practicable & hope every thing will be to your Satisfaction & in Expectation of your Further Favours & directions by your Said Brigantine, I Most Respectfully Remain &c.

ADDRESSED: "Per Capt. Saltus alliis Hinson & Copie per Capt. Howard"

TO GEDNEY CLARKE
Barbados

Charles Town, 19th January 1744 [1745]

SIR:

The preceeding of the 20th Ulto. per your Sloop *Merimack*, Capt. Donavan, for Antigua is Copie of my last & Since have your Favours of the 29th November with your Directions for ordering Capt. Donavan for your Island directly which would have been duely Comply'd with but that your Said Sloop had been Sail'd ten days before your Letter Came to hand & hope by this you may have account of his safe arrival there.

I have Sold your Rum at 17/6 per Gall. & by my next you may Expect Account Sales thereof & your Sugar per your said Sloop, & I Wait your orders how the Neat Proceeds is to be Remitted. Naval Stores are Still High & every thing else low & in plenty.

We have no Material News here at present, am Very Glad to hear that you are Likely to have So Very Good a Crop in your Island. We have a Very Great Crop of Rice, but in no Demand any where & is now at 20/ per Ct. The prices of Goods the Same as in my last. I most Respectfully Remain &c.

ADDRESSED: "Per Capt. Saltus alliis Hinson & Copie per the Sloop *Postilion*, Capt. Howard"

TO ANDREW PRINGLE
    London
                            Charles Town, 19th January 1744 [1745]
SIR:

I have already writ you at Large of the 17th Current per this Oppertunity of Capt. Trenchard who is Still in the Road & am now to acknowledge both your most acceptable Favours Yesterday of the 26th September & 1st October with the Packett from Mr. Conyers (being the only Letters from you since the 27th June, Capt. White & Wilkinson not being yett arrived) all Received at the Hands of James Ogilvie in Capt. Crossthwait with Receipt for Suit of Cloaths & Stationary per said Crossthwait for which you have my kind thanks.

The Concerned in the *Recovery* wonder that there is no letter from you later than [793] that Inclosed of the 25th July per Crossthwait which ocassions Grumbling especially about the Account Current which dont Seem to Give Satisfaction notwithstanding you have been Considerably in Advance for the privateer. Some here, who are no Well Wishers to Mr. Crokatt especially, think that they are not Well used & Seem to be a Sort of a party here. Two of the managers dont much like Mr. Crokatt, Vizt. James Reid & William Stone & also the Shubricks on account of their friend Mr. Nickleson, & some Seem to Insinuate tho' falsly that the *Recovery* is kept in Europe purposely that Mr. Crokatt & you may have the Commissions on the prizes, the Contrary of which doubt not you will make fully appear. So that you have Need to be Very Circumspect in the Management & Rendering & an Exact & fair account of every thing as Some of the Concern'd here are odd Sort of people & you ought to make them sencible in the Strongest Light of the Service done them which they dont Seem to be at all Sencible of. I observe that Mr. Crokatt Lays all the Trouble on you. It would be proper for to write to Some persons here to give them a Hint thereof & of how little Service he has been in the affair, Suppose to Mr. Reid or to Mr. George Austin that the Concern'd here may know it & it would Come much Better from them than from Me.

Our planters here, for as low as Rice is, have not the Courage any them to Ship it on their account & will Rather take 20/ per Ct. as it now is than to pay freight & Insurance, &c. The prize brought in by the *Rose* is Condemn'd here & Valued at One hundred thousand pounds Sterling. The Bulk of Her Cargoe (besides Gold & Silver which is the Cheif) is Cocoa & is said to be very Good. If it sells a Bargain at Vendue intend to be a purchaser especially as you Encourage me to draw on you upon any Good Adventures.

I wish you had been so Good as to have mention'd the prices of Indigo, Cocoa, Chocolate, Coffee, Sugar, &c. & how far I might Venture to goe in the purchase of those Commodity's, we being in the dark here as to the prices at home, which am again to pray you may never omit to advise me of.

I am Very Sencible of your affabillity & Hospitaly to Mr. Abercrombie & a Great many others Which they are but Two apt to Forgett when they Come on this Side the Water. I have late advice from Barbadoes & the Leeward Islands that provissions & Rice Especially are very plenty, tho' not much Gone from this Lately.

Shall make it my Business to look out for & procure if possible the Young plants and Seeds you are pleased to mention in order to be sent you. Most of the Shipping here are Loaded & preparing to goe, so that we shall have But a Dull Time this Season. Hope to have more full advices from you by Capt. White & Wilkinson in the mean time beg Leave to Remain &c.

P. S. Have heard nothing as yett from the Gentlemen in Geurnsey. I understand by Mr. Evance that Mr. Nicholson wont allow the Interest Charged in our account with J. Hunter & Co. Please acquaint Capt. Conyers Brother that as the Commission about his Brother's Negro is but just arrived it Cannot be finished here to be Return'd to London by the 1st of

February next as therein ordered so that Longer time must be allowed & of the Six Commissioners appointed here One is in England, Vizt. Mr. Abercrombie & two are Dead Vizt. Richard Wright & John Houghton so that three only Remain to Act, Vizt. James Graham[2] & James Wright,[3] Esqr. (both Gentlemen of the Law) & my self & I find the Charge must be paid by me. I am Supprized you have had no letters of mine of late as I miss no Conveyances from this. Have Sent you under the Care of Capt. Trenchard a Summer Drake & Duck which he has promised to take great Care of & which youll please to make acceptable & Ruff Rice for their food.

ADDRESSED: "Per Capt. Trenchard & Copies per Capt. Waddle & Capt. Scott & Copie per Capt. Baber Via Bristoll"

[794]
TO PETER WESTERMAN
　　Barbados
　　　　　　　　　　　　　　Charles Town, 25th January 1744 [1745]
SIR:
　　Capt. Boaz Bell of Bermuda advises me that he left in your Hands An India workt Sattin Counterpine for a Bed of mine at the Same Time when he put into your hands Twenty four Barrells Rice & Six Barrells Tar, belonging to me for Sale, the Account Sales of which you were pleas'd to Send me Dated March 26th, 1743 but the Counterpine is not mention'd or Accounted for in said Account Sales as Same has been omitted.
　　Capt. Bell desires me to Remind you thereof, And am to desire you'll please to Ship me the Value in Good Coffee if Reasonable By the Return of this Conveyance of Mr. Manigaults Sloop, Capt. Howard, or any other Bound this Way. Shall be always Very Glad to Render you any acceptable Service & I am &c.

　　[2] James Graeme.
　　[3] James Wright was a Charleston lawyer who became Attorney General of South Carolina, an agent in London, and later the royal governor of Georgia. HL, I, 7n.

25th January 1945

Rum 17/6 per Gall., Muscovado Sugar £12.10/ per hundredweight, Rice 20/ per Ct.

ADDRESSED: "Per the Sloop *Postilion*, Capt. Howard"

WILLIAM MACKAY
Cape Fear, North Carolina

Charles Town, 25th January 1744 [1745]

SIR:

I did my Self the Pleasure to write You of the 10th Current by Mr. James Thomson, who hope with Mrs. Mackay & Familly are Safe arriv'd with you after a Good Passage, & to which please be Refferr'd. Since my Last Mr. John Hume & I have attatch'd & taken into Our Custody Some Effects which we have Good Ground to beleive & are well Inform'd belong & were Intended to be Sent to Richard Caulton & were Ship'd on Board the Schooner *Molly* for Cape Fear, & for which the Bearar Capt. John Frazer had given a Receipt to the Shippers (who are Two Young Women that keep a shop here). However we are not Certain if we will be the better for Our Attatchment as there are Two Attachments on Coultons Effects that were taken out here before Ours, tho' not Serv'd on the Said Effects.

The Shippers Refuse to give Capt. Frazer up his Receipt for the Things put on board intending we imagine to make use of it (if they Can) to his disadvantage. We have therefore Indemnified him of the Consequences & given him a Copie of the Cheif Justices Writt of Attachment for his Further Satisfaction, & to Clear him in Case they may want to bring him to any Trouble on Said Account & it is at his desire that I have taken the freedom to write you this to Inform you of the Affair. Shall be Glad Youll be so good as to advise me if you are Likely to Recover the Money of Coulton, as it is Uncertain, if can have any Effects here. Please present my best Respects to Mrs. Mackay & I am &c.

ADDRESSED: "Per Capt. John Frazer"

[795]
TO EDWARD PARE
Barbados

Charles Town, 29th January 1744 [1745]

SIR:

The above of the 19th Current is Copie of my last per Capt. Saltus, to which please be Refered, & have only now to advise that your Brigantine *Charming Sarah* does not yett appear but am in dayly Expectation of her, & as I advised in my last have provided the Several things you order'd for her Loading in order to give her Good dispatch. I add not at Present, but that I am With very great Respect &c.

ADDRESSED: "Per the Sloop *Postilion*, Capt. John Howard"

TO ANDREW PRINGLE
London

Charles Town, 2nd February 1744 [1745]

SIR:

My last to you was of the 19th Ulto. per the *Ann Galley*, Capt. Trenchard, who sail'd over the Bar the 23d, also two Copies thereof to which please be Refer'd & on the 24th Received your Sundry most agreeable Favours per Capt. White of the 15 June, 18th & 30th August, & 22d October, also yours of the 28th July Via Philadelphia & duely Remark the Contents.

Mr. Stead being just arrived in Capt. White, I understand by Dr. David Caw that he has possitive Directions from Messrs. Moore & Hurthwaite to Sue him, & As I have as I formerly advis'd you given him a Bond of Indemnity when he paid me the money, so I must defend the suit here for him as well as I can & bear him harmless, & am very Glad to be advised that you keep the money I have Remitted on said account in your hands till the Isue of the Law Suit is known as perhaps I may be cast here, & so be obliged to Refund the money by drawing on you for itt besides a Considerable Charge that may attend the Suit. Dr. Caw seems more to favour Messrs. Moore & Hurthwaite in the affair than his Cousin

2nd February 1745

William Caw & in the mean Time it will be Very proper that you send over all the proofs you can about the affair & Especially if they proved there Debt after Caw was a Bankrupt & please advise that in Case I may be cast in the Suit here If I must appeal home to London. Mr. Stead Says he Saw Messrs. Moor's Books & they have Charg'd Dr. David Caw for the Goods in their Books & not William Caw, & doe not Imagine they have Two Setts of Books.

I am greatly oblig'd to you for your kind offers of a share in your Privateer *Queen of Hungary* & doe Very Willingly accept of one Share in Same accordingly, which doubt not You'll be so Good as to Interest me in. The Cocoa of the *Roses* prize Sells of so dear that it wont answer to purchase any as the prices you advise are in London. Shall take Care to Ship Mr. James Henderson of Jamaica the Value of Tann'd Leather as you Direct per first Conveyance.

There are but three Commissioners on the Spott to Actt in Mr. Conyers affair about the Negroe besides my self, Vizt. James Grame & James Wright, Esqr. & said Two Gentlemen dont seem inclinable to accept or act in said Commission. Mr. Grame is stil'd Merchant in said Commission which he says is not his profesion or Calling, being a Gentleman of the Law & at present our Judge Admiral & he writes his Name Grame, not Graham as mention'd in the Commission & James Wright, Esqr. is Mr. Grames Brother in Law & Likewise a Gentleman in the Law & at present our Attorney Generall in the absence of [796] Mr. Abercrombie. Those Gentlemen don't like to be Concern'd in affairs that may take up their Time or Give them Trouble unless they are Well paid for Same, so that am afraid said affair must Lye Dormant till have further Directions about same & other Commissioners appointed, who am of opinion would be proper to insert in Same some Merchants who are known to be here on the Spott & will accept of said Commission.

There is one Mr. Archbald McIlvray[4] who has been here for these Twelve or Fifteen years in the Indian Trade, & has gott by his Industry (with a Good Caracter in said Trade) Two or Three Thousand pounds Ster. who went passenger for London about a fortnight agoe in the Ship *Triton*, Capt. Mcfarland, & am informed intends out here again after he has Seen his Relations in the North of Scotland. Itt is likely that he may want a Corespondent in London & it may be worth your while to gett acquainted with him. I intended to have writ to you by him to Introduce

[4] The firm of Archibald McGillivray and Co. had a virtual monopoly on the Creek Indian trade after 1747. *HL*, I, 284n.

him to your acquaintance as I told him, but the Hurry I was in dispatching the Guernsey Ship when this their Ships went prevented me till it was two late, tho' this you may take the oppertunity to mention to him with my Service. He Is a Good plain sort of a Man & always kept his Creditt exceeding well here. I beleive he is Recommended to Messrs. Samuel & William Baker to whom all his Deer Skins Goe Consign'd of which he has Shipt a Good Quantity.

I understand by Mr. Stead that he has full Instructions from Mr. Nicholson about Messrs. Hunters Account in order to have it Settled & he has prepos'd that it may be Refered to two persons, which we have agreed to rather than to goe to Law & be thought Litigeous. He Gives Mr. Nicholson a Very Indiffrent Caracter, & says that If he had not been pressed by Messrs. Baker to gett it settled he would have no Concern in it, as desireing to have nothing to doe with Mr. Nicholson in any shape.

Mr. Thomas Elliott desires me to acquaint You of the Receipt of your Last favours & the great obligations he Lye's under to You for your great Care of his Son, & is Willing that he may goe to holland this Spring for the Space of a Month or two, but upon no Account to lett him goe any further or out of holland, which he Recommends to you in the Most particular manner, being Apprehensive that he has Some inclinations for the Army from an Expression he seem'd to Hint at Relating thereto in one of his Letters which seems to give his Father not a Little Concern, & which would be much averse to his Way of thinking. Therefore hopes You'll be Very Watchfull & have a Very Strict Eye over him if you discover his Inclination any ways tending that way that you may take proper measures to divert him from such away of thinking & this he Very Earnestly Recommended to me to write to you about. My wife & I Return you our joint thanks for your kind present of the Copper Cooler. I am to Request youll be so good as to pay Mr. Glen for the Suit of Cloaths sent me which fitt Very well. My Wife joyns in Best Respect & I Remain &c.

ADDRESSED: "Per Capt. Baber Via Bristoll & Copie per Capt. Jackson Via Bristoll"

9th February 1745

[797]
TO JAMES HENDERSON
Kingston, Jamaica

Charles Town, 9th February 1744 [1745]

SIR:

The above of the 29th November is Copie of my last, Since have Not the Pleasure of any of your Favours. By late advice from My Brother in London he Informs Me of Your Departure from Thence for Jamaica & desires me to keep a Corespondence With You, which doubt not Will Find to our Mutual Advantage & Towards which shall with Great Pleasure very Readily Contribute all in my Power. My Brother likewise advises me That Tann'd Leather will answer Very well with you & desires I may ship some to you for a Tryal per first Conveyance. Please therefore Receive Inclos'd Bill of Loading & Invoice of One Hundred Sides Tann'd Leather Shipt on board the Sloop *Elizabeth*, John Rains, Master for Kingston, Jamaica on my Brother & my joint Risque & account & to your Good self Consign'd, Amount as per Invoice Being £209.7.6 this Currency, being for a Tryall, which you'll please to Receive & to Dispose of to our Best advantage, & the Neat Proceeds you'll please to Remitt to London to my Brother or to ship the Same Here to me in Good Muscovado Sugar in Teirces or in Flour Barrells. You may have an Opportunity of Shipping here by this Sloop, which Returns here again Directly & Capt. Rains has promis'd me to Take on Board what ever may be shipt to me on freight. By another Sloop nam'd the *Mary*, David Marshal, Masster which will sail from this for your Island in Fourteen days, You may expect One hundred sides more of Tann'd Leather which You'll please Likewise to Dispose of & make Remittance for same as already Directed.

As for your Rum and Lime juice it will by No means Answer here & is not worth the freight, Neither any thing else from your Island will answer here excepting Good Muscovado Sugar & a Small Quantity of Coffee if Cheap with you, & Sometimes Molassis, No Cocoa, being very Cheap & plenty here. Please be so Good as to advise me the prices of Goods with you & provisions, &c., & what may be most Suitable to send from this for your Markett & The proper Seasons. If this first Esay Turns to Good account it may Encourage a Further Corespondence which shall be Very Glad to Improve & Cultivate, & hope to have the Pleasure of

15th February 1745

hearing from You by all Conveyances this Way. Mean Time I salute you & am Most Respectfully &c.

Exchange To London £700 per £100 Sterling.

ADDRESSED: "Per the Sloop *Elizabeth*, Capt. John Rains, & Copie per Capt. Dickinson"

[798]
TO EDWARD & JOHN MAYNE & EDWARD BURN
   Lisbon
                    Charles Town, 11th February 1744 [1745]
GENTLEMEN:
   The above of the 17th October is Copie of my last to which Please be Reffer'd, & Since have not the Pleasure of any of your Favours. This goes per Capt. Rose for your Port. Our Commodity of Rice is Low here being at 20/ per Ct., there being but little Demand for Exportation & no Late Advices of the Marketts with You, the want of which Discourages Adventures, the prices with You being very Low by former Advices. I Most Respectfully Remain &c.

ADDRESSED: "Per Capt. Rose"

TO THOMAS HUTCHINSON & THOMAS GOLDTHWAIT
   Boston
                    Charles Town, 15th February 1744 [1745]
GENTLEMEN:
   Since my last to You of the 7th November per Capt. Bangs I have your most Esteem'd Favours of the 29th October at the Hands of Mr.

15th February 1745

Jeremiah Osborne and shall always with Great pleasure Render said Gentleman all the Good offices in my Power, or any other Friend that you may be pleased to take notice of to me. I was in hopes of having the pleasure of hearing from you by the Return of Capt. Bangs by whom this Goes, but none of Your Favours does yett appear. Said Capt. Bangs Informs Me that a Sloop one Chadock,[5] Master was Coming here from your Good selves to my address & it is Reported has Run ashoar & been beat to peices, near Port Royall, & altho' it is Ten or Twelve days agoe since said accident happened, have no advice from the Captain thereof, neither any of Your Letters, notwithstanding there are daily opportunitys from Thence. I have not further to offer at present as being without any of your offers, but That I Remain in haste &c.

ADDRESSED: "Per Capt. Bangs"

TO THOMAS HUTCHINSON
Boston

Charles Town, 15th February 1744 [1745]

SIR:

I have your Favours of the 29th October and Inclosed please Receive Invoices of Two Hogsheads Deer Skins shipt on board the Ship *Ann Galley,* Capt. John Trenchard, for London on your proper Risque & account & to Messrs. Burryau & Schaffer Consign'd, Amount as per Invoice being £699.11.9 this Currency which hope will Goe safe to hand & to a Good Markett. I took Care to Give said Gentleman previous advice of same in order for Insurance by four or five Diffrent Conveyances.

I take due notice of what you are pleased to Mention in Relation to making Remittances to said Gentlemen on your account & what has been Remitted on Your account has been Chiefly in Deer Skins & Silver which I apprehend you can have no Reason to Complain of or that they have Turned out worse then Bills of Exchange as I had occasion to ship in Both at the Same Time With Yours. I find by account Sent that Both Deer Skins & Silver turn'd out Better than Bills, & by latest Account

[5] Chadock is Joseph Chadwick. See RP to Joseph Chadwick, 16 February 1745.

16th February 1745

Deer Skins are much preferable & indeed Bills are now so Scarce that none are to be had at any Rate, the Course of our Trade having of late very much alter'd, our Commodity of Rice being now in no Demand in Europe so that no Bills are now Drawn for Same as has been formerly for some Time past.

Shall Loose no Opportunity as Conveyances offer to Remitt said Gentlemen in whatever may be most for your Interest for which shall always have the utmost Regaurd & I am most Respectfully &c.

ADDRESSED: "Per Capt. Bangs"

TO JOSEPH CHADWICK
    Port Royal, South Carolina
                    Charles Town, 16th February 1744 [1745]
SIR:
    I Received a Few hours agoe your's of the 14th Current per the bearer of this Mr. Latter & am Sorry for your Misfortune & loss as well as for the Gentlemen my friends who I am informed are yours Employers. I am not a little Supprized that you did not think proper to advise me thereof before this, (the former Letter you mention has not Come to hand) especially as there has been frequent opportunitys from Port Royall & if you had sent a person by Land on purpose to Inform me, would very willingly have paid the Charge. I am likewise supprized you did not at same Time with your own Letter forward what Letters you may have for persons in this Town & any letters for me, the Want of which has prevented from advising my friends of your misfortune, as not having heard anything from your self.
    You advise of your selling off where you are (what things you have Saved) on Munday the 19th Instant tho' am of opinion they would turn out to Better Advantage in Charles Town. I have heard with no manner of Certainty of your misfortune. The Sloop that it Seems was the occasion of your Running ashoar is now in this harbour & proves to be a Bermuda's Sloop from Providence. If you Can prove that the Master of said Sloop has done any thing that he Ought not, or Cannot answer to have

16th February 1745

done towards You, You may oblidge him to make Satisfaction so that the Sooner you Come to Town to Clear up the matter it will be the Better, in Case he may Goe from this Soon. Shall be Glad to See you in Charles Town and I am &c.

P. S. hope you have Taken Care to make a Regular Protest &c.

ADDRESSED: "Commander of the Sloop from Boston per Mr. Letter from Georgia"

TO JAMES HENDERSON
Kingston, Jamaica

Charles Town, 21st February 1744 [1745]

SIR:
The Preceeding on the other side of the 9th Current is Copie of my last to which please be Reffered. And agreeable thereto, please Recive Inclos'd Bill of Lading & Invoice of One Hundred and thirty Six Sides Tann'd Leather which shipt on board this sloop *Mary*, David Marshall, Master for Kingston, Jamaica on the Joint Risque & Account of my Brother & my self, & to you Consign'd, Amount as per Invoice being £269.17.2 this Currency which hope will Come safe to Hand & which you'll please Receive & dispose of to our Best Advantage, & the Neat Proceeds You'll please to Remitt here in good Muscovado Sugar, or to London as Directed in my last. The Leather has been Shipt in very Good order, is very Good in Quality, & hope will be Deliver'd in the same Good order accordingly. I have not further to offer at present, but that I am with very Great Respect &c.

ADDRESSED: "Per Capt. Marshall & Copie per Capt. Williams"

21st February 1745

[800]
TO DON DOMINGO
 St. Augustine

Charles Town, 21st February 1744 [1745]

SIR:
I have the Honour of your most Esteem'd Favours from Providence which Received at the Hands of the Bearer of this Very Worthy & agreeable Senor Don Fransisco de Castilla.[6] It Gives me Great pleasure to be Inform'd of Your Good Health & am very sorry for your Misfortune by being Taken in Your passage to Florida but it is the fortune of War which all those that have occasion to Goe by Water are Lyable To in these precarious Times, & all Well wishers to Mankind ought to pray for a Speedy peace which is one of the most Desirable & agreeable things we enjoy in this world. You have done me a Very Singular pleasure in Recommending to me the Very agreeable Senor Don Fransisco de Castilla, who is Very much of a Gentleman, & what Good offices I have been Capable of Rendering him here doe assure you has not been wanting, As I shall be always Very Glad to have it in my power to be of any Service to any friend you may be pleased to take Notice of or Recommend to me. And I hope when it pleases God to send us peace to have the pleasure of hearing often from you, than which Nothing Can be more agreeable.

I am to pray the favour You'll please be so Good as to present my most Humble Respects to his Excellency Senor Don Manoel de Montiano, Governour of Florida, which province Cannot fail of happiness & prosperity while under the Direction & Government of so Very Worthy a Gentleman. My Wife Joins in Best Respects, & I truely am With very Great Respect &c.

P. S. I hope your Goodness will pardon my Writing to you in English, as not being so much Master of the French Language, as to Express myself so well to you in it as it is my Desire.

ADDRESSED: "Per Don Fransisco de Castilla Contrador de Floride in Capt. Julian, Flagg of Truce"

[6] Fransisco de Castilla, Contrador de Floride, departed on the ship of truce commanded by Capt. Julian De La Vega. SCG, 11 March 1745. In 1747 Pringle while on his way to England was taken by a Spanish privateer and carried into St. Augustine whence he made his way back along the coast to Charleston. While in St. Augustine he gave presents to Don Francisco de Castilla, his son, and his servants, which presents must have eased his stay. "Journal of Robert Pringle, 1746–1747," annotated by Mabel L. Webber, SCHM, XXVI (1925), 107–112.

816   THE LETTERBOOK OF ROBERT PRINGLE

23rd February 1745

TO JAMES HENDERSON
    Kingston, Jamaica
                    Charles Town, 23rd February 1744 [1745]
SIR:
    Since writing the Preceeding on the other side of the 21st Current, Severall Sloops are arriv'd from Jamaica by which I writt you, & not having any of Your Favours I imagine that you was not arriv'd from London, otherways was in hopes of having the Pleasure of hearing from you. I understand that Muscovado Sugar is very high with You. If so, it will not am afraid answer here as it will come cheaper from the Leward Islands, so You'll please Remitt the Neat Proceeds of the Tann'd Leather to my Brother in London, or if Course Linnins that are Prize Goods are plenty With you & Come Cheap, Such as Plattilaes,[7] Silesias, & Britanias[8] may Send here the Neat Proceeds in Said Articles being very Scarce here at Present & am Inform'd are to be purchas'd with you for Less than the first Cost in England. I hope this will find you Safe arriv'd & I am &c.

ADDRESSED: "Per Capt. Marshall & Copie per Capt. Williams"

[801]
TO DAVID CHESEBROUGH
    Newport, Rhode Island
                    Charles Town, 23rd February 1744 [1745]
SIR:
    The Preceeding of the 17th December per Capt. Dudley Hilton, is Copie of my last to which please to be Refferred & yesterday have your Favours of the 26 January per Capt. Silas Cook, & am Much supprized that you have not Received Mine per said Capt. Hilton, who I understand by Capt. Cook Was arrived. Inclosed please Receive Copy of account Sales of your Soap, & account Current sent you per Capt. Hilton also 2d Bill of Loading for Seventy Six Spanish Dollars sent by him, being

---
[7] Platiloes was a sort of silesian linen.
[8] Britanias cloth was linen.

Ballance of your account which hope you have Received before this, if not you must have Your Recourse on Capt. Hilton for Same.

This Goes by Capt. Oliver Via Boston & hope will Come safe to hand, & that I shall have the Pleasure of hearing from you Soon in Expectation of which I most Respectfully Remain &c.

Rice 20/ per Ct., Rum N. E. 16/ per Gall., Ditto West India 20/ per Gall., Exchange to London £700 petr £100 Sterling.

Please to advise me the Prices of Goods with you.

ADDRESSED: "Per Capt. Oliver Via Boston"

TO JOHN ERVING
    Boston

Charles Town, 23rd February 1744 [1745]

SIR:

My last to you was of the 17th December & this day have Your most Esteem'd Favours of the 23d December & 22 January per Capt. Langstaff[9] & duely Remark the Contents. I shall doe myself the pleasure, according to your Directions, to write you by all opportunities of what occurs here worth your Notice. Rice is at present at 20/ per hundredweight & Freight for London at £6 per Ton & for Holland at £7 per Ton. Naval Stores are Low at present, Pitch 35/ per bbl., Tarr 40/, Turpintine 10/ per hundredweight, but how long may Continue So is very uncertain. However as there are but few Shipping here, there is not much liklyhood that Naval Stores will be Higher, especially as freight will be High which Naval Stores Cannot afford.

I intimated to Messrs. Peronneau what you are pleased to Mention in Relation to them, who Tell me they Are Likewise favour'd with one from you. I have not yett seen Capt. Jelf but shall take Care to Deliver Mr. Apthorpes Letter to him & to whom please to present my Humble Service. Capt. Jelf lives Chiefly at Hobcaw about four miles from Town on the

---

[9] Capt. Bethel Langstaff, sloop *Prosperity*, arrived from Boston. *SCG*, 4 March 1745.

23rd February 1745

other side the River. He has Lately had the Misfortune to Lose the Snow *Swallow*, Among the Bahama Islands.[1]

My Wife & I are much concern'd to be Inform'd of Mrs. Erving's Indisposition. Hope this shall find her Restored to perfect health & which heartily Wish may long Continue. My Wife Joins in Best Respects to Good Lady & all the pritty Familly. Capt. Oliver being Just agoing I add not at present but that I am With Very Great Respects &c.

Exchange to London £700 per £100 Sterling.

ADDRESSED: "Per Capt. Oliver & Copies per Capt. Langstaff & [*Blank*]"

[802]
TO THOMAS HUTCHINSON & THOMAS GOLDTHWAIT
  Boston

Charles Town, 23rd February 1744 [1745]

GENTLEMEN:

The preceeding on the other side of the 15th Current is Copie of my last, & Just now have your Esteem'd Favours of the 7th & 15th January (per Capt. Chadwick, late Master of the Sloop *Betty*) & Not before, who is Just Come to Town from Port Royall & Gives me account of his Misfortune in having Lost the Sloop & Cargoe, near Port Royall. Am very Sorry for your Loss of Sundry's you were pleased to Consign to my address as per Bill of Loading Inclosed, which it Seems are all Intirely lost. Capt. Chadwick Tells me that he has Saved Nothing, excepting a Sail or Two & Some part of the Rigging, & was Chas'd ashoar as he says by a Sloop which he took for a Spanish privateer, but proves to be a Sloop Bound here from Providence & at present in this Harbour. Rice is at present at 20/ per hundredweight, Freight to London £6 Ster. per Ton, & to Holland £7 per Ton. Naval Stores are Low at present, Pitch at 35/ per bbl., Tarr at 40/ per bbl., Turpintine 10/ per hundredweight, But how Long may

[1] HMS *Swallow*, Andrew Jelfe, was wrecked on 24 December 1744 on the Abaco Keys. Captain Jelfe and part of his crew had returned to Charleston in a large sloop. May, p. 165; SCG, 21 January 1745.

Continue So is Uncertain. However, as there are but Few shipping here, there is not much Likelyhood that Naval Stores will be much higher especially as freight will be high, which Naval Stores Cannot afford.

I observe what you are pleased to Mention Relating to the Oranges. They will Keep a Considerable Time from Spoiling in Which they have the Advantage of the fruit from the Islands & hope by this, they may be all Disposed of & the Remainder at a Better price than you mention. Some Lately Shipt to Philadelphia, have advise keep Very well & Sell off at 20/ per Hundred that Currency. Have Disposed of most part of the Brandy, but have not been able to gett more than 25/ per Gallon. It is Very unsaleable here. None of the Florence Wine is Yett disposed of. It is a Wine not us'd or much Lik'd here. Capt. Oliver by whom this Goes, being just upon his Departure prevents me from Enlarging at present, so must begg Leave to Conclude in haste &c.

Rum N. E. 16/ per Gall., Ditto West India 20/ per Gall., Single Refind Loaf Sugar 6/ per lb., Exchange to London £700 per £100 Ster.

ADDRESSED: "Per Capt. Oliver & Copies per Capt. Langstaff per Capt. Bangs"

TO JOHN HOBBS[2]
London

Charles Town, 23rd February 1744 [1745]

DEAR SIR:

I have your very agreeable Favours of the 8th January from Boston per the Bearer Capt. Oliver, which Gives me Great Pleasure to be Inform'd of your Health, Wellfare, & Success, which heartily wish may long Continue. I have had the pleasure with Capt. Oliver to Remember all absent Friends and Shall be always Very Glad to have the Pleasure of hearing from you. I am uncertain If I shall Goe for London this Summer unless a Good opportunity offers. We are inform'd that the Kings ships

[2] Dr. John Hobb's address was at Mr. John Cargill's, the Surgeon's Instrumentmaker, in Lumbard Street, London. RPC, p. 820.

on this Station are order'd to Goe & assist in an intended expedition against Cape Britoon.[3] Please to present my Compliments to the Very Worthy Capt. Philip Durell.

My Wife Joins in Best Respects, & I am with much Esteem &c.

We have no Material News at present.

ADDRESSED: "Per Capt. Oliver"

[803]
TO ROBERT ELLIS
Philadelphia

Charles Town, 25th February 1744 [1745]

SIR:

Above is Copie of my last, & Since have Yours Favours of the 20th December not Sign'd with Bill of Loading & Invoice of Bread & Beer per Capt. Willson, Amount £59.1.10 Philadelphia Currency which have Received and shall Take Care to dispose of to your Best advantage & Carry the Neat Proceeds to the Credit of your account. Some of the Bread has Received Some Damage, but whether before or after it has been Shipt Cannot Determine. Hope youll be so Good as to make Further Remittances this Spring as you mention in order to Ballance your account now of so long standing. My Wife Joins in Best Respects to Good Mrs. Ellis & Self & I am &c.

P. S. I understand that Good Chocolate is Sold at 20/ & 22/ per lb. your Currency. If so, a Quantity would answer well here at that price.

ADDRESSED: "Per Capt. Buckmaster"

---

[3] A force of New England men with the assistance of ships of the royal navy captured the French fortress, Louisbourg, on Cape Breton Island, in 1745, but it was restored to France by the Treaty of Aix-la-Chapelle in 1748.

TO RICHARD ROWLAND
St. Kitts

Charles Town, 25th February 1744 [1745]

Sir:

The preceeding on the other side of the 22d November is Copie of my last, Since have not the pleasure of any of your Favours. I was Very Glad to be inform'd by Capt. Harraman of this Place & Lately at your Island of your Good Health & by whom should have been Very Glad to have heard from you. I am to pray the Favour you'll Please be so good as to Lett me have a few lines in Return to this per the Bearer Capt. Beek or any other Conveyance Bound this Way. I hope your Goodness will Excuse the Trouble I Give you in this affair, & if in the Like or any other occasion I Can be of any Service to You here, You may always most Truly Command &c.

ADDRESSED: "Per Capt. Beek"

TO ANDREW PRINGLE
London

Charles Town, 27th February 1744 [1745]

Sir:

My last to you was of the Second Current Via Bristoll To Which please be Reffer'd, & since have not the Pleasure of any of your Favours, your last being of the 22d October per Capt. White, & no Vessells from England Since. Capt. Wilkinson does not yet appear. Inclosed please Receive Copie of Two Invoices of Tann'd Leather Shipt per Two diffrent Conveyances to Mr. James Henderson in Jamaica as you direct'd on our Joint account. It Seems he had not Lately been arrived from London, but hope he may by the Time the Tann'd Leather Getts there, Amount of Both Invoices being £497.3.9 Currency. I have directed him to Remitt the Neat Proceeds to you, or here as he may Judge most for our Interest.

The privateer *Recovery* does not Yett appear which Gives Great Uneassiness & the Privateer Snow *Assistance* built here & Intended for a Consort to the *Recovery* is now in the Road Wind bound on a Cruize by her Self[4] which is a fine Vessel & Well fitted. Said Vessel has Come to a Considerable Charge here & for which we that are Managers are at present Greatly in advance & we Intend as agreed to Reimburse our Selves by the Shares of the Prizes Taken by the *Recovery* that may be due to the Concern'd here in your hands, & who have not paid their proportions here for the Cost & outsett of the Snow. So that altho Some of the Concern'd here may perhaps Send Letters of Attorney to their friends in London to Receive their Dividends of the Prizes in your hands, Hope [804] That Mr. Crokatt & You will be So Cautious as not To take any Notice or pay any Money to any of the Concern'd without Particular Directions from us that are Managers here, & of which we Intend to Write You by next Conveyance & ought to have done now, or Before this. But as there are So Many of Us, things are not Transacted with that Dispatch & Unanimity as if it was in one Persons hands & Management which is Generaly the Case in afairs of that Nature. The Managers here intend to Draw a Sett of Bills of Exchange to pay the Defeciency of the Cost of the Snow out of the Concern'd, their Dividends Due on the prizes per the *Recovery*. I hope you have been so Good as to Insure my Share in the Privateer *Queen of Hungary*, which I advised you in my last That I was Very Willing to accept a Whole Share of according to your kind offer, & I leave it to you to Insure the said share or not as you Judge proper, & to Doe the Same as you doe with your own.

Our Friend Mr. Thomas Elliott is lately Married to a Widow Lady nam'd Bellinger,[5] a Very agreeable Lady but not much Fortune. Please my Service to the Young Gentleman his Son. Our Governour Mr. Glen told me sometime agoe that he Intended to Give me a Letter for you to be forwarded under my Cover. I told him you would be very Glad to be Honour'd with one from Him, & that I Writ to you by every Conveyance But he has not Since thought proper to give me as Yett any Letter. There is not much Confidence to be put in him. He is a Weak Man & begins to Loose himself here pretty much and has not Near the Respect show'd him as at first. My Wife Joins with me in Best Respects, & have not further to

---

[4] The privateer snow *Assistance*, Richard I'On, and the privateer sloop *Famed Revenge*, Clement Lempriere, sailed together on a cruise. SCG, 4 March 1745. For their prizes see SCG, 13 May 1745.

[5] He married Mrs. Elizabeth Bellinger, the widow of Edmund Bellinger. *SCHM*, XI (1910), 59.

offer at present, as being without any of Your Favours but that I Remain Most Affectionately &c.

Rice 20/ per hundredweight, Exchange to London £700 p £100 Sterling.

ADDRESSED: "Per Capt. Jackson Via Bristoll"

TO HENRY LASCELLES & CO.[6]
London

Charles Town, 27th February 1744 [1745]

GENTLEMEN:

Inclosed please Receive a Letter for you from Edward Pare, Esqr. of Barbadoes which Came by his Brigantine *Charming Sarah*, Capt. John Davison, who arrived here from Barbadoes a few days agoe, & which he directed me to forward you as Soon as possible to acquaint you of the arrival of said Brigantine here, & that you'll be pleased to make Insurance on Same and Cargoe on his account at & from this back to Barbadoes. The Brigg is Burthen about 100 Tons a New Vessell, & Capt. Davison tells me has Cost his owner Mr. Pare £700 Ster. & the Cargoe I ship on board for him may be about £300 Ster. However I imagine he has advis'd you, in Relation to the Sum, to be Insur'd on Vessell & Cargoe which he has not made mention of to me. Shall be Very Glad to Render You any agreeable Service here & I am Most Respectfully &c.

ADDRESSED: "Per Capt. Jackson Via Bristoll & per the *Flambro's* Prize"

---

[6] Henry Lascelles, who preceded Gedney Clarke as collector of customs in Barbados, was associated with Lascelles & Maxwell, sugar factors of Mark Lane, London. He was M.P. for Northallerton 1745–1752. *HL*, I, 316n; Namier & Brooke, II, 22.

27th February 1745

TO FITTER & TYZACK
London

Charles Town, 27th February 1744 [1745]

GENTLEMEN:

The above of the 16 January is Copie of my last, & Since has Come to Hand Mr. John Lightfoot his Third Bill of Exchange for Fifty Pounds Sterling as above Mention'd, which please Receive Inclosed. I am Most Respectfully &c.

ADDRESSED: "Per Capt. Jackson Via Bristoll"

[805]
TO DAVID GLEN
London

Charles Town, 6th March 1744 [1745]

SIR:

I Received your Favours of the 24th August with My Suit of Cloaths which are Very much to my likeing & fitt me Exactly excepting that the Coat Slevees are an Inch or an Inch & a half Two Long. I Received also your Bill, amount of the whole being £9.7.6 Ster. for which you'll please to apply to my Brother, who I have Desired to pay you the Money. I am also to Desire you'll Gett made for me a Suit of Black Cloaths, Vizt. a Coat of Best Super fine Black Broad Cloath, of a Good Black Colour, full Trimm'd & Lined with Black Allepine & a Jackett for Same, & two Pair Breeches of Figur'd or Rais'd or Cut Velvett. I mean the Jackett of Cut Velvett & the Two Pair Breeches of Plain Black Velvett, & pray dont make the Coat Slevees so Long as the last, & Lett them be done & Carried to my Brother's that they may be sent per first oppertunity.

I am uncertain as yett Wether I Can Come for London this Summer, but Wether I do or Not, desire the Suit of Cloaths may be made & Sent. I Deliver'd your Letter to Mr. Duty,[7] who Tells me that he will Pay the money Soon & when he does Shall Take Care to Remitt it You. I am with much Esteem &c.

ADDRESSED: "Per Capt. Jackson Via Bristoll & Copie per Capt. Willson Via Cowes"

[7] James (Duty) Duthie was a Charleston peruke-maker. SCHM, XL (1939), 137.

14th March 1745

TO EDWARD PARE
Barbados

Charles Town, 14th March 1744 [1745]

SIR:

My last to you was of the 29th January & Since have both your Esteem'd Favours of the 18th January per your Brigantine *Charming Sarah*, Capt. John Davisson, who arrived here the 22d past with Inclosed Bill of Loading & Invoices of sundries which have Received & am to Acquaint you that the Muscovado Sugar happn'd to Come to a Dull & Low Markett, there being a Great Deal here at present which has Come Chiefly from Jamaica. Rum had been Much Better than Sugar, however my best Endeavours shall not be wanting to Dispose of every thing to your best Advantage. Capt. Davisson Informs me that he hath your orders to Sheath the Vessell which has been accordingly Done, & is now Ready to take in her Cargoe, which is Chiefly Ready to Take on board, & shall take Care to Ship every thing as Near as Can be to your Directions, But as I advis'd in my Former Am apprenhensive the Cedar you order, Cannot be procur'd in the province, being of so Extraordinary Large Dimensions. Black Ey'd Pease are not to be had & Corn Very Scarce & dear, So that Capt. Davisson advises me that it will be more for your advantage to Ship you good Rice in the Room thereof, it being very low in price at present.

I writt to Henry Lascelles & Co., Esqrs. according to your Directions, & at Same Time forwarded both your Letters to them Inclos'd by Different Conveyances & Your Two Bills to Capt. Davisson shall be Duely Honour'd. As for his Disbursments here, it is the first Time that I have ever known any Commander of a Vessell address'd to me that their Disbursments where Disputed by their owners. However think Capt. Davisson's are Certainly very Reasonable, & Who I take to be a Very Honest Carefull Man whose Disbursment need no Attesting further then my sending you the account of same, as I always Do to the owners of Every ship Consign'd to me & if Capt. Davisson is not be be Confided in as to his Disbursments Do not think he ought to be intrusted with your Brigantine & Cargoe. Shall take Care that all the Charges shall be Managed with the best Oeconomy. As I shall doe my self the Pleasure to write you again soon by your Brigantine *Charming Sarah* which hope will be Loaded & Ready to Sail in three Weeks if Weather Permitts, I add not at Present but that I most Respectfully Remain &c.

ADDRESSED: NO ADDRESS

16th March 1745

[806]
TO DAVID CHESEBROUGH
Newport, Rhode Island

Charles Town, 16th March 1744 [1745]

SIR:

The Two annex'd Letters of the 17th December & 23d February are Copies of my last to which please be Reffered, & this Goes by Capt. Silas Cook to Whom I show'd Copie of Bill of Lading in my Bill of Loading Book for the Spanish Dollars Sent you per Capt. Hilton which if he has been so base as not to Deliver, you must Take Your Recourse on him. Inclosed please also Receive Copie of Your Account Sales of Soap & Account Current. I have not further to offer at Present but that I Remain Most Respectfully &c.

ADDRESSED: "Per Capt. Silas Cook"

TO OSBORNE & OXNARD & THOMAS GUNTER
Boston

Charles Town, 16th March 1744 [1745]

GENTLEMEN:

I have both your Most Esteem'd Favours of the 24th December & 4th January with Inclosed a Certificate for the Brigantine *Dolphins* Cargoe which has Clear'd the Bond. I have paid the Bearer of this Mr. Jeremiah Osborne on your account the Outstanding Debt on said Cargoe of Henry Sherriff[8] being Twenty Eight pounds 8/ Currency Since Received. The other Debt of Stephen Hartley's[9] of £26.6.1 is still Outstanding, & When

---

[8] Henry Sherriff of James Island in Berkeley County willed money for the support of the Presbyterian minister at Will Town. Moore & Simmons, II, 137.

[9] Stephen Hartley, Charleston school-master, advertised in 1741 that he wanted payment from "all persons indebted to me for schooling." In 1744 he opened a school in St. Thomas Parish about twelve miles from the city. SCG, 5 February 1741; SCHM, XXXI (1930), 314. Later in 1751, RP sued Stephen Hartley of St. Thomas Parish for £97 because Hartley had defaulted on his bond, dated 18 May, 1747. Judgment Rolls, 1751 B-H, 22A.

18th March 1745

Recover'd shall be imediately Remitted. Shall be always Very Glad to Receive Your Commands & to Render you any agreable Service as being most Respectfully &c.

ADDRESSSED: "Per Capt. Silas Cook Via Road Island"

TO JOHN ERVING
    Boston
Charles Town, 16th March 1744 [1745]

SIR:

    The above of the 23d February is Copie of my last, Since which have not the Pleasure of any of your Favours & have only to add at Present that Rice is now Very low in price being at 15/ per Ct., there being few or No Shipping in the Place & Freight is at Six pounds Ster. per Ton for London & Seven Pounds Ster. for Holland & Believe will keep up & be wanted as few Shipping are Expected this Season. Naval Stores are the Same as in my last. Capt. Jelf has Dispos'd of his Bill on Mr. Charles Apthorpe. This Goes by Mr. Jeremiah Osborne with whom have frequently had the Pleasure to Drink to all absent Friends. My Wife Joins in Bestt Respects to Mrs. Erving & all the pritty Young ones & I most Respectfully Remain &c.

ADDRESSED: "Per Capt. Silas Cook Via Road Island"

[807]
TO ANDREW PRINGLE
    London
Charles Town, 18th March 1744 [1745]

SIR:

    My last to You was of the 6th Current with Copies advising about my being Concern'd with Mr. Inglis, in a Cargoe of Goods (& of his Good

18th March 1745

Behaviour Since he has Liv'd with me, so much to my Satisfaction & of the Great Regaurd & Esteem I have for him) which Intended to write you for to Supply us with against next fall of the Year, & Inclos'd please Receive Invoice or List of an Assortment which will be very Suitable, & desire may be to the Value of about £1,500 or £2,000 Sterling & shoud be very Glad to have you one third part Concern'd in Same with us, which doubt not will be agreeable to You. I also hinted to You the Branch of Trade which we Intend the Said Goods for, which doubt not will Turn out to Our Mutual advantage, & the sooner they Come the better, to be here the first or Earliest Goods in the fall & hope may be here by September or October next & whither I Come for London this Summer or not am to Request the Said Goods may be Sent.

Inclos'd please Receive the Managers of the Two Privateers *Recovery* & *Assistance* Their Joint Bill of Exchange for £250 Ster. in my favour on Mr. James Crokatt & your good Self & Payable to your Order as per advice from them of this Date, to which please be Refferr'd & which doubt not will be duely Honour'd & for which please to Creditt my Account Current. They have also Drawn on Mr. James Crokatt & you three Setts more of £250 Ster. each makes in all £1,000 Sterling, To the Order of Mr. James Buchanan £250 Ster., To the Order of William Pomroy & Sons £250 Ster., To the Order of George Mackenzie £250 Ster., all payable at 40 days Sight, Being for Our advance on the Cost & Outsett here of the Privateer Snow *Assistance,* the Subscriptions here having fallen greatly short thereof. As it is with the Generall Consent of the Concern'd here that we Reimburse Our Selvs in that Manner & have Impower'd us so to doe, as they have not advanc'd or paid in their Proportions here for the Cost & Outsett of the Snow, & we are to Receive no Share or Dividend of Prizes 'till we are Reimburs'd for Our advance, & hope you have Cash Sufficient in your Hands due from the Prizes to answer Same, & we shall have Occasion to make other Drafts on you for what may be due to the Concern'd here, & if anything shou'd happen which we Cannot foresee, that Our Said Bills on You should not be Honour'd, we have agreed to write to Our Friends that they may not be protested, but keept in Our Friends Hands in London.

There is still Great Discontent that the *Recovery* has been Detain'd in Europe, & most of the Concern'd Declare that if they had thought the Vessell had been keept in Europe they had never been Concern'd. I am sorry to Observe they Seem more to Blame Mr. Crokatt & Your Self for it than Capt. Anderson. As the *Recovery*'s not Coming out Directly has

18th March 1745

Broke & Disappointed the Whole design & Scheme in Purchasing such a Vessell which has Occasion'd Great Discontent & Reflections from most People here, & those that are Concern'd are the jest & Sneer of those that are not Concern'd.

Have sent under the Care of Capt. Alexander Pearson, Commander of the Ship *Grayhound* a Box of Young Plants of Laurells[1] & Bays,[2] as you Order'd, which I had of our Friend Mr. Thomas Elliott. He Rang'd the Woods (he tells me) for the Fringe Tree,[3] but Could find none, neither any seeds to be had at Present. I have put on Board a Cask of Water for Watering the Plants & Capt. Pearson has Promis'd to take Great Care thereof & hope they will Come safe to hand.

I Omitted to advise you that in Case Capt. Douglas comes this Way again this Summer it might answer very well for him to touch at Madeira in the Way for Some Wines, as they are likely to be very Scarce here this Summer, & beleive will turn out to a very Good Account. As Scots Cheqs may be Scarce in London & pretty much in Demand, as there will be pretty Large Orders for them from this Place the Sooner you Secure them the better, as Likewise the Garlix. Per my next you may expect a Remittance on Account of Mr. Inglis. I have not further to Offerr at Present, as being without any of your Favours, but that My Wife Joins in Best Respects & I Sincerely Remain &c.

P. S. Am of Opinion it may be very Proper & most for Our advantage that you Charter or Take up a Vessell for to bring the Goods if you can on easie & Moderate Terms & at Good time for Lye days in case you may have no Vessel of your own to send the Goods by.

[808] A Postcript to Mr. Andrew Pringle's preceeding Later, Vizt.

The Managers are in hopes that no Demur will be made to the payment of Our Bills as you are in Cash for the *Recovery's* Prizes & is the only way we have to Reimburse our Selves for Our advance in fitting out the Privateer here, as the Concern'd have not paid their Proportions of the Charge,

---

[1] The "laurels" referred to could have been either the Carolina Laurel Cherry, or more probably mountain laurel. William Chambers Coker and Henry Roland Totten, *Trees of the Southeastern States* (3rd. ed.: Chapel Hill, 1945), pp. 191–195, 254, 359.

[2] The "bays" could be any one of a number of flowering trees, including members of the magnolia family. Coker and Totten, *passim*.

[3] The "Frenge Tree," Flowering Ash, or Old Man's Beard is "very showy in the spring and often cultivated for ornament." Coker and Totten, p. 385.

& doubt not You will be so Circumspect as not to pay any Money on Account of any of the Concern'd for their Dividend or Shares to their Attorneys as no Money is Due to them till the Cost of the Privateer Snow is paid here, which we have advanc'd for them, and they agreed we Shou'd first Reimburse Our Selvs, & yet we are Inform'd, that Some of them, unknown to us, Sent Powers of Attorney to Receive their Shares of the Prizes, which is not using us well, & the which the Other Managers Request that I shoud make mention of in my Letter to You, as we shoud be in a bad Situation for what we have advanc'd here If there was not Money in Your Hands, Yours &c.

ADDRESSED: "Per Capts. Willson, White, & Brown Via Cowes"

TO ANDREW PRINGLE
London

Charles Town, 21st March 1744 [1745]

SIR:

I have writt you of the 18th Current per three Diffrent Conveyances still in the Road to which Crave Refferance & am to accknowledge the Receipt just now of your most Esteem'd Favours of the 4th & 6th December at the Hands of Mr. Kenneth Michie being the only Letters from you since that of the 22d. October and Duely Remark the Various Contents.

Shall take Care to Deliver the Inclos'd for Mr. Elliott, & duely notice what you mention in Relation to Indigo, & doubt not will be much Improv'd in Time.[4] Colonel Lucas & his Familly Live now in Antigua (he being Lieutenant Governour there) & Charles Pinckney, Esqr. is Married to his Daughter & is the only One of his Fammilly now here.

I hope Mr. Murray will be Sensible & Gratefull for the very Singular peice of Service you have done him. He bears an Honest Character here & believe you run no Risque in being his Security, either in the Discharge of

---

[4] In 1744 Eliza Lucas Pinckney made seventeen pounds of indigo and sent six to England for comparison with the French product. Initially, the judgment of English tradesmen was favorable, but as indigo began to be exported in quantity there were complaints in London about the quality of the South Carolina product. The uneven quality was due primarily to a lack of experience and inspection. Wallace, I, 384.

21st March 1745

his Duty, or in his Remitting £90 Ster. Annually. It is much that he Could not find a Person among his Friends, Mr. Clelland's or Mr. Seaman's Friends to do that part for him & think he has been greatly Oblidg'd to You. It is with much Concern that I have to advise you that we have heard nothing of the Privateer *Recovery*, so that as you advise in Yours, She had been Sail'd two Months, she must be either Loss't or taken, & as what you mention of the Portuguse Vessel, am afraid will Occasion great Discontent here. Am to Caution You not to pay any Money on Account the Prizes to any of the Concern'd, but by Order from the Managers here.

His Majestys Ship the *Aldburough* does not yet appear, by whom expect Your further favours.[5] I am again to pray You'll endeavour to Recover the Money due me from Michael Thomson. Mr. Michies goods will Come to a very good Markett, being Scarce here at Present. It is pity we had not over a Good Sorted Cargoe this Spring. It would have sold well, & have been able to have made Returns for Same this Summer & in the fall in Gold & Silver. I Observe you are So good to Advise that you Desire to be Concern'd in what ever Goods I may Order, & you may depend that the Trade we propose them for will yeld Returns as you mention, & within the Year & Run no Risque, & am to desire that the assortment order'd in my Last may not be Less in all than £2,000 Ster. & Shipt in a Charter'd Ship & dispatch'd as Quick as possible. As by coming by themselvs on a Charter'd Ship, they have a Good Chance of being more Vendable & the Quick Sale will much Depend on their being here early in the fall, & if the Vessell they Come in shou'd have the Misfortune of being taken Youll please to Order [809] immediatly another Vessel with the Same Assortment making Insurance on the whole Value of the Cargoe, & doubt not of making You Considerable Returns by the Same bottom the Goods Come in.

I have writt Severall times to Mr. James Henderson in Jamaica who it seems is not yet arriv'd there, but his Brother who is there has not thought Proper to give me any Return. I in haste Remain &c.

P. S. Please not to fail getting a License for Portugal for the Vessell You Send & Charter'd at as Long Lye days as You Can, as perhaps She may arrive Long before Our New Rice is Ready to Ship. We have no Good Madeira Wine in Town at present, hope you have Order'd Some this Way. Pray Lett Two or three pieces of the Chintz Patterns for Beds be of

[5] HMS *Alborough*, Ashby Utting, arrived on the Carolina station 25 May 1745. May, p. 165.

21st March 1745

a very Good Figure as I intend it a Bed for my Self, & Lett my Wife's Gown & my Cloaths be sent with the Goods.

Twenty five Tons of Coals, if Reasonable.
Twelve Iron Bound Cask of 15/ Beer, about 32 Gallons per Cask.
Mr. Hume had Some Over answ'd very well.

Since writing have seen a Letter of Yours to the Managers here of the 4th December about the Privateer, & it gives me much Concern to find that every Letter gives more & more discontent. Two things are found Great fault with in Same, Vizt. One that you seem to hesitate in being Concern'd in the Privateer here, as the Proposalls Sent were to be both One Joint Concern, which they say you accepted of, & the other that you wish we had put it in Your power to have had Capt. Anderson under your Directions, & upon looking at the Copie of the first Letter to You, they say it appears that we writt You that we had given Capt. Anderson Instructions to be entirely under Your Directions, & which Directions were to Come here Directly, & which Instructions of His, they & I imagine he must have Show'd You. Said affair is like to be attended with a Good deal of Ill will, which gives me not a Little Concern, & it will be very Proper for you to make it appear, if there is any blame in Conducting the Affair, at whose Door it Lyes, & am very well Convinc'd you will be able to make every thing You have had the Management of appear to Satisfaction. Mr. Michie it Seems gives no Satisfing Account to the Concern'd, & I understand says you did not Lett him know any thing of the Affair, altho' one of the Concern'd, & a Manager here, which they seem much to admire at.

ADDRESSED: "Per Capts. Willson, White, & Brown Via Cowes, & per Capt. William Willson for London"

TO WILLIAM PITT[6]
Island of Rattan, on the Mosquito Coast
Charles Town, 29th March 1745

SIR:
Having had occasion to have the Pleasure of Some Corespondence with you by Your Sloop, John Babb, Master who was here in the Year 1741, I therefore take the Liberty to Recommend to You the Bearer of this my Good Friend, Mr. Henry Kennan, a Young Gentleman who is partner with Mr. James Reid of this Place Merchant. Mr. Kennan Comes with a Cargoe to Your Island of Rattan[7] to Try if there is Encouragement to Carry on Trade from this to your said New Settlement & What Good Offices & Civilities you may be pleas'd to Render said Gentleman Shall Esteem a Most Particular Favour done Me, & on the Like or any other occasion Shall be always Very Glad to Receive your Commands, & to Render you any agreeable Service, as being Most Respectfully &c.

ADDRESSED: "Governour of the Island of Rattan, per Henry Kennen"

[810]
TO ANDREW PRINGLE
London
Charles Town, 4th April 1745

SIR:
My Last to You was of the 21st Ulto. with three Copies to which please be Refferr'd, & Since have your Most Acceptable Favours of the 14th November, 4th & 28th December at the Hands of Murray with *Aldbrough*, Capt. Utting, who arriv'd here the 26th Ulto. Inclos'd please Receive the 4th Bill of Exchange the Managers of the Privateers for £250 Str. on Mr. Crokatt & Self, And to Your good Self payable having already forwarded three Bills, & hope some of them will come to hand.

I am to Return you my kind Thanks for the Perewigg you have been so

---

[6] William Pitt, a merchant in Black River near Cape Comorin on the Musketto Shoar, was addressed by RP as "Governor of the Island of Rattan." RPC, p. 819.
[7] Rattan was an island in the Gulf of Honduras "which was a starting point for illicit trade with the Spaniards." HL, I, 61n.

good as to send me per Mr. Murray which happens to be a Great deal too Large & too full for me & too much hair in it, but will be no Dissappointment as I can dispose of it here, & am again to pray You'll be so good as to excuse the Trouble of Sending You the Size of my head for another Wigg of the Same Sort or Make, but much less in the Caul & of a much Lighter Colour of the Gray Sort, & not Inclinable to Yellow which the Sun & Heat of the Climate is very apt to take Effect upon, & to Spoil the Colour especially if any ways inclinable to the Yellow Cast.

There is as yet not a Word of the Privateer *Recovery*, which Occasions a Great many Reflections & Murmuring amongst the Concern'd who give her Over for Losst or Taken, & Seem to Complain much of not having the Satisfaction of ever Seeing the Vessel here. The Law Suit of Dr. Caw's with Messrs. Moore & Hurthwait is not yet Comenc'd. Mr. Stead their Attorney apply'd to a Lawyer here to bring an Action, but not being Satisfied with the Account, as not being proof enough for the Debt or a Regular Account Charg'd to Dr. Caw, it Seems Can't do nothing with it till a more Regular Account appears from them, & which am in hopes they Cannot produce from their Books, & which Mr. Stead it Seems (as Dr. Caw tells Me) writt to Said Gentlemen for, which will Occasion Some Delay. Meantime have been Oblidg'd to give Mr. Grame Twenty Pounds Currency as a Retaining Fee in the Affair. I hope you wont part with the money till the affair is Adjusted, otherways we bring it upon Our Selvs, in which we have no Benefitt or Interest further than to Serve the Creditors of William Caw's Estate, So that we ought to take Care not to be Sufferers in Said Affair purely to Serve other People.

You may Depend on my Particular Attention in Relation to Indigoe, as You Advise, which Your Letter Relating thereto gives a Great Sanction to the Value thereof, & which I intimated to Colonel Pinckney & Severall other Gentlemen which gives them Great Joy & Encouragement to goe heartily upon the Improvement thereof, which however will yet Require Sometime to bring to Maturity or to produce any Quantity. But there is at Present a Necessity to push for it & to Stimulate Our Planters, as they See the Rice is in no Demand or Value being at 10/ Currency per Ct.

Inclos'd please Receive a few Things as an addition to the Assortment of Goods already sent you, which Disire may be Chiefly in the Cheq Linnens & Garlix to make up to the Value of Four or Five Hundred Pounds Sterling more, so that the whole may be about £2,500 Ster. There never was so Great a Demand or Encouragement for Dry Goods here, which formerly were at a Long Creditt, but are now Cash Commoditys, the

4th April 1745

Course & Channell of Our Trade being alter'd, & in another way. As I advis'd in my Former, Mr. Michie Sells his Goods to Shopkeepers at 6 per Cent.

Mr. Inglis has paid me One Hundred & Eighty Pounds [811] Sterling, which You'll please to Charge to my Account, & for which he is to have Creditt on Account of his proportion of the Goods we are to be Concern'd in, & which You'll please to Note accordingly.

This I hope will be Deliver'd You by Our Friend & Old Accquaintance Capt. William Willson, Commander of the Snow who put in here in his passage from Jamaica for London, having Losst both his Masts. His owner & Employer Capt. Peirce being Dead, he Desires that I wou'd make mention of him in my Letter to You as he may stand in need of a Friend & be at a loss to gett again in to Good Employ. As he is a very Worthy Honest Man of much Meritt & Equally as well known to your self as to me doubt not of your good Offices to him, & Shall be very willing to be part Concern'd in any undertaking or Adventure you may be Inclinable to be Concern'd with Capt. Wilson in, & wish he was fix'd in a Good Ship in this Trade, which doubt not might be agreeable to him, & hope wou'd turn out to Our mutual Advantage. If a Cliver small Ship or Snow can be purchas'd at his arrival Reasonable to come out here with Our Goods & a Licence for Portugal, it is Likely he may be Willing to Embrace the Opportunity, & am of Opinion we shall be very happy in a Good Commander, & wou'd be very proper to Touch at Madeira for Some Wines (which are Likely to be very Scarce here) in Case You may have no Advice to the Contrary. There is no Madeira Wine now in Town to be Sold, & beleive very Little be here this Season.

I am afraid I shall not have the wish'd for happiness of seeing You in England this Summer. The *Rose* Man of Warr goes in a Month for England & will be the only King's Ship that Goes Home this Season, & no Likelyhood of any other Good Opportunity. Mr. John Watsone, Senior Goes Home passenger in the *Rose* & is the only Passenger that Capt. Frankland will carry with him. He has Refus'd a passage to Severalls which is not Handsome in him. Mr. Watsone has gott in to Capt. Frankland's Good Graces thro' the means of his Cousin Mr. Rind,[8] who is his Doctor, & he & George Austin has been Agents for his Rich Prize which has been a Great deal of Money in their Way. I understand there is a Missunderstanding between Mr. Watsone & his Correspondant Mr. George Udney. The *Rose* will be a Very Rich Ship as she Carries Home a

[8] Dr. William Rind.

4th April 1745

Very Great Quantity of Gold & Silver to the Value of (its Thought) £100,000 Ster. which will make her a Very Rich Prize if taken, & is said will goe North about.[9] I have not further to Offerr at Present but that I Remain &c.

P. S. It will be a Main Matter to have the Goods Out the first of any in the Fall, & if Possible in all August or September as the Profitt on the Adventure will Cheifly Depend on Dispatch. And to have a Ship or Snow Bought Out Right, may answer better than Chartering &c.

I Desire that all the Goods may be fully Insur'd.

ADDRESSED: "Per Capt. William Willson & Copies per Capt. Ladd"

[812]
TO NICHOLAS RIGBYE
Savannah

Charles Town, 1st April 1745

SIR:
I have not been favour'd with any from you for Some Time. Shall be Glad to be advis'd if it may now Suit you to Discharge your Bond which has been now Due Six Months agoe, also if you have yett Received Mr. Dormers money, both which you'll please to advise me off by the Return of the Bearer Mr. Emery, & hope You'll now Soon make Remittance for Both. There is one John Delagal,[1] Patroon of an open Periaugua of mine that Carries about Seventy barrells Rice. Said Delagal has been Gone up to the southward with said Periaugua for Near three months & have heard nothing from him, so that have Some Reason to think he has Run away with my said Boat, being my Sole Right & property. And in Case he may have Come your way, am to Request the favour You'll please be so Good

---

[9] HMS *Rose*, Thomas Frankland, sailed 1 June 1745. May, p. 164; SCG, 1 June 1745.
[1] Philip Delegal of St. Peters Port in the island of Guernsey mentions in his will (written 22 January 1762) a son John of South Carolina, mariner. He also mentioned three other sons who were all planters in Georgia. SCHM, XI (1910), 129–30.

9th April 1745

as to Secure him & my boat & acquaint me thereof, & in Case he should offer to put my boat to Sale or want to dispose of her, Youll please to put a Stop to it & prevent it, the Boat being Solely & intirely mine & he has no manner of Claim Right or property in her. I hope you'll please to excuse this Trouble, & hoping to hear from you Soon I Remain &c.

P. S. The Boat is Nam'd the *Sea Nymph* & has Two Masts being a Small Schooner.

ADDRESSED: "Per Mr. Emery"

TO PETER WESTERMAN
Barbados

Charles Town, 9th April 1745

SIR:
I did my self the Pleasure to write you of the 24th January last, & Since have Your Favours of the 18th Ditto & observe by yours that Mr. Thomas Lake & you are parted, & Doe assure you what service I may be Capable to Rendering you upon all occasions you may Depend on & with the Utmost Pleasure.

The workt India Silk Coverlid belonging to me that you are so Good as to make mention of, You'll please be so kind as to dispose of for whatever it will fetch. It was Charged at Twenty five Pounds or Thirty Pounds this Currency the same as I sold the Rest for. However please to sell it for the Most you Can & Remitt me the Neat Proceeds in Good Coffee, If Reasonable with you or Clay'd Sugar. I intimate to Messrs. Lamboll & Allen What you are pleas'd to Mention about the Ballance you Received for them from Mr. Daniel Moore, & Remitted to them per Capt. Lightwood which they are well Satisfied with, and advis'd you thereof (they Tell me) per three Diffrent Conveyances Which however it Seems has not Come to your hands, & they Tell me they intend to Write you again in Relation to Same per this Conveyance of Capt. Davison.

Rice & Naval Stores are Very Low here, there being no Shipping at Present, and Sugars are in Great Plenty, there being a French Prize Load-

9th April 1745

ed with Sugars Lately brought in by his Majestys Ship *Aldburough*.[2] Shall be always Very Glad to Render you any agreeable Service, & I am Most Respectfully &c.

Rice 10/ per Ct., Pitch 35/ per bbl., Tar 25/ per bbl., Rum 17/6 per Gallon.

ADDRESSED: "Per Capt. Davison"

[813]
TO GEDNEY CLARKE
    Barbados

Charles Town, 10th April 1745

SIR:

The above of the 19th January is Copie of my last and Since have your Most Esteem'd Favours of same Date. It has Given me not a Little Concern that Capt. Donavan Could not be Dispatch'd here so Expeditiously as you Limited, but as I advis'd you in my former, Doe assure you that Same was then impracticable. I take Due Notice of your Taking Mr. Edward Winslow into Partner Ship in all your Business from North America & to whom please present my hearty Compliments, & most heartily wish you all Success & Felicity, & you may assuredly Depend on what Business any of my Friends or I may have your Way, which shall be always addres'd to your house only.

Please Receive Inclosed Account Sales of Rum & Sugar per your Sloop *Merrimack*, Neat Proceeds being £1,767.19.3. You have also Inclosed your Account Current, Ballance in your Favour being £439.1.10 this Currency, which hope you will find Right. I presented Your Compliments to Capt. Frankland as you Injoin'd me. He is preparing to Goe for England in three or Four Weeks and has been here ever since he took the Rich Prize in December Last. Rice & Naval Stores are Very Low, there

[2] HMS *Aldborough*, Ashby Utting, captured 15 January a French schooner *Les Deux Amis*, Master Laffitte, with 270 hogsheads of brown and white sugars. SCG, 1 April 1745.

being No Shipping here at Present, & the Place is full of Sugars from a french prize taken & brought in by his Majesty's Ship *Aldburough*, Capt. Ashby Utting, in his Pasage from England to this Station. As under please Receive the Prices of Goods. Shall be always Very Glad to Receive your Commands, as being with Very Great Respect, &c.

P. S. Rum 17/6 per Gall., Muscovado Sugar Low & in no Demand, Rice 10/ per hundredweight, Pitch 35/ per bbl., Tar 25/ per bbl., Turpintine 12/6 per hundredweight, Exchange to London £700 per £100 Ster., Corn 10/ & Scarce, Pork £10 to £12 per bbl.

ADDRESSED: "Per Capt. John Davison"

TO SETH PILKINGTON
   Bath Town, North Carolina

Charles Town, 10th April 1745

SIR:

The Preceeding of the 23d November is Copie of my Last to which please be Reffer'd, Since am not favour'd with any from you, neither have I as Yett heard from Mr. James Blount of Edentown. Shall be Glad to have the Pleasure of a Line from You in Return, that My Letters have Come to Your hands. I add not at present but that I am Respectfully &c.

Rice & Naval Stores very Low at present.

ADDRESSED: "Per George Nicholas"

13th April 1745

[814]
TO EDWARD PARE
Barbados

Charles Town, 13th April 1745

SIR:

The preceeding on the other Side of the 14th Ulto. is Copie of the Last I did myself the Pleasure to write you & this per your Brigantine *Charming Sarah*, Capt. John Davison, being now Completely Loaded and Clear'd & Ready to Sail, & Inclosed Please Receive Bill of Loading & Invoice of Sundries shipt on Board Your said Brigantine on Your proper Risque & Account & to Your Good Self Consign'd, Amount as per Invoice being £1,359.0.6 which wish safe to hand, & hope will be to Content, everything being Very Good in Quality and as Near to Your orders as was practicable, & Some of the things mention'd in your order that have not been shipt are not to be procur'd here at any rate, particularly the Cedar as I advis'd you in my former Cannot be had in the Province. As for the Bricks per Capt. Davison did not think them Good enough, So that he has Taken No More than 3,500. The Bricks that are Made here being but Very ordinary. The Salt I bought & provided according to your Directions Before Capt. Davison arrived, as there happened an oppertunity of Getting it Cheap, there being None to be Sold at first hand, neither under 15/ per Bushell. But as you desired in your Last to have it omitted, have Sent very Little More than one half of what you order'd being 120 Bushels and have kept the Rest to my Self, tho' it is a thing out of my way.

Youll please observe I have shipt 60 barrells of very Good Rice (by Capt. Davison's advice) in the Room of the Corn & pease which are Very Scarce & Dear, & Capt. Davison assures me it will be most Agreeable to You as the Rice Comes Very Low in Price & is Very Good in Quality. There is Now No Good Beef here fitt to Ship, so did think it proper to Send you any. Your Gun Powder happens Not to be Good & would not answer here at the price Charg'd in your Invoice, so thought it Most proper to Return it to you again, & if it was to Lye on hand any time, it would Spoil, as we have a Very Bad Magazine.

If you should at any Time happen to Send any Negroes here for Sale, I am to take Notice to You that all Plantation Negroes are Lyable to a Duty of Fifty pounds this Currency per head, unless a Certificate is Sent with them to make it appear that they have been Lately Imported from Africa,

13th April 1745

& have not been Six Months in any of our Plantations. In Such Case they pay only a Duty of Ten Pounds Currency per head.

Please also Receive Inclosed Account Sales of your Two Negroes & Lime juice, Neat Proceeds being £388.3.3 this Currency. The Negroes I was obliged to Send to the Island of Providence, otherwise must have paid a Duty here of £100 per head. It is with Concern that I have to acquaint you that Your Sugar proves a Meer Drugg here, & when it Can be dispos'd of at any Rate is very uncertain, having only as yett been able to dispose of three or four Barrells of itt, & now the Town is full by a French Prize, Lately brought in here by his Majesty's Ship *Aldbrough*. I propos'd to Capt. Davison if he thought it would be agreeable to You to put up all Your Sugars at publick Vendue that he Might leave No Effects behind him, but as they would Sell to Great Disadvantage & but for a Triffle, he told me that You will better approve of my keeping them to Dispose of to Your best advantage.

Not Doubting of Your Remitting me Speedily for the Cargoe now advanc'd & Shipt per your Brigantine which am well Satisfy'd You will very Readily Reimburse me for. I have paid Capt. Davison Your Two orders on me for £24.14.2 & £10 Barbadoes Currency, & Inclosed Please to Receive Account of the whole Disbursements I have paid on your Said Brigantine here, Amount being £828.5.10 Currency for which you have Inclosed Capt. Davisons Receipts & altho You'll observe it Comes to a pritty Deal of Money, doe assure You every [815] Thing has been Managed with the best oecunumy & Capt. Davison Carries all the Tradesmens Bills with Him & their Receipts on them as you order & tells we have done Nothing More to the vessell than you directed & was Necessary.

Inclosed please also Receive Your account Current, Ballance in my favour being £1,533.7.2 this Currency which am at Present in advance for, & When Your Sugars are Sold & in Cash You may be Sencible will fall much Short of said Sum Which doubt not of your Reimbursing me with Honour. Rum is pritty Scarce at present & is at 20/ per Gall. If it comes low with You this Crop, doubt not it will answer very well, & if you think proper to send back Capt. Davison with a Quantity of said Commodity, am of opinion you will find your Account in itt & in Case You may order your Brigantine otherways, you may Please to Remitt the Ballance of Account in Good Rum on my own Account & Risque, giving me proper advice for Insurance, which in Such Case am to pray the favour you'll not omitt to Give me due Notice thereof in order that I may Insure Accordingly. Please to Send me a Certificate of the Delivery of Your Brigantine's

Cargoe as soon as it may Suit your Conveniency in order to Clear the Bond at the Custom house. The wind being now fair, hope Capt. Davison will soon be with you, So that I add not, but That I most Respectfully Remain &c.

Exchange to London £700 per £100 Sterling.

ADDRESSED: "Per Capt. Davison"

TO JAMES BLOUNT
Edentown, North Carolina

Charles Town, 15th April 1745

The Preceeding on the other Side of the 23 November is Copie of my Last & Since have not heard anything from You at which am Much Surpriz'd, which does not answer the Good opinion I had of You, & will oblige me to take Such Measures as may Neither be agreeable to You nor to me to procure Payment of Your Bond, now So Long Due. This will be Deliver'd you by Enoch Hall,[3] Esqr. who comes Chief Justice of Your province, & am again to Desire you may acquaint me when I may Certainly Depend on payment of your said Bond, & if you have Made any Remittances to any of the Places that I mention'd in My Last, & I must insist on Your Speedy & full Answer to this, which will Determine me on taking proper Measures for the Recovery of my Money which You doe not Seem to take Care to pay as I expected, which however hope You will Discharge very Soon, & in expectation of your Speedy Answer & to my Satisfaction, I Remain, &c.

ADDRESSED: "Per Enoch Hall, Esqr."

---

[3] Hall was evidently more than an acquaintance of RP's for he sent the North Carolina judge one dozen bottles of claret and later some oranges. *SCHM*, XXVI (1925), 24, 27.

24th April 1745

[816]
TO JAMES HENDERSON
Kingston, Jamaica

Charles Town, 24th April 1745

SIR:
The above of the 23d February is Copie of my Last, & So Which please be Reffer'd, & about a Week agoe Came to hand per Capt. Rains Your Favours of the 19th March advising of your safe arrival after So Long a Passage on which I heartily Congratulate You. I observe You have been so Good as to enquire into Capt. Wimbles affairs, but am afraid there will be nothing obtain'd, however hope Your Good offices Wont be Wanting in Case any part of the Debt Can be Recover'd. I Likewise take Notice That you have sold the 100 sides of Tann'd Leather per Rains at 2/ per lb. which is a Good price. Hope the other Leather Shipt you per Marshall is also arrived, & am to acquaint you that Sugars are Very Low here on account of a French Prize Lately brought in here, & if the Prize Goods Mention'd in my Last as above are Still plenty & Cheap with you, am to desire you may Shipt the Neat Proceeds of the Leather, in said Articles, if not in Sugar.

I Duely Remark that you are willing to be Concern'd one third, or one half in a Cargoe Consisting in the Articles according to the List sent me Inclosed & when an oppertunity of Freight Can be Gott Reasonable your Way, you may expect a Vessell with Same accordingly.

Our Beef & Pork is now all exported & Cannott be procur'd till next fall Neither potatoes. Please be particular as to the Potatoes, if you mean in Yours the price to be 20/ per Bushell as they are always sold by the Bushell & in your List you put Down potatoes 1 M. Please Explain if you mean One Mille or 1,000 Bushels of Potatoes in the Cargoe. As for Deer Skins we have None Dress'd here fitt for Gloves or Seats for Saddles, being only what we Call Indian Dress'd. Shall send You one or Two for a Sample for a Tryall. Several Vessells have Gone from this Lately for your Island, with Beef, Pork, & Rice, which last is Very low at Present.

We have Very few Shipping here at Present. If a Good Sloop or Schooner, Can be Hir'd on easie Terms with you to Come here by Next October You may expect her Loaded back with the Articles you Mention, but desire you'll send nothing in her but Sugar & dry Goods, if Low with you & a Little Coffee. Shall be always Very Ready to Cultivate & Continue

24th April 1745

a Constant Correspondence, which doubt not will be to our Mutual advantage. I Remain Most Respectfully &c.

ADDRESSED: "Per Capt. Mackey & Copie per Capt. Diamond"

TO WILLIAM MACKAY
   Cape Fear, North Carolina

Charles Town, 24th April 1745

SIR:

I have both your Esteem'd Favours, of the 13th February And 31st March & am to Return you my hearty thanks for Your Good offices in Coultons affair & am Much Concern'd, to have given you so Much Trouble therein. Said Person is Come here again, & is in Jail at the Suit of Severalls here, the affair of our Attachments not being Yett Determin'd, We Cannot Yett know wether we shall Recover any thing of him or Nott. It Was very odd in Your Sheriff to lett him have his Liberty by which Mr. Graeme says he has Taken the debt upon himself, for Suffering him to Escape, & ought to be Lyable for Same & all the Charges, attending itt. In such a Case here our Marshall would Certainly be obliged to pay the Debt. The Sherrif does not Satisfie at Least the Charge yet have been at, as he ought the whole Debt. You'll please to Send me Account of Same which shall be punctually paid to your order. Youll please also to Send me back by a Sure hand Coultons Note, & in Case there may be any Likelyhood of Recovering the Debt or any Part thereof, which however appears Very uncertain. I am Sorry to Hear of your Indisposition, hope this shall find you Restor'd to perfect health. Please to present my Best Respect to Mrs. Mackay & Mr. Thompson & I am &c.

ADDRESSED: "Per Cape Fear Sloop"

29th April 1745

TO ENOCH HALL
Charles Town

Charles Town, 24th April 1745

SIR:

I have Taken the Liberty to Trouble you with the Inclosed Letter for Mr. James Blount in Edentown, in North Carolina, which am to pray the favour You'll please be so Good as to have Deliver'd to him. Said Blount is Indebted to Me by Bond, Eighty four Pounds Sterling which with the Interest due thereon makes it Amount to £100 Ster., & have Not Yett Received any part thereof, or heard From him for a Considerable Time past. I am therefore to Request You'll be so kind, as to make Mention of it to him, & to desire to know of him, when I may Certainly Depend on payment, thereof, & favour me with a Line, in Relation to Same. I hope Your Goodness will pardon the freedom I take in Troubling You in This Manner. Shall be always Very Ready to Receive Your Commands, & to Serve You in the Like or any other Occasion. I most heartily Wish you health & Felicity, & I am Most Respectfully &c.

ADDRESSED: "Deliver'd him in Charlestown"

TO JOHN ERVING
Boston

Charles Town, 29th April 1745

SIR:

The above of the 16th March is Copie of my Last which went Via Rhoad Island, & Since have not the Pleasure of any of Your Favours. We are inform'd there is an Embargo Laid on all your Shipping by Reason of your Expedition against Cape Bretoon, & which has prevented any advices from your parts (pray God Grant Success). There are Still Very few Shipping here, freight the Same as in My Last, Rice at 12/6 per hundredweight, Naval Stores also Low, & in No Demand at present. This Goes by Mr. Jeremiah Osborne, who should have been the Bearer of my last. My Wife joyns in Best to Self, Mrs. Erving, & all your pritty

29th April 1745

Familly. I have not further to offer at Present, as Being without any of Your Favours, but That I most Respectfully Remain &c.

No New England Rum here.
Linnens of all sorts very Scarce & dear.

ADDRESSED: "Per Mr. Jeremiah Osborne"

[818] Messrs. Verissime & Clarisseau, Merchants in Madeira.
Alexander Strachan, Merchant in Kingston, Jamaica.
Colonel Alexander McKensey at Hampton in Virginia, Correspondant with Richard Bennett in Maryland.
Colonel Henry Scarburgh in Accomack, Virginia, Correspondant with Richard Bennett in Maryland.
Don Gasper Ruiz, Lieutenant of His Catholic Majesty's Ship of War the *Princise*, Capt. Coronell, Commander of 70 Guns, at the Havanna.
Mr. John Livingston, Merchant in New York.
Mr. Jacob Franks, Merchant in New York.
Andrew Pringle's Correspondants at Sundry places May 1744.
Mr. James Henderson at Jamaica.
Mr. Isaac Duport at St. Kitts.
Mr. John Blane at Antigua.

[819] Capt. Alexander Heron in Generall Oglethorpe's Regiment of Foot in Georgia.
Alexander Stewart, Ensign in Generall Oglethorpe's Regiment.
Clemens Chapman, formerly a Commander from London to St. Kitts now Settled at Raneymund in Virginia.
William Pitt, Merchant in Black River near Cape Comorin on the Musketto Shoar.

A List of Correspondents

Mr. Colquhon, Merchant in St. Kitts, Correspondant of Andrew Lessly.
Messrs. Cuningham, Merchants in St. Kitts.
Bruning Osborn, Attorney in Nevis.
Alexander Andrew, Merchant in Rotterdam.
John Dunn, junior, Merchant in Antigua.
Ralph Payne, the King's Attorney Generall in St. Kitts.
Capt. William Lithgow at New Brunswick, Cape Fear.
Capt. Edward Friend in Williamsburg, Virginia to the Care of William Parks, Printer in Williamsburg, Virginia.
Mr. Alexander Grant, Merchant in Newport, Rhode Island.
Mr. Gidney Clark, Merchant in Barbadoes.
Mr. John Esdale, Merchant in St. Kitts.
Richard Bennett, Esqr. on the River Wye in Maryland in Queen Anne's County.
Mr. Tench Francis, Attorney at Law in Philadelphia, is Richard Bennett in Maryland his Correspondant there.
Richard Howell at Howell's Point on Sasafras River in the Province of Maryland.
Edward Lloyd in Maryland Suppos'd will be Executor to Richard Bennett, Esqr. on Wye River there.
Brother A. P. in his Letter of the 26 June 1743 advises to Consign Rice to Mr. James Archibold, Merchant in Oporto, being a better Markett for it then at Lisbon.
Dr. John Hobb's at Mr. John Cargill's Surgeons, Instrument Maker in Lumbard Street, London.

[820] Capt. George Collcott in Lee's Court St. Catharines near the Tower, London.
Capt. William Mitchell & Capt. Stephen Haven from Bellfast.
Mrs. Elizabeth Edgley in Ayliffe Street, Goodmans Fields, London.
Hugh Pringle, Merchant in Belfast.
James Trotter & John Ross in Edenton, North Carolina.
David Coltrane & John Cowan, Storekeepers in Edenton Ditto.
Mr. Joseph Huggins, Merchant near the Hermitage Stairs, Wapping London to Address for Capt. Jacob Ayers.

A List of Correspondents

The Reverend Mr. John McAlaster, Minister in Pond Pond.
James Humphrey at Mr. James Slater's, Gold Smith at the Crown in Foster Lane, London.
Mr. James Henderson, Merchant in New York, is my Brothers Correspondant & Attorney there.
Mr. Stephen Byard in New York, Merchant.
Charlestown, So. Carolina April 19th, 1739 This day Capt. Robert Screech, Commander of the Brigantine *Rochelle*, Sail'd over the Barr Bound for Bristol & Consign'd to Mr. Freeman Partridge, Merchant there.
Mr. William Stead, Merchant in London.
Messrs. Stewart & Ferguson, Merchants in London.
Mr. Seth Pilkington, Merchant at Pamplico near Bath Town, No. Carolina.
John Gressier, Merchant in Rotterdam.
Andrew Reid, Esqr. at Old Tom's Coffee house in Burchin Lane, London.
Archbald Ramsay, Surgeon of His Majesties Ship *Squirrell*, Capt. Peter Warren, Commander at Boston.

INDEX

INDEX

Names of vessels and captains mentioned in the text, footnotes, and Address Notes are indexed. After the name of each vessel the type of vessel and the name of the captain, when known, have been added as information. The material in the Address Notes has been indexed, but that in the front matter has not. Charleston, London, and South Carolina are not indexed as they are referred to on almost every page. After street names, the city in which it is located has been included in parentheses as, Tradd St. (Charleston). Merchants' places of residence have been added following the names of the more prominent ones (except for Charleston merchants). Wives are indexed under husbands' names with maiden names given in parentheses, as Pringle, Jane (Allen).

Abaco Keys, Bahamas, 818n
Abany (Clarke), 596
Abatement, 78, 85, 467, 596, 711
Abercrombie, Capt., 484–486, 489, 492, 630, 688
Abercromby (Abercrombie), Alexander, 778, 778n (biog.), 779
Abercromby, James, 379, 379n (biog.), 380, 382, 387, 587, 690, 701, 709, 778n, 804, 805, 808
Abigail, a sloop (Batchelder), 717, 719–721, 731, 732, 753
Academy, in Eng., 634
Accomack, Va., 610, 846
Accoumpting house, 280
Accusors, 353
Ackworth, a ship (Jones), 584
Acts of Parliament, 438, 675, 776. *See also* individual acts
Addis, Capt., 793
Administrators, 105, 177, 521n, 663n
Admiralty, the, 608, 613
Affidavit, 352, 415, 792

Africa, 156n, 181n, 684, 686, 763, 840.
  See also Angola; Calabar; Guinea
Agent, for Ga., 805n; for Ga. Trustees, 26n, 729; for Grenada, St. Vincent, & Tobago, 342n; for Mass., 32n; for privateers, 455, 456, 467; for prize ship, 675; for R. I., 463n; for S. C., 309n, 478, 577, 588, 776; for S. C., assistant to, 776; for S. C. merchants, 350n, 498n, 700. *See also* Correspondents; Factors; Managers
Agars, Edmund, 657, 658, 671
Aithen, Henry, 680, 693–696, 698, 702–705, 718
Albany (White), 65
Albertson, Gilbert, 791
Alborough, HMS (Utting), 831, 833, 838, 839, 841
Ale, 181, 257, 262, 299, 338; Windsor, 305
Alepine, 63, 423, 706, 824; price of, 249
Algarve, kingdom of, 747

851

Index

Allen, Andrew, 23n, 26n, 418, 470n, 474, 497, 550, 563
Allen, Capt., 288, 585, 665
Allen, James, 569
Allen, William, 26, 26n (biog.), 147, 178, 418, 474, 497, 563, 837
Alloway, Nathaniel, 379, 382, 387
Almanac, for 1743, 234n
Ambergris, 261, 386, 467, 576
Ambuscade, 430. *See also* Battle of Bloody Marsh
America, 219, 243, 615, 639n, 774. *See also* North America
America, a ship (Gerald), 85n
American Philosophical Society, first president of, 108n
Americans, 478n
America stations, 135, 177, 181, 183, 185–187, 190, 193, 194, 197, 200, 230, 380; commodore of, 177n. *See also* Bahama station; Cape Fear station; Carolina station; King's ships; Port Royal station
Ammunition, 196, 759. *See also* Bullets; Shot
Amoretta (Crode), 259n
Amsterdam, Holland, 104, 236, 241, 382
Amyand, Claudius, 64
Amyand, Isaac, 64, 64n (biog.)
An act for the encouragement of the trade to America, 473n, 492
An act . . . governing Negroes and other slaves, 352; punishment under, 351, 354, 357
An act . . . granting . . . taxes . . . on Negroes imported, 174, 175, 182, 186, 190, 211, 241–242, 259–260, 263, 448, 542, 683–685, 715, 724, 763, 775
An act for regulating the buildings . . . to be erected . . . in Charles Town. . . . , 282
An act for the relief of poor debtors, 92, 792
An act to prevent frauds and deceipts in selling rice, pitch, tar, rosin, turpentine, beef, pork, shingles and firewood, 70, 270; penalty under, 40
Ancell, Stephen, 270, 271
Anchona (Marvin), 302n
Anchor, 545, 546, 619, 620; bower, 530, 578

Anchovies, 605
Anderson, Alexander, 599
Anderson, Andrew, 262
Anderson, Capt., 450, 513, 625, 627
Anderson, John, 260, 264, 265
Anderson, Mark, 636, 639–643, 654, 728, 746, 748, 761, 771, 772, 828, 832
Anderson, Robert, 403, 404
Andover, Lord. *See* Bowes, William Howard
Andrew, Alexander, children of, 359, 528
Andrew (Andrews), Alexander, of Rotterdam, 358, 358n (biog.), 377, 408, 439, 440, 527, 530, 847
Andrew and Betty, a ship (Patton), 323, 358, 501, 528
Andrew, Mrs. Alexander, 359, 528
Andrew, Peter (Patrick), 358, 377, 408, 527
Angola, Africa, 51, 121, 282, 284
Anguilla, W. I., 191
Ann Galley, a sloop (Barnard, Falla, Trenchard), 713–715, 722, 723, 730, 735–737, 741, 742, 773, 775, 777, 778, 789, 792, 794, 797–801, 807, 809, 812
Anstruther, Scotland, 222
Antigua, W. I., 11, 13, 14, 31, 36, 38, 43–46, 69–72, 91, 119, 122, 123, 125, 127, 129–131, 133, 134, 136, 179, 180, 182, 183, 189–191, 211, 224, 229, 231, 232, 237, 238, 244, 251, 252, 266, 267, 281, 283, 284, 289, 315, 318, 360, 410, 447, 451, 497, 498, 503, 515, 517, 518, 520, 556, 569, 578, 589–591, 609, 624, 633, 644, 662, 701, 705, 719n, 723, 724n, 725, 752, 756–758, 764, 765, 770, 773–775, 784–786, 793, 802, 830
Apoplexy, 62
Apothecary, 289, 543, 688
Apothecary shop, 543
Apples, 275, 318, 503, 564n, 652, 754
Appraisement, of vessels, 414, 697, 703, 753
Appraisers, of vessels, 386, 753
Apprentice, 387n, 404
Apprenticeship, 404
Apthorp, Charles, of Boston, 666, 666n (biog.), 679, 817, 827
Archard, Mr., 148

Index

Archbold (Archibold), James, of Oporto, 622, 622n (biog.), 769, 771, 847
Archer, John, 487, 501, 510, 511, 520, 559, 585, 586, 688, 747–749
Arent, a ship (Heysham), 329n
Argile, a ship, 6
Argyle, a ship (Stedman), 653
Armstrong, John, 129, 133, 134, 136, 191
Army, British, 11n, 809. *See also* Troops, British
Arrack, 39, 155, 440
Arras, gold, 63
Arroba, 509
Ashley River, S. C., 117, 121n, 140, 388n, 416, 818
Assembly, of Antigua, member of, 591n
Assembly, of Bahamas, speaker of, 297n, 333n
Assembly, of S. C., 174, 175, 190, 265n, 272, 276, 282, 379, 550, 577, 699, 776; clerk of, 64n; members of 131n, 350n, 379n, 579n, 588, 700; speaker of, 175n, 227
Assignees, 584
Assistance, a snow (I'On), 740, 761, 772, 790, 796, 821, 828–830
Assistant judges, 379n, 418n
Atkin, Edmund, 488, 488n (biog.)
Atkinson, Peter, 215–220, 311, 350, 398, 420, 423, 424, 442, 524, 654, 655, 657, 658, 671, 687
Atkinson St. (Boston), 489n
Atlantic Ocean, 488
Atlee, John, 73
"A True and Historical Narrative of the Colony of Georgia in America," 171n
Attorney. *See* Lawyer
Attorney-general of St. Kitts, 847
Attorney-general of S. C., 80, 379, 382, 587, 590, 632, 705, 778, 805n, 808; fees of, 688; perquisites of, 688
Audibert, Moses, 113–115, 146, 146n (biog.)
Auditor, 542
Aughram, Ireland, 296n
Austin Friars (London), 431n
Austin, George, 187, 187n (biog.), 533, 660, 804, 835
Austin, Robert, 379, 379n (biog.)
Axes, 22, 66, 82, 84, 391, 429, 507, 508, 539, 567, 645, 704
Ayers, Jacob, 4, 8, 12, 13, 28, 58–62, 64, 67, 89, 90, 93, 98, 99, 162, 164, 166, 167, 186, 207, 208, 211, 221, 225, 228, 229, 233, 256, 257, 262, 292, 298, 299, 332, 334, 335, 351, 356, 358, 409, 413, 467, 541, 542, 552, 553, 561, 562, 571, 615, 687, 688, 707, 715, 723, 847
Ayers, John, 410
Ayers, Mrs. Jacob, of London, 90, 99, 187, 208, 229, 410
Ayliffe St. (Goodman's Fields, London), 88n, 375n, 847

Babb, John, 833
Baber, Capt., 797, 805, 809
Baccle, Eng., 585
Back country, 299
Bag (cloth), 31, 82; middling, 783
Bags (containers), 252, 338, 797
Bahamas, 280n, 293n, 298, 333n, 455, 735, 818. *See also* New Providence
Bahama station, 143, 568, 663
Bail, 351–355, 357, 708; special, 581; forfeiture of, 798
Baird, Peter, 359, 360
Baird, Thomas, 461
Baize (Bays), Colchester, 398, 421, 524
Baker, John, 51
Baker, Mr., 54
Baker, Samuel, 809
Baker, William, 89n
Baker, William, of London, 639, 639n (biog.), 641, 643, 663, 748, 772, 790, 809
Balchin, Sir John, 173, 175
Bales, of cloth, 259, 338
Balieul (Baileaul, Bailleul, Baillou), Peter, of Guernsey, 69, 69n (biog.), 70, 270, 521, 522, 526, 527, 530, 532, 652, 714
Ballast, 94, 195, 236, 586, 604, 608, 662, 732; bricks, 32, 283, 399, 400, 616; coals, 32, 288; gravel, 224; salt, 32, 215, 399, 400, 440; shingle, 223; slate, 399; stone, 176, 224, 616; tiles, 400
Ball, Papillon, of London, 153, 153n (biog.), 401, 402, 409
Baltic Merchant, 173
Bangs, Benjamin, 745, 748–755, 781, 795, 811–813, 819
Banker, 467
Bankrupt, 808

Index

Bankruptcies, 316
Bankson, Andrew, 255, 255n (biog.), 565
Bankson, Peter, 255n
Bant, William, of Boston, 23, 199, 206, 316, 389
Barbados, W. I., 61, 331, 371, 407, 408, 416, 418, 432, 439, 440, 447, 448, 467, 474, 475, 481, 511, 513, 517, 528, 529, 531, 545, 551, 563, 575, 590, 591, 609–610, 624, 627, 638, 662n, 666, 667n, 670, 682, 685, 686, 715, 716, 728, 756, 760, 764, 767, 774, 784, 786, 787, 802, 804, 805, 807, 823, 825, 837, 838, 840
Barber, 146n
Barnes, James, 177, 185–189, 276, 277, 291
Barnard, Mrs., 800
Barnard (Bernard), Mathew, 713, 714, 722, 730, 736, 743, 777, 795, 799, 801
Barnes (Barns), Thomas, 719
Barrels, 605, 618, 675; flour, 511, 738, 754, 810; pitch, 40; price of, 32; rice, 754; small, 744; tar, 40
Barrett, Capt., 483
Barry, Mr., 600
Bartlett, John, 760, 763, 771, 773
Barum, a snow (Daymund), 587n
Barus, Capt., 168
Bassnett, John, 362, 579, 579n (biog.), 599, 600, 623, 755
Bassnett, Mrs. John, 623
Bassnett, Nathaniel, of London, 124, 124n (biog.), 181, 257, 262, 362
Batchelder, Daniel, 702, 703, 705, 717–719, 721, 731, 753
Bathing, 211
Bath Town, N. C., 142, 418, 383, 411, 412, 709, 711, 765, 839, 848
Battle of Bloody Marsh, Ga., 387n, 396, 397, 399, 400, 404, 406, 409, 414, 430
Bay, Charleston, 6, 10, 64, 82, 84, 85, 89, 91, 95, 98, 112, 113, 115, 118, 124, 138, 142, 173, 212, 265, 268, 280, 296, 297, 314, 352, 354, 361, 368, 392, 398, 405, 413, 466, 471, 472, 486, 490, 496, 504, 506, 514, 520, 530, 545, 561, 566, 571, 578, 593, 616, 665, 685, 701, 703, 718, 742, 755, 773, 780–783,

789, 807, 848; St. Augustine, 217, 219, 225
Baynton, Peter, of Philadelphia, 504, 514, 514n (biog.)
Baynton, Mrs. Peter (Paris), 514n
Bay of Honduras. *See* Gulf of Honduras
Bay of Mexico. *See* Gulf of Mexico
Bayonets, 90, 333, 334
Bay, on the (Charleston), 271, 275, 288, 293, 466n, 698n
Bays, Colchester. *See* Baize, Colchester
Bay St. *See* Bay, on the (Charleston)
Bay (tree), 829
Beach, Henry, 229, 379, 401, 402, 405, 407–410, 413, 467, 477, 479, 544. *See also* Vezie, Hugh
Beale, Capt., 162
Beale, Othniel, 279, 279n (biog.), 360, 388, 519, 688, 708
Beans, 237, 252
Beauchamp, Mr., 39
Beaufort, S. C., 296n, 512n. *See also* Port Royal, S. C.
Beaufort Town, N. C., 380, 412, 556, 557, 710
Bedford, Eng., 262n
Bedon, Mr., 54
Beds, field, 660
Bed tickings, 170, 258
Beef, 11, 282, 346, 348, 724, 767, 840, 843; price of, 192, 320, 321, 460, 500, 509, 625, 626, 757, 758, 765, 766, 787, 788; smoked, 744
Beek (Beake), Capt., 756–758, 821
Beer, 26, 161, 276, 596, 820; Matlock's Best, 737; ship, 254; price of, 675; price of, in London, 832
Bell, Boaz, 369, 416, 417, 474–477, 481, 513, 563, 756, 805
Bellgarde (Bellegarde), Capt., 613, 623
Bellinger, Edmund, 822n
Bells, of St. Michael's, 203n; ship's, 800
Belt, 5
Bennett, John, 193, 374
Bennett, Richard, I, of Maryland, 385n
Bennett, Richard III, of Maryland, 385, 385n (biog.), 393, 413, 414, 609, 610, 653, 778, 846, 847
Berkeley County, S. C., 19n, 255n, 826n
Bermuda, 333n, 614, 662n, 756, 758, 805
Bermudian sloop, 813

Index

Berry, Mr., 623
Bertie Countie, N. C., 328
Best, Capt., 202–204
Beswicke, Anne (Wigg), 494
Beswicke, John, 500, 708
Beswicke, Mary (Hill), 708
Beswicke, Thomas, 494, 494n (biog.), 500, 708
Bethel (Presbyterian) Church (Pon Pon), 134n
Bethesda Orphan Home (Savannah), 629n
Betsey, 407n
Betties, 605
Betty, a schooner (Everton), 5n
Betty, a ship (Ragles), 237n
Betty, a sloop (Chadwick), 812, 814, 818
Betty, a snow (Jenny), 374n
Bills of exchange, 15, 27, 34, 44, 45, 57, 58, 63, 64, 66, 78, 79, 81, 84, 86, 89, 90, 107, 111, 112, 115, 118–120, 124, 127, 130, 141, 147, 155, 156, 174, 182, 183, 185, 187, 189, 192, 204, 205, 218, 223, 225, 229, 232, 233, 237, 238, 257, 263, 266, 268–270, 272, 275, 276, 281, 286, 287, 290, 292, 293, 295, 299–303, 308–310, 312, 314, 316, 323, 325, 330–332, 337, 338, 350, 352–357, 366, 372, 375–377, 380, 382–384, 389, 395, 396, 400, 404, 408, 409, 412, 413, 418, 422, 431, 435, 438, 439, 444, 454–456, 459, 467, 473, 482, 483, 487, 491–494, 496, 497, 499, 501, 506, 507, 510, 515, 520, 523, 526, 533, 538, 541, 544, 545, 547, 549, 554, 557, 558–561, 565, 585, 586n, 591, 598, 600, 614, 629, 634, 639–643, 647, 649, 652, 655, 657, 661, 671–674, 678, 680, 682, 685, 686, 687, 689, 691, 696, 698, 699, 703, 714, 718, 722, 731, 737, 740, 742, 743, 750, 752, 760, 761, 765, 767, 770, 771, 783, 784, 786, 793, 795, 796–799, 812, 813, 822, 824, 825, 827, 828, 829, 833; protested, 28, 194, 313, 342, 480, 495, 543, 758, 759; with protest, 615, 620, 665, 679, 689, 763, 768. *See also* Drafts; Letters of advice; Rate of Exchange; Sola bills
Bills, tailor's, 58, 824; tradesmen's, 469, 795, 841
Binford & Osmond, 689n

Binford, Thomas, of Exeter, 689, 689n (biog.), 708
Bird cages, 620, 654, 773, 774, 788; price of, in Eng., 585; trapp, 585; wire, 585
Bird, Capt., 653, 654
Bird, James, 281, 283, 292
Birds, 705; rare & curious, 620. *See also* Bluebirds; Non-pareils; Redbirds
Birot, Peter, 129
Birst, Peter, 483
Birt, Samuel, 618, 619n
Biscuit, milk, price of, 291. *See also* Bread
Bishop, John, 162, 164
Bishopgate St. (London), 43n, 153n
Bishop of London, 169n, 239
Bishop of St. David's, 549n
Bishop of Salisbury, 169, 212, 542
Bishop of Sarum, 169, 212
Blackader, Christopher, 6, 7
Blackburn, Capt., 497
Blacker & Fenwicke, a ship (Kitchingman), 654n
Blackie, Mr., 297
Black River, Mosquito Coast, 833n
Black River, S. C., 579n
Blacksmith, 255
Black, William, 386, 408
Bladwell, William, 589, 594, 595, 597, 603, 608, 609, 663
Blake, Capt., 70
Blake, Joseph, 197
Blanchard, Thomas, 55, 56
Blane, John, of Antigua, 662, 757, 846
Blanketing, duffel, 31, 139, 202, 218, 351, 395, 646; ship, 31
Blankets, bed, 31, 351, 423; duffel, 423, 552 (Bristol-made), 552 (London-made)
Blount (Blunt), James, of Edentown, 142, 142n (biog.), 377, 382, 383, 411, 412, 483, 673, 709, 712, 766, 767, 839, 842, 845
Blubber, 391, 393, 645, 669, 676, 721
Bluebirds, 10
Blunt, James. *See* Blount, James
Blunt, Samuel, 388–393, 403, 405, 432, 434, 644, 645, 647, 664, 668, 669, 720, 721
Blyth, Nathaniel, 657
Board of Trade, 159, 421n, 489n, 666n
Boards, 144, 320, 346, 348, 391, 392,

Index

491, 506–508; definition of, 421. *See also* Wood
Boat, decked, 489, 493, 500, 504; man of war's, 473; pilot, 386, 414
Boatswain, 736
Boddicott (Boddicot), Richard, 92, 770, 784, 793
Boehm, Charles, of London, 6n (biog.)
Boehm, Charles & Edmund of London, 6, 14, 142, 154, 168, 176, 184, 185, 196, 197, 209, 211, 214, 330, 478, 667
Boehm, Edmund, of London, 6n (biog.)
Boggy Swamp, S. C., 755n
Boiltins, Handrina, 198
Bonaventure, a sloop (Blunt), 645, 647
Bond, 48, 49, 78, 79, 153, 187, 194, 255, 285, 304, 312, 378, 384, 419, 450, 511, 523, 546, 554, 556, 564, 565, 580, 600, 649, 650, 651, 654, 684, 686, 702, 709, 710, 713, 731, 734, 764–767, 836, 845; marriage, 339n; of indemnity, 699, 807; plantation, 12, 35–37, 53, 80, 114, 142, 155, 202, 209, 219, 234, 280, 311, 312, 337, 405, 432, 434, 476, 482, 491, 492, 537, 558, 571, 573, 589, 590, 593, 594, 596, 597, 607, 615, 632, 647, 662, 693, 705, 741, 749, 785, 786, 796, 826, 842; plantation, instructions of governor on, 741, 796. *See also* Note
Bonamy, Capt., 70
Bonomy, Peter, 736, 777, 799, 800
Bookeeper, 613; RP's, 121, 122, 136, 752; salary of, 121
Books, 82n, 212, 262, 468, 469, 577, 601, 619, 658, 724n; bill of loading, 826; custom house, 280, 596, 786; of accounts, 254, 272, 275, 280, 291, 394, 395, 408, 410, 437, 494, 708, 808, 834; popularity of, 262n. *See also individual authors and titles*
Bookseller, 618–619
Boone, Capt., 613, 623
Boscawen, Edward, 193, 193n (biog.)
Boston, Mass., 5, 6, 13, 14, 20, 21, 23, 25, 28, 34, 52, 65–67, 81, 82, 86, 87, 90, 94–96, 99, 102–104, 107, 114, 115, 118, 128, 129, 131, 132, 134, 142, 143, 147, 165, 167, 169, 173, 175, 176, 178, 184, 187, 195, 197–200, 203–206, 208, 211, 212, 220, 223,
226, 233, 239, 241, 243, 250, 254, 255, 260, 263, 270, 272–274, 286, 297, 300, 302, 309, 315–318, 330, 335n, 362–364, 375, 377, 382, 385, 386, 388–390, 392, 403–406, 429, 430n, 433–435, 438–440, 442–444, 446, 458, 462, 464, 465, 467, 468, 470, 484, 485, 493, 502, 503, 505–508, 514, 520, 525, 530, 535, 537–541, 548, 549, 566–569, 575, 580–582, 593, 596, 602, 609, 614, 615, 616n, 617, 634, 635, 637, 643, 644n, 645, 661–666, 668, 669, 674–677, 679, 680, 682, 683, 689, 696–698, 702, 703, 717–720, 722, 726, 731, 733, 745, 749, 750, 752, 763, 778, 781, 786, 789, 793, 795, 811, 812, 814, 817–819, 826, 827, 845, 848
Boston Regiment, 20n. *See also* Troops, New England
Bottles, broken, 637, 646, 753; pint, 486, 508, 605; quart, 604–605; three pints, 605
Botts, 565
Bounty, on pitch, 162n; on rosin, 162n; on tar, 162n; on turpentine, 162n. *See also* Certificate, bounty
Bours, Peter, 643, 665, 680, 780
Boutin, Capt., 693, 702
Bowes, William Howard (1714–1756), Lord Andover, 544, 550
Bowler, Capt., 607
Bowls, china, 424, 592, 780; wooden, 508. *See also* Punch bowls
Bowman, Mr., 477
Box, 509; garden, 512, 565, 653; mahogany, 335
Boyd, Thomas, 127, 179
Boyes, Capt., 436, 441, 442, 446
Bracey, Capt., 166, 229
Bradford, Capt., 562
Bradgate, Christopher, 49, 152
Bradshaw, Mr., 54
Brand, maker's, 40
Brandy, 81, 130, 155, 156, 174, 430, 440, 780, 783, 785, 789; price of, 752, 781, 819
Branscombe, Arthur, 95, 158, 159, 617, 618, 621, 622, 630, 634
Brazil, 247n
Braziletto wood, 30, 32, 86, 95, 240, 246, 270, 314, 336, 349, 364, 388, 460,

Index

544, 603, 605, 609, 688; price of, 32, 175, 186, 217, 242, 294, 317, 421, 602, 606
Brazil-wood, 30n
Bread, 12, 255, 277, 282, 538, 556, 564, 653, 739, 820; brown, 254; midling, 291, 737–738, 744; price of, 125, 291, 320, 323, 452, 508, 766; ship, 125, 291, 320, 323, 329, 452, 508, 511, 515, 744, 766. See also Biscuit
Breakers, 486
Breast plates, brass, 90; gilt, 452, 453; price of, in London, 452, 453
Breden (Breading, Breeding), Andrew, 364, 429–434, 443, 444, 447, 503, 505, 508, 534–536, 642, 655, 660
Breeches, 63, 188, 658, 706, 824
Bremen (Bremin) Factor (Tisehurst), 431, 454, 459, 461, 472, 487, 489, 541, 545, 559, 585, 635, 688
Brest, France, 479
Bricklayer, 169n, 276, 282
Brick maker, 301
Bricks, 22, 282, 399, 400, 491, 506, 507, 654, 655, 661; English, 32, 28, 301; New England, 84, 243–244, 301, 616; price of, 283, 301, 616; S. C., 301, 840
Bridgetown, Barbados, 335n, 346
Brigantine, 6, 304, 326, 454; Spanish, 216, 533n
Bringhurst, John, 108
Brislington, a ship (Whitfield), 73n
Brislington, a ship (Purnell), 660n
Bristol, Eng., 30, 32–34, 103, 173, 194, 253, 259, 263, 273, 299, 323, 329, 418, 422, 454, 456–458, 512, 552, 585, 603, 604, 609, 613, 617, 624, 642, 660, 670, 728, 739, 760, 763, 771, 776, 777, 797, 805, 809, 821, 823, 824
Britania, a ship (Trimble), 295
Britania, a snow (Armstrong), 129, 202
Britanias, 816
Brittania, a ship (Franklin), 86, 113, 114
Broadcloth, 31, 63, 170, 398, 422, 524; superfine, 351, 423, 706, 729, 824
Broad Seal of S. C., 578
Broad St. (Charleston), 92n, 314n, 466n, 714n
Broad St. (London), 350n
Brock, Henry, of Guernsey, 70, 70n (biog.), 522, 526n, 652

Brock, Henry & John, of Guernsey, 713, 722, 735, 741–743, 776, 777, 795, 798
Brock, John, of Guernsey, 70n (biog.), 526, 526n, 652
Brock, Mary, of Guernsey, 70, 70n (biog.), 526
Broker, 169
Bromadge, Capt., 237, 239
Brooks, Edward, 663
Broughton's Battery (Charleston), 714n
Broughton, Thomas, 265n
Brown, Capt., 830, 832
Brown, John, 253, 259n
Brown, Mathew, 541, 543
Brown, Rev., 143
Brown, Robert, 478n, 521, 626, 637, 638
Brozett, James, 342
Bruce, Henry, 332, 333
Bruce, Peter Henry, 293, 293n (biog.), 298
Brune, Capt., 373, 374
Brunet, Henry. See Burnet, Henry
Brunswick. See New Brunswick, N. C.
Buchanan, James, of London, 282, 282n (biog.), 292, 385, 544, 551, 553, 554, 559, 562, 563, 570–573, 575, 828
Buckle, Thomas, 755, 755n (biog.), 756
Buckmaster, Capt., 820
Buckram, 361, 398, 421, 442, 446, 525
Buckskin, a snow (Collcock), 261n
Budge Row (London), 124n
Bullard, Edward, 149, 196, 206, 663n
Bullets, 31, 189, 252, 424, 646. See also Ammunition; Shot
Bullock, Samuel, 147, 177, 177n (biog.), 254, 291, 329, 451, 452, 596
Bull's Bay, S. C., 665n
Bull, William I (1683–1755), 239n, 265, 272, 276, 377, 379, 387–388, 390, 395, 542, 577
Bull, William II (1710–1791), 239n
Buoy, 578
Burchin Lane (London), 848
Burleigh, Benjamin, 450, 463
Burn, Edward. See Mayne, Edward & John & Edward Burn
Burnet, Henry, 412, 412n (biog.), 712
Burrill (Burrell), Thomas, of Hull, 32, 106, 106n (biog.), 115, 118–120, 139, 204, 216, 217, 223, 237, 287, 290, 293, 302, 310, 311, 350, 396–398,

Index

400, 419, 420, 423, 450, 482, 523, 589, 593, 595, 607, 615
Burrill, Mrs. Thomas, 218
Burroughs, Edward, 784
Burryau (Bourryau) & Schaffer, of London, 431, 441, 468, 470, 484, 489, 506, 533, 539, 545, 547, 549, 567, 617, 647, 720, 763, 789, 792, 812
Burryau & Spooner, of London, 431n
Burryau, John, 431n
Burryau, Zachary, of London, 431n (biog.), 618
Butter, 253, 277, 371, 600; Irish, 667, 670, 685, 775; price of, 667
Buttons, gold, 63; hair, 706; horsehair, 63; mohair, 706; neat, 63
Butts, water, 800
Byard, Stephen, 848

Cabbot, George, 365
Cabbott, Capt., 168, 170
Cabinet maker, 755n
Cabin. *See* Stateroom
Cables, 31, 578
Cabot, Capt., 502
Caesar, a snow (Keith), 551–554, 559, 562, 563, 570, 571, 573, 574
Calabar, Africa, 259, 262
Calico, 31, 56
Callendar, Mr., 370
Callow, John, 17
Calvert, Charles, Lord Baltimore, 385n
Camblets, silk, 31
Cambric, 31, 724, 783, 788; middling, 776, 785; price of, 592
Cambridge St. (Boston), 22n
Cameron, Mr., 158
Campbell, Charles, Robert, & William, of Gibraltar, 579, 604, 608
Campbell, Joseph, 561
Campbell, Mr., 54
Campbell, William, 709, 715, 723
Candles, 282, 451; Bayberry, 461; Myrtle wax, 291, 381, 452; New York, 39, 529; Philadelphia, 39; price of, 596; tallow, 596, 738, 744
Cannisters, 270
Cannon, Mr., 80, 125
Cannon St. (London), 99, 163n
Canock, 338
Cantey, James, 19n

Canvas, 31, 270, 424, 480, 634; Russian, 538, 648, 655. *See also* Duck; Sail cloth; Sail makers; Sails
Cape Breton Island, 820n. *See also* expedition, Cape Breton
Cape Comorin, Mosquito Coast, 833n, 846
Cape Fair. *See* Cape Fear, N. C.
Cape Fare. *See* Cape Fear, N. C.
Cape Fear (Fair, Fare), N. C., 95, 102, 103, 112, 128, 129, 133, 134, 136, 142, 144, 159, 165, 218, 234, 242, 325, 397, 523, 594, 720, 791, 806, 843, 847
Cape Fear sloop, 844
Cape Fear Station, 608
Cape Finisterre, Spain, 472n. *See also* License, to ship rice south of Cape Finisterre
Cape Francois, St. Domingo, 665, 689
Cape Romain, S. C., 643
Capes, the, 504, 514
Carabines, 90
Carabineers, of Antigua, 122n, 179n
Caribbean Sea, 173n
Carboys, 440
Cargill, John, 819n, 847
Carolina, a brigantine (Murray), 447, 516
Carolina, a brigantine (Wilkinson), 244n
Carolina, a ship (Meshard), 634n, 660
Carolina, a sloop (Schermerhorn), 648
Carolina, a sloop (Sheddon), 294
Carolina, a sloop (Roome), 738n, 744
Carolina Coffee House (London), 105, 152, 216, 219, 305, 378, 771, 801
Carolina Galley, a ship (Campbell), 561n
Carolina Merchant (Atkinson), 420
Carolina Packett, a ship (Summersett), 46n, 97, 226, 306, 308, 310, 327, 532
Carolina Station, 10, 42n, 98n, 135n, 186n, 260, 264, 323, 331, 332n, 367, 371, 497, 569, 587, 613n, 639n, 640, 662n, 737n, 762, 831n, 839; commodore of, 430. *See also* King's Ships on Carolina Station; Port Royal Station
Carpenters, 339n, 792; house, 272, 276, 282, 412; ship, 270, 412, 493, 777. *See also* Joiners
Carpet, 158. *See also* Rugs
Carrol, Mr., 592

Index

Cartagena, Colombia, 170n, 193n, 230n, 231, 262, 663n, 782, 783, 785, 787, 788, 790
Carteret (Cateret) County, N. C., 380
Carter, John, 17, 18
Carter, Samuel, of Barbados, 449, 475, 513, 528, 531, 625
Cartouch boxes, 5
Caruthers (Curruthers), James, 227, 790
Cases, 226, 249, 473, 753
Cash, 226, 459, 478, 510, 520, 546; ready, 325, 337, 453, 487, 501, 571, 573, 686, 704, 776. *See also* Currency; Money
Cask, 31, 68, 153, 163, 166, 192, 223, 226, 252, 336, 417, 459, 464, 481, 486, 508, 509, 596, 602, 605, 611, 675, 717, 719, 737, 797; ironbound, 832; quarter, 579; rice, 422
Castilla, Francisco de, 815, 815n (biog.)
Castilla, Señor de, 815n
Castle Alley (Cornhill, London), 339n
Caswall, John, 115n. *See also* Lane, Smethurst, & Caswall
Cateret County. *See* Carteret County, N. C.
Cater, Mr., 522
Cateton St. (London), 360n
Catherine, a ship (Collock), 369n
Cathcart, Lord Charles, 230, 231, 269, 270, 288
Cattell, William, 126
Caulton, Richard. *See* Coulton, Richard
Causton, Thomas, of Georgia, 26, 26n (biog.), 729
Cavanagh, Charles, 39
Caw, David, 543, 543n (biog.), 587, 688, 699, 807, 808, 834
Caw, William, 587, 688, 699, 740, 808, 834
Caygill (Caygell), Mr., of Halifax, 216, 223
Caygill, Mr., of Hull, 106
Cedar, 802, 825, 840
Cedar Valley, Antigua, 122n
Certificate, 28, 303, 353; bounty, 9, 107, 141, 162, 166, 208, 466; for pilotage, 98; for wages, 67; of hypothecation, 375–377, 392, 406; of origin, for imported slaves, 684, 686, 840; of registry, 414; of survey, 338, 417; plantation, 12, 22, 35–38, 53, 80, 94, 113, 114, 142, 143, 155, 197, 201, 202, 209, 214, 234, 280, 311, 337, 432, 447, 476, 482, 490, 492, 537, 558, 589, 590, 593–597, 607, 615, 624, 632, 647, 662, 684, 688, 693, 705, 741, 749, 754, 760, 785, 786, 796, 826, 841. *See also* Cocket
Chad, Capt., 564, 565, 576, 579
Chadock, Joseph. *See* Chadwick, Joseph
Chadwick (Chadock), Joseph, 812–814, 818
Chagres, Castle of, Panama, 231
Chairs, 601, 657, 672, 772. *See also* Chaise
Chaise, 263, 383, 745, 761; furniture, 468; harness for, 301. *See also* Chairs
Chaise, Dinnis, 489
Chaise maker, 468
Chalder, 170
Chamber of Commerce (Charleston), 83n
Champain, John, 100
Chapman, Clemens, 846
Chapman, Thomas, 452, 460
Charing Cross (London), 613
Charity House (Rotherith, London), 473
Charles, a ship (Harramond), 222, 322
Charleston Bay, S. C., 6, 276, 283
Charleston Library Society, members of, 210n, 240n, 365n, 543n
Charleston Neck, S. C., 144n, 519n
Charlestown, Mass., 444n
Charming Bettey, a sloop (Crossthwaite), 108, 149, 150
Charming Betty, a brigantine (Swain), 677
Charming Betty, a ship (Anderson), 265
Charming Betty, a ship (Whitman), 244
Charming Betty, a sloop (Cowie), 196, 198, 203, 206, 212, 240
Charming Molly, a schooner (Murray), 191
Charming Sarah, a brigantine (Davison), 802, 807, 823, 825, 840, 841
Charming Sarah, a schooner (Davison), 682, 683, 685, 716, 786, 802
Charming Susan, a ship (Scott), 370n, 477n, 587, 604, 606, 617, 621
Charter party, 210, 211, 220, 222, 290, 302, 338, 353, 355, 396, 433, 594, 655. *See also* Lye days

Index

Check, John. *See* Cheek, John
Checks, 400; cotton, 31; ell-wide, 246, 258; linen, 31; paper, 258; Scots, 829; ¾'s, 246, 258. *See also* Linen
Cheek (Check, Chick), John, 230, 232, 233, 568, 585
Cheese, Cheshire, 31
Cheever, Bartholomew, of Boston, 22, 22n (biog.), 23, 83, 84, 197
Chellos, Indian blue, 488
Cherokee nation, 588n, 628n
Cherokee Mountains, S. C., 588
Chesebrough, David, of Newport, 717, 717n (biog.), 719, 767, 768, 779, 816, 826
Chests, 742
Chests of drawers, mahogany, 469
Chickasaws, 387
Chick, John. *See* Cheek, John
Chief Justice, of N. C., 842; of S. C., 169, 227, 351–353, 355, 357, 550, 619n, 708, 744n, 806
Childsbury, S. C., 723, 736, 800
Chillingsworth's *Works*, 654
Chillingsworth, William, 654
Chimes (cask), 338
Chimney backs, 50
Chimney hearths, 50. *See also* Grates
Chimney hooks, 252
China ware, 31, 145, 146, 545, 592, 635, 637, 646, 688, 709, 729, 776, 780, 781, 783, 785, 788; enamelled, 473; price of, 722. *See also* Bowls; Dishes; Earthenware; Plates
Chintz, 831
Chocolate, 804; price of, in Philadelphia, 820
Cholic, Bilious, 264
Christie, Thomas, 599
Chronological History of New England, 569n, 751
Church St. (Rotherith, London), 473
Churchwarden, 211, 271, 543n
Cinnamon, 447, 517
Cistern. *See* Cooler
Citron, dry'd preserv'd, 509, 520
Clackmannanshire, Eng., 690n
Clarke & Gutteridge, of Boston, 21, 22, 24, 52, 66
Clarke (Clark), Capt., 250, 502, 581, 583, 596
Clarke, Gedney (Gidney), of Barbados, 335, 346–348, 356, 370, 371, 407, 416, 436, 439, 440, 449, 450, 476, 529, 545, 551, 614, 624, 627, 638, 661, 666, 667, 670, 671, 674, 685, 715, 716, 756, 760, 764, 766, 767, 774, 784, 787, 802, 823n, 838, 847
Clarke, Mr., 669
Clark (Clarke), Thomas, of Wilmington, 128, 129, 235, 277, 297, 328, 368, 522, 555, 711
Cleland & Wallace, 162, 249, 251, 298, 392
Cleland, John, 162n, 169, 831
Clearance, 389, 414, 422, 786
Clergyman, 239, 575, 848; Presbyterian, 826n. *See also* Missionary; Rector
Clerk, 127; of the court in Mass., 695n, of the crown, 240; RP's, 774, 786; to the president and assistants in Ga., 598n. *See also* Assembly of S. C., clerk of; Council of Ga., clerk of; Council of S. C., clerk of; Court of Common Pleas, clerk of
Climate, change of (to Boston), 175, 177, 187, 203; of Boston, 242, 243, 251, 254, 389, 754 (effect on oranges); of Europe, 465; of S. C., 188, 211, 242, 389
Climate (S. C.), effect of, on drunken sailors, 736; on metal, 460, 465; on rice, 130, 187, 210, 218, 236, 241, 391, 592, 597; on soap, 779; on stored produce & provisions, 385, 568, 676, 685, 694; on woolens, 525. *See also* Weather
Clinton, George, 587, 587n (biog.)
Cload, Roger, 312, 417, 436, 440, 441, 442, 453, 549, 561, 562, 571–575
Clockmaker, 522
Cloth, 25, 77, 147; checked, 164; coarse, 31, 139, 259; Negro, 33, 261; Yorkshire, price of, 148. *See also* Alepine; Arras; Bag; Baize; Colchester; Britanias; Blanketing; Blankets; Broadcloth; Buckram; Calico; Camblets; Cambric; Canvas; Checks; Chintz; Damask; Diaper; Dimity; Dowlas; Drabb; Drapery; Duck; Duroys; Flannel; Garlix; Gauze; Gulix; Half thicks; Huckaback; Kendal cottons; Linen; Manchester goods; Osnaburg; Plains; Platiloes; Sagathy; Sail cloth; Serge;

Index

Shalloon; Silesias; Silk; Velvet; Woolens
Clothes, 57, 58, 63, 188, 272, 275, 731, 796, 832; Negro, 31; ready made, 524; silk, 267, suit of, 706, 709, 803, 809, 824; women's, 317; woolen, 525. *See also* Belt; Breeches; Coat; Gloves; Gown; Hats; Jacket; Shirts; Stockings; Stocks; Waistcoat
Clothing. *See* Clothes
Clubs, 707
Coach Founders, 468
Coals, 116–118, 169, 170, 228, 299, 832; New Castle, 32, 664, 666, 682; price of, 170, 299, 664
Coast, 815; of Africa, 775; of America, 243, 380; of Eng., 264; of Fla., 662; of Mass., 300; of S. C., 264, 265, 323
Coasting vessel, 702
Coat, 63, 188, 706; cloth, 658; fly, 63; riding, 63; sleeves of, 824. *See also* Jacket; Waistcoat
Coatam, Thomas, 514, 515, 518, 564, 652
Cochran (Cockran), James, 40, 40n (biog.), 41, 87, 88
Cocket, 401, 648, 738. *See also* Certificate
Cockfights, 92n
Cocoa, 87, 645, 669, 676, 720, 779, 804; price of, 87, 182–183, 590, 592, 780, 808, 810
Cod, dried salted, price of, 500
Coe, John, 27, 32, 33
Coffee, 44, 45, 69, 145, 189, 202, 407, 780, 804, 805, 810, 837, 843; price of, 44, 87, 182, 190, 192, 268, 301, 369, 590, 592, 625, 626, 632, 633
Coffee Houses, 551. *See also* Carolina Coffee House; Forrest's Coffee House; Jamaica Coffee House; Lloyd's Coffee House; Old Tom's Coffee House
Coffin, John, 73, 74
Colcock, Deborah (Milner), 748
Colcock, John, 748, 748n (biog.)
Colchester (Simons), 173, 186, 187
Colebatch, Capt., 187, 189, 271
Collcock, John, 156, 246, 250, 259, 261, 271
Collcott, George, 3, 4, 9, 10, 25, 53, 80, 91, 94, 847
Collector of Customs, in Barbados, 335n;
in Bermuda, 662n, 823n; in Boston, 432; in Charleston, 29n, 418n, 447; in London, 337; in New York, 738; in Va., 610n. *See also* Commissioner of Customs; Customs Officers
Collector of Revenues, 385n
Colleton County, S. C., 42n, 521n
Colleton, John, 533
Collingwood, Capt., 248n
Collins, Ann (Farril), 11n
Collins, Henry, of Newport, 86, 86n (biog.), 113, 137, 144, 146, 202, 211
Collins, Thomas, of Antigua, 11, 11n (biog.)
Collock (Kolleck), Philip, 368, 369, 565
Colonies, British, 841; in America, 51, 662, 761, 776; new, 700; northern, 154, 177, 180, 227, 282, 366, 390, 393, 438, 455, 501, 533, 538, 722, 732, 739, 742, 744, 747, 751, 783; Spanish, 7n, 663
Colors, popular, 224, 487
Colquhon, Mr., 847
Coltrane, David, 847
Comeur (Commeur), Mr., 489, 490, 493, 494
Commerford, James, 471
Commissioner of Customs, 280. *See also* Collector of Customs; Customs officers
Commissary of N. C., S. C., & Bahamas, 239
Commissioner of Quit Rents, 293n
Commission, mercantile, 13, 53, 54, 84, 162, 164, 166, 167, 221, 223, 267, 292, 293, 310, 322, 330, 357, 361, 394, 418, 423, 468, 474, 549, 571, 572, 603, 630, 646, 699, 752, 753, 797, 803, 804; rate of, 30, 32, 39, 52, 141, 295, 337, 378, 455, 541, 795, 799
Commission, military, 379
Committee of London merchants, 488
Committee to distribute relief in Charleston, 478n
Common law court. *See* Court of Common Pleas
Company of Merchants Trading to Africa, 156n
Comptroller of the Country Duties, 379
Comrin, John, children of, 318
Comrin (Camorin, Cameron), John, of Boston, 82, 203, 217, 219, 221, 222,

225, 226, 273n, 274, 317, 364, 365, 389, 393, 403, 733
Comrin, Sarah, of Boston, 273, 273n (biog.), 302, 318, 364, 388, 403, 404, 733
Conception, a ship (De Marcan, Piedro De Lessagrate), 780n, 781–783, 785, 787–790, 796, 804, 808, 835
Concerts, 92n
Concord, a ship (Young), 210n, 280
Congregational Church (Charleston), 76n, 314n, 696n
Constable, 148, 353, 756
Congregation Beth Elohim (Charleston), 147n
Content, a sloop (Fuller), 132, 133
Contrador de Floride, 815
Convoy, 163, 265, 530, 533, 568n, 701, 797
Conyers (Conyears), David, 758, 759, 768, 804
Conyers, Mr., of London, 803, 804, 808
Cook, John, 523–526
Cook, Silas, 816, 826, 827
Cook, William, 309, 468
Cookson & Welfitt, of Hull, 296n, 324, 332, 336, 349, 352, 354, 357, 361, 370, 398, 418, 419, 421, 442, 443, 445, 450, 483, 524, 544, 601, 609, 796, 797
Cookson, William, of Hull, 116n, 287, 339, 687, 797
Cooler, copper water, 585, 620, 654, 751, 809
Cooper, 129, 414, 417, 422
Cooperage, 694, 717, 737
Cooper & Gerald, 185
Cooper, Brewton, 366, 366n (biog.)
Cooper, Capt., 104–106, 756, 757, 758, 764, 765
Cooper River, S. C., 83, 117, 140, 334, 407, 416, 441, 723, 736
Cooper, Thomas, 144, 144n (biog.), 155, 192, 313, 316, 366
Copybook, 602
Cordage, 25, 31, 40, 41, 187, 228, 338, 440, 602, 776; price of, 351; twice-layed, 208. *See also* Cables; Hawsers; Hamburg lines; Rope; Twine
Core (Corse) Sound, N. C., 380n, 557, 710, 712, 765
Cormell, Theod., 8

Corn, 11, 282, 415, 475, 610, 638, 710–713; crop of, (N. C.), 410, 412; crop of (S. C.), 26, 38, 408, 410–412, 416, 476, 590, 591, 609, 630, 631, 651; Indian, 22, 23, 26, 45, 320, 509, 513, 562, 579, 627; in Europe, 238; price of, 22, 24, 125, 191, 320, 321, 385, 408, 416, 448, 450, 452, 460, 474, 483, 509, 513, 529, 612, 624–626, 632, 633, 716, 719, 721, 724, 725, 734, 757, 758, 766, 785, 787, 788, 825, 839, 840. *See also* Grain
Cornhill (London), 55n, 339n
Cornish, Capt., 152, 155, 533
Coronell, Capt., 846
Coroner, 736
Coroner's jury, verdict of, 736
Correspondence, 31, 50, 51n, 57, 80, 81, 86, 106, 122, 131, 181, 183, 190, 193, 206, 216, 219, 224, 225, 297, 303, 307, 365, 385, 389, 397, 436, 514, 526, 527, 544, 579, 583, 604, 606, 627, 628, 652, 717, 779, 810, 833, 843
Correspondents, 545; in Amsterdam, 575; in Antigua, 846; in Boston, 177, 382, 458; in Cape Fear, 419, 423, 450; in Hamburg, 225, 235n; in Jamaica, 662, 689, 763, 846; in London, 385, 635, 808; in New York, 648n, 848; in Philadelphia, 847; in Rotterdam, 575; in St. Kitts, 846, 847; in Va., 610n, 846. *See also* Factors; Merchants
Corse Sound. *See* Core Sound, N. C.
Cossett, Field, family of, 474
Cossett, Field, of Frederica, 473, 577, 614, 619, 635, 689, 731
Cossett, John, 473, 577, 614, 635
Cossett, Miss, 635
Cossett, Mrs. Field, 474
Coulter, Edward, 92
Coulton (Caulton), Richard, 792, 806, 844
Council of Bahamas, members of, 591n; president of, 297n
Council of Ga., clerk of, 649n; president of, 629n
Council of Mass., members of, 5n, 20n, 489n
Council of S. C., 272, 275, 276, 377, 388, 715n, 726n; chamber of, 700, 714n; clerk of, 332n; eldest councilor of, 265n; members of, 83n, 162n,

Index

169n, 196, 488, 533, 588, 619n, 724, 725; messenger of, 8n, 9; president of, 279n, 418n. *See also* Grand Council
Counterpane, India satin, 481, 756, 805; price of, 481, 837
County Essex, Eng., 591n
County Fife, Scotland, 222n
County Galway, Ireland, 296n
County of Gloucester, Eng., 4n
Courtier, 578
Court of Chancery, 550, 635
Court of Common Pleas, 379n, 418n, 635; clerk of, 240
Court of General Sessions, 352, 353, 355, 357, 398, 421, 442, 525, 603, 748, 798
Court of Vice Admiralty (Pa.), judge of, 108n
Court of Vice Admiralty (S. C.), 675, 679, 682, 689, 691, 699, 726, 753; charges of, 385, 414; decrees of, 413, 414; judge of, 619, 808
Court room, 92n
Coverlid. *See* Counterpane
Cowan, Capt., 251
Cowan, John, 847
Cowes, Eng., 84, 85, 89, 119–121, 167, 173, 181, 196, 202, 203, 204, 222, 223, 225, 245, 262n, 278, 279, 281, 290, 295, 312, 313, 315, 322, 323, 344, 362, 374n, 380, 381n, 387, 422, 436, 439, 441, 442, 446, 455, 456, 471, 477, 479, 482, 484–486, 492, 498, 519, 530, 533, 558, 559, 587, 592n, 622, 637, 638, 656, 659, 661, 664, 674, 789, 791, 794, 824, 830, 832
Cowie, James, 149, 196, 198, 206, 233, 240, 300, 301, 302, 317, 318, 323, 325, 331
Cows, 299
Cox, Florentia (Florentius), 333, 333n (biog.), 334, 358, 386, 420, 460, 583, 628, 656, 727
Crammond, Robert, 240
Cranberries, 754
Cranck, Capt., 315
Cranes, 338
Cranston, Col., 248n
Craven County, S. C., 42n
Credit, 30, 57, 86, 90, 92, 159, 189, 264, 281, 325, 396, 440, 459, 487, 504, 507, 510, 520, 577, 636, 637, 646, 686, 809; long, 24, 367, 578, 834

Creditors, 20, 115, 199, 206, 234n, 521, 620, 834
Creeks, 121, 808n
Crew. *See* Sailors
Crode, John, 259n
Crokatt & Michie, 433, 613, 655
Crokatt, James, 156n, 210n, 310, 310n (biog.), 313n, 455, 551, 639, 643, 656, 663, 699, 701, 739, 746, 748, 761, 772, 790, 791, 803, 804, 822, 828, 833
Crokatt, James, & Co., 310n, 350n
Crokatt, John, 313, 313n (biog.), 433, 678, 726, 735n
Crokatt, John (d. 1740), 210, 313n, 332
Cromwell, a ship (Nicholson), 644, 662, 664, 666
Crops, 14, 82, 86, 122, 123, 125, 126, 130, 131, 155, 184, 210, 724n; in Antigua, 319–321, 340–344, 346, 348, 448, 449, 632, 706, 782, 783; in Barbados, 346, 349, 417, 476, 661, 664, 803; in Leeward Islands, 368, 502, 517, 664, 691; in St. Kitts, 38; in West Indies, 645. *See also* Corn, crop of; Grain, crop of; Rice, crop of; Weather, effect on crops
Crossthwaite (Crossthwait), Thomas (James), 108, 109, 150, 151, 174, 269, 437, 438, 614, 803
Crump, Elizabeth (Burke), 126, 127, 180
Crump, George, 126, 126n (biog.), 127, 180, 321
Crutched Friars (London), 282n, 455
Cuba, W. I., 663. *See also* Havana
Cullender, hard metal, 59
Cuningham, Messrs., 847
Cunningham, Capt., 418
Currants, 424, 579, 605
Currency Act of 1751, 776n
Currency, Antigua, 44; paper, issuance of, 550, 776; S. C., 269, 281, 292, 293, 295, 303, 308–310, 474, 530
Currie, George, 513
Currie, Mr., 514
Curruthers, James. *See* Caruthers, James
Custom House, at Antigua, 590; at Boston, 405, 537, 693, 749; at Charleston, 272, 283, 337, 389, 401, 405, 571, 573, 586, 596, 605, 608, 648, 684, 714, 786, 842; at Hull, 311, 482, 593;

Index

at London, 155, 280, 490, 492, 558, 589, 597, 794, 801; at New York, 738. *See also* Books, Custom house
Customs officers, fees of, 432; in America, 662; in Barbados, 186n, 662n; in Charleston, 13, 143, 337, 414, 430, 432, 575, 596, 605n, 738, 741; in New York, 596. *See also* Collector of customs; Commissioners of customs

Daily, John, 267
Dalby, Francis, of London, 539, 541, 557, 558, 561, 566, 589, 619, 646, 647, 673
Dalby, Mr., 289
Dale, Richard, 532, 532n (biog.)
Damask, Italian, 245; silk, 262; worsted, 31, 63
Daniel, Mary, 126
Darien, Ga., 157n
Dartmouth, Eng., 278n
Davis, Caleb, 171
Davis, Capt., 35, 665, 666
Davis, James, 123, 135, 183, 211, 224, 229, 231, 232
Davis, John, 702
Davison (Davidson, Davisson), John, 682–686, 716, 786, 823, 825, 837, 838, 839, 840, 841, 842
Davis, Zachary, of Limerick, 127, 127n (biog.), 130, 131
Dawson, Mrs. (Hamilton), 315
Daymund (Diamond), John, 167, 587, 844
Deas, David, 136, 136n (biog.)
Debby, a brigantine (Coatam), 515
Debtor, 54, 92n, 339, 663n
Debts, 53–55, 58, 76, 88, 89, 92, 97, 101, 105, 109, 110, 152, 219, 220, 228, 254, 257, 294, 304, 305, 311, 327, 329, 330, 339, 362, 372, 374, 378, 382, 455, 456, 459, 461, 478, 479, 486, 487, 513, 521, 532, 547, 554, 563, 564, 570, 575, 580, 584, 598, 599, 607, 615, 620, 623, 643, 649, 651, 655, 663, 665, 668, 688n, 690, 693, 702, 713, 729, 731, 755n, 765, 794, 797, 807, 826, 834, 843, 844; book, 607n
Deeds, 42
Deer, 45, 268
Deer skins, 16, 17, 22, 30, 32, 86, 106, 114, 141, 144, 145, 147, 287, 297, 313, 364, 410, 419, 431, 451, 462, 466, 484, 489, 506, 526, 533, 547, 548, 556, 562, 564, 567, 570, 572, 574, 575, 584, 587, 600, 604, 616, 617, 621, 630, 643, 644, 670, 671, 685, 699, 739, 776, 777, 789, 792–794, 798, 799, 809, 812, 813; heavy, 23, 291; Indian dress'd, 605, 843; price of, 32, 87, 125, 154, 156, 165, 175, 178, 186, 190, 201, 202, 209, 217, 227, 242, 254, 288, 291, 313, 317, 452, 508, 525, 582, 583, 594, 601, 603, 606, 653, 657, 766; price of, in London, 477; quality of, 566, 617; stout, 672
De la Pierre (Delapee), Elizabeth (Lloyd), 13
De la Pierre, George, 13
De la Vega, Julian, 815
Delaware, a ship (Rivers), 674, 737
Delegal (Delagel), John, 836, 836n (biog.)
Delegal, Philip, 836n
DeLessagrate, Piedro, 780n
Delight, a snow (Law), 503n
DeMarcan, Capt., 780n
Demurrage, 142, 337
Dennis, John, 312, 533, 534
Deposition, 37
DeSalis, Pierre, 377
Desks, 469
Deserters, from merchant ships, 513, 531, 557; from Royal Navy, 473n, 492n; from St. Augustine, 231
DeVas, Francis Luis, of Madeira, 363, 373, 376, 377, 392
DeVeaux, Andrew, 740n
Dial, Horizontal, 469
Dial, Verticle, 469; south, 551
Diaper, 31, 55, 246, 258, 776
Dickinson (Dickenson), John, of Beaufort Town, 380, 380n (biog.), 382, 412, 556, 557, 650, 651, 710, 712, 713, 764, 765
Dickinson, Capt., 811
Dickinson, Christopher, 144–146
Didicott (Didcott), Abraham, 148, 532, 668
Dillon, Peter, 246
Dimity, 399, 658; India, 63
Dinwiddie, Robert, 662, 662n (biog.)
Disease. See Fever; Pringle, Robert, illnesses of; Smallpox; Yellow fever

Index

Dishcovers, hard metal, 59; tin, 470
Dishes, china, 249, 424, 592, 780; pewter, 31, 249, 298; pewter water, 59
Dispatch, a ship (Cheek), 568n
Dobree & Harris, 729
Dobree family, of Guernsey, 722
Dobree, William, of London, 737, 777, 795, 799
Dobrug, Mr., 54
Doctors. *See* Physicians
Dogs, 268
Doharty, Cornelius, 588n
Dollars, 788, 826. *See also* Pieces of Eight; Rate of Exchange, with dollars
Dolphin, a brigantine (Evans), 489n, 493, 500, 502, 504, 505, 514, 534, 536, 678, 693, 749, 826
Dolphin, a ship (Erwin), 82, 103, 206
Dolphin Court (Tower Hill, London), 667n
Dominions. *See* Colonies
Domingo, Don, 815
Donovan (Dunavan, Dunovan), Francis, 760, 764, 765, 774, 775, 782, 784, 785, 787–789, 802, 838
Dorchester, S. C., 121n, 305, 544
Dormer, James, of Savannah, 47, 47n (biog.), 48, 49, 100, 101, 124, 146, 328, 598, 599, 629, 649, 734, 836
Dorset, a snow (Thompson), 247
Doubloons, 740
Doughty, Thomas, 339, 339n (biog.)
Douglas (Douglass), Archibald, 235, 277
Douglass, James, of London, 123, 182, 224, 229, 266, 285
Douglas (Douglass), William (captain), 11, 308, 310, 313, 321, 322, 323, 331, 334, 335, 344, 356, 480, 642, 655, 661, 670, 674, 700, 722, 746, 747, 748, 762–764, 769–771, 773, 775, 776, 778, 789, 796, 829
Douglas, William (physician), 234, 234n (biog.)
Dove, a brigantine (Ford), 530, 534, 535, 537
Dove, a sloop (Sigourney), 21, 23
Dover, Eng., 250, 302, 549
Dover, William, of London, 360, 360n (biog.), 465, 603, 617, 621
Dowlas, 31
Downs, the (English Channel), 734
Drabb, 63

Drafts, 107, 118, 128, 218, 223, 457, 566, 701, 733, 777. *See also* Bills of Exchange
Drake. *See* Ducks, summer
Drapery, 55
Drawback, 54. *See also* Duty
Drewry, Capt., 120
Drink, 490
Druggist. *See* Apothecary
Drum, 6
Drummey, Capt., 230, 232
Drummond, James, 179, 238
Drummond, John, 266–268, 283, 589, 590
Dry goods, 32, 44, 57, 84, 116, 238, 249, 295, 422, 440, 455, 530, 549, 578, 633, 634, 708, 709, 784, 834, 843; prices of, 243, 317, 337
Dry goods trade, 30, 50, 238, 440, 578, 794; glutted, 317, 320, 332, 367, 372, 392; nature of, 57, 269, 396
DuBois, John, 777
Duck (cloth), 98, 372, 727. *See also* Canvas; Sail cloth; Sail maker; Sails
Ducks (fowl), summer, 805
Dudding, Capt., 237, 239
Duke of Cumberland, a ship (Bishop), 161–162
Duke of Newcastle, a snow (Ancell), 270
Duke of New-Castle. *See* Pelham-Holles, Thomas
Dunbar, Charles, 569, 770
Dunbibin, Daniel, of Wilmington, 296, 296n (biog.), 326, 397, 410, 412, 419, 450, 463, 556
Dundass, Alexander, 270
Dung, horse, 565
Dunnage, 162, 392, 439, 454, 536, 799
Dunn, John, Jr., of Antigua, 179, 179n (biog.), 341, 517, 847
Dunn, Mrs. John, Jr., 341, 517
DuPlessis (Du Plissis), Peter, 554, 554n (biog.)
Duport, Isaac, of St. Kitts, 662, 757, 765, 767, 846
Durell, Philip, 519–521, 529, 530, 533, 820
Duroy, 31
Durour (Durreau), Col., 434, 441, 443, 444
Dutch, 365n, 382. *See also* Amsterdam; Holland; Rotterdam

Index

Dutch goods, 430. *See also* Brandy; Claret; Gin; Lace; Spices
Duthy, Capt., 737–739, 791
Duthy (Duthie, Duty), James, 824, 824n (biog.)
Duty, 13, 401; additional, on: flour, madeira, molasses, rum, sugar (clay'd), sugar (muscavado), 699n; extraordinary, on Negroes, 684, 686; on Negroes, 174, 182, 186, 190, 211, 241–242, 247 (at Lisbon), 260, 263, 284, 684, 686, 841; on pitch, 710; on pork, 411, 556, 577, 710; on plantation Negroes, 840; on rice (half-subsidy in Eng.), 459, 487, 510; on sugar, 253; on sugar, French, 738; on tallow, 710; on tar, 710; on turpentine, 710; on wax, myrtle, 710; on wines, 571
Dye-wood, 30n

Eagle, a sloop (Anderson), 636n
Eagle, a sloop (Fennell), 533
Eagle (Long), 295, 299, 309, 584
Eagles, Richard, 128, 326
Earthenware, 31, 147, 402. *See also* China ware
Eastern cardinal. *See* Redbirds
East India Co., 382; director of, 212
Ebsworthy, Mr., 34
Edentown, N. C., 380, 411, 412, 483, 673, 709, 712, 766, 767, 839, 842, 845, 847
Edgely, Elizabeth, of London, 88, 88n (biog.), 151, 847
Edinburgh, Scotland, 62n, 382
Education, abroad, 519, 520
Edwards, George, 461
Elfe, Thomas, 755n
Elfreth, John, 731
Eliza, a sloop (Newton), 35–38
Elizabeth, a ship (Hammat), 195n, 316n
Elizabeth, a ship (Lee), 123n
Elizabeth, a sloop (Bell), 369
Elizabeth, a sloop (Rains), 810, 811
Elizabeth, a snow (Douglas), 308, 322, 331
Elliott, Buleah (Law), 519n
Elliott, Claudia (McKewn), 519n
Elliott, Elizabeth (Bellinger), 519n, 822
Elliott, Mary (Bellinger), 519n
Elliott St. (Charleston), 272n
Elliott, Susannah, 519n

Elliott, Thomas, Jr., 519, 519n (biog.), 520, 634, 640, 655, 659–661, 663, 761, 794, 809, 822
Elliott, Thomas, of Long Point, 519n, 642n
Elliott, Thomas, Sr., 519, 519n (biog.), 520, 634, 640, 642, 654–656, 659–661, 663, 688, 745, 761, 772, 794, 809, 822, 829, 830
Ellis, Catherine (Abbott), 26, 255, 512, 565, 652, 653, 675, 738, 791, 820
Ellison, Mr., of Boston, 203
Ellis, Robert, children of, 518
Ellis, Robert, of Philadelphia, 19, 19n (biog.), 25, 26, 28, 48, 49, 146, 156–158, 160, 161, 171, 193, 255, 256, 359, 511, 515, 518, 538, 564, 565, 652, 653, 674, 675, 737, 738, 767, 768, 791, 820
Embargo, effect on trade, 397, 399, 400, 720; in Eng., 135, 538; in Mass., 845; in S. C., 11, 273, 389, 390, 393, 402, 404–405, 408, 410, 414, 477, 715–718, 722–725
Emery, Mr., 836, 837
Emery, Mrs., 599, 629
Emigrants, for Ga., 157n
Emma Susannah, a ship (Watts), 176, 184, 185, 195, 200–202, 204, 206–209, 211, 212, 214, 227, 330
Empress of Russia, 674
Endeavor, a sloop (Bell), 474, 481
Endeavor, a sloop (Dickinson), 145
Endeavour (Hope), 151, 152
England, 18, 23, 26, 28, 30, 45, 72, 85, 92, 105, 116, 119, 124, 169, 170n, 181, 187n, 190, 192, 196, 216, 239, 241, 259, 276, 287n, 298, 304n, 305, 310, 312, 380, 383, 384, 387, 418n, 472, 486, 493, 498n, 510, 520, 530, 531, 532n, 542, 544n, 550, 585, 586, 594, 606, 613, 624, 634, 640, 644, 663n, 681, 700, 701, 706, 720, 729, 732, 747, 749, 760, 772, 777, 805, 815n, 821, 835, 838; west of, 790
England, James, 127, 130, 131
English (language), 247, 815
Enumerated goods, 590
Erving, Abigail (Phillips), 5n, 35, 66, 84, 113, 133, 144, 167, 197, 205, 212, 233, 234, 242–244, 251, 274, 276, 302,

Index

317, 366, 390, 430, 431, 445, 503, 535, 570, 582, 593, 616, 665, 676, 695, 705, 719, 734, 751, 781, 827, 845
Erving, Ann, 66n
Erving, Edward. *See* Erwin, Edward
Erving, Elizabeth, 66n
Erving, George, 66n
Erving, John, children of, 66, 84, 113, 133, 205, 242, 276, 302, 317, 366, 390, 431, 445, 503, 535, 570, 582, 593, 616, 644, 665, 676–677, 695, 705, 719, 734, 751, 781, 818, 827, 845–846
Erving, John, Jr., 66n
Erving, John, of Boston, 5, 5n (biog.), 13n, 21, 23, 28, 34, 35, 52, 65, 67, 79, 81, 82, 86, 87, 90, 95, 102, 103, 104, 112, 113, 120, 131, 133, 136, 142, 144, 154, 165, 167, 168, 176, 177, 184, 185, 195, 197, 198, 199, 201, 203, 205, 212, 216, 223, 225, 226, 233, 234, 235n, 241, 243, 249, 250, 274, 278, 300, 315–317, 362, 365, 366, 388, 389, 392, 429, 431, 433, 434, 443, 445, 502, 522, 534, 568, 570, 580, 582, 592, 607, 615, 616, 635, 643, 644, 662, 664, 665, 676, 680, 690, 693, 695n, 696, 702, 704, 718, 719, 733, 750, 765, 768, 781, 817, 818, 826, 845
Erving, Sarah, 66n
Erving, William, 66n
Erwin (Erving), Edward, 82, 103, 206
Escott, Gabriel, 259n
Escritoire, 469
Esdale, John, 847
Estates, 234n, 239, 254, 255n, 296, 321, 373, 385n, 392, 418, 451, 461, 474, 497, 546, 550, 563, 620, 642n, 653, 656, 755n, 759, 834. *See also* Administrators; Assignees; Executors
Estates, Aston Hall, 533n; Great House, 591n
Europe, 30, 116, 117, 145, 196, 210, 211, 215, 216, 219, 236, 238, 241, 245, 249, 262, 265, 266, 269, 290, 301, 330, 367, 371, 398, 401, 405, 436, 465, 487, 523, 525, 527, 534, 535, 538, 607, 641, 674, 681, 717, 728, 729, 730, 735, 736, 739, 742, 744, 761, 772, 774, 779, 803, 828
European goods, 729, 776, 783, 785, 788; price of, 781

Europeans, 143
Evance, Branfill, 287n, 634, 641, 656, 728, 804
Evans, Edward, 46, 529
Evans, John (Jonathan), 489, 493, 500, 504, 505, 514, 534–537, 693, 749
Everleigh, Samuel, 552, 552n (biog.)
Everton, a ship (Hall), 123
Everton, Samuel, 5
Executors, 89n, 203n, 267, 304, 305, 312, 363, 365n, 376, 378, 397, 418n, 542, 546, 601n, 623n, 847
Exeter, Eng., 689, 707
Expedition, Cape Breton (1745), 820, 845
Expedition, Lord Cathcart's, 269, 270, 288
Expedition, St. Augustine (1740), 42n, 196, 202, 212; effect on trade, 228; failure of, 230, 231, 234, 248, 266, 268; mismanagement of, 228, 230, 231, 232, 248, 266, 268; S. C. assistance for, 169–170, 175, 177, 181, 183, 184, 186, 187, 190, 193, 194, 197, 200, 216–217, 219, 220, 222, 225, 231, 232, 248. *See also* "The Report of the Committee of Both Houses of Assembly of the Province of S. C."
Expedition, to assist Ga., 407, 410, 415
Exports, printed account of, 17, 73, 74, 248

Factors, at Cape Fear, 419, 423, 433; at Charleston, 287, 292, 298, 301, 308, 730; at London, 375–377, 498n; at Wilmington, 296n; responsibility of, 423, 437; sugar, 823n; wronged by English merchants, 603. *See also* Correspondents; Merchants
Fadree, Capt., 678
Fairchild, John, 407, 408n, 479, 544, 551
Falla, John, 714, 730, 736, 777
Falmouth, Eng., 471n, 530, 532, 746
Famed Revenge, a sloop (Lampriere), 822n
Fan Church St. *See* Fenchurch St.
Fan Court (Fenchurch St., London), 801
Fandina (Fandino), Juan de Leon, 382, 382n (biog.)
Faneuil, Andrew, 81n
Faneuil Hall (Boston), 81n

Index

Faneuil, Peter, of Boston, 81, 81n (biog.), 83, 96, 118, 129, 200, 204, 211, 286, 300, 362, 503
Fanshawe, Charles, 260n, 265, 323, 325, 327, 331n
Faris & Walker, 131–132
Faris, John, 277, 278, 297, 419
Faris, William, of Wilmington, 128, 128n (biog.), 228, 234, 242, 397, 419
Farrington, Thomas, 296
Farrow, William, 67
Fashions, women's, 568
Faucheraud, Gideon, 105
Faucheraud, Mary, 105
Fenchurch St. (London), 159n, 801
Fender, Brass, 50, 245, 252
Fennell, Edward, 533
Fenwicke, John, family of, 640
Fenwicke, John, 514n, 640, 640n (biog.), 655, 776
Ferrell, Mr., 267
Ferrol, Spain, 260n
Ferry, 39n. See also Parker's Ferry; Skrine's Ferry
Fessenden, Hephzibah (Worth), 115n
Fessenden, Nicholas, 115, 199, 206
Fever, 404, 408, 431, 709; fever & ague, 122; nervous, 736. See also Pringle, Robert, illnesses of; Yellow fever epidemic
Field, John, 473
Fifeshire, Scotland, 215n
Fire (1740), 273, 280, 282, 284, 292, 293, 377, 401, 543; causes fear of insurrection, 273; damages & losses caused, 271–72, 275 (fig.), 276, 277, 279, 283, 284 (fig.), 285, 288 (fig.), 289, 304, 330, 364, 478n; effect of, on price of rice, 281, 288; effect of, on trade, 276, 279, 280, 289, 307; parliamentary relief for sufferers of, 478, 484, 655, 661, 688; sufferers by, 271, 272, 275, 276, 279, 300, 330, 478. See also Fire ticket
Fire ticket, 407, 408n, 439, 479, 544, 545, 551, 642, 655, 659, 661, 745, 760
First cost. See Prime cost
First Regiment of S. C., 144n; officers of, 227, 239n. See also Troops, S. C.
Firth of Forth, Scotland, 215n
Fish, 81, 96, 130, 275, 568; salted, 507. See also Cod; Herring

Fishbourne, Capt., 288, 290
Fisher, William, 27, 27n (biog.), 64
Fishing rods, 307
Fitter & Tyzack, of London, 591, 770, 770n (biog.), 773, 783, 793, 824
Five Fathom Hole, 530, 578. See also Harbor, Charleston
Flag of truce, 708, 726, 728, 731, 733, 778n, 815
Flamborough (Flambro), HMS (Pearce), 177n, 365n, 367, 369, 517, 755, 762, 775, 782, 796, 823
Flanders, 440
Flannel, 63; strip't, 270, 351, 424
Flasks, 221
Flax, experiments with, 724n
Fleet, British, 173, 175, 288, 488; French, 304; Spanish, 260, 387, 389, 390, 392, 396, 397, 399, 400, 404, 414, 430, 663n; Spanish treasure, 173n, 663n
Fleetwood, Capt., 29
Flemming, William, 549
Fletcher, Henry, 544, 550
Fletcher, Mrs. Henry, 544
Flooring, 6, 439, 454, 536
Florida, 254, 815. See also St. Augustine
Flour, 216, 220, 255, 277, 282, 329, 452, 493, 494, 500, 502, 504, 514, 515, 534, 536–538, 556, 564, 653, 699n, 739; Aesopus (Esopus), 291, 744; price of, 125, 228, 254, 291, 320, 323, 452, 508, 766
Flower, Henry, 20, 25
Flux, the, 19, 627
Fob, 706
Ford, Robert, 534, 535, 537, 538
Fordyce, John, 549, 549n (biog.), 558, 614
Fore, John, 385
Forks, London-made, 473; with buckhorn handles, 423; with ivory handles, 423
Forrest, Arthur, 594, 597, 613, 615, 616
Forrest, Mr., 613
Forrest's Coffee House (London), 613
Forrest, Thomas, 262
Forsyth, Alexander, of Boston, 569, 569n (biog.), 581, 582
Forsyth, Robert, 569, 580–583
Fort Frederick, S. C., 388n
Fortifications, of Charleston, 8, 488, 518;

Index

damaged by fire, 276; need repair, 387, 407; strengthening of, 388n
Fort Johnson, S. C., 388n, 405
Forty-Second Regiment of Foot, 40n, 41, 158, 231, 487n; officers of, 468n, 495n, 846; provisions for, 255n; recruits for, 255n
Foster, Capt., 339, 351, 358
Foster Lane (London), 15n, 848
Fowler, James, 242, 242n (biog.), 243
Fowler, Martha, 242
Fowling pieces, 5
Fowl, 788
Frames, for buildings, 276; for pictures, 299, 417, 438, 468, 688; for plans and prospects, 503, 512, 565, 653
France, 113, 304n, 396n, 714, 722, 820n; desires Atlantic port in America, 488
Francis, a bilander (Walker), 442–446
Francis, Capt., 611
Francis, Tench, 847
Frankland, Thomas, 280n, 323, 382, 383, 385, 408, 413, 569, 663, 664, 668, 673, 682, 698, 699, 726, 780–783, 785, 787, 788, 790, 835, 836n, 838
Franklin, Benjamin, 108n
Franklin, Peter, 86, 87, 98, 113, 114, 145
Franks, Jacob, 744, 846
Fraser, Capt., 388
Frazer, John, 321
Frazer, John (captain), 792, 806
Frederica, Ga., 40, 41, 157, 158, 387, 390, 392, 473n, 494, 541, 731
Freeman, Elizabeth (Pringle), 4n, 365n
Freeman, William, 4n
Free school, in Dorchester, commissioner of, 175n; in North Carolina, 95n
Freight, 9, 22, 41, 43, 45, 66, 80, 84, 109, 110, 116, 134, 136, 144, 145, 154, 162, 167, 201, 203, 204, 207, 212, 234, 239, 244, 257, 263, 269, 277, 278, 280, 293, 294, 304, 310, 323, 336, 343, 345, 347, 352, 353, 355, 370, 391, 393, 407, 417, 432, 433, 435, 436, 446, 453, 459, 467, 529, 533, 546, 562, 571–574, 586, 596, 604, 605, 608, 611, 626, 627, 630, 631, 632, 633, 646, 647, 662, 671, 674, 696, 723, 729, 736, 737, 741, 744, 754, 795, 796, 799, 800, 804, 810; at Antigua, 320, 321, 331, 335–336, 340–349, 356, 362, 370; at Barbados, 319, 321–323, 335–336, 340–349, 356, 368–370, 449; at Cape Fear, 120, 132; at Jamaica, 441; at Leeward Islands, 331, 341, 347–349, 356; at Montserrat, 347; at Nevis, 347; at St. Kitts, 347; at West Indies, 331, 347, 367, 437; for Amsterdam, 103, 124; for Barbados, 625, 683; for Boston, 112, 196, 365, 431, 504, 534, 536, 678, 690, 693, 695, 732; for Bremen, 34, 62; for Bristol, 81, 83; for Charleston, 173 (from Lisbon), 509 (from Madeira); 511 (from Philadelphia), 520 (from Madeira), 575 (from Holland), 579 (from Gibraltar); for Cowes, 108, 124, 331, 676, 679; for England, 762; for Europe, 102, 112, 123, 133, 136, 320, 321, 340–347, 368, 638, 678, 684, 722, 727, 738; for Hamburg, 34, 62, 215, 218, 220, 222, 236, 238, 242, 313, 324, 525, 616, 622, 638, 641, 714; for Holland, 34, 62, 108, 156, 166, 215, 218, 220, 222, 236, 238, 242, 281, 288, 298, 300, 301, 303, 308, 309, 313, 316, 318, 320, 324, 335, 358, 359, 367, 437, 493, 501, 503, 505, 507, 520, 524–527, 534, 535, 537, 539–541, 616, 622, 625, 638, 641, 653, 657, 664, 676, 679, 714, 736, 742, 763, 773, 777, 798, 817, 818, 827; for Hull, 215, 216, 220, 224, 290, 422, 602; for Lisbon, 374, 454, 487, 510, 625, 657, 677; for London, 7, 12, 13, 62, 65, 83, 86, 88–91, 93, 94, 96, 97, 104, 107, 108, 129, 156, 163, 165, 166, 173, 174, 176, 178, 181, 184, 185, 187, 189, 192, 194, 195, 200, 208, 215, 218, 220, 222, 230, 231, 236, 238, 242, 251, 259, 261, 274, 275, 281, 288, 290, 295, 298, 299, 300, 301, 303, 308, 309, 313, 316, 318–320, 335, 363, 365, 367–369, 371–373, 376, 392, 437, 452, 458, 462, 464, 465, 471, 476, 485, 486, 493, 503, 505–507, 520, 523–527, 530, 534, 535, 537–541, 551, 552, 554, 565, 566, 569, 581, 602, 606, 614, 616, 621, 622, 624, 625, 638, 641, 644, 653, 656, 657, 661, 664, 666, 669, 672, 676, 680, 684, 685, 694, 697, 700, 714, 736, 742, 748, 750, 760, 762, 763, 770, 771, 773, 776, 777, 779, 781, 785, 797–

Index

798, 817, 818, 827; for New York, 739; for Oporto, 748, 762, 770; for Portugal, 748, 750; for Rotterdam, 331, 358, 367, 530; for St. Kitts, 150; for Va., 609, 778; for West Indies, 438; price of, 3, 5, 6, 12, 34, 65, 81–83, 85, 86, 88–91, 93, 94, 96, 102, 103, 107, 113, 114, 120, 132, 156, 159, 163, 165, 166, 168, 173, 174, 176, 178, 181, 184, 185, 187, 189, 192, 194–196, 200–202, 204, 208, 209, 210, 211, 215, 218, 220, 222, 227, 230, 231, 236, 238, 242, 246, 248, 249, 251, 259, 261, 274, 275, 281, 288, 290, 295, 299–301, 303, 308, 309, 313, 316, 318–321, 324, 330, 331, 335, 337, 340–342, 346–349, 358, 359, 363, 365, 367, 371, 372, 374, 376, 392, 407, 418, 422, 429, 437, 438, 441, 452–454, 458, 462–465, 471, 476, 483, 485–487, 493, 501, 503, 505–507, 510, 520, 523–527, 530, 534–541, 551, 552, 554, 564–566, 569, 570, 575, 581, 602, 606, 614, 616, 619, 621, 622, 625, 635, 638, 641, 644, 653, 655–657, 661, 664, 666, 668–670, 672, 674, 676–680, 682–685, 693, 694, 697, 700, 713, 714, 716, 719, 722, 732, 736, 738, 742, 743, 746–748, 750, 760, 762, 773, 775, 777, 779, 781, 785, 797–798, 817–819, 827, 845
Freighters, 45, 114, 142, 222, 352, 357, 571, 573. *See also* Shippers
French, 488, 722, 782, 790; ambassador, 674; casualties, 785, 787, 788 (language), 815
French church (Charleston), 272n
French, John, 345, 345n (biog.)
French, Nathaniel, 122, 122n (biog.)
French, Valentine, of St. Kitts, 12, 12n (biog.), 13, 35–38, 69, 151, 631
Freshes, the, 694, 700, 714, 723, 727, 728, 735, 740. *See also* Ashley River, S. C.; Cooper River, S. C.
Fresh rivers. *See* Freshes, the
Friday St., (London), 15n
Friend, a brigantine (bilander) (Slater, Wood), 116, 117, 137, 140, 215, 217
Friend's Goodwill, a ship (Glegg), 576n
Friendship, a ship (Mackay), 644n
Friendship, a ship (Story), 290, 293, 295, 311, 589

Friendship, a snow (Steinson), 661n
Friend, Edward, of Williamsburg, 172, 172n (biog.), 394, 415, 847
Frost, 282, 732n
Fruit, 39. *See also* Currants; Lemons; Limes; Olives; Oranges; Raisons
Fryer (Fryor), Mr., of London, 249, 261, 282, 554
Fuller, Joseph (John), 130, 132, 133, 285
Funeral, 177, 254
Funnels, hard metal, 59
Furniture, 729; household, 271, 275, 277, 283, 284
Fury, Peregrine, 309, 309n (biog.), 478, 577, 588, 776

Gadsden, Thomas, 29, 29n (biog.), 169, 194
Galleys, fitted out by S. C., 265, 407, 708; furnished by Eng., 265n, 662
Gaol. *See* Jail
Garden, 724n. *See also* Pringle, Robert, garden of
Garden, Alexander, 239, 239n (biog.)
Garden seeds, 389, 804
Gardner, Mr., 489
Garlix, 9, 55, 147, 162, 706, 788, 829, 834; holland, 148; middling, 776; price of, 592; ⅞'s, 24, 31, 154, 225, 227, 330, 592; ¾'s, 31, 148, 154, 202 (coarse), 225, 227, 330, 592, 776 (coarse), 783, 785; yardwide, 227
Garnet. *See* Canock
Gatman, Capt., 695
Gauge, for pitch barrel, 40; for tar barrel, 40
Gauze, Italian, 224, 487, 605; silk, 605, 660; price of, 487
Geare, Capt., 564
Geekie, David, 57, 58
Geese, 788
Gelding, 564, 711; price of, 564n. *See also* Horses
Gelly, Capt., 612
Gentlemen, country. *See* Planters
George, a ship (Campbell), 709n
George, a snow (Raitt), 643n
George II, 121, 265n, 273, 379, 588, 700
George Town, S. C., 169n, 503, 541, 599
Georgia, 19n, 26, 29, 40n, 41n, 43, 45, 47n, 48, 87, 100 147, 153, 161, 171n, 193, 197, 200, 216, 219, 252n, 255,

Index

387, 526, 586, 596, 598n, 599, 649, 712, 713, 814, 846; charter of, 16n; law & justice in, 101; malcontents in, 157n, 171n. *See also* Oglethorpe; Spanish invasion of Ga.; Trustees of Ga.
Georgia Bills. *See* Sola bills
Georgia Office (London), 729
Georgia Packett, a brigantine (McClean), 437n, 494n
Germans, 249, 262, 299. *See also* Palatines
Germany, 203n. *See also* Bremen; Hamburg
Gerrald (Gerald), John, 6, 7, 85, 90, 144n, 192, 269, 313
Gibbon, Capt., 674
Gibraltar, 604, 605, 608, 642, 656
Gibraltar, HMS (Durell), 519–521, 529–531, 533
Gibson, William, 67, 98, 187, 355
Gin, 430, 440
Ginger, preserved, 481
Gladoe, Mary, 579, 580
Glasses, 585
Glegg, John, 576, 586, 739, 741–743, 745–747
Glen, David, 57, 57n (biog.), 58, 63, 188, 549, 706, 709
Glen, James, 18n, 51, 51n (biog.), 58, 121, 170, 188, 253, 280, 289, 293, 332, 333, 358, 369, 372, 378, 466n, 468, 488, 588n, 589, 605, 618, 622, 636, 664, 732n, 741, 745, 796, 809, 822, 826
Glen, Mrs. David, 58, 64, 188, 707
Gloves, 107, 117, 139, 843; lamb, 31; London-made, 524
Godfather, 365n, 473
Gold, 86, 137, 141, 144, 202, 431, 487, 501, 506, 510, 520, 533, 673, 678, 723, 742, 782, 783, 785, 787, 788, 804, 831, 836
Goldsmith, at the Crown (London), 15n, 848
Goldthwait (Goldthwaite), Thomas, of Boston, 458, 463, 464, 467, 485, 489, 506, 507, 540, 542, 548, 549, 566–568, 635, 637, 646. *See also* Hutchinson & Goldthwait
Golightly, Cultcheth, 514n
Goodchild, James, of London, 97, 99, 99n (biog.), 225, 306
Good Hope, a ship (Turell), 555, 538–541, 547–549, 552, 557, 558, 566
Good Intent, a brigantine (Cook), 523n
Good Intent, a brigantine (Thornton), 616n
Good Intent, a sloop (Blunt), 388, 390–393, 403, 405, 647
Goodman's Fields (London), 88n, 375n, 847
Gooseberries, 403
Goose Creek Friendly Society, 212n
Goose Creek, S. C., 146
Gordon, Alexander, 332, 332n (biog.), 333
Gordon, Alexander, family of, 333
Gordon, Mr., 40, 373
Gordon, Roger, 755, 755n (biog.)
Gore (Goore), Charles, of Antigua, 71, 123, 180, 190
Gorlitz, Prussian Silesia, 10n
Gosport, HMS, 461
Gough, Mr., 43
Gould, Capt., 643
Gould, Thomas, 467
Government, of Antigua, 43; of Ga., 16; of Great Britain, 163, 170; of S. C., 7, 11, 102, 122, 135, 441, 443, 444, 498; of S. C., weak, 265, 289–290. *See also* Ministry
Governments, of North America, 613, 728
Governor, 134, acting, of S. C., 272, 276, 377, 379, 387–388, 390, 395, 542, 577; needed, in S. C., 122, 188, 259, 265, 280, 289, 388, 488, 577; of Bahamas, 280, 293n, 298, 333, 334, 358, 386; of Fla., 815; of Ga., 629n, 744n, 805n; of Island of Rattan, 833; of Mass., 363n; of N. C., 235; of N. Y., 587; of S. C., 18, 51, 58, 121, 170, 188, 253, 280, 289, 293, 332, 358, 369, 372, 378, 418, 587, 618, 622, 700, 701, 741, 745, 796, 822
Gowen, Elizabeth, 444n
Gowen, Joseph (John), 444, 507, 647
Gowen, Joseph, children of, 444n
Gown, 832; Banyan morning, 63, 188; silk, 470
Graeme, James, 442, 619, 619n (biog.), 688n, 805, 808, 834, 844
Graham, Patrick, 655

Index

Graham, William, of Antigua, 46, 71, 107, 124
Grain, 11, 321, 330; crop of, 448–450; price of, 321. *See also* Corn; Rice
Grand Council of S. C., 39n. *See also* Council of S. C.
Grant, Alexander, 847
Grant, Capt., 510, 511
Grant, Ludowick, 628, 628n (biog.), 734
Granville County, S. C., 47n, 296n
Granville's Bastion (Charleston), 714n
Grappling, 800
Grate, 245, 283; price of, 169, 252. *See also* Chimney hearth
Gravel, 224; black heath, 796
Gravener, Sharnell, 475, 476, 513, 528, 529, 531, 624, 625, 661, 662, 664, 667, 668, 670–674, 682, 683, 685, 689, 760
Gravener, Mrs. Sharnell, 682, 683
Gravestones, 754
Grayhound, a ship (Pearson), 829
Grayhound, a ship (Perkins), 574, 577
Gray, Mrs. Robert, 521, 586
Gray, Robert, 147, 147n (biog.), 521, 586, 620, 663n, 668
Gray, Robert, children of, 521, 586, 620
Gray, Sibella, 521, 586, 620
Great Britain, 158n, 367, 371, 383n, 396n, 446, 535, 537, 662, 722, 747; northward of, 223. *See also* England; Scotland
Great Marlow, borough of, Eng., 418n
Great Market Square (Charleston), 714n
Greaves, Capt., 165
Green, Daniel, 304, 311
Green, John, 213, 304, 305, 311, 312, 546
Greenhill, Richard, 53
Greenleaf, Daniel, 316n
Greenleaf, Stephen, of Boston, 316, 316n (biog.), 695n, 717
Green, Mrs., 213
Green, Young, 460, 583
Gregory, Ranier, 68, 69, 149, 150
Gregory, William, 162, 167, 231, 243, 246, 248–252, 254, 256–264, 270, 280, 319–321, 330, 335, 336, 340–346, 348, 349, 356, 360, 368, 370, 371, 407, 408, 416, 417, 436, 439, 447–449, 462, 464–467, 469–477, 480, 482–484, 486, 517, 530, 545, 546, 578, 590, 603, 620, 621, 632, 794

Grieg, William, 210, 212, 213, 222–225, 229, 230, 238, 260, 269, 380, 467, 576
Gressier, John, 848
Griffin (Griffen), a ship (Sutherland), 282, 284, 295, 544, 551, 553, 554, 559, 563, 570, 571, 574, 575, 674
Griffin, Mr., 178
Grimké, Frederick, 203
Grimké, John Paul, 105n, 314, 314n (biog.)
Grind stones, 117, 216, 220; New Castle, 667, 671, 685, 775
Grocers, 364
Guarda Costa, 382
Guerard, John, 186n
Guernsey, Eng., 69n, 521, 522, 530, 652, 713, 722, 723, 735, 741–743, 763, 775–777, 794, 795, 798, 801, 804
Guichard, Francis, of St. Kitts, 35, 35n (biog.), 36, 68, 69, 150, 631
Guichard, Hubert, of St. Kitts, 68, 68n (biog.), 69, 149, 150, 630, 631
Guinea ships, 16n, 230, 232, 259, 262, 724
Guinea trade, 156, 190, 238, 498, 542
Guinea traders, 701
Gulf of Honduras, 668n, 669, 833n
Gulf of Mexico, 533
Gulix, 31, 82
Gun carriages, 276
Gun flints, 31, 226
Gunpowder, 31, 80, 82, 117, 132, 170, 176, 186, 188, 192, 196, 209, 214, 226, 244, 246, 247, 289, 424, 467, 575, 646, 781, 840; allowance on ballast, 244; glazed, 241; pistol powder, 132; price of, 82, 148, 173, 189, 241, 270, 301, 317; single fine, 545, 776, 780, 783, 785, 788
Guns, 85, 102, 307, 621, 688; carriage, 6; great, 102, 121; Indian trading, 5, 31, 77, 85, 189, 226, 360, 465, 603, 646; naval, 167, 195; price of, 5, 77, 85, 189, 226. *See also* Carabines; Fowling pieces; Muskets; Pistols; Small arms
Gunter, Thomas, of Boston, 489n (biog.), 490, 502, 504, 514, 534, 536, 678, 693, 749, 826
Guyn (Gwyn), Mr., 459n

Habersham, James, 629, 629n (biog.)
Halfhide & Willson, 5

Index

Half thicks, 438
Halifax, Eng., 216, 223
Hall, Enoch, 842, 845
Hallen (Hallin), Samuel, 462, 464, 465, 470, 471, 474, 480, 484–486, 489–493, 496, 497, 501, 505–507, 535, 539, 540, 548, 549, 566, 567, 578, 589, 607, 645, 721
Hall, Peter, 108, 116, 118–120, 123, 124, 180, 181, 190, 257, 262, 546, 565
Hallyburton (Halliburton), William, 538
Halsey & Hanbury, 682, 689, 691, 692, 697–699
Ham, 565
Hamar (Hamor), Joseph, 755, 762, 782
Hamburg, Germany, 64, 66, 73–75, 79, 84, 235, 302, 538, 689–691, 697, 699, 703, 721, 726
Hamburg lines, 31–32, 440
Hamilton, William, 8, 8n (biog.), 315, 324
Hammat (Hamett, Hammett), Benjamin, 195, 316–318, 364, 365
Hammers, 50
Hammerton, John, 370, 370n (biog.), 689–690
Hammock, 533n
Hampers, 250, 262
Ham, Peter, 740, 760, 789, 791, 794
Hampton, Va., 609, 778, 846
Hancock, Mr., 666
Handkerchiefs (Handkes), 31; Barcelona, 82
Handkes. *See* Handkerchiefs
Handles, brass, for saws, 488
Hands. *See* Sailors
Hannah-Bella, a ship (Vaughn), 473
Hanson, Mr., 631–633
Harbor, Charleston, 193n, 332, 530, 643n, 676, 749, 818; Port Royal, 608
Harbour Island, Bahamas, 460, 583
Harding, Thomas, 386, 619
Hardison, John, 765–767
Hardman, John, 181, 181n (biog.)
Hard metal, 59, 298
Hardware. *See* Handles; Hinges; Locks; Nails; Plates; Screws
Hardwareman, 99n
Hardy, Charles, 323, 380, 406, 430, 473, 497, 529, 569, 580–582, 639, 640
Hardy, John, of London, 53, 53n (biog.)
Hardy, John & Co., 53n

Hardy, William, 15
Hare, William, 335, 336, 348
Harramond (Harraman, Haramon), Henry, 222, 225, 230, 296, 299, 303, 313, 315, 322, 410, 582, 583, 614, 732, 733, 821
Harris & Crosshold (Croshole), of London, 314, 323
Harris, Charles, 629n
Harris, Mr., 54
Harrison, Capt., 144
Hartley & Foster, 153
Hartley, Stephen, 826, 826n (biog.)
Harvard College, 316n
Harvests, in Europe, 435, 447. *See also* Rice, harvest; Corn, harvest
Harvey, Robert, 792
Hats, 3, 93, 117, 224, 306; beaver, 61, 97; Beveritt, 783; castor, 783; felt, 31, 107, 218, 424; for Negroes, 218; gold laced, 97, 221; price of, 61, 97, 218, 221, 222
Hatters, 53n
Haurney, Capt., 585
Havana, Cuba, 7, 8, 193, 260n, 380, 518, 528, 530, 533n, 636, 673, 712, 713, 716, 718, 720, 722, 724–726, 728, 731, 733, 755n, 762, 775, 778n, 780–783, 785, 787, 790, 846
Haven, Stephen, 847
Hawding, Thomas, 433
Hawk, a brigantine (Fennell), 533
Hawk, HMS (Bruce, Forrest), 332, 333, 594, 597, 613, 615, 618
Hawkins, Mr., 5
Hawsers, 31
Hay, 644, 666; New England, 66, 95, 176, 196, 214
Hay, Charles, 560, 561
Hayden, James, 634, 635, 637, 646, 741
Hayes & Canham, of London, 339, 339n (biog.), 350, 357, 418, 421, 422
Haynes, Samuel, 295
Hector, a snow (Rodgers), 437n, 574
Hemp, experiments with, 724n
Henderson, James, of Jamaica, 662, 662n (biog.), 759, 763, 768, 808, 810, 814, 816, 821, 831, 843, 846
Henderson, James, of New York, 80, 80n (biog.), 100, 124, 174, 177, 178, 244, 253, 276, 291, 329, 381, 451, 455, 460, 595, 848

Index

Henderson, James, of New York, child of, 595
Henderson, Mr., 831
Henderson, Mrs. James, of New York, 178
Henderson, Walter, 177, 254, 291, 329, 451, 461
Henning, Thomas, 69
Hermitage Stairs (Wapping, London), 20n, 409, 847
Heron, Alexander, 158, 255, 255n (biog.), 260n, 846
Herring, red, 299
Hewlett, John, 519, 520, 655, 659
Hext, John, 379
Heysham, Thomas, 329, 330, 381
Hicks (Hickes), William, of Hamburg, 225, 235, 238, 302
Hides, 410, 533n, 762. *See also* Leather
Hill & Guerard, 51n, 121n, 186, 360, 763
Hill, Humphrey, of London, 15, 15n (biog.), 16, 17, 62, 76, 91, 92, 239, 268, 289, 545, 546
Hill, John, 186n
Hill, Richard, 369, 533, 542, 708
Hilton, Dudley, 750, 751, 755, 779–781, 789, 816, 817, 826
Hilton Head Island, S. C., 296
Hinges, brass, 50, 469; garnet, 50
Hinson, Capt., 625, 627, 802, 803
Hiscox, a ship (Saunders), 121
Hispaniola, W .I., 304
Hitchcock, William, 27, 34
Hoare, Thomas, 439
Hobbs, John, of London, 521, 529–531, 533, 819, 847
Hobcaw, S. C., 473n, 817
Hockely, Mr., 194
Hodge, John, of Jamaica, 42, 43, 126, 134, 191, 321
Hodge, Mrs. John, 191
Hodges, James, 665, 666, 676, 679, 680
Hodshon, Theodorus, of Amsterdam, 85, 85n (biog.), 103, 104, 153, 154
Hodshon, William, of London, 85, 85n (biog.), 103, 104, 153, 155, 165, 197, 635, 643, 661, 704
Hoes, 117, 495; Crowley's best, broad & narrow, 50, 351
Hogg, Robert, 326
Hogs, 10. *See also* Shoats
Hogsheads, 579, 728

Holland, 29n, 66, 73–75, 79, 84, 132, 155, 167, 225, 233, 312, 317, 323, 440, 574, 634, 809
Holland (cloth), 31, 82, 243, 317, 783, 785, 788; fine, 452, 453; price of, in London, 452, 453
Holmes, Ebenezer, 439n
Holmes, Francis, 439n
Holmes, Isaac, 439, 439n (biog.)
Homans, Thomas, 67
Home, Archbald (Archibald), 381, 381n (biog.), 455, 575
Home, James, 369, 370, 372, 377, 379, 381, 382, 418, 438, 451, 452, 455, 575
Home, Mr., 330
Home. *See also* Hume
Honeyman, George, of London, 163, 163n (biog.), 164, 166, 170, 246, 250, 258, 261, 289, 454, 484
Hoop poles, 475
Hoops, 192, 596, 694; iron, 694
Hope, Alexander, 151–154
Hope, a sloop (Branscombe), 95
Hope family, of Amsterdam, 323, 323n (biog.), 382
Hope, Mr., of Cowes, 223
Hopewell, a schooner (Prout, Martin), 385, 386, 394, 413, 414, 416, 609
Hope (White), 61
Hopkinson, Thomas, of Philadelphia, 108, 108n (biog.), 160, 172, 256, 359, 511, 653
Hopton & Smith, 466
Hopton, William, 466n
Horses, 301, 512, 565, 644; carriage, 383; N. C., 710, 711; northern, 66. *See also* Gelding; Stallion
Horsey, Samuel, 18, 51
Hose. *See* Stockings
Hospital ship, 701n
Houghton & Webb, 3
Houghton, John, 3, 3n (biog.), 305, 459n, 479, 498, 521, 641, 805
Houghton, Mary (Sheppard), 479, 479n (biog.)
Houghton, Webb, & Guyn (Gwyn), 459
House. *See* Pringle, Robert, house of
Houston, Mr., 709
Howard, John, 251, 802, 803, 805–807
Howell, James, of New Providence, 297, 297n (biog.)

Index

Howell, John, 303
Howell, Richard, of Howell's Point, 172, 172n (biog.), 393, 394, 415, 511, 610, 653, 847
Howell's Point, Md., 172, 415, 847
Hubbard, Capt., 28
Hubbard, Thomas, of Boston, 669, 675, 689
Huckaback, 31
Huggins, Joseph, of London, 20, 20n (biog.), 64, 67, 98, 207, 208, 211, 256, 262, 847
Huguenots, 350n, 550n, 696n
Hull, 29, 32, 106, 115–117, 139, 140, 214, 217, 223, 228, 237, 287, 295, 302, 310, 311, 314, 323, 324, 332, 336, 337, 339, 349, 351, 352, 354, 356, 357, 365, 370, 395–400, 403, 418–422, 442, 443, 445, 450, 482, 523–525, 589, 593, 594, 600–602, 607, 615, 629, 630, 657, 658, 670–673, 687, 688, 741, 762, 796, 797
Hume, Alexander, 212
Hume, John, 438n, 530, 742, 743, 748, 806, 832
Hume, Peter, 212, 212n (biog.)
Hume. *See also* Home
Humphrey, James, of London, 5, 15, 15n (biog.), 78, 84, 848
Humphrey, Mrs. James, 15, 16
Hunnyford, John, 362
Hunt, Capt., 760, 771, 773, 776, 778
Hunter, James & Co., of London, 7, 7n (biog.), 9, 21, 22, 24, 51, 65, 79, 84, 90, 94, 96, 111, 132, 144, 184, 185, 192, 201, 211, 271, 276, 281, 286, 290, 292, 294, 295, 309, 313, 316, 584, 635, 728, 804, 809
Hunter, James, of London, 656
Hunt, John, 101, 330, 381
Hunt, Joseph, 259n, 273
Hunt, Thomas, 541
Hurricane, 635, 714, 735; at sea, 607; in Antigua, 251; season, 83, 407
Hurthwaite, William. *See* Huthwaite, William
Husks. *See* Breast plates
Hutchins, Joseph, 590–592, 650, 653, 654, 775, 787
Hutchinson & Goldthwait, of Boston, 462, 489, 491, 541, 557, 566, 620, 635, 637, 643, 645, 668, 669, 673, 675, 679, 682, 686, 688–692, 695, 697, 698, 699, 702, 719, 731, 741, 749, 750, 752, 762, 811–813, 818
Hutchinson, Thomas & Co., of Boston, 390, 405, 429, 458, 465, 539, 619
Hutchinson, Thomas, of Boston, 363, 363n (biog.), 373, 375–377, 382, 389, 390, 431, 434, 435, 438, 440, 444, 445, 464, 467, 468, 470, 484, 485, 489, 493, 505, 535, 538–541, 547–549, 567, 616–618, 647, 674, 675, 689–691, 717, 719–722, 726, 753, 763, 789, 793, 812
Huthwaite (Hurthwaite), William, of London, 688, 688n (biog.), 699
Hutson, Capt., 102
Hutting, Ashby. *See* Utting, Ashby

Ils (Iyles), Joseph, 105
Imports, printed account of, 17, 73, 74, 248
Impressment, 10, 206, 491, 492, 529
Imprisonment, false, 581
Independent church. *See* Congregational Church (Charleston)
Independent Companies of Foot, 379, 487, 662. *See also* Troops, S. C.
India goods, 367, 776, 783, 785, 788
Indian goods, 31, 144; demand for, 202. *See also* Blanketing, duffel; Guns, Indian trading; Plains; Strouds
Indian King, a ship (Philips), 775n
Indians, 109n, 588; North American, 218. *See also* Chickasaws; Creeks
Indian trade, 218, 551, 552n, 646, 808; monopoly of, 808n
Indian traders, 131n, 328n, 465, 467, 551, 588n, 628n
Indigo, 512, 545, 779, 804; experiments with, in S. C., 724n; French, 830n; produced in S. C., 740, 762; S. C., quality of, 830; S. C., value of, 834
Industrious Sally, 433
Inglis, Andrew, 250n
Inglis, Capt., 96
Inglis, George, 335n, 407, 407n (biog.), 479, 480, 577, 827, 829, 835
Innes, James, of Cape Fear, 95, 95n (biog.), 159
Inns, Mr., 655, 659, 661
Inoculation, 16n, 26, 28, 33, 38, 44, 56. *See also* Small pox epidemic

Index

Insanity, 521, 607, 714, 722, 736
Instrument of hypothecation. See Certificate of hypothecation
Insurance, 159, 162, 163, 165–167, 184, 202, 204, 207, 257, 261, 313, 322, 348, 350, 353, 356, 361, 373, 374, 380, 381, 396, 422, 438, 454, 456, 462, 468, 470, 471, 477, 483, 484, 487, 493, 501, 506, 520, 539–541, 545, 547, 554, 570, 572–574, 584, 587, 604, 606, 607, 611, 658, 661, 670, 672, 682, 686, 689, 697, 698, 704, 717, 720, 723, 729, 736, 742, 743, 748, 749, 754, 760, 762, 772–774, 776, 777, 789, 795, 804, 812, 823, 831, 836, 841
Insurrections. See Slave insurrections
Interest, 17, 27, 47, 48, 79, 187, 219, 278, 328, 329, 415, 487, 511, 578, 623, 650, 711, 712, 759, 804, 845; rate of, in Ga., 598, 599; rate of, in Eng., 599; rate of, in S. C., 30, 39, 52, 295, 337, 357, 584, 598, 599, 686, 752, 795, 799
Invasion. See Spanish invasion of Ga.; Spanish invasion of S. C.
Inverness, a ship (Comrin), 82n
I'On, Richard, 727, 761, 822n
Ireland, 400, 498, 682n
Iron, bar, price of, 654
Iron mine, 728
Iron monger, 252
Irons, 357
Iron ware, 49, 206, 272, 465. See also Pots, iron
Island of Rattan, on the Mosquito Coast, 833
Isle of May, 215. See also, Salt, Isle of May
Italian Merchant (Smithson), 106, 107, 115, 399–400, 403n

Jacket, 63, 658, 824
Jacks, Capt., 743, 746
Jackson, Capt., 809, 823, 824
Jackson, Challoner, 64
Jackson, Henry, 58, 59
Jail, 299, 351–353, 355, 357, 708, 712, 765, 844
Jamaica Coffee House (London), 761
Jamaica, W. I., 13, 30, 42, 43, 127, 167, 169, 191, 270, 304, 313, 367, 382, 434, 435, 443, 454, 458, 471, 482, 497, 533, 538, 607, 663, 665, 669,
678, 701, 735, 758, 759, 768, 808, 816, 821, 825, 831, 835. See also Kingston; Spanish town
James Island, S. C., 826n
James, John, 600, 706
Japanning, 335
Jars. See Jugs
Jason Galley, a ship (Bartlett), 763n
Jasper, Edward, 27, 64
Jarvis, Elias, 66, 67
Jauncey, Capt., 539, 540, 542
Jeffries, Capt., 447, 517, 518, 530, 533
Jelfe, Andrew, 817, 818, 827
Jenkins' ear, 382. See also War, of Jenkins' Ear
Jenkins, Robert, 382
Jenkins, Thomas, 297
Jenny, a ship (Staples), 530n
Jenny, John, 374, 520
Jenys, Paul, 175, 269, 431, 495
Jenys, Thomas, 541, 543
Jerseys. See New Jersey
Jews, in Ga., 41n; in S. C., 147; "Scotch," 551
John and Edmund, a ship (Coffin), 73n
John and Isabella, a ship (Warden), 270, 280, 281, 289, 294n, 295, 297–299, 303, 308–310, 313, 323, 332–334, 367, 371, 408, 440, 454, 462, 471, 480, 486, 488, 520, 575, 584, 606, 607, 614, 620, 655, 656, 729, 776, 794
John and Jane, a bilander (Ward), 324, 332, 336, 338, 339, 349–353, 355, 356, 370, 398, 421, 602
John and Mary, a sloop (Lillybridge), 380, 382, 438
John and Thomas, a ship (Brooks), 663
John, a snow (Palmer), 363, 373–377, 379, 392, 404, 406, 429, 508, 589, 689, 754
John Gally, a ship (Patterson), 82, 85, 89, 92n, 95, 102–104, 165, 167, 195, 241, 243, 251, 433, 502, 644
Johnson, Capt., 539, 540, 542, 544, 669
Johnson, Mr., 649
Johnson, Thomas, of Barbados, 449, 475, 513, 528, 531, 625
Johnston, Gabriel, 235
Johnston, John, 304, 311, 312, 378, 546
Joiners, 276. See also Carpenters
Joists, 320

Index

Jolliffes Adventure, a ship (Archer), 487, 501, 510, 519, 559, 747
Jolliffe, William, of Poole, 454, 487, 722
Jones & Oliver, 601, 657, 672
Jones, Rebecca (Holmes), 288
Jones, Samuel (Captain), 584
Jones, Samuel, of S. C., 220, 288, 601
Jones, William, & Co., 642
Jopson, Laurence, of Hull, 399n (biog.). *See also* Turner & Jopson
Judges. *See* Assistant judges; Chief Justice; Vice admiralty court, judge of
Jugs, earthen, 579; stone, 605
Juryman, 748
Justice of the peace, in Mass., 432; in S. C., 19n, 100 ,383, 495, 543n

Kay, John. *See* Keys, John
Keets, John, 385
Kegs, 252
Keith, Alexander, 551–554, 559, 563, 564, 570–573, 589, 597, 607, 611, 741
Keith, Capt., 15
Keith, John, of London, 159, 159n (biog.), 363, 373–377, 404, 408, 429, 435, 438, 508, 551, 552, 571, 572, 589, 597, 607, 611, 615, 741, 796
Kellaway, John, 54
Kelsal, (Kellsall, Kelstahl), Roger, 239, 239n (biog.), 577
Kelsal, Roger, Rev., 239, 577
Kelty, Capt., 331
Kendal cottons, 244
Ken, James, 494, 495
Kennan, Henry, 613n, 619, 833
Kent County, Md., 172n
Kettles, 59
Keys, John, 407, 408n, 479, 544, 551
Kilay, Thomas, 702
Kilner, Capt., 685, 686, 716
Kilsworth, a ship (McHugh), 172n
King, Benjamin, 770
King George, a bilander (Ayers), 4n, 58, 64, 166, 187, 208, 228, 332
King George, a ship (Cabbot), 365n
King, Jasper, 623, 623n (biog.)
King's attorney. *See* Attorney-general
King's beam, 166
King's bench, 708
King's share, of contraband, 29n; of silver mine, 588
King's ships, 7, 67, 434, 435, 835; assist
St. Augustine expedition, 134–135, 177, 181, 183, 185–187, 190, 193, 194, 197, 200, 202, 212, 217, 219, 220, 222, 225, 230; on Carolina station, 10, 86, 89, 260, 265, 281, 323, 332, 371, 380, 406, 492, 493, 497, 529, 755, 782, 819–820. *See also* Carolina station; Men of war
Kingston, Jamaica, 626, 735, 759, 768, 810, 814, 816, 843
King St. (Boston), 22n
King's Tree, S. C., 579n
Kinloch, James, 39n
Kingsloe (Kinsloe), Capt., 718, 719, 721, 731
Kirkwall, Orkney Islands, 5n
Kitchingman, Joseph, 654
Knives, clasp, with buckhorn handles, 423; with ivory handles, 423, 473
Knott, Edward, 604
Knox, Capt., 8
Knox, Andrew, 52, 84, 94, 95, 112, 113, 132, 144, 201
Kolleck, Philip. *See* Collock, Philip

Laborers, 498
Lace, 515, 653, 675, 785; bone, 440, 545, 788; gold, 63, 783, 785, 788; price of, 440; silver, 783, 785, 788
Lace merchants, 6n
Lacy, Samuel, 157
Ladd, Capt., 836
Laffitte, Capt., 838
Lake, Thomas, 837
Lamb, Capt., 227n
Lamboll, Thomas, 418, 418n (biog.), 497, 563, 837
Land, 72, 299; grants in Ga., 171n; grants in S. C., 42n, 47n; improvements on, 126; plat of, 125; price of, 42; title of, 125
Land Bank of 1740 (Mass.), 696n
Landlady, 288, 456, 457
Lane & Smethurst, of London, 115, 118, 119, 130
Lane, Smethhurst & Caswall, of London, 200, 204, 211, 286, 300
Lane, Thomas, of London, 115n (biog.)
Langdon, Samuel, 262, 273
Langstaff, Bethel, 817–819
Lappits, 440
Lard, hogs', 723

Index

Lark, a snow (Knox), 84, 94, 111, 132, 201
La Roche, Daniel, 673, 673n (biog.).
Lascelles & Maxwell, 823n
Lascelles, Henry & Co., of London, 823, 825
Lascelles, Henry, of London, 186, 186n (biog.), 823
La Sendre, a ship (Seguinard), 755n, 762, 775, 782, 796, 823
Lasserre, William, 89, 98, 228, 295
Latter (Letter), Mrs., 813, 814
Laurel, 829; Carolina Laurel cherry, 829n; mountain laurel, 829n
Laurens, Henry, 27n, 42n, 418n
Lavenham, Eng., 574
Lavers, Hercules, 632, 633
Lavington, Samuel, 44, 44n (biog.), 45, 70–72, 107, 122
Lavington, William, 44, 72
Lawrence, a snow (Crossthwaite), 437n
Laws (Law), David, 503
Laws, of S. C., 105, 599. *See also* individual acts
Laws of the Province of South Carolina, 262
Laws, William, 143n
Law, the, 731, 756
Lawyers, 51n, 108n, 369, 370, 555, 619, 688n, 700, 708, 755, 805, 808, 834; fees, 47, 48, 328, 329, 414, 705; in Nevis, 847; in Philadelphia, 847; RP's, 442
Leacraft, William, 12, 727
Leapidge, Edward, 456, 457, 468, 497–500, 544
Leapidge, John, 468
Leapidge, Mrs. Edward, 457
Leather, price of, in Jamaica, 843; red, 533n; tanned, 346, 348, 475, 536, 537, 808, 810, 814, 816, 821. *See also* Hides
LeBay, James, 521
LeBrasseur, Ann (Splatt), 78, 78n (biog.), 272n, 285
LeBrasseur, Francis, 78, 78n (biog.), 79, 285, 286
Lee's Court (St. Catharine's, London), 847
Lee, Edward, 122, 123, 183, 668
Leeward Islands, 310, 321, 323, 517, 804, 816. *See also* Anguilla; Antigua; Montserrat; Nevis; St. Kitts

Lefebure (Lefebore), John, 96, 102
Leith, Scotland, 6
LeMarchant, Mr., 69, 70
Leman, John, 354, 361, 362, 368, 371, 437
Lemons, 182, 677, 747; fresh, 586
Lempriere, Clement, 822n
Lennox, James, 365, 365n (biog.)
Leopard, a snow (Homans), 67
Les Deaux Amis, a schooner (Laffitte), 837–839, 841, 843
Lessende, Mr., 20
Lesslie, George, 595
Lessly, Andrew, of Antigua, 42, 42n (biog.), 125, 128, 133, 136, 191, 237, 238, 244, 252, 281, 320–322, 335, 343, 348, 356, 370, 447, 503, 516, 578, 589, 624, 632, 705, 763, 770, 774, 784, 787, 788, 847
Lester, Capt., 661
Letter of administration, 105
Letter of advice, 27, 45, 58, 63, 111, 112, 118, 119, 156, 229, 286, 287, 293, 309, 314, 323, 350, 353, 357, 456, 467, 541, 543, 559, 560, 575, 634
Letter of attorney. *See* Power of attorney
Letter of credit, 45
Letter of dismission, 544n
Letter of license. *See* License, for debtors
Letter of marque, 134, 184, 185; effect of, on price of freight, 195
Letter of recommendation, 455–457, 497, 499, 545
Letters of reprisal, 134
Levy, Simpson, of London, 40, 40n (biog.), 41, 87, 109, 313
Lewis, David, 669, 726, 731–734, 752
Lewis (Francis), 611
Leyden, University of, 126n
Leyton, Eng., 591n
Library, 82n. *See also* Books; Charleston Library Society
License, 29n; for debtors, 20, 54, 115, 199; to ship rice south of Cape Finesterre, 454, 472, 487, 773, 796; to ship rice to Portugal, 737, 831, 835
Liddall, Capt., 567, 568, 570
Lieutenant governor, of Antigua, 11n., 830; of S. C., 239n, 265n; of Va., 66n. *See also* Governor, acting, of S. C.
Lightfoot, John, 770, 784, 793, 824

Index

Lightwood, Edward, 563, 638, 666
Lignum vitae, 54
Lillybridge, John, 380, 382
Lime juice, 683, 716, 786, 810, 841
Limerick, Ireland, 131
Limes, 71, 108, 179, 182, 369; price of, 46
Lime St. (London), 32n
Lindsay (Lindesay, Lindsey), John, 256, 512
Linen, 10, 21, 22, 24, 25, 31, 51, 52, 63n, 66, 79, 90, 105, 132, 144, 154, 176, 201, 214, 225, 330, 479, 592, 633, 724; checked, 157, 164, 189, 258, 259, 776 (¾), 776 (yardwide), 783, 785, 788, 834; coarse, 816; price of, 164, 243, 331, 846; Russian, 31; Scotch, 202, 246; sheeting, 31, 55. *See also* Checks
Linen draper, 55n
Lion, the, 43n
Lipelly, Capt. *See* Pollie, Capt.
Liquors, 250, 277; spirituous, 736
Lisbon, Portugal, 74, 78, 79, 159, 175, 188, 192, 210n, 247, 270, 313n, 453, 455, 459, 461, 472, 489, 493, 501, 520, 521, 538, 541, 575, 585, 586, 614, 623, 747–749, 754, 760, 769, 789
Lithgow, William, of New Brunswick, 325, 325n (biog.), 384, 847
Live Oak, 105n
Liverpool, Eng., 30, 181, 184, 257, 262
Livestock. *See* Ducks; Fowl; Geese; Hogs; Horses; Shoats; Turkeys
Livie, Alexander, 364, 507
Livingston, John, of New York, 648, 648n (biog.), 655, 727, 738, 743, 767, 768, 846
Livingston, Mr., 382
Livingston, William, 521n, 663n
Lloyd, Edward, 847
Lloyd, John, 115n
Lloyd, Peter, of Philadelphia, 109, 109n (biog.), 160, 256, 359
Lloyd's Coffee House (London), 546
Lloyd, Thomas, 663, 663n (biog.)
Logwood, 30, 86, 141, 162, 166, 217, 314, 421, 544, 602, 605, 606, 663, 668, 674, 675, 682, 691, 697, 699, 703, 726; price of, 6, 32, 242, 317, 687; price of, in London, 686, 689, 697
Loadstone, 212

Locks, brass, 469; stock, 50. *See also* Padlock
London, a ship (Russell, Reid), 383, 385, 386, 401, 402, 405, 408, 409, 413, 415, 418, 753
London Bridge, 53n
London Frigate, 16n
London Packet (McHugh), 313
Long, Adam, 294, 295, 299, 309, 584
Longboat, ship's, 800
Long, Jonathan, 270, 271
Loo, HMS (Utting), 587, 592, 595, 608, 662, 740
Louisbourg, Cape Breton Island, 820n
Louisiana, 488
Lovell, Michael, of Antigua, 43, 43n (biog.), 46, 70, 72, 108, 119, 124, 149, 181, 189, 267, 283, 289, 319, 322, 344, 345, 347, 356, 360, 370, 448, 515, 578, 591, 633, 723, 756, 763, 766, 767, 783
Lovell, Mrs. Michael, 268
Lowder, Samuel, 311, 314
Loyal Judith, a ship (Lemon), 437n
Loyall Judith, a snow (Drummond), 267, 268, 321, 370, 447, 516, 589, 590, 632, 705, 784, 785
Loyal William, a brigantine (Anderson), 636n
Lucas family, 518, 830
Lucas, George, Jr., 724, 725, 764, 783
Lucas, George, of Antigua, 11, 11n (biog.), 126, 128, 134, 340, 518, 724, 725, 830
Lucas, John, 11n
Lucy, a bilander (Lindsay), 512n
Ludlow, Lambert, of London, 455, 456, 467, 473, 543, 545, 559, 560, 585, 759
Lumbard St. (London), 819n, 847
Lumber, 134, 136, 319–322, 336, 341, 342, 348, 362, 416, 436, 438, 450, 475, 476, 632, 669. *See also* Wood
Lumsdaine, Capt., 307, 309, 310
Lusher, Capt., 81, 84
Lusitania, a ship (Gravener), 475, 476, 513, 528, 529, 545, 624, 625, 627, 638, 661, 666–668, 670–674, 685, 760, 775
Luttrell, Richard, 303
Lye days, 210, 290, 324, 325, 332, 337, 829. *See also* Charter party

Index

McCallister, John, 134, 134n (biog.), 143, 848
McClean (Macklellan, McClellan, M'Clellan), John, 437, 494, 530, 534
McCulloch, Henry, 293, 293n (biog.), 298
McCulloch, Henry, family of, 298
McDaniel, Hugh, 680, 702, 704
McDonald, Adam, of Frederica, 252, 452, 453, 494
McDonald, Mr., 761
McDowall (Mack Dowell), James, of N. C., 143, 235, 277, 297, 328, 383, 411, 483, 522, 555, 711, 765
Mcfarland, Mr., 808
McGillivray, Archibald, 808
McGillivray, Archibald & Co., 808n
Machannis, Capt., 411, 419
McHugh (Mackew), Patrick, 172, 313, 332
McIver (McIvar), John, 579, 580, 600, 623
Mackay (Mackey), Æneas, 644, 656, 661, 662, 664, 670, 844
Mackay, Mr., 316, 500
Mackay, Mrs. William, 792, 806, 844
Mackay, William, family of, 792, 806
Mackay, William, of Cape Fear, 791, 791n (biog.), 806, 844
Mackellan, Capt., 670
Mackellan (McClellan, M'Clellan), John. *See* McClean, John
Mackenzie (McKensey), Alexander, of Hampton, 609, 778, 846
Mackenzie (McKenzie), Capt., 495, 687, 700, 707–709, 722, 723
MacKenzie (McKenzie), George, of Cowes, 223, 477, 828
McKenzie, John, 12n, 194
McKenzie, Serjeant, 40, 41
Mackew, Patrick. *See* McHugh, Patrick
Mackord, Mr., 148
Mackrae, Capt., 286, 287
Madeira, 7, 8, 29, 34, 50, 95, 116, 117, 158, 159, 163, 186, 289, 295, 363n, 373, 374n, 375–377, 498, 508, 511, 527, 551, 552, 571, 572, 597, 613, 624, 674, 829, 835
Magazine, powder, 317, 840
Magazines, monthly, 438
Magistrate. *See* Justice of the peace
Magnolia, 829n

Maid, Mr., 267
Maintru, (Maintree, Maintrue), James & Co., 61, 93, 221, 224, 305, 327, 478
Maitland, Richard, of London, 342, 342n (biog.)
Malbone, Evan, 316, 389
Maltby, Anthony, 403
Manchester, Eng., 395n
Manchester goods, 351, 480, 629; price of, 395
Manesty, Joseph, of Liverpool, 181, 181n (biog.)
Manigault, Gabriel, 550, 550n (biog.), 758, 805
Manson, Mr., 356
Marblehead, Mass., 279n
March, a sloop (Conyers), 758, 759
Margaret and Mary, a sloop (Morgan), 291n
Margaret, a ship (Dillon), 246n
Mariners. *See* Sailors
Marital infidelity, 252n
Market, Antigua, 321; Boston, 365; European, 320, 330, 405; foreign, 34, 52, 66, 408, 498; Holland, 225; Hull, 421; Jamaica, 810; Lisbon, 73, 439, 459, 487, 612, 769, 811, 847; London, 144, 225, 313, 401, 550, 732n; Oporto, 622, 623, 769, 847; Portuguese, 408, 538, 655
Market (S. C.), 831; for bread, 323; for cloth, 82; for gunpowder, 192; for limes, 46; for molasses, 68, 69, 86; for Negroes, 182, 190, 284, 716; for rum, 86, 238, 284, 504, 618, 717, 720; for sugar, 284, 618, 684, 825; for wines, 30, 284; pitch, 714, 720; rice, 60–62, 102, 245, 257, 258, 261, 293, 316, 319, 322, 324, 325, 331, 371, 416, 421, 433, 436, 443, 445, 446, 590, 592, 594, 595, 597, 601, 604, 606, 743, 746, 750, 769
Mark Lane (Crutched Friars, London), 282n, 314n, 823n
Marquand, Capt., 245
Marr, Timothy, 420, 460
Marshall, Charles, 560, 678
Marshal, David, 810, 814, 816, 843
Marshall, John, of Cape Fear, 218, 234, 397, 419, 450, 523, 594
Marshall, the, 581, 844
Martin, Capt., 336

Index

Martin, Mr., 305
Martin, Samuel, 385, 386, 413–416
Martin, William, 41
Martyrs, the (Las Martyrs), Fla., 662
Marvin, William. *See* Mervin, William
Mary, a brigantine (Chapman), 460n
Mary, a brigantine (Mason), 274
Mary Ann, a ship (Webber), 269n
Mary Anne, a ship (Shubrick), 94
Mary, a sloop (Marshall), 814
Mary, a sloop (Schermerhorn), 461n
Mary, a snow (Ougier), 592n
Mary Gally, a ship (Nicolson), 102, 112, 113, 132, 165
Maryland, 172, 385, 393, 394, 413, 415, 846, 847
Maryland, a snow (Langdon), 262n
Mary (Nicolson), 234
Mason, John, 234, 274, 372, 652, 791
Mason, Samuel, 647
Master, of a vessel, 249–250, 252n, 277, 302, 326, 333n, 350, 367, 382, 386, 413, 417, 461, 473n, 570, 575, 586, 596, 605, 608, 635, 644, 669, 675, 708, 723, 743, 761, 763, 784, 813, 825, 846; freight privileges of, 800, 801; wages of, 463, 794–795, 800, 801. *See also* Officers, of the Royal Navy
Masts, 250, 298, 835, 837; fore, 323; main, 323, 385, 607; mizzen, 323
Mate, of a vessel, 162, 207, 248, 252, 263, 265, 302, 351, 353, 357, 361, 385, 440, 461, 666, 680, 714, 736, 743, 759, 777, 795; wages of, 799
Mathews (Matthew, Mathew), a mariner, 248, 252, 263
Mathews, James, 314, 314n (biog.), 395
Maubray, Arthur. *See* Mowbray, Arthur
Mauduit (Manduet), Jasper, of London, 32, 32n (biog.), 77, 111, 112, 576, 578
Manduit, Jasper & Co., 32n
Maxwell, James, 588n
May-flower, a sloop (Peat), 326n
Mayne, Edward, of Lisbon, 73n (biog.), 210n, 439, 559, 585
Mayne, Edward & John & Co., of Lisbon, 73, 173, 186, 188, 245, 247, 270, 454, 455, 467, 487, 501, 509, 510, 520, 538, 541, 612, 614, 635, 688
Mayne, Edward & John & Edward Burn, of Lisbon, 458, 461, 472, 510, 559, 585, 612, 623, 677, 746–49, 760, 769, 811
Mayne, John, of Lisbon, 73n (biog.), 210n, 439
May River, S. C., 296
Mazyck, Isaac, 350, 350n (biog.)
Measures, wooden, half bushel, 508
Medcalf, William, 610
Medicine, practice of, 171n, 543. *See also* Physicians; Surgeon
Medley, Jonathan, of London, 3, 55, 56, 75, 110, 487
Memorandum, 55–57, 267
Memorial, on 1740 fire, 272; on silver mine, 588
Men of war, British, 29, 292, 690; French 304; Spanish, 260, 668n. *See also* King's ships
Merchants, British, of Amsterdam, 85n, 323n; of Antigua, 42, 43n, 347, 766, 767, 847; of Barbados, 325n, 345n, 346, 418n, 766, 847; of Belfast, 847; of Black River, Mosquito Coast, 833n, 846; of Boston, 5n, 20n, 22n, 81n, 177, 216, 278, 316n, 373, 376, 421, 439n, 489n, 522, 569n, 691, 765, 767–768; of Bristol, 105, 153n, 171n, 431, 552n, 848; of Charleston, 3n, 23n, 29n, 41, 47n, 51n, 83n, 86n, 89n, 105, 156n, 171, 175n, 176, 179, 181, 183–185, 187n, 190, 193, 200, 210n, 216, 219, 269, 287, 288, 298, 304, 305, 308–310, 312n, 323, 335n, 365n, 438n, 439n, 466n, 488, 497n, 498n, 521n, 533, 547n, 550, 552n, 569, 613, 636, 639, 640n, 663n, 689n, 696n, 700, 706, 708, 761, 797, 808, 833; of Edentown, 142n, 380n, 382; of England, 492, 497, 498, 588, 708; of Ga., 387; of Georgetown, 673n; of Guernsey, 70n, 270, 526n; of Hamburg, 225, 235n, 238, 682, 692, 698; of Hull, 29n, 106n, 116n, 118, 119, 137, 287n, 395n, 399n; of Kingston, 626n, 846; of Limerick, 127n, 130; of Lisbon, 73; of Liverpool, 181n, 190; of London, 4n, 6n, 7n, 9n, 10, 15n, 20n, 27n, 32n, 40n, 51n, 85n, 86n, 107n, 111, 116, 118, 123, 124, 142, 155, 159n, 186n, 216, 219, 223, 224, 229, 265, 266, 270, 286, 300, 303, 310, 314n, 339n, 346, 350n,

Index

357, 375, 385, 412, 431n, 455, 483, 488, 490, 515, 522, 527, 550, 639n, 648, 651, 667, 672, 691, 737, 757, 759, 765–767, 770, 773, 777, 783, 798, 799, 801, 847, 848; of Madeira, 29n, 95n, 846; of New England, 421n; of Newport, 86n, 717n, 767, 768, 847; of New York, 80n, 648n, 744n, 767, 768, 846, 848; of North Carolina, 148, 433; of Oporto, 622, 847; of Pamplico, 142n, 148, 848; of Philadelphia, 19, 27n, 108, 514n; of Rotterdam, 358n, 641, 847, 848; of St. Kitts, 12n, 68n, 765, 767, 847; of Savannah, 69n, 153n; of Southhampton, 367; of Wilmington, 296n; orange, of London, 742; West India, of London, 268n, 342n, 431n, 549n, 591n
Mercy, a ship (Wright), 269n, 313, 315, 322, 417, 453, 458, 463
Meredith, Capt., 286, 287
Mermaid (Willson), 51
Merrimack, a sloop (Donovan), 760, 764, 774, 775, 782, 784, 785, 787, 788, 802, 838
Mervin (Marvin), William, 237, 302
Meshard (Miznard), Stephen, 634, 656, 658–661
Messlin, George, 565
Metcaff, Messrs., 225
Metcalf, family, 538
Merriweather, William, 20
Michie, Kenneth, 433, 434, 797, 797n (biog.), 830–832, 835
Middleton, Arthur, 418, 418n (biog.)
Middleton, Henry, 418, 418n (biog.)
Middleton, William, 418, 418n (biog.)
Midnight, a sloop (Barnes), 719
Midway, (Hunt), 259n
Midwifery, 544
Miles Lane (London), 163n
Militia, in Antigua, 591n; in New Hanover, 95n
Millechamp, Timothy, 544, 544n (biog.), 550
Milner, Jeremiah, 47, 47n (biog.), 48, 148
Minas, Abraham. *See* Minis, Abraham
Mincing Lane (London), 9n
Minerva, a ship (Cload), 312n, 417, 418, 436, 439–442, 453, 549, 562,
564, 571, 574
Minerva (Meredith), 287
Mines. *See* Iron mine; Silver mine
Minet, Mr., 142
Minett, William, 497, 550
Minis (Minas), Abraham, of Savannah, 40n, 41, 41n (biog.), 87
Minis & Salomons, 41
Minis, Philip, 41n
Minister. *See* Clergyman; Missionary; Rector
Ministry (British), 230, 231; change in, 362–363, 366, 367, 371, 379; effect on trade, 366, 367, 371
Minson, John, 339n
Miscarriage, 705
Missing, Capt., 122
Missionary, 549n
Mitchell, William, 847
Mississippi River, 121, 488, 755n
Mitford, Mr., 761
Miznard, Stephen. *See* Meshard, Stephen
Moidore, 247
Molasses, 11, 23, 31, 45, 68, 69, 86, 87, 114, 145, 149, 150, 301, 507, 699n, 810; price of, 87, 125, 150, 151, 201, 242, 268, 508, 626, 631
Mollo, David, 252
Molly, a schooner (Frazer), 806
Moncreif, George, 133, 136
Money, ready, 52, 481, 485, 504, 507, 634, 636, 637, 646, 729; scarcity of, 530; silver, 681. *See also* Cash; Currency
Monro (Monroe), Capt., 616, 676, 677
Montiano, Manoel de, 815
Montrose, a ship (Nicolson), 22, 142, 155, 209, 214
Montserrat, W. I., 267, 713
Moon, Alexander, 495
Moone, Mr., 298
Moony, Mr., 756
Moore & Hurthwait, of London, 699, 807, 808, 834
Moore, Daniel, 418, 418n (biog.), 474, 497, 563, 837
Moore, John, 418n
Moore, Mary, 158
Moore, Rebecca (Axtell), 418n
Moore, William, of London, 688, 688n (biog.), 699
Morgan, Benjamin, 178, 254, 291

Index

Morley, George, 369, 370
Morson, Thomas, of London, 55, 55n (biog.), 56, 110, 487
Mortgage, 299, 731
Mosquito Coast, 833n, 846
Moss, Capt., 655
Moths, 33, 525
Motte, Jacob, 378, 550
Mouncie, Mr., 294
Mowbray (Maubray), Arthur, 479, 521, 521n (biog.)
Mowbray, Mary (Stanyarn), 521n
Moyer, Moses, 303, 309
Mulryne, Capt., 713, 725
Murphy, Capt., 654, 655, 670, 674
Murray, Alexander, 709, 709n (biog.), 830, 833, 834
Murray, John, 191, 192, 242, 297, 326, 410, 419, 447, 448, 449, 451, 515–518, 556, 582, 589, 590, 592, 653
Muskets, 43, 45, 334, 358, 386, 420, 460, 583, 656; guinea trade, 189; price of, 333
Musketto Shoar. *See* Mosquito Coast
Mutiny, 666; in Ga., 43, 45

Nails, 117, 261, 272, 367, 480; clasp, 31, 50, 351, 424; sheathing, 371
Nairne, Capt., 306
Nancy, a schooner (Marr), 460n
Napkins, 31
Nassau, Bahamas, life in, 293n. *See also* New Providence
Naval office, 571
Naval officer, Barbados, 786; Charleston, 709, 786
Naval stores, 6, 102, 320, 334–335, 341, 347, 350, 579, 722, 736, 742, 782; demand for, 140, 714, 782, 783, 785; prices of, 750, 764, 774, 781, 800, 803, 817–819, 827, 837–839, 845; quality of, 787. *See also* "An act to prevent frauds..."; Pitch; Rosin; Tar; Turpentine
Nazareth, a brigantine (Bennett), 374n
Negroes, 12, 26, 35, 37, 38, 42, 44, 52, 56, 71, 122, 153, 175, 186, 194, 206, 241, 247, 263, 267, 274, 283, 490, 498, 599, 656, 681, 683, 684, 708, 716, 731, 755, 756, 763, 786, 804, 808, 841; cargoes of, 19, 51, 295; clothing, 31, 218, 244; plantation, 840; price of, 247, 282, 284, 469, 751; sales of, 51, 259, 282, 284, 512. *See also* Duty, on slaves; Guinea ships; Guinea trade; Guinea traders; Slave insurrections; Slave trade; Slave traders; Weather, effect on slaves
Nevis, W. I., 847
New Brunswick, N. C., 325, 384, 419, 792, 847
Newcastle upon Tyne, Eng., 662, 664, 666, 682
Newcomin (Newcomen), William, 278, 279
New Court (Broad St., London), 350n
Newell, Andrew, 104–107, 109–112
Newell, Ebenezer, Jr., of Boston, 696, 696n (biog.)
Newell, Ebenezer, Sr., 696, 696n (biog.)
New England, 215, 236, 279n, 301, 421n, 446, 516, 616, 622, 769; goods of, 81. *See also* Boston
Newfoundland, 614
New Hanover, N. C., 95n
New Jersey, 418, 575
New London, 28, 34
Newnan (Newnham), James, 730, 737, 740, 741
Newport, R. I., 86, 87, 113, 137, 144, 145, 178, 242n, 717, 779, 780, 816, 826
New Providence, Bahamas, 125, 170, 171, 212, 246, 261, 270, 280, 294, 295, 297, 298, 303, 304, 308, 333, 334, 357, 386, 420, 460, 523, 543, 559–561, 583, 585, 614, 615, 620, 628, 656, 662n, 678, 681, 684, 716, 722, 727, 759, 813, 815, 818, 841
New South Sea Company, 640n
Newspapers, from West of Eng., 790; London, 15, 17, 85, 181, 237, 544, 690, 797. *See also* South-Carolina Gazette; Virginia Gazette
Newton, John, of London, 27, 27n (biog.), 53–55, 75
Newton, Samuel, of St. Kitts, 12, 35–38
New York, 4, 5, 8, 10, 16, 17, 21, 25, 26, 29, 34, 50, 51, 53, 64, 66, 73, 74, 79, 80, 82, 88, 101, 102, 124, 158, 168, 173, 177, 178, 180, 195, 244, 253, 254, 276, 289, 291, 301, 323, 329, 330, 365n, 381, 451, 460, 461n, 502–505, 507, 508, 512, 515, 534–536,

Index

587, 595, 596, 634, 648, 655, 660, 691, 727, 731, 738, 742–744, 752, 778, 796
New York Coffee House (London), 660
Nicholas, George, 839
Nickleson, Shubrick & Co., 162, 371
Nickleson, John, of London, 162n (biog.), 440, 584, 634, 636, 639, 655, 728, 746, 748, 803, 804, 809
Nicolson, Capt., 65, 67, 155
Nicolson (Nicholson, Nickleson), James, 6, 6n (biog.), 7, 14, 22, 40, 55, 57, 102, 103, 112, 120, 128, 132, 142, 165, 188, 197, 203, 209, 213, 233, 234, 242, 243, 251, 644, 662, 664
Nightingale, a sloop (Barnes), 276
Nisbett, Alexander, 169, 169n (biog.)
Nisbett, Mary (Rutherford), 169n
Non-pareils, 10, 773, 775, 788
Non so pretties, 31
Normans, 743
Norris, Isaac, of Philadelphia, 161, 161n (biog.)
Northabout, 265, 682, 692, 697, 836
Northallerton, borough of, Eng., 823n
North America, 99, 838; struggle for, 396n. *See also* America
Northamptonshire, Eng., 3n
North Carolina, 143, 148, 218, 219, 235, 278, 296n, 302, 326, 328, 380, 382, 411, 416, 433, 438, 523, 556, 610, 650, 764. *See also individual towns*
North Carolina Station (Cape Fear), 663n
Northforeland, 244
Northward [*colonies*]. *See* Colonies, northern
Notary, 305; public, 493
Note, 36, 69, 146, 151, 158, 171, 194, 255, 328, 372, 407, 451, 467, 512, 541, 596, 607n, 713, 764, 765, 766, 792. *See also* Bond

Officers, military, 90, 298; of the Royal Navy, 281, 380, 492, 497, 569, 595, 608, 640, 662, 709, 740, 742, 790; Spanish, 663, 668, 726, 846
Ogelvie, Robert, 57
Ogilvie, James, 387, 387n (biog.), 404, 407, 408, 435, 553, 597, 803
Ogle, Sir Chaloner, 663, 663n (biog.)
Oglethorpe, James Edward, 29, 29n (biog.), 33, 34, 40n, 42n, 43, 45, 121, 158, 169, 170, 175, 177, 181, 183, 184, 186, 187, 190, 193, 194, 197, 200, 216, 219, 220, 222, 228, 230, 231, 232, 248, 266, 268, 332, 387, 389, 390, 392, 396, 397, 399, 400, 404, 406, 407, 409, 414, 430, 435, 441, 443, 445, 468n, 480, 487n, 495, 541, 543, 577, 586, 598, 614, 649, 655, 661, 846
Oglethorpe's Regiment. *See* Forty-second regiment of foot
Oil, 306; Florence, 31, 221, 224, 605, 776, 780, 781, 783, 785, 789; linseed, 31, 424; price of, 221; salad, 82; train, 645
Old Church St., (Charleston), 714n
Old Tom's Coffee House (London), 848
Olive Branch, a sloop (Hilton), 779–781
Oliver, Capt., 817–820
Oliver, Richard, of Antigua, 591, 591n (biog.), 770, 771, 773, 783
Oliver, Thomas, 601n (biog.), 657
Olives, 605
Olive trees, 747
Oporto, Portugal, 73, 74, 250, 322, 331, 454, 612–614, 623, 634, 769, 771, 789, 796
Oranges, 742–745, 750, 753, 754, 842n; exported, 732, 739, 742, 747, 751, 778; European, 732; from the islands, 819; price of, 732; price of, in Philadelphia, 819; produced in S. C., 253, 732, 739, 786; Seville, 732; sour, 732; West Indian, 732
Orange trees, 732, 739, 742, 751, 778
Orkney Islands, 5n
Orr, Elizabeth Isabella (Scott), 188
Orrock, Capt., 104, 109–112
Orr, William, 57, 58, 188, 188n (biog.)
Osborn, Bruning, 847
Osborn (Osborne) & Oxnard, of Boston, 490, 502, 504, 514, 534, 536, 678, 693, 749, 826
Osborn, Jeremiah, 812, 826, 827, 845, 846
Osborn, John, of Boston, 489n (biog.), 781
Osmond, James, 521n, 689, 689n (biog.), 701, 707, 709
Osmond, James, family of, 689
Osmond, Mrs. James, 706

Index

Osnaburg (Osnabrig, Ozenbrigg), 31, 60, 93, 202, 227, 244, 252, 351, 424, 545, 729, 776, 783
Oswald, Mr., 162
Ougier, Peter, 592, 783, 784
Outlaws, in N. C., 219
Out ports, 215, 264, 288, 422, 498, 602, 801. See also Bristol; Cowes; Dover; Falmouth; Guernsey; Halifax; Hull; Liverpool; Newcastle-upon Tyne; Poole; Portsmouth; Southampton; Topsham
Overcharge, 54
Overseer, 239n, 474, 575
Ownership, of Vessels, 6, 7, 9, 22, 35, 36, 38, 52, 62, 66, 73–76, 79–82, 86, 90, 94, 95, 102–104, 112–114, 123, 129–130, 132, 142, 143, 164, 167, 187, 195, 207, 208, 226–228, 240, 243–245, 251, 254, 261, 265, 270, 311, 313, 317, 321–323, 331, 334, 345–347, 353, 356, 358, 364, 368, 370, 376, 382, 385, 407, 413, 414, 420, 433, 441, 447, 463, 466, 474, 475, 481, 486, 489n, 490, 491, 493, 494, 496, 501, 506, 507, 514, 516, 520, 522, 529, 533, 538, 539, 541, 549, 551, 553, 554, 557–559, 563, 566, 570, 571, 574, 575, 589, 590, 593, 607, 611, 614, 616, 620, 633, 638, 642, 655, 657, 658, 661, 662, 664, 666, 667, 669, 671, 674, 676, 679, 681, 690–692, 703, 715, 716, 719, 721, 722, 726, 730, 731, 735, 736, 742, 743, 752, 764, 775, 776, 794, 795, 801, 825, 833, 835, 836
Oxnard, Thomas, of Boston, 489n (biog.). See also Osborn & Oxnard
Ozenbrigg. See Osnaburg
Ozmond, Dr., 51

Packaging, 249, 338
Padlock, 50
Pails, wooden, 508
Painted bunting. See Non-pareils
Painter, 417, 468
Painter (Paynter), Richard, 26, 39
Painter's colours, 424
Paints, 62, 117
Palatine, of S. C., 39
Palatines, 249, 498. See also Germans
Palatine ships, 430, 791

Palatine trade, 498
Palmer, George, 363, 364, 373–379, 390, 392, 404–406, 429, 432, 435, 437, 438, 589, 597, 607, 682, 686, 689–692, 697, 698, 702, 703, 726, 754
Palsy, 62
Pamphlets, 237
Pamplico, N. C., 142
Panama, 773n
Panther, a ship (Hodges), 665, 666, 676, 679
Paper, brown, 31; Dutch, 380; price of, 380; writing, 31, 84, 380, 424, 614. See also Stationery
Pare, Edward, of Barbados, 683, 716, 786, 802, 807, 823, 825, 840
Parish, a charge of, 270, 271; at Roxbury, (Mass.), 696n; business, 271; Christ Church, 177n, 190n; country, 239; of Clifton (Eng.), 4n; of Stow (Scotland), 62n; Prince Frederick, 579, 600n, 623; records of, 239; St. Andrew's, 494n, 740n; St. Helena's, 255n, 494n, 500n; St. James Goose Creek, 26n, 212n; St. James Santee, 19; St. John's (Antigua), 122n; St. Thomas, 383, 826n. See also Churchwarden; Rector; Vestry; Vestryman
Parker, Daniel, 777
Parker, Joseph, 455, 456, 543, 559
Parker's Ferry, S. C., 494
Parks, William, 172n, 847
Parliament, grant to Ga., 649; members of, 29n, 158n, 418n, 690n, 823n
Parham Pink, a ship (Alloway), 387n
Parmyter, Capt., 7
Parr, John, of Liverpool, 181, 257, 258, 262
Partington, George, 289
Partners, 3n, 12n, 115n, 116n, 126n, 128n, 158n, 162n, 186n, 259n, 305, 313, 420, 431n, 433n, 438n, 458, 464, 467, 480, 507, 530, 540, 547n, 548, 585, 619, 629n, 634, 641, 688, 689n, 708, 728, 747n, 833
Partnership, 71, 124, 350n, 828; indenture of, 262. See also Pringle, Robert, partnership, with Inglis; with Reid
Partridge, Freeman, 848
Partridge, Richard, of London, 463, 463n (biog.), 465, 471, 489–491, 493, 496, 501, 506, 578, 589

Index

Passage, 129, 134, 146, 174, 177, 185, 196, 206, 210, 243, 250, 263, 294, 298, 319, 323, 370, 404, 416, 436, 444, 449, 502, 530, 549, 564, 581, 583, 607, 644, 662, 709, 741, 773, 797, 815, 835, 839, 843; 7 weeks from Lisbon, 747; 38 days from Cowes, 173; winter, 140

Passengers, 95, 116, 173, 240, 263, 297, 332, 333, 382, 408, 441, 479, 489, 498, 499, 519, 520, 531, 533, 587, 593, 613, 640, 647, 662, 663, 701, 709, 808, 835; French, 369

Patterson, John, 65, 67, 82–85, 88–91, 93–95, 98, 102–104, 112, 165, 166, 196, 243, 249, 258, 493, 496, 498, 563

Patton, William, 313, 323, 331, 358, 359, 367, 440, 471, 483, 498, 501, 508, 509, 520, 527, 528, 530, 612

Patty, Thomas. *See* Petty, Thomas
Paul, Capt., 54, 583
Pavillions, 487, 605; ready made, 660
Payne, Capt., 237, 246, 250, 253
Payne, Ralph, 847
Paynter, Richard. *See* Painter, Richard
Peace, 28, 51, 56, 121, 144, 145, 175n, 779, 815; of Paris (1763), 487n
Pearce, James, 51, 51n (biog.)
Pearce, V., 177, 231, 254
Pearson, Alexander, 829
Peas, 11, 68, 69, 149, 630, 631; black eyed, 825; price of, 191, 320, 321, 385, 448, 450, 452, 460, 474, 625, 626, 632, 633, 757, 758, 766, 785, 787, 788, 840
Peat, Robert, 326, 410
Peggy, a ship (Newell), 109, 110, 112n
Peggy, a sloop (Webster), 681
Pelham-Hollis, Thomas, Duke of Newcastle, 587n, 588
Penn, John, 109n
Pennsylvania, 385n, 430n, 654; politics in, 161n
Pepar, Capt., 44
Pepper, black, 31, 424; price of, 722
Percival, James, of Liverpool, 181, 181n (biog.)
Periaugua (Periagua, Perrigua). *See* Pettiauga
Periwig, 3, 43, 45, 110, 833, 834; fashionable, 729; price of, in London, 76, 729. *See also* Wigs
Periwig maker, 57, 146. *See also* Peruke maker
Perkins, Capt., 303, 304
Perkins, Joseph, 543
Perkins, Samuel, 468, 468n (biog.)
Perkins, Thomas, 574–577, 579
Peronneau, Alexander, 696, 696n (biog.), 718, 733, 750, 817
Peronneau, Elizabeth (Hall), 696n
Perroneau, Henry, 696, 696n (biog.), 718, 733, 750, 817
Perroneau, Mary (Pollock), 696n
Perth Amboy, New Jersey, 7
Peruke maker, 824n
Petition, for Three Independent Companies, 379, 487; from RP to Ga. Trustees, 729; of New England merchants to Board of Trade, 421n, 489n, 666n; to change psalm version used, 696n. *See also* "The Humble Petition of the Council and Assembly. . . ."
Pettiauga (Periaugua, periagua, perrigua), 157n, 260, 493, 836, 837
Petty coats, 155, 260
Petty (Patty), Thomas, 125, 170
Pewter, 283, 468, 486; common, 298; composition, 298. *See also* Dishes; Pewterer; Plates; Spoons; Tankards; Tureens
Pewterer, 58n, 456, 468, 497, 499
Philadelphia, Pa., 12n, 18, 25, 26, 28, 49, 71, 87, 107, 109, 159–161, 171, 172, 189, 193, 195, 216, 220, 243, 255, 256, 267, 270, 299, 302, 320, 323, 329, 344, 358–360, 381, 382, 386, 393, 415, 416, 418n, 430, 440, 448, 502–504, 507, 512, 514, 515, 518, 520, 525, 537, 538, 556, 564, 607, 609, 610, 631, 652, 653, 674, 675, 737, 739, 743, 767, 768, 778, 791, 807, 820
Philips, Samuel, 747, 769, 770, 775, 776, 778
Phillips, Capt., 586
Phillips, Eleazer, 255
Phoenix, HMS (Fanshawe), 260n, 265, 323–325, 327, 331
Physicians, in Boston, 205; in Charleston, 175, 296, 714, 835; in Eng., 574–575;

Index

in New Providence, 297n. *See also* Medicine, practice of; Surgeon
Pichard, Alexander, 420
Pichard, Anna Catharine, 420
Pichard (Picard), Charles Jacob, 386, 420, 420n (biog.)
Pichard, Sussannah (Bourget), 420n
Pickering, Michael, 740–742
Pickles, 187, 618, 637, 646, 753; price of, 187, 228
Pictures, 299; India, 688, 723
Pieces of eight, 717, 762. *See also* Dollars
Pierce, Capt., 835
Piercy, Hugh, 28, 29, 32, 33, 156
Pigot, Mrs., 39
Pilkington, Seth, of Pamplico, 142, 142n (biog.), 148, 328, 383, 411, 412, 483, 709, 711, 765, 767, 768, 839, 848
Pilot, at Charleston, 67, 98, 138, 173, 352, 355, 357, 361, 439n, 486, 490, 504, 530, 545, 578, 619; at Tybee, Ga., 47n
Pilotage, 98, 187, 270
Pinckney, Charles, 226, 227, 369, 724, 725, 830, 834
Pinckney, Charles, children of, 724n
Pinckney, Elizabeth (Lamb), 227
Pinckney, Eliza (Lucas), 11n, 724, 724n (biog.), 725, 740n, 830
Pinckney, Mr., 155, 339
Pine Apple, a brigantine (Sigourney), 137
Pipes, hunting, 31, 252; long tavern, 252; tobacco, 117, 252, 289, 299
Pipes (wine), 322, 486, 508
Pistole, 45, 228, 673, 740, 741.
Pistols, 285n, 603, 604, 736; holster, 5, 218, 226; price of, 5, 77, 465
Pitch, 6, 30, 32, 40, 70, 86, 99, 106, 116, 117, 140, 141, 145, 161, 162, 185, 195, 196, 206, 207, 211, 228, 242, 270, 278, 287, 293, 314, 325, 346, 348, 373, 391, 396, 406, 407, 462, 522, 534, 536, 609, 610, 690, 702, 710, 721, 723, 764, 768, 774, 784, 786; price of, 32, 87, 118, 125, 154, 156, 160, 163, 165, 175, 178, 186, 190, 191, 201, 202, 208, 209, 217, 227, 242, 254, 268, 290, 291, 300, 313, 317, 320, 321, 397, 398, 400, 408, 418, 422, 439, 448, 450, 452, 460, 466, 474, 503, 508, 509, 525, 526, 582, 583, 594, 601, 603, 605, 606, 608, 621, 641, 644, 645, 653, 657, 680, 694, 696, 700, 703, 704, 714, 724, 725, 750, 757, 758, 765, 766, 773, 780–783, 785, 787, 788, 817, 818, 838, 839
Pitt, William, of Island of Rattan, 833, 833n (biog.), 846
Plague, the, 642
Plains, 31, 139, 218, 351, 395, 423; Welch, 170, 244
Planks, 348, 528, 628, 794, 799; definition of, 421; madeira (mahogany), 386, 391, 392, 421, 462, 606, 671, 685; price of, 606. *See also* Wood
Plans, 468, 469; of Boston, 503, 568, 751; of Charleston, 377; of Philadelphia, 512, 565, 653; original, of Beaufort, 512n
Plantations. *See* Colonies
Plantations, Dean Hall, 169n; in N. C., 557; in S. C., 11n, 247; Longpoint, 519n; Rat Trap, 144n; Thorowgood, 26n; Wappoo, 11n, 724n.
Planter, a ship (Lavers), 632n
Planters, of Antigua, 289; of Ga., 836n; of S. C., 30, 52, 60–62, 102, 177n, 190n, 210, 212n, 227, 239, 247, 269, 270, 292, 296n, 305, 311, 315, 316, 319, 322, 324, 331, 335, 337, 371, 407, 418, 422, 490, 520, 530, 538, 550, 554, 564, 579n, 588, 601n, 623n, 639, 656, 663n, 686, 700, 703, 762, 781, 788, 804, 834
Plants, 804. *See also* Trees
Plate covers, hard metal, 59
Plates, brass, 469; china, 249, 424, 592, 780; pewter, 31, 249, 298; pewter water, 59, 688
Platiloes, 816
Plowden, Edward, 600, 600n (biog.)
Plymouth, Eng., 332, 333, 541
Point Pleasant, N. C., 95n
Polder, Capt., 159
Pollie (Lipelly), Capt., 412, 712
Polly, a snow (Bird), 272, 281, 283, 292
Pomeroy, Henry, of London, 164, 164n (biog.)
Pomeroy, William, 164, 164n (biog.)
Pomeroy, William & Sons, 828
Pon Pon (Pond Pond), S. C., 134n, 848

Index

Poole, Eng., 163, 168, 454, 487, 635, 722
Pork, 11, 277, 282, 414, 415, 686, 710, 716, 724, 725, 767, 843; price of, 192, 320, 321, 385, 411, 509, 556, 557, 624–626, 632, 633, 757, 758, 765, 766, 787, 788, 839
Port charges, 9, 107, 167, 209, 263, 338, 349, 454, 459
Porteridge, price of, 447
Port Lewis, Hispaniola, 304
Porto Bello, Panama, 170n
Porto. *See* Oporto
Port Royal, Jamaica, 784
Port Royal, S. C., 127, 239, 296, 388n, 489, 493, 500, 512, 587, 592, 595, 723, 811, 813, 818
Port Royal Station, S. C., 592, 595. *See also* Carolina Station
Ports, American, 217; North Carolina, 380. *See also* Outports
Portsmouth, a schooner (Seavey), 733n
Portsmouth, Eng., 292, 541, 734
Portsmouth, N. H., 463n
Portugal, 113, 195, 247n, 472, 674, 764. *See also* Lisbon; Oporto
Posstillion, a sloop (Lightwood), 638, 737, 803, 806, 807
Postage, 134, 377, 615; double, 450; rate of, 384
Postmaster, 255
Post, 297, 302, 384, 419, 451, 555, 557; subscription, 255n
Potatoes, 66, 133, 234, 243, 277, 430, 431, 445, 616, 754; price of, 843
Pots, 645; iron, 50, 391, 429, 508, 567
Powell, Capt., 6, 7
Powell, Rev., 239
Power of attorney, 42, 47, 48, 58, 100, 101, 105, 108, 146, 172, 180, 213, 218, 219, 235, 240, 282, 295, 304, 305, 328, 342, 364, 378, 393, 394, 397, 407, 415, 418, 419, 439, 450, 473, 474, 479, 495, 498, 543, 544, 545, 551, 555, 560, 584, 587, 599, 642, 650, 651, 655–657, 659, 661, 679, 688, 689, 702, 704, 711, 731, 758, 759, 763, 766, 768, 791, 792, 822, 830
Pretty Betty, a sloop (Evans), 46n
Pretty Betty (Trimble), 173, 308
Price, John, 127

Prices, 145, 213, 244, 290, 447, 449, 615, 716, 803. *See also each commodity*
Price's Inlet, S. C., 665n
Price, Thomas, 14
Prime cost, 3, 162, 259, 269, 337, 367, 422, 453, 480, 488, 511, 816
Prince, Moses, 95
Prince, Thomas, 751
Princess Amelia (Haurney), 585
Princess St. (Rotherith, London), 482n, 589
Principal, 329
Princise, a ship (Coronell), 846
Pringle & Reid, 219, 282, 362, 408, 584
Pringle, Andrew, of London, 4, 4n (biog.), 5, 7, 8, 10, 16, 17, 21, 22, 25, 26, 34, 50, 51, 53, 61, 64, 66, 73–80, 84, 85, 89, 91, 96, 100, 111, 119, 121, 125, 133–135, 152, 155, 156, 159, 160, 161, 163n, 164, 165, 167, 168, 172, 173, 175, 177, 178, 185, 188, 192, 205, 206, 209, 213, 216, 219, 222, 229, 231, 232, 235, 237, 240, 243–245, 247, 248, 251, 254, 257–261, 264–268, 271, 280, 285, 289, 294, 296, 297, 300, 303, 307–309, 312, 315, 316, 320, 321, 331, 333–336, 341, 343–350, 354, 356, 358, 366–369, 371, 375, 376, 378, 379, 381, 387, 390, 397, 401, 406, 412, 417, 436, 437, 453, 454, 457–459, 461–464, 466, 471, 472, 477, 479, 482–486, 492, 496, 499–501, 503, 507, 509, 510, 515, 519, 522, 527–529, 531–533, 537, 540, 541, 543, 545, 546, 549, 555, 558–562, 565, 566, 570, 571, 574, 576, 583, 586, 587, 595, 601, 605, 606, 611, 613, 617, 618, 621–623, 634, 638, 640n, 642, 645, 646, 648, 651, 652, 654, 659, 661, 662n, 665, 670, 672, 677, 686, 687, 697, 699, 706, 707, 710, 715, 722, 727, 728, 732, 737, 739, 740, 742, 745, 747, 757, 759, 760, 764–767, 769–771, 775, 777, 778, 789, 794, 798–801, 803, 807, 810, 814, 816, 821, 824, 827, 829, 830, 833, 846–848
Pringle, George, 655
Pringle, Hugh, 847
Pringle, Jane (Allen), 23, 23n (biog.), 26, 35, 66, 70, 84, 90, 113, 133, 144, 156,

Index

158, 163, 168, 170, 173–175, 177, 178, 186, 187, 196–198, 200, 201, 203, 204–208, 212, 220, 223, 226, 227, 230, 233, 239, 241–243, 254, 255, 260, 263, 270, 272–274, 276, 283, 299, 300, 309, 317, 318, 323, 332, 359, 363, 365, 366, 368, 371, 372, 378, 380, 389, 390, 403, 408, 430, 431, 441, 445, 456, 463, 469, 470, 474, 489, 497, 498, 503, 512, 521, 528, 530, 534, 535, 538, 542, 546, 550, 552, 561, 565, 570, 575, 579, 582, 588, 593, 607, 608, 615, 616, 621, 622, 636, 642–644, 652, 653, 656, 662, 664, 665, 675, 676, 690, 694, 701, 705, 709, 719, 723, 730, 733, 734, 738, 741, 751, 763, 781, 790, 791, 796, 809, 815, 818, 820, 822, 827, 829, 832, 845
Pringle, John, 169
Pringle, John, of Madeira, 158n, 508, 611
Pringle, John Julius, 4n, 470n
Pringle, Robert (1755–1811), 4n
Pringle, Robert (of Stow, d. 1738), 62
Pringle, Robert (1702–1776), 4n, 12n, 15n, 23n, 42n, 58n, 62n, 70n, 82n, 83n, 138, 155n, 162n, 172n, 203n, 211n, 224n, 265n, 296n, 335n, 338n, 355, 365n, 381, 406n, 407n, 418n, 442n, 469, 470n, 479n, 521n, 554n, 564n, 579n, 605n, 607n, 663n, 688n, 707n, 751n, 755n, 815n, 826n, 833n, 842n; builds a new house, 293, 457, 469, 470, 551; churchwarden, 211, 271; desires peace, 779, 815; garden of, 224, 253, 293, 512, 742, 751, 196; honesty questioned, 84, 196, 249; illnesses of, 43, 52, 53, 60–62, 65, 71, 75, 88, 122, 143, 147, 265, 293, 295, 624, 627; library & books of, 82n, 751; motto of, 469; on arbitrary taxation, 700; on bathing, 211; on Charleston merchants, 761; on copybooks, 602; on council, of S. C., 388, 488; on Dutch, 382; on Esther, a slave, 247; on evils of easy money, 662–663; on Glen, John, 745, 822; on Hardy, Charles, 406–407, 430, 497, 569, 580–581, 640; on impressment, 10, 491–492; on Middleton family, 418; on N. C., 219; on placemen, 701; on planters in S. C., 269, 418; on Pringle, Jane, 205; on responsibilities of a factor, 423, 437; on vendue, 480; on Walpole's fall, 367, 371; optimism of, 272, 289; orders clothes, 63–64, 706; petition of, to trustees of Ga., 729; partnership with Inglis, George, 407n; partnership with Reid, James, 156, 162, 176, 181, 183–185, 190, 193, 197, 200, 216, 219, 237, 257, 262, 286–288
Pringle, William, of Antigua, 14, 123, 179, 182, 224, 229, 266, 284, 318, 340, 448, 725, 782
Printer, 847
Prints, 468, 469
Prioleau & Crokatt, 735
Prioleau, Samuel, 735n
Priscilla, a ship (Ham), 760n
Prison. *See* Jail
Prisoners, English, 726, 778n; French, 785, 787, 788, 790; of the Spaniards, 385–386, 444, 728; Spanish, 663, 708, 726, 728
Pritchard, Mary, 64
Privateering, 134, 765
Privateers, 377, 408, 456, 560, 583, 808; English, 455; Jamaican, 272, 533, 678, 689, 763, 780, 796; New York, 262, 739; R. I., 248, 585, 665; St. Kitts, 765; share in, 822; Spanish, 193, 243, 255n, 260, 264, 265, 302, 382, 385, 636, 665, 815n, 818. *See also* Privateers (S. C.); Prizes
Privateers (S. C.), 410, 773, 808, 821; agents and managers for, 636, 639–641, 643, 663, 673, 728, 739, 740, 761, 772, 790, 803, 822, 828–833; instructions for captain of, 761, 772, 832; subscribers of, 636, 639–641, 656, 673, 728; subscription for, 640, 772, 828. *See also Assistance*, a snow (I'On); *Recovery*, a privateer (Anderson)
Privy council, 273, 379, 588, 700
Prize goods, 689, 816, 843
Prizes, 135, 456, 486, 560, 615, 620, 686, 720, 746, 759, 763, 785, 790, 803, 828–831; brought to Charleston, 143, 193, 197, 200, 212, 215–216, 248, 262, 382, 383, 385, 386, 394, 402, 408, 413, 415, 533, 663–665, 668, 669, 674, 675, 755, 762, 775,

Index

780–782, 785, 787, 788, 790, 796, 804, 808, 835, 837–839, 841, 843; captain's share of, 790; dividends of, 822; French, 701, 738, 755, 762, 775, 780–782, 787, 788, 790, 796, 804, 808, 823, 835, 837–839, 841, 843; sunk, 197, 212; value of, 197, 200, 212, 248, 332, 762, 775, 780n, 782, 788, 790, 804, 836; share of, 796. *See also* Privateers
Produce, of N. C., 765; of S. C., 86, 140, 144, 145, 195, 419, 422, 525, 528, 607, 609, 686, 778; of W. I., 150, 183; price of, 27, 150, 183, 288, 407, 526, 694 (fluctuating), 734, 803; trade in, 238. *See also individual commodities*
Profit, 33, 188, 255n, 306, 367, 440, 542, 575, 588n, 608
Prospects. *See* Plans
Prosperity, a brigantine (Selew), 593, 602, 616
Prosperity, a sloop (Langstaff), 817n
Protest, regular, on damaged goods, 246, 248, 493, 504, 814; validity of, 251, 263. *See also* Bills of exchange, protested
Prout, Joseph, 385, 413
Providence, a ship (Agars), 658
Providence, a ship (Newcomin), 278n
Providence. *See* New Providence
Provinces. *See* Colonies
Provisions, 11, 22, 23, 26, 38, 51, 268, 270, 277, 281, 282, 298, 329, 400, 411, 412, 478n, 490, 556, 557, 564, 586n, 612, 630–633, 656, 727, 759, 765, 768, 804, 810; from the Northward, 282; in Barbados, 417; price of, 239, 320, 417, 483, 675, 714, 777. *See also individual commodities*
Provost marshal, 353, 369
Prussian, 293n
Psalm versions, New England, 696n; Tate & Brady, 696n
Public house, 43n, 146. *See also* Tavern
Public treasurer, 550
Pulsifer, Mr., 214–216
Punch bowls, 31
Puritan, 32n
Purnell, John, 660n, 670

Quakers, 27n, 519n, 520

Quarentine, 656
Quebec, 396n
Queen Anne's County, Md., 385, 414, 415, 609, 847
Queen Carolina, a ship (Snelling), 6n
Queen of Hungary, a privateer, 808
Queen of Hungary, a ship (Blackburn), 441, 442, 450, 454, 458, 471, 497, 533, 538, 607
Quarm (Quarme), Capt., 570, 572–574

Rae (Ray), John, 328, 329, 648, 649
Ragles (Raggles), John, 237, 276, 300
Rains, John, 810, 811, 843
Raisons, 424, 579, 605
Raitt, Alexander, 643, 644
Ramsay, Archibald, 168, 177, 178, 254, 848
Raneymund, Va., 846
Rate of exchange, 145, 269; on Antigua, 44, 126, 321; on dollars, 779; on London, 17, 32, 76, 89, 101, 107, 116, 126, 130, 155, 178, 183, 186, 201, 202, 209, 229, 236, 248, 257, 266, 268, 270, 281, 287, 290–292, 299–301, 303, 307, 310, 314, 317, 323, 338, 350, 371, 377, 378, 384, 396, 397, 399, 401, 402, 405, 406, 409, 411, 414, 417, 420, 423, 432, 438, 448, 450–452, 456, 457, 459, 466, 475, 482, 485, 489, 491, 496, 500, 503, 508–510, 516, 525, 526, 528, 529, 532, 549, 553, 557, 561, 567, 575, 582, 583, 590–592, 601, 603, 604, 606, 608, 610, 612, 615, 617, 618, 621–623, 625, 626, 632, 633, 638, 644, 654, 657, 658, 671, 672, 677, 681, 684, 685, 687, 693, 695, 716, 718, 725, 727, 741, 747, 755, 757, 758, 765, 766, 770, 771, 780, 782–784, 787, 788, 799, 811, 817–819, 823, 835, 839, 842; on New England, 444, 503, 696, 718, 731, 733, 752; on New York, 101, 277, 451; on Philadelphia, 161; on pieces of eight, 717, on pistareen, 779; on pistoles, 740; on Portugal, 635; reduced, 270, 281, 287, 290, 292, 299, 301, 303, 308
Rawlins, Lt., 608
Ray, John. *See* Rae, John
Rebecca, a schooner (Anderson), 403n
Rebecca, a schooner (Watson), 197

Index

Rebecca, a ship (Lowder), 311, 314
Rebecca, a sloop (Bangs), 748, 749, 752–754, 781, 795
Rebecca, a sloop (Schermerhorn), 253
Rebellion Road, 67, 84, 94, 95, 133, 136, 227, 265, 318, 324, 329, 349, 351, 352, 354, 356, 357, 364, 387, 418, 434, 442, 462, 472, 473, 477, 479, 480, 482, 533, 569, 573, 581, 641, 642, 697, 698, 703, 745, 775, 803, 822, 830
Recovery, a privateer (Anderson), 739, 740, 743, 745, 746, 748, 761, 771, 772, 789–790, 796, 803, 822, 828, 829, 831, 832, 834
Receiver general of the quit rents, 588n
Receiver general of the revenues, 370n
Recognizance, 353
Rector, assistant of St. Philip's, 188n; of Prince Frederick's, 549n; of St. Helena's, 188n; of St. James Goose Creek, 544n; of St. James Santee, 554n; of St. Paul's, 188n; of St. Philip's, 239n. *See also* Clergyman; Missionary
Redbirds, 10, 705, 788
Re-exchange, rate of, 665
Register in chancery, 370
Register of Mesne Conveyances, 370, 372, 378, 379; deputy, 370
Reid, Andrew, 848
Reid, Dorothy, 498, 520, 542, 554, 570, 608
Reid, James, 162, 163, 166, 176, 179, 181, 183–186, 190, 193, 197, 200, 210, 211, 216, 219, 222–224, 229, 237, 238, 242, 243, 252, 257, 271, 276, 282, 284, 286, 288, 292, 301, 302, 310, 322, 362, 383–386, 394, 395n, 405, 408–410, 413, 417, 418, 441, 453n, 477, 479, 498, 520, 542, 544, 551, 553, 554, 559, 570, 572, 584, 608, 615, 619, 629, 653, 674, 675, 680, 709, 803, 804, 833
Reid, Mr., 229, 709
Reid, Patrick, 350n, 613, 613n (biog.), 615
Reid, Thomas, 554n, 570
Remick, Abraham, 669, 675, 682, 726
Remittances, 49–50, 53, 56, 59–61, 74, 76, 78, 81, 86, 88, 89, 93, 94, 130, 135, 145, 153, 155, 159, 169, 171, 172, 174, 185, 191, 194, 198, 200, 203, 204, 207, 211, 228, 238, 246, 252, 257, 258, 261, 312, 372, 374, 377, 396, 397, 444, 446, 455, 470, 474, 477, 479, 485, 507, 520, 522, 532, 538, 540, 544, 547, 548, 554, 564n, 565, 566, 568, 572, 575, 586, 598, 602, 604, 607, 608, 614, 628, 629, 652, 663, 674, 675, 682, 690, 710, 720, 723, 728, 740, 741, 763, 766–768, 773, 774, 779, 783, 786, 790, 791, 793, 810, 812, 820, 831, 836
Returns. *See* Remittances
Revenge, a bilander (Wimble), 455
Revenge, a sloop (Wimble), 455, 456, 560, 585, 758, 759, 780
Rhode Island, 143–146, 178, 202, 211, 227, 248n, 316, 380n, 403n, 463n, 557, 581–583, 585, 615, 616, 620, 643, 650, 665, 669, 675–677, 680, 719, 750, 751, 755, 781, 827, 845. *See also* Newport
Ribbons, 429, 508, 568, 645, 721; frequently imported, 392, 592; Spanish, 592
Rice, 29, 39n, 54, 58, 59, 66, 68, 71, 78, 79, 81, 86, 95, 106, 114, 136, 140, 144–146, 149, 155, 163, 167, 196, 206, 207, 210–215, 218, 223–225, 229, 272, 282, 286, 287, 289, 295, 298, 306, 312, 314, 329, 332, 336, 350, 351, 364, 373, 375, 376, 377, 388, 389, 403, 409, 421, 431, 438, 443, 445, 455, 462–467, 469, 475, 477, 489, 498, 504, 508, 518, 528, 529, 532, 533, 536, 546–548, 553, 562, 563, 566, 567, 571–575, 578, 579, 584, 600, 603, 610, 643, 658, 666, 667, 671, 679, 683, 690, 694, 698, 702, 705, 756, 769, 776, 798, 799, 805, 836, 845, 847; a bad investment, 301; beat out, 245, 251, 260, 261; broken, 633; contracting for, 269; crop of, 3, 4, 6, 8, 16, 17, 19, 21–24, 26–28, 30, 32–34, 38, 43, 45, 46, 49, 51, 52, 56, 60–62, 65, 69, 70, 73, 74, 77, 83, 85, 88, 89, 91, 93, 102, 103, 107, 109, 112–114, 116–118, 121–123, 125, 126 (fig.), 130 (fig.), 131 (fig.), 132 (fig.), 135, 136, 138, 139, 141, 143, 145, 146, 150–154, 156, 159, 163, 165, 173, 174, 181, 184,

Index

189, 192, 216, 220, 225, 227, 228, 230, 231, 234, 236, 237, 238 (fig.), 241, 245–247, 251, 254, 257, 258, 260, 261, 263, 266, 268, 269, 274, 275, 279, 285, 301, 313, 316, 318, 319, 321, 325, 330, 331 (fig.), 335 (fig.), 340–342, 346, 347, 349, 358, 362, 363, 366, 367, 371, 374, 379, 393, 396–398, 400, 401, 405–412, 416, 417, 420, 423, 429, 430, 432, 433, 435, 436, 447–450, 452, 459, 468, 479, 497, 517, 522, 526, 527, 534, 535, 537, 554, 570, 582, 586, 590 (fig.), 591 (fig.), 592 (fig.), 594, 595, 597, 601, 602, 605 (fig.), 606, 609, 612, 613, 616, 622, 623, 625, 626, 630, 631, 635 (fig.), 651, 660, 676, 700 (fig.), 715, 719, 723, 727, 729, 732–734, 736, 738, 740, 749, 750, 753, 754, 757, 760, 762, 765, 770, 774, 775, 783, 785, 786, 803, 841; crop of, in Italy, 73; in N. C., 410, 412; demand for, 269, 287, 290, 292, 301, 308, 367, 398, 401, 523, 534, 535, 607, 774, 779, 782, 783, 785, 786, 793, 797, 811; harvest, 24, 30, 33, 38, 136, 143, 145, 156, 238, 248, 250, 251, 420, 423, 736, 740; new, 151, 152, 245, 416, 439, 446, 453, 454, 458–460, 474, 476, 484, 506, 509, 510, 528, 589, 590, 592, 595, 604, 606, 607, 612, 614, 617, 638, 645, 672, 678, 695, 743, 747, 748, 750, 753, 757, 758, 762, 766, 771, 777, 778, 794, 831; old, 245, 261, 439, 460, 474, 528, 595, 606, 704; price of, 3–6, 8, 23, 30, 32, 51–53, 60–62, 65, 70, 73, 74, 80, 84, 87, 88, 90, 91, 93, 94, 96, 97, 99, 103, 104, 107, 109, 110, 112, 114, 118, 125, 130, 150, 151, 154, 156, 159, 160, 163, 165, 166, 173–176, 178, 181, 184–187, 189–192, 194, 195, 200–202, 204, 209, 216–218, 222, 227, 228, 230, 231, 234, 236, 238, 241, 242, 245, 248, 251, 254, 258, 265, 268, 269, 274, 275, 279, 281, 285, 288, 290–292, 296, 299–303, 308, 309, 311, 313, 315, 316–322, 324, 325, 330, 331, 335, 340–342, 346, 348, 358, 359, 367, 371, 372, 374, 380, 391, 392, 396–398, 400, 401, 405–408, 416, 418, 422, 423, 429, 430, 435, 437, 439, 446–450, 452, 453, 459, 460, 471, 472, 474, 476, 483, 485, 486, 487, 493, 501, 503, 506, 508–510, 513, 520, 522–528, 530, 534, 535, 538, 551, 554, 564, 570, 575, 577, 582, 583, 586, 589, 594, 601, 602, 606, 608, 612–614, 616, 621–626, 632, 638, 641, 644, 653, 656, 657, 668, 670, 672, 673, 676–678, 687–689, 691, 693, 700, 703, 704, 713, 716, 720, 723–725, 727, 743, 747, 750, 754, 757, 762, 765, 766, 770, 773, 775, 780–783, 785–788, 797, 803, 804, 806, 811, 817, 818, 823, 825, 827, 833, 837–840, 843; price of, in Amsterdam, 103; price of, in Antigua, 516; price of, in Europe, 293; 485; price of, in Lisbon, 73, 454, 458, 509, 541–542, 559, 585–586, 612, 614, 677, 746, 811; price of, in London, 310; price of, in Madeira, 612; price of, in Portugal, 642, 748, 769–770; quality of, 5, 151, 153, 218, 236, 336, 391, 421, 459, 510, 528, 549, 564, 566, 570, 577, 586, 592, 595, 597, 693, 720, 840; small, 11, 656; weighing of, 337; whole, 633
Rice, Capt., 587, 591, 613, 621
Rice trade, 73n, 372
Richard, a brigantine (Hallen), 462–465, 470, 471, 474, 480, 484–486, 488, 490–493, 496, 505, 506, 540, 589, 721
Richards, John, of London, 7, 50, 75, 121, 134, 149, 183, 211, 224, 229, 231, 232, 324
Richards, Travers, 324
Rigbye (Rigby), Nicholas, of Savannah, 598, 598n (biog.), 628, 648, 734, 836
Rigby Hole, a brigantine (Mulryne), 725
Rigg, Alexander, 240
Rigging, 385, 818; running, 31
Rind, William, 616, 616n (biog.), 835
River Club. *See* Goose Creek Friendly Society
Rivers, Joseph, 674, 687, 690, 737
River, the, 475
Robert and Jane, a snow (Douglas), 642, 747, 762, 769, 771, 773, 775, 789, 796
Roberts, George, 11
Robertson, Capt., 122–124, 126, 128, 131, 134, 626

Index

Robertson, William, 302
Robinson, Alexander, 494, 495
Robinson, Capt., 735
Robinson, Mr., 155n, 480
Rochelle, a brigantine (Screech), 81, 83, 130, 200, 848
Rochelle, France, 755n
Roche, Jordan, 131, 383n
Roche, Matthew, 384
Roche, Mrs., 383
Roche, Rebecca, 383n
Roche, Rebecca (Brewton), 383n
Rodger, James, 105n
Rodgers (Rogers), James, 437, 453, 471, 559, 574, 575
Rolfe, Daniel, 14
Romme (Romar), Cornelius, 738, 739, 744, 745
Rood Lane (London), 159n
Rook, Capt., 290, 293
Rope, bolt, 372; buoy, 578; white, 440
Rose, Capt., 322, 612, 811
Rose, HMS (Windham, Frankland), 10, 280, 292, 296, 298, 308, 323, 382, 385, 408, 413, 414, 567–570, 572, 575, 580, 615, 616, 663, 668, 669, 673, 675, 682, 691, 692, 698, 726, 780–783, 785, 787, 788, 790, 796, 804, 808, 835
Rosin, 30, 86, 140, 162n
Ross, Capt., 304
Ross, John, 847
Ross, Mr., 610
Rotherith (Rotherheth) (London), 473, 482n, 589
Rotherith Church, 614
Rotterdam, Holland, 377, 439, 440, 527
Rowland, Richard, of St. Kitts, 650, 713, 764, 821
Roxbury, Mass., 696n
Royal Exchange, 455, 468; insurance director, 153n
Royal Exchange Assurance Co., director of, 549n
Royalist, 316n, 695n
Royal navy, 473n, 492n. *See also* King's ships; Men of war; Officers, of the royal navy
Royall Ranger, a sloop (Burroughs), 784
Rugs, Negro, 351, 423. *See also* Carpet
Ruiz, Gasper, 726, 846
Rum, 18, 22, 23, 31, 114, 127, 155, 161, 174, 181, 183, 198, 211, 224, 229–231, 233, 246, 277, 284, 285, 345, 349, 370, 441, 449, 458, 464, 467, 475, 485, 494, 495, 514, 539, 551, 556, 557, 589, 616, 661, 699n, 754, 756, 770, 771, 784, 825; Antigua, 39, 46, 70, 123, 129, 135, 148, 237, 238, 244, 281, 321, 444, 516, 589; Barbados, 39, 148, 238, 407, 431, 434, 436, 444, 471, 476, 500, 507, 508, 535, 589–591, 594, 608, 614, 626, 684, 686, 773; consumption of, 31, 87, 123, 429, 430, 436, 446, 449, 626 (fig.), 684 (fig.); glut of, 485, 502, 504, 505, 513, 516, 528, 534–536, 548; Jamaica, 217, 337, 626, 810; New England, 82, 84, 86, 87, 130, 132, 145, 178, 201, 242, 300, 301, 317, 382, 389, 391, 393, 406, 411, 429–431, 434, 444, 446, 460, 476, 500, 505, 508, 548, 567, 568, 644, 645, 653, 688, 691, 696, 703, 704, 717, 718, 721, 722, 727, 750, 766, 780, 781, 817, 819, 846; Philadelphia, 46; price of, 11, 39, 45, 46, 84, 87, 90, 123, 138, 148, 150, 151, 178, 184, 189, 190, 192, 201, 217, 238, 242, 253, 266, 268, 282, 284, 285, 291, 300, 301, 317, 320, 321, 380, 389, 393, 406, 407, 411, 412, 416, 417, 429–431, 434, 436, 444, 447, 448, 450, 452, 460, 471, 474, 476, 485, 500, 502, 504, 506, 513, 516, 528, 535, 548, 590–592, 594, 601, 603, 606, 608, 624–626, 632, 633, 638, 653, 680, 686, 688, 691, 694, 696, 703, 704, 713, 715–722, 724, 725, 727, 732, 750, 757, 758, 765, 766, 774, 780–783, 785, 787, 788, 802, 806, 817, 819, 838, 839, 841; price of, in Antigua, 516; price of, in Barbados, 481, 684, 691; price of, in W. I., 656; retailers of, 281, 285; St. Kitts, 618; trade in, 440; W. I., 87, 150, 178, 201, 232, 242, 254, 317, 411, 429, 430, 452, 460, 535, 548, 567, 644, 653, 694, 696, 703, 704, 717–721, 727, 732, 750, 766, 780, 781, 817, 819
Russell, Mr., 305
Russell, Daniel, 386, 408
Russell, William, 76
Rust, 391, 460, 465
Ruth, a ship, 385, 415
Ryan, Edmond, 380, 381

Index

Ryan, John, of Philadelphia, 18, 18n (biog.), 25, 26, 168, 193
Rye, Eng., 202
Rye (*Rye Gally*), HMS (Hardy), 323, 380n, 430, 473n, 569, 580, 582, 583, 639, 640–642

Sack. *See* Wine
Saddler, 213n, 218, 305
Saddlery, 305
Saddles, 3, 213, 305, 420, 843
Sagathy, 31
Sail cloth, 31, 367, 424, 440, 753, 776; English, 372. *See also* Canvas; Duck; Sail makers; Sails
Sailmakers, Charleston, 372; London, 409. *See also* Canvas; Duck; Sailcloth; Sails
Sailors, 22n, 51n, 250n, 272, 361, 375, 379n, 385, 489, 496, 497, 504, 523, 607, 608, 674, 675, 731, 736, 777, 818n, 836n; hire of, 473; shortage of, in Boston, 173; shortage of, in Charleston, 471, 491, 492, 506, 513, 529, 531, 557, 558, 566, 680, 777; sufficient number of, in Charleston, 407; wages of, 356, 492, 777, 799. *See also* Boatswain; Impressment; Master, of a vessel; Mate, of a vessel; Officers, of the royal navy
Sails, 385, 818. *See also* Canvas; Duck; Sailcloth; Sail makers
St. Andrew, a ship (Greig), 210, 222, 380
St. Andrew, a ship (Steadman, Brown), 479, 482, 493, 521
St. Andrew, a sloop (Webster), 726n, 778n
St. Andrew's Society, 707n
St. Augustine, Fla., 11, 34, 38, 51, 121, 143, 163, 175, 177, 178, 212, 230, 302, 332, 435, 441, 443, 445, 518, 528, 530, 708, 739, 777, 815; a threat to S. C., 135, 163; garrison of, 231; siege of, 231, 232, 578. *See also* Expedition, St. Augustine
St. Catharines (London), 847
St. Christophers. *See* St. Kitts
St. George, a ship (Hallyburton), 538n
St. Helena's Sound, 489n, 500, 502, 504, 514, 520

St. John Baptiste, a snow (Fandino), 382n
St. John, James, 19, 19n (biog.), 115, 169, 211, 212, 542
St. John, Miller, 542
St. Kitts, W. I., 12, 35, 36, 68, 69, 149, 301, 316n, 326, 431n, 590, 592, 618, 630, 631, 650, 651, 662, 710, 713, 756, 757, 764, 821
St. Lucas, a snow (Robertson), 626
St. Margret Pattens (London), 4n
St. Michael's Alley (London), 761n
St. Michael's Church, bells of, 203n; interior carving of, 412n
St. Peter, a brigantine (Hunt), 101
St. Peter's Church (Philadelphia), 12n
St. Peters Port, Guernsey, 836n
St. Simon's, Ga., 309, 386, 390
Salem, Mass., 696
Salomons, Coleman, of Savannah, 40, 40n (biog.), 88
Salt, 129, 133, 136, 173, 191, 398, 399, 400, 512, 520, 553n; English, 32, 215, 440; Isle of May, 215, 323, 520; large, 440; price of, 134, 173, 323, 411, 440, 520, 660, 667, 683, 840
Saltus, Capt., 802, 803, 807
Salvage, 619, 682, 697–699, 703, 721; captor's ⅛ share, 385, 668, 675, 679, 689, 690–692, 726
Sam and John, a ship (Atkinson), 215n
Samuel, a ship (Prince), 95n
Sandwell, Stephen, 149, 642, 664, 670
Sanders, Samuel. *See* Saunders, Samuel
Santee River, S. C., 39n, 255, 296
Sarah and Elizabeth, a snow (Breden), 364n
Sarah, a ship (Callcott), 3, 4, 7, 9
Sarah, a ship (Remick), 669, 679. *See also Thomas*, a ship (Palmer)
Sarah (Knox), 8
Sarah, a sloop (Blackader), 6, 143
Sarah, a sloop (Lefebore), 102
Sarah, a sloop (Mason), 233, 234n
Sarah, a snow (Breden), 430n
Sashes, price of, in London, 452, 453; silk, 90, 452, 453
Sassafras, 336, 349, 688
Sassafras River, Md., 172n, 415, 847
Saunders, Mrs. Samuel, 155, 156, 175, 260, 309, 368, 622

Index

Saunders (Sanders), Samuel, of London & Southampton, 121, 155, 156, 174, 210, 213, 230, 239, 246, 250, 259, 261, 269, 271, 283, 294, 295, 298, 307, 310, 366, 368, 371, 377, 454, 455, 462, 477, 479, 480, 488, 544, 587, 614, 621, 622, 648, 655, 670, 674, 727, 776, 794, 795, 797
Saunders, Samuel, children of, 155, 156, 175, 260, 308, 309, 368, 622
Savage, Benjamin, 82, 82n (biog.), 102, 105, 173, 259n, 323, 503, 569, 615, 642, 702n, 740
Savage, Benjamin & Co., 206, 259, 263, 530, 763
Savage, John, 83, 83n (biog.), 105
Savage, Martha (Pickering), 740
Savannah, a ship (Wood), 157n
Savannah, Ga., 40, 41, 47, 48, 69, 156, 157, 171, 255, 328, 598, 628, 648, 649n, 734, 836
Savannah River, Ga., 47n
Saws, 488
Saxby, George, 550, 588n
Scannell, David, 71, 190, 190n (biog.), 267
Scarborough, HMS (Tucker), 698, 701, 706, 709
Scarbrugh (Scarburgh), Henry, of Accomack, 610, 610n (biog.), 846
Schermerhorn, John, 253, 253n (biog.), 254, 460–461, 503, 505, 508, 511, 596, 648, 691, 727
Schoolmaster, 826n
Schools. *See* Academy; Free Schools
Schooner, 495; converted into a brigantine, 802
Schuyler, Andrew, 651
Scotland, 62n, 136n, 170n, 222n, 682n; north of, 808
Scots, 29n, 58, 169, 179, 183, 223, 227, 235, 293n, 323n, 350n, 381, 797
Scott & Pringle, of London, 29n, 158n
Scott & Pringle, of Madeira, 158, 163, 373, 375–377, 597
Scott & Watson, 354
Scott, Ann (Harleston), 238
Scott, Henry, 98
Scott, James, of New Providence, 297, 297n (biog.)
Scott, John, of Madeira, 95, 95n (biog.), 158n, 508
Scott, John, Rev., 262
Scott, Jonathan, 238, 239, 280
Scott, Patrick, 370, 479, 587, 588, 604, 606, 614, 617, 618, 621, 622, 634, 655, 689, 740, 745, 746, 760, 797, 798, 800, 805
Scott, Pringle, & Scott, of Madeira, 29n, 95n, 158n, 501, 510, 520, 551, 552, 571–573, 611, 613, 660
Scott, Richard, 238
Scott, Robert, of Madeira, 29, 29n (biog.), 158n, 509
Scott, Robert (d. 1808), of London, 29n
Screech, Robert, 81, 83, 130, 200, 848
Screws, brass, 469
Scrutor. *See* Escritoire
Sea Flower, a schooner (Cossett), 473n
Sea Flower, a schooner (Gregory), 68
Seaford, HMS (Scott), 98n
Sea Horse, a snow (Woodwell), 693, 695, 749
Sea Nymph, a pettiaugua (Delegal), 836, 837
Sea Nymph, a ship (Beach), 229n
Seaman, George, 312, 312n (biog.), 323, 331, 358, 359, 377, 378, 408, 498, 501, 520, 527, 530, 546, 699, 701, 830
Sea stores (sea stock), 243, 407
Seavey, Stephen, 733
Secretary for Indian Affairs (Ga.), 598n
Secretary of the Province, deputy, of Pa., 381n; of Ga., 629n; of Montserrat, 267; of S. C., 227, 267, 297, 573, 690
Secretary to Ga. trustees, 598n; to Gov. Glen, 332, 333; to Gov. Tinker, 333n
Security, 219, 299, 352, 353, 370, 376, 409, 433, 573, 579n, 580, 594, 595, 597, 598, 623, 649, 651, 699, 738, 743
Seguinard, Elias, 755n
Selew, Priam, 593, 602, 616, 643
Selwyn (Selwin), Henry, 420, 420n (biog.)
Serge, German, 424
Sermon, farewell, 239n
Servants, 339, 394, 512, 521, 815n; indentured, 272, 282, 598n
Settlements. *See* Colonies

Index

Settlers, 11
Sewee Bay (Seewee Harbour), S. C., 665, 666, 676
Shalloon, 423
Shell, silver, Charleston-made, 203
Sheddon, R., 294n
Shepheard, Charles, 64, 92, 92n (biog.)
Sherlock, Thomas, 169, 169n (biog.), 212
Sheriff, in N. C., 844; in Suffolk County, Mass., 316n
Sherriff, Henry, 826, 826n (biog.)
Shingle (or River of Thames Ballast), 223
Shingle maker, 528
Shingles, 784, 787; broad, 529; cypress, 528; narrow, 529; price of, 716, 725, 757, 765
Shippers, 308, 309, 331, 678, 680, 684, 685, 700, 773, 806. See also Freighters
Shipping, 22, 26, 28, 30, 132, 135, 154, 175, 183, 185, 195, 225, 227, 230, 263, 273, 281, 282, 290, 292, 293, 301, 303, 308, 309, 331, 332, 379, 389, 390, 393, 397, 400, 402, 405, 410, 414, 423, 525, 534, 538, 562, 570, 581, 694, 701, 720, 724, 725, 728, 736, 739, 762, 770, 773, 775, 781, 798, 804, 843; at sea, 134, 264, 346, 413, 490, 692, 801; effect on price of freight, 34, 65, 88, 89, 91, 93, 96, 107, 109, 176, 181, 184, 185, 189, 192, 194, 200–202, 204, 207, 208, 215, 218, 220, 231, 316, 318, 319, 321, 324–325, 330, 331, 335, 340–342, 362, 363, 365–367, 371, 372, 408, 417–418, 422, 429, 430, 432, 433, 437, 439, 445, 453–454, 458, 471, 493, 501–503, 507, 520, 523, 524, 526, 534, 535, 537, 540, 541, 552, 566, 569, 574, 602, 606, 661, 664, 666, 669, 676, 719, 734, 738, 747, 749–750, 760, 796, 817, 819, 827; effect on price of naval stores, 315, 783, 817, 837–839; effect on price of rice, 6, 30, 73, 74, 80, 84, 88, 93, 96, 97, 107, 112, 166, 173, 174, 181, 184, 185, 187, 189, 192, 194, 200–202, 204, 208, 218, 231, 241, 248, 258, 310, 311, 315, 324–325, 330, 422, 454, 458, 459, 471, 493, 503, 507, 510, 520, 523, 524, 526, 527, 564, 691, 721, 749, 782, 783, 785, 786, 819, 827, 837, 838–839; in Charleston fire (1740), 271, 275, 277, 279, 284, 285; in Mass., 845; numbers of, 429 (fig.), 430 (fig.), 439 (fig.). See also War, effect on shipping; Weather, effect on shipping
Shipping charges, 25, 32, 41, 49, 400, 515
Ships, built in Boston, 83, 168, 169; merchant, 491; of truce, 815n. See also Vessels
Shirts, 31; linen, 658
Shoals, 643
Shoats, 212, 788. See also Hogs
Shoes, 533n; coarse leather, 31
Shopkeeper, 147, 392, 601n, 835; young women, 806. See also Storekeeper
Shop, retailing, 221
Shoreham, HMS (Boscawen), 434, 435, 441, 443, 444
Shot, 252, 325, 338, 351, 424; lead, 117, 797, 524, 602; small, 31, 398, 422, 602; swan, 31. See also Ammunition; Bullets
Shovel & tongs, 50
Shropshire, Eng., 187n, 533n
Shubrick, Richard, 162n, 639, 746, 748, 803
Shubrick, Thomas, 94, 116, 118, 119, 162n, 246, 250, 259, 261, 639, 746, 748, 803
Shute, Atwood, of Philadelphia, 12, 12n (biog.), 320, 360, 448
Siddall, William, 295, 296
Sigourney (Sygourney), Charles, 21, 23, 24, 135–137, 202
Silesias, 227, 783, 785, 788, 816
Silk, culture of, 724n
Silks, 70; Italian, 267; for women's wear, 783, 785, 788; price of, 267; stuffs, 189, 320, 344, 360, 448
Silver, 23, 25, 75, 83, 86, 89, 91, 96, 113, 141, 143, 182, 183, 196, 205, 206, 240, 272, 294, 386, 431, 506, 533, 615, 678, 689, 699, 782, 783, 785, 787, 788, 804, 812, 831, 836; money, 681; plate, 86, 105, 272, 275, 468; "scheme" in Mass., 489n;

Index

Spanish, 132, 198, 223, 243, 587, 617, 620, 621, 647. See also Shell, silver; Tankard, silver
Silver mine, in S. C., 588, 728; Spanish, 662
Silversmith, 314n, 365n, 702n
Simmons, Smith & Co., 350, 747
Simonds (Simmons), Ebenezer, 288, 350n, 747n
Simonds, Mary (Jones), 288
Simons (Symonds), Capt., 173, 186, 187
Simpson, John & Thomas & Co., of London, 107, 107n (biog.), 116, 118, 119, 223, 237, 302, 310
Sise Lane (London), 6n
Skillets, 59
Skrine, Jonathan, 39, 39n (biog.)
Skrine's Ferry, S. C., 39
Skutt, Capt., 185–189
Slate, 282, 283, 399
Slater, Edward, 116–118, 137–141, 217, 338, 339, 350
Slater, James, 15n, 85, 848
Slatters, William, 351, 353, 355, 357
Slave conspiracies, 163, 175n
Slave insurrections, in Antigua, 122; in St. Kitts, 69; in S. C., 135, 143, 163n, 175n, 273
Slaves, 121n, 155n; kidnapped, 351–355, 357; sales, 259n. See also Negroes
Slaves' names, Jack, 241; Cudjoe, 681; Esther, 247; Jack, 681
Slave trade, 121; monopoly of, 7n. See also Guinea trade
Slave traders, 181n
Sloops, 84, 382, 449, 518, 557; altered to a snow, 179, 283; Spanish, 215, 533n
Small arms, 121, 628, 727. See also Guns; Pistols
Smallpox, epidemic, effect on trade, 16, 18, 19, 21, 22, 25, 26, 33, 34, 38, 52, 60, 61, 66, 93; in Antigua, 44; in S. C., 121n. See also Inoculation
Smallwood, James, of Wilmington, 327, 410, 450, 463
Smallwood, Mrs. James, 463
Smethurst, Joseph, 115n
Smith, Capt., 456, 457, 523
Smith & Co., of London, 175
Smith, Benjamin, 350n, 747n
Smith, Charles, 27
Smithers, Mr., 412

Smith, John, 146
Smith, John, of London, 213, 304, 311, 378, 546
Smith, John, of New York, 596
Smith, Mr., 220, 494
Smith, Mrs. John, of London, 312, 547
Smith, Mrs. Samuel, 456
Smith, Samuel, of London, 58, 58n (biog.), 59, 456, 457, 468, 497–499, 544
Smithson, John, 106, 107, 115, 116, 118, 138, 139, 218
Smithson, Samuel, 395–401, 403, 420, 421, 524, 525, 600
Smith, Thomas, of Broad St., 466n
Smith, Thomas, Sr., 466n
Smuggling, 173, 241, 247, 411, 430, 440, 575, 579, 586, 605, 608
Smythe, Alexander, 168
Snelling, Abraham, 6, 164, 242–244, 301, 304, 309, 389, 392, 406, 429, 721, 759, 768
Snow, 282
Snow, Capt., 424
Snow Hill (London), 58n, 456, 497, 499
Snow, John, 333
Snows, 149, 510, 530; altered from a sloop, 179, 238; built in Boston, 52, 66, 79, 80, 90; built in Charleston, 740, 761, 772, 796, 821
Snuff, 762
Soap, 282, 452, 461, 596, 717, 744, 779, 816, 826; New York, 39, 254, 291, 381
SPG, treasurer to, 549n, 614
Sola bills, 89, 252, 255, 257, 262, 308, 366, 614, 663, 741
Solebay, HMS (Warren), 42n
Sommers, Thomas, 770
Southampton, Eng., 155, 367, 440, 480, 621
South-Carolina Gazette, 176n, 237n, 260, 273, 282n, 301, 332n, 383n, 497, 607; circulation of, 255n; editor of, 255n; publisher of, 255n
South Carolina Society, 314n
South Sea Company, 7
Southward, the, 410, 836
Spain, 16, 113, 331, 396n, 663n
Spaniards, 134, 181, 183, 184, 186, 187, 190, 194, 217, 219, 220, 222, 230,

Index

326, 344, 383, 385, 403, 407, 408, 471, 659, 662, 668, 673, 674, 682, 691, 692, 708, 722; captured, 193, 197, 200, 212; encourage runaway slaves, 135
Spanish invasion of Ga., 389, 392, 402, 407, 429–430, 434, 435, 441, 443, 444, 449, 488; effect on trade, 387, 390, 393, 396, 414; failure & retreat from, 396, 397, 399, 400, 404, 406, 409, 414, 430, 449; rumors of, 8, 16, 33, 34, 38, 712, 713, 715–718, 720, 722, 724, 725, 728
Spanish Invasion of S. C., preparations for, 387–390, 393, 396, 400, 402, 404, 409, 414; rumors of, 7, 8, 16, 34, 38, 387, 389, 393; 488, 498, 516, 518, 528, 530, 577, 712, 713, 715–718, 720, 722, 724, 725, 728
Spanish Town, Jamaica, 42, 126n, 134, 191
Speaker (Flower), 20
Spectacles, 138
Spence, HMS (Laws), 143n
Spices, 29n, 31, 424, 430, 447, 729, 776, 780, 781. See also Cinnamon; Pepper
Spithead, Eng., 739
Spoons, pewter, 31
Spring, Hans, 249, 262, 299, 549
Spring tide, 408
Spy glasses, 74
Spy, HMS (Newnham), 434n, 435, 441, 443, 444, 730, 737, 740–742
Squadron. See Fleet
Squirrel (Brown), 259n
Squirrel, HMS (Warren), 42n, 143n, 168, 173–174, 177, 212, 848
Stallion, 711. See also Horses
Standiford St. (Boston), 22n
Stanton, Ward, 278
Stanton, Mrs. Ward, 279
Stanton, Ward, family of, 278, 279
Stanyarn, John, 521n
Staples, Samuel, 530, 533
State lottery, ticket for, 761
Stateroom, 243, 263
State St. (Boston), 22n
Stationer, 468
Stationery, 84, 468, 708, 803. See also Paper, writing
Staves, 348; white oak, price of, 192

Staymakers, 361
Stays, 399
Stead, Evance & Co., 237n, 287, 290, 372, 471, 584, 656, 688
Stead, Benjamin, 86n, 86n (biog.), 106, 138, 223, 287n, 420, 523, 524, 584, 594, 634, 641, 728, 807–809, 834
Stead, William, of London, 86, 86n (biog.), 114, 137, 144, 145, 202, 211, 848
Stedman, Capt., 293, 479, 671, 672, 674
Stedman (Steedman), Charles, 358–359, 359n (biog.), 653
Steedman, John & Co., 641
Steel, Mr., 112
Steill, Hume, & Co., 369, 438n, 469, 530, 547n, 635, 742
Steill, Robert, 438, 438n (biog.), 530, 578, 743, 748
Steinson, John, 656, 659–661, 677, 747
Stephens (Stevens), William, of N. C., 710–712, 767
Stevens, Carter, 326, 327
Stevens, Mr., 364
Stevens, William, of Ga., 598n
Stevenson, Capt., 544, 546
Stewart & Ferguson, 136, 848
Stewart, Alexander, 495, 495n (biog.), 846
Stewart, Mr., 294
Stiles (Styles), Ephraim, 453, 496–501, 544, 615
Stobo, William, 148
Stockings, cotton, 776; coarse worsted, 31; thread, 31, 776
Stocks, 658
Stone cutter, 117, 470
Stone, ornamental, 469
Stones, 176, 244, 616, 654, 655, 661
Stone, William, 498, 498n (biog.), 501, 527, 530, 803
Stono River, S. C., 135
Storage, charges, 400; cost of, 32, 602
Storekeeper, 498; for Ga., 729n; in Edentown, 847; in the country, 127, 521, 586, 702. See also Shopkeeper
Stores, 280, 292, 293, 305, 335n; in the country, 521, 586, 702; RP's, 272, 571
Storke, Samuel & Son, of London, 637, 646, 681, 689, 691, 692, 697–699, 703, 720, 741, 747, 749, 753, 754

Index

Storke, Samuel, of London, 375, 375n (biog.), 376, 377, 392, 406, 635, 686
Story, John, 290, 295, 311, 478–480, 482, 589, 593, 594, 615, 688, 741
Story, John, of London, 482
Stoutenburg, Luke, Jr., 363–365, 365n (biog.), 366, 389, 390, 433, 502
Stoutenburgh, Luke, Sr., 365n (biog.), 366, 433
Stoutenburgh, Sarah (Beating), 365n
Stove, chimney, 565
Stowage, 162, 248, 251, 263, 336, 462, 489, 536, 537, 720, 754, 799, 800
Strahan (Strachan), Alexander, of Jamaica, 626, 626n (biog.), 735, 846
Straits of Gibraltar, 113, 642
Straits, the. *See* Straits of Gibraltar
Strand, the (London), 57, 619
Stray, Francis, 305
Street, Philip, 409, 413
Strouds, 31, 218, 552, 646
Stuart & Reid, 613n
Stuart, John, 350n
Success, a ship (Commerford), 471n
Suffolk County, Mass., 316n, 574, 585
Sugar, 18, 22, 31, 39n, 45, 46, 83, 84, 113, 122, 127, 150, 174, 195, 238, 277, 301, 319, 321, 336, 340–344, 346, 348, 368, 412, 475, 476, 556, 598, 607, 618, 628, 661, 802, 804, 839, 841; brown, 838; clay'd, 481, 563, 699n, 774, 837; double refined, 253, 254, 507, 716, 718, 721, 724, 725, 729, 732; French, 738; loaf, 23, 31, 83, 130, 132, 139, 170, 233, 244, 289, 424, 507, 508, 545, 568, 596, 616, 635–637, 645, 646, 709, 715–722, 724, 725, 727, 729, 732, 733, 738, 739, 744, 750, 754, 766, 776, 780, 781, 783, 785, 788–789, 819; muscavado, 11, 18, 38, 69, 266, 268, 284, 285, 320, 345, 349, 407, 411, 448–450, 474–475, 481, 516, 528, 563, 590, 592, 614, 624–626, 632, 633, 684, 686, 699n, 715, 716, 721, 724, 725, 738, 757–759, 765, 766, 780–783, 785, 787, 806, 810, 814, 816, 825, 839; price of, 39, 45, 83, 87, 148, 150, 151, 182, 190, 192, 201, 254, 266, 268, 320, 407, 411, 416, 417, 448, 450, 474–475, 508, 590, 492, 624–626, 632, 633, 686, 715–722, 724, 725, 727, 729, 732, 733, 752, 757, 758, 765, 766, 774, 781–783, 785, 787, 806, 819, 839, 843; price of, in Barbados, 481, 684; price of, in Jamaica, 816; price of, in Leeward Islands, 816; price of, in New York, 738; price of, in W. I., 656; single refined, 31, 170, 253, 254, 424, 507, 508, 545, 715–721, 724, 725, 727, 729, 732, 738, 744, 750, 754, 766, 776, 780, 781, 783, 785, 788–789, 819; white, 838
Sugar Islands. *See* West Indies
Sugar house, 22n
Sugar refiner, 22n
Suicide, 285n, 730, 736; attempted, 521
Suit (law), 80, 153, 590, 807, 808, 834, 844; chancery, 169
Sullivans Island, S. C., 84n
Sulpher, 12, 13, 36, 38
"Summary, History and Political, of the British Settlements in North America," 234n
Summer goods, 30
Summersett (Sommersett), Thomas, 46, 50, 51, 53, 56, 58, 97–99, 122, 173, 185–187, 189, 194, 217, 219, 221, 222, 224–226, 240, 263, 292, 304, 305–310, 327, 331, 332, 334, 410, 498, 520, 530–532, 682, 687, 690
Superintendent of Indians Affairs for Southern District, 488
Suppliers of provisions, 40n. *See also* Victuallers
Surgeon, 168, 177, 461, 521, 529–531, 848. *See also* Medicine, practice of; Physicians
Surgeon's instrument maker, 819n, 847
Surry, Capt., 245, 246
Survey, 338
Surveyor & auditor general of the plantation revenues, 169n
Surveyor general of American customs, for the southern part of America, 662
Surveyor-general of S. C., 19n, 125, 542; deputy of, 551n
Susanna, a snow (Styles), 453n
Susannah, a ship (Pringle, Gregory), 62, 66, 73–76, 143, 157, 162–164, 166, 167, 211, 225, 239, 243–246, 248–252, 254, 256–265, 268–270, 272, 280, 283, 289, 310, 319–322, 331, 332, 334–336, 340, 342–349, 356, 360, 367, 368, 370, 371, 377, 407, 416, 417,

Index

436–441, 453–456, 458, 462–467, 469–473, 480, 482–484, 486, 488, 520, 545, 546, 549, 551, 574–578, 590, 607, 614, 619, 620, 655, 670, 673, 674, 729, 794, 796
Susannah, a sloop (Hunt), 381n, 382
Susannah, a sloop (Willson), 651
Susannah, a snow (Partington), 289n
Sutherland, John, 282–284, 295, 544, 575
Swallow, HMS (Jelfe), 728, 818
Swan, a schooner (Cox), 333, 334
Swanzey, a schooner (Hutchins), 787n
Swayne (Swain), John, 677
Sweetman, Capt., 589
Sweetmeats, 369, 481, 563
Swift, HMS (Bladwell), 589, 595, 597, 601, 603, 604, 606, 608, 609, 613, 663
Switzerland, 377, 420n

Tablecloths, 31
Tailor, 57n, 252, 709
Talifer, Patrick, of Savannah, 153n, 171, 171n (biog.), 255
Tallow, 278, 483, 710
Tankards, pewter, 298, 332; silver, Charleston-made, 203, 365n
Tar, 9, 30, 32, 35, 37, 40, 70, 86, 99, 106, 107, 116–118, 129, 133, 136, 140, 145, 162n, 278, 287, 314, 325, 346, 348, 392, 396, 406, 407, 452, 475, 522, 609, 610, 710, 714, 764, 768, 774, 784, 805; price of, 32, 87, 118, 125, 154, 156, 160, 165, 175, 178, 186, 190, 191, 201, 202, 209, 217, 242, 254, 268, 288, 290, 291, 313, 315, 317, 320, 321, 397, 398, 400, 408, 418, 422, 448, 450, 460, 474, 503, 508, 509, 525, 526, 582, 583, 594, 601, 603, 605, 606, 608, 621, 625, 644, 645, 653, 657, 721, 750, 757, 758, 765, 766, 773, 780–783, 785, 787, 788, 817, 818, 838, 839
Tare, 337, 422
Tartar (*Tartar Pink*), HMS (Townshend), 134, 135, 207, 260, 313, 618, 622
Tavern, 92, 599n. *See also* Public house
Tavern keeper, 92, 339n.
Tax bill of 1744, 699–700, 728; effect on trade, 701
Tax collector, 755, 756
Taxes, arbitrary, 700

Taylor, Richard, 88, 89, 151, 152
Tea, 249, 545, 596, 635, 637, 646, 709, 776, 780, 781, 783, 785, 788; Bohea, 31, 424; green, 270, 424, 729; Hyson, 253, 270, 276; price of, 270, 722
Teneriffe, Canary Islands, 248n
Thames St. (London), 100
Theatre, 92n
The Christian Life, 262
"The Humble Petition of the Council and Assembly of Your Majesty's Province of South Carolina on behalf of the Distressed Inhabitants of Charles Town in the Said Province," 272, 273, 276
"The Report of the Committee of Both Houses of the Assembly of the Province of South Carolina," 577–578
Third communion, 285n
Thistle, a snow (Aithen), 680, 690, 693, 694, 696, 704, 705, 718
Thread, 31
Threadneedle St. (London), 29n, 158n
Thomas, Andrew, 66, 79
Thomas and Ann, a brigantine (Blanchard), 55n
Thomas, a ship (Palmer), 663, 668, 673, 675, 679, 682, 686, 689, 690–692, 697–699, 702, 721, 726, 752. *See also Sarah*, a ship (Remick)
Thomas, Edward, 383, 383n (biog.), 554, 574, 575, 584
Thomas, Joshua, 113–115
Thomas, Samuel, 383, 574, 575, 584
Thompson, Capt., 375, 376, 378, 387
Thompson (Thomson), James, 463, 792, 806, 844
Thompson (Thomson), Michael, of London, 45, 70, 78, 115, 119, 120, 189, 285, 642, 659, 660, 745, 762, 831
Thompson, Richard, of Hull, 29, 29n (biog.), 116, 117, 137, 139, 140, 214, 220, 224, 288, 311, 314, 323, 339, 350, 397
Thompson, Robert, 247, 248, 620
Thornton, Christopher, 593, 616
Three Tun Court (Miles Lane, London), 163n
Tiles, 282, 283, 301, 400
Tillers, for saws, 488
Tillidge, Capt., 677

Index

Tillotson, John, 262
Tillotson's *Works*, 262
Timber, 319, 320, 334, 346, 475, 513, 528; square, 348, 476. *See also* Wood
Timber trade, 475
Timothy, Lewis, 255n, 262n
Timothy, Peter, 171n, 578n
Tinker, John, of Barbardos, 280, 280n (biog.), 293, 298, 333, 334, 357, 367, 386, 460, 656
Tisehurst, Thomas, 431-434, 454, 459, 461, 506, 535, 567
Tobacco, 22, 66, 84, 147, 195, 277, 278, 287, 336, 385, 412, 483, 711, 762, 766, 767; box, 335; country, 287; common mixed, 31; hand mixed, 31; leaf, 141, 380. *See also* Snuff
Tobias, Joseph, 147, 147n (biog.)
Tod, Mr., 282
Toddy, 683
Topham, Ann, 104, 105n, 106
Topham, Christopher, 105
Topsham, Eng., 30, 706, 709
Torres, Rodrigo, 260n, 663, 668, 674
Tower Hill (London), 107n, 667n, 770n
Tower St. (London), 463n
Tower, the (London), 847
Townshand, Rebecca, 302
Townshend, George, 134, 135n, 207, 260
Tradd St. (Charleston), 224n, 365n, 470n, 702n
Trade (Carolina), 106n, 155n, 259, 423, 478, 488, 513, 608, 662, 708, 770, 799; altered, 281, 308, 310, 797, 813, 834; description of, 30-31, 49-50, 52, 57, 66, 116, 117, 210, 223, 338, 380, 468, 504; dull, 530, 538. *See also* Ministry (British), effect on trade; Smallpox epidemic, effect on trade; Spanish invasion of Ga., effect on trade; Yellow fever epidemic, effect on trade
Trade, Carolina-Boston, 197, 240n; Carolina-New Providence, 358; Carolina-Philadelphia, 359n; Carolina-Portuguese, 73n; Carolina-St. Kitts, 713; illicit, with Spaniards, 708, 833n; London-New England, 115n; of Great Britain, 701; Savannah, monopoly of, 153n, 171n. *See also* Dry goods trade; Guinea trade; Indian trade;

Ministry (British), effect on trade; Palatine trade; Slave trade; Smuggling; Trade (Carolina); Triangular trade
Tradesmen, 469, 498; English, 830n. *See also* Bills, tradesmen's
Transom, 332
Transports, 29, 255, 269, 434, 435, 441, 443-445
Travers, Samuel, of London, 9, 9n (biog.), 51, 122, 142, 148, 149, 315, 324
Treaty of Aix-la-Chapelle (1748), 820n
Trees, flowering, 829n; frenge (Flowering Ash, or Old Man's Beard), 829. *See also* Bay; Laurel; Magnolia
Tregagle, Nathaniel, 599, 599n (biog.)
Trenchard, John, 739, 743, 773, 775, 777, 789, 792-794, 796-798, 800, 801, 803, 805, 807, 812
Trenn, Capt., 566
Trial, 353, 355, 357, 442, 603, 679
Triangular trade, 30-31, 400
Trimble, John, 173, 188, 192, 208, 209, 247, 295, 308, 310, 367, 467
Trinity House (Hull), 399n
Triton, a ship (McFarland), 808
Troops, British (Regulars), 173, 175, 434, 435, 441, 443, 444, 488, 498; Ga., 387, 390, 393, 586n; New England, 820n; S. C., 175, 177, 183, 186, 187, 190, 193, 194, 197, 200, 202, 212, 217, 220, 222, 225, 228, 231, 234, 407; Spanish, 387, 389, 392, 397, 399, 400, 404, 406, 414, 430, 518, 712. *See also* Boston Regiment; First Regiment of S. C.; Forty-Second Regiment of Foot
Trotter, James, 847
Trott, Nicholas, 262n
Trumpery, 299
Trunks, 259, 515
Trustees of Ga., 16n, 28, 157n, 598, 614, 729
Tryon, Thomas, of London, 549, 549n (biog.), 558, 614
Tryon, William, of London, 549, 549n (biog.), 558, 614
Tub, 249, 562
Tucker, James, 101
Tucker, Joseph, 180
Tucker, Thomas, 698, 701
Tureens, pewter, 332

Index

Turkeys, 788
Turpentine, 30, 70, 86, 106, 154, 162, 166, 201, 202, 209, 278, 287, 314, 325, 346, 348, 522, 610, 710, 720, 764, 765, 768, 774, 784; price of, 32, 87, 156, 160, 163, 175, 178, 186, 190, 191, 217, 242, 254, 268, 288, 291, 313, 317, 320, 321, 416, 503, 508, 509, 525, 526, 594, 601, 603, 605, 606, 608, 625, 653, 657, 721, 750, 766, 773, 781, 785, 787, 788, 817, 818, 839
Turner & Jopson, of Hull, 399, 525, 600, 657, 661, 670, 671, 673, 762
Turner, Lawrence. *See* Turner & Jopson
Turner, Lewis, 11, 13
Turner, Mr., 203
Turrell (Turill, Turril), Joseph, 538–541, 545, 547–549, 551–553, 555, 557–559, 561, 566, 567, 589, 619, 646, 673, 695, 698
Turrell, Joseph, Jr., 695, 695n (biog.), 698
Turtles, 10, 212, 234, 377, 389, 392, 403, 535, 551, 562, 571, 705, 721
Twine, 372, 424, 776; Hamburg, 440
Two Brothers, a brigantine (Vezie, alias Beach), 401, 402
Two Brothers, a ship (Ryan), 381n
Two Sisters (Rice), 591

Udney, George, of London, 350, 350n (biog.), 835
Udney, Robert, 350n
Union, a ship (Sandwell), 670n
Upholsterer, 792
Utting (Hutting), Ashby, 587, 608, 662, 740, 831n, 833, 838n, 839
Ulysses, a ship (Hayden), 634n, 637

Vallaint, Paul, 619
Varelst, Harman, 541, 543
Vaughan, John, 169, 169n (biog.)
Vaughan, Francis, 465, 466, 470, 472–474, 477–479
Vellars St. (London), 57
Velvet, 63, 317, 783, 785, 788; cut, 824; price of, 241
Vendue, 26, 267, 297, 320, 326, 480, 530, 592, 629, 645, 658, 669, 676, 685, 721, 780, 804, 841
Vendue master, 466n
Venus, a ship (Snelling), 768n

Verissime & Clarisseau, 846
Vernon, Edward, 170, 230, 231, 288, 304, 441, 458, 488, 663n
Vessels, 533; Assiento Company's, 7; Portuguese, 831. *See also* Bermudian sloops; Brigantines; Galleys; Guinea ships; Hospital ships; King's ships; Men of war; Palatine ships; Pettiaugas; Privateers; Prizes; Ships; Sloops; Snows; Transports
Vestry, 211n, 623n
Vestryman, 211n
Vezie, Hugh, 401, 402, 405. *See also* Beach, Henry
Vice Admiralty Court. *See* Court of Vice Admiralty
Victuallers, 47n, 339n, 371; agent, 414. *See also* Supplier, of provisions
Vintner, 47n
Virginia, 172, 186, 187, 195, 239, 317, 364, 386, 403, 408, 414, 514n, 577, 709
Virginia Gazette, 172n

Waddle (Waddel), Capt., 727, 793, 797, 798, 800, 805
Wadge, Nicholas, 517, 762, 796
Wages, rates of, for workmen, 301; ticket for, 581, 583. *See also individual occupations*
Waistcoat, 63
Walker, John, 68, 69
Walker, Richard, 434, 443–446, 505, 507, 647
Walker, Robert, of Cape Fear, 128, 128n (biog.), 129, 326, 410, 451
Wallace, William, 162n, 282, 298
Wallace, William & Co., 282, 363, 376
Wallnuts, 621
Walpole, Horatio, 169, 169n (biog.), 542
Walpole, Robert, 169n, 363n, 367, 371
Wansell, Edmond, 309
Wanton, Capt., 176
Wapping (London), 20n, 847
War, 28, 42, 121, 140, 144; apprehensions of, 138, 139, 141, 143, 145, 150; apprehensions & uncertainty of, with France, 183, 195, 223, 228, 265, 268, 468, 488, 523, 525, 527, 530, 535–537, 588, 594, 602, 605, 607, 612, 614, 622, 625, 626, 660, 676, 677, 680,

Index

686, 690, 697, 706, 719; declaration of, 714n, 722, 728; effect on prices, 138, 183, 266, 411, 696, 709, 714–717, 719, 720, 722, 724, 725, 742, 748; effect on shipping, 139, 141, 143, 218, 220, 265, 266, 268, 602, 605, 607, 612, 622, 625, 626, 715, 716, 719, 721, 734; fortunes of, 815; of Jenkins' Ear, 7n, 156, 159, 163, 165, 193n, 195n, 215, 216, 265, 602, 663n, 734, 753, 777; with France, 714–717, 720, 721, 724, 725, 797. *See also* Wartime
Ward, Capt., 677–681
Warden, William, 36, 38, 43–46, 70, 71, 189, 292, 294–299, 303, 308, 318, 333, 336, 348, 356, 367, 371, 377, 379, 382, 387, 471, 479, 615, 618, 660
Ward, John, Jr., 324, 325, 336–339, 349–357, 361, 370, 398, 421, 423, 442, 525, 602, 603, 798
Ward, John, Sr., 351, 354
Warehouse, 22n
Warner, Samuel, 9
Warrants, 352, 355, 357
Warren, Peter, 42, 42n (biog.), 125, 126, 143, 174, 177, 197, 200, 212, 701, 848
Warring, Dr., 168
Wartime, 137, 212, 264, 346, 413, 490, 801
Watch, 761
Water, 829
Water Lane (Tower Hill, London), 463n
Wathen, James, 532
Watkins, Capt., 194
Watlington, Samuel, 60, 93, 97, 532
Watson, Capt., 696
Watson, Charles, 649, 649n (biog.)
Watsone & McKenzie, 12n, 166, 173, 187n, 194n
Watsone, John, 12, 12n (biog.), 187, 228, 314, 350, 571, 698, 699, 835
Watson, Samuel, of Hull, 395, 395n (biog.), 629, 658
Watson, William, 179, 180, 182–184, 190, 197, 266, 267, 284, 285
Watts, Alexander, 90, 91, 184, 185, 195, 196, 200–204, 207–209, 211–214, 222, 227, 241, 285, 286
Watts & Fuller, 763, 783
Wax, 780; myrtle, 483, 710, 766, 794

Weather, bad, 303; effect on crops, 16, 17, 19, 21–24, 26, 28, 34, 103, 104, 107, 109, 112–114, 116, 118, 121–123, 125, 126, 130–132, 136, 143, 227, 228, 230, 234, 241, 247, 250, 251, 253, 393, 420, 423, 710–712, 719, 729, 732n; effect on shipping, 106, 167, 196, 251, 297–299, 453, 464, 465, 479, 486, 506, 539, 540, 667, 762, 785, 825; effect on slaves, 282; effect on trade, 116, 118, 224, 325. *See also* Climate; Frost; Snow; Winds
Weaver, 532n
Wearing apparel. *See* Clothes
Webb, Capt., 149
Webber, Robert, 269
Webber, Samuel, 630–633, 723, 724, 758
Webb, Nathaniel, 267
Webb, William, 3, 210, 459n
Webster, John, 460, 626, 678, 679, 681, 726, 735
Wedderburn (Widerburn), Alexander, 319–322, 340, 343, 344, 542, 544, 551, 562, 571, 615, 618, 620
Wedderburn, James, 240, 240n (biog.)
Weevils, 210, 218, 236, 391. *See also* Worms
Welfitt (Wellfitt), William, of Hull, 116, 116n (biog.), 117, 118, 138–141, 147, 217, 220, 287, 325, 337–339, 350, 422. *See also* Cookson & Welfitt
Wells, Capt., 768
Wendell, Jacob, of Boston, 20n (biog.)
Wendell, Jacob & John & Co., of Boston, 20, 115, 199, 206, 316, 503, 661
Wendell, John, Jr., of Boston, 20n (biog.)
Wentworth, Thomas, 170n, 230n, 441, 443
Westerman, Peter, of Barbados, 474, 563, 756, 805, 837
West Indies, 7n, 18, 46, 102, 113, 230, 260, 288, 289, 297, 308, 310, 322, 334, 356, 360, 378, 400, 412, 451, 461, 485, 498, 502, 504, 506, 538, 548, 556, 656, 663n, 669, 686, 689, 694, 704, 719, 720, 767. *See also* Anguilla; Antigua; Cuba; Hispaniola; Jamaica; Leeward Islands; Montserrat; Nevis; St. Kitts
West Indian trade, 431
Westminster (London), 729

Index

Wethered, Henry, 433
Wey River. *See* Wye River, Md.
Whale, a sloop (Jarvis), 66
Wharfage, price of, 447
Wharves, 292, 337, 461, 546, 616; common, 244; Elliott's, 335n; Motte's, 282n
Whately (Price), 14
Wheelwright, John, of Boston, 421, 421n (biog.), 442, 446, 602, 666
Whitaker & Hannington, of London, 661, 667, 670, 674, 685, 760, 774, 775
Whitaker, Benjamin, 169, 169n (biog.), 227, 351, 478n, 550, 708, 790
Whitaker, Sarah (Godfrey), 227
White, Capt., 227
Whitefield, George, 242, 285n, 629n
White people, 52, 56, 135, 143, 498
White, Samuel, 60, 61, 65, 67, 323, 379, 382, 383, 498, 519, 615, 618, 620, 803, 804, 807, 821, 830, 832
Whitfield, James, 73, 74
Whitman (Wightman), William, 244, 250, 265, 268
Widerburn, Alexander. *See* Wedderburn, Alexander
Wigg, Edward, 500
Wiggins, Edmund, 599
Wigg, Mary (Hazzard), 500
Wigs, bob, 76, 729; bob major, 729; caul of, 834; ramillie, 76. *See also* Periwig; Periwig maker; Peruke maker
Wilkinson, Thomas, 244, 803, 804, 821
William and Mary (Hunnyford), 362
William, a sloop (Webber), 630n, 758n
William (Carter), 17, 18
Williams, Anthony, 19
Williamsburg Township, S. C., 579, 599, 600, 755
Williamsburg, Va., 172n, 394, 415, 847
Williams, Capt., 213, 590–592, 632, 814, 816
Williams, Elizabeth (Stevens, Cantey), 19
Williams, Lawrence, 28
Williams, Robert, of Savannah, 153, 153n (biog.), 171, 255, 512, 723
Williams, Thomas, of London, 4, 15, 19, 77, 85
Williamson, William, 369
Wills, 3n, 4n, 26n, 212n, 267, 296n, 418n, 473, 521n, 623n, 640n, 799, 836
Willson, Capt., 330, 636–638, 651, 791, 820, 824, 830, 832
Willson, George, 51
Willson, Major, 439n
Willson, Mr., 85
Willson, William, 51, 832, 835, 836
Will Town, S. C., 147, 826n
Wilmington, N. C., 235, 277, 296, 297, 326–328, 410, 419, 463, 522, 555, 556; board of town commissioners of, 128n
Wimble, James, 455, 467, 473, 523, 543, 545, 559–561, 585, 615, 620, 643, 665, 678, 680, 689, 758, 759, 763, 768, 780, 843
Windbound, 7, 95, 118, 133, 136, 329, 349, 573, 641, 697, 703, 822. *See also* Winds
Windham, Charles, 10
Winds, 315, 480, 617; contrary, 352, 354, 356, 387, 593, 698; easterly, 434; fair, 469, 471, 492, 537, 558, 559, 647, 842; fan Charleston fire (1740), 271, 275, 284; NE, 479, 775; northerly, 473; NW, 472, 773; southerly, 214, 227, 472–473
Wine, 7, 8, 29, 95, 100, 158, 159, 186, 248n, 277, 282, 285, 322, 335, 377, 498, 520, 551, 571–573, 636, 748, 762, 770, 771, 799, 829, 831, 835; Bordeaux, 605; canary, 22, 30, 364, 486, 508, 721; claret, 262, 430, 440, 575, 605, 752, 773, 780, 783, 785, 789, 842; color of, 611; consumption of, 30, 159, 372, 374, 377; Florence, 82, 605, 819; Frontenac, 70, 605; glass of, 455; Madeira, 30, 31, 39–40, 85, 116, 117, 148, 160, 161, 163, 174, 178, 201, 228, 254, 268, 284, 291, 295, 317, 320, 321, 323, 329, 337, 372, 374, 380, 405, 406, 411, 417, 440, 448, 450, 452, 460, 471, 475, 483, 501, 508, 520, 530, 550, 594, 601, 603, 606, 608, 625, 638, 641, 653, 660, 699n, 716, 718, 721, 724, 725, 727, 766, 781–783, 785, 787, 788; mountain, 579, 604; Oporto, 250; price of, 148, 159–161, 201, 254, 268, 291, 295, 317, 320, 321, 323, 329, 337, 372, 374, 380, 405, 406, 411, 417, 440,

Index

448, 450, 452, 471, 475, 498, 501, 508, 509, 550, 553, 594, 601, 603, 606, 608, 612, 625, 634, 638, 641, 653, 716, 718, 721, 724, 725, 727, 752, 766, 781–783, 785, 787, 788; price of, in Gibraltar, 579; price of, in Holland, 575; price of, in Madeira, 611; sack, 486, 508, 605; trade in, 440
Winnyaw (Winyaw). *See* Winyah Bay, S. C.
Winslow, Edward, 838
Winter (1740–1741), 301
Winyah Bay, S. C., 503, 505, 508, 523, 697, 750, 754
Winyaw, a sloop (Painter), 26n
Wise, John, 149
Withy, Hilborn, 74
Withy, Mrs. Hilborn, 75
Witnesses, 375, 495, 640n, 651, 660, 661, 759
Wood, 79, 114, 294, 799. *See also* Boards; Braziletto; Brazil wood; Cedar; Joists; Lumber; Planks; Shingles; Staves; Timber
Wood, Anne (Bax), 158, 158n (biog.), 252, 255
Wood, Capt., 735
Wood, Nicholas, 137, 140
Woodrope, Capt., 27
Woodropp, William, 156, 156n (biog.), 157, 251, 252, 263, 314, 571, 572, 611, 735
Woods, the, 268, 829
Woodwell, John, 691, 693, 695, 696, 698, 749
Wood, William, of Frederica, 157, 157n (biog.), 158n, 193, 252, 255, 495
Woolens, 30, 139, 162, 276, 295, 325, 351, 395, 525, 526; price of, 400. *See also* Blanketing; Baize. Colchester; Drabb; Durays; Flannel; Plains; Shalloon; Strouds
Wooley, John, 493
Work house, 271
Worlond, Anthony, 682
Worms, parasitical, 565; rice, 210, 236, 391; ship, 83, 96, 140, 572, 714, 735. *See also* Weevils

Wragg family, 102
Wragg, John, 196, 212, 531
Wragg, Joseph, 83, 83n (biog.), 102, 111, 196, 212, 498, 503, 531, 607, 751
Wragg, Joseph, Jr., 196n
Wragg, Joseph & Co., 321
Wragg, Judith (DuBose), 196
Wragg, Mr., 293, 302, 310
Wragg, Samuel, 102, 102n (biog.), 497, 550
Wragg, Samuel (son of Joseph), 196n
Wright, Charles, 744, 744n (biog.)
Wright, James (captain), 269, 312, 313, 315, 322, 417, 453, 458, 462, 463, 466, 469, 471
Wright, James (lawyer), 744n, 805, 805n (biog.), 808
Wright, James (storekeeper), 702
Wright, Jermyn, 547, 547n (biog.), 744, 763
Wright, Richard, 805
Wright, Robert, 744n
Wright, William, 702, 702n (biog.)
Writ, 581; of attachment, 806, 844
Wye River, Md., 394, 610, 653, 778, 847
Wyrill, Roger, 106

Yawl, 7, 9
Yellow fever epidemic, 132, 135, 138, 145, 146, 151, 156; effect on trade, 139, 140, 143
Yeomans & Escott, 259, 263
Yeomans, William, 259n, 521, 521n (biog.), 646, 711
York Buildings (London), 57
York, Eng., mayor of, 329
Yorkshire, Eng., 32, 237
Yorktown, Va., 396n
Young Queen, a ship (Young), 174n, 472
Young, James, 210, 211, 280, 283, 545, 547, 548, 555, 558, 559, 561, 562
Young, Robert, 174, 175, 458, 472, 510
Yucatan, Mexico, 773n
Yverdon, Switzerland, burgesses of, 420n

The Letterbook of Robert Pringle

Composed in Linotype Electra by Heritage Printers with selected lines of display in Goudy Old Style. Printed letterpress by Heritage Printers on Warren's University Text, an acid-free paper watermarked with the University of South Carolina Press colophon. Three-piece binding by Kingsport Press with GSB natural finish fabric on spine and Elephant Hide paper over .080 boards on sides. Designed by Robert L. Nance.